Mrs. J. Sadlier

The confederate chieftains

A tale of the Irish rebellion of 1641

Mrs. J. Sadlier

The confederate chieftains
A tale of the Irish rebellion of 1641

ISBN/EAN: 9783742831514

Manufactured in Europe, USA, Canada, Australia, Japa

Cover: Foto ©Thomas Meinert / pixelio.de

Manufactured and distributed by brebook publishing software
(www.brebook.com)

Mrs. J. Sadlier

The confederate chieftains

THE

CONFEDERATE CHIEFTAINS:

A TALE

OF

The Irish Rebellion of 1641.

BY

MRS. J. SADLIER,

AUTHOR OF "NEW LIGHTS," "BLAKES AND FLANAGANS," "WILLY BURKE,"
"RED HAND OF ULSTER," ETC.

Rebellion! foul, dishonoring word,
  Whose wrongful blight so oft has stain'd
The holiest cause that tongue or sword
  Of mortal, ever lost or gain'd.
How many a spirit born to bless,
  Hath sunk beneath its withering name;
Whom but a day's, an hour's success,
  Had wafted to eternal fame!
                          MOORE's *Lalla Rookh.*

NEW YORK:

D. & J. SADLIER & CO., 31 BARCLAY STREET;

BOSTON:—128 FEDERAL STREET;

MONTREAL:—COR. OF NOTRE DAME & ST. FRANCIS XAVIER STREETS.

1864.

PREFACE.

It is a common saying, even amongst Irish people, that Irish history is about the driest history known to us. There may be some truth in the remark, for the fact is that Ireland of all countries, has never yet been fairly represented on the page of history. In this she has had reason to complain, for although her sons have done much for the historic fame of other countries, they have, for the most part, wholly neglected that of their own. If Goldsmith had but done for Ireland what he did for England, then the personages of Ireland's eventful drama would be as familiarly known as are those of English history,—our O'Neils and O'Donnels would bear comparison with the Russels and the Sidneys, and the Hampdens,—our Desmonds, and Geraldines, and Butlers would stand on a level with the Warwicks, the Percys, and the Douglases of British story, and Brian Boromhe and Art McMurrough would shine out from the darkness of their times with as true a lustre as that which gilds the names of the English Alfred and the Scottish Bruce. The sons and daughters of Ireland in foreign countries would not then have to ask: "Who on earth is Owen Roe?—who is Hugh O'Neil?—who is Oliver Plunket?—What in the world did they do that people keep talking so about them?" Oh! what wonder is it that such ignorance prevails, such deplorable ignorance, with regard to the history of Ireland? What effort has ever been made to invest it with charms for the rising generation to whom history is of itself a dry study?

We of the Irish race owe a debt to our departed worthies which we cannot too soon set about paying. Their efforts to redeem the land of their love were unhappily for the most part unsuccessful, but the fault was not theirs—they were great and noble in their generation—they did great things for Ireland—they have left us their fame as a legacy—shall we not avail ourselves of it to ennoble our country and give her that place amongst the nations to which the glory of her sons entitles her? No country under heaven has had more heroic deeds done for her—no country holds a higher place in the martyrology of nations (so to speak)—no history more chequered than hers, or marked by more striking vicissitudes, more stirring events, deeper shadows or more radiant lights. How then is it so little known, and when partially known so little cared for? Precisely because the romance of our history is left in the background,—the facts, even when told over, are presented to the reader in the driest and least attractive manner possible. What young person will think of reading the Four Masters, McGeogegan, Lanigan, Keating, or O'Halloran? The very sight of those ponderous volumes would deter most people from opening them in search of "Irish story," and, even though they did summon courage to "look in," the formidable array of long (and apparently) unpronounceable Milesian names would be more than enough to damp their curiosity and give them a distaste for further research.*

The annals of Ireland have been not inaptly likened to a skeleton; a heap of dry bones, which require the prophet's breath to infuse life into them, and clothe them with the vesture of humanity. To follow up the comparison—as the student of anatomy takes, bone by bone, and joint by joint, the wonderful piece of mechanism which forms our body, in order to arrive at a perfect knowledge of the whole, so would I endeavor to dissect the *corpus* of Irish history, and presenting it piece by piece to the reader, give a knowledge of each in detail. This is what I have done in the work now placed before the reader. I have taken the Religious War—commonly called the Great Rebellion—which convulsed Ireland from 1641 to 1652, and clothed the dry bones of the principal actors on both sides with the flesh of their mortality, and breathed into them the breath of life, so that they might speak and tell their own story to all who are disposed to listen. I have woven a thread of fiction—a slender thread, too—through the stirring events of that "hero-age," just enough to keep the *dramatis personæ* grouped together. In adhering so faithfully to the historical narrative, I may have rendered the book less interesting to those who love mystery and crave excitement, but it was not to pander to morbid and unhealthy appetites that I undertook a work requiring so much patient research; nor is it for the mere novel reader that I write now or at any other time. To those who love Ireland and can appreciate her fidelity to her ancient faith, the sufferings she has endured, and the heroic efforts which her children have made in times past to free her from civil and religious bondage, I make no apology for the undue proportion of historical matter in this story, they will value it all the more for being "an ower true tale."

* The Popular History of Ireland now appearing from the pen of our distinguished countryman T. D McGee, bids fair to supply this want.

CONFEDERATE CHIEFTAINS.

CHAPTER I.

" Is Iran's pride, then, gone for over,
   Quenched with the flame in Mithra's caves ?—
No—she has sons that never—never—
   Will stoop to be the Moslem's slaves,
   While heaven has light, or earth has graves."
                                    MOORE'S *Lalla Rookh.*

THE long dreary reigns of Elizabeth and James, her successor, had passed over bleeding, suffering Ireland like a hideous dream, and the persecuted Catholics of that country hailed the accession of Charles I. to the throne of his father, as the dawn of a day that was to bring them peace and rest. For the king spoke them fair and made many soothing promises, and they, in their exuberant loyalty, and in the gush of newly-awakened hope, believed every word he said, nor dreamed that the faithlessness of all his race had descended upon this young prince, whose precocious gravity of demeanor and affected generosity of sentiment were alike calculated to impose on the credulous and unsuspecting. But the king wanted money, as the Stuart princes always did, and who so ready as the Irish Catholics to supply it, hoping thereby to secure the monarch's favor, and to obtain from his gratitude at least, if not his justice, those concessions which might raise them nearer the level of the other subjects of the realm. Plundered and dispossessed of their estates by the wholesale confiscations of the previous reigns, it is matter of astonishment to us at this day that anything was left them to give. Undoubtedly the native chieftains were many of them landless men, stripped of their immense possessions by the crying injustice of English sovereigns and their willing agents, the Lords Deputies of Ireland. But the Catholics of the Pale were not so bankrupt in this world's goods—they being of English descent had been somewhat more leniently dealt with, and the fairest and richest portion of the island was still in their hands. They, then, were better able to advance money, and it is probable the greater portion of the subsidies came from them—who but they had it to give? However it was, no less a sum than *one hundred and twenty thousand pounds*—an enormous sum in that age—was sent over by the Catholics of Ireland as a peace-offering to the king. The money once received, Charles thought no more of the promised "graces," and the work of persecution and spoliation went on in Ireland with undiminished violence, under the truculent and remorseless Strafford, the devoted henchman of the faithless king. The Catholics, amazed and disappointed, petitioned and remonstrated—reminded the king of the gracious promises which had beguiled them into hope, and of the solemn contract into which he had entered with them, but Charles gave them no sort of satisfaction, and his minister in Ireland silenced their just complaints with insult and mockery, and proceeded, with that diabolical ingenuity which was characteristic of the man, to invent new schemes of robbery for the benefit of his unworthy master. The Commission of Defective Titles was appointed for the modest and laudable purpose of dispossessing the Chieftains of Connaught of their remaining lands and hereditaments—the pretence was to examine into the titles of all the estates of the Province, but the examination was only a legal farce. The juries were in every instance coerced by the tyrant Strafford into finding for the king. In fact, no alternative was left them. If they declared in favor of the owners of the property, their own goods were confiscated, and their persons dragged to Dublin to undergo the tortures of the hell-devised Star Chamber, so that no alternative was left them but to *find* the existing title *Defective*, and by their verdict to turn an ancient family out of its possessions, to swell the ranks of the landless and beggared men who formed the great bulk of the native gentry.

But the work of iniquity did not prosper with either Charles Stuart or his *factotum*, Strafford. The Irish nation was bound hand and foot, as they thought, and the remaining inheritance of its loyal and long-suffering sons transferred in cash to the coffers of the English king, but the all-seeing eye of a just God was on them and their deeds of darkness were registered above. Even when their power seemed at the highest, their doom was recorded, and the crash of their fall resounded through the civilized world. The same party whom the king, in his selfish blindness, permitted to harry and distress his faithful subjects in Ireland, in England and in Scotland, rose up in arms against him, and by a signal stroke of retributive justice Strafford first, and himself at a later period, suffered death at the hands of the ruthless fanatics who were armed with power to smite them. When the king's affairs became desperate, his enemies many and powerful, and his friends few, he was forced to recall Strafford from Ireland, hoping that his tried fidelity, indomitable courage, and known ability, might help to extricate him from the toils in which his own duplicity had ensnared him. Vain and short-sighted calculations! The measure of Strafford's iniquity was full, and the hands which had exercised such cruelties on the long-enduring Irish Catholics were soon manacled by the fierce Puritans and rendered powerless for evil or for good. His subsequent fate is well known to all readers of history, but before his haughty neck was laid on the block, the king his master replaced him in Ireland by two joint governors named Lords *Justices* (strange perversion of terms!). Of all the Popery-hating, plunder-loving rulers ever sent by the *paternal* government of England to soothe the woes and sufferings of Catholic Ireland, these two men, Sir William Parsons and Sir John Borlase, stand out in the light of history as amongst the most odious robbers and persecutors. Even the bold, blustering, barefaced villany of the royalist Strafford was better than the smooth, hypocritical, all-grasping, and no less ferocious dealings of these truculent agents of the Covenanting rebels, styled by themselves and others the Parliament of England. It was a dismal day for poor bleeding, prostrate Ireland, when this pair of associates were sworn in as Lords Justices, the actual Lord Lieutenant, the Earl of Leicester, being then and long after resident in England.

Amongst other atrocities of those penal days in Ireland was the famous Court of Wards, established some years before with the avowed object of protecting all heirs and heiresses, but in reality for the double purpose of depriving them not only of their patrimony, but of what was far more important, their faith, for, be it known to the reader, that *Catholic* wards were the special care of this precious *Court*. That such was the case Ireland knew to her cost, for the working of this institution was more fatal to her cherished faith than all the open persecution of the times. Many of the descendants of her noblest and most ancient families were in this way snatched from the fold of truth, and brought up in rancorous hatred of that religion for which their fathers suffered and died. Of this number was the famous James Butler, Earl of Ormond, the representative of one of the oldest Anglo-Irish houses of the Pale, who, being an orphan from his childhood, was of course laid hold of by the Court of Wards, taken at nine years old from a Catholic school near London, transferred to the *care* of the Protestant Archbishop of Canterbury, and "trained up in the way" the English government "would have him go," till he became the able and unscrupulous minister of the crown, and one of the most dangerous—because insidious —enemies the Catholics of Ireland ever had. But worse than Ormond—worse than the fiercest blood-hounds of the Parliament, was another of these royal wards, viz., Murrough O'Brien, Earl of Inchiquin, a man who outdid all his colleagues—the fanatical persecutors of the Catholics—with the single exception of the monster Sir Charles Coote—in implacable enmity towards the religion of his fathers. Even Coote himself did not exceed this degenerate descendant of the great O'Briens in savage cruelty towards the unhappy professors of the proscribed faith, when they fell into his hands.

Truly was Catholic Ireland then passing through the sea of affliction, enveloped in the darkest gloom of the penal days.

Her religion proscribed by law, its professors styled *recusants*, exposed with the poor remains of their possessions to the tender mercies of such men as we have been describing, at the head of infuriate bands of English soldiery.

Prostrate and helpless the whole country seemed to lie before them, terrified into passive obedience, with no sign or symptom of life save the convulsive thrill of agony which ever and anon passed through the tortured frame when some honored head was smitten by the oppressor's sword, or some fresh outrage was perpetrated on the general body. But was this apathy real or only apparent?—was there not, in all the land, one patriot soul to conceive a thought of freedom?—where were the sons of those martyred chiefs who had lost fortune, and lands, and life itself for conscience' sake?—where the O'Neills and O'Donnells, were there none to inherit their wrongs?—where the O'Moores of Leix who in preceding reigns had lost every foot of their princely possessions, and were driven forth as wanderers on the earth?—where the O'Byrnes of Wicklow whose noble spirit of independence, and undisguised hatred of the foreign foe,* had drawn down on them the fiercest vengeance of tyrannic rulers for ages past, so that they were made to endure every evil that malice could invent or power execute?—were they all dead, or slept they in their chains, that no murmer of complaint was heard, nor threat of vengeance? Ah the time for complaints had passed away—they were tried all too long, and had been found only to excite ridicule and contempt. Threats and menaces would have seemed nothing short of madness, for all power was in the hands of the pitiless enemy, and no hope of redress or liberation could quicken the pulse or warm the heart of a nation in which life was almost extinct. No sound, then, was heard from the despised masses of " the mere Irish" to indicate either hope or fear—a sullen silence reigned in all the Catholic provinces—the native tribes and the descendants of the Norman settlers were alike sunk in stolid hopelessness, to judge from what was visible on the surface. What was passing in the

---

* The daring exploits of the famous Wicklow Chief Feagh McHugh O'Byrne " and his hard-riding men" only a generation or so before, are already celebrated in song and story—if not in history.

1*

secret depths, amongst those slumbering masses, it is for us now to show.

Somewhere about the middle of September, in the memorable year of 1641, a party of gentlemen were assembled around a festive board in the back parlor of a house in Bridge street, Dublin. The room was comfortably but plainly furnished, and the black oak table with its pewter plates and dishes and earthen drinking-cups denoted but moderate means on the part of the entertainer, yet there was that about him which savored of a different order of life, and though all his guests—they were four or five in number—were not, in manner at least, of the same high polish as himself, they were all evidently of a class entitled, if not accustomed, to costlier fare and more humble service than that which fell to their lot on the present occasion. They were all habited alike in the gay and not ungraceful costume of the native Irish chieftains, though it required not *truis* or *cochal*, to prove that such they were. Their ages were different, though all might be called young, for the oldest could not have seen forty, while the junior of the party was still in the summer of life. As they quaff their Spanish wine and idly while away in cheerful chit-chat the half-hour after the *viands* were removed, let us tell the reader in confidence who they were. The handsome and high-bred host, with his long and silken hair so smoothly parted on his high white forehead and falling on either side in the most exquisite of *cooluns*, is no other than Roger O'Moore, the disinherited heir of the domains of Leix, although none might trace on his frank, engaging countenance even the faintest shadow of the stormy passions which wrongs like his are apt to foster in the soul. Near him on the right sat a younger man of prepossessing appearance, his manners marked by that careless ease which indicates the consciousness of rank, together with a certain assumption of superiority which might, or might not, give offence according to the dispositions of the company. This was Connor Maguire, Lord Enniskillen, more commonly known then, as since, by the name of Lord Maguire. Next to him sat a personage of more mature years, whose face and form were cast in a rougher mould, while his bushy whiskers and thick short hair of sandy hue gave an air of fierceness to the contour of his head that did not belong to his broad, honest face, which was more indicative of good-nature than anything else. This was Tirlogh O'Neill, brother of the famous Sir Phelim, and as true a clansman as ever trod Tyrone heather. On the opposite side of the table were two other gentlemen, both in the prime of life, one of whom it was easy to distinguish as O'Reilly of Cavan, for his was the tall, thin, yet sinewy frame, the fair and rather delicate features, and the calm dignity of mien which ever characterized that far-descended line of chieftains. The other gentleman was a promising scion of the noble house of McMahon of Monaghan, and he, too, carried about him the most prominent marks of his race—their frank sincerity, their earnestness of purpose, and a shrewdness which eminently fitted them for elbowing their way through life.

The distinctive peculiarities of each were more or less subdued on the present occasion, and the wine appeared to circulate more slowly than might be expected, notwithstanding the frequent challenges of the host.

" Why, gentlemen," said O'Moore at length with sudden vivacity, " I marvel much at your disregard of wine which I have taken some pains to provide of such quality as I thought likely to make you merry at heart. How is it?—are ye thinking to conform to Puritan ways of godliness ?"

" Nay, my very good friend," made answer Lord Maguire, " if it be with others of your guests as it is with me, their thoughts are too big for much speech."

O'Moore's assumed vivacity suddenly vanished, but a glow of satisfaction overspread his features. " You have been thinking, then, friends and noble gentlemen, of the matter concerning which I spoke to you severally as occasion offered heretofore. I trust I see you all in the same mind, resolved to lend what power in you lies to the relief and comfort of our suffering country."

The guests exchanged glances, and a certain embarrassment was visible amongst them. Maguire was the first to break silence. He assured O'Moore that no one felt more keenly than himself the galling yoke of the oppressor, " but," said he, " it would be worse than useless for us to make any show of resistance at the present time, seeing that we have neither arms, ammunition, money, nor anything whatsoever to fit an army for the field."

"It is even so," said McMahon bitterly; "between confiscations, fines and subsidies, and what not, they have left us bare as whipping-posts. We have nothing to start us in the trade of war —all is in their hands!"

"Nothing!" cried O'Neill with ill-concealed impatience; "call you nothing, Costelloe McMahon, the strong arms and stout hearts who follow the standards of our chiefs? Why, man, we could raise an army in a month—ay! and shorter time—fit to sweep the cut-throat Englishers into the sea!"

"Spoken like a true son of the Hy-Nial!" said O'Moore, reaching across Lord Maguire to grasp the rough hand wherewith Tirlogh had made the table quiver to the tune of his fiery speech.

"All well so far as it goes," observed Maguire drily, his dignity being somewhat hurt by his host's momentary forgetfulness of the respect due to his person; "men we have in great plenty, but who will put arms in their hands, and clothes on their backs, and find them wherewithal to live while they fight the country's battles? Would ye send them into the field as droves of sheep without means of offence or defence, to be butchered at will by the fanatic soldiers of the English Parliament?"

"No need of that," replied O'Neill with increasing warmth; "there be iron and wood enough, for small purchase, to make most excellent pikes, which will serve, I opine, till better weapons come within reach, and I tell you, Connor Maguire," he added significantly, "the smiths of Tyrone have not been idle this time back, and moreover I can answer for one chieftain at least——"

"Ay! and who may that be?"

"PHELIM O'NEILL!" said the haughty clansman with stern emphasis, and a contemptuous glance at his neighbor; "he at least is ready when his country calls him to the rescue—he will offer no excuses—I tell you that, Roger O'Moore!—you may reckon on my brother whensoever and howsoever you need his aid in this matter."

Had Maguire been as hot-blooded as O'Neill it might have given their host some trouble to prevent a quarrel, but happily the chieftain of Fermanagh was not of such choleric temperament, and with a somewhat higher degree of polish had a certain amount of caution which enabled him to control his feelings when he deemed it expedient.

The other guests were visibly alarmed for the effect of O'Neill's taunt, and O'Moore was about to interpose with his most winning smile, but Maguire set them all at rest by saying in a good humored way :

"I call ye all to witness that Tirlogh here took me up over quickly. If I did express some doubts concerning our present state of readiness, I had no thoughts of dallying behind when others were of a mind to go forward. Right glad am I to hear that my good friend of Tyr-owen is pushing matters on. Heaven knows there be no time for delay—but for me I do hope to see some other thing besides pikes in the hands of our men when they come to blows with an enemy so well armed and otherwise fitted out for war."

"You are in the right, my good lord," said O'Moore, glancing with evident relief at the restored good humor visible on Tirlogh's broad face; "much caution is needful in a matter of so great import, but the provision of all things requisite for the maintenance of warfare has been well considered before now. There be those of our friends beyond seas in divers countries, as ye all know, who have much skill in these matters, and they wait but the signal to be with us with good store of all things needful which, through God's mercy and the royal charity of Catholic princes, they have in speedy expectation."

"*Lamh dearg aboo !*" shouted he of Tyr-owen, jumping to his feet with a suddenness that made the others start, "I knew it, Rory !—I knew *they* wouldn't fail us !"

"It is even so, Tirlogh," replied his host smiling at the other's *capricole*, "the Red Hand is working for us even now—not only amongst the hills of Tyr-owen, but in the courts of Europe and in the councils of kings."

"**Tyrone*** will be a host in himself," observed O'Rielly, who had

---

* The Tyrone here alluded to was the son of the great Hugh O'Neill. He was the friend and counsellor of Roger O'Moore in his bold not as yet taken part in the conversation; "his father's great deeds are in all men's minds, and his name will be enough of itself to stir up the northern clans."

"OWEN ROE is worth a dozen of him!" said the rough-spoken Tirlogh; "fighting is no novelty to Owen—he's well used to it, and can teach us all we want to know!—Lamh dearg aboo!—there's not a man of the O'Neills but will follow Owen Roe!"

"You forget Sir Phelim, Tirlogh!" said Costelloe McMahon with a meaning smile; "he has been so long now the first man in Tyr-owen that I fear me much he will not take bidding even from the hero of Arras or the belted Earl himself!"

"Oh! *that's* another story," said O'Neill somewhat more coolly; "there's no need for him to take bidding—they can pull together—and they will too, please God on high!"

"Never was more need," said O'Moore, fixing his thoughtful eye on each of his guests in turn, "there be news now to set us on if we ever mean to do anything!"

Maguire's anxious interrogatory was seconded by the startled look of the others. "What worse news can there be than those which daily come to our ears? Thank Heaven! matters cannot be worse with us than they are!"

"They *can* be worse, my lord, and they *will*, if we do not something before long. Have ye heard of this letter lately intercepted?"

"What letter?"

"Why, one from Scotland to a *planter* in the north, one Freeman by name, apprising him that the Scotch covenanting army is coming over anon in full strength to massacre every Papist in this unhappy country."

"It is true, then, what Parsons said at the banquet,"* said Maguire with a quivering lip, "not content with taking all our substance, they must needs take our lives, too. Truly they treat us as wolves——"

attempt to free the country. Their connection was formed abroad, O'Neill being in exile.

* A little before this Sir Wm. Parsons had declared at a public entertainment that the Irish Papists should and would be exterminated.

" Yet we submit as lambs to their bloody oppression," said O'Moore eagerly; "let us but turn on them with the strength that God gave us, and you shall see them wither as grass before our righteous anger!—make but a gallant show—rise in union and in strength—stand before them as men resolved—and they will not dare to smite ye! The first news of our rising will bring over supplies of all we want from the friendly courts of Europe —our exiled countrymen will rush to aid us with the skill they have gained in foreign wars, and before many months go by, if we but keep together as we ought, we may hunt from our shores the ferocious beasts who fatten on our spoils and on our blood, stand as free men on the soil that is ours by right, and worship God after the manner of our fathers in the way we deem safe for our soul's weal!—what say ye, friends and gentlemen? Chief- tains of the north! shall we still lie motionless under the enemy's armed heel, and suffer him to sweep our race from the face of God's earth without striking even one blow for freedom or re- venge? Which one of us is there whose father they have not robbed—ay, and *murdered!*"—his deep, impassioned voice sank to a thrilling whisper as he spoke the hideous word, and whether by accident or design he turned his eloquent eyes full on McMa- hon, whose immediate ancestor, McMahon of Dartrey, had ac- tually been hung in front of his own door* in the stormy days, yet fresh in all men's minds, when Hugh O'Neill was waging his heroic but unequal war against the giant power of Elizabeth.

McMahon rose, and with flushed cheek and flashing eye gave his hand to O'Moore : " Such aid as I can give, Rory, you shall have— the cause is just, and the God of justice will bless our arms—we were no men, either you or I, could we forget Dartrey or Mullaghmast.†

---

* Could Philip O'Reilly have looked into the future but a few years, he would have seen a venerable chieftain of his own race hanging from a tree, within sight of his own castle windows, during the bloody Cromwellian period. These horrible tragedies are, and will ever be, traditional in Ulster.

† Every reader of Irish history is familiar with the story of the treacherous murder of the O'Moores at the Rath of Mullaghmast. It is one of the blackest pages in the annals of British rule in Ireland.

When the banner of our country is again unfurled, the men of
Uriel will be found in the right place and at the fitting time.
O'Reilly, what say you?"

"I say this, Costelloe McMahon, that there beats not in Irish
bosoms hearts more true than those of Breffny-O'Reilly. Let the
clans of Ulster once raise the war-shout and the Red Hand
point the way, the O'Reillys will not be hindmost, take my
word!"

"Uriel and Breffny for ever!" shouted Tirlogh O'Neill; "I told
you the truth was in them, Rory O'Moore!—now for Fermanagh!"
and he turned his fierce eyes on Maguire, who appeared to take
the matter rather coolly for his liking.

"Fermanagh is not an ass, to be driven at will," said Maguire
haughtily and coldly. "If Roger O'Moore, or any other man,
can show me any fair prospect of success, I am ready to join a
cause which I know is just and righteous, but as yet, I have
heard or seen nothing to change my opinion, namely, that as
things stand now with us of the old faith it would be madness
to make a show of fight. Idle boasting will do nothing, Roger
O'Moore!"

O'Neill's hand was on his *skene* in an instant, and the other
gentlemen, although habitually more self-possessed, could not
conceal their surprise. O'Moore laid his hand on O'Neill's arm,
and admonished him by a gentle pressure to listen patiently.

"Nay, Tirlogh," said Maguire with a calm smile, "if others'
feathers were but as easily ruffled as yours, you should have hot
work of it, let me tell you! By what I said, I meant no offence
to any gentleman of this good company. What I want, Rory
O'Moore, is this: Before we take any rash step in a matter which
concerns all men of Irish blood, or professing the Catholic faith,
let us see what the lords and gentlemen of that religion in other
parts of the country have a mind to do. The chain is as heavy on
them as it is on us—they have as many wrongs as we to rouse
their ire—of a surety, then, they will lend a hand—let us do
nothing till we acquaint them and make an agreement with them
as to what share of the work they will take!"

"Your lordship must surely forget," said O'Moore, his hand
still resting lightly on the arm of his refractory neighbor, "what

I told you a few days since when I saw you at your lodgings, to wit, that I have journeyed much of late through several parts of the Irish country, and have talked the matter over with many of the first men as to name and standing—they are all well affected towards this thing, as far as I could see, and, with God's blessing, are determined to join us. There is not a man of the ancient race, I do think, in Ulster, Connaught, or Munster that will not rise at the first news of an attack on the government forces. Nay more, my good Lord, there be those of English blood—ay! within the borders of the Pale itself, who are only waiting for us to strike a blow in defence of religion, when they will join us heart and soul!"

"Well, there is some encouragement in that," said Maguire, "especially as regards the Connaught and Munster tribes—as for the Palesmen, it will go hard with them when they strike a blow on the same side with us Irishry, as they choose to style us. However, Roger, I will not be the man to stand by and see others fighting my battle—it would ill become one of my name—so, in due time—nay, nay, no fierce looks, Tirlogh O'Neill!—I say in due time—that is, when fitting preparation be made here at home and our countrymen abroad are in the way of joining us with their well-tried swords—then, I and mine will not be found wanting!" He had spoken all along with a sort of nervous trepidation, that was but too visible, but as he reached the close, his voice gathered strength and firmness, and he spoke the last words in a tone as firm as even O'Moore himself could wish, though he relished not the qualified consent which ought to have come, he thought, without reserve or exception.

But O'Neill in his thoughtless, headlong generosity felt none of this, and he was the first to grasp the young nobleman's hand, which the others all did in their turn.

"Nobly said, Connor Maguire," said the warm-hearted son of the O'Neills, and his voice quivered with emotion; "I shamed to see the Chieftain of Fermanagh throwing cold water on so good a cause. Now you speak like a Maguire!—Let's have a bumper, most sage Rory, to drink Maguire's health!"

"And success to the cause in which we are all embarked!"

the host added, as the brimming tankards gleamed aloft in every hand.

There was a momentary pause, during which one looked at the other, and all, as if by a common impulse, turned their eyes on Maguire. That chieftain saw the doubt, and a smile of cheering import lit his manly features. He was the first to raise the goblet to his lips, and he drained it to the patriotic toast, as given. The others followed his example, and O'Moore felt that something had been done—the representatives of four powerful houses stood pledged to the common weal when they parted that evening.

CHAPTER II.

" In vain did oppression endeavor
      To trample that green under foot ;
  The fair stem was broken, but never
      Could tyranny reach to its root.
  Then come, and around it let's rally,
      And guard it henceforward like men ;
  Oh ! soon shall each mountain and valley
      Grow bright with its verdure again.
  Meanwhile, fill each glass to the brim, boys,
      With water, with wine, or potheen,
  And on each let the honest wish swim, boys,
      Long flourish the Gael and the Green !"

M. J. BARRY.

EIGHT or ten days after the dinner party at O'Moore's lodgings
two gentlemen stood together at a window in an old weather-
beaten castle amongst the heath-clad hills of Tyrone. The scene
without was wild and rugged, bare, bleak hills of every variety of
shape stretching far and away, with brown moors and patches of
stubble-fields here and there between. Few traces of human habitation were at first sight visible, but a closer examination
showed the district thickly inhabited. The hill-sides and the
valleys, the moors and the meadow-lands were all dotted with
cabins and cottages, whose time-darkened clay walls were brown
as the withered herbage or the arid soil around them. Even
while the eye endeavored to distinguish these hut-like dwellings
from amid the drear monotony of the scene, smoke began to ascend in many a spiral column from every imaginable point, giving
life and animation, if not grace or beauty, to the scene. But it
was not the brown autumnal hills, or the smoke from cottage-
fire giving note of the evening meal, that arrested the wandering

gaze or occupied the minds of the two individuals who stood in
earnest conversation at a window of the great hall in yon gray
old keep, whose solitary tower, surrounded by high, strong walls
of rough stone, looms dark and menacing over the adjacent moor-
lands. Both were in the prime of life, and their sinewy proportions showed to full advantage in the close-fitting *truis*, and what
we would call *jacket*, of the Irish chiefs of that and former ages,
as they stood in the flickering, glaring light of a bog-wood fire
blazing and crackling behind them in the wide, open chimney of
the hall. The short cloak or *cochal* which invariably completed
the costume, hung more gracefully from the shoulders of one,
while the broad chest and stalwart form of the other would have
furnished a model for one of the Athletes of old. His voice, when
he spoke, too, was rough and strong, with something imperious
in its tone; while that of his companion was soft and well-modu-
lated, as one who had lived long in cities, it might be in courts.
They talked in characteristic fashion of the great scheme then
in agitation for the country's weal, and he of the courtly mien
was urging on his not very patient auditor certain reasons which
he himself deemed conclusive for a speedy and general demonstration of strength. Surely we have heard those mellifluous
accents before, and as surely it is Roger O'Moore that speaks.
His companion is a stranger to us, but we all at once remember
having lately seen a face like his and a burly form of just such
muscular proportions. Putting one thing with another, the Tyrone fortress, the authoritative tone of this stalwart chieftain, and
the eagerness wherewith the astute Leinsterman labors to convince him, we venture on a shrewd surmise, eventually found
correct. With a start we recognize Sir Phelim O'Neill, at that
period the chief man of his race in Ulster, and the old gray fortalice under whose smoky rafters he appears before us is, then, no
other than Kinnard Castle, made memorable to all aftertimes by
the valorous exploits of its martial lord.

O'Moore had been watching through the misty light from
without, the lowering brow of the northern chieftain and the
fiery glances which shot at intervals from his half-closed eyes.

"I say they count on our forbearance, Sir Phelim—or mayhap
they name it cowardliness. Those men of blood and rapine have

doubtless made up their minds that our lives and what holdings we still have are theirs when they list to seize them, and that the spirit of our fathers is squeezed out of us by the load of misery they have put upon us—they have done what men could to cool our blood by keeping us on low living and divers other expedients——"

Sir Phelim interrupted him with a grim smile. "They may find it too hot for their liking, an' they wait a little. But name them not, Rory—I confess to a want of patience, at all times, but the black villany of these canting knaves is something I cannot even think of without feeling for my skene. By our hopes of happiness hereafter, Rory O'Moore, I would barter my chance of that earldom of Tyrone of which you spoke but now, ay! and the broad lands that called the great Hugh master, could I but see the green flag waving from Dublin Castle, and Parsons and Borlase swinging from the battlements! Before God, I would this very night!"

"I doubt it not, my friend," said O'Moore, with undisguised satisfaction, "but, now that you mention that accursed Castle, I must tell you a thing which has come into my mind concerning it. Come a little farther this way—I see your people are making ready for the evening repast."

"Pooh, man, heed them not—the Sassenach tongue is a dead one to them—so should it be to us all—and as for treachery—did they catch the meaning of our words—there be no such poisonous weed amongst our heather. Still, an' it please you better, let us move somewhat farther from the gillies'* lugs."

O'Moore then unfolded to his astonished host, in as few words as might be, a plan which had been projected by himself and others yet to be named for the seizure of Dublin Castle with its stores of arms and ammunition, as the first grand move in their military tactics. He was proceeding to enlarge in his clear and lucid style on the incalculable advantages likely to follow this bold stroke, if successfully carried out, but O'Neill broke in very curtly with——

* Gillie was the Celtic word equivalent to our *follower* or *attendant.* Hence the prefix *Gill* or *Gilla* to some of the old names, such as *Gilpatrick, Gil-macuddy,* &c.

"What!—take the Castle!—without men or reasonable arms!
—why, before Heaven, man, I think your wits are failing you!"

"It may be so," replied O'Moore with a quiet smile, "though
before I leave you I may prove myself sane enough. But, I pray
you tell me what you mean by *reasonable* arms?—what manner
of arms be they?"

"Nay, Roger O'Moore," cried the fiery northman, "this, I take
it, is no laughing matter; you know well that by reasonable arms
I mean arms of sufficient quality and in sufficient numbers,
which, if so be you had, where are the men and the leaders to
carry out such a measure? Sdeath, man, where be all these?"

"If you will but hear me, Sir Phelim, I will make this matter
plain to your comprehension. You have heard, doubtless, of certain instructions lately sent over by the king's majesty concerning
forces to be raised here for the Spanish and other continental
services——"

"Yea, surely I have heard the thing spoken of, but what is
that to us, or rather will it not be hurtful to us in this matter to
have our best men sent abroad, if it so happen that we need
them here at home?"

"Ay, but suppose,"—he lowered his voice almost to a whisper
and drew still nearer his companion—"suppose, Sir Phelim, these
regiments—drilled and trained by royal permission—might lend
us their good swords and muskets—ay! and their stout arms to
boot—what think you of that, son of the Hy-Nial?"

At this hint Sir Phelim's countenance brightened up, and he
turned eagerly towards O'Moore: "What! do you mean to
say——"

"I mean to say, O'Neill, that the colonels of several of those
regiments—two or three I can answer for—have another end in
view besides that of aiding the King of Spain; think you, my
good friend, that *our* cause is not nearer and dearer to Colonel
Hugh O'Byrne—for to such command is he named—than any
other in the wide world?——"

"He were no man, Rory, an' he were not so affected towards
us!" and honest Phelim rubbed his hands right gleefully.

"Well! there be others of the officers of rank in that service
no less willing to join us than Hugh O'Byrne. There be Plun-

ketts and Dillons there, too, Sir Phelim!—men with Catholic
hearts though of English blood!"

"I have no faith in them," said the blunt Ulsterman, with a
doubtful shake of the head.

"Nay, I tell you, Sir Phelim! there are good men and honest
men among them—ay! and some who have suffered long and
much for the ancient faith—they are branded by the penal laws
as well as we—why should they not join us in rending asunder
a chain which binds us all alike?"

"Well, well, Rory, I believe you know best; I will take your
word for the good faith of these Norman churls——"

"How, Sir Phelim! you forget, surely, that some of these lords
and gentlemen are my friends and kinsmen!—Norman churls! I
like not the phrase."*

"Ha! ha!" laughed O'Neill, "I did not think to see such a
frown on Rory O'Moore's smooth forehead—an' it were me, now,
none might wonder; but you, Rory!—for shame, man! clear
your brow, and keep your temper, I advise you, in Kinnard
Castle, or your Norman friends and kinsmen, as you call them
may fight the battle on their own account!"

O'Moore, by this time sensible of his error, and partly ashamed
of a display of petulance very unusual with him, applied himself to
soothe the chafed Ulsterman, and with that end asked him if his
brother had mentioned to him a certain matter appertaining to
the dispositions of a powerful nobleman in the Western province.

"Something of the kind he said you hinted to him and the
other gentlemen at your lodgings, but darkly and in a way they
could make nothing of——"

"I told them further," said O'Moore, "that I was kept from
naming that lord by a promise of secrecy which he needs would
have of me; still, as you now seem to doubt the good dispositions of
the Catholics of English blood, and as it behoves us to put the Red
Hand in motion at any cost—for without its aid our cause were
hopeless—I will tell you, on condition that you tell no man with-

* It is agreed by historians of all parties that Roger O'Moore was
connected both by kindred and affinity with many of the first houses
of the English Pale.

out my consent—that this nobleman is no other than the Lord
Mayo, whose power, and authority, and good credit amongst all
men you know as well as I!" This speech was a master-stroke
of dexterity, and told well on more accounts than one.

"Did Miles Burke give you his word that he will join us in
this matter?"

O'Neill fixed his fiery eyes on the Leinsterman as though he
would read him through.

"So help me Heaven and our dear Lady, he promised in all
sincerity to do his utmost in our behalf, when once our standard
is on the wind!"

Every trace of displeasure, not to say suspicion, vanished at
once from Sir Phelim's open countenance, and grasping his guest
by the right hand he gave it a hearty squeeze as he led him to
the dais at the head of the table where Lady O'Neill, with one or
two female friends, already awaited them. "Take your seat,
man, and forgive my rough speech! Nora!" to his wife, "you
know Roger O'Moore before now—the greatest man of his name,
I take him to be!"

O'Moore smiled and bowed with the graceful suavity peculiar
to himself. Some other gentlemen of the O'Neills entered and
took their seats, and the meal began with a clatter of knives and
plates and dishes which boded no good to the substantial viands
on the board.

The repast was not yet over when a bustle in the court without attracted the attention of those within, and before Sir Phelim's inquiry as to the cause of the tumult had time to be
answered, the door at the lower extremity of the hall was thrown
open, giving admission to an elderly man of portly mien, who
walked up the hall to where the hostess sat, with the smiling air
of a man who feels himself at home, every one present rising to
greet him as he passed with some word of joyous welcome.
O'Moore, though he rose with the others, was at first somewhat
puzzled, but his surprise was at an end when Sir Phelim presented the new-comer as

"Bishop McMahon of Clogher!"

"What! HEBER MCMAHON!" cried O'Moore joyfully.

"The same, good sir," said the patriotic prelate, with a good-humored smile, as his quick eye ran over the face and figure of O'Moore.

"Then I am better pleased to meet you, my lord of Clogher, than if you were the Pope of Rome, to whom be all reverence! The name of Heber McMahon is as a trumpet-note heralding victory!"

"I joy to hear it, Mr. O'Moore," returned the Bishop, "for in sooth my heart is on fire at the present hour with hopes and wishes for speedy action on behalf of our oppressed people, and far in the solitude of my poor dwelling my ears have been gladdened of late by the tales of Roger O'Moore's heroic efforts to rouse the chief men of the nation from their fatal lethargy! Heaven bless you, my son! you are worthy of your noble race!" And the layman and the bishop, then meeting for the first time, clasped each other's hand with the fervor of old friends for long years parted.

Lady O'Neill, being in poor health at the time, so far from taking any interest in the contemplated movement, shrank with nervous apprehension from the possibility of a rising which her dread of the English made her regard as likely to draw down swift and sure destruction on all concerned. She was a pious and devoted Catholic, and felt, in common with all others, the crying injustice wherewith those of the ancient faith were treated year after year by every successive ruler, still she feared that any attempt to throw off the cruel shackles which bound the people would only increase the general misery, and, sure to end in defeat, make matters worse instead of better. She had seen, for months before, all manner of secret meetings and consultations going on within the precincts of her dwelling, and well knowing that her husband had more ambition than prudence, and was naturally fond of excitement, she feared his being drawn into the assumption of a responsibility which would be sure to make him a prominent mark for that judicial vengeance which never spared any one. In the beginning she had remonstrated warmly with her husband against the making a general *rendezvous* of Kinnard Castle, urging him if those meetings *were* to be held, to arrange it so that some of the other chiefs and nobles of the province should have them occasionally at their several houses in

2ᴀ

order to avoid fixing suspicion on him.* But Sir Phelim was
little in the habit of taking counsel of women, so he only laughed
at his wife's fears, and, at length, cut her short with an order to
mind her own business, nor dare for the future to meddle in his.
The lady knowing by long experience that further interference
on her part would do no manner of good, contented herself ever
after with showing a cold countenance to the gentlemen who frequented the Castle on this, to her, obnoxious business. She had
no difficulty in distinguishing them, for they were all, without exception, heads of the old Irish families, men who had severally
and separately long accounts of insult, and outrage, and robbery
to settle with the government. In her heart the Lady Nora sympathized with these injured chieftains, for she herself was of the
old blood, but still, as I have said, she abhorred the idea of open
insurrection, dreading its results, and so it was that her cheek
paled and her rounded form wasted day by day under the pressure of fears which were necessarily pent up within her own
bosom. She had personally a great respect for Roger O'Moore
and a still greater for Heber McMahon's high office, yet it was
not without alarm that she saw them together at her board, for
the part they were both acting in the way of stirring up the
chiefs was well known to her. It was with difficulty that she
could show even ordinary civility to her husband's guests, notwithstanding the not very gentle hints from time to time thrown
at her by Sir Phelim, and the still more powerful influence of
O'Moore's polished manners. On the plea of indisposition she
left the table early with her companions, having first ascertained
from the bishop his intention of saying Mass next morning.

" But where, my lord?—surely not here—not in the castle ?"

" Assuredly no, my daughter,—if you are afraid of running
such risk !"

* That this advice was a wise and salutary one, we see from the
fact that in the famous letter of Sir Wm. Cole, governor of Enniskillen,
to the Lords Justices, apprising them of some unusual stir amongst the
Ulster chiefs, he founds his opinion on the number of visitors going
and coming, as he heard, all summer, to and from Sir Phelim O'Neill's
house at Kinnard.

" In the Castle-chapel, my lord !" interrupted Sir Phelim, with a wrathful glance at his wife, of whose timidity he was heartily ashamed. " With God's help, we will soon have Mass when and where we wish."

" But that time is not come, Phelim !" pleaded Nora ; " oh ! bethink you ere it be too late. Think of the danger to the bishop—yourself—all of us !"

" Woman ! hie you to your chamber !" cried Sir Phelim, starting to his feet, " not another word, now—begone ! I say !—too long have we worshipped in caves and huts through slavish fear—from this day out, Mass shall be duly said here in the castle—that is," he added bitterly, " when we can get priests to minister to us —let me see who shall intrude on our sacred rites !"

Although Sir Phelim spoke in English, the substance of what he said seemed well understood by all present, for as Lady O'Neill retired sad and sorrowful, she heard from all parts of the spacious hall, from retainers as well as guests, one long continued burst of applause.

" But on second thoughts," said Sir Phelim, turning to the bishop, " it may be that I go too far in this matter without authority. Will you have any fears, my lord ?"

" Fears !" cried the prelate contemptuously, " fears to say Mass in Kinnard Castle, protected by the chief of Tyr-Owen ! Were I sure of death I would not shrink,—it were worth a hundred lives such as mine to see one such step taken in advance,—and by Sir Phelim O'Neill ! I would I were within sight of Parson's ill-favored countenance and the news reach him at the council-board that Mass was said on a certain day in Kinnard Castle by one Heber McMahon, a titular popish bishop ! ha ! ha !" The bishop's derisive laugh was echoed from all parts of the hall, and then the host called for a general bumper to the discomfiture of all tyrants and oppressors.

" I pledge you in *Spanish wine*," said O'Moore pointedly.

" Not so, Rory, not so," quickly rejoined his host, " our own usquebaugh and no other—foreign wines are good in their way, but at a time like this, my friend, I say the *native whiskey* warms the heart—ay ! and nerves the arm !"

O'Moore gracefully assented, saying as he filled his goblet from

the steaming bowl: " I believe you are in the right, our worthy
host, in more senses than one—strength and power are from *within*
the nation, whatsoever may come from *without*."

Here the bishop excused himself from farther potations as the
evening was wearing late, and soon after withdrew to his appointed sleeping place, preceded by a tall henchman of the clan
O'Neill, bearing an oil-lamp in which a rush-light glimmered
by way of wick. It was never willingly that Rory O'Moore lingered long over the punch-bowl or the wine-cup, but on that occasion he found it no easy matter to escape the determined attack
of Sir Phelim on his temperate habits. Fearing to exasperate the
choleric chieftain by an obstinate refusal to continue the carouse,
he sat much longer than was his wont, and at last succeeded only
in effecting a timely retreat by the aid of a violent headache,
which, indeed, was partly real, owing to the share he had been
compelled to take in the fiery libations so plentifully "poured" by
O'Neill, to the cause of freedom and justice. With a very contemptuous expression of pity, Sir Phelim returned his guest's
courteous salutation, while O'Moore, as he, in turn, marched to
his chamber after a stately follower of the O'Neill's, pathetically
murmured to himself :

" Phelim O'Neill!—honest Phelim O'Neill! your drink is good,
and your heart better, but I would your hospitality were less
urgent."

Next day was Sunday, and hours before the lingering dawn,
the bishop's man was in the chapel, preparing all things for the
celebration of the divine mysteries. The gloom of the place was
broken, not dispelled, by the fitful glare of a pine-torch standing
in an earthen socket close by the temporary altar,* making the
damp walls and the rafters of black oak dimly visible. The cold
autumn wind whistled dolefully around the narrow windows,
which were, indeed, loop-holes filled up with thin sheets of horn,
through which even the day-beam made its way but faintly.
There was a ghostly look about the place, and the wailing of the

---

* An altar could not then have existed as a fixture in any building,
public or private. It would have been as much as any nobleman or
gentleman's life was worth to have such a thing on his premises.

wind was like the voices of perturbed spirits. It is probable that Malachy McMahon would have shrunk from braving the loneliness of the place and the hour had he been without a companion, but he had taken the precaution of securing over-night the valuable company of Shamus Beg, no less a person than the foster-brother of Sir Phelim. This individual, fully conscious of the dignity arising from his intimate connection with so great a chief —the greatest, *he* thought, in the whole island—gave himself little trouble to assist Malachy, deeming his presence there quite a sufficient stretch of condescension. So he lay at full length in luxurious ease on a bench near the scene of Malachy's labors, with the flickering light of the torch shining on his well-formed though somewhat stolid features. He evidently listened with much relish to Malachy's oracular discourse, as that grave and half-clerical functionary suspended operations now and then to deliver himself of an opinion. From his long attendance on priests, dating, in fact, from his very boyhood, Malachy had acquired a certain gravity of demeanor amounting at times to a solemnity that was somewhat ludicrous. His claims to superior wisdom were, however, cheerfully admitted by all the Clan McMahon, amongst whom he was known by the *soubriquet* of Malachy na Soggarth, or Malachy of the Priests, and the stoutest McMahon in Farney, the boldest McKenna in Truagh would not raise a finger for the king's crown against that privileged individual. Malachy always knew, or appeared to know, more than any of his fellows, and amongst the simple clansmen with whom he lived his *dictum* on any subject was almost as much respected as though he had drank from the mystic fountains of knowledge in the halls of Louvain or Salamanca. It was natural that at such a time, when all men's minds were filled with portentous thoughts of coming events, the confidential servant of a bishop, a man so gifted withal as Malachy, should be in much request amongst the lower orders of the Catholics as an expounder of things past, present, and to come.

"As sure as you're a living man, Shamus O'Hagan," said Malachy, stopping for the twentieth time or so in front of his companion, "as sure as you're a living man, we'll have a hard fight for it, if God is pleased to give us a victory over them thieving foreigners. You see they have the whole power of England at their back, and what's more, they have their general, the black devil below, to fight for them, Christ save us! for sure wasn't it him that put it in their hearts and in their heads to harass, and plunder, and slaughter poor creatures as they're doing ever since the time of old Harry."

"Never mind, Malachy," said Shamus, half raising himself from his recumbent posture, "we'll pay them back for it some of these days. When Sir Phelim and the rest of the chiefs once get at them—as they will soon, please God on high!—they'll settle them for ever and a day—I'll go bail it's little hurt or harm they'll do, the murdering villains, when once we're done with them."

To this Malachy shook his head doubtingly : "We couldn't do it, Shamus, we couldn't do it—it's a thing impossible, any way you take it, unless the Sassenachs of the Pale would stand to us—as they ought—for to be sure they're of the same religion as ourselves, and for that reason they don't know the day nor the hour they'll be stripped of lands and livings as we are ourselves, glory be to God!—if they'd only come out like men and fight for their country and their God, we mightn't care what day we'd hoist the green flag, as I've heard the bishop say many a time. But sure I'm afeard, and so is the bishop, that *that's* what the Sassenachs will never do—as long as they can live shut up in their big stone castles, and hear Mass of an odd time down in a vault, or any place out of sight and hearing of the bloody Englishers and Scotchmen from beyond seas, they don't care a straw if all the Irishry in the country, man, woman and child, were roasted alive or turned out to starve on the wide world, as thousands of them are every year, and them the flower of the old blood, more's the pity!—no, no, Shamus, if ever you see us gaining any of our rights, it'll be with good help from France and Spain—and sure the ancient prophecies tell us that plainly."

"Ah, then, do they, Malachy?" asked Shamus with renewed interest, and he quickly raised himself to a sitting posture.

"Indeed they do, Shamus—they make it as clear as the sun at mid-day, that when Ireland rises to her feet again, and the race of Heber and Heremon gets back their own it will be with help from the King of France and the King of Spain—and the Pope himself, Shamus!" he added by way of climax.

" See that now !"

" Ay, and there's great mention made, too, of the Irishmen in foreign countries—heroes of great fame, and strength, and courage, like the mighty men of old, Fin MacCool, and Ossian——"

" And Hugh of Tyr-Owen," suggested the clansman of O'Neill. " If he could only come himself with his warriors, now, from the cave of Aileach where they're enchanted*—and who knows, Malachy—who knows but he may ? Isn't it prophesied that he's to rise and head the men of Ireland when the country's at a great pinch ?——"

It was evident that Malachy had not much faith in the great Earl's timely re-appearance, for he cut the other's rhapsody short with——

" There's a man in this very house, now, that'll be at the head and foot of everything."

" Oh, to be sure—you mean Sir Phelim !"

" No, I don't—Sir Phelim will be a great help, I know—but the man I mean is Rory O'Moore !"

A dissenting grunt and a surly shake testified the foster-brother's disapproval, but what he might have said was prevented for that time by the entrance of the bishop, whereupon Shamus betook himself to the vast dormitory allotted to the retainers and male domestics of the house, to apprise his fellows that the hour of Mass was at hand.

---

* The peasantry in the northern parts of Ulster cherish as fondly tho belief of Hugh O'Neill's being enchanted with his warriors under tho hill of Aileach as tho people of South Munster do the continued presence amongst them, in a similar state of enchantment, of *their* great champion, *Garret Earla*, as they familiarly style Gerald, the last Earl of Desmond.

CHAPTER III.

" Joy, joy, the day is come at last, the day of hope and pride—
And see! our crackling bonfires light old Bann's joyful tile,
And gladsome bell, and bugle-horn from Newry's captured tow'rs
Hark! how they tell the Saxon swine, this land is ours, is OURS!

*   *   *   *   *   *   *   *   *

" They bann'd our faith, they bann'd our lives, they trod us into earth,
Until our very patience stirr'd their bitter hearts to mirth ;
Even this great flame that wraps them now, not *we* but *they* have bred,
Yes, this is their own work, and now, THEIR WORK BE ON THEIR HEAD.

*   *   *   *   *   *   *   *   *

" Down from the sacred hills whereon a SAINT* communed with God,
Up from the vale where Bagnal's blood manured the reeking sod,
Out from the stately woods of Truagh, McKenna's plunder'd home,
Like Malin's waves, as fierce and fast, our faithful clansmen come."

C. G. DUFFY's *Muster of the North.*

IT were tedious to describe the several meetings that took place
during the next two weeks amongst the native lords and gentry
of the northern province. The newly-awakened thirst for freedom increased from day to day, and quickly spreading from the
chieftains to their friends and followers, infused life and vigor
and swelling hope into hearts long plunged in the torpor of
despair. Before O'Moore quitted the confines of Ulster to return
to his post in Dublin, he had contrived to visit all the principal
chiefs at their widely-scattered dwellings, and on more than one
occasion had the satisfaction of bringing them together to concert
measures for the grand and simultaneous effort to be forthwith
made throughout the province. He had seen the fiery spirit of

---

* St. Patrick, whose favorite retreat was Lecale, in the county
Down.

Phelim O'Neill and his brother Tirlogh applied to the work of sober and earnest deliberation, in concert with the calmer O'Reilly and the haughty Maguire, and the bold, high-spirited McMahon. Nay, so vast and so potent was the spell of that auspicious hour, that even those who had been bitter enemies for years before, then met in peace to deliberate on the means of righting their common wrongs, and extended to each other the hand of fellowship across the council-board. O'Moore's influence was all-powerful amongst them, and lay at the bottom of their league, although none of them was made to feel it. They had all in turn felt the force of his persuasive eloquence, and bowed to the wisdom of his suggestions, but not one amongst them would have acknowledged his superiority. This the sagacious Leinsterman well knew, and his enlightened patriotism being happily proof against that puerile vanity which makes men desirous of public homage, he was quite willing to let O'Neill and Maguire and the other Ulster chiefs have all the merit of the work—provided it was done, he cared not who did, or appeared to do it. Yet somehow, by a sort of poetical justice that must have been purely instinctive, the share he had in the great movement was both understood and appreciated by the people who, as often happens, were more enthusiastic in the cause than most of those who undertook to be their leaders. No sooner did the glad tidings of life and hope extend to any locality, no matter how remote, than the name of *Rory O'Moore* was whispered at the same time as the great magician beneath whose wand the slumbering masses were to start into life endued with sudden power. The short glimpses which the people had of his handsome and graceful person during his flying visits to their chiefs, the little they had heard him speak, his extreme devotion to the national cause, the mystery which enveloped his comings and goings, the high repute in which he was held, and though last, not least, the well-known misfortunes of his ruined house, all conspired to inflame the minds of a lively imaginative people with a romantic interest in whatever concerned him: by common consent he was made the hero of the stupendous drama then in preparation, and his name became the watchword of freedom amongst the clans.

Even when O'Moore went back to Dublin, which he knew

2*

must necessarily be made the centre of operations, the charm
of his presence lingered amongst the clansmen of the north, and
when at length they came together armed and determined for
the struggle, and planting their feet on their native soil vowed
that it should be theirs and their children's, as of old it was their
fathers', the name of the Leinster chief mingled with the war-
cries of their respective leaders, and was heard above the din
of many a battle-field where Irish arms prevailed—

> " On the green hills of Ulster the whi'o cross waves high,
> And the beacon of war flames each night to the sky—
> The taunt and the sneer let the coward endure,
> Our trust is in God, and in Rory O'Moore."

Weeks and weeks did the chiefs and people of Ulster await
some symptom of co-operation, or even word of encouragement
from their equally oppressed brethren of the South and West
—from the East they had no hope of sympathy or succor, for
there lay the English Pale with its sluggish Norman lords and its
well-trained bands of stalwart yeomen, more ready ever to do
battle for the autocrats of Dublin Castle, because they were English, than for their fellow-sufferers in the cause of religion,
because they had Irish blood in their veins. But except the
few Leinster Catholics whom O'Moore succeeded in animating with
a portion of his own spirit, the tribes of three provinces either
were or appeared to be buried in the dullest apathy. Whether
this was real or apparent, it disheartened the patriots of Ulster,
but could not deter them from making an attempt to which they
had braced up every nerve, and made what preparation their
poverty allowed. O'Moore, well-knowing the effect which the
rising of the northern province would have on the other native
tribes, and fearing the tepidity that might grow out of procrastination, sent trusty messengers to Sir Phelim O'Neill, urging him
to fulfil his part of their engagement, viz., the taking of London-
derry and some other northern strongholds, and to effect a general rising of all the Ulster clans, on an appointed day. Sir
Phelim, once into the affair, was, to do him justice, nothing loath
to help it on by every means in his power, so that the work of
preparation went bravely forward wherever his influence reached;

and where his could *not* reach, other chieftains took it up, and
sped it on, and all worked together for a happy completion of
the herculean task which of hard necessity they undertook. The
twenty-third day of October was fixed on for striking a grand
and simultaneous blow in the cause of civil and religious freedom,
and the very appointment of the day gave a new and strong
impetus to the movement.

Secrecy was, of course, observed as far as might be, yet such
preparations could not be made without coming in some way
under the observation of keen eyes all through the province,
whose very consciousness of guilt, and of foul wrong done their
neighbors, made them watchful and suspicious. They saw that
the forges were a-going early and late, and the smiths ever ham-
mering away at work which they might not see. Crowds of
natives were seen loitering in and around the forges, and the
snatches of songs wherewith the field and the workshop began
suddenly to resound were all of a martial or patriotic kind, chiefly
borrowed from the strains of the old bards. There was a certain amount of independence, too, in the bearing of old and
young—a firmness of step and an erectness of mien little common heretofore among the down-trodden children of the soil, and
this the Scottish and English colonists took to be the worst
symptom of all. A presentiment of coming evil darkened many
a thrifty household which had grown rich and prosperous on
the spoils of poor Popish recusants. The oppressors began all at
once to pale with a nameless fear, and the bustle of preparation
stealthily going on the province over, suddenly extended itself to
the bawns and castles of "the planters." Couriers were dispatched to Dublin from divers "loyal gentlemen" of Ulster,
acquainting the Lords Justices that something dreadful was in
contemplation amongst the Irish Papists, which they implored
them to look after while it was yet possible to avert the evil.

The night of the 22d October came on dark and moonless.
The earth was wrapt in the double veil of gloom and silence, and
the warders on the English Castles of Ulster, as they walked to
and fro on the bleak battlements exposed to the piercing damp
of the atmosphere, amused themselves not seldom, for lack of
better employment, with heaping curses on the cowardly Papists

and "wood kerne," who, hidden away in huts and holes, kept
them shivering there in the cold night breeze, though for what
earthly use they could not see, as the rascally crew were too careful of their wretched hides to come within range of musket or
reach of whip.

Such, too, might have been the amiable cogitations of certain
troopers belonging to the military command of Captain Lord Blayney, of Castle Blayney, in the county of Monaghan, as they rode at
a brisk trot along the high road through the barony of Farney,
about ten of the clock on that same night. They had been
escorting some members of the Blayney family to Dundalk
on their way to England, and were now returning post haste to
the Castle full charged with divers rumors relating to the supposed treacherous practices of the Irishry, which they had heard
amongst the Palesmen in the old borough.

All at once the foremost riders blasted out a military oath, with
a vociferous " who be you?"

The party addressed consisted of two individuals mounted on
the rough nags of the country, whose approach had attracted no
attention, in the greater noise and clatter of the cavalry. At
first, the soldiers were half inclined to let the strangers pass unmolested, being quite sure that they must be "the right sort" to
venture so near a troop of Blayney's horse, the only cavalry to
be met in that wild country. The answer to their rough challenge quickly undeceived them.

" We're peaceable men going about our business—pri'thee let
us pass!"

" Peaceable men!" repeated the cornet in command, " that is
no answer—be ye friends or foes?"

" Foes we are not, but fain would be friends to all men,"
replied the larger and more prominent of the two. " I pray thee,
good sir, detain us not, for our business brooks not delay!"

" Ay! they say there is much business of that kind now going
on hereabouts," said the officer, and he planted his horse full in
the other's way. " Let us hear who you are that we may know
whether you be a loyal subject or one Popishly affected."

"I am Heber McMahon, Bishop of the Catholics in these
parts——"

" For God's sake, my lord !" cried his companion in low smothered accents, " don't—don't—they'll be the death of us—you
know they will—they'll hang us without judge or jury !" An
exulting shout from the troopers gave fearful confirmation of the
justice of his fears.

" Be still, Malachy," said the Bishop with stern dignity ; " they
cannot slay us unless God wills it, and if He does, we cannot die
in a better time. Sir," said he, addressing the officer, " I am
going to administer the last rights of religion to a dying sinner—
detain me not, I adjure you by the Holy Name of that God who is
to judge us all !"

" Now, by the Book !" cried the cornet, sternly enjoining his
men to keep back, " this impudence of thine, McMahon, passes
belief. A man whose life is forfeited by his own confession—
openly avowing himself a Papist bishop, and caught, as one may
say, in the act of practising unlawful rites—here, soldiers !—
advance and seize him—but see that you harm him not till we
place him in the captain's custody. He is a pestilent recusant—
a snake in the grass, and his capture will fill our pockets—seize
the two and ride on at full speed—we have lost too much time
in parley with the wretch !"

The bishop made no further attempt at remonstrance ; indeed,
he was suddenly seized with a fit of coughing, just as the half
drunken soldiers rode up on either side of him and his servant,
the latter being, by this time, well nigh paralyzed with fear,
though he kept repeating his *Ave Maria* in a voice inaudible to
the ruffian crew around him.

The bishop's cough seemed to annoy the troopers wonderfully,
and the fellow who rode on his right hand taking him by the
shoulder gave him a hearty shake—" Stop your coughing, you
old Popish thief, or I'll choke you as dead as a herring."

It seemed as though the fellow's savage threat acted as an incan-
tation, for in an instant the thick darkness was, as it were, instinct with life, and resolved itself into human beings. The cry of
" McMahon aboo" arose—from what seemed a thousand voices—
on every side, before, behind, and all around the terrified troopers,
men started into sudden existence, armed, they could see, with
weapons that assumed fearful shapes in the darkness. The wild

clan shout of the McMahons, which startled even the well-
trained cavalry horses, was suddenly succeeded by a fierce and
vengeful cry of "down with Blayney's bloody cut-throats!" and
instantly the clash of weapons was heard on every side, and
the horsemen, almost forgetful of their prisoners, thought only of
effecting their escape, or if that were not possible, of selling their
lives as dearly as they could, when a loud authoritative voice
made itself heard above the tumultuous din—it was that of Heber McMahon, commanding his friends and kinsmen to shed no
blood.

"Let them go, in God's name," said he, "or rather, Eman," addressing the leader of the bold Farney men who, guided by his
voice, was now close at his side, "or rather, take them prisoners
to your chief—but see they are kept safe – it would be an ill beginning to slay them, and they so few in number."

Some grumbling voices were heard amongst the crowd reminding the bishop of divers outrages committed by Blayney's troopers, but the stern prelate silenced all objections by repeating
his orders to Eman McMahon to take the soldiers in charge.

The latter was easier said than done, for, as if actuated by a
common impulse, and with a cry of "Save who can!" the score
of troopers set spurs to their horses, and, drawing their sabres,
dashed furiously through the amazed and frightened multitude
which, falling back on either side, from the horses' hoofs, left a
passage open, and before the shouts from the rear of "Seize them!
seize them!" could be made intelligible to those in front, the opportunity of obeying the command was lost, and the troopers
were dashing at headlong speed along the road far beyond the
reach of pike or musket. Not a sound escaped them during the
few moments of their detention or even when they succeeded in
effecting their escape. The joy of finding themselves again at
liberty, so far safe in life and limb, coupled with their uncertainty
as to whether other and more fatal obstacles might not still impede their progress, gave them little inclination for indulging in
idle bravado, and it was not till they came within sight of Castle
Blayney that they ventured to slacken rein. The account which
they gave of their adventure with the McMahons was wholly inexplicable to their captain. It was something so remote from the

range of probability that the Irish should be abroad in such numbers at that hour, or that the notorious Heber McMahon should
thrust himself, as it were, amongst English bayonets—for his boldness amounted to nothing less—that Blayney was completely
mystified. At length a bright thought shone upon his mind, and
he started to his feet and flung back his chair with a vehemence
that made the silver tankards on the table before him dance and
quiver :

"I have it, Trellingham! by h— I have it! These Popish
hounds are not so bold without good reason—what if this night
were—let me see—it is on the stroke of midnight!"

"Hark! heard you that savage shout?—you are right, captain! There be mischief brewing this very hour."

A tumult was now heard within the castle, and soldiers and
domestics crowded unbidden to the captain's presence with tidings that the country was up in arms, and bonfires blazing on
every hill. Measures were promptly taken to secure the castle
against a sudden assault, but its defences were not much to
boast of, and after doing all they could to strengthen it, the small
garrison awaited in fear and trembling the moment when "the
bloody Irish Papists" should take it by storm and burn it over
their heads—which, by the dread law of retaliation, they had but
too much reason to expect.

When the bishop found his enemies gone, and none but friends
around, he stated his intention of resuming his journey, so roughly
interrupted. A couple of miles were yet to be travelled, and
the sick man lay in imminent danger of death.

"But are they *gone?*" put in Malachy; "are you *sure* they'll
not come back?"

"No fear of that, anyhow," laughed Eman, "you may take
my word for it, Malachy!—what would you say, my lord, to an
escort—a dozen or so of our Farney men?"

"Not one, Eman, not one—thanks for your kindness. I do
not think I shall meet any more such obstacles between this and
my journey's end, and it ill beseems a minister of the Lord to go
guarded to the sick bed."

"As you will, my good lord, there be friends enow on foot to
keep you from harm; and I warrant the English will stay within

doors for this night. Now, friends, up to the hill there and light
your bonfire—an' ye wait longer, our signal will be far behind
the others—haste for the honor of Farney!"

Hundreds ran to do his bidding, but ere yet the crackling,
smoking brushwood had burst into a flame, a joyful shout from
the assembled clansmen rent the midnight sky. From every hill
northward a column of flame was shooting up, one following the
other in quick succession till the country far and near was tinged
with a ruddy light, and even the blackness of the heavens was
partially broken by the thousand prophet-fires of earth heralding
the dawn of freedom.

To those who ascended the brow of Slieve-gullian that night at
midnight a glorious spectacle presented itself, if haply they who
looked were of the proscribed class, the ancient dwellers in the
land. The hills and the mountains to the north were in a blaze,
and along the margin of the rivers the signal-fires were shooting
up one by one. At first it was but the hill country of Tyr-Owen
that sent up its flaming protest to the heavens above, then most
of Tyr-Connel followed—the hills of Antrim were shrouded in
darkness, except a few along the borders of Donegal, so, too,
were those of Derry, but Down and Armagh quickly caught up
the illumination, and onward like wildfire it passed through
Monaghan and Cavan, and westward through all Fermanagh, to
the very gates of Enniskillen. And the shouts which came
swelling on the gale, some full and distinct, others faint and far
like the murmur of ocean-shells, were the voice of a newly-
awakened people, tribe answering to tribe, and county to county,
even as hill flashed electric news to hill that the children of the
soil had at length risen in their might to throw off the incubus
that had paralyzed their existence. As that light of hope, so
long expected, broke athwart the darkness of the winter's night,
the persecuted ministers of religion, hiding away in secret places,
raised their hands in thankfulness to Heaven that they had lived
to see that sight, and floods of joyful tears streamed from many
an eye long unused to weep.

But the bristling castles of the strangers, whose prosperity was
based upon the ruin of the native chiefs, were dark and dismal
that busy night. Terror and confusion had suddenly taken the

place of insolent security, and Castle Blayney was not the only one where swift and terrible vengeance was anticipated. Had the Catholic people of Ulster been what their enemies delight to represent them, few Protestants would have lived next day amongst its hills and valleys to tell the tale of retributive justice. As it was, not one single murder stained their hands throughout that general insurrection.* Long before noon of the following day, Castle Blayney was garrisoned by Eman Oge with his stout Farney men, and Blayney's troopers, "in durance vile," marvelling much, it may be, at the unlooked-for mercy shown them, especially as they had wounded some few of the insurgents before the castle was given up.

Lord Blayney's wife and children were also captured, but he himself escaped to Dublin Castle with the news.

It was understood among the chiefs that, for the present at least, Sir Phelim O'Neill was to act as commander-in-chief of the Ulster forces. As the head of the O'Neills he deemed himself entitled to the office, and flung himself with right good will into the stormy arena where its duties called him. Had he been a man of finer or more tender feelings, it would then have been a painful task, for but few days before he had laid in the grave the once-beloved wife of his youth. The terror of the approaching event, with all its fearful contingencies and possibilities, had hastened the progress of disease, and the gentle, but too timorous spirit of Lady O'Neill had fluttered out of its mortal tenement just in time to avoid the tumultuous warfare which so long after convulsed her native province. She was borne to the grave amid the loud wailing of her kinswomen from the plains of Iveagh, followed by a long and imposing array of O'Neills and Magennises, the latter headed by her two brothers, Sir Con and Bryan Magennis. Sir Phelim's mourning was not from his heart—his wife had latterly been more of a restraint on his actions than any-

* All Protestant historians admit that during the first week of the rebellion—that is to say, in the first glowing outburst of recovered liberty, not one individual was put to death by the Irish. It was only when murders and massacres perpetrated on themselves drove them to it, that they adopted a system of retaliation

thing else, and such being the case he viewed her death at that
particular juncture as a capital stroke of good luck. When her
coffin was placed amongst the mouldering remains of her lordly
ancestors in far Iveagh, and the tomb of the Magennises shut her
for ever from his view ; when he knelt in prayer with her brothers
and other near relatives for a short space before quitting the
graveyard, his " *requiescat in pace*" was breathed in all sincerity,
for internally he added, " now, indeed, may *I* rest in peace, or
rather do *in peace* that which it behoves me to do for myself and
others !   The great dread secret which gives me present rank and
future riches came never to your ear.   I kept *that* from you,
Nora ! because I knew it would neither gladden your heart nor
smooth your last journey ! God rest you, then, Nora Magennis !
heaven to *you* this day—name and fame to *me*, and freedom to
all our race ! Up, brothers, clansmen of Iveagh !" he shouted,
starting to his feet, " grief and affection have had their hour—
now for freedom and revenge !"

Anger was at first mingled with surprise on the faces of Nora's
kinsmen, as they slowly arose and blessed themselves after their
devotions.   Even his own friends and followers looked surprised
at the sudden, and, as it appeared, indecorous change in Sir Phelim's manner.   Sir Con Magennis, after eyeing the other sternly
for a moment, at last spoke: " Your words were more seemly,
methinks, at another time.   Neither the hour nor the place befits
such discourse."

" Nay, Sir Con Magennis, you shall hear what I have to say,
and then judge if the tale be not one for churchyard bounds—
ay ! by my sacred hopes, it is one to make the dead clansmen of
Iveagh start from beneath our feet, into vengeful life, their eyes
charged with heaven's lightning to blast and burn the whole
treacherous brood of robbers and murderers !"

" Sir Phelim O'Neill," said the elder Magennis coldly, " we
would have, if it so please you, this fresh count in the indictment
—of what nature may it be that we are called on to hear it over
our sister's dead body, as one may say ?"

O'Neill, folding his arms, wrapped his long cloak around him,
and turned on his interlocutor an eye wherein his natural impetuosity struggled with the stern coldness which he deemed most

fitting the occasion : "You pledged your word, Sir Con Magennis, to join us with all your clan so soon as Tyrone came in person to head the northern army—did you, or did you not ?"

"Surely I did, and with God's help, I mean to do what I said I would do—at the first news of the Earl's landing on Irish ground the banner of Magennis is flung to the breeze."

"Chieftain of Iveagh," said O'Neill in a voice hoarse with suppressed passion, "that news will you never hear—the son of the great Earl will you never lay eyes upon."

"How so, man!—speak out and tell us what your words—your looks portend—what of Tyrone?"

"They have murdered him, Con Magennis! The Sassenach has put him out of the way in the nick of time—oh! doleful news for me to tell!"

A cry of horror escaped from every listener, but Magennis by a sign commanded silence : "Murdered him—did you say ?—when? where?—they dare not—no, by St. Columb! they dare not!"

"I tell you they did—choked like a dog was he in his bed by night—yea, even in Brussels where of late he had been awaiting the summons home!"

"Sir Phelim O'Neill! are you sure—*sure*—that this maddeuing news is true ?"

"As sure as that yon sun is clouded in the heavens. The carrier who brought me the sad tidings from Rory O'Moore in Dublin is still under my roof—you may see and speak with him when you list."

Magennis made no answer, but the convulsive working of every feature, and the swollen veins on his white forehead, told a tale of mighty passion, beyond the power of words to express.

"Your hand, O'Neill!" he faltered out, after a pause of deep meaning; "who talks of delay *now* is an enemy to our just and holy cause—the axe is ready—before God it shall be laid to the root of the accursed tree ere many days go by. Brother!—kinsmen what say ye?—shall we longer hug our chains?—shall we longer pocket wrongs and insults?—shall the blood of our slaughtered kindred longer cry to heaven unavenged?"

A shout of execration, both loud and long, resounded through the graveyard, and each stout clansman grasped his skene, and muttered a stern vow, as Bryan Magennis bent his knee before his brother and chief and swore from that day forward to wage unceasing war against the common enemy.

"Home, then," cried the chieftain of Iveagh, "home, friends and kinsmen all, and speed ye in making all things ready—fare you well, O'Neill!—men of Tyr-Owen! fare ye well!—God give us all stout hearts and strong arms to fight His battle and our own!—send me word, Sir Phelim, when the day is fixed on—as early as you will, let it be—and, on the faith of Magennis, you shall hear of me and mine full soon!" So the chieftains parted, each declining the other's proffered hospitality; even the funeral festivities then deemed indispensable were for that time laid aside.

Magennis kept his word, for in less than twenty-four hours after the receipt of Sir Phelim's fateful message, news was brought to the assembling clans that "NEWRY WAS TAKEN BY SIR CON MAGENNIS." The words were like an electric shock, animating the tepid and the dull, giving life and warmth to the cold and passionless, and sending a thrill of hope through the hearts of all. At midnight the beacon of freedom blazed on the hill-tops, and by the morning light the stout clansmen of the north were trooping in armed bands over highway and by-way to the place appointed for the general muster, viz., the plain in front of Kinnard Castle.

It was a clear frosty day, and the sun shone down on the crusted earth with a brightness seldom seen in that season of "melancholy days." But more cheering than autumn's rare sunbeam to the roused spirit of the clansmen—was the snow-white flag so proudly floating from the castle-keep with the Red Hand of the O'Neills emblazoned on its centre. That time-honored banner was ever a sign of hope to the tribes of Ulster, but that generation had never before seen it flung in defiance to the breeze. Now as band after band arrived, it was the first object on which their eyes rested, and the joyful "*Lamh dearg aboo!*" echoed far over hill and valley, at every fresh recognition of the well-loved ensign—and the stalwart head of the O'Neills, "Stout Phelim," as the clansmen loved to call him, stood just without his courtyard gate, surveying with a proud and swelling heart the ever-increasing multitude from which he was to form an army of offence and defence. Near and around him stood some half dozen of the principal gentlemen who had already arrived, all habited like himself in the Celtic garb, with the addition of a green scarf encircling the waist, and hanging almost to the knee in graceful folds. Tirlogh O'Neill was not amongst this group, but his burly form might be seen bustling here and there amongst the clansmen, his red face glowing with excitement, as he grasped the hand of friend and neighbor, and welcomed each with exuberant glee.

Every moment some fresh arrival called forth a shout of welcome, and as chieftain after chieftain joined the group in the shadow of the old gateway, the air rang with his proper war-cry, caught up from mouth to mouth by way of welcome. Only portions of the different clans, however, followed those leaders to the muster, the others remaining for the present with the Tanist, or chief man on their own soil, to secure as many of the strong places as possible, and take what spoils they could from the enemy. But long before the sun began to decline there was hardly a clan that had not sent its quota to swell Sir Phelim's army. O'Reillys were there from far Breffni, McMahons from Uriel, headed by the gallant Eman, stout Maguires from the lake* shore, O'Cahans from the hills of Derry, O'Hanlans from the plains of Ardmacha, and tall McKennas from the song-famed "Green woods of Truagh," but as yet the banner of Magennis was nowhere to be seen, the men of Iveagh were still wanting. It was just when their tardiness was beginning to be noticed that a solitary horseman was seen spurring swiftly over the waste from the western country. Coming near he was quickly recognized as a follower of Magennis, but the anxious inquiries addressed to him as he sped his way towards the castle-gate were all met by the single question of "Where may Sir Phelim O'Neill be found?" Once in the chieftain's presence, he was not slow in delivering his message :

"The Magennis greets you well, Sir Phelim, and sends you

_____
* Lough Erne, around whose broad bosom lay the ancient domains of the Maguires.

word by me, that if he and his are backward in showing themselves here, it is because they were not idle all day at home—
the men of Iveagh were up betimes this morning, and have
taken Newry from the enemy!"

It was then that the shout of "Magennis for ever!" went
up into the air from thousands of manly voices, and the wild
war-chorus had not yet died away amongst the neighboring
hills, when Sir Phelim gave the word: "Let us march to Dungannon—that and Charlemont shall be ours before to-morrow's
sun sets!"   And so they were.   Stout Phelim kept his word.

CHAPTER IV.

"Amid their joyous merriment, a cloud sails slowly o'er the sun!
They start up as the shadow falls; they look; it loometh dreadly dun;
And tho', not e'en the slightest leaf is by the slumbering breezes stirr'd,
Advancing bodefully afar a Pyramid of gloom appear'd!"

"If it feel nothing else, it will feed my revenge!"
SHAKSPEARE'S *Merchant of Venice.*

On that memorable night when "the beacon of war" was
flaming in triumphal brightness on the hills of Ulster, and a
whole province awoke into life, and the activity which springs
from sudden hope, while the chieftains of the north were exulting
in the gushing enthusiasm of the people, how did it fare with
their equally-devoted friends in Dublin? O'Moore, and Maguire,
and McMahon were all there in person to direct and carry out
the hazardous design—the success of which would be almost a
guarantee for the ultimate triumph of their cause. They were
well acquainted with the state of affairs in the Castle, and knew
that skill and caution more than force were required for its capture. They had, therefore, wisely abstained from making their
intention known within the city, except to the few gentlemen whose
honor and patriotism they had had too many and convincing
proofs to doubt. Their plan was well devised, and promised fair
for success. A hundred chosen men were to enter the city by
ten different gates on the following day, which, being market-
day, the ingress or presence of so small a number would attract
no attention. While the citizens were engaged about their market-
business the all but unguarded gates of the old fortress were to
be taken by the several small parties appointed for the task,
under the leadership of the chieftains already named, with Colonel

Plunket and Colonel O'Byrne. Arms were secretly provided, and hid away in safe places ready for use.

The leaders of the enterprise had all supped together at Lord Maguire's lodgings in Castle street, and although each one strove hard to appear gay, or, at least, easy in mind, still the effort was too visible, and the attempt was, consequently, unsuccessful. It was hard for men with such a perilous step before them to drown the thought of the coming morrow, with all its dread possibilities, in the sense of present enjoyment. Failure was not to be thought of—the thought would have been too dreadful—success they did and would anticipate, rejecting with scorn all the chances that lay against them, with a spirit worthy their heroic blood, and the noble cause in which they had embarked, suppressing, as it rose within them, every thought of the personal danger to be incurred. Yet, even in that final hour, when their daring scheme was drawing to its completion, and all had girded their loins with strength and courage for the neck-or-nothing venture, the distinctive features of their respective characters were broadly marked and clearly visible. O'Moore was still calm and collected, earnest, firm, and full of that high-souled confidence which springs from a consciousness of innate resources and capacities yet undeveloped, together with a strong conviction of supernatural aid and assistance. Maguire, on the other hand, though apparently devoted heart and soul to the success of the cause which he stood pledged to advance by every means in his power, still showed symptoms, involuntary on his part, of a nervous anxiety as to the result, (shrinking, as it were, from the approach of actual peril,) which was little in keeping with his usual character. Men were wont to speak of Lord Maguire as a young nobleman who lacked prudence and was noways given to calculation, who, in short, had suffered a large portion of his patrimony to slip through his fingers, because and by reason of his reckless habits. It was passing strange; and the bold brave chieftain of Uriel, who had known Maguire from earliest boyhood, found it hard to believe him the same man, or to repress the words of contemptuous surprise which ever and anon rose to his lips as he marked the unwonted paleness, not to say agitation, of his friend from Fermanagh.

O'Byrne, a tall, broad-shouldered mountaineer, of some thirty odd years, with a frank and cheerful countenance, hale, hearty, and good-natured, was the very beau-ideal of a dashing, daring, high-handed soldier, little disposed to harm others without special good cause, and just as little likely to bear wrong or insult tamely. A genuine Milesian was Hugh O'Byrne, proud yet not stern, brave even to rashness, seldom pausing to calculate results, warm and impulsive in all his feelings, somewhat apt, at times, to give offence by over-free speech, yet always willing to make reparation when conscience or good sense convinced him of having erred. Independent of the manifold wrongs sustained by his own family at the hands of robber-rulers, O'Byrne's generous heart bled for the woes of all his nation, and if his was not the fierce, insatiable ardor wherewith Phelim O'Neill threw himself into the struggle, his hostility to the foreign oppressors was none the less strong or determined. Take him for all in all, O'Byrne was a fair specimen of an Irish chieftain of that day, high-spirited, straightforward, honest and patriotic, with a certain dash of chivalry in his composition that served to soften and refine his outward bearing, especially in the presence of ladies. He, too, had noticed the, to him, unaccountable depression of Maguire, but, unlike McMahon, he was touched by a sadness with which he yet could not sympathize—his own heart revelled in the thought that the work of liberation for the country and the people was so soon to commence, and that he was to aid in striking the first blow. He had an intuitive sense of delicacy, however, that prevented him from making any allusion to a feeling which he plainly saw was involuntary, and he more than once restrained McMahon by a look or a sign when that gentleman seemed disposed to address his lordship in terms more candid than polite.

As for Plunket, he sat looking from one to the other through half closed eye-lids, a singularly humorous smile on his thin features, mingled at times with the slightest possible expression of contempt, for Richard Plunket, although a patriot at heart, and, moreover, a zealous Catholic, was still a Norman by descent, and as such looked down upon "the mere Irish" with a sense of superiority which in his case, however, was good-natured and rather patronizing than otherwise. Still he had quite enough of

3A

Norman superciliousness to enjoy in a sly way what he justly termed "the old Milesian crustiness and thin-skin" of his companions. Notwithstanding all that, Richard Plunket was a man of honor and probity, clear-headed and far-seeing, who deserved well of his countrymen as being the first man of English blood who joined the ranks of the native Irish in that memorable struggle for freedom. His first adhesion was owing to the influence of O'Moore, between whom and himself a strong and sincere friendship had been growing for years. Connected by family ties, and pretty nearly of the same age—they had been boys together, and in their case, at least, the distinction of races was obliterated, and the feuds of past times voluntarily forgotten. The high-bred descendant of the princes of Leix had many friends within the English Pale, but none so true, so steadfast as Richard Plunket.

The long evening passed away, the stilly night wore on apace, and still the party lingered as if loath to separate, when the measured tread of armed men was heard echoing through the deserted street,—near and nearer the sound came, and some of the gentlemen, becoming alarmed, rushed to extinguish the lamp. Maguire, smiling at their fears, pointed to the time-piece on the wall, which was just on the stroke of ten.[*]

"It is the city watch, my friends!—do but keep quiet, and they will pass on!"

The room-door opened softly, and a lank, thin-visaged individual in a bob-wig protruded his head cautiously through the aperture. The leaden eyes fixed themselves on Maguire's face and there they rested.

"Sdeath, man!" cried his lordship, half angrily; "what's amiss that you look so frightened?"

"My lord, it's Sheriff Woodcock that wants to know why there be lights in my house at such an untimely hour——"

"Sheriff Woodcock!" cried Maguire with a start; "wherefore comes he here?"

---

[*] It is hardly necessary to remind the reader that ten o'clock was as far in the night in the seventeenth century as *twelve* is in the nineteenth.

"That I know not," replied Nevil the surgeon, "but he seems marvellously curious to know who we have within——"

"Let him travel farther in quest of knowledge, the hangman!" said McMahon in a voice so loud as to excite the apprehensions even of O'Moore, who admonished him by signs to keep quiet.

"Nay, my very good sir," quoth Nevil, "we may not answer law-officers in that fashion—at least here in the city. I told him it was only the Lord Maguire making merry with some noble gentlemen——"

"You did!" exclaimed Maguire, starting from his seat with a flushed and changing countenance. "You told him so, Nevil?"

"Surely I did, but be not wrothful, my good lord—I told him you were all civil, well-behaved gentlemen, and that I would answer for your peaceable ways, though I couldn't deny but what you were from the Irish country, and come of the old blood, all excepting Master Plunket——"

Some of the company laughed, but others, seeing more in the affair than the ordinary vigilance of the night-watch, were in more humor to give the pragmatical chirurgeon an occasion to test his skill on his own bones, than to relish the quaintness of his words or the oddity of his demeanor.

"Let us throw him out to his sheriffship as a love-token!" said one.

"Nay, rather, let us tie him to the pump near at hand," said another, "till he learns to keep his tongue from wagging——"

"Jest an' you will at my poor expense, noble sirs," said Nevil with sly emphasis, "but were it not for my promise that you should all be in your beds within the space of half an hour you might have been taking the air by this time in company with the worshipful Sheriff Woodcock—I pray ye all to mark well my words, and straightway betake yourselves to your proper lodgings, ere your laughter be turned another way. Now do as you list, and blame not Peter Nevil, if evil befall ye!"

The bob-wig vanished, the door closed, but somehow the mirth of the company had departed with Peter, and after a short and whispered consultation it was agreed that Nevil's warning was not to be slighted, inasmuch as none of them had any particular

reason at that particular time for desiring to make the acquaintance of the worshipful Woodcock.

"They be birds of ill omen in this quarter," observed Plunket,
who could never resist the temptation to give utterance to what
he considered a good thing; "any cock were better than a *woodcock* here within the city limits!"

"Until such time as we have a cage ready for him in Birming-
ham Tower,*" added Roger O'Moore, with his expressive smile.

This allusion was well-timed, and served to restore a portion of
the cheerfulness so lately lost. The high hopes, the daring con-
ceptions cherished so long, and for one short moment partially
dimmed, darted again into life and glowing fervor at the mention
of the hated prison, the Irish Bastile, where so many of the na
tion's noblest and best had languished, suffered—and died.

"Let us hence to our lodgings, friends and comrades," said
O'Byrne, gayly, as he tightened his leathern belt around him and
threw his cloak over his shoulders; "we have glorious work in
hand for the morrow—nay, our noble host, ask us not to dip
farther into that charmed bowl—we need steady hands, ay! and
cool heads for the task before us——"

"You say truly, colonel," said O'Moore, with an approving
nod; "our game is a bold one, and the stakes are fearfully high,
but if well played, it will give back the heart of Ireland to its
dissevered members, and set the life-blood flowing once again
from end to end of the old land. Your hand, my lord!—
McMahon, yours!—the touch of an Ulsterman's hand sets my
pulses throbbing this night, when I bethink me of what is passing
in that north country by this—no, not by this—" he added,
glancing at the time-piece, which barely indicated the tenth hour
—"no, not by this—at midnight the signal-fires are to blaze on
northern hills—Fermanagh and Monaghan are busy scenes by
now—and the O'Reillys are stirring in Breffny, and the men
of Tyr-Owen are not idle—St. Bridget! an' we were there at this
hour, to see those bold clansmen throwing off their shackles——"

---

* The principal tower of Dublin Castle, in troublous times, used
as a State-prison. This portion of the edifice was, therefore, as may
well be supposed, peculiarly obnoxious to the native Irish.

" No need to go so far for a sight, Roger," said his friend Plunket; " before the morrow's sun sets behind our own Ben-Edir, we may see the green flag waving over Dublin Castle——"

"*May!*" repeated the fiery Wicklow-man ; " say rather we *shall* and *must*——"

" If God so wills it, O'Byrne," rejoined Plunket.

" Oh, surely, surely—that is understood, but——"

" But nothing is certain," put in Maguire, in a low, earnest tone, as he accompanied his friends to the stair-head ; "if our eyes see not the sight you mention, friends and loyal gentlemen, others whom we wot of will see *us* in doleful plight——"

" Hear the raven croak !" said McMahon with good-humored irony ; " where learned you that dismal note, Connor ?—methinks it was not by Erne's banks or in those old Fermanagh woods where you and I chased the fallow deer so oft together——"

Maguire's answer was prevented by O'Moore, who laid a hand on the arm of each of the northern chieftains as they stood together. " Enough for the present," said he, in a low, impressive voice, his eyes glistening with strange brightness through the dim light of the lampless lobby, " to-night our friends in the north will stand on their own soil as freemen—*midnight* is *their* hour of freedom —shall not to-morrow's noon be ours ?"

Every voice answered in the affirmative, and each clasped the other's hand with the energy of determination ; then one by one Maguire's guests departed and went their several ways, unnoticed in the darkness of the narrow streets, as they confidently believed.

Their host, left alone, turned moodily back into the room they had left, muttering to himself : " *Midnight !*—it is a dreary hour for those who fear—but what should I fear more than the others ? —fear ! it is an ill-word—no, I do not fear—wherefore should I ? Saints above ! who is here ?"

" Only a poor brother of the Order of St. Francis !" said a meek voice from the depth of a high steeple hood, and a figure, which had taken possession of a chair in front of the now expiring fire, rose to its feet and slowly, very slowly, turned towards the interrogator a pale emaciated countenance, looking ghastly and spirit-like in the deep shade of the hood.

" But how came you here ?" stammered Maguire, strangely

agitated; "what is your business with me—speak, friar! I charge you speak!"

"There be danger abroad," said the friar with solemn emphasis, in a low muffled voice; "I know a noble quarry for which a pitfall is in waiting, an' it move many paces from where it stands."

"In God's name, speak plainly," said Maguire, with increasing agitation.

"Leave this house, an' you love your life," said the Capuchin, with a warning motion of the finger; "lose not a moment, or it may, even now, be late!"

"Friar!" said Maguire, solemnly, "I know you not, and I marvel much at the nature of your speech. Wherefore should I fly as a felon?"

"As a felon you will be judged, full soon, an' you do not a friend's bidding!"

"But what—what is the danger?"

"The Sheriff has set a watch on this house—you know best in how far that may concern you. Heaven grant you may even now escape; and should ill befal you, Connor Maguire, there be those within the city walls whom the news will sore afflict!"

Maguire started and fixed his eye on the haggard face before him—much of its character he might not see.

"Stranger, I *will* do your bidding—but tell me first, who they be that sent you hither, at the risk of your own life?"

A scornful smile flitted over the ghostly visage. "I care not, an' I save yours—that is—a poor Capuchin's life is of small value weighed against the Lord Maguire's—but why tarry so long—give me but one word of kindness—gratitude for those who take so deep an interest in your welfare, and I lead you hence by a secret way!"

"Now, out upon you, Capuchin!" Maguire exclaimed, with a vehemence as sudden as unaccountable; "you a priest of God's Church, and holding communion with—nay, I name no names, but say to those whom it concerns, that what I said before I say now again—my mind is still the same on the matter they and I wot of—and say further from me that Connor Maguire would not take the boon of life at such hands——"

"This is your final answer," said the friar, very, very calmly.

" It is, and let me tell you, father, that I am much surprised, and no little afflicted to see a man of your holy state herding with like company, and doing their will, moreover, in slavish fashion!——"

" It is well," said the preternaturally calm voice from beneath the hood; " I marvel not that the lofty feeling of gratitude which cast at your feet a heart which the proudest and noblest have sought in vain, should be a stranger to your flinty bosom—it was said of old that nothing good could come out of Galilee—fool—fool that *I* was to look for good where good never yet was found. But the dream is past—ay! and for ever—and *love*—" the voice ceased a moment—a low, strange sound like hysteric laughter was heard—then was added, in a hissing tone, the figure approaching the astonished nobleman till it placed itself within a few feet of where he stood, " love will be henceforward *hate*—ay! hate—stay or go now—as you will—the toils are around you, go where you may—and I pray the just and righteous God that the doom of traitors may fall soon and suddenly on all concerned in your foul plot!—should that thing come to pass, Connor Maguire! you will think of—*the Capuchin friar*—ha! ha! ha!"

A name was on Maguire's lips when he could command his voice to utter a sound, but whatever he might have purposed to say, in the overwhelming surprise of the moment, was now too late to reach the ear of the strange visitor—gliding through the half open door he had vanished in the obscurity of the passage without.

At first, the whole seemed to Maguire like a hideous dream, and, hastily pouring out a goblet of wine, he swallowed it at a draught, hoping that its generous warmth might overcome the dreary chillness which was creeping over him, but all in vain—nor wine, nor reason, could dispel the gloomy impression left on his mind by the parting words of the strange being whose identity he was at no loss to establish, any more than he could reasonably doubt of the dread reality of what he had seen and heard.

In the silence and loneliness of the place—for no sound was heard within the house—Maguire could not divest himself of the thought that he *was* surrounded by danger—his morbid imagination peopled the very air with hostile creatures—spies, it might be, and from Nevil's manner, during his brief appearance, his suspicions settled on him. He was alone, without any friend to consult, and the dark presentiment within him, had other motives been wanting, was, to a mind like his, sufficient to make him decide on some step that might possibly avert the imminent peril in which he began to fancy himself, though of its exact nature he could form no idea. Strangely enough, he forgot what his mysterious visitor had said, that there was a watch set on the house, and believing that a change of quarters might ensure his safety till morning light—or even till the hour appointed for the great attempt—he softly made his way down the dark stair-case, and, taking the key from its usual place, let himself into the street, without any clear or definite idea as to whither he should steer his course. Not unseen of Sheriff Woodcock's understrapper walked Connor Maguire through the shades of night. From under the archway which had sheltered his precious body, stepped forth John Steeples, and after the Irish lord paced he at safe and respectful distance, anxious, no doubt, to see him safely and snugly housed again for the comfort and satisfaction of his worshipful principal. Now had Master Woodcock any definite or special charge against Lord Maguire or his late guests, it would have saved honest John Steeples some trouble, for nothing would have been easier than to procure a few of his comrades and "grab them" on the spot, but, unluckily, no instructions had been issued for their arrest, they were only suspected in a general way, as it were, and hence the necessity for John Steeples' continued *surveillance*, without any further steps in aggression. So on walked Lord Maguire, and on followed John Steeples, past the old Church of St. Nicholas, down through Christchurch Lane, past the dark dead walls of the old Cathedral, under the frowning arch of Ormond's Gate, and so on into Cook street, where the young nobleman was soon lost to John's sight, but not before the sharp eyes of the latter had marked the humble domicile into which three gentle knocks had gained him admission. Having taken due note of the house, John Steeples moved his bulky *corpus* with quickened paces towards the place where he knew his employer was likely to be found in snug quarters that cold raw night.

While the chieftain of Fermanagh was taking his lonely way

through the upper streets of the old city, he little dreamed of
what was passing by the water side in one of the mansions on
Merchant's Quay.* Within the last two hours there had been
quite a commotion amongst the inmates of the house, from the
dark-browed, sinister-looking personage enveloped in ample robes
of grave official character, whose air and bearing expressed the
consciousness of high authority, to the humblest lackey who rendered service to the great man's great man. Alone in solemn
state the master of the mansion paced a spacious chamber to and
fro, muttering to himself dark and incoherent sentences, and
chuckling with strange mirth at times the while he waited with
nervous impatience for some intelligence which was evidently
delayed too long for his liking. Every now and then he stopped
and listened, then rang a hand-bell, which lay on a large table in
the centre of the room, covered with crimson cloth, and strode to
the door to meet the tidings half way, but it was long before any
came. Always to his question of "Any of them come yet?"
the same unsatisfactory answer was returned. A fierce imprecation, spoken withal in godly phrase, was on the man's lips, in
anticipation of a like reply to his last imperious query, when the
serving man hastily put in: "There's one waiting without to
see your lordship's honor."

"Who is it, sirrah? Not one of the lords-councillors surely?"

'Not so, my lord, it seems to me that the man is habited like
the devil's birds named by the recusants, *friars* or something of
the kind!"

A sudden change passed over the heavy, puritanical features
of Sir William Parsons, for he it was. "Admit him quickly."

---

* To those who know anything of the Dublin of our day it will seem
strange to hear of aristocratic dwellings on the "Quays," and yet
they were as numerous there two hundred years ago—perhaps more
numerous—than the commercial buildings. It is now hardly credible
that some of the first legal functionaries and literary celebrities of
those days, together with many distinguished members of the gentry
and even the nobility, had their town dwellings in Bridge street, Winetavern street, and all around that neighborhood, which seems to have
been quite a fashionable locality at that time.

3*

The servant vanished. "Friars! ay! he must needs be one of our own friars—ha! ha!—godly men they be, too, for all the heathenish fashion of their garments!—ay! so I thought," as the monk of St. Francis glided in, cautiously closed the door after him, and advanced to the very centre of the room.

"How is this?" cried the Lord Justice; "fellow, you are a stranger—why enter here in that garb?"

"Ha! ha!" laughed the monk, "as though such mummers never appeared in this most godly house! Fear not, however, Sir William Parsons, I be no enemy for all my frieze robe. I came hither with good intent, as you will presently see—moments are precious. You received certain depositions this night from one Owen O'Conolly, a servant of Sir John Clotworthy."

"Surely I did," said Parsons, eyeing the other as closely as the deep hood permitted; "know you aught appertaining to that matter—an' you do, good payment will not be wanting——"

"Your gold I seek not, Sir William Parsons," said the monk sternly, "but there be those amongst these Romish traitors whom I would see brought to justice, and that full speedily—an' you wait till morning light, you will stand but poor chance of taking them."

"But how—where can we come at them now!"

"Leave that to Sheriff Woodcock—he knows ere now where the conspirators lie hidden."

"So there is a plot," said Parsons musingly.

"Can you doubt it when you have O'Conolly's sworn evidence of the fact?"

There was a keen touch of irony in this question which the Lord Justice well understood, and he bristled up accordingly.

"Nay, nay, Sir William," said the monk in a tone half jeering, half soothing; "what matters it to you or me that your deponent be a drunken serving-man—his deposition is none the less clear —it will serve your turn and mine, too—it will help to build up your fortune, and it will give the balm of revenge to my heart— revenge!—ay! truly—but this is folly—Sir William Parsons! you have the germ of a great rebellion between your fingers— crush it, I tell you! crush the poisonous growth ere it crush and destroy you—all——"

The Lord Justice had been listening in silent wonder to the vehement and most bitter speech of the friar, but at the last words uttered in a somewhat softer tone, he started and fixed his eyes anew on the mysterious personage before him.

"Surely I have heard that voice ere now—say, am I right ?"

" I came not hither to answer questions of that nature," said the monk haughtily, " but to refresh your lordship's memory concerning the traitorous doings of Connor Maguire, Costelloe McMahon, and others of their associates. You have heard that to-morrow's *morn* is fixed for the execution of their plot—look to it now, or the morrow's *ere* may find you a headless man——"

" You are right, good monk—if monk you be——"

"Good me no goods—nor monk nor priest am I—God forbid I were !——"

" Well! let us not quarrel on that head," said Parsons in no small trepidation ; " an' you think there is real danger, friend ! I will repair to the house of my honorable colleague, Sir John Borlase, and there await the assembling of the Council—being without the walls, it may be safer——"

" As you will," said the stern voice from the hood, " but what you do, do it quickly !" The monk was gone ere Parsons could summon a servant to see him out. The Lord Justice, happily for his own peace, heard not the malicious laugh which echoed through the vaulted halls below as the Capuchin roused the porter from his nap to give him egress.

A little while after, and Sir William Parsons was engaged in deep consultation at the house of Sir John Borlase, in College Green,* with that functionary and some three or four members of the Privy Council, over the sworn depositions of the drunken servant, O'Conolly, who was secured and brought back for further examination.

At midnight, Lord Maguire was arrested† at the house of his

---

* College Green was then outside the city limits.

† To commemorate the capture of Lord Maguire, the bells of St. Audeon's—in which parish it took place—were rung at midnight on the 22d—23d October of every succeeding year. This custom is said to have been continued down till the year of Emancipation, 1829.

tailor in Cook street, just, as he bitterly thought, when the hills and dales of Fermanagh were blazing with the signal-fires of freedom, and his faithful clansmen were eagerly looking forward to news of victory and noble exploits from their absent chief. As the guard dragged him roughly along in the direction of the prison, a voice, which the unhappy nobleman well knew, addressed him in mocking tones from a deep archway: "My benison on thy head, Connor Maguire—*benedicite*, my son!" The chieftain shuddered, but made no answer.

CHAPTER V.

"Such which breaks the sides of loyalty, and almost appears in loud
rebellion."   SHAKSPEARE'S *Henry VIII.*

"Then up starts the lord of Rathgogan, and fierce is the flash of his eye,
As he glares on the dark brows around him with bearing defiant and
high."   *Ballad of* "SIR DOMNALL."

THE Lords Justices and the Council passed a sleepless night
at the house of Sir John Borlase, and the morning light found
them still in solemn conclave, with O'Conolly's depositions before them. The master of the house, old and somewhat inert by
nature, lay fast asleep in an easy chair, oblivious of plots, massacres and conflagrations, nay, even of fines and confiscations, as
the discordant music of his nasal organ from time to time bore
witness, to the no small annoyance of the other "grave and reverend seigniors" who were still on duty, and wide awake. Of
these some were disposed to make merry over the whole affair,
regarding O'Conolly's evidence as a capital joke. Of this number was Sir Robert Meredith, the Lord High Chancellor, a man
of prudence and sagacity, if possessed of no higher quality. He
had from the first ridiculed the idea of arresting a peer of parliament on the sole testimony of a low-born varlet who, from drunk-
enness, could hardly make himself intelligible. When Sir Robert
joined the council on the previous night he did not attempt to
conceal his surprise on finding that such depositions were being
acted upon in a matter of such moment, while the "scurvy fellow,"
as he styled him, who gave the information, had not even been
detained as security for the truth of his allegations. Parsons, who
had received the depositions, and also discharged O'Conolly on
his sole responsibility, was somewhat nettled by the Chancellor's
stinging comments on the proceeding, but seeing, at the same

time, the utility of having his informant at hand, he immediately sent messengers in pursuit of him all through the city. When the fellow was at length secured and conveyed to the mansion on College Green, Sir Robert was not the only one who was moved to mirth, for the witness, being brought before the Council, was found wholly incapable of answering any question put to him. He had been taken from the hands of the watchmen who were about consigning him to the Black Dog,* and, when introduced to the august presence of the nation's rulers, was unable to stand without support. Still there was an attempt made by some of the Lords, at the suggestion of Parsons, to examine him. His deposition on the preceding evening was read over to him; he listened with drunken gravity, steadying himself on his feet by the aid of the two servants who had effected his capture. Being asked at the conclusion of the documentary reading, whether what he had heard read was his real evidence, he asseverated with a vulgar imprecation on his soul that it was true, every word of it.

"And you spent the early part of the evening at the Lion Tavern in —— street drinking beer with Mr. Costelloe McMahon?"

"I' faith I did, your honor's lordship, and if any noble gentleman here wants a can of prime quality, if he finds not the beer in that same Lion Tavern as good as any in town, let him call me a liar—hic—hic!"

"A likely story truly," observed Meredith aside to Sir Thomas Rotherham, "that a gentleman of McMahon's standing made a pot-companion of that varlet."

Sir Thomas smiled his incredulity, but being a friend and *protege* of Parsons, thought proper to make a show of believing the ridiculous statement. Prefacing his question with a small judicial cough, he addressed himself to the witness:

---

* The Black Dog was the lowest of the city prisons in those days, its dungeon corresponding to the "Black Hole" of modern towns and cities. It had formerly been a castellated private mansion, known in Dublin as "Browne's Castle," and being subsequently converted into an inn, received its name of the "Black Dog" from the innkeeper's sign of a mastiff or large dog.

"And you came up to Dublin, Mr. O'Conolly, on a written invitation from this McMahon to meet him, Lord Maguire, and other gentlemen for the purpose of consulting anent this treasonable plot?"

"I said not that, did I?—(hiccup)—I wrote to Mr. McMahon—"

"Which of them—there are two brothers, you know?"

"I know—Joseph—Joseph and—Tim—*two*—surely there is."

The members of the Council looked at each other, and Sir William Parsons, detecting a smile on certain of their visages, hastened to interpose:

"You mistake, Mr. O'Conolly,—I think the names are Costelloe and Art——"

"Surely, my lord, surely—Costelloe and Art—it be all the same——"

"Which of them wrote to you?"

"Cossloe, I think—no, it was the other——"

"And he invited you to go to his house on this business——"

"Just so, my lord."

"Nay, Sir William Parsons," said a nobleman present, speaking for the first time, "it is sheer folly for this honorable body to sit here listening to such evidence—the man is drunk—that is clear—he knows not what he says, and I, for one, do protest against receiving his information—until such time, at least, as he be sober——"

"Who says I'm *not* sober?" cried O'Conolly, setting his arms a-kimbo.

"Silence, good fellow!" said the clerk of the Council.

"Remove him!" said Sir Robert Meredith, "his presence here is an insult to the Council."

"Sir Robert Meredith! you shall answer for this," said Parsons doggedly, his coarse dark features swelling with rage and vexation; "this be no time for cavilling at the evidence of loyal men——"

"I *am* a loyal man," broke in O'Conolly, "an' your lordship gives me a can of that same beer I told you of, I'll drink confusion to all Popish—Popish traitors (hiccup!)—I will, before your eyes—hurrah!—Parsons and Borlase for ever! What the puck! —this head of mine is playing the d——l with me!—your hand, old fellow!"—and making a grab at something to hold by, he caught Sir William Parsons by the nose, that dignitary of the State having unluckily approached him at the moment for purposes of general admonition. A roar of laughter from his brethren of the Council exasperated the already irritated Justice, but as he did not choose to make an open show of resentment towards the real offenders, he discharged a portion, at least, of his venom on the unlucky witness, ordering him to be placed in close confinement until the effects of his night's carousal had passed away and he could speak like a Christian man.

"And that's what I'll do, your lordship (hic!—hic!)—after I get a sleep. I'll tell you all as true as the Gospel, and we'll hang them all, Sir William, ay! every mother's son of the rascally Papists—I had a brace of them for father and mother, but never mind 'that—I'm all right myself—I am—that is, I *will* be, when I get paid for this job—hic! hic! hiccup!"

In the midst of this harangue, the witness was dragged from the presence, vociferating in smothered accents his staunch adherence to loyal principles.

Before the other members of the Council had succeeded in smoothing away the wrinkles from the lowering brow of Parsons, a violent knocking at the gate without gave rise to serious alarm amongst the deliberative body. Even Borlase awoke with a grunt, and asked what was the matter.

"It is well an' the rebels be not upon us," said Parsons; "it were a just judgment to some among us, an' the Lord delivered us unto them——"

The door opened, and a tall, dark-visaged, soldierly man made his appearance, wrapped in a military riding-cloak. Even before his keen eye had run over all the noblemen and gentlemen present, a chorus of gratulation welcomed the new-comer as Sir Francis Willoughby, all the way from Galway, of which fort he was governor. He had ridden post-haste to Dublin at the urgent request of Sir William Parsons, to assist in the deliberations of the Council on this momentous occasion, and his appearance at that juncture was most welcome to the Puritanical members of the body, for his military experience and known hatred of the Papists, together with much real or supposed ability, gave him a

certain influence in their councils. Even those of the Council
who were neither friends nor admirers of Sir Francis Willoughby
were, on the present occasion, well pleased to see his stern visage
rather than that of some wild Irish chieftain, with eyes of fire,
all a-thirst for English blood.

"In the foul fiend's name," was Willoughby's salutation; "what
may all this mean?—I am summoned to town with all dispatch,
and when I *get* to town, I find every gate locked and double
locked against me."

"Not against you, Sir Francis! surely not against you," said
Parsons, eagerly advancing with a most deprecatory countenance.

"I tell you there was no admission for *any one*," repeated Sir
Francis, roughly; "after much parleying with your halberdiers,
through the key-hole, I got word of the Council's whereabouts,
and betook myself hither with all speed. I pray ye inform me,
lords and gentlemen, wherefore all this commotion?—has the
city, then, lost its wits, that it has turned itself inside out?"

"Nay, nay, Sir Francis! be not wroth," said Parsons in as
soothing a tone as he could command; "the Papists are up in
arms, they are within the city we know not in what strength."

"And the honorable Council and the Lords Justices fearing for
their precious lives have locked themselves out—ha! ha! ha!—
i' faith, a good joke!—here ye be in an unfortified house outside
the walls, open to all the country round, and the enemy, as ye
say, left in snug possession of the premises within—whoever before heard of men locking themselves *out* for safety!" And
Sir Francis, albeit little given to mirth or merriment, threw himself into a chair and laughed full heartily, regardless of the
frowns and menacing looks of his brother councillors, who
winced individually beneath his biting sarcasm.

"I rejoice," said Meredith, "to see the gallant Sir Francis
Willoughby make so light of this matter—methinks it is over
grave for jesting, seeing that a leading man amongst the Papists
is already in custody, and other arrests are hourly looked for."

"I knew nought of that," said Willoughby, "but this I know,
to wit, that from Galway hither I have seen no signs of this
mighty rebellion whereof ye speak. And yet methinks if there
were any such movement on foot amongst the Irishry that coun-

try would not lie still. There be as arrant Popish knaves where
I come from, ay! and in as great numbers, as you would find in
any part of this island. An' you take my advice, Sir William
Parsons, you will move back to our old quarters bag and baggage ere the day be an hour older—for our own credit do this
that our name and authority fall not into disrepute even amongst
those who be well disposed—first of all, however, I would break
my fast, an' it please our honorable host——"

" Ay, surely," cried Borlase, endeavoring to get rid of the
drowsy god by a vigorous shake and a most energetic yawn; "ay,
surely, Sir Francis, men do assuredly fight better and talk better
when the stomach is in good condition, to wit, well supplied with
wholesome food. I never prospered on anything I took in hands
fasting—" he had just reached for the hand-bell to summon the
steward of the house, when bang at the outer gate came a new
series of knocks, or rather blows, as of heavy sticks.

" There," said Parsons, addressing Willoughby, half in fear half
in exultation, " what think you of that?—who be they that demand admission in such fashion as that?".

" That will I tell you full soon," replied the stout soldier, as he
made for the door, while Meredith and Rotherham approached
one of the high narrow windows looking on the small court, hoping to discover by the help of the dawning light the cause of this
new commotion.

No one ventured, however, to follow Willoughby to the hall,
and when, after a very brief absence, he again entered the room,
his first words were anything but satisfactory.

" The rebels, my Lords Justices! the rebels are upon us!"

" The rebels!—how say you, Sir Francis?—surely—surely
they have not attacked the house—why it would not stand an
hour's siege!"

" I know that, Sir John—I know it full well, but the dwelling
is safe for this time—I see but one recusant on the premises, and
he is in good hands——"

" How?—who?"

" Be not alarmed, Sir William—your fellows have taken another
of these wasps—it was their truncheons that battered the gates

so lustily even now—are your lordships in readiness to examine the rascal, whose name I know not ?"

" I say nay," put in Borlase quickly ; " let him e'en cool his heels till we have answered the demands of our several stomachs —I'll warrant him not over anxious for the meeting——"

This proposition was unanimously adopted, and the morning meal being happily announced at the moment, the two Lords Justices and the five Privy Councillors proceeded, nothing loath, to the discussion of the good things awaiting their attention. This important affair took up the best part of an hour, during which time the Irish chieftain, the descendant of a lordly line, was left shivering on the stone bench in the fireless hall, whose low arched roof was dripping with damp, for Sir John Borlase grudged all expense which had not his own comfort for its immediate object, and hence a fire in the outer hall would have been a superfluity.

It were hard to describe the feelings of the prisoner during that dreary time of expectation, which, however, he turned to some account, for when at length he was summoned to the presence of the Council, the stone walls of the vacated hall were found ornamented in strange fashion. Ghastly visages of tortured men, figures dangling from gibbets, and other such quaint and horrible devices were sketched on either side with a master hand and of life size.* This audacious act was duly stated to the worshipful assembly at the moment when *Costelloe McMahon* was ushered by the sheriff's officers into the judicial chamber. Seven pairs of eyes were immediately turned on him, some in wrath, some in contempt, some in mere curiosity, but the Tanist of Uriel shrank not from the darkest scowl of all, even that of Sir William Parsons.

Drawing his short cloak around him, and shaking back the long curled locks from about his face, he walked to the foot of the Council-table with a step as light and as proud a mien as though he trod his native plains at the head of his martial clan. His clear blue eye met in turn the searching glance of each of

* This fact is historically true. It is strikingly illustrative of the bold and reckless character of the brave but unfortunate McMahon.

his judges, but the lid never drooped for a moment, nor did the spirit-light of that eye grow dim.

"Good faith, he were a gallant leader this," muttered Willoughby to himself, as his soldier-glance scanned the fair proportions of the prisoner and marked his dauntless bearing.

"What is this I hear, McMahon?" said Parsons at length, as he disposed his clumsy members in the chair of presidential dignity at the upper end of the long table; "how came you so far to forget the respect due to this house as to disfigure the walls thereof with foul daubing?"

"Ask your fellows, rather, how it came that they did not see it done—methinks it was for them to keep watch on my evil propensities?"

"So please your lordships," cried the three bailiffs in a breath, "we did but go into the steward's room near by to warm our hands, the which were well nigh frozen!"

"Even so it was with mine," said McMahon carelessly; "I found the vault over cold for my liking, and being, moreover, left to my own wits for company, I was moved to exercise my fingers in the delineation of certain pleasant fancies which came into my head."

"An' the churl had only clothed his unsightly criminals after the manner of his own barbarous tribe," said Borlase, entering the room, after a critical inspection of the obnoxious images; "I might easier overlook the injury done me, but as I am a living man this day, they are clothed in decent English garb—ay! every one of them!"

While some of the Council turned aside to conceal a smile, Parsons again fixed his scathing glance on the prisoner, who was smiling too. "This surely heightens the offence, McMahon! The meaning of this bloody riddle we can all of us see——"

"It was my purpose that you *should* see it," said McMahon haughtily; "men do say that Sir William Parsons is not over quick of comprehension, but he were duller than one of his own donkeys an' he could not read so plain a lesson!"

A livid hue overspread the massive features of the Lord Justice, and a gleam of lurid fire—a single gleam, shot from his eye, as though charged with the lightning's destructive power. But he

was not the man to give way to violent emotion, at least in outward show, and so terribly calm was the tone in which he next
addressed the prisoner—that the latter looked at him in some
surprise, a surprise which was not shared by Parson's brethren of
the Council who knew the man better.

" It is well, it is very well," he said with a sort of portentous
smile, " you have shown us at once the full extent of your malig-
nity, and thereby saved much trouble. You appear to be somewhat plain spoken, and may, therefore, throw some light on this
matter, to wit, the traitorous rising up of the Irishry against the
King's majesty——"

" That the rising will take place, nay, has taken place in many
parts of this Kingdom of Ireland, I freely admit," said McMahon,
calmly ; " that it is against the King's majesty I deny—and I desire that your scribe yonder put this my solemn denial on record.
If his highness were left free to deal with his Irish subjects,
according to his own royal clemency and justice, there would be
no discontent among us."

" Most like not—an' ye had your way in all things, ye might
be content to give the King his. His grace is much beholden to
you. Pity it is, though, that so gracious a sovereign and such
loyal subjects should so little understand one another."

" It well becomes Sir William Parsons to talk in that fashion,"
said McMahon, with bitter emphasis ; " none knows better than
he the causes which keep our liege lord and his faithful Irish
subjects from coming to an amicable agreement. Your lordship
and some others whom we wot of may live to feel that we are
over loyal for your liking, though you speak the word now in
scorn. Our lord the king, likewise, may learn all too soon—pray
God it be not to his cost—that treason and rebellion lurk full
often under robes of state !"

This home-thrust told so well on the thick hide of Sir William's conscience that the purple tint faded from his dark visage,
and was replaced by an ashy paleness. He rose from his seat,
sat down again, drew a long convulsive breath, then coughed
slightly once or twice as though to clear away the last lingering
remnant of emotion, and was finally about to address the prisoner,

who was all this time engaged in adjusting his girdle, when Willoughby stood up:

"My Lord Justice," said he, "I crave your pardon. This insolence exceeds the bounds of toleration. We cannot allow farther speech before this Council to a man who can so far forget the respect due to such authority——"

A scornful laugh from McMahon elicited a dark scowl from Parsons and a fierce threat from Willoughby. Some of the other members urged dispatch, as, from certain sounds outside the house, they had reason to believe that either some other prisoners or at least fresh intelligence had arrived.

"Pray God it be not Maguire!" murmured McMahon, half audibly, enlightened by a sudden presentiment. It was Maguire, and before any further question could be put to his friend he was brought in looking as

"——— Ghastly, pale, and wan
As he who saw the spectre-hound in Man."

And yet there was nothing craven or cowardly in the manner with which he confronted the imposing array around the table. He was still the Irish peer, the chieftain of Fermanagh, looking down, as it were, on his upstart judges from an elevation all the greater for the misfortune which had placed him in their power. With him indeed the flesh was weak, but the spirit strong, and so McMahon felt as their eyes met in melancholy greeting.

After a short whispered consultation amongst the councillors as to whether the prisoners should be examined apart or face to face, the former was decided on. Lord Maguire was removed to an adjoining chamber until such time as McMahon's examination was brought to a close. Again the friends exchanged glances.

"Courage, Connor!" said McMahon in Irish; "all is well that ends well!"

"True, Costelloe," returned the peer dejectedly; "but *this* cannot end well——"

"Why not," called McMahon after him, as he was conveyed to the door; "what can they do but take our lives, and surely you would not shrink from a patriot's death——"

" Silence, prisoner!" cried a stern voice from the table ; "you presume on our indulgence !"

A contemptuous laugh was McMahon's answer, as Parsons rose in wrath to examine him.

" You are cognizant, are you not, of a deep-laid conspiracy amongst certain individuals to overturn the existing government and——"

" To destroy rather the ferocious and tyrannical reign of despotism in this island——"

" Note well his answers!" said the galled Puritan Justice to the Clerk of the Council.

" Ay! note them well," replied the prisoner; "put them down in black and white ; they will soon be copied in my blood!"

" Silence!"

" You admit a knowledge of this traitorous plot!"

" I admit that your government is in danger!"

" And you were a party to the design concerning the seizure of the Castle?"

" I was—I came up to Dublin, with other lords and gentlemen, with intent to take that fortress!"

" Be so good as to name some of these lords and gentlemen!"

" Not one of them will I name!"

" We can force you—there be persuasive arguments at our command—ay! arguments to overcome even *your* contumacy!"

"I deny it," said McMahon firmly; " I know the arguments you mean—the rack, the thumbscrew, and other such appliances for Popish flesh and blood—you may use them on me, an' welcome——"

" Sirrah!" cried Willoughby, starting from his seat, " your *life* is forfeited even now——"

" I know it, *sir!*—I scorn to give back your scurvy *sirrah*— I know I stand here alone and helpless in the power of those who never spared or pitied one of my race or creed—but, nevertheless, I pledge ye my word as an Irish gentleman, my Lords Justices, and ye of the Council, that not one drop of my blood shall fall unrevenged—there be those in arms, ay! and in *power*, who will settle the score with ye all!"

Further attempts were then made to induce McMahon to

impeach some of his "fellow-conspirators," but not another question would he answer, and some of the Council being anxious to get rid of the affair, besought that this contumacious rebel might be remanded for further examination, and the other prisoner brought in at once.

"Keep him in the hall," said Borlase, "till the other is disposed of. Let him e'en study his morning's work—but, hark you, Milman! see that his hands be made fast—no more sketching, an' you value whole bones!"

Maguire's examination occupied but little time. With characteristic caution and timidity he persisted in denying all knowledge of a conspiracy against the government. Unlike McMahon he neither boasted nor threatened—he knew nothing, and hence could tell nothing, or criminate any one. The only outburst of feeling that escaped him was when the Lord Chancellor Meredith, on the part of the Council and the King's majesty, held out to him hopes of pardon if he would name some of the lords and gentlemen implicated in the plot. On this, the blood of the Maguires took fire.

"Plot!" cried the chieftain indignantly; "I have said I know of no *plot*, but suppose I *did* know that all the chief men of our persecuted native race, and all the tribes who look up to them as rulers, were resolved no longer to be crushed as worms, but to cast off, come what may, the intolerable burden laid upon them for their destruction—suppose I were to tell you *that*, which, perchance, your wisdom may see without hint of mine —it were needless to name any—all being of the same mind. Work your will on the children of the soil collectively, for assuredly we are all of the one mind in regard to your doings, but that is all I have to tell you, though you tore me to pieces on the rack."

"It is very well," said Parsons, with his gloomy smile; "summon hither the Constable of the Castle—I believe he is in attendance." That functionary quickly appeared, and to him were delivered the two prisoners, with a delicate hint from the Lord Justice that it might be necessary hereafter to initiate them into the mystic rites of the Star-chamber. Maguire changed countenance on hearing this, though he tried to force a smile. McMahon answered with a gesture of haughty indifference and a careless laugh.

" Do you affect Irish music, Sir William ?" said the reckless Tanist of Uriel ; " if so, you may have a serenade full soon from the pipes and clairseachs of Ulster. I hear them even now—far off as in a dream—and *vengeance* breathes in every tone !"

" Take them hence," cried Parsons, almost speechless with anger, and the prisoners were accordingly conveyed to the dungeons of that Castle which in a few hours was to have been their own.

4A

CHAPTER VI.

"What I do next, shall be, to tell the king of this escape, and whither
  they are bound."   SHAKSPEARE'S *Winter's Tale.*

> " As spiders never seek the fly,
>   But leave him of himself t' apply,
>   So men are by themselves employ'd
>   To quit the freedom they enjoy'd,
>   And run their necks into a noose,
>   They'd break 'em after to get loose."
>
> BUTLER'S *Hudibras.*

HALF an hour or so after Lord Maguire and his friend were
committed to the Castle-prison, a small wherry might have been
seen, floating idly down the Liffey's turbid stream, not far from the
Old Bridge. Its only occupant was a lubberly boy of that amphi-
bious class, midway between the seaman and the landsman, then
as now to be found about the water side in sea-port towns, well
content to do nothing, yet able to take a hand on either element
at any species of work which required only bone and sinew. His
bullet eyes were gazing listlessly on a crowd of persons assembled
at the corner of Bridge street, around an officially-clad personage,
who was reading aloud from a manuscript document in his hand.
Stolid as the youth was he could not but perceive that some
unusual bustle was going forward. All along the quay, and in
the various streets opening on it from the city, men were hurrying to and fro, exchanging significant words as they passed
each other, as if all were bent on a common object.

" I'm thinking there's some news abroad this morning," said
Perry to himself, but without any troublesome feeling of curiosity,
" an' it were not that master bade me keep the boat here about
the bridge-foot till I'd light on a fare, I'd be ashore before

this to see what's in the wind. Hillo, master!—do you want a boat?"

This was in answer to a signal made him by a sailor on the bridge-steps. Another sign in the affirmative brought the boat close alongside, and the sailor jumping in, stretched himself with a lazy yawn on a bench in the stern. In answer to the boy's question, as to where he wished to be rowed to, the sailor, with a drunken hiccup, pointed to some three or four of his fellows who had joined the crowd on the quay and seemed listening intently to the reading aforesaid.

"Hang the lubberly knaves, what an itching they have for news!" grunted their comrade in the boat; "we have got but this one day a-shore, and they e'en clip it shorter than it be—(hiccup!)—hearkening to some fal-de-ral not worth a brass farthing. Hark ye, Watty!" raising his voice to the utmost, "what the plague's got into your noddle?"

His voice appeared to set Watty and his mates in motion, for they instantly detached themselves from the crowd and walked towards the boat with that shuffling gait peculiar to their craft. They were all more or less under the influence of liquor, and laughed uproariously at the angry rebuke of their companion.

"Time enough, Bill! time enough," cried one of the last arrivals; "your old dame's porridge will keep hot, never fear!"

"But, what—what the puck made you stand there gaping?"

"We were a-listening not a-gaping, Bill!" said the man addressed as Watty; "yonder fellow is reading what they call a proclamation, so as we never chanced to hear the like before, Launcelot and the rest of us had a mind to listen."

"A proc——, what did you say it was?" demanded Bill.

"A proc-la-ma-tion! do you hear it now?"

"Ay, marry, do I—(hiccup!)—but I be nothing the wiser for the hearing. What is it like, that proc——, hang the word!—"(hic —hiccup!)

"Hang your scurvy memory," retorted Watty, with a hoarse laugh; "the word is well enough. An' you want to know what it's all about, why, it's a chance for somebody to win five hundred gold marks by delivering up to justice one Roger O'Moore, a certain wild Irishman who, it seems, has been raising the old d—l in these parts. An' the fellow is only half as bad as they make him out, his whole carcass be not worth the money, though any one who brings in his *head* will get it. Strike me dumb if these great folks on shore be not greater fools than any we have on sea!—pull out now, my lad, we'll lend a hand an' you give us oars!—up, Bill, up—take an oar, you lubber! or the dame's cookery may go for nought!" Bill's intoxication did not prevent him from both taking and using the oar, which he did, however, so awkwardly that Perry grinned from ear to ear as he inquired : "Where to, master ?"

"Up the river a piece —we'll show you where to stop. Be alive now and you shall have a trifle to drink our health over and above your fare!"

Before the lad could turn his boat's prow up the stream, he was hailed by another voice from the shore—"Where is that boat bound for ?"

"Can't say, master!" and Perry shook his head with a puzzled air.

"*Can't say*, you blockhead," cried the other angrily ; "I'll teach you to *say*, an' I come within reach. Are you going up or down, sirrah ?"

"Up!" said the boy very gruffly, muttering to himself, at the same time : "You may go seek a passage for all Perry cares, my fine gentleman!"

"Stop, stop, that's my way, too!" shouted the stranger; "stop, I command you!"

But this was not so easy done, had Perry been ever so well inclined, for the sinewy arms of the four sailors had been speeding the boat with all their might, and the little craft was already some distance from the shore skimming the water with amazing swiftness for the lumbering thing she appeared to be. The boy grumbled somewhat about losing another fare, but his good humor was quickly restored when Watty assured him, on the part of himself and his mates, that he should be no loser on the occasion.

"Ay! but he'll have a grudge against me on account of it," said Perry ; "that's Sheriff Woodcock, and a dark man they say he is!"

"Sheriff Woodcock!" repeated one of the sailors carelessly; "Lord! who'd have thought it. He's as arrant a churl as ever I laid my eyes on!"

"Take your time now, lads!" said Bill in an under tone, "no hurry—you understand? till *the worshipful* is out of sight!" and thereupon Bill raised his voice to its highest pitch, and sang, as the boat moved slowly up the stream, a verse of a street-ballad then much in vogue amongst the anti-Irish population of the metropolis :

"Proud and poor,
  Lank and lean,
With matted locks,
  And face unclean,
Owner of a pike and skene—
  Here's your native Celt, O!"

"Pike and skene!" he muttered, exchanging a fierce look with his comrade opposite; "better that than nothing!" Aloud he repeated once again: "Here's your native Celt, O!"

"All is right in that quarter," said the sheriff on the quay; "there can be no deception in the good will with which the fellow gives *that* out, and no man of the Irishry would sing it."

"I think your worship is well shot of such company," spoke a shrill voice at his side, and turning quickly the official personage encountered the flabby face of his subordinate John Steeples; "the fellows are as drunk as swine! Let them e'en go their way—though they be loyal, too, as my ears tell me—howsomever, worshipful sir, an' you'll step this way, I have a word for your particular hearing. I pray you heed not the boat, good master! for though the song be not bad, and so well sung that I could share a can of beer with the singer, an' I had him near me at a leisure hour, still the hearing of it will put no gold in your worship's pocket, nor would the sail to Island Bridge, for that matter, but an' you'll come with me to a private place, I can tell you something that may fill every pocket you have with gold pieces!"

Anxious to hear this lucrative secret, the sheriff followed his familiar to a small house in Winetavern street, where John had

a back room at command. "You know, John," said the employer, with a very serious face, as he took his seat near the
blazing hearth; "you know, John, gold is nothing to me—
nothing—but the duties of mine office are—I need not tell *you*,
John—are—*everything !*"

"I know it, your worship! I do know it," quoth John, with a
look which he intended to convey honest conviction; "hence it is
that I am so urgent in this matter." Then lowering his voice to a
whisper, he stepped over on tip-toe, and stretching out his short
neck till his face almost touched the grave official countenance:
"I have found out the chief plotter in this rebellion!"

"What—whom do you mean?" cried the sheriff with a start.

"I mean *Roger O'Moore !*" said John, drawing himself up with
an air of superlative exultation.

"You do, John!" and the sheriff started to his feet; "you
know where to lay your hand on him ?"

"Of a surety, I do !"

"Then, my dear John, give me your hand!—fifty of the gold
marks shall be yours—for the rest, you know, I care nothing,
but the credit of the thing, John !—that is what I prize the most
—with Maguire and McMahon in custody, and now the arch-
traitor, O'Moore—why, man it will make our fortune—let's go,
now, my trusty and right faithful John!"

Taking with them a trio of stout constables whom they met
on the way, they went accordingly to the dwelling of Patrick
Moore, merchant, in the upper part of what is now Lower Bridge
street, where undoubtedly Rory O'Moore had been wont to lodge,
for it was the identical house wherein we first found that chieftain
entertaining his friends. Unluckily for Sheriff Woodcock's professional glory, though the cage was there, the bird was flown.
Master Patrick Moore, being informed of the object of their
search, politely expressed his regret that they had not come a
few hours earlier.

"How so ?" asked the sheriff, with a sad misgiving smiting his
heart.

"Why, because, worshipful sir," said the urbane man of com-
merce, "Mr. O'Moore left his lodgings here before daylight this
morning—to my sorrow, I needs must say, for he is a man of

princely generosity and thinks no more of money than he does of the sand on the floor. I crave your pardon, honored sir, for making free to speak of my own affairs in your presence, but the loss of a good lodger whom one has had on his floor, off and on for three years, is something not easy to get over. You can walk up stairs, gentlemen—assuredly!" seeing some of the constables in the act of ascending.

As for the sheriff, he saw all too clearly that the man spoke in the best of faith, and with a groan that came from the region of his bowels, he called to John Steeples, who was already near the top of the narrow stairway, that he thought it were but losing time to search the house.

"No matter for that, your worship," cried John from above, "I'm determined to see it out—it's something I can't stand to be tricked by a scurvy Irishman, and I *won't* be either, an' I can help it. I'll have him out, an' he's in the house, though I ripped open every bed in it. I'll not leave a hole where a mouse could hide, but I'll know what's in it! An' your worship has a mind to go elsewhere, we can e'en see this matter out—myself and these good fellows."

"And if so be you find him, John! you will bear in mind that you act for me—will you not?"

"Of a surety, sir, I will—make your mind easy on that head!"

With a very polite obeisance, Master Moore let the sheriff out, and with slow and heavy step that interesting specimen of the ornithological tribe took his way to the Castle, where the Lords Justices, and their privileged advisers, were by this time re-established for dispatch of business. Before we enter with his worship those gloomy portals so justly dreaded by the natives of the country, it may be worth while to have another peep at John Steeples as he steps on tip-toe into the apparently deserted sitting-room of Rory O'Moore.

John appeared to have a good understanding with the other members of the search-committee, for the street-door had no sooner closed after their common employer, than that worthy, hearing Master Moore's step on the stairs, hastened to prevent his entrance by double locking the room-door, which having done, he tipped a sly wink at each of his companions, and smiled a grim smile, and nodded his head in a way peculiar to himself, but well understood, it would seem, by those for whom the gesture was meant.

"Sit down now, my mates, and make yourselves at home for a brief space," said the fat constable, in an easy confidential tone, having first taken care to stuff the key-hole; "or perchance it were the better thing for you to make some noise in the way of knocking things about, even as though we were searching with all our might."

Having set his comrades to work pulling furniture hither and thither in the noisiest manner possible, John approached an alcove in the sitting-room, saying with a most complacent air: "If so be we find not Roger O'Moore, we may find somewhat in the shape of a cordial for our empty stomachs this cold morning. These Irish gentlemen, to give the devil his due, are most excellent judges of liquor, and I warrant me this same 'arch-rebel,' as they call him, is not without good store of it in his cupboard!"

This hint was not lost on his companions, and, amid the arduous and laudable employment at which John had placed them, many a wistful look was cast towards the deep recess into which that ingenious personage had dived. Hopes were raised to the highest pitch as flask after flask was drawn forth, to the number of half a dozen, some of them labelled with foreign names which no one there could decipher. These being duly ranged on the table, together with a few goblets, at a signal from John the whole party gathered around like so many cormorants over their prey, their frost-pinched noses and blue cold lips, indicating the need they had of some warming draught.

"Here's the real usquebaugh," said John, taking up a stone flask, and proceeding, as he thought, to pour out some of its precious contents; "there be nothing like it, they do say, for keeping out the cold." Alas! the cruel usquebaugh refused to come, the still more cruel rebels had not left one solitary drop. This first disappointment was bitter, but still hope remained. There were others to be tried, and some of them must needs be full, they were so heavy. With convulsive eagerness, and imprecations not a few, one after one was tried and found wanting—their weight was deceitful—they were all empty as the prophet's gourd,

and with a vengeful oath John Steeples flung the last on the
stone hearth, and shivered it into a thousand fragments, amid
a chorus of shouts from his companions, some angry, some
derisive.

"May the foul fiend fly away with them, boat, and all!" cried
honest John; "an' I thought he would play such a scurvy trick
as to leave his cupboard in this wise, Sheriff Woodcock might
have had his five hundred marks by this time."

"How is that, John?" asked one of the listeners, but John all
at once remembered that in his anger he was committing himself,
so he made an evasive answer, and wisely kept to himself the fact
that he had bargained with a certain Master Dillon, (to wit, Sir
James of that name,) to connive at O'Moore's escape, he being
found cognizant of his whereabouts. The trusty follower of Sheriff Woodcock well knowing that in case he delivered the rebel
chief to justice, his employer would contrive to pocket the lion's
share of the reward, thought it more to his real advantage to
pocket the sum offered by Sir James Dillon, and let the sheriff,
look after his own interest. If truth must be told, too, he had a
trifling grudge against the same gentleman, for and on account
of certain former transactions wherein John had been the dupe
of his master's superior cunning. Hence John's timely appearance on the quay, and the pains he had taken to draw off the
sheriff's attention from the boat which, having said so much, it
is needless to say, contained Rory O'Moore, Colonels Plunket and
Byrne, with the friend who had engaged the boat, and otherwise
provided for their escape.

Having demolished the principal articles of furniture within the
rooms, by way of venting their disappointment, the jackals of the
law, thinking it time to evacuate the premises, made to open the
door, taking it for granted that they had nothing to do but
walk down stairs. Here, however, another and still worse disappointment awaited them: the door was locked and also fastened on the outside, the bailiffs and constables were caught in
a trap of their own making. Threats and promises were alter-
nately addressed by the chafed and angry captives to Master Moore
or some other imaginary personage without, but no word or sound
could their straining ears hear in reply—all within was noise and

4*

clamor, all without silent as the grave. Hungry and cold as the
prisoners were, the keenest pangs of their misery arose from the
recollection of the rich harvest to be reaped that day in the city—
a harvest on which each of them had been building all manner of
speculations. Every expedient that ingenuity could suggest was
tried on the door, and at length the lock yielded to the skill and
perseverance brought to bear on it. Alas! freedom was as far
off as ever—the outward fastening still remained. Hope at length
vanished, and as grim despair began to take its place, the general excitement amounted almost to frenzy, discharging itself in
a torrent of angry abuse on the conscious head of John Steeples,
whom his worthy associates accused as the sole cause of their
misfortune. John defended himself as best he might, alleging
that what he had done was with a view to the common good, and
that no one could charge him with selfish motives. If jars and
flasks were found empty, when they ought in all reason and in
fair play to have been full, surely no one could blame *him*, inasmuch as he was himself a joint sufferer with the rest. His
rhetoric was, however, thrown away—hunger, and cold, and thirst
—yea, even the thirst for gold were all clamoring fiercely against
him, and as time passed brows scowled darker and words came
forth fiercer and more ominous, till, at last, John Steeples' professional hardihood failed him, and he began to shiver with bodily
terror, when affairs took a turn as lucky as unexpected. In a
fit of desperation John's fellow-prisoners made a combined attack
on the door, rushed against it with all their might, and went head
foremost into the corridor without, one over the other in ludicrous
confusion, while the whole venerable fabric shook with the force of
their fall, and a peal of distant laughter echoing from room to
room proved, with provoking clearness, that the mishap was not
the work of chance. Stunned and bruised as they were from
their fall, and mortified beyond endurance at the trick which had
been put upon them, still the sense of recovered liberty was paramount over all, and as John Steeples, with most meritorious
gravity, assisted them in turn to regain the perpendicular, there
was less of anger than of sheepish embarrassment in the general
expression of their faces. Vengeance they, indeed, vowed against
the Moores, young and old, kith and kin; but the desire of car-

rying it out was, for the time, subordinate to the corporal wants before alluded to, and the no less craving longing for a share of the government gold, likely to be flung that day with a liberal hand amongst their honored fraternity. Great in proportion to the peril from which he believed himself to have escaped, was the joy of John Steeples when he trundled down stairs in the rear of his company, free to seek his morning meal at the nearest eating-house, and free, too, from the bodily fear which had been oozing in cold sweat from every pore.

Meanwhile all was confusion amongst the high functionaries of the realm. Entirely ignorant as to the actual extent of the rebellion, fear magnified it into universal, and, in the absence of all reliable information, the very worst was apprehended. It was something, to be sure, that the design on the Castle had been frustrated, (for the hour appointed, according to O'Conolly, for the attack, was now past, without any appearance of insurrection within the walls,) yet that afforded but small consolation when there was no knowing what moment the rebels might come, in overwhelming numbers, to invest the city. Several other members of the Council had made their appearance, including two of the episcopal body by law established. A proclamation was prepared, announcing to the country, in exaggerated terms, the wicked plot which had been so happily frustrated, together with the capture of some of the chief conspirators. Couriers were sent with this document to all the principal lords and gentlemen throughout the provinces, requesting that all possible publicity might be given to it, and this with a view to discourage and prevent any further attempts on the part of the Irish. The city was all bustle and excitement, confined, however, to the officials and hangers-on of the government, for, whether it was that timely warning had been sent over night to the different parties who were to have combined for the attack on the Castle, or that the arrest of Maguire and McMahon was told them before they entered the city, it is certain that they were all invisible during the day, even to the lynx-eyed cormorants of the law.

As the day approached its meridian, and yet nothing heard of the rebels, the vague terrors of the night and of the morning began to clear away somewhat, and by the time Sheriff Woodcock

made his bow before that august body—the zodiac of his solar
system—announcing the continued quiet of the city and its
neighborhood, the Council, and even the Lords Justices, waxed
quite facetious, and many a dull grave jest was bandied about
at the expense of "the beggarly Irishry," who, as Parsons
jocosely observed, "had not mettle enough in them to raise a
stir that might perchance give honest men their own."

"But what of O'Moore, Master Sheriff?" demanded the Bishop
of Meath.

"No word of *him* yet, my reverend lord," returned the obse-
quious official, carefully keeping his morning's adventure out of
sight; "I warrant me has e'en betaken himself out of our reach
in time——"

"Ay, marry," put in Parsons, "they say he is cunning as a
fox, and can shift *himself* out of difficulty let who may get the
worst of it."

"I am well acquainted with his prudence and sagacity," observed the prelate, and he shook his head with a very serious
air; "hence it is that I am ill at ease so long as he remains at
large. I would, for the peace of the country, he were in as safe
keeping as the other two."

"Caged, eh?" cried Willoughby from an arm-chair in a remote
corner; "all in good time, my Lord of Meath! We'll have
them all time enough for the plucking—what say you, Sir William? There be scores of the Popish fowl better worth than
this gallows-bird, O'Moore, who, as I hear, is bare as a picked
bone—let him e'en go, he will bring others into the nest whose
feathers will make soft pillows—ha! ha!"

This demoniacal hint was sharply rebuked by one of the bishops,
while Parsons himself thought it decorous to reprimand his
friend, accompanying the words, nevertheless, with a side glance,
which more than contradicted their meaning.

Willoughby laughed in his usual boisterous way, saying: "I
knew not that any here were so squeamish as regards a joke
—however, an' ye do not relish mine we can e'en let it pass——"

His discordant laugh had not yet died away amongst the arches
of the old oaken roof, when the Council was again thrown into
perturbation by the arrival of Lord Blayney, who, travel-stained

and weary from his long night's ride, suddenly appeared before
the assembled lords in that same room, so memorable in Irish
story, where half a century before

"Silken Thomas flung
King Henry's sword on Council-board the English thanes among."

To the hurried and anxious question of "What news from the
north?" simultaneously put by several voices, Lord Blayney replied in tremulous accents:

"The worst that could be brought—all Ulster is up in arms
under Sir Phelim O'Neill, O'Reilly, McMahon, and other chiefs
of note."

"Merciful Heaven!" cried Sir Robert Meredith, "are you sure
of this, my lord?"

"Sure of it, Sir Robert!" answered Blayney with some indignation; "think you I would travel from Castle Blayney hither on
an idle rumor? Am I sure of it! when all I hold dearest—wife,
children—all—are prisoners in the hands of the fierce McMahons.
God only knows if they be not butchered ere now!"

"And your Castle?" asked Parsons eagerly.

"My Castle, too, is in their possession—oh! that I live to
tell it!"

Lord Blaney's evil tidings, if the first, were not the last of that
eventful day. Towards evening, the Council was brought together again by a message from Sir Arthur Tyringham, governor
of Newry, to the effect that the garrison had been taken by the
Magennises, together with a large quantity of military stores—
the latter was deemed even the greater loss, inasmuch as it furnished the rebels with what they most wanted, and, moreover,
what the government could but ill spare at the time.

The courier from Newry was quickly followed by another
from Dungannon, announcing the capture of that fort by Sir
Phelim O'Neill.

"What! Dungannon taken, too?" cried Willoughby.

"Yea, my lord!" replied the soldier who had brought the
news; "but that is not all—Charlemont is likewise in the hands
of the rebels—the same crew that took Dungannon made straight
for Charlemont."

"Charlemont! well nigh the strongest place in Ulster!—surely you mistake, good fellow! they can have no artillery—no siege-engines—by St. George! an' they took *that* fort so easily, it is foul shame to the garrison—I would shoot every man of them, my lords and gentlemen!—I would—or worse death—yea, even hang them like dogs for arrant cowards as they be!"

"I warrant O'Neill will save us the trouble, Sir Francis!" observed Parsons, while the others talked apart in low, eager whispers. "How is it, soldier! did the rebels kill all before them?"

"Not that I heard of, my lords! As yet they have but taken prisoners." This almost incredible news elicited no word of commendation, softened no heart on behalf of "the Irishry." Leaving the Council to digest the astounding intelligence hourly pouring in from the north, we must hasten to relieve the reader's anxiety for the fate of Rory O'Moore and his faithful friends. Acting their assumed parts with consummate skill, so as to keep Perry under the impression that they were nothing more than they seemed, they managed to get safe on shore some miles up the river. After dismissing the boat with the promised gratuity to Perry—so small as not to excite his suspicions, they took their way inland, and when once out of sight of the river, shook hands and parted, each one betaking himself to the house of an acquaintance in the neighborhood, lest they, remaining together, should attract attention. The future steps to be taken had all been previously arranged. As for O'Moore, he found a safe and pleasant asylum at the house of his daughter, then lately married to a certain Mr. Sarsfield,* and residing at Lucan. There he remained for a day or so until he effected his escape to the north.

* And these were subsequently the parents of one of Ireland's most illustrious sons—Patrick Sarsfield.

CHAPTER VII

" Yet hadst thou thy vengeance—yet came there the morrow,
    That shines out, at last, on the longest dark night—
When the sceptre that smote thee with slavery and sorrow,
    Was shiver'd at once like a reed in thy sight."

                                    MOORE'S *Irish Melodies.*

" He rose the first—he looms the morning star
    Of the long, glorious, unsuccessful war—
England abhors him! Has she not abhorr'd
All who for Ireland ventured life or word ?
What memory would she not have cast away,
That Ireland hugs in her heart's-heart to-day ?"

                                    T. D. McGEE.

A WEEK had produced unhoped-for changes in Ulster. As if
by magic, all the land had changed masters, and from Lough
Sheelan's waters in O'Farrel's country,* to the shores of Lough
Swilly and Lough Foyle, in the far north, the banners of the native chiefs floated in triumph over fortress, tower, and town. In
all the province of Ulster, from the green hills of Cavan to Antrim's rugged coast, with the single exceptions of Derry, Carrickfergus and Enniskillen, there was not one stronghold in stranger
hands. Over Charlemont and Dungannon, Benburb, Mountjoy,
and Portmore, the Red Hand waved as in days of old, side by
side with the royal banner of England, for it was Phelim O'Neill's
proudest boast that he and his warred not against their sovereign,
but only to resist the further aggressions of his government in Ireland, regarded by the whole Catholic body as traitors to the royal

* Now the county of Longford.

cause, as well as ruthless oppressors of themselves. Ever blindly attached to the house of Stuart, the native Irish were but too ready to make excuses to themselves for the ungrateful and perfidious conduct of Charles, and to throw the blame on his officials in Dublin, who were consequently the avowed objects of their undying hostility. Parsons and Borlase with their host of satellites constituted the actual scourge of Catholic Ireland at that day, and they, with the system of robbery and persecution which they represented, must be swept away, as the chieftains thought, before the king could carry out his merciful designs in their favor. Hence it was that the banner of England floated on the northern breeze wherever the native arms prevailed, and so it was all through what is strangely called the great *Rebellion*. But to return. Tyr-Owen, as I said, was Phelim's own—ay! every rood of it. Newry, and all the Ban country were subject once again to the ancient lords of Iveagh. The strong fort of Tanderagee was taken from the enemy by the brave O'Hanlons; the venerable city of Patrick, the Primatial See of Ireland, was captured by Phelim O'Neill after a fierce and protracted resistance; the gallant McDonnels of the Glynns did their duty well in Antrim, notwithstanding the threatening proximity of the Scotch garrison of Carrickfergus; the McMahons, roused to tenfold fury by the news of their brave Tanist's imprisonment, swept over their entire country, within the first few days of the insurrection, so that not one place of refuge remained to the enemy in all the county of Monaghan.

In Fermanagh, for a similar reason, the arm of vengeance fell with deadlier force. The Maguires were a stern and a warlike race, men of Spartan courage and iron will, and it grieved them sore to think that *their* lord should languish in dungeon vile when other clans marched to battle with their chieftains at their head.

When the news of Maguire's capture first reached his own domains, his brother Roderick assembled the men of his name who had not as yet joined Sir Phelim's army, and announced the disaster which had come upon them. A roar, or rather a mighty groan, was heard, like that of the angry ocean, when its waves are lashed into sudden fury,—the crowd heaved to and fro as though agitated by one common instinct, then all was ominously still, save the voice of one who cried aloud—

"What can be done, O Roderick, for the chieftain of our race ?"

"Nought can we do," made the brother answer, in a sorrowful tone ; "nought can we do, for Connor,—the fangs of the serpent are in his flesh, and while life is left him he will be their prey—justice neither he nor McMahon can expect, and word or act of ours were alike powerless on their behalf—to God's mercy, then, must we entrust them, hoping that ere it be too late, we may win freedom for them with our strong arms—but this can we do—" he paused and surveyed the breathless crowd with a kindling fiery glance—" an' we cannot save them from ignominy, torture, and, perhaps, *death*—we can gloriously revenge them—we can do what I am well assured they would wish us to do—yea, what will gladden their sorrowful hearts to hear of—we can drive the foreign herd like swine from this land of ours—we can do unto them that which they have for ages done unto us—we will do *our* part of what needs must be done, if we would longer breathe God's air and live above ground !"

A wild shout of approbation denoted the kindred sentiments of the people, and the lake shore resounded with the ancient war-cry of the Clan Maguire, announcing to the English garrison, shut up within the walls of Enniskillen, that all the country round was in open rebellion, that the fierce sept, whom even in repose they feared, were now girding on the weapons of war. And they did gird them on with a vengeance, and the Tanist kept his stern vow, for annalists tell that Rory Maguire, "brother of the Lord Maguire," ruined and devastated the English possessions in Fermanagh, and carried fire and sword to the very walls of Enniskillen. He had an uncle, too, a valiant gentleman, one Lorcan More Maguire, who did good service all during those trying times, and between them they made Fermanagh too hot for the enemies of their race and creed. Lorcan was a great lover of the marvellous, and to him were made all the spiritual " warnings." and other like manifestations affecting the fate of the Maguires. Accordingly, the news of his nephew's imprisonment had no sooner reached him than he declared it had all been foreshown

him by dreams and divers remarkable omens, not to speak of
the Banshee, whose doleful cries had been nightly ringing in his
ears for weeks. And still her voice haunted his slumbers, Lorcan
said, but her wail was mingled with beseechings for revenge, and
the old man vowed she should have enough of it, or be his race
"unwept" for ever more. And yet by a strange anomaly, characteristic, however, of the Irish people, there was comparatively
little blood shed during that first memorable week even in Fermanagh. With the sole exception of Enniskillen—which, for
want of artillery, the Irish were unable to take—every town and
fortress in the county was seized by the Maguires, the well-filled
barns of the strangers furnished provisions for the patriot soldiers,
and their owners were most terribly frightened by the wild and
vengeful threats which those who uttered them had no intention
of carrying out. By a singular stretch of mercy and forbearance,
English and Scotch Protestants were permitted to betake themselves, which they did in droves, to the sheltering walls of Enniskillen, Derry, or Carrickfergus, as the case might be, and instances were not wanting of their being allowed to take with them
what valuables they could collect.*

In Cavan the O'Reillys were up and stirring, but their warfare
was marked by that calm, yet firm moderation, which we have
seen manifested in the speech and bearing of their chief on his
first introduction to the reader. When once his mind was made
up on the necessity, as well as justice of the war, no man entered
into its details more minutely, or carried out its operations with
greater energy than he. Still the gentleness of his nature gave
a peculiar character to his share of the military transactions of
the time, and even the most prejudiced Protestant historians bear
honorable testimony to the clemency wherewith the O'Reillys of
Cavan tempered the horrors of civil war in *their* part of the
country. With Philip, their worthy chief, was associated in

---

* This was especially the case at one of the northern castles taken
by Sir Phelim O'Neill, of much-slandered memory, on which occasion the occupants of the fort were seen in broad day carrying off
with them trunks of rich clothing, plate, and even money, the Irish
forces looking on without offering to molest them.

command his cousin Miles O'Reilly, who, at the time of the northern "rising," was High Sheriff of the county. This gentleman
is specially mentioned as heading the first rising of the men of
Breffny, and his gallant spirit sustained and cheered them on
through many a trying scene of the eleven years' war. One of
the first acts of the O'Reillys, after sending their quota to the
general army, and taking possession of all the strongholds of
their territory, was to restore the churches to their rightful
owners, and this they did in the coolest and most business-like
way imaginable. The usurping clergy were in every parish duly
warned to quit without further notice, as the churches and glebes
were required for the use of those whose fathers built them.
Where any remonstrance was attempted or an appeal made to
the pity of the unwelcome visitors, the latter generally cut the
matter short with a peremptory order to pack up and go, saying it
was only fair that they should have their turn of the hardship
which God's anointed ministers had been made to endure for ages
by them and their friends. The example set by these high-souled
Breffny men was quickly followed throughout the province; the
clergy of the people, hitherto wandering about on sufferance
amongst their flocks, were now publicly installed in the glebe-
houses, and the churches, so long profaned by heretical worship,
were purified and solemnly opened again for the celebration of
the divine mysteries.

Thus within the second week after the rising, the whole aspect
of affairs was changed in Ulster; the native tribes were again in
possession of the soil; the flags of their chieftains floated free
over tower and town;—Religion, so long occult and concealed,
now raised her stately head as of old, and planted her royal
standard on the high places—in Ulster, at least, she was again "the
city on the mountain" seen of all men;—the Cross, her beloved
emblem, for ages hidden away in the caverns of the earth and
the inaccessible fastnesses of the hills, was now brought forth in
triumph and placed on the steeples and on the altars, amid the
exulting shouts of the faithful people, and the loud *hosannas* of
the clergy. It was a proud day when Hugh O'Neill, primate of
Ireland, stood once more at the altar of Patrick on the holy hill
of Ardmacha, and when Heber of Clogher appeared before the

warlike clans of Uriel in full episcopal costume, and offered up
for them in the cathedral which their own valor had recovered
the divine sacrifice of the New Law. When we remember that
these scenes were going on either simultaneously or in rapid succession all over the northern province, while the heretical clergy
who had so long usurped the ancient seats of piety were hud-
dled together within the walls of the few fortresses remaining to
their party in Ulster, we can imagine the wild enthusiasm of a
people in whom the religious sentiment was stronger than all
others, and in whose hearts the triumph or debasement of religion was ever inseparably associated with that of their country.

Of the chieftains who led the people almost everywhere to victory during those eventful weeks, Sir Phelim O'Neill holds the
first place—the traditional reverence in which the name was
held, the position he occupied amongst the native chiefs, and,
above all, the fiery and impulsive vehemence of his character—set
down as *valor* by his compatriots—placed him just where he desired to be, at the head of the Ulster forces. He had established
his head quarters at Newry, a day or two after the general muster of the army, and thence he issued orders with supreme authority, commanding and countermanding as occasion required with
that ceaseless activity which belonged to his character. From
the upper borders of Breffny to the wild capes and headlands of
Innisowen, from Slieve-Gullian and the Mourne Mountains,
to the Western Marches, where Fermanagh stretched into Connaught, Sir Phelim's authority was recognized and his word
obeyed as law; at his command castles and forts were stormed
and taken, protection given, withheld or withdrawn, supplies
levied, and commissions issued. Others of the chiefs, associated
with O'Neill, might have, and undoubtedly had, abilities superior
to his, but so sincere was their general devotion to the cause that no
petty jealousy appears to have arisen amongst them—had they
not been united heart and soul as one man under one head, their
fair province could not have thrown off the shackles of ages in
one single week, giving an example to the sister-provinces which
in due time they followed.

Considering, then, the leading part which Sir Phelim O'Neill
took in this magnificent revolution in the north, it is easy to un-

derstand the detestation with which he was regarded by the generation of robbers whom he dispossessed—very uncivilly, no doubt—of the lands and livings from which the lawful owners had been driven out to make room for *their* fathers in a bygone age. It was very unpleasant, to be sure, for the bloated "planters" of Ulster, to be forced to disgorge the six counties swallowed with so much unction in the days of bountiful King James, and little wonder it is if they looked upon Stout Phelim as a very ungracious leech. Hence the massacres and wanton cruelties which they delighted to lay to his charge, magnified by the traditional hatred of their descendents into the blackest and most atrocious crimes, so that Phelim O'Neill is represented to the world as a monster stained by every crime that can disgrace humanity. That he had a heart-hatred of English tyranny, and resented with all the intensity of a fierce and passionate nature the system of spoliation and religious persecution of which his whole race had been for centuries the victims, is as true as that the eight or ten first days of the war so actively carried on by him in Ulster were marked by no massacre or even personal outrage beyond what was incidental to the violent transfer of a whole province from one set of masters to another.

But, leaving this digression—which, after all, is no digression —let us see what has become of Rory O'Moore, and how the news of the Ulster rising is received in the other provinces. As yet all seemed quiet in Leinster, and the government proclamation, duly read in the proper places, and duly posted on church and other public doors, seemed to have the desired effect—the Palesmen were as peaceable and "well-affected" towards the powers that were as even Parson's heart could wish, when suddenly the border parts of the south were found to be in quite an alarming commotion, and before the loyal could tell what it meant, within a mile or so of the then strong fortress of Ardee, almost within range of the guns, a suspicious gathering of the people was observed, occupying a decidedly suspicious position on the slope of one of the few hills in the vicinity—if hills we may call the occasional undulations of a vast plain. Rumors got afloat, and penetrated even to the English garrison of the castle, that one of the rebel leaders was there in person, and, in great excitement, the governor dispatched a troop of horse, under the command of his lieutenant, Sir John Netterville, to ascertain whether the report were true, and, in any case, to send the people about their business, seeing that they had no business there.

When the young noble of the Pale approached the multitudinous assembly on the hill, he was much surprised to perceive them fully equipped with such arms as country people could improvise, to wit, pikes, bludgeons, scythes, and other such unsoldierly implements of warfare, and so unsightly did these appear that Netterville could not refrain from smiling, while his men laughed outright. There was that, however, in the resolute air of the peasants as they drew together at the approach of the cavalry, firmly grasping their formidable weapons, which instantly checked the unseasonable mirth of the soldiers, and made their leader himself look grave. He immediately ordered one of his troopers to the front with a white flag, calling out himself at the same time:

"Peace, peace, good people!—we come not as enemies!—who is in command amongst ye?"

"An old acquaintance of yours, Sir John Netterville!" said a gentleman in a Spanish hat and an Irish cloak, advancing from a farm-house in the centre of the crowd, the people giving way respectfully as he passed. It was no other than our friend Watty, the drunken sailor of the Liffey, though Perry would have had some difficulty in recognizing him, as he exchanged a graceful salute with the royal officer.

"What! Roger O'Moore! or do mine eyes play me false?" the latter cried in amazement.

"Surely no, Sir John!" said O'Moore with his bland smile; 'methinks those gracious orbs of thine were much at fault, an' they knew not my lineaments!—how fares the good lord your father."

"Well in body, Roger," replied Netterville with a meaning smile, "but wofully afflicted in spirit because of the doings of these—ahem!" he stopped abruptly, and glanced at the motley array before him.

"I understand you, Sir John," said O'Moore in Irish, and he spoke with a bitterness all unusual; "I heard of my lord

Netterville, with the other chief men of the Pale, hastening
many days since to offer their services at the Castle—they asked
for arms, too, it would seem, to use against their poor countrymen of the same faith, who are fighting *their* battle as well as
their own—faugh! they stink in our nostrils, those magnates of
the Pale—for all many of them *were* my good friends and kinsmen—inasmuch as that, with noble blood in their veins, and
the profession of faith on their lips, they crouch like hounds at
the feet of those who have wronged the Catholics of this nation
beyond forgiveness, as beyond reparation—yea! who are sworn
to cut us off root and branch—ah! Sir John Netterville! I shame
to hear of these craven doings, and trust me! my heart is sore
oppressed with grief to see *you* in such livery—you, of whom I
had better hopes!"

"So said my Lord Moore but yester-eve," cried Sir John
with a gay laugh, speaking fluently the same tongue. "He and
his family have betaken themselves to Drogheda for shelter—fearing, God wot, to trust the strength of his own walls—he seems to
have no great opinion of my loyalty, for, as I was saying, he told me
over night, as you did but now, that he had thought me a loyal
gentleman and a true son of a noble father—i'faith an' I am
doubted on every side, I must e'en doubt myself——"

"Sir John Netterville!" said O'Moore, advancing a step or two
with outstretched hand, "what am I to think—what brings you
hither in such guise if, indeed, you be what my heart would
fondly hope?"

"Stand back, Roger! not a step farther, an' you value my head
and your own! For your thoughts of me, I would have them favorable—what brought me hither was to disperse this tumultuous ·
gathering—so the order runs—an' you take a friend's advice, ye
will move from here, and thereby show that I did my errand—but
hark you, Roger! keep your men together, and march northward—a little way beyond the borders into Farney—there let
them remain in arms till you have concerted measures with those
you know in the far north!"

"Thanks, Sir John, thanks! That course is surely safest and
best—but you?"

"Oh! leave me to my own wits"—and again Netterville laughed

as he turned his rein, and made a sign to his subordinates to ride on —" suffice it for the present, that I *feel* as you do, and will *act* accordingly, when occasion serves, so help me God and my good patron St. John!—nay, doubt me not, Roger!—I have plans in my head of which you may hear ere long to your satisfaction— but name me not in the councils of your friends—the time is not yet come—farewell! and I pray you to bear this in mind, that all the Catholic gentlemen of the Pale are not so pliant, or so oblivious of past and present wrong as my honored father and his peers *would seem to be !*"

The last words were uttered in a tone so significant that O'Moore could not help laying them up for future reflection. One doubt, however, remained to be solved.

"A word with you, Sir John," he called after Netterville, in a subdued tone, " I am to conclude that your people do not understand our language —but how is it that you seem to have no fear of exciting their suspicions by such lengthened parley with me ?"

" Why, man! from the distance at which we stood," said the other, riding back a few yards, " they would have had good lugs an' they heard what passed—for the rest I have no fears —not one of them would harm a hair of my head for Lord Moore's estate ! go your ways, Roger, and God have you in care till we meet again—by then you may know many for friends whom you now, perchance, esteem as foes !"

" Heaven grant it be so !" murmured O'Moore, as he gazed a moment after the gallant cortege, his eyes resting with pride and no small degree of hope on the light and graceful form of the young Norman noble. Many questions were by this time buzzing in his ears, from the curious and eager listeners around him, and to answer them satisfactorily he took the principal men amongst them into the farm-house before-mentioned, where, after a short consultation, the march into McMahon's friendly country was agreed upon, until such time as orders could be received from head-quarters. It is needless to say that while O'Moore rode post-haste to join the northern chieftains at Newry, the sturdy Louth men were welcomed with joyful acclamation by their neighbors "over the border," in the Irish country, who naturally hailed their accession as the first instalment from the Pale.

On his way from Ardee to Newry, O'Moore's patriot heart was gladdened by the tidings that Longford and Leitrim were up in arms—Leinster and Connaught were at length stirred into action, though as yet only on their outskirts. "I knew the O'Farrels would not long remain inactive," said O'Moore to a Louth gentleman, who, with two of his followers, accompanied him to the camp; "I knew they would speedily snap their chain, for all their officious loyalty—loyalty, indeed! defend us, heaven! from the loyalty which is treason to our bleeding country! But the O'Farrels were in former times such very loyal gentlemen that they must' needs prove their adhesion to the government by fighting their best against Hugh O'Neill, for which, forsooth! they received government commendation, together with a small matter of toleration, by virtue of which they have retained some shreds of their ancient patrimony—they have lately, as I hear, got some kicks and buffets from the Castle-folk, which, most like, spurred them on to make cause with us."

"Ay, marry!" said the Louth man, "I have ever heard the O'Farrels of Longford, marvellously well spoken of within the Pale—good Lord, Mr. O'Moore! what may that mean?" He pointed as he spoke to a bulky object suspended from a tree some twenty yards before them. O'Moore answered not, but rode forward at a more rapid pace, closely followed by the others, till he reached the object in question. It was the body of a man comfortably clad in the English costume.

"It is e'en one of the blood-hounds of the law," said O'Moore with indifference, that was partly assumed, "and look!" pointing to a printed paper on the breast of the corpse, "look you, there is the insolent proclamation lately issued from the Castle —he would read it, doubtless, for some of these fierce border chieftains! methinks that will be the last of such readings this side the march!"

"It is an awful sight!" said Callan, with a heavy sigh; "after all, Mr. O'Moore, war is a direful trade to take up!"—and he spurred his horse to a gallop so as to get out of sight of the hateful object.

5A

" What, man," cried O'Moore, rather more sternly than was his
wont, " you must, ere now, be well used to such sights, or there
be no ' Popish recusants' in your country. I warrant me, these
gallant gentlemen will teach them to dance to another tune ere
long, and moreover, to keep their proclamations for those who
value them !"

They were here challenged by a warder from ·the battlements
of a castellated building, some perches from the high road, and his
husky voice made the Palesmen start. But O'Moore made answer quickly in Irish, telling who they were and on what business,
when a prompt " Pass on, in God's name !" sent the travellers on
their journey with renewed hope and confidence. Even the half-
fearful Louth man exclaimed in a cheerful tone: " Marry, but
times *are* changing—something *may* come of it yet!"

" Never doubt it, man, never doubt it," cried O'Moore, slapping him gaily on the shoulder ; " every step you take now is on
free soil, and by the time you reach O'Neill's camp, you will be
as sure of victory for our arms as I am !"

While O'Moore and his companions were thus beguiling the
weary way to Newry, exchanging friendly greetings ever and
anon with straggling parties from O'Neill's force, the brave
O'Rourkes of Western Breffny were rapidly clearing their ancient territory of the savage brood of vipers who had been so long
preying on their life-blood. One of the most atrocious miscreants
of the robber-race, Sir Frederick Hamilton, was, unhappily for
that county, located in Leitrim, in the midst of princely possessions, which, of right, belonged to the plundered O'Rourkes, and
his stately mansion of Manor Hamilton was nothing better than
a den of marauders, who, under pretence of keeping the Papists
in subjection, periodically issued forth and committed all manner
of depredations (of which robbery was the least offensive) on the
unoffending natives. Any attempt at resistance had hitherto but
provoked still greater cruelty and oppression, for Hamilton and
his hell-hounds, as the people called them, were far too useful to
the Lords Justices to be restrained in their harmless sport of robbing, torturing and murdering such illicit animals as native Papists.
What fell out in Breffny-O'Rourke in those days of retribution
we shall presently see.

CHAPTER VIII.

"The tyrannous and bloody act is done."
SHAKSPEARE.

"The greatest attribute of Heaven is mercy,
And 'tis the crown of justice and the glory,
Where it may kill with right to save with pity."
BEAUMONT AND FLETCHER.

THE torch of freedom had shone but few days on the hills of Leitrim when, as in the neighbouring counties of Ulster, the most brilliant success attended the bold attempts of the native tribes to recover their independence, or rather to free themselves from the iron fangs of the fanatic government, for it never entered into the hearts of any amongst them to reject the authority of King Charles. Many of the chief strongholds of the country were already in possession of the O'Rourkes and other tribes of lesser note, but as yet no attempt had been made on Manor Hamilton, partly on account of the extreme terror in which its freebooting lord was held, and partly, because of the exaggerated ideas entertained regarding the strength of the fortress.

But although this stronghold of fanaticism was still unassailed, many places of equal, or almost equal, importance were snatched from the enemy by the brave and chivalrous Owen O'Rourke, the chosen head of the Leitrim clans—chosen not more on account of his princely lineage than the admirable qualities of his head and heart. Handsome, like most of the chieftains of his race,*

---

* Most of our readers are doubtless acquainted with the story of that O'Rourke of Breffny who, visiting London in the time of Queen Elizabeth, the Royal virgin became so struck with his extraordinary

brave as man could well be, accomplished in all the knightly arts
of war, and withal generous in the highest degree, the O'Rourke
of that day was a man who commanded the respect of all—even
his enemies were forced to acknowledge his high deserts, while
by his own party he was universally loved and esteemed. Such,
then, was the man whom the fate of war opposed to the brutal
and overbearing Hamilton in the wild guerilla warfare of that
remote country. It so chanced that in capturing the various castles and manor-houses of the county, many distinguished persons
of both sexes had fallen into the hands of O'Rourke, and for
some days these were entertained in the dwelling of the chief
with that princely hospitality which became his noble ancestry
rather than his present fortune. Amongst the prisoners were a
few ladies of high rank, either belonging to, or connected with
some of the first English families in Ireland. Now the terror
with which these dames of quality had at first regarded the Irish
chieftain speedily wore away in the genial influence of his presence, surrounded as he was, too, by a most interesting family-
circle—and what with the novelty of their situation, the polite
attentions of the chieftain and his family, and the soothing strains
of the old harper who nightly made his harp discourse most sweet
music from an oaken settle in one of the wide chimneys of the
great hall, the prisoners—at least the female portion of them—
almost forgot their captivity, and learned to love the chains which
the chivalrous O'Rourke contrived to interweave with flowers.

A week had flown away—the number of English in the Castle
was every day increasing, as fort after fort was taken by the
sept, and yet no diminution in the respectful demeanor of the
household, including often whole parties of the fiercest and most
formidable of O'Rourke's followers. The latter, in conformity
with old customs, still took their place at the further end of the

---

personal beauty that she conceived a violent passion for him, and long
detained him near her. It is characteristic of the woman that when,
after a time, her passion cooled, she much desired to have O'Rourke
made away with; and the ill-fated chieftain was accordingly brought
to the scaffold for some frivolous political pretext. This Teige was
not the only one of his race distinguished for personal attractions.

spacious board extending the full length of the hall, the family and their guests occupying the dais or raised portion at the upper end.

It was the middle of November and the wild northern blast was sweeping angrily over the frost-clad hills and moors around the Castle, when about midday word was brought the chieftain that his brother had been taken prisoner that morning by a party of Sir Frederick Hamilton's horse. At first a chillness like that of death crept over the stout warrior, for imprisonment in the gloomy vaults of Manor Hamilton was, to a Catholic, sure to end in death —most likely a death of torture and ignominy.

"Great God!" cried Owen O'Rourke, the cold sweat oozing from every pore of his body, "can it be true that my own—my only brother—the brother who is to me more than a son—that my fair-haired Tiernan is in the power of that blood-thirsty demon?—an' it be so, his chance of life is not worth a straw!"

Suddenly a gleam of hope illumined the darkness of the chieftain's soul, and he bounded from his seat with the lightness of a mountain-deer. "Glory and honor to thy name, my God!" he said almost aloud as he darted to the chamber of his wife to communicate the tidings but late so heart-rending, now of less painful import.

"Bad news were mine to tell you, Eveleen!" said Owen as he threw himself on a cushioned bench beside his still lovely mate, "were it not for one thing."

"How now, Owen," his wife exclaimed with a look of anxious surprise; "there be much in your words and more in your eyes —what has fallen out?"

"Our Teague is a prisoner in the hands of Hamilton!"

"Holy St. Bridget! Owen! can that be true?" and the lady crossed herself devoutly, "an' it be, I marvel at your gaiety!"

"So you might, sweetheart, an' I were thus lightsome without good cause. Bethink you of the number of persons of prime quality who are prisoners here with us—ha! you smile now—the rose returns to your cheek—yes, Eveleen, my faithful wife, let us thank the Lord of hosts who has placed these dames and gentlemen in our hands, for they are hostages for the safety of our brother!—giving *them*, we shall receive *him!* Rejoice with me, oh my beloved!"

But Eveleen did not, could not rejoice. A dark presentiment of evil took possession of her mind, and fears, which she might not utter, lay heavy on her soul. She strove to appear as though she shared her husband's hopes, but beneath the assumed cheerfulness of her outward showing lay the fearful thought that the generous, high-hearted youth, whom all the Clan O'Rourke looked up to as their future chief, was in the power of an incarnate fiend who seemed to revel in bloodshed as the joy of life.

Neither were the gentlemen of his kindred so sanguine as their chief, regarding Tiernan's safety, and if O'Rourke had taken their advice he would have assembled all his forces, and marched at once to storm Manor Hamilton. But the chieftain was confident, having, as he supposed, the guarantee of his brother's safety in his own hands, while, on the other hand, it was his opinion that a sudden attack on a fortress which, without artillery, they could hardly hope to take, would but exasperate Hamilton and perhaps accelerate the catastrophe which by fair means he hoped to avert.

A messenger bearing a flag of truce and accompanied by a suitable escort was accordingly sent without loss of time to Manor Hamilton to inform Sir Frederick that Owen O'Rourke having in his custody a number of prisoners of high standing amongst the English of the Pale, and having just learned that his brother Tiernan O'Rourke had been captured that morning by a troop of cavalry from the Manor, he was willing to deliver all the prisoners before-mentioned into Sir Frederick's hands without ransom or other condition than his brother's release.

Sir Frederick stood on the battlements surrounded by his archers to hear O'Rourke's message. As he listened, a smile of savage ferocity gleamed on his swarthy face, and his great black eyes shone with a lurid light.

"Ho! ho!" he laughed, and his laugh rang strangely out on the moaning wind; "ho! ho! release his brother—ay! marry will I—it were hard to refuse the first favor so good a neighbor ever asked of me. Where be your chieftain now?"

"He waits our return some miles hence at the Haunted Hollow."

"And the prisoners?"

" They are of his company there, Sir Frederick, ready to make the exchange forthwith."

" Pity it is to have such noble dames shivering in the blast. What, ho! there, bring up the prisoner O'Rourke——"

" Is it your pleasure, Sir Frederick," said Manus O'Rourke through his trumpet, " is it your pleasure that we bring the English prisoners hither?"

" As ye will,—stay first to have a sight of your pretty Tanist—bless the boy!" he jeeringly added as the youthful warrior was brought before him by a winding staircase leading from the donjon-vault. " A nice captain, forsooth, for savage rebels."

A joyful shout from the O'Rourkes beyond the moat hailed the appearance of their young lord, who turned and smiled his grateful recognition. Sign he could not make, for his hands were closely manacled. He was going to speak, however, for he advanced a step or two towards the parapet, his soul-lit face beaming with the joy of seeing friends once more, but suddenly his eye caught sight of some strange preparations going on amongst the brutal soldiers near him, and the words died on his lips.

Having once seen him, and being naturally anxious to have him again in their own safe keeping, the faithful clansmen were moving hastily away, in order to bring the English prisoners, when an agonized voice of entreaty reached their ears, high above the wail of the wintry blast. It was that of Tiernan O'Rourke—their hearts told them so—and the words it uttered were " For God's sake, stay!"

Manus O'Rourke and his little party turned quickly back, and again faced the fortress just in time to see their idolized young Tanist launched from the lofty parapet, his body swinging in mid-air above their heads, his death-shriek drowned in a yell of savage mockery from Hamilton and his brutal archers. Alas! the presence of his clansmen, so urgently invoked, afforded no protection to the unhappy victim—they had the horror of witnessing his murder without the power of doing aught on his behalf, when there was not a man amongst them who would not have given his heart's blood to save him. It was a fiendish device, worthy of Hamilton himself, to secure such witnesses for such a spectacle. And oh! the agony which wrung those faithful hearts as with a wild shriek they covered their faces to avoid the maddening sight! Rage and despair filled their souls, and for a moment they could think of nothing but the dread calamity which had come upon them. They were speedily aroused from this torpor by the harsh voice of Hamilton overhead:

" Why dally ye now, men of Breffny?—surely ye have got your message!"

" Ah! you devil's limb!" cried Manus as loudly as his choking passion would permit. " There will come a day for this—an' you had a thousand lives we'll have them all—they say the devil has you bodily, but if all his legions took your part, we'll have revenge for this deed—ay, for every hair in Tiernan's head!"

" Go to h—l!" shouted Hamilton; " an' ye remain a moment longer, these fellows will send ye a shower of arrows—but stay, ye shall have Tiernan home with ye in regard to the prisoners whom your chief holds!"

Before the bewildered followers of O'Rourke could guess his meaning, the rope was severed above, and down amongst them came the lifeless body of poor Tiernan. Reverently and with tender care the precious remains were placed in front of Manus on the horse, and clasping the corpse close to his bosom, that faithful vassal slowly turned and rode away, followed by his comrades, each one of whom registered a vow in his inmost heart that Hamilton should suffer for that day's work if the Lord spared them life.

Shouts of derisive laughter from the battlements followed the mournful cavalcade on its way. Once, and once only, Manus turned his head.

" Ye may laugh now," he said sternly, " at the load you have given us to carry home, but remember, Hamilton, we can send you ten to one!"

An arrow whizzed past his head as he spoke, missing its fatal aim by little more than a straw's breadth; following its slanting course, it struck his horse in the neck, but happily, with little hurt to the animal, its force being well nigh spent ere it reached him.

" Ride on, my comrades," said Manus quickly, " or the hell-

hounds will not leave a soul of us to bear these woful tidings!
—ride on for Tiernan's sake that we may live to revenge, since
we could not save him! Woe for our valiant chief this day, and
woe, woe for us who bear him such a burden!"

The responsive wail which burst from the mourning band was
kept up with little intermission till they came within sight of
the towering oaks which clothed the sides of the Haunted Hollow. Bare, and bleak, and gaunt they were as they waved and
shivered in the blast, but still they afforded a sort of shelter to
the cloaked and hooded forms of the English ladies who were
seated on palfreys belonging to various members of the family
of O'Rourke. Their male companions were no less decently
mounted, and all seemed well satisfied with the treatment they
had received from their Irish captors. Little cared the bold
clansmen of O'Rourke for the blustering blast, and they would
not long have confined themselves to the limits of the dell, were
they not kept there by duty as a guard to the prisoners. They
were all more or less, sharers in the anxiety with which their
chief kept watch for the return of his messengers, and the delay
of Manus and his companions excited no small discontent.
O'Rourke himself was becoming impatient, and had just resolved
to move nearer to Manor Hamilton for the purpose of expedi-
ting the joyful meeting to which he looked forward. He had
barely intimated his intentions to the prisoners—who, to say the
truth, seemed no way anxious to be delivered to Hamilton,
whose character was well nigh as odious amongst those of his
own race and creed as it was amongst the Irish—when his quick
ear caught the distant sound of wailing in the very direction
from which he expected his own people. His attendants, too,
heard the mournful sound, and a simultaneous rush was made to
the mouth of the glen, all looking at each other with ghastly faces,
but no one daring to give utterance to the fearful thought which
filled heart and brain. But near and still nearer came the dismal
sound, faintly heard at times in the louder howling of the blast,
then rising to a wild cry when the winds were still a moment.

"It is—*it is*," cried O'Rourke at last, and a paleness like that
of death came over his handsome features; "it is our own

5*

caoine—oh, Tiernan! oh, my brother! Heaven grant it be well
with you!"

A few moments more of racking suspense, amounting to all
but certainty of coming evil, and on the brow of a hill, scarce a
hundred yards distant, Manus and his party were seen advancing
with that funereal slowness which denoted the presence of death,
while louder and wilder rose the dirge as though to give warning of what had happened.

By this time even the strangers had noticed the change in the
demeanor of those around them, and as most of them were
either Irish by birth or had lived long enough on Irish soil to
know the peculiar customs of the natives, they were at no loss
to associate the visible agitation of the chief and his followers
with the now distinct death-cry. As their own fate was just then
interwoven with that of the young O'Rourke, they, too, became
fearfully anxious to know whether evil had befallen him in his
dangerous captivity.

Notwithstanding O'Rourke's previous intention of advancing to
meet his messengers, he now stood still as a statue, his eyes
fixed with stony immobility on the approaching cortege. One of
his kinsmen suddenly laid his hand on the chieftain's arm, and
asked in a thrilling whisper what the load might be that Manus
carried so carefully.

" I know not, but I partly guess. Philip!" said O'Rourke half
unconsciously, and not another word was spoken till the party
from Manor Hamilton approached. With a scream of anguish
Owen O'Rourke threw himself from his horse, and received in his
arms the cold, stark body of his fair haired Tiernan, his one brother, the swollen and distorted features hardly recognizable, alas!
not at all, save to the unerring eye of agonized affection.

"I knew it!" murmured the wretched brother as he clasped
the beloved remains to his bosom and gazed with tearless eyes on
the face but late so beautiful, now so revolting; " I knew it—
something told me it was for you, Tiernan! for you, brother of
my heart! that the sons of Breffny raised the cry!—oh, Manus!
Manus! where were you—where were all the others—oh! God!
where were we all—all—when Tiernan O'Rourke was butchered?"

" My eyes saw the deed done," was Manus's stern reply, " and

I shame to live and tell it—but blame us not, my chief! blame not your faithful clansmen, for the height of Hamilton's accursed battlements was between us and the incarnate fiends who did it—from that height, O'Rourke, was he flung to our arms even as you see him—think then if we could save him—no, we could not, but we can avenge him—we have sworn it every man of us!"

O'Rourke, sunk in a lethargy of woe, heeded no more what was passing round him; neither the vengeful threats, nor the moans and lamentations of his retainers, the increasing wildness of the storm, nor aught but his own misery noted he. The first sound of which he was conscious was a vehement appeal to himself by name from his English prisoners, and raising his head suddenly he saw Manus and some others of his men engaged in the singular work of suspending their leathern girdles in the form of nooses from the branches of the trees above them. Manus appeared to be directing operations generally, for, having reckoned the number of nooses already arranged, he called for three more.

"There are nine of them," said he, "and we may as well string them all up at once."

"Manus," cried O'Rourke, "what, in God's name, are you about?"

"Why, making ready to hang the prisoners, to be sure—we have no place at home better than this, and it be nearer the Manor for the sending of them to Hamilton."

"Take down those belts!" was the chieftain's stern rejoinder, "and go make a litter of branches without loss of time that we may take my brother home!"

Some of his men went immediately to execute the latter command, but the order regarding the girdles was not so promptly obeyed. The clansmen looked at each other, and then at their chief, then furtively eyed the prisoners with no very friendly aspect.

"Chief of the Clan O'Rourke!" said Manus with a sullenness, not his own; "do you, or do you not, mean to revenge your brother's blood?"

"I do, and if life is spared me I will," said O'Rourke,

'but not by *murder*, Manus, not by the murder of innocent persons——"

" An' their lives are worth anything," said Manus still unconvinced; " it is to their own they be of value—when Hamilton set no store on them, why should we ?—what were five score of them to us compared with him who lies *there ?* Owen O'Rourke, mine eyes saw him hung—hung like a dog—ay! even Tiernan, the pride of our name—these arms caught him when he was flung like rotten carrion from their walls, when they had worked their devilish will on him. I told Hamilton we would have revenge—and first of all send him back *our* prisoners in such wise as he sent *his*—I tell *you*, now, that with my good will these dainty Englishers shall never go to him with life. Men of Breffny, what say ye ?"

" Blood for blood!" was the fierce response from every man of O'Rourke's party. " An' every one of them had as many lives, let the nine die as did our Tanist!——"

" Justice! justice on the Hamilton brood!"

" Mr. O'Rourke!" said a venerable gentleman of the prisoners, Sir Robert Hanna by name, " Mr. O'Rourke, your people are in error—I thank God there is no connection of any kind whatsoever between any one of us here present and this bloody-minded man, Hamilton! Whether you carry your generosity so far as to send us to our friends—for what ransom you may please to name —or whether you yield us to the vengeance of your people—and assuredly their demand is not unnatural—but be that as it may, I beseech you, noble sir, to believe all of our company your humble debtors, and, as in duty bound, much grieved for the heavy woe which has come upon your house!"

" I believe you, Sir Robert," said O'Rourke sadly, " and you say truly—this *is* a heavy woe!—still no harm must come to you or yours because of it—God forbid! Manus! as the nearest of kin, to you will I give this precious charge to bear homeward——"

" And you, our chief ?"

" I, with Philip and ten more of our party, will see these strangers safe to the Manor—at least within sight of it." There was a quiet dignity in Owen's manner that impressed even his equals, and inspired his clansmen with a feeling deeper than respect. Independent of his authority, his word had absolute power over them, because of the high qualities of which they saw him possessed, amongst others a certain firmness of purpose, amounting at times to sternness. There was a meaning in his words and in his looks which his followers well understood, and notwithstanding that their own convictions remained unshaken, and the fierce instinct of their warlike nature urged them to persist in their clamorous cry for what they considered justice as well as revenge, still there was no resisting the stern command and the still sterner look of their chief.

"Be it as you will, O'Rourke!" said Manus, spokesman for the rest, but his lowering brow and sullen tone showed the struggle which it cost him to obey.

Meanwhile the litter was prepared, and the body of the young Tiernan being carefully placed upon it, was slowly conveyed homewards, amid the renewed lamentations of the brave clansmen who had so often followed him to danger, both by flood and field. When the final moment came, O'Rourke, with all his firmness, looked irresolute, as it became necessary to turn his back on the body of his murdered brother.

"Manus," said he, "I have never known you to deceive or disobey me in aught. May I trust you to convey these prisoners *safe* to Manor Hamilton?"

"At your bidding, Owen, I will do it, though my heartstrings broke asunder, to do that which may pleasure Hamilton. *You may trust me*, Owen MacBryan."

Some of the prisoners looked aghast at the prospect of such an escort, for whatever might be Owen's confidence in his kinsman they had but too much reason to shrink from being left in his power. One of the ladies, a stately matron of mature years, was on the point of imploring the chieftain either to keep them in his own hands till such time as they could communicate with their friends, or, if not that, to carry out his original purpose of conveying them himself to Manor Hamilton, the only fort within many miles then in the hands of the English, but Sir Robert Hanna, better understanding the people with whom they had to deal, gave her an admonitory look, and hastily addressed the chief.

"Your pleasure is ours, Mr. O'Rourke!—we have seen enough

110 THE CONFEDERATE CHIEFTAINS.

of your gallant clansmen since we came into your hands, to trust our lives to their honor—cold-blooded murder is foreign to their nature, we feel assured. Therefore, good Mr. Manus, we are ready to place ourselves in your keeping, though well content with our treatment in the hospitable halls of Drumahair, and no ways anxious to see the inner parts of Manor Hamilton, which house is not in over good repute amongst honest or peaceable men, even of our own nation. But, concerning the ransom, Mr. O'Rourke, in what way can we send it that it may come safe to your hands in these unhappy times?"

"Name it not, I pray you, Sir Robert!" said the princely O'Rourke, waving his hand with a commanding air; "the chieftain of Breffny were hard driven, an' he could not afford to be generous without hope of reward. An' ye feel yourselves under an obligation to me or mine, you may have occasion during these troublesome times to discharge it by a similar act of kindness to some poor Irish prisoners who may, perchance, stand much in need of your good offices. By saving from death or torture even one poor kern or gallowglass of ours, ye will render to O'Rourke the ransom he most esteems. Go now with my best wishes for your safe and speedy arrival in your own homes, and may ye find them far otherwise than the desolate home of O'Rourke!"

"And be it our prayer, most generous and noble sir," said the lady before mentioned, who was indeed the daughter of Sir Robert Hanna, "be it our prayer to the throne of grace that the chances of war may never throw us into worse hands than those of the chieftain of Breffny! This is the second priceless boon for which I and mine are indebted to the nobles of your nation,— it will go hard with me an' one bitter enemy, at least, be not softened towards you. If Sir——"

A simultaneous sign from the chieftain and her father arrested the name hovering on the lady's lips, and O'Rourke, by an almost imperceptible gesture, urged immediate departure. A last courteous salute was exchanged between the chieftain and his late prisoners, and then the parties dividing took their separate way.

Few words passed between Manus and the liberated prisoners. He and his men were dark and sullen to the last degree, yet nor word nor sign gave any amongst them, during the miles which they had to traverse, of any ill intent towards those whom they had in charge. When, at length, they came in sight of the towers of the fortress, and Sir Robert, on the part of himself and his friends, offered them a sum of money, the offer was sternly, contemptuously rejected.

"No, no, Sassenach!" cried Manus, with passionate warmth, "not so—gift from you would dye our hands crimson—it were *blood-money*, O stranger! which men of Breffney might not take, and live!"

Such were Manus's parting words, as he shortly turned and rode away, unwilling to remain longer in sight of a place for ever hateful to him and his.

CHAPTER IX.

" It was no fire from heaven he saw,
       For, far from hill and dell,
    O'er Gobbin's brow the mountain flaw
       Bears musket-shot and yell,
    And shouts of brutal glee that tell
       A foul and fearful tale,
    While over blast and breaker swell
       Thin shrieks and woman's wail.

" Now fill they far the upper sky,
       Now down mid air they go,
    The frantic scream. the piteous cry,
       The groan of rage and woe;
    And wilder in their agony
       And shriller still they grow—
    Now cease they, choking suddenly,
       The waves boom on below."
                                    SAMUEL FERGUSON.

It was a wild bitter night in the early part of November,—it might have been about the very day so loved of English mobs, when the veritable Guy Fawkes appears again at their bidding in all the dark-lanthorn horrors of his Popish identity. The winds were whistling drearily over the snow-clad earth along the bleak shore of Antrim, and the billows of that boisterous sea were lashing the dark spectral rocks with as much fury as though they gave vent to some stormy passion long pent up within their secret depths. The gloomy towers of Carrickfergus rose dark and massive at no great distance, and the ancient town which nestles in their shallow lay silent, and, as it were, wrapped in slumber around the huge old fortress. A wild pastoral tract of land inhabited at that time chiefly by fishermen, shepherds and goatherds, stretched out for miles into the sea from the near neighborhood of the city. It is a long, narrow peninsula, girded on one side by a range of rocks whose crags assume the strangest and most weird shapes imaginable. These are known to the country round as the Gobbin Cliffs, and many a tale of superstitious horror is connected in the minds of the surrounding peasantry with their jutting shelves and gloomy caves. Superstition has ever had a fitting home amongst these geological phantoms of the coast, and bold were the man or woman esteemed who would venture after nightfall within their haunted precincts.

It was at all times a dismal sound, or rather a chorus of dismal sounds, to hear, when the winds rushed to and fro amidst the clefts and caverns of the Gobbins, but on that dark stormy November night in the memorable year of '41 there came such unearthly cries, and groans, and screams from amid the haunted cliffs that it seemed as though a thousand demons were doing their accursed will on myriads of tortured souls.

"God bless us all, it is a fearful night!" ejaculated in the Irish tongue a patriarchal old man, who, in the simple luxury of humble life, occupied a straw-backed chair of ample dimensions in the right-hand chimney-corner of a small cottage about midway on the peninsula, and so close to the rocks that not a sound from thence escaped the ears of its inmates.

"You may say that, Corny!" responded his aged dame, who in high-cauled cap and kerchief white sat directly opposite plying her wheel. "It *is* a fearful night sure enough—God pity all poor souls who are at sea in weather like this!" And in her sympathy for those who were so perilously exposed, old Rosh Magee looked round with a grateful heart on the snug and cozy little spot which contained at that moment all her nearest and dearest, to wit, her venerable partner before mentioned and a numerous family of sons and daughters of every age between thirty and eighteen,—the latter a blooming, bright-eyed lass who seemed on the high road to matrimony, judging by the tender glances of unmistakeable meaning interchanged between her and an individual whose leathern girdle displayed on its clasp the well-known cognizance of the Red Hand as his voice was marked by the peculiar intonation of the "land of Owen."

"God grant there be none on sea to-night making their way to *us!*" said the follower of O'Neill. "An' there be, granny, I'd offer up a Pater and Ave myself for all sea-faring people, though the devils in Dublin above may be getting help too!"

"Shamus aroon!" said old Corny with a fatherly smile, "there be nothing in *your* head but the wars. But, sure, agra! we needn't wonder at that—it's as natural for Tyrone men to fight as it is for a fish to swim. Our boys here be not much better, an' they had their way, though God only knows how they got such wild notions in their heads—except they come down to them from their grandfather—God rest him! who was out with the great Hugh. For my part, I declare I never had any turn that way, and I'm sure I'd make a poor hand at a scrimmage——"

"To be sure you would *now*, father," said his eldest son, a fine young man of some eight-and-twenty or thereabouts, and his eyes twinkled with sly meaning.

"Any time, Phelim!—any time, even the youngest day ever I was, I'd run a mile of ground sooner than I'd see blood shed—the Lord be praised, they say there's not many lives lost yet since *these* troubles began—that's a great thing entirely, for if we could get our rights civilly and peaceably, it would be a blessing from God. But sure, sure that's what we needn't expect anyhow!—the Lord save us, children, did you ever hear such fearsome cries from the cliffs abroad?"

"It's for all the world, Corny," said Shamus Beg, for Aileen's favored suitor was none other than that notable person, who having some relations in that neighborhood made an excuse to go there occasionally; "it's for all the world as if every Banshee in Ireland was gathered about the Gobbins this night—or maybe they're spirits from beyond the water crying the Englishers that are to fall in these wars."

"Or witches from Scotland, Shamus," suggested Aileen with her mirthful smile; "who knows but they followed the Scotch red-coats here abroad in the Castle—Christ save us," she added, with a shudder, "they have a bad look about them—the same red-coats—myself never meets one of them when I go into town with eggs or butter, or anything that way, but I feel in a hurry to get past him—a kind of a weakness comes over me somehow—isn't it strange, mother dear?"

"Take me with you, when you go," said Shamus jocosely, "though I'm in hopes it isn't long they'll be in it to frighten you —we'll scatter the nest some of these days and make the place too hot for them as we did at Charlemont and Dungannon, and all the rest of them. When the money, and the big guns, and everything comes to us from foreign parts—and that will be soon now, please the Lord!—you'll see how we'll send Monroe and his villainous looking cut-throats about their business—just wait a little, Aileen, and it's me and the like of me you'll see mounting guard at the Castle within, and maybe it's myself won't be watching for the pretty girls coming in and out with baskets on their arms, when I'm standing at the gates with my musket at my shoulder—and the boys here—faith we'll make corporals and sergeants of them at the very start—eh, Rosh?—won't them be the times—and you and Corny and the girls will be coming in to Mass, Sundays and holidays, to our darling fine chapel where the blackguard Scotch ministers spend their time on God's holy day cramming murder and robbery and all sorts of wickedness again Catholics down the throats of their bearers! Lham derg aboo! but it's ourselves will send them where they came from in double quick time, when once we get the cannon!"

The caper which Shamus cut at the conclusion of this harangue made the girls laugh, but the young men, catching a share of his enthusiasm, swallowed every word with avidity, and testified by unequivocal signs their intense desire to be with and of that grand army of Sir Phelim's which was doing, and would yet do, such wonders on behalf of the oppressed Catholics. Seeing this, the old couple took the alarm at once, and Corny hastened to put a damper on the martial ardor of his sons.

"War is a fine thing," he observed with a discouraging shake of the head, "when people have it all their own way, and so long as it stays far off—but God keep it away from us, that's all I say!"

"Why, Corny, man!" cried Shamus, more than a little nettled by this show of indifference—which, had he seen the old man's heart, he would have placed to its proper account, viz., the natural affection of the father struggling with the hopes and wishes of the patriot—"why, Corny, man, what's come over you at all—you talk for all the world like one of the Sassenachs in the Pale above—sure you ought to know as well as we do that there's nothing left for us but to fight the battle out—things could'nt go on as they were—every one knows that—and, as I have heard Rory O'Moore, and Sir Phelim, and other great, long-headed men saying a hundred times over, fair means were tried long enough, and when *they* didn't do,—when things were getting worse from day to day in place of better, what could the people do, or the chiefs—tell me that, now, Corny?" This was a "clincher," and the old man having no such answer ready as he would willingly give, hesitated and looked at Rosh, as though expecting aid from her in so great an emergency, while Shamus glanced around with a triumphant air to gather the suffrages of his younger auditors, all of whom, but especially the young men, appeared to enjoy the old man's discomfiture.

But Rosh was a powerful auxiliary, a host in herself, and she stopped her wheel to pronounce her opinion, which she did in a very dictatorial manner :

"I never want to see the face of a soldier, Shamus Beg—do you hear that now? And it's thankful I'd be if you'd leave your game-cock notions behind you when you come to Island Magee—where you're always welcome only to do as I tell you—the wars are keeping away well from *us*, thanks be to God for that same! and I tell you what it is, Shamus, as long as they let *us* alone, we'll let *them* alone! Girls! isn't it time some of you was seeing about the supper? Shamus will be none the worse for something to eat!"

These words put Aileen and her sister Cauth in motion, and under their hospitable cares, Shamus's wants would doubtless have been well provided for, but the meal they went about preparing was never ready,—the oaten cakes which Aileen's taper fingers shaped and placed before the peat fire were never tasted by Shamus, nor yet the fresh eggs which Cauth put down to boil, for, just as their culinary labors had reached that stage, a roaring, rushing sound swept past on the land side, screams of anguish and of terror were heard mingling with shouts of wrath and execration, and the clashing of sharp weapons and the report of musketry or other fire-arms—all near enough to be distinctly audible in Corny Magee's cottage, the terrified inmates of which started to their feet and held their breath to listen.

"Rosh!" said Shamus Beg in a hurried whisper, "if the troubles never came before, they're on you now—God in heaven save ye all!"

"Why, Shamus, dear," cried the old man, "what can it be at all? Oh Lord!—oh Lord! hear them shrieks—oh Rosh!—oh children! what will we do—what will we do, if it's the bloody Scotch red-coats that are out?" And the old man wrung his hands in piteous agony, while his aged wife fell on her knees before a rude picture of the Virgin which graced the wall near her.

"As sure as God's in heaven, Corny, it's them and no other," again whispered Shamus, whose practised ear had already distinguished the foreign tongue amid the horrible din of slaughter which came every moment nearer.

"Father," said the eldest son Phelim, as he shudderingly glanced at his old mother and his fair blooming sisters, "father, it were not so bad to be a soldier now—a score or two of the O'Neills or Magennises with pikes in their hands were worth their weight in gold this night."

"Alas! alas!" groaned Shamus, "if Sir Phelim did but know of this—but och! there's many a long mile between him and us this miserable hour—oh holy St. Columb! hear ye that? Why, they're not a hundred yards off!—oh! the treacherous, bloody villains to come in the night and murder all before them without rhyme or reason—creatures, too, that never done or said them ill—boys! boys! have ye no arms of any kind?" He cried in despair as the tumult came rushing on. No weapon either offensive or defensive did the house contain, but each of the four sons laid hold of some household implement which might answer the purpose—even the old man snatched with the energy of despair a sickle from under the thatch, and placed himself with his sons in front of the trembling, fainting group of females, his shaking hand clutching the weapon with a desperation that was fearful to look upon.

"I tell you all," cried Shamus wildly, "that there's no earthly use in your staying here—you'd be butchered, every soul of you, like sheep—and even that were perchance not the worst of it!" His heart sickened at the hideous thought that presented itself to his mind, and seizing Aileen by the arm, he opened the back-

door—which he knew led to the shore—calling on the others to
follow for life or death.

"There may yet be time to get among the rocks," he muttered,
as, clasping the sinking form of Aileen he dashed out—not into
the darkness he fondly hoped to find, but a light more glaring than
that of day, the lurid light from homesteads burning in all directions. At this sight a wild shriek burst from one of the affrighted
damsels, and old Rosh dropped on the threshold.

"Mother of God! we're done for now!" whispered Shamus in
despair, and still holding fast by Aileen, he seized the benumbed
and paralyzed old man by the arm, and attempted to drag him
onwards. But Corny would not go without Rosh, and jerking
himself out of Shamus's grasp with a strength and agility little
to be expected from his seeming frailty, he stooped over the
senseless partner of forty years, and with the help of one of his
sons had succeeded in raising her to a sitting posture, when a
wild shriek from some of the fugitives made them start, and
roused the old woman to sudden consciousness. It was only to
see her husband and son struck down by the butt end of two
muskets, and the next instant her scream of agony was silenced
by a bayonet thrust down her throat—she fell back a lifeless
corpse against the wall of her cottage, her snowy kerchief crimsoned with her own blood and that of her aged husband. Shouts
of fiendish laughter followed, as some half dozen of the murderers trampling over the dead bodies rushed to set fire to the house,
while twice as many of their comrades darted off in pursuit of
the fugitives. Alas! the chase was of short duration—encum-
bered with the weight of their shrieking sisters, the brothers could
make but little progress, and in their vain efforts to save

"―――― from outrage worse than death"

the pure and loving ones who clung to them as their last
and only hope, they fell one after another. But where,
meanwhile, was Shamus Beg—had he basely deserted his
betrothed in that moment of death and danger, and left
her a prey to the savage fury of incarnate demons rioting in
blood? No, sooner might the lioness abandon her young to

the pursuing hunter than Shamus Beg O'Hagan leave the girl of
his heart under such circumstances. Neither turning to right nor
left, nor once casting a look behind, on, on he dashed with a speed
more than human across the level snow-plain which lay between
him and the rocks, his left arm still encircling the now senseless
Aileen, while his right hand grasped the trusty skene, which he
meant to plunge into her bosom should their ruffian pursuers once
come within reach. In his heart he thanked God for Aileen's happy
unconsciousness, as he heard the oaths and threats and hideous
laughter of the infuriated soldiers, their heavy footsteps crushing
the frozen snow as on they dashed—near and more near they
came till poor Shamus fancied he could hear the laboring breath
of the foremost, and by that time his own strength was failing
fast. Oh, God! how wildly he scanned the space yet lying
between him and safety—or if not safety, at least escape—every
cranny and cleft of the rocks thereabouts was known to him, and
already his straining eye was fixed on a certain point right
before him—it was only a few yards off—a second or two would
bring him there, but, alas! a gully lay between—a brackish,
briny streamlet or creek, which a thousand times he had leaped
across in boyish sport—but now—now—when death—and maddening danger were close upon him—when the most hideous
of all fates was about to fall on her for whom he would have
given an hundred lives—now when the breath of the pursuing
savages was unmistakeably in his ear—faint and exhausted with
the weight of his precious burden and the superhuman exertions
he had made, he felt that the attempt was beyond his utmost
strength, and his blood ran cold as he reached the brink. There
was no time for hesitation—not even an instant, and breathing
from his heart a fervent " Mary Mother! now or never!" he
sprang over the chasm with a lightness that amazed himself, and
drew a shout of admiration even from the ruthless Scotchmen
—three or four of whom reached one bank as he gained the
other.

"Saul! but that's a braw lad for a wild Irishman! 'twas a
bold leap that, I tell ye!"

"But the lassie—the bonnie lassie, Alick, pitch *him* to the
de'il, but we'll have *her* or I'm no Lindsay! Here's for her!"

and the fellow was about to spring over the chasm when one
of his comrades caught him by the arm.

"Hoot awa! Jamie Lindsay, are you gone daft or what?—see
you no that the boiling sea is ahint them rocks—*that* callan
kens the place weel—he may chance to lead you an ill dance
there awa. The spot is no canny, ye see weel!"

"Canny or no, I'll see it out!" cried Lindsay, "I'm bent on
having that lass, an' the tramp we hae had after her!"

"I tell you, Scot, you'll never lay a hand on her!" cried Shamus, from the elevated point which he had now gained; "though
every devil's imp of your crew was there on that bank, I could
dare ye all now—a drop of my blood you'll never spill, nor nearer
shall one of you ever be to this 'bonnie lass,' as you well call
her! *Death before dishonor* is a word with us Irish. I'll leave
my chief, *Sir Phelim O'Neill*, to settle with you for this—you'll
pay dear for this night's work—take my word for it—ay! every
egg and bird of your accursed brood!"

"Hear till him now," shouted the enraged Scots, "hear till the
senseless braggart!" and loudly they laughed in scorn and hate
but louder laughed Shamus Beg, when seeing his savage foes
about to overleap the ravine, he sank down behind the rock with
his still unconscious burden, and a heavy plash in the waters far
below reached the ears of the awed and terrified Scotchmen, even
amid the roaring of wave and wind. Warned thus of the fate
which awaited themselves if they ventured to scale the fearful
barrier, and awed in spite of themselves by this episode in the
night's bloody tragedy, they said little to each other on the subject, as they turned to retrace their steps to the burning cabin of
Corny Magee. There, however, they found none of their comrades—the work of destruction being completed, the place was
left to the silent dead and the crackling flames. It was meet
cause for mirth to the disappointed ruffians that the body of
poor Rosh was well nigh consumed, and as one of them gave a
kick to the venerable head of Corny, where it lay across the path,
with its white locks dabbled in gore, it furnished him with a
ribald jest for the present and future entertainment of his companions.

When the bugles called the marauders together, an hour after, they presented a hideous sight; smutted and begrimed they were with the smoke of many dwellings, and marked like Cain with the murderer's brand stamped in the blood of their victims.* They had glutted their national and religious hatred of the Irish to their hearts' content, and were drunk with the fulness of their bloody feasting. Yet they talked in Scriptural cant of the good work they had been doing, and the salutary terror which such an example would strike into the Moabitish rebels. And it did seem as though the Lord had abandoned his faithful people into the hands of those merciless executioners, who came upon them when least expected in the darkness and storm of night. Of all the gallant chieftains who were then in arms with their legions of brave followers, to repel the aggressions of bigotry and legalized rapine, not one was near in that dark hour to save the unoffending peasantry of Island Magee from the exterminating sword of fanatical ruffians. Where were O'Neill and O'Reilly, McMahon and Maguire, on that fatal night, when the maids and matrons of that old Catholic race were shrieking and struggling in the grasp of Munroe's soldiers? Ah! they were far, far away, little dreaming of the foul butchery which, on that night, commenced the work of slaughter in the northern province. But, if they were not within ken, there was an eye that witnessed all, and a power that armed those leaders with might and strength to revenge that massacre. If blood could wash out the stain of blood then was the torrent that flowed that night, on the wild Antrim shore, effaced from the soil it saturated, for the memory of that atrocious deed, thenceforward, nerved the arms and steeled the hearts of the Ulster chieftains, and if ever wanton slaughter was avenged it was that of Island Magee.

---

* The number of those slain in the massacre of Island Magee is so variously estimated, that it is hard to arrive at any accurate conclusion respecting it. By Catholic writers it is said to have amounted to three thousand, while no respectable Protestant historian attempts to make it less than "thirty families." The victims must, in any case, have numbered many hundreds, from the actual extent of the district, viz., seven miles. Even the ultra-Protestant, Leland, speaks of the affair as an " infernal massacre.'

6A

Next morning the wintry sun rose over the peninsula, with a keen and frosty radiance, **and it shone** on black roofless walls and the shattered remains of household furniture, and, sadder than all, on unburied corpses, some of them partially, others wholly, charred and burnt, while others still lay singly or in heaps on the highway, where they had been overtaken in their attempted flight, these last bruise l and shattered by the iron-shod boots of their slayers trampling them to and fro. Terror and consternation, at this dreadful news, had so far overcome the Catholic people of the adjoining country, that the day was far advanced before any of them ventured to approach the scene of the slaughter, either to seek the living—if life were yet to be found there—or to give sepulture to the dead.

In the early morning, long before the first of these parties visited the place, two men had appeared there at different times, coming stealthily and slowly from opposite directions. Each in turn made his way to Corny Magee's cottage, now a pile of smoking clay walls and smouldering thatch. The first who came was Phelim, the eldest son of the murdered family. He had escaped almost by a miracle the fate of all his kindred, though his bandaged head and his right arm supported in a sling showed that he had not been altogether forgotten in the distribution of the Scottish favors. No thanks to them that Phelim was not still under the mangled corpses of one brother and two sisters, where he had been left for dead. At midnight he recovered his senses, and with much difficulty extricated himself from his fearful position, for the death-grasp of his sisters held him as in a vice, and the unnatural weight of three dead bodies was a crushing load for a living man, wounded, too, as he was. But at last he rose to his feet, his clothes stiff upon him with the blood of his murdered relatives, as he saw by the flickering and uncertain light from the still burning ruins. His first thought was one of gratitude to Heaven for so signal an interposition of its mercy, his next to seek some place of shelter from the bitter northern blast until morning's light should enable him to look after the remaining members of his family, of whose fate he had little doubt. Before he left the spot, however, he stooped and turned over in succession each of the three before him, in order to as-

certain whether life remained in any of them. Alas! they were
all dead—dead, stiff and cold as death and frost could make
them. With an instinctive horror that almost froze his blood,
poor Phelim then moved towards the cottage, and who may describe his feelings, who may even imagine them, when right
across his path he beheld the mangled corpse of his father, and
a step or two farther on, by a portion of the brown-drugget gown,
which still covered her lower limbs, he recognized the half-con-
sumed body of his mother! No sigh, no groan escaped the son
as he bent over the ghastly remains of his beloved parents—the
grief and the horror and the sense of desolation which paralyzed
his being left but one feeling acute—one passion dominant—who
cannot guess what that feeling, that passion was—the feeling was
hatred, the passion *revenge*, and from that hour Phelim Magee
lived but to gratify both. All softer emotions were thenceforth
banished his heart, and his nature, hitherto so genial, became
hard, hard as stone.

On the following morning when Phelim emerged from the
sheltering walls of a neighboring cottage which had escaped the
fire, he found an individual whom, even at a distance, he knew to
be Shamus Beg, standing with folded arms looking down on his
father's dead face. It was a joyful surprise for each of the young
men to see the other, and the silent greeting which they exchanged was as glad as it was sorrowful. By a common impulse
they knelt on the bloody snow, but neither heard what the other
uttered. When they arose, sad and stern, Phelim said:

"What of Aileen, Shamus?- is *she* gone, too?" A dismal
shake of the head was O'Hagan's answer, and Phelim covering
his face with his hands, groaned aloud. But Shamus did not
suffer him to remain long in his lethargy of woe. Laying his
hand on his arm, he said briskly:

"What's to be done with these?" pointing to the bodies.
"And these?" added Phelim, leading the way to where his brother and sisters lay. "And Aileen and the others, wherever
they are."

It was then agreed that they should go up on the mainland
and seek assistance amongst their friends there, in order to perform the solemn rite of burial.

"There's one thing to be done before we leave the spot," said Shamus with stern emphasis, "and after that we'll go look for our poor Aileen and the rest!" He extended his hand to Phelim across the old man's body, and the son, at no loss for his meaning, joined him in a solemn vow to do battle against the Scotch murderers and all who took part with them as long as breath remained in their bodies. By way of ratifying their solemn compact, each laid his hand on the face of the corpses, and then rising they stood a moment silent, surveying the awful scene.

"That will do now!" said Shamus at length, as he turned to commence his journey. "When we have found the others"—here his voice trembled—"I must leave you to do the rest—Sir Phelim must have word of this before the sun sets, and I would that my tongue should have the telling of it! Let us off now on our search, and first for Aileen!"

CHAPTER X.

"Superior worth your rank requires;
For that, mankind reveres your sires,
If you degenerate from your race,
Their merit heightens your disgrace."

GAY's *Fables.*

"Me glory summons to the martial scene;
The field of combat is the sphere for men,
Where heroes war, the foremost place I claim,
The first in danger, and the first in fame."

POPE's *Iliad.*

It was a grand and stately edifice, dating from mediæval times, turreted and castellated for purposes of defence, as became the dwelling of a princely house, with crenellated walls and lofty curtains uniting the various towers, and tall, narrow windows, most of them splayed so as to give much more light to the interior than might be expected from their outward dimensions. This noble old building, old even in the seventeenth century, stood in the midst of a spacious park, whose venerable woods of oak, and birch, and hazel, were in keeping with the lordly character of the dwelling. The neighborhood, too, was rich in picturesque beauty, for the matchless valley of the Suir lay spread beneath, and the noble river rolled its silvery waters seaward through the lovely scene, the whole enlivened by the even then prosperous town of Carrick-on-Suir.*

In a spacious apartment of the baronial dwelling thus situate,

---

* "I know of few finer prospects," says Mr. Inglis, the famous traveller, "than the valley of the Suir presents as it opens upon one from the heights above Carrick. . . . . I do not think it is equalled by the vale of Clwyd."

about the last days of October, in the year of 1641, the noble owner first received the intelligence of the great rebellion in Ulster, transmitted to him in all haste from the terrified and vacillating officials of Dublin Castle. A gentleman of Sir William Parsons' household bore the despatches, and the number of his well-armed escort, while it showed the fears of the Lords Justices, made the lord of the Castle smile, knowing as he did that however things might be in Ulster—by this official showing—there was not an illegal mouse stirring in that part of Munster.

But the tidings brought were grave and important, and with a very grave countenance the nobleman heard them. No one knew better than he the many and grievous causes of complaint on which the native chiefs based their rebellion, and no one knew better, either, than he the persevering resistance of which they were capable, and the trouble they were likely to give the government when banded together in the sacred names of Religion and Justice. His fine countenance darkened more and more as he read of the rapid success of O'Neill and his friends in Ulster, and when at length the official document closed with an earnest hope that his lordship would hasten to Dublin without delay in order to assume the chief command against the rebels, an ironical smile flitted across the darkness, giving a strange expression to his features.

Turning towards the expectant envoy, he was about to speak, when the latter, bowing lowly, said by way of appendix: "Their chiefest hope is in my Lord of Ormond!"

"My Lord of Ormond is much beholden to them," the nobleman replied, with the same cold, calm smile; "their lordships are well aware that for the king's necessity they may command my poor services, and I thank them for so signal a mark of their good opinion. With God's help, I will do what in me lies—after I have heard from the king's majesty!"

"But, my lord, the affair is urgent," ventured to suggest the messenger, "an' the rebels go on as they are doing, Dublin itself will not be safe ere many days go by!"

"How is it with the Catholic English of the Pale?" demanded Ormond suddenly, without at all heeding the remonstrance so humbly offered; "I find no mention of them in these despatches."

"They have not joined the rebels—*as yet*, my good lord!—but I have heard said that the Lords Justices trust them none the more. The chief men amongst them were at the Castle betimes on the first day after the news of the rebellion came in——"

"They were?—on what business, I pray you?"

"Making a tender of their loyal services to the government, my lord, and soliciting arms for the defence of their castles against the rebels."

"And they doubtless got them?"

"Ay, marry, did they," and the gentleman shrugged his shoulders and looked up with a half quizzical expression into the dark, passionless face above him, where nothing was to be read save dignified attention. "But how long they may have them passes my poor ability to say. I did hear Sir William Parsons say but yesterday that they were all traitors at heart, and that he would as soon trust Maguire or McMahon—whom God has even now delivered unto us—as Dunsany or Netterville, or Gormanstown himself, for all their smooth speeches!"

"But Maguire and McMahon—be they, then, in prison?"

"Even so, my lord! they be safe as bolt and bar can make them—they were trapped like bag-foxes even in their own lodgings in Dublin the night before the rising in Ulster. There was a nest of them gathered in the city with intent to seize the Castle next day when their wretched kerns got in from the north. But the Lord—even the Lord of Hosts—saw their bloody designs and His arm smote them and gave them bound and manacled into our hands——"

"Who waits without?" demanded the Earl, and when one of his pages appeared at the door he commanded him to give the gentleman in charge to the steward of the household so that all proper attention might be paid to his wants and those of his attendants. "Meanwhile, sir, I will prepare my answer to the Lords Justices," and so saying he dismissed him with an imperious gesture, whereat the follower of Parsons wondered mightily and was much abashed, saying to himself as he followed the page through the ante-room where numerous attendants were in waiting:

"Of a surety he bears him grandly, this earl—an' he be the king's *servant*, it were ill standing before the master!"

And he was, too, a grand and stately personage, that same
Earl of Ormond—a man of commanding presence and imposing
manners, high and haughty in his ordinary bearing, above all,
where undue assumption on the part of others, or any approach
to familiarity made him deem it requisite, yet no man of his
order could condescend with a loftier grace, a more bland or
winning courtesy. Accomplished in all the arts of dissimulation,
and well versed in courtly wiles, prudent, too, beyond most men
of his time, it was little wonder that Ormond's sentiments and
opinions on public events were often a mystery both to his colleagues at the council-board and his subordinates in the field.
Allied to the Catholic party by every near and dear tie, he
was naturally suspected by the Puritans, while the Catholics,
especially those of English blood, gave him credit for a secret
sympathy with them and their cause which was, in reality, foreign
to his heart. Like all apostates he hated the religion he had
left, and thought it quite right to restrict its growth by penal
enactments, yet, having just as little, or it might be even less
sympathy with the fanatical Puritans, he held their exterminating
doctrines in utter abhorrence, and for very hatred to them might
at times appear less determined in his hostility to Catholic interests than he really was. Outwardly he professed the religion of
the king to whose fortunes he was every way bound, but at heart
James Butler was a self-worshipping, worldly-minded man, bent
upon turning to his own advantage some at least of the conflicting
elements around him, and not over scrupulous as to the means of
building up a yet greater fortune, and attaining to yet greater
power than that which he already possessed. Still his religious
profession was sincere, that is to say, his sympathies were all
with the Anglican Church, and to a certain extent he was also a
loyal subject of King Charles, always providing that the monarch's interests and his own ran in the same channel.

Such a man must necessarily have wielded a powerful influence
in the complicated machinery of the state at that momentous
period when all was anarchy, strife, and contention, in the great
councils of the empire. And so, in fact, he did, for all through
the storms and convulsions of those turbulent times, his grand
figure stands out in strong relief from the chaotic mass of medi-

ocre statesmen, intriguing politicians, and truculent, unprincipled leaders. With all his faults—and they were partly the effect of early training, partly of non-training, and the absence of all salutary restraint on a wild and spirited youth, brought up in the corrupt atmosphere of the court of James the First—with all his faults, Ormond had some redeeming qualities which challenge our respect, and although we may not love, we cannot help admiring the lofty, ambitious. courtly Earl of Ormond, who, handsome and accomplished, wise in council, great in camp and field, presented to a dissolute and faithless age the rare spectacle of immaculate purity of morals, with the strictest observance of all domestic ties.

For the part which James Butler took in frustrating the efforts of the Confederate Catholics, we owe him small liking, the more so as his powerful influence should, by right, have been thrown into the scale in their favor, whereas he proved himself throughout their consistent enemy, while, at times, professing friendship for the most sinister motives. If his giant shadow fell darkly across the most brilliant effort ever made by the Irish people to obtain redress, it was the fault of those who trusted him blindly and against all experience—had he never obtained an influence in the Catholic councils, he never had power to betray, and in fair fighting he could never have conquered.

Such as he was, however, the Lords Justices were but too happy to avail themselves of his recognized abilities at that critical juncture, and hence their urgent request for his speedy attendance in Dublin, for the purpose of assuming the chief military command.

Left to himself, the Earl took some turns up and down the spacious apartment, pausing now and then at one of the windows to look out upon the gray lowering sky and the misty rain which drearily veiled the fair landscape.

" The season is a bad one," he muttered, " for military operations, but it is no better for them than it is for us. And yet—I know not but it may—they be used to hard living, these wild kern and gallowglasses, and are wont to battle with the elements."

Again he paced the room to and fro, then stopped before a grim old portrait which hung in a deep recess between the two

6*

centre windows. The Earl folded his arms on his broad chest, and gazed with an eye half sad, half defiant, on the dark, stern face which seemed to look reproachfully down from the time-worn canvas. Gradually a dreamy look settled down on Ormond's face, and he stood riveted to the spot in utter abstraction. Once more his full rich lips parted, and many words of strange import escaped them as he apostrophized the mailed warrior.

"You need not look so grim, Thomas Butler, for there be too much of your own haughty spirit in me to quail even before *your* frown. For all you were a stern old Papist, given to mumbling over beads like my grandfather,* good, easy man, it does not follow that I, your descendent, should serve the Pope of Rome in preference to my lawful sovereign. Men may upbraid me, if they will, with my Popish ancestry, and some seek, on that account, to hold me to Romish ways of thinking, but I tell you, Thomas Dhu, *I'll none of them*, and they do me foul wrong who cast my Popish blood in my face, for there be none of it in my heart. An' my Elizabeth were once in a mending way,† and his highness's commission come to hand, this old house of yours‡ should not long hold me within its walls. The voice of duty calls me to crush these audacious rebels—ay, doth it, Thomas! —and crush them I will, so help me heaven!"

Here there came a message from the Countess, craving a few moments' speech of her lord, and immediately Ormond recollected the despatches, which he must needs send off without delay. Still his thoughts followed him as he repaired to the apartments of the Countess, situate in another wing of the Castle, and on the way he soliloquized in this wise

"McGuire and McMahon in prison—humph—McGuire would never have given us much trouble, but McMahon served in Spain

* His grandfather, Earl Walter, whom he immediately succeeded in the title, was known by the *soubriquet* of Walter of the Rosary.

† It was the illness of his Countess that then detained him at Carrick.

‡ This Tipperary Castle of the Butlers was built by this Thomas Dhu, one of the lineal ancestors of the great Earl

for a short time, and for the little I have seen of him, I am well content to hear of his speedy capture. But this Phelim O'Neill, who has, they say, overrun the major part of Ulster with his allies within a week—as a military leader his name is new to me, though I have seen the man more than once in Dublin—a genuine Celt I took him for, rough and somewhat hasty withal —and yet, if what I have heard be true, he did profess the Reformed doctrines while studying the law in London* —it matters not, he must have returned to the fold, as the Papist's phrase it, else would he never go headforemost into this treason. A plague on them for O'Neills, they be ever brewing mischief—I thought the late mishap which befel young Tyrone might, perchance, keep them quiet a space, but they be a hydra-headed race—no sooner one lopped off, than up another starts, and what is worse, all Ulster starts up with them. I would that Bloody Hand of theirs was in the Red Sea, never again to beckon men on to treason and foul rebellion—an' the Flemish hero of the family take it into his noddle to come and have a finger in this precious pie, we may find it over hard of digestion for our stomach's health. There be others of the old blood, too, who have won laurels abroad, an' they all flock around the standard of rebellion, *we* may look to *our* poor laurels, such as they be. As for the Palesmen, I value them little, one way or the other—their lip-loyalty is not worth a straw, for of a surety they have but small cause to relish this government—still it will go hard with them an' they make common cause with the natives—no, no, their Norman stomachs could never brook *that*—their Papistry and their English sympathies will keep tugging them in opposite directions, till it be too late to give effective aid to either party. Ha! ha! their estates begin to shake under them—poor Fingal and all the rest of ye, what a quagmire ye have got upon since the unlucky *twenty-third*. And of all men living it is to Parsons and Borlase ye must needs reach out your hands for succor!—oh blood of our Norman

---

* If this be true, and many credible authorities say it is, we have only to say that Sir Phelim nobly atoned for this temporary apostacy of his earlier years. All through the long struggle for religious free dom, he did what in him lay to advance the Catholic cause.

fathers, do you indeed fill the veins of these Plunkets, Prestons, Nettervilles and Dillons! Ye call yourselves Papists, yet have not the manhood to stand up for your party—better, surely, to be as James Butler!"

This contemptuous sarcasm brought the keen-witted nobleman to the Countess's ante-chamber, whence he dispatched one of her women to apprise her that he waited admission. Meanwhile a short digression may not be amiss.

Elizabeth Preston, Countess of Ormond, then lying on a bed of sickness, the effect of a long and tedious confinement, was a woman of great beauty and of many fine endowments of mind. Like her husband she had been brought up in the noxious atmosphere of the English Court, for she, too, was the orphan daughter of a noble house,* and being so, was, of course, under the fatherly care of the Court of Wards, and brought up in the orthodox religion of the state, though her veins, like Ormond's, were filled with the purest Catholic blood. It so happened that the Lady Elizabeth's large possessions were made up in great part from the domains of the house of Ormond, seized at various times by the hypocritical rapacity of James, and by him, for some consideration, unjustly transferred to his new Earl of Desmond. Drawn together not only by similarity of position, but also by the ties of blood,—for they were cousins,—the two noble wards early began to regard each other with more than common attention, and it was not strange that the all but portionless heir of the Butlers should do homage to the peerless charms of the fair daughter of Desmond, or that she, on her part, should feel what all admitted, that the young Lord Thurles was the handsomest and most accomplished cavalier about the court. Mutual admiration quickly grew into mutual love, and much was the plotting king disconcerted to find that the wealthy heiress of Desmond, whose hand he had promised to his unworthy favorite Buckingham, for a nephew of his, son of the Earl of Denbigh, was about to bestow herself and her possessions on her cousin Lord Thurles,

‖ Her father, Sir Richard Preston, was endowed by James the First with the earldom of Desmond, long vested in the crown under various political pretexts and thereby to build up again the broken fortunes of the house of Ormond, for whose prosperity Scotch Jamie cared very little. Finding, however, that the nearest relations on both sides were favorable to the union, the king could not for shame withhold his consent, and so it was that young Butler bore away in triumph the fairest lady, and, perchance, the richest heiress of King James's Court. Their first married days were spent amid the shades of Acton, the beautiful seat of the bridegroom's maternal grandfather, but after a brief season, Earl Walter of Ormond, being far advanced in years, " shuffled off this mortal coil," leaving his title and his castles, and the remnant of his domains, together with his blessing to the grandson whose auspicious marriage had brought back into the family the bulk of its princely possessions. So the youthful bride of Ormond was removed from her quiet English home, and installed as a Countess in the lordly halls of Kilkenny, and in that stately Castle by the silvery Suir, near Carrick's walls, where we have first seen the great Earl, and when the pipers and harpers of Ormond put forth their joyous strains of welcome, the lady of Desmond won their hearts by declaring that never music sounded half so sweet to her, albeit that her ears were attuned to the melody of courtly minstrels. From that day forward the bards were loud in the praise of Ormond's bride, and she ruled like a queen in beauty and in grace, over the hearts and homes of the thousands who called the Butler lord.

The Countess, although brought up under the same pernicious influence as her husband, was no sharer in his anti-Papist prejudices. Her clear sound judgment and her strong sense of right made the justice of the Catholic claims apparent to her mind, while the gentleness of her nature made her prone to pity the sufferings, which, for conscience' sake, they bore, and to sympathize with the hardships of their ruined and plundered state. Not that she regarded their religion with any more favor than others of the royal perverts, but as a clear-headed, soft-hearted woman she viewed their cause and entered into the feelings which impelled them to this struggle when from Ormond's lips she heard of it that day.

" My lord, my lord," said she, " bethink you well what you do

ere you take upon you to carry out the views of the Lords Justices in regard to these poor misguided people ?"

"Why, Elizabeth," said the Earl with a sportive smile, "methinks you be more than half a rebel yourself to hold such speech
in their behoof. I little thought ever to hear wife of mine plead
in favor of the king's enemies !"

"Nay, Ormond," replied the lady, "you know full well that
the king's enemies are not the Irish Papists—marry, he has his
worst enemies nearer home, and I have it from our gracious
queen herself that if his highness dared he would do somewhat
to lighten the burden which weighs so heavily on his subjects in
this realm who hold to the old faith——"

"Hush, Bess, hush, I pray you !" said the Earl in a low earnest
tone, " such words be neither safe nor prudent—heard and repeated by tattling tongue they might reach those who would be
right glad to use them to his grace's detriment. However it be
in that matter, my duty is plain, and if God spares me life to
do it, I will put down this rebellion before it gathers more
strength."

"But, Ormond," persisted the generous Countess, and she
raised herself on her elbow the better to urge her remonstrance,
" no fair means have been tried to conciliate these poor natives—
not one of their just demands hath been conceded—why, then,
have recourse to force and bloodshed, ever odious in the sight of
heaven, before any attempt hath been made to win them from
their treasonable practices by gentler means ?"

"Truly, Bess, their own ways are gentle!" quoth the Earl,
sharply; " they be dealing softly, of a surety, with the loyal Protestants whose goods and substance they lay hold of with so little ceremony. Your womanly softness leads you into error!"

"Surely, no, James, I bear all their treasonable doings in
mind, and, all things taken into account, I marvel they be not of
a bloodier nature—but your lordship knows right well that these
Papists, hunted, and robbed, and persecuted for their religion
though they be, have made divers efforts to soften the flinty
hearts of their rulers, and obtain even a small portion of that
justice which is due to them—nay, in the late affair of the
Graces—have they not been treated with most base and cruel

treachery —interrupt me not, I beseech you, till I speak my
thoughts once for all on this pitiful subject—why it was but the
other day, in a manner, that a large body of these much-wronged
poor people had a remonstrance written for them by that godly
prelate, Bishop Beddell, of Kilmore, urging upon the government their many grievances, and humbly asking for redress—
think you that good bishop and most loyal subject would have put
pen to paper on behalf of knaves and plotters of rebellion ? —nay,
never tell me, it was hard necessity that drove them to their
present courses—whenever they complained or remonstrated
ever so humbly, Sir Charles Coote and such like men were sent
into their territories to silence their clamor with fire and sword."

The Countess sank on her pillow exhausted, and the Earl
laughed—a low deep laugh peculiar to himself—as he rose to
proceed to the writing of his despatches. The look of discontent
on the fair brow of Elizabeth quickly vanished as he stooped and
whispered some words of tenderness, and smoothed with his
hand the fair silken tresses which had made their way from under
her cambric coif. "Rest you softly, sweet wife," he said very
gently, as he beckoned to her women, who had merely retired on
his entrance to the farther end of the spacious chamber; "trust
me, the rebels will not thank you for taking up their cause, and
good Doctor Delamere will find you none the better for what you
have spoken."

The following day brought the royal commission, written by
the monarch's own hand, appointing his "trusty and well-beloved
Ormond" lieutenant-general of all the army in Ireland, with an
urgent request—meaning, of course, a command—to take the
field immediately. Fortunately the Countess's health was so far
improved that in two days more the leech pronounced her out of
all danger, and, his mind thus lightened of its heaviest load, the
Earl proceeded at once to Dublin.

The Lords Justices, in their puerile terror, hailed Ormond's
appearance with exuberant satisfaction, as, in times of trouble
and confusion, weaker minds ever throw themselves on the
stronger for support, and Ormond was even then famous amongst
the men of his time for readiness of wit as for promptness and
decision of character. He was known to both friends and foes

as one who could practise as well as plan, and plan as well as practise. He was the man, in short, on whose genius, energy, and courage, both the Irish government and the king himself relied in every emergency.

A council was immediately summoned to meet the Earl, who belonged, of course, to that dignified body whose privilege it was to advise the executive. Great was Ormond's surprise to find that the small force actually at the disposal of the government was already brought into Dublin from the different garrisons of the adjoining country, leaving the whole island, as one might say, open to the incursions of the rebels, as, to be sure, the Catholic forces were styled. In the Earl's eyes this amounted to little less than encouraging the rebellion, and so he broadly hinted, but Parsons was ready with his answer, that the seat of government must needs be protected at all hazards.

"And the Lords Justices above all!" Ormond added within himself, and he smiled, but made no remark.

Here one of the many doors of the Council Chamber opened, and another remarkable personage made his appearance.

CHAPTER XI.

"Nurtur'd in blood betimes, his heart delights
In vengeance, gloating on another's pain."
                              BYRON's *Childe Harold*.

" Torture thou mayest, but thou shalt ne'er despise me ;
The blood will follow where the knife is driven ;
The flesh will quiver where the pincers tear ;
And sighs and cries by nature grow on pain :
But these are foreign to the soul ; not mine
The groans that issue, or the tears that fall ;
They disobey me ;—on the rack I scorn thee."
                              YOUNG.

THE person who now made his appearance was a man of large
proportions, considerably above the middle height, and far beyond the middle age. His form and demeanor might have been
called commanding, were it not for the fleshy redness of his face
and the large, fierce-looking gray eyes, which, protruding far
beyond the surrounding surface, gave a fierce and somewhat
brutal expression to the whole visage. His hair and whiskers
were already silver gray, and his massive forehead bald to the
crown. He was clothed in the undress military uniform of the
British army of that day, and his brawny, sinewy neck, in utter
defiance of the chill November rain, was bare almost to the col-
lar-bone. Altogether there was a look of ferocious energy and
inlomitable courage about the whole man, that, with his huge
muscular frame, and the sensual appearance of his eyes and
mouth, made a strong and very disagreeable impression even on
the casual beholder. To the native Irish, and, indeed, to all the
Catholics who fell in his way, the man was an object of fear and
abhorrence, and well he might, for he was no other than Sir

Charles Coote,* the Dalzell of the Irish wars, one of the bloodiest and most inhuman generals that ever drew sword in execution of a tyrant's will. With the Lords Justices Coote was in high favor, higher far than Ormond or any other captain of that day, and that not on account of any superior excellence as a general, or any superior knowledge of military tactics, but solely because of his entire subserviency to their will, and utter disregard of the means by which it was accomplished. The more cruel, in fact, the means, the better pleased was Coote, and where cupidity had little to look for or expect from the utter wretchedness of the victims, another and still stronger motive had he in his unquench- able hatred of the Irish Papists. Like Hamilton of Leitrim, Sir Charles Coote was disliked by all the moderate and humane even of his own party, and the general impression amongst them was that when any strong temptation offered, or his brute pas- sion impelled him on, it would cost him no more to give them cold steel or short shrive than the veriest Papist or merest Irish kern in broad Ireland. Between Coote and Ormond there was little sympathy and just as little liking—heartless as the Earl was in regard to Catholics, he was utterly opposed to the savage policy of Coote and Parsons, and with all his intense devotion to his own interests, he could never have stooped to advance his fortunes by the harsh and brutal means which they, from choice, adopted. There was hardly one bond of union between the two generals, if we except that of hatred to Catholics—for while Ormond was the friend and servant of King Charles and honestly fought in his interest, Sir Charles Coote was by all recognized as the henchman of the Lords Justices, and consequently of the refractory Parliament of England, a far more rebellious body even then than the insurgent Catholics of Ireland.

"How now, lords and gentlemen," said Coote, in a deep gruff voice, as he advanced to a vacant seat near Parsons, scarcely

---

* This Sir Charles Coote was the founder of a race which has left its bloody mark on many a page of Irish history—above all others they have been distinguished for cruelty, love of plunder, and the grossest sensuality. The Queen's County and that of Cavan were specially given over to their rapacious rule.

deigning to make the customary salute to the other members of
the Council, though it numbered two or three Bishops ; " ye do
take things easy here, nothing mindful, it would seem, that the
rascally Papists are overrunning the whole country !"

" What would you have us do, Sir Charles ?" asked Parsons in
what he meant for a gracious tone ; " until such time as your new
levies are fit to take the field, we are, as it were, powerless to
smite those Philistines—here is my lord of Ormond, newly appointed by his grace's highness to the chief command—he would
have us give him what forces are here in town—and our Lord
knows they be all too few to protect the place—and to let him
march northwards in quest of the enemy, when Heaven knows
but they might give him the slip and by another route come upon
us here in town and burn and slay all before them after their savage manner. We were of hard necessity driven to refuse his lordship's demand, how then can we answer your question, otherwise
than by saying that the lack of troops is our misfortune rather
than our fault."

" It is even so, Sir Charles," said Ormond with his bland and all-
concealing smile ; " here have I been summoned to town in all
haste to proceed against the rebels, and being come, I am like a
man with his hands tied—men, money, and arms are all wanting,
so that I am a general without a command--was there ever such
provision made for such an emergency ?"

" Go to work and make an army as I do," was Coote's rough
answer ; " Sir William is right, strength must be kept up here,
come what may, and the king's trust is much misplaced in your
lordship an' you cannot raise forces to serve your turn."

" Were I inclined to bandy words with a gentleman *so polished,*'
said Ormond with lofty scorn and keen irony, " I might say to
Sir Charles Coote that what man can do that will Ormond do, an'
means are given him, but a carpenter can ill work without tools,
or a *butcher*, either, as some here present may bear witness."

There was something in the last words that brought a smile to
many a grave face around the table, though all cast down their
eyes to avoid making any application.

" I understand you, my lord of Ormond," said Coote with a
smile half humorous, half ferocious, " but I would have you to

know that butchery, for all your sneer, is the best trade going now that wild cattle are out in droves—an ounce of sharp steel will go farther with *them* than a bushel of fair words. Hang them up and rip them open—make scare-crows of them to frighten their accomplices—that's all you can ever make them good for, and that's how I treat them whenever they come into my hands, egg or bird of them!"

With the exception of Parsons and his surly old colleague, there was hardly one around the council-board who did not shudder at this brutal declaration, but all knew the speaker too well to attempt either censure, ridicule, or remonstrance. By general consent, little or no notice was ever taken in the council-room of Coote's characteristic blustering, and Ormond, to whom he had specially addressed himself, vouchsafed no reply but turned with cold contempt to the Lords Justices.

"I have heard," said he, "that the English Papists of the Pale have asked and received arms from the government. Your lordships, then, believe them trustworthy?"

Some members of the Council, amongst others the Archbishop of Dublin, were eagerly professing their belief in the loyalty of those lords and gentlemen, when Coote roughly interposed:

"I wouldn't trust them the length of my nose"—here there was a very perceptible titter amongst the younger members, for the general's nose occupied a large portion of his facial surface, and was moreover of very remarkable *length*—"ay! ye may laugh," he continued, with a fierce glance around the board, "especially as the rebels are at safe distance—an' they come within pike's length of any of your noble lordships, the laughter, I fear, will be the other way. As for these white-livered and most dainty gentlemen of the Pale, I tell you they be worth watching—the lying spirit of Rome is in them to the back-bone, and ye know it too—if ye trust them, ye are no better than they, and another thing let me tell you concerning them, lords and gentlemen, which perchance some of ye know not—" here the speaker paused and looked around with a leer so expressive and at the same time so diabolical as to make the majority of his hearers turn away their eyes in disgust—" rich lordships they have and hold, and fair manors, and barns and bawns well stored—little wonder is

it, then, that they would fain pass for most loyal men, but great
wonder it is to me that you, my Lords Justices, and you, honorable members of the Council, should suffer those knaves to throw
dust in your eyes, and thereby keep what they have until such
time as their friends the northern rebels can, with *their* secret
aid and abetment, take *your* houses over your heads, ay! and
ornament the tops of their pikes with those same sculls—num-
skulls we might well call them then, seeing that they had not
sense enough to protect themselves! By the ——," and he swore
a dreadful oath, striking the table with his ponderous fist at the
same time, "an' ye leave these arms in the hands of such traitors
as Gormanstown, Dunsany, and the rest of that crew, ye deserve
all that will come upon ye! Some even of this Council may seek
to persuade you in courtly speech that these mongrel hounds
being of English blood, and, moreover, in divers ways connected
with *them*, must needs bo loyal gentlemen, but I give you my
word I would not trust them an' they were *Charles Stuart's*
kinsmen!"

"CHARLES STUART!" Ormond repeated with stern emphasis,
"who may that be, Sir Charles Coote?" and rising, he drew
himself up to his fullest height.

"Go northward and ask Sir Phelim O'Neill," was the insolent
answer; "they do say he shows a license from an individual of
that name!"

"I insist on knowing what you mean!" said the Earl in his
loftiest tone and manner; "I will not, cannot suppose that our
sovereign lord the king is alluded to in such wise by one of his
own generals and in such presence as this——"

"Suppose what you please, my lord of Ormond," said Coote
with vehemence, "I say the arch-rebel and traitor, Sir Phelim
O'Neill—whose head I look to see on one of our city gate-posts
some of these days—does publicly and openly exhibit to his
ruffianly followers a commission for his present work, signed by
no less a personage than 'our sovereign lord, the king.' Hear
you that, my lord?"

The insolent imitation of his own tone and manner would at
another time have irritated the proud earl, but at that moment

the astounding news* which he then heard for the first time
engrossed all his attention, and leaving Coote to exchange triumphant glances aside with Parsons and a few others of the members, he eagerly turned to the Bishops and Sir Robert Meredith
to ask if what he heard could possibly be true. The report was
common in town, they regretted to say, and however idle or improbable it might seem to be, there were but too many who believed it.

"It were strange an' they did not," said Borlase, disregarding
the nods and winks of his more wily partner in office, "when
they have it from the mouths of the sufferers who flock hither for
shelter from the ravenous fury of the Ulster Papists who have
stripped them of all they had and turned them adrift like shorn
sheep, to die in the fields and highways of cold and hunger."

"It is but too true, my lord," said Bishop Loftus in reply to
Ormond's look of wonder and interrogation; "we have for the
last two or three days witnessed sights of that nature fit to melt
our poor hearts within us. Shoals of the loyal and God-fearing
Christians of Ulster—men, women and children, are daily flock-
ing hitherward for succor and protection—ay! some of the foremost people of that unhappy province, too glad to escape with
their lives from the bloody hands of those godless Papists who
have stripped them of all they had—alack! alack! but our
bowels yearn over those suffering confessors for the faith of
Christ!"

Hearing this, Ormond could not keep from smiling: "Well! it

* There is no doubt that Sir Phelim O'Neill did exhibit such a document in order to induce a belief that he and his army fought under
the royal sanction. Amongst a people so loyally disposed as the
Irish, this pretended commission did undoubtedly strengthen Sir
Phelim's hands considerably. Our condemnation of such an act as
the production of a spurious commission would be much more severe,
did we not know that Sir Phelim expiated the deed with his life, and
that his last words declared the king entirely innocent and ignorant of
such a document being in his hands. The history of this famous commission with the mystery in which its origin was involved, the reader
will find in a future chapter.

is very moving, I do confess," said he, "but still I see not how the rebels can have such bloody hands as your lordship speaks of, seeing that they do not make martyrs of these pious confessors—surely, an' they were so much given to bloodshed, these 'shoals' of Protestants could not escape their fury? But methinks we are losing much precious time in idle chit-chat—what news from the west, the south I know to be quiet?"

"Ay, marry, is it?" quoth Parsons curtly; "thanks to good St. Leger——"

"Little fear of rebellion where *he* rules," put in Coote with a fierce laugh.

"And as for Connaught," continued Parsons, taking no note of the interruption, "the men of Belial there have not dared to stir a finger—they are quiet as——"

"As muzzled bears," suggested Coote again; "who thanks them?"

"Nay, Sir Charles, said Rotherham coldly," much thanks are due to the Lord Clanrickard for the good disposition manifested in those parts. Papist though he be, he is a most loyal and excellent nobleman, and writes us in such wise as we might expect from a true friend to law and order!——"

"Of a surety that Earl is doing good service," said one of the Bishops, "and deserves most honorable commendation."

"Well! well!" said Coote impatiently, "let it pass—Clanrickard and the other Papists of that country are none the worse for Willoughby being there to watch them. Having Galway city under his thumb he can keep it screw tight on them. But as regards this royal commission to the rebels—be there no way left us of getting at the proof?"

The sinister look which accompanied the words was well understood by Parsons, and he smiled exultingly as he replied: "That have we, Sir Charles! I thank God, we are in a fair way to bring out the truth—grievous as that may be to loyal subjects —though I see not but we have only too much proof even now —however, lest any doubt remain, Sir Charles, we will have recourse to the safe and secure means which the God of justice has placed within our reach."

Ormond and most of the other members exchanged significant

glances, for they all guessed what Parsons had in view. Disgusted
as many of them were by the blasphemous hypocrisy which yet
was characteristic of the man, and perhaps condemning in their
hearts the cold-blooded cruelty which made so little account of
the sufferings of others, like Pilate they shrank from inter-
posing between the tyrant and his victims, fearing to em-
broil themselves in an affair which no way concerned them.
Even the Bishop who talked so feelingly of the hardships endured
by the Protestants of Ulster had not a word of remonstrance to
offer on behalf of fellow-creatures about to undergo the extremity
of human torture.

So without having formed one resolution, or framed one salutary measure to check the progress of the rebellion, the Privy
Council adjourned its sitting in favor of the noble and right honorable stomachs of its members. This first and most pressing
duty discharged, Parsons and Coote proceeded together to sift
the matter of Sir Phelim O'Neill's commission.

Ormond was no way surprised to hear that evening that Lord
Maguire and Mr. McMahon had been both put to the torture,
and that even the rack which strained and twisted every bone
and sinew of their body could not draw any confession from
either which went to inculpate the king as privy to the designs of
the insurgent chieftains. The Earl had made up his mind that
the document was a forged one, and he knew enough of the
Irish generally to be well assured that chieftains such as the two
in custody would not be induced by any amount of suffering to
criminate their sovereign wrongfully.

The heroic fortitude displayed by both prisoners, and their
generous refusal to obtain a release from torment on a false pretence, might have softened many a hardened heart, but it could
not soften either Coote or Parsons, who alone witnessed the examination (as the torture was technically styled). Standing by,
they directed the fiendish operation, plying the sufferers at short
intervals with such questions as they would have had them
answer affirmatively. Maguire being deemed the most hopeful
subject, was first placed on the rack. And, in sooth, his appearance when first introduced to the fatal chamber, and, surveying
the various instruments of torture, was such as to inspire his

fiendish persecutors with hope. But the deathly pallor of his fine countenance, the tottering of his limbs, and the clammy sweat which bedewed his face were merely outward symptoms, the natural effect of extreme bodily terror, suddenly excited. Those who judged of the chieftain's spirit by these manifestations of weakness did him foul wrong, as they speedily found to their no small amazement. As for Coote, he missed the sight of the first application. He was summoned from the room just as the unfortunate nobleman was stretched on the rack. What detained him from the luxurious feast of cruelty for full ten minutes neither Parsons nor any one present could guess, but when he returned and hastily took his seat near the Lord Justice, that personage noted with surprise that his whole frame trembled, and his every feature was convulsed by some strong emotion, most probably of anger, judging from the livid hue which pervaded the whole. Had any one been bold enough to question him, he would hardly have told that two persons of high estate, and whose solicitations even he had found hard to refuse, had been pleading with passionate earnestness that the prisoners might not be subjected to the torture. Threats and persuasions had been tried, and reasoning so cogent that few men could have resisted it. Sir Charles Coote, however, was not the man to give in to reason—and, at last, as the agonized groans of the sufferer fell on the ears of the petitioners, and still no sign of obtaining mercy for him, the tones of entreaty were suddenly changed to that of solemn denunciation, and one of the two, as with the sudden inspiration of a prophetic spirit, exclaimed with fearful energy :

" No mercy for him who showeth not mercy—as we judge, so shall we be judged—doom dark and dreadful awaits the merciless tyrant—away—let's away—I cannot listen to those sounds of agony—oh, God! wilt not Thou—*Thou* have pity ?"

There was a rush of sweeping garments down the long stone passage, the other individual, after another fruitless entreaty, followed at slower pace, and Coote, without turning his head to look after either, pushed in the iron-studded door of the torture-room with a muttered imprecation of fearful import, and glancing with hellish exultation at the panting, fainting form writhing on the rack, he

7A

took his seat near Parsons with as much composure as he could assume, although that was very little. It soon became evident that nothing satisfactory was to be elicited from the prisoner— nothing, at least, but what was already patent to the whole country. As to the royal commission alleged to be in the hands of Sir Phelim O'Neil, Maguire heard of it then for the first time, and although it was made the chief point of his examination —although bone, and nerve, and sinew, were stretched almost to rending asunder, still he assured them with a voice almost extinct, that he knew nothing whatever of such a document, or had never heard of its existence. At last the unfortunate victim fainted away, and his two examiners concluding there was nothing to be made of *him*, ordered the ministers of their vengeance to remove him, and bring in the other prisoner.

McMahon, true to his own character, and having, doubtless, braced his mind for the first effect of the gloomy chamber and its dismal apparatus, betrayed no sign of fear as he glanced around, and when his eye settled on Coote and Parsons, its expression was that of calm defiance, mixed with a stern resolution that was anything but encouraging to the worthy pair, especially after their experience of the weaker and more timorous Maguire, whose "stature tall and slender frame," were also strongly con- trasted by the more athletic proportions of the Tanist of Uriel. They were not deceived in their calculations, for if the peer proved an unsatisfactory subject, the commoner was still worse. Even the rack could not quench the fire of his free spirit, and so far from gaining any admission from him detrimental to the cause for which he suffered, they heard many words of biting sarcasm, and many home-truths which stirred them to the very quick. Not the least provoking thing was that, increase the amount of torture as they might, they could not extract an ex- pression of pain from McMahon. Like the son of Alknomook " he scorned to complain," and although his members were strained till the joints and sinews cracked, and the big drops stood on his pallid brow, yet, pressing his lips together, he resolutely kept from uttering even the slightest groan. When the officials had exercised upon the brave prisoner the full measure of torment prescribed by the disappointed rage of the examiners, McMahon was taken from the rack more dead than alive, though still conscious, and consigned once more to his dark and silent dungeon without remedy or soothing application of any kind to his bruised and aching limbs.

Like inhumanity was shown to Lord Maguire, but, more fortunate than his friend, he was not without one sympathizing heart to compassionate his sufferings. All through the long and dismal night a figure muffled from head to foot in a sort of military cloak sat weeping in silence at the door of his cell, crouched up in a shapeless heap, listening ever to the piteous moans and half-suppressed groans of the lonely sufferer within. And yet though some mighty passion at times shook the frame of the solitary watcher without, not even one sigh, one whisper of sympathetic sorrow escaped its lips. No turnkey's tread broke in on the mournful vigil, for the golden key which had obtained admission "for some moon-struck Irish damsel," as the jailor phrased it, kept the passage which contained Maguire's cell from all official visitation that night. It was enough for the turnkey in charge to glance down the dimly-lighted corridor as he passed its entrance, and seeing the dark, motionless bulk still there, he would mutter something about "strange tastes" and pass on his round.

CHAPTER XII.

"Pity! no, no, you dare not, Priest,—not you, our Father, dare
Preach to us now that godless creed—the murderer's blood to spare ;
To spare his blood, while tumbles still our slaughter'd kin implore
'Graves and revenge' from Gobbin-cliffs and Carrick's bloody shore !

"Pity! could we 'forget—forgive,' if we were clods of clay,
Our martyr'd priests, our banish'd chiefs, our race in dark decay,
And worse than all—you know it, Priest—the daughters of our land,
With wrongs we blush'd to name until the sword was in our hand !"
                                                    C. G. DUFFY.

ALL was bright and cheerful in the Irish camp at Newry.
Roger O'Moore and Hugh McMahon and Rory Maguire and
Lorcan, Sir Con Magennis and many others of the chief leaders
were there with Sir Phelim O'Neill, and Sir Phelim, now tacitly
recognized as *the O'Neill*, and, moreover, the head of an all-
conquering army—if army his multitudinous force could yet be
called—was in the best possible humor with himself, his brother
chiefs, his brave followers, and, in short, all the world, with the
trifling exception of the Lords Justices and their adherents, and
the sluggish Normans of the Pale. Even the usurping English
and Scotch within his own borders Sir Phelim could, in his gracious mood, somewhat excuse, inasmuch as restitution had been
exacted from them, and that, on the whole, with less trouble
than might be expected. In fact Sir Phelim could have almost
sympathized with them on their losses, in the exuberance of his
good-nature, and the other chiefs were no little amused by his
unsoldierly bearing in their regard. The Irish of that, as of former days, had an instinctive dislike to be shut up in walled towns,
and thus it was that although the neighboring stronghold was

theirs, they chose to keep outside rather than inside its walls,. leaving merely a small garrison to keep the place in possession. But their flag was floating from its towers, and their sentinels walked its ramparts, and they knew themselves masters of Bagnal's fortifications, so they rested content in their encampment close by on the Newry-water, well supplied with provisions by the country-people around, and little heeding the rain and snow beating in at times through the frail coverings which were merely apologies for tents.

The sixth day of November arrived and Sir Phelim spoke of making another attack on the strong walls of Lisnagarvey,* which had some days before repulsed a detachment of his forces with considerable loss. Some few castles, too, were yet in the hands of the foreigners, and these must be gained, if possible, without further delay. The following day was fixed on for the attack on Lisnagarvey, and all things were to be put in readiness over night for an early start.

This arranged, the chieftains met by invitation in Sir Phelim's tent to partake of the evening meal. While it was still in preparation they talked over the general prospects of the war, what had been already done, and what remained to do before freedom could be established on a fair basis. O'Moore marvelled much that nothing was heard from his friend Owen Roe O'Neill to whom he had straight sent off a trusty messenger on hearing of Tyrone's assassination.

"An' he were but come," said Rory, "he would organize our forces and teach them the art of war——"

"What's amiss with them at this present?" demanded Sir Phelim snappishly; "I see not that they have need of new-fangled modes of fighting—what could they do more than they have done here in the North, an' they had fifty Owen Roes to head them?"

"I said not to *head them*, Sir Phelim," replied O'Moore very gently, "but only to train them in the military art, and thereby make them more efficient soldiers——"

"Such teaching were well enough for the Englishers of the Pale," said O'Neill with increasing petulance, "but the clans-

* Now Lisburn.

men of Tyr-Owen and Tyr-Connell—ay! and others whose valiant chiefs are here present, have but small need, I think, of such lessons. Trust me they can use their pikes and skenes, not to speak of other instruments of that kind, as prettily as heart could wish!"

Most of the other chiefs, however, were clearly of O'Moore's opinion that a leader of foreign reputation, and of tried prowess, like Owen Roe, was much to be desired.

"I would you had a score of such," cried Sir Phelim passionately, "an' I warrant me, chiefs of Ulster, you would soon be sick of them, and wish them back again in France or Flanders, or wherever they came from—who did you say was come?" to one of his gillies who had been waiting at his elbow for some minutes vainly trying to get a hearing.

"It's Shamus Beg," said the youth quietly, "at least he says so, though, for my part, I'd hardly know him; he wants to see you, Sir Phelim—why, here he is himself—well! sure enough he must be in the d—l of a hurry!" he added looking back over his shoulder as he moved away.

"Well, Shamus, my man," said his chieftain with restored good humor, as he held out his hand to his foster-brother, for whose return he had, to say the truth, been much more anxious than he would wish to acknowledge; "well, Shamus, my man, what news from the Island—I hope you've brought the colleen back this time—I can ill spare you these busy times running after a colleen bawn—but how are all in Corny Magee's?"

"Not one of them breathes the breath of life," said Shamus, speaking with difficulty, "in *that* house anyhow," he added in an under tone.

"Why, how is that?" asked the chieftain in surprise.

"They're all dead, Sir Phelim, dead—*dead*—and their house is a heap of burned rubbish—and so is most every house on Island Magee—and the whole place is like a graveyard with corpses, only that *there* they're above ground——"

"Shamus O'Hagan," said O'Neill with increasing agitation, "what is this I hear?—have then the whole people been massacred?"

"Ay, every soul of them—I may say—it was a miracle from

God that I escaped myself—and it's little I'd care to do that same only to bring the news to *you* myself——"

"Great God!" cried O'Neill, as he leaped from his seat, "*who* did this horrible deed?"

"Monroe's bloody *sassums* from Knockfergus—last night, in all the storm they marched out to the Island and murdered and burned, and robbed and plundered all before them—by this morning's sun, when I stole back to see what harm was done, I found only one living being in the place—and he groping like myself among the dead!—oh! the curse of God villains!—the black, blood-thirsty hell-hounds!" cried Shamus, warming up at his own recital, "it was them that did their work well!—*farcer gar*, but they did!"

"Chieftains of Ulster!—Catholics! gentlemen! hear ye that?" shouted O'Neill, now thoroughly roused to that passion which was always fearful.

"We do, O'Neill!" said Magennis, who had been sitting next him, but all now rose from their seats, and stood looking on each other and on their host with faces of horror and blank amazement; "we hear the black tidings, and mournful it comes to our ear, O son of the Hy-Nial!"

"By my faith, they'll be worse for the foreigners than they are for us!" exclaimed Maguire in a voice quivering with passion. "It's all over now with the poor victims on Island Magee, but *they* have it all before them——"

"And if it do not overtake them in every corner where our arms can reach," said McMahon sternly, "may those same arms fail us in our sorest need!"

"Ay," said O'Neill in a half-stifled voice, grinding his teeth at the same time, "we were all over generous with the brood of vipers—we were sparing them, forsooth—ay, were we—sparing them for our own destruction—now, Mr. O'Moore," he exclaimed, turning suddenly to that gentleman, "what have *you* to say for yourself?—this milk—and—water work—this clemency and generous forbearance, and what not, was a pet scheme of yours—are you satisfied now that they deserve nor mercy nor pity at our hands—these scorpious—*these*—oh! that my single arm could deal destruction to them all—but if my life be spared, I will give them enough of this bloody work—ay! they shall have it to their hearts' content!"

"I knew it," cried Shamus, his eyes gleaming with exultation and the burning anticipation of revenge; "I knew O'Neill would stand by us—*lamh dearg aboo!*" and he leaped some feet from the ground, "it's ourselves will pay them back with heavy interest for their last night's work—I told them Sir Phelim would see justice done!—*lamh dearg aboo!* friends of my heart, but it's many a proud Sassenach we'll bring down as low as these eyes saw you!" And so saying, he darted from the room, eager to spread the doleful news.

"Sir Phelim," said Rory O'Moore in a tone of deep emotion, "believe me there is no one amongst you all who feels more deeply for the victims of this inhuman massacre, or more detests the cruel treason which wrought so foul a work, but ere we do aught by way of revenge, I would have you think whether, as Christians, we can follow in the bloody track of our enemies without danger of drawing down on ourselves and our cause the wrath and malediction of the God who claimeth vengeance as His own right. Shall we, by indiscriminate slaughter, imbrue our hands in innocent blood, after the manner of these ruthless fanatics, and stain with foul crime the cause now so holy and so just? Friends! Brothers! shall we forfeit our high character as Christian gentlemen, and worse still, our hopes of heavenly guerdon? —speak!"

More than one of the chieftains was about to make reply, but Sir Phelim broke in with thundering voice, and fierce gesticulation:

"Ay, speak!—speak all of ye!—tell our smooth-tongued Leinster friend that ye will close your ears to the cry of kindred blood—that ye will obligingly banish from your minds the memory of last night's slaughter, and in all Christian charity join hands with the murderers, and humbly thank them for what they have done! Talk of staining our cause by punishing those miscreants whom no other power can or will punish! By St. Columb of Hy! Rory O'Moore, you're not the man I took you for—an' you were, Island Magee would stir up the memory of Mullaghmast!"

It required all O'Moore's self-control to bear this taunt. The hot warm blood of the princes of Leix took fire at the insult, and his generous heart, conscious of its own fervent sympathies, was deeply wounded by a sarcasm which more than hinted a want of feeling on his part for the unhappy victims of fanatic cruelty. His face, pale and flushed by turns, and the fitful light flashing from his deep blue eyes, showed at once the struggle going on within and the depth of the emotion which he would fain repress. Sir Phelim himself seemed to expect an angry retort, for he turned his fierce eyes on Rory with a sort of dubious expression as though prepared either to defy or conciliate as occasion might require. If he expected an outburst of passion from O'Moore he was much mistaken, for the latter, after a few moments of obvious self-combat, to the surprise and no small admiration of those present, turned calmly to the other chiefs :

" I know not if I merit this reproach," said he, " mayhap I do —although there be none that I know of—not even Sir Phelim O'Neill—who hath had this matter more at heart from the first hour in which it was planned. What I have *felt* and do *feel* for our nation's wrongs my own heart knows, what I have *done* for the cause, it beseems not me to say. Gentlemen of Ulster, I perceive there be some amongst you with whom I could never agree on the mode of warfare to be pursued—my presence is of small import here, and much work is to be done in other parts of the country—I will, therefore, take my leave of you all for a time, wishing you all success and beseeching you, not for my sake, but for that of the great cause in which we have all engaged, to cherish a brotherly feeling amongst yourselves and avoid all unnecessary bloodshed——"

" Why, surely, you are not going without your dinner ?" put in Sir Phelim, with a ludicrous change of manner, while the other gentlemen crowded around with eager solicitations.

But O'Moore, having once made up his mind, was not to be moved from his purpose, although when he shook Sir Phelim's hand at parting, there was not the slightest trace of ill feeling visible on his face or in his demeanor. Cullen and his followers were well pleased to return to their own country, where all was comparative peace, and in very few minutes the small cortege was ready for the start. Sir Phelim, in high dudgeon, lounged in

7*

his tent while O'Moore was setting out, but his absence gave
little concern to Rory or the other chiefs, all of whom were assembled in front of McMahon's tent to wish him God speed.
Glancing his keen eye over the stately group, O'Moore bent from
his saddle and softly whispered :

"Heed not his wayward humors—keep together, and work for
the common good—as Christians—till God sends you a fitting
leader, wanting whom but little can be done. Such a man ye
all wot of, and, with God's good aid, he will soon be with you—
of that I am well assured. Heaven guard ye all, friends and
gentlemen, till we meet again!" These last words were said
aloud, and, after exchanging a cordial salute with his friends,
O'Moore was just starting, when up, at full speed, rode Bishop
McMahon, followed, as usual, at a respectful distance by his
faithful Malachy.

"Well met, Mr. O'Moore," said the prelate hastily, after exchanging salutes with his cousin of Uriel and the other chieftains ;
"it was but last night I heard of your being here, and as I have
many things of moment to treat of with you, I hurried off this
morning betimes, the rather," he added with a smile, that was
not of mirth but sadness, "the rather as our good Malachy was
anxious, likewise, to have speech of you."

I am truly happy, then, that your lordship arrived in time,'
said O'Moore courteously ; "a few minutes later and I should
have been on my road southward."

The Bishop appeared surprised. "Why, I thought you purposed making longer stay with us here, an' it were but to see
how our brave clansmen move in war-harness."

O'Moore explained in few words what had happened, adding
that his presence was really more needed elsewhere. The prelate then lowering his voice, and drawing as near as their respective steeds would go, inquired if there were any recent news
from Colonel O'Neill, and whether he was soon to be expected.
Being answered in the affirmative, he appeared much pleased.

"Well," said he, "Mr. O'Moore, as you have given me good
tidings, it is but fair that I do the same by you. I have got word
but yester-eve from my reverend friend, Father Luke Wadding,
whom you doubtless know—at least by name."

" Surely I do, my good lord," said O'Moore joyfully ; " when in
Spain I saw much of that worthy priest and true patriot, and
there be few men living whom I hold in higher esteem. My poor
friend, Hugh O'Neill—now, I trust, with God—was first moved
to hope and work for our country's freedom by the glowing eloquence of that great and good man. I warrant me he is taking
note of our poor efforts——"

" That is he and more, too, which you will hear of before long—
he desires to know what truth there is in the reports current
throughout Europe concerning our rising here—he says, an' it
be true that we have already done so much as he has heard, that
we shall have no lack of succor, and that right speedily. I am
able to give him good accounts of this northern country, but
what shall I say regarding the other provinces and the English
Catholics of the Pale ?"

" As regards our own tribes in the south and west," said
O'Moore, " I am daily in hopes of their rising—portions of both
Connaught and Leinster are even now in action—as for the Palesmen, I must say that my hopes of succor from them have dwin-
dled into nothing—they are too wedded to those fat lands of
theirs to gainsay the government in aught."

" Ho ! ho !" laughed Sir Phelim O'Neill, who had just come
within hearing, " you were ready to measure swords with me,
but late for saying no worse thing of your Norman ' friends and
kinsmen.' I joy to think that you have found them out in time
—how goes it with my good lord of Clogher?—have you heard
the news from Carrick side ?"

While Sir Phelim, with some of the other chiefs, horrified the
Bishop with the fatal story of the last night's butchery, Malachy
approached O'Moore, who merely waited to take his leave of the
prelate, and begged permission to say something very particular.
The permission being given with an encouraging smile, Malachy
opened his large mouth and spoke as follows :

" It's in regard to the heavy load that's on my heart these days
that I make bold to speak to you, Mr. O'Moore. I can't sleep
by night or rest by day only thinking of our noble Tanist that's
a prisoner with the bloody villains in Dublin Castle above. The

Lord save him from worse harm, but somehow I'm troubled
entirely with fearsome dreams and visions concerning him."

"Oh! that is all but natural, my good Malachy," said O'Moore
with assumed gaiety; "your faithful heart is sore grieved for your
young lord's misfortune, and I do not wonder that your dreams
should be wild and gloomy!"

Malachy shook his head. "There's more than that in it, sir,—
ochone! I know there is, and as we're entirely in the dark about
him, with the blessing of God I'm determined to make my way
to where he is before I'm many days older."

O'Moore was touched by the self-forgetting devotion of the faithful follower, and his voice trembled as he replied: "Alas! my
poor friend, the journey to Dublin is long and toilsome, and
supposing even you got there in safety, it might profit you
little. How could you hope to get speech or even sight of Mr.
McMahon?"

"Well! as for the journey, the Bishop says you know every
foot of the way, and that if you'd let me follow you when you're
going back, I'd get so near Dublin that I could make out the rest
of the way easy enough - if I was once in the city, God and the
Blessed Virgin would do the rest, and who knows but I might be
able to get to do something for Mister Costelloe."

O'Moore could not help laughing at Malachy's grave simplicity,
whereupon that individual opened his eyes very wide and looked
somewhat offended: "You needn't laugh, sir," he said in a very
serious tone, "for it's not me alone that's troubled in mind about
this matter – there's his honor Lorcan More Maguire has got
warnings to no end about my lord Maguire and our Tanist, and
he wouldn't believe even the Bishop but something very bad has
happened to them both—or *will* happen, if God hasn't said it,
before long."

The person thus alluded to hearing his own name mentioned,
—and Malachy, whether by accident or design, spoke it in a raised
voice,—quickly detached himself from the group around the
Bishop, and came eagerly forward. He was much excited, for
he had been warmly combatting some rash proposal of Sir
Phelim's, but on hearing of Malachy's purpose, he became calm
in a moment, and strenuously recommended the visit to Dublin.

" An' it were not," said he, " for the press of work put upon us
by these bloody Scotch I'd be up in Dublin myself before now,
for I know well there's something amiss with my poor Connor.
Not to speak of all the signs and warnings I have got of late, it
was only the other night I was told by one that came to me in
my sleep that the Maguire was in sore bodily distress at that
hour, an'l that unless something wonderful turned up he'd never
stand on green grass. It is ease to my mind to think that
Malachy here may be able to bring us some word of Connor, and
if he didn't go, I'd go myself, for, after all, I know there's enough
here to settle accounts with the enemy—ha! ha! if there was
none but Sir Phelim and our Rory yonder, they'd do that between
them !"

" I believe you," said O'Moore in all sincerity, " heaven only
grant they go not too far with this thing of revenge. However,
my duty lies elsewhere, and if the Bishop be content to spare
Malachy, he can journey with us—let me see—to the very
borders of Dublin county, whence I can send a trusty messenger
to guide him to the city !"

The Bishop, being appealed to, declared himself quite willing,
albeit that he feared Malachy's simplicity and inexperience, yet,
as he said apart to O'Moore, such persons often fared better in
trying contingencies than those of sharper wit, so in God's name
he dismissed Malachy with his blessing, commending him earnestly to the guiding care of his Leinster friend. Not so McMahon,
who, when informed of Malachy's project, ridiculed the whole
scheme, and scouted as something altogether impossible the
notion of his reaching Dublin in safety, or, at all events, of his
seeing his brother. His chieftain's mockery disturbed poor
Malachy not a little, but with the Bishop's blessing and consent
he consoled himself, and started hopefully for the unknown re-
gions of the English Pale, not, however, without giving the prelate sundry charges relating to the care of their slender stock of
altar linen and other matters of a like nature.

While Rory O'Moore was rapidly retracing his way to the confines of the Pale, and thence over the rich plains of Louth to the
neighborhood of Dundalk, where he expected to meet Colonels
Plunket and O'Byrne, the Red Hand was smiting in wrath and

vengeance the terror-stricken settlers in the northern parts of
Ulster. On the very day after the receipt of Shamus's fateful news,
Sir Phelim led a strong force against Sir William Brownlow's
Castle of Augher, situate in the county of Tyrone, and the
place being taken after some resistance, the garrison and household servants—all, in short, who were found in arms, were put to
the sword. At the intercession of Lady Brownlow, however, she,
her husband and family, were spared, and suffered to quit the
Castle, of which Sir Phelim immediately took possession. During
that first scene of slaughter on the part of the Irish troops, and
in many a bloody act of retributive justice in after days, their
watchword was " Island Magee!" and when pity touched their
hearts or unnerved their arms, the recollection of that wanton
and most savage massacre silenced the voice of compassion.
From that time forward, the war in Ulster assumed a fiercer and
more sanguinary character, and its horrors were daily, hourly
increased by mutual acts of retaliation. Roused to fury by the
savage cruelty and base treachery of Monroe's Scotch fanatics,
and conscious that his own forces had previously been almost too
sparing of bloodshed, Sir Phelim O'Neill gave full rein to his
fierce passions, and thenceforward treated the enemies of his
country according to what he believed their deserts.

CHAPTER XIII.

"A great man struggling in the storms of fate,
And greatly falling with a falling state."

POPE

"Full many mischiefs follow cruel wrath,
Abhorr'd bloodshed, and tumultuous strife,
Unmanly murder, and unthrifty scathe,
Bitter despite with rancor's rusty knife,
And fretting grief the enemy of life."

SPENSER.

WHEN the new order of things began to extend into Breffny, and the clansmen were more or less imbued with the fierce spirit of revenge coming southward on every breeze from the north country; when every tongue was busy with the horrors of the Antrim massacre, and many a stout Breffny-man was heard to mutter a stern regret for past clemency thrown away, it was then that Philip O'Reilly was called upon for the display of those high qualities which have since won the admiration of all. Like his friend O'Rourke, he knew how to battle for the right without staining his soul with murder or degrading the noble profession of arms by unnecessary cruelty. O'Reilly and O'Rourke, generous, noble and warm-hearted, were neither of them insensible to the wrongs and outrages committed on their people—they felt, as brave men could not but feel, their hearts swell with indignation and disgust at the atrocious massacre which had stirred up Catholic Ulster from end to end, and they, too, panted for revenge, but their revenge took a higher range with more solid advantages in view. Little gratification would it be to either of these Breffny chieftains to see Protestant blood shed in torrents, or to know that every foreigner in the land was put to cruel torture; these things were foreign to their nature, and they never could delight in human suffering, but to crush the power of the stranger, to smite the oppressor in honorable warfare, and raise the old tribes everywhere to that position which they ought to hold in their own land—finally, to re-establish the true faith in all its pristine glory, and to humble the haughty crest of heresy even to the dust—such was the revenge for which O'Rourke and O'Reilly thirsted, such were the ends which they had in view in raising their respective standards.

During the stormy days, and weeks, and months which followed the massacre of Island Magee, the clans of Breffny O'Reilly were not idle any more than their neighbors of Uriel and Breffny O'Rourke. They had their musters, and marches and counter-marches amid the swelling hills and pastoral knolls of their ancient principality. The several chieftains who looked up to O'Reilly as their head had all more or less contributed to the general success of the northern army, and each, in his own district, dispossessed the English planters in a summary manner of the castles with which they had studded the country. The Protestant inhabitants, necessarily regarded as adherents of the government, and, therefore, not to be tolerated,—were ejected with very little ceremony, and sent to seek winter-quarters elsewhere. In some places, where an obstinate resistance was made, and the native forces suffered, the power of the chief was not able to withhold his people from taking revenge in their own hands, although even then the executions were confined to the most prominent and rabid of the enemy.

There was one house, however, in O'Reilly's country—one Protestant dwelling which no hostile force ever attacked, no random shot ever reached. It was an old-fashioned glebe-house, of plain yet respectable exterior, surrounded by pleasant woods and fertile, well-tilled fields. Here the Anglican bishop of Kilmore had dwelt in peace for many a year; a man of peace he was, a venerable man, devoted to study and the care of his flock, meddling not with his Catholic neighbors, in their spiritual affairs, but serving them when occasion required, to the utmost of his ability. A good man of quiet, unostentatious habits, kind and benevolent to all, was Bishop Beddell, of Kilmore, the same whom our readers will remember as so favorably mentioned by the Countess of Ormond, when pleading the cause of the proscribed Catholics with her husband. Respecting the religious convictions of others, this exemplary man was himself respected in times when religious rancor was at the highest, and his house was a sanctuary never violated by the generous and grateful clansmen of Breffny. By it they marched at all hours of the night and day with banners flying, and weapons gleaming, often in all the flush of victory, and again, smarting under some recent provocation, yet never was their anger directed against the house of Bishop Beddell, although it was well known that many Protestants driven from other parts of the country were sheltered within its walls. Had the Anglican prelate been other than he was, and more like to his brothers of the established episcopate, his snug glebe-house would have passed into other hands as his cathedral and parish churches had done before, but, as it was, he lived there in peace, with his friends and his numerous household, protected by the noble-hearted O'Reilly and other influential Catholics of the country.

On a certain day when the good Bishop had the numerous occupants of his house assembled in his best parlor for some religious exercise, word was brought him that the Catholic bishop had come to visit him, and was then waiting in an adjoining apartment. This announcement was heard with dismay by the little congregation who naturally feared that it boded no good to them. Bishop Beddell, however, calmed their fears and assured them that Dr. McSweeny was not the man to take advantage of their misfortunes or betray them to the Philistines of the northern country.

"Howsoever," said the good Doctor, "I will go and see what the gentleman's business may be with me, and when I have had speech of him I will straightway return hither. Meanwhile, rest ye here in peace, supplicating the Lord on behalf of his poor dispersed flock, that he keep them from the hands of Sir Phelim O'Neill and such like men of blood."

The meeting between the two bishops was characteristic of the times. In Dr. McSweeny, a tall dignified man of middle age, the

polished bearing of the foreign ecclesiastic, the graduate of Royal
Salamanca, was blended with the somewhat patronizing air of a
man suddenly raised from an outlawed and hidden life to one of
triumph and jubilation,—from a position of constant dependence
to one of absolute command and all but unlimited power.

In the bent form of the old Protestant bishop, and on his mild
but wrinkled brow, there was deep sorrow, but nothing of deference or deprecation. On the contrary there was in his aged eyes
when he raised them to the face of his visitor a look of something
like reproach which the other was at no loss to understand, although quite conscious that he did not deserve it at Bishop Beddell's hands.

The two had met but once before, and the memory of that long-
past meeting was fresh in the mind of each, giving, it might be,
a sort of constraint to the demeanor of both.

"Times are changed with us, Dr. Beddell, since last we met,"
observed the Catholic bishop after they had exchanged a somewhat distant salute.

"Fear not that I forget the change," the other replied with
more warmth than he commonly displayed, "the Lord hath humbled us, we trust for our good!—will it please you to sit?"

"My time is short," the Bishop replied, "for, in these unhappy
days, my avocations are many and arduous."

"Unhappy days!" repeated Beddell with some sternness, "and
whose be the fault, Owen McSweeny?"

"I came not hither to dispute a question which the sword
must decide and the might of armies," said the Bishop coldly,—
"Dr. Beddell, I respect you beyond all men of your persuasion—
you once served me, too, in a matter of great moment, which I
wish not to forget – our people are moved to wrath at the present
time by the recent bloody act of Monroe's soldiers at Island Magee—so that even these kindly men of Breffny, who have hitherto
respected your name and character, may in some moment of
frenzied irritation forget all else but your connection with that
establishment which truly they have no reason to love—nay, hear
me out, Doctor! Even O'Reilly's power may not always be able
to protect you—that is, when other portions of our army come
to pass this way—*mine* will never fail with Catholic soldiers—

would you that I send a small party hither who, wearing my
cognizance and colors, may secure you against all attacks from
our troops.?"

"I pray you, good brother, excuse my compliance," said Beddell hastily ; "I fear me much that the presence of your armed
followers would do more harm than good in my quiet household.
And, moreover, if the rebel hordes—excuse me—if the army of
Sir Phelim unhappily comes this way, our chance of life or
escape were small, indeed, even under favor of your reverence's
cognizance and colors, which I pray you to believe I hold in all
respect."

The grave caustic irony of these last words was keenly felt by
Bishop McSweeny, who, conscious of his own good intentions,
could not help being somewhat nettled. Taking his hat to depart, he coolly observed :

"My reverence's cognizance may serve you yet, Master Beddell, for all you seem to set so slight store on my poor ability to
befriend you. It may be that Philip O'Reilly, on whose protection
you now depend, may one day fail you—should that ever come
to pass, you will find a friend in the Bishop of Kilmore."

"Nay, nay, good sir," cried the old man, following his visitor
to the door, "if you mean yourself, assuredly the Bishop of
Kilmore stands not in your shoes—the Cathedral maketh not
the Bishop, Owen—I pray you, remember that !"

"I remember, John, I remember," said the Bishop looking
back over his shoulder with a humorous expression of countenance, "I stand beholden to you for that new lesson in theo-
logy. But, man, King Charles himself cannot make a Bishop
here now, and as for Cathedrals, there be no one in all Ireland
more expert at making them than the O'Reilly, Heaven bless
him!—except it be Sir Phelim O'Neill, who has, I hear, turned
stone mason of late for the building of such like fabrics !"

"Ay ! they may laugh and jest that win," cried Bishop Beddell,
still more excited, and raising his cracked voice to the utmost ;
"but forget not that I am and will be Bishop of Kilmore, while
God spares me life !—of that title no man can rob me, Dr. Mc-
Sweeny, for it came to me from God himself !"

"From his late Majesty King James you mean—howsoever,

Dr. Beddell, keep your temper an' you may not keep your title
—my humble service to you!"

" But you will bear me witness," shouted the excited old man,
" that I gave not in to your unlawful assumption of my dignity !"

" I pray you, shelter yourself from the cold !" was the Bishop's
good-humored answer as he mounted the horse which one of his
attendants held for him at a little distance down the avenue, and,
waving his parting salute, he rode away at a brisk trot, wilfully
closing his ears to the vehement protestations of the superseded
dignitary of King Charles's church.

But, alas! while the good Bishop of Kilmore and the chivalrous chieftains of Breffny were thus shielding from harm the
venerable man who, in his better days, had shown himself the
friend of the persecuted Catholics, far different scenes were being
enacted in various parts of the same province, where the lurid
flame of civil war burned more fiercely and made greater havoc.

Far amongst the wild mountains of Tyrone, where one of the
rude castles of the O'Neills stood in its strength defending an
important pass, one of the saddest episodes of that sad drama had
lately taken place. When Charlemont Castle was taken by Sir Phelim O'Neill it was by a clever stratagem, and the chief, well disposed
towards the veteran soldier, who was at once its owner and the
commander of its garrison, strictly forbade his followers to harm
him or his, and, after some deliberation, (during which he had
been removed more than once for greater security from one
stronghold to another,) finally resolved on sending him to the
mountain-fortalice above referred to until such time as he might
turn his capture to account by obtaining other prisoners in exchange for him.   Thither, then, Lord Caulfield was conveyed,
with his family, in the early part of November, escorted by a
party of O'Neill's men.   Lady Caulfield and her children were
safely lodged in the Castle, her husband was already on the
threshold when, unluckily for himself, he made some imprudent
remark concerning Sir Phelim O'Neill, little complimentary to
that chieftain's honor or good faith.   He was passing between
some six or eight of O'Neill's clansmen at the moment, and their
hot blood could ill brook words derogatory to their chief.

" Say that again," cried one of them, "and you pass not that threshold with your life!"

Caulfield, unawed by this threat, repeated what he had said, and with increased bitterness—another moment and six skenes were in his body : he fell across the threshold a lifeless corpse, the victim, surely of his own imprudence, rather than of premeditated treachery on the part of his captors. The cry of terror and dismay which arose from their comrades was not needed to alarm the culprits, who had hardly done the deed when they would have given worlds to recall it. They knew that their chieftain's wrath was terrible and that he would exact a rigorous account of the blood they had just shed.

When Sir Phelim heard of what had happened, he acted with a coolness little to be expected from his fiery nature. He neither blustered nor stormed as was his wont when laboring under great excitement, but he ordered the offenders to be brought before him, and waited their appearance with a calmness more terrible to those around who knew him well, than the most violent manifestation of anger.

Some minutes elapsed without the offenders making their appearance, and Sir Phelim began to wax impatient, especially as, from certain significant looks and gestures passing rapidly amongst his officers, he concluded that the delay was not accidental. Pacing to and fro in front of his tent, he repeated his command in a louder and more threatening tone—still no prisoners appeared, and the angry chief was about to proceed on a quest that would likely have proved fatal to those concerned, when a stir was noticed in another direction, and round a projecting angle of a wall rode up to the general's tent a young gentleman of grave and sedate aspect, with an elderly lady in a cloak and riding-hood, mounted on a pillion behind him. They were followed by a couple of serving-men whose composed demeanor, round ruddy faces, and smooth, well-combed locks pointed them out as of Saxon rather than Gaelic origin. It was English, too, that the party spoke, when they came to exchange salutations with those of the camp.

Sir Phelim advanced hastily to assist the lady from her elevated seat, though his greeting manifested anything but pleasure.

"In God's name, mother, what wind blew you hitherward—surely this be no place for hoods or kirtles!"

"I know it, Phelim, and I come not from choice, believe my word, but pressed by sore trouble and anxiety on your account I prayed Alexander to conduct me hither that I might hear from your own lips the truth which will either give me rest or a heavier load of sorrow to bear for evermore."

"Why, what in the d——'s name is she driving at, Alick?" cried Sir Phelim with ill-concealed discontent as he turned to the gentleman, who was no other than his half-brother, by a second marriage. "What *does* it all mean?"

Alexander Hovenden only smiled and said : "she will tell you that full quickly!"

"I came hither, Phelim," said the aged matron, dropping her voice so as to reach only her son's ear, "to know from yourself in person whether you be chargeable with the death of that good man, Lord Caulfield, as people say you are—tell me, my son! what am I to believe concerning this foul deed, for since I heard of it, I cannot eat, or drink, or sleep!"

"Mother," said Sir Phelim O'Neill, and opening his large eyes wide he fixed them full on those of his parent, "mother, as I hope to be saved, I solemnly assure you that I knew not of this murder—for murder I do call it—until it was too late to do aught but punish the guilty—which that I do in all sincerity, you may see in a few minutes' time. Why, Mistress Hovenden, my good mother, I had hoped much from the imprisonment of my Lord Caulfield, whose death I look on as a heavy loss, not to speak of the good esteem in which I held him as a right valiant old soldier and a jovial, hearty neighbor—but stay—what is this —how—do mine eyes see right, or is that Shamus?"

Alas! it was Shamus, the beloved foster-brother, the trustiest vassal that ever followed chief to the field—and there he stood, one of the *six* whom Sir Phelim had already doomed to death. Seeing him thus, O'Neill struck his brow with his open palm, and turned away in violent agitation. Turning again he walked close up to Shamus, whose downcast eyes scarcely appeared to notice his presence.

"Shamus!" said the chief, in a voice trembling with emotion,

"Shamus, are *you* a murderer—did *you* aid in slaying a prisoner entrusted to your care—a prisoner of rank and note?—speak, Shamus, did you do this deed?"

"My chief, *I did not*," said the foster-brother, raising his eyes for the first time, "I have made my death-shrift but now, and I tell you—believe me or not—that I am innocent of this crime, which Modder and the rest can tell you as well as I."

But Modder O'Neill, a fierce-looking mountaineer with fiery red hair, when questioned by his chief, declined to answer, alleging that he knew nothing more than that Shamus Beg was on the spot—whether he struck the Sassenach lord he could not tell.

"God forgive you, Modder!" cried Shamus, in a reproachful tone, "you know well I had neither act nor part in it, only that I helped to lift the corpse when them that ought to be in my place took to their heels——"

"And who is *that?*" demanded Sir Phelim.

"If you dare——!" cried Modder, with a look of savage ferocity.

"I would dare," replied Shamus, returning the look with one of stern defiance, "only that what I never done before, I'll not do now—that is turn *informer*—Sir Phelim, if you *think* me guilty, I'm ready to bear whatever punishment you lay on me!"

"You must die, then, Shamus, though it breaks my heart to say it——"

"Son! son!" exclaimed Mistress Hovenden, coming forward with clasped hands, "the same milk nursed you both—for the sake of his dead mother who loved you as her own, spare his life—spare poor Shamus, I beseech you!"

"Mother, I cannot spare *him* without sparing the others, and I have sworn by the soul of the great Nial that the murderers of Toby Caulfield shall die—*die!*" he repeated with fierce emphasis, stamping his foot at the same time; "if it were my *own* brother, he should share the same fate——"

"More shame for you, O'Neill," said Modder suddenly, "it was on your account we did it—an' it were to do over again, you might do it yourself——"

"Silence!" cried the chieftain in a voice of thunder; "you have left a stain upon my name which your heart's blood can

never wash out—here, you, Teague, take twelve of the best
shots in your company, and shoot these six there behind—behind—" he strove to keep up a show of stern indifference but
it would not do—his rough voice sank to a whisper, and at last
failed him quite—pointing with his hand to the fatal spot which
he would have mentioned, he rushed away, followed, however, by
several of the chieftains who, hearing of what was going on,
hastened to intercede for the unhappy culprits.

But Sir Phelim, who had already rejected his mother's intercession, was little likely to hear them with more favor, and in a
very few minutes all would have been over with the prisoners,
when a duplicate image of Modder O'Neill was seen making his
way through the doggedly silent and discontented crowd, and
seizing Shamus by the arm as fiercely as though he would have
torn him to pieces, he dragged him back to the presence of their
chief, crying with the fury of a maniac:

"It was I did it, Sir Phelim, and not him—he wouldn't *inform*
on me, so I will!"

A cry of anguish from Modder brought all eyes on him, and
the ghastly visage with which he stared on his twin brother, thus
throwing himself on death, was a piteous sight to behold. How
that wild, fierce man must have loved that no less uncouth brother of his, and the despairing look with which he regarded him,
moved every heart. But Phadrig heeded him not at all, so intent
was he on carrying out his wild idea of justice.

"I did it, Sir Phelim, and not Shamus—I stabbed the Sassenach chief—he said you were a base traitor—and I silenced his
lying tongue with my skene—*I* did it, and I'm willing to die for
it, but let Shamus go!—for he's innocent!"

"Thank God!" murmured Mistress Hovenden, and her younger son advancing shook Shamus warmly by the hand.

"It is well," said Sir Phelim, the ruddy tinge returning suddenly to his cheek and brow, "release Shamus, Teague, and
take Phadrig O'Neill in custody. I am sorry for you, Phadrig,
my honest fellow! by the sounding *Lia Fail*, I am, but justice
must be done——"

It was now Shamus's turn to sue for "poor witless Phadrig,"
and other mediators of higher rank were not slack in their sup-

plications for a general pardon of the six,—even his own chaplain adding his entreaties,—but Sir Phelim silenced them all with a ferocity that was partly assumed, and having allowed time, as a special grace, for Phadrig to receive the last rites, he consigned the prisoners to their fate,* with as much coolness as though they were so many of the hated Scotch troopers.

The other chieftains, with the sole exception of Rory Maguire, withdrew to their quarters in displeasure, and even Mistress Hovenden, albeit that she rejoiced to know her son innocent of Lord Caulfield's murder, refused to partake of any refreshment at his hands, and left the camp immediately. As for Shamus, he hardly knew, he said, whether to be glad or sorry, for, after the way in which poor Phadrig acted, he would as soon have died himself in a manner, as see *him* die—to be sure, whatever Sir Phelim did was right, but somehow he could not help thinking that the black looks and lowering brows of the clansmen were not without good cause, considering that the unlucky old Sassenach had brought his death on himself if ever man did.

* It is said, in justification of Sir Phelim, that, on hearing of Lord Caulfield's murder, he caused six of his men to be put to death in punishment of that crime.

8ᴀ

CHAPTER XIV.

"Experience, wounded, is the school
Where men learn piercing wisdom."
                                        LORD BROOK.

"Those that fly may fight again,
Which he can never do that's slain ;
Hence, timely running's no mean part
Of conduct in the martial art."
                                        BUTLER's *Hudibras.*

THE last days of November had come on, and, although the
insurgent forces had, as I have shown, overrun nearly all Ulster,
with some counties of Leinster and Connaught—for great part
of Sligo had recently followed the example of Leitrim—still,
strange to say, they had never yet encountered the enemy in
open field. For so far, they had it all their own way, as one
might say, the few troops who were at the government's disposal
being kept so selfishly and at the same time so imprudently
within the limits of the capital. Owing to the unaccountable
supineness of the Lords Justices, Ormond's military talents were
comparatively useless, for, under one pretence or another, he
was kept inactive in Dublin, waiting for forces which were not
forthcoming, his proud spirit chafed and mortified by the powerless condition to which he was reduced, and the little regard
paid to his proposals, which, had they been acted upon, would
speedily have arrested the progress of the rebellion. To crown
his mortification, he saw Sir Charles Coote entrusted with whatever operations *were* carried on, and empowered to levy forces
almost at discretion, while he, with his consciousness of superior
ability, possessing, too, the confidence of his sovereign, and vested
in some degree with his authority, was yet, through the narrow

jealousy and suspicious bigotry of the Lords Justices and their party in the Council, compelled to a most disgraceful inactivity.

Much was expected by Ormond and what might be called the royalist party in the Council from the opening of Parliament, which, adjourned in the previous August, was to meet in this month of November. But, to the utter astonishment of all, except those who were in the confidence of Parsons and his colleagues, a few days before that fixed on for the opening of Parliament, a proclamation was issued declaring it prorogued till the following February. This arbitrary and most insane step excited such a storm of indignation and drew forth such angry remonstrances from almost all parties, that the Lords Justices agreed to have the Parliament sit for *one day*, provided the two estates would unite in a strong protestation against the rebels. This was agreed to, and the Parliament assembled, as was its wont, within the walls of the Castle, guarded by the whole available force of the government, and further secured from unwelcome intrusion by the exclusion, by proclamation, of all strangers from the city.

The Lords and Commons after much deliberation agreed on a form of protest which, though not at all strong enough for the liking of the Executive, was gladly received and industriously scattered throughout the country. A parliamentary commission, consisting of nine lords and twelve commoners, was then appointed to treat with the rebels about laying down their arms, and this done, the assembly was prorogued in the most arbitrary and tyrannical manner possible by Parsons himself, notwithstanding that a numerous deputation from each of the two houses was sent to him to request that the session might continue a little longer that measures might be taken to suppress the rebellion. This was peremptorily refused, and the Parliament was forced to dissolve at the very moment when its deliberations were most necessary for the country, and its counsel and direction most required by the bulk of the people.

Meanwhile the Lords of the Pale were in no enviable position. Keeping entirely aloof from the rebels, and taking all possible care to avoid anything that might appear like sympathy with them or their cause, they did all that in them lay to attach themselves to the government party, and to obtain even a share of government confidence. Their application for arms on loyal pretences was, as we have seen, successful, but only in a very moderate degree, for the five hundred stand of arms granted to them was not more than sufficient for the defence of a single county, much less the five inclosed within the Pale. A short way would it have gone against the pikes and muskets and hatchets of the northern clans, as the Norman lords bitterly said amongst themselves.

Small, however, as the supply was, it was rather encouraging to the Palesmen, as showing a certain amount of confidence on the part of the Executive, and Lord Gormanstown, to whom the arms were sent, lost no time in distributing them as far as they went, amongst the border castles of the Pale. It is probable that the exaggerated reports concerning these military stores would only have excited the Ulster chiefs to attack those castles all the sooner with a view to obtain, if possible, what they stood most in need of, but almost before the news had time to reach them, a peremptory order was sent to Lord Gormanstown from the Castle to send back the arms without delay. Great was his lordship's discomfiture and bitter his mortification, for, of course, he and his friends had been making a great parade of the trust reposed in them by the powers that were. But even this new insult they were forced to pocket, and the arms were duly returned to the arsenal in Dublin to the no small amusement of Lord Ormond and men of his stamp, amongst whom it was jocularly remarked that the arms aforesaid having been for days in Popish hands must needs undergo some process of purification ere they were given for use to godly Protestants.

Certain of the lords thus insulted repaired forthwith to Dublin to offer their humble remonstrances to the Lords Justices, but, even there they found a trifling difficulty in the way, for, on reaching the metropolis, they were denied admission, the gates being closed, they were told, against all persons residing at a certain distance from the city. But they went on business of importance to the government. It mattered not, the orders were peremptory. So the magnates of the Pale, the ultra-loyal supporters of Parson's government, and the determined foes of all rebellion—right or wrong—were under the painful necessity of turning their backs on the viceregal city in which all their hopes were centred. Like the false knight in the old roundelay

" *They* love and they ride away,"

ride away from government patronage and all its soothing hopes and prospects, which, to such very loyal gentlemen, was a sore affliction. Blank was the comely oval face of Gormanstown, as he turned his horse's head for home, and Dunsany's thin, sharp features grew wofully wan, whilst Netterville, who was also of the party, was half inclined to laugh at a rebuff which, of all the Norman lords, he regretted the least, for reasons known unto himself.

"It passes belief," said Lord Gormanstown, "that any administration should so goad men on to rebellion——"

"So far does it outstrip credibility," put in Dunsany, "that I will never believe this rejection of our services to proceed from the Lords Justices or the Council, unless I have it from Parsons himself, or some other member of the government. Why, the thing is wholly impossible when we bethink us of the favor wherewith the first tender of our services was received——"

"I think as you do, my Lord Dunsany," said Gormanstown gravely, "and we will not give up our hopes of being rightly understood without another trial. What say your lordships to our meeting—I mean the chief men of the Pale—at Killeen Castle, as the more central, three days hence, and then after holding counsel together, to name one or two of our number to repair to Dublin and there assure the Lords Justices in a still more solemn manner than heretofore of our entire devotion to the royal cause, and our anxious desire to be employed in any way their lordships may deem fitting for the suppression of this dangerous rebellion ?"

Dunsany eagerly caught this new idea, and although Netterville was clearly of opinion that sufficient pains had been already taken to demonstrate their loyalty, he agreed to be present at the meeting, and to advertise the noblemen and gentlemen of his vicinity where and when it was to be.

So the over-loyal magnates of the Pale met at Killeen Castle, enjoyed Lord Fingal's princely hospitality, railed at the hot-headed folly of the " mere Irish," and appointed Lord Dunsany to convey their loyal and most submissive sentiments to their mightinesses of the Castle, with their humble prayer to be allowed to serve the state and defend their own possessions at the same time against the savage hordes who were already encroaching on their domains.

Much was expected from this embassy of Dunsany, who, well pleased with the office, set out in high spirits for Dublin, pondering, doubtless, as he went on the perspective advantages likely to accrue to himself and his brethren of the Pale. But Patrick Plunket, like many another very sagacious individual of his stamp, reckoned without his host, and so did those who sent him. It was long ere they saw his face again—some of them never on earth—and the gracious reply and warm commendation of their good dispositions, which they fully expected him to bear back, never reached their longing ears, for Sir William Parsons, having heard what Dunsany had to say, was so charmed by that nobleman's loyal sentiments and so grateful for the same, that he must needs treat him hospitably, and with that laudable intention, doubtless, sent him to share the imprisonment of the northern chiefs in the dungeons of the Castle.*

Alas! for the would-be loyal Catholics of the Pale when these tidings reached them! how blanched their cheeks, how ghastly the look which they turned one on the other, and how hollow the voice in which each made his brief comment on the strange announcement.

"Dunsany in prison!" cried Fingal.

"The loyalest noble of the Pale!" echoed Gormanstown.

"Parsons must be mad!" said the courtly Louth.

"There be more than Parsons so," quoth Netterville bluntly; "methinks all Ireland will set us down as crazy-pates, and, by mine honor, not without good reason!"

"Who knows," said a stout elderly gentleman of martial aspect, "but they may send Sir Charles Coote amongst us some

---

* Burke, in his British and Irish Peerage, says that this imprisonment of Lord Dunsany lasted for several years—in fact, till after the Restoration. So much for the gratitude and honor of Parsons.

of these days—an' they do, the Tyrone man's countenance and succor were worth having—there be no man on Irish ground to meet Coote in due form save O'Neill!"

"O'Neill is no general," said Lord Slancy in a contemptuous tone; "if he wins it is by good luck and brute force, not by skill or prudence."

"Ay, but there be others of the northern chiefs more skilled in warcraft than he," observed Lord Netterville, "and there is Roger O'Moore, with whose prudence and sagacity, not to speak of other rare qualities, we are all well acquainted."

"Surely yes," said Lord Trimbleston, who had not yet spoken; "Roger O'Moore is well fitted for courtly diplomacy—no man more wise or discreet, or of more winning tongue than he, but I have no faith in his military skill—an' it come to a trial of strength, as it soon will, no doubt, there be no man *as yet*, amongst the insurgent leaders, able to cope for one hour with Ormond, or even with Coote—brave men and gallant chieftains they have—I deny it not—such as O'Rourke, O'Reilly, and McMahon—men who would do honor to any cause, but they have not that knowledge or experience in the art of war which might give them a chance of success."

"By my faith, Trimbleston," said Louth with a significant smile, "your speech savors of more interest in their affairs than becometh a loyal gentleman——"

"Loyal!" repeated Trimbleston with emphasis, "I know not but these gallant chieftains of the old stock who have boldly taken up arms for country and religion be the *loyal* men rather than we—excuse me, lords and gentlemen—who have been offering incense to bigotry and injustice—before God this day, I shame to think of how we have humbled ourselves before these upstart Puritans, the bitter enemies of our faith and all who profess it!"

Lord Trimbleston rose as he spoke these words with honest warmth, and many a pale cheek amongst his hearers waxed red with the glow of a new-born spirit, and many a knightly gentleman laid his hand on his sword-hilt as he joined in the shout of applause which greeted the Baron's short but significant address. Still, there was amongst the Palesmen there assembled too much

of the time-serving and timorous spirit which had of late characterized the degenerate sons of the Norman knights of old for
any genuine act of patriotism to be elicited from their worldly
and over-cautious minds—all the experience of the past months
was not sufficient, it would seem, to show them that their duty and
their true interest pointed in the same direction. They had ever
regarded the native Irish with contempt, as a race wholly inferior,
and only fit for that serfdom which *their* fathers imposed on the
conquered Saxons of England, and in viewing them still in that
light they could not or would not make common cause with them,
until every vestige of hope was taken from them by the acts of
that government to which they clung with the blindest infatuation.

Meanwhile, the Ulster forces, unwilling longer to be cooped
up within their own limits when so much was to be done in the
other provinces, began to penetrate in large bodies into the adjoining counties of the Pale. Crossing the borders with banners
flying, they attacked and took several strong Castles ; at length
growing bolder from success, the O'Reillys and McMahons laid
siege to the house of Lord Moore at Mellifont, within a few miles
of Drogheda, and succeeded in taking it by storm, to the extreme mortification of its noble owner, who was justly considered
as one of the best officers in the government service. With his
family, however, he retreated to Drogheda, leaving his lordly
manor in the hands of the Catholics, and what was far more of
triumph to them the sacred vale of Mellifont, at whose ruined
and desecrated shrines the chieftains knelt with swelling hearts
to give thanks for their success, and invoke the blessing of God
and His saints on their future efforts to redeem His suffering
people. Where the ill-starred Dervorgil wept and prayed of old
in penitential mood, the brave defenders of their country and
their creed, catching fresh enthusiasm from the mournful yet
hallowed scene, vowed to do yet greater things for the holy cause
to which their lives were pledged, nor sheath their swords till
freedom and justice were established in the land on a firm basis.

So long as the native chieftains kept within the bounds of the
northern province, the government were clearly well content to
let them work their will on the king's lieges, godly and ungodly,
as the case might be, but when once they crossed the marches

and began to clear the bawns of the Pale of the fat beeves which were wont to supply magnificent sirloins for Dublin boards, and still worse, when their rebellious flags began to appear on castle-keeps within a score of miles of the metropolis, as in the case of Mellifont, then, indeed, it was time to bestir themselves, or there was no knowing how soon the very gates of Dublin might creak and shiver beneath their ponderous axes. Word was even brought them at the council-board that the rebels meditated a speedy attack on Drogheda, headed by Sir Phelim himself with the chosen men of his army.

Immediately a commission was issued to raise four regiments in the vicinity of Dublin, and with one of these, a thousand strong, and a goodly troop of horse, Sir Charles Coote was sent to scour the counties of Meath and Louth and drive the rebels back into Ulster, giving no quarter to such as fell into his hands.

The latter part of the instructions Coote heard with a sardonic smile, believing the order somewhat superfluous in his case.

A strong reinforcement was, at the same time, sent to Drogheda under the command of Sir Patrick Wemyss. These troops, on the eve of their departure, were reviewed by Lord Ormond, who pronounced them hardly sufficient for the purpose, but the Lords Justices would not consent to any further reduction of the metropolitan forces, and Sir Patrick had nothing for it but to set his column in motion, while the Earl bowed with lofty grace and a smile of forced acquiescence.

Wemyss and his men were alike disheartened by the Earl's opinion of their insufficiency in point of numbers, and, to make matters worse, the day was dull and misty, threatening rain. More experienced soldiers would have probably exulted in the prospect of meeting a superior force of the wild Irish in hopes of signalizing their powers, but Sir Patrick's command was composed entirely of raw recruits from the new levies; men, for the most part, to whom the smell of powder was less trying than the glitter of an Irish skene. On they marched, however, with as great show of military ardor as though their valor had stood the test of an hundred fields. The level plains of Dublin were soon passed, and many a mile of the rich lands of Louth, and already the confidence of the Palesmen began to revive when Balbriggan

8*

and Balruddery were left far behind, and they found themselves nearing the place of their destination. The picturesque heights on the Nanny-water were already in sight, or ought to be—for the cold, thick mist rested cheerlessly on every object—when a horse was heard approaching at full gallop across the fields, and, Sir Patrick sending a scout or two to reconnoitre, they returned with a courier sent by Lord Gormanstown to apprise the officer in command that a strong detachment of the Irish army was stationed at Julians-town bridge, only a little farther on, awaiting their approach.

At this confirmation of their worst fears, the men were at first seized with trepidation, and were more disposed to retreat than to go forward, but Sir Patrick, himself a brave soldier, representing to them in brief but stirring terms the disgrace which was sure to follow such a step, and, moreover, the heavy punishment which they might expect, the column again turned its head towards Drogheda and marched steadily down the gentle slope leading to the bridge. It was little wonder if the stoutest heart there beat more quickly, and the bravest held his breath, for they knew not but death awaited them all in the misty depth of the valley. Urged on, however, by their gallant leader, they gained the bridge, crossed it, and marched in good order up the opposite acclivity without any other obstacle opposing their way than the mizzling rain which now began to beat in their faces.

Elated by this agreeable disappointment, the men were with difficulty kept from expressing their joy in a loud "hurrah," but they said one to another with bounding hearts and gleeful eyes : " Now for Drogheda—the cowardly rebels will scarce venture so near the guns of Millmount !"

But their commander was far from sharing their confidence, and as he rode on at the head of his column, his face had a stern and determined look, his keen gray eyes piercing the mist in all directions as though seeking some expected object. Without noticing his ominous silence, his men kept laughing and talking amongst themselves, in anticipation of the guardroom fire and the foaming tankard, when, just about a quarter of a mile beyond the bridge, they were struck dumb by the fierce clan-shouts of an Irish host, as it seemed to them, and the equally terrific sound of pipe and war-trump striking up a martial strain. At the same moment, the rain ceased, and the mist clearing partially away, disclosed to the affrighted soldiers of the Pale what appeared to them a whole army of the enemy, the foot drawn up in five battalions, flanked on either side by a troop of horse.

Immediately the English bugles sounded a charge, and Wemyss and his officers tried hard to get their men in order of battle. Just, however, when they seemed to have succeeded, another shout from the Irish ranks, and a slight forward movement, struck new terror into the hearts of the amateur soldiers, and with scarcely a glance at the formidable array before them, they fairly turned their backs and fled, notwithstanding that their commander and others of his subordinates threw themselves from their horses and did what men could to bar their retreat. Maddened by the yells of derisive laughter from behind, and yet not daring to turn on the fierce foe whom they fancied in full pursuit, the Dublin men rushed with headlong speed towards the bridge, little recking that they turned their backs on Drogheda and left its garrison to their fate.

Well for them that the mist closed in behind them thick and heavy, so as to prevent the possibility of pursuit—else had they never reached Dublin with the news of their own disgrace. As it was they effected their retreat without any loss, leaving the enemy a bloodless victory, and what they well loved, a standing joke in relation to " the battle of Julians-town."

They had reached Swords on their way back when, cowering in the shade of the old round tower, with a view to protect himself from the now pelting rain, they found an individual mounted on a shaggy pony and enveloped from head to waist in the many-folded scarf of home-made woollen then generally worn by the lower orders of the native Irish, after the manner of a Highland plaid. This personage, having his back turned towards them, was wholly unconscious of the approach of the soldiers till a loud halloo, coupled with the epithet of "Irish dog," made him turn his head just as a heavy grasp was laid on his shoulder. The ludicrous mixture of 'surprise and terror depicted on his lank features made the Palesmen laugh heartily, and well it was for him that he presented so woe-begone a spectacle as to move even the mortified and crest-fallen Wemyss to mirth.

"What do you here, you pitiful d——l?" said the sergeant whose clutch was on his shoulders; "be you a spy or what?"

"Dominus Vobiscum" was the reply,—"no, no, God forgive me for saying the like to—to—ahem! I'm no spy, an' it please you, sir!—I'd scorn the like."

"Where do you come from, then, and who the foul fiend are you—quick, for we cannot stand here in the rain waiting on such a scarecrow!" This was from one of the officers.

"I come from McMahon's country, and if you're curious to know my name I'll tell you, and welcome—my name is Malachy McMahon. There's another name they give me at home, but that's the right one."

"McMahon's country!" repeated Wemyss, "why the man's a fool—what brought you here all alone if that be your dwelling-place? Answer me, fellow!"

"Well, it's a little business I had in Dublin," said Malachy, "if I could get there—but dear knows when that will be, except your worship or some of these good-looking *sassum dergs* would be pleased to direct me, for I'm wandering like a ghost hither and thither in search of it, and never seems to be coming any nearer! There's a great man there that I'd wish to have a word with."

"And who may the great man be, you numscull?"

The first name that occurred to Malachy was that of Ormond, but luckily for himself, and perhaps for the Earl, too, he cunningly changed his mind; "I don't know if you know him," said the keen Monaghan man with a look of great simplicity; "but anyhow his name is Sir William Parsons, a very fine gentleman and a great lord besides, at least people say so, down where I come from!"

Many of the soldiers laughed outright, but not so Sir Patrick Wemyss.

"Why not tell us at first that your business was with him?" he said shortly.

"Well, because you didn't ask me the question!"

"Take him along!" cried Wemyss, "and march!" an order which was promptly obeyed, for the men were on thorns while they stood, and had they dared would have made short work of the " d——d Irish fool," as they very erroneously styled Malachy.

" Take me along !" echoed McMahon, " why, it isn't a prisoner I'd be ?"

" You want to have speech of Sir William Parsons," said Wemyss sternly; " no more talk, but come with us !"

It would have fared harder with poor Malachy had not Sir Patrick set him down in his own mind as an informer, a class of persons then largely employed and liberally encouraged by the government.

In such company and under such circumstances it was that our friend from Uriel made his entry into Dublin, but he knew Parsons too well by reputation to let the joke go so far as appearing in his presence. Passing under the gloomy arch of one of the city gates, he contrived to detach himself from the soldiers who, confused and ashamed of their ignoble conduct, had little attention to bestow on him. Even Wemyss thought no more of him till he was about to appear himself before the Lords Justices to give an account of his unlucky expedition. It is unnecessary to say that the man from McMahon's country was nowhere to be found. Sir Patrick finding himself thus duped, looked blank enough, but he little thought how often Malachy na Soggarth made merry amongst the clansmen of Uriel over the trick he played on the Sassenach chief, whom he got so cunningly " to show him the way to Dublin !"

CHAPTER XV.

"Ah me! what perils do environ
The man that meddles with cold iron!
For tho' Dame Fortune seem to smile
And leer upon him for awhile,
She'll after show him, in the nick
O. all his glories, a dog-trick."

BUTLER'S *Hudibras.*

'Tis necessity
"To which the gods must yield; and I obey,
Till I redeem it by some glorious way."

BEAUMONT AND FLETCHER.

BUT whilst the Catholic arms were beginning to command
fear, if not respect, within the territory of the Pale, how was it
with Sir Phelim and the vast multitude who followed his standard? Alas! the flush of conquest which attended his first career had subsided into a dull, cheerless state that was neither
life nor death—it was partly struggle and partly the inaction of
failing hope. The castles he had won were for the most part
still in the hands of his friends, so, too, were the smaller and less
important towns, but some of the principal forts had unhappily
been retaken by the enemy, and that through no want of bravery
or perseverance on the part of the Irish, but because leaders of
greater skill than any they then had to boast of were sent from
Carrickfergus and other places against them with artillery and
other war equipage of which they were wholly destitute. Even
powder and other ammunition would have long since failed them
had it not been for the supplies which they succeeded in wrest-
ing from the enemy. Now when the remaining fortresses were
too well garrisoned and supplied with military stores, and tho

Scotch forces increased by a strong reinforcement under Lord Leven were scattered in large bodies over northern Ulster, there was little chance of continued success for an inexperienced general like Sir Phelim, with a raw, undisciplined host, badly armed and badly accoutred in every way.* In fact, when the first enthusiasm began to die for lack of any substantial encouragement, and obstacles, not at first foreseen, began to arise and went on increasing in magnitude from day to day, the very numbers of Sir Phelim's forces became an incumbrance of which he knew not well how to dispose, for with abundance of animal courage and the most sincere devotion to the cause, he was unhappily wanting in those other qualities which constitute an able general. He was, moreover, too much under the control of passion to acquire much influence over others, or command that respect to which his position entitled him. Many of his associates in command were repelled by his harsh, overbearing demeanor, and mortified by seeing the boyish gusts of passion to which, on the slightest provocation, he gave way. With heavy hearts they acknowledged to each other that with such a leader there was little prospect of success, especially as no succor was coming from abroad, and no solid or lasting advantage had been gained at home after the first weeks of the rebellion.

Newry, so early taken by the impetuous valor of Magennis, was retaken by Scotch troops under Lord Conway, after being but a few weeks in possession of the Irish. Other cities which yet remained in their hands were expected to share the same fate as soon as a reasonable force presented itself with proper provision for a siege.

Yet still Sir Phelim fought on, wherever fighting was to be done, his temper, as may well be imagined, no way improved by the discouraging aspect of his present affairs, but his courage and activity, if possible, increased by the reverses he had lately encountered. The clouds were gathering darkly around him,

* Lord Ormond, writing to the King about this time, makes the following remarks: "The rebels are in great numbers, for the most part very meanly armed with such weapons as would rather show them to be a tumultuary rabble than anything like an army." See Carte's *Ormond.*

and no gleam of hope illumined his soul—no aid came from abroad, no sign of life amongst the noble or wealthy of the land at home, yet stout Sir Phelim was undismayed, and bravely holding his head above the surging waves, resolved by a bold effort to recover the ground he had lost, and with it the prestige of success so necessary to revive the drooping spirits of his followers.

"We will march eastward and besiege Drogheda," said Sir Phelim to his friend Magennis, as they strode to and fro together in the winter twilight in the neighborhood of the camp. "We must do something, Con,—it may go hard with us, an' we rest longer on our oars."

The gallant chieftain of Iveagh was never the man to throw obstacles in the way of a bold attempt promising any degree or chance of success, and, moreover, he had been for several days urging upon his impracticable leader the necessity of pushing the war beyond their own borders. He was, therefore, well pleased with this proposal, the full merit of which, however, he was content to leave with Sir Phelim as a healing unction for his wounded vanity. A council of the principal officers was immediately summoned, and the siege of Drogheda being proposed, met with their entire approbation. As "the key of the north," and commanding the Boyne, the old town was, in itself, valuable as a military port, and as being directly on the road to Dublin, and within less than half a day's march of the capital, it became of the last importance to secure it.

The success at Julianstown and the capture of Lord Moore's house at Mellifont—both localities in the immediate neighborhood of Drogheda—had contributed to inspire Sir Phelim with what seemed otherwise an over-bold design, considering the pusillanimous neutrality, to say the least of it, observed by the Lords of the Pale. The country around Drogheda was all in their hands—there was no reason to hope for sympathy, much less actual assistance from them, and, as the chiefs bitterly said amongst themselves, it was a good prospect for the Catholic army of Ulster to have probably to fight its way through the domains of the Catholic nobles of Leinster.

It *was* hard to see those degenerate Normans, if not openly

arrayed against the defenders of their faith, at least disposed to
stand aloof with folded arms while the tyrannical power of the
government was brought to bear upon them, unaided and alone
as they were left to oppose it with the scanty means at their
command. Where, alas! was the boasted chivalry, the lofty
spirit of the old Norman knights who were wont to style themselves the champions of the faith—they whose magnificent foundations of piety still covered the soil of Ireland—they who had
done such great things for the *Church* of Ireland, in atonement
for their oppression and spoliation of its native tribes ? Had the
sons of the Fitzgeralds, the Plunkets, the Cusacks and the Dillons, the Burkes and the Butlers, all lapsed from the faith which
their fathers loved, and fallen so low as to worship at the shrines
of Moloch and Mammon with the other creatures of the government ? There were moments when the high-souled Catholics of
Ulster could believe even that of them, from the tales which constantly reached them concerning their base truckling to the
powers that were. It might be that they did them injustice, but
of that there seemed little probability.

It was just when the northern chieftains had given up all hope
of any patriotic movement, or friendly co-operation on the part
of the Palesmen, that a bleak December day found a gallant show
of lords and gentlemen of high degree with a numerous train of
their respective followers assembled on the hill of Crofty, in the
fair county of Meath. The rounded crest of the gently-swelling
eminence commanded a view far and wide over plains extending
into the adjoining counties of Louth and Cavan, and ever as the
chief men of this assembly rode to and fro on their elevated plat-
form, they cast many an anxious, scrutinizing glance into the far
distance on every side as though expectation were becoming tedious. The while they conversed amongst themselves with the
gravity of men engaged, or about to engage, in some affair of
great moment. Yet, considering the troubled aspect of the times,
the whole array, although imposing, was wonderfully void of
martial show. Neither banners nor music were there, nor weapon
of any kind, and even the numerous company of men in attendance were characterized by the same staid and sober gravity
which marked the demeanor of their lords. The calm patience,

too, with which all waited, hour after hour—whatever their purpose might be—was worthy of admiration, and sufficiently denoted, were there no other mark of distinction, that it was not
the hot Milesian blood of the natives which flowed in their veins.

As the mid-day hours wore on, the stillness was broken from
time to time by the arrival of some lord or gentleman, with his
band of retainers, when a grave salute being exchanged, and
perhaps some brief inquiries between friends or acquaintance,
the new comers took their station according to their respective
grades, and like water broken by some falling pebble, the ripple
presently subsided and all was still again. The scene was impressive as well from the high bearing of the chiefs as the vast
number and respectable appearance of their followers.

After some hours had thus passed, a stir was visible amongst
the anxious watchers on the hill, and a murmur of " They come !
they come !" was heard passing through the crowd below. Presently the sound of martial music came floating on the breeze—
near and nearer it came—and more distinct, then approaching
the hill from the northward was seen a gallant band of soldier-
men arrayed in the picturesque costume of the native troops, with
many-colored woollen scarfs of ample dimensions wrapping their
brawny shoulders, their lower limbs encased in *truis* and buskins,
and on their heads the graceful hanging cap traditionally dear to
the Celts of Ireland. A banner they had, too, a gay, green banner,
with the royal sunburst emblazoned on one side and Ireland's harp
flaunting on the other. With a light, quick step and a buoyant
mien they marched up the slope, those bold borderers from the
Irish country, and the younger gentlemen on the hill catching, as
it were, a gleam of their bright and hopeful spirit, gave vent to
sundry exclamations of pleasure and glad surprise as they rode
to the front to watch the approaching cavalcade.

"By my faith," cried Sir John Netterville, for he, with his
father, was of the expectant party; " by my faith and honor,
these be men to stand by one's side in tented field—ha, there I
see my old friend Roger—why, man"—he called out at his topmost voice, as O'Moore, with some four or five other gentlemen, all
in military costume, detached themselves from their company and
rode up the hill—" why, man, you must count largely on our

patience, for I swear we have been here—some of us at least—
since morning hours. Well for you that it is your own body and
bones we see, or belike trouble might come of this delay !"

O'Moore apologized in his usual brief yet forcible manner for a
delay wholly unintentional on his part or that of his friends, whom
he severally introduced to the crowd of Norman lords and gentlemen as Colonels McMahon, O'Byrne, Plunket, the O'Reilly of
Breffny, and Captain Fox. These officers, arrayed in a costume
half Irish, half Spanish, presented a remarkable contrast to the
soberly-attired gentlemen of the Pale in their black broadcloth
cassocks, broadly edged with plush, and loose, long riding-cloaks,
all of the same, or some other almost equally sombre hue. Their
broad-leaved hats, too, were more akin to those worn by the Puritans than any other head-gear of that age, so that, what with the
cold reserve of their manner and the cheerless character of their
personal attire, these proud Normans of the Pale were to all appearance the very opposite of the gay, light-hearted, soldierly men
who came there to represent the native Irish.

On the part of the Palesmen, seven of their chief nobles rode
forward to treat with O'Moore and his friends. There was Gormanstown who, as Governor of the County, had drawn this assembly together by his warrant; Fingal, the premier peer of the
Pale; Louth, Trimbleston, Slaney, Netterville, and the gallant
son of the latter. There was one wanting of the seven great
lords—Plunket of Dunsany was far away the tenant of a vault in
Dublin Castle, but though absent he was not forgotten, the
thought of his wrongs, and the outrage committed on their order
in his person, rankled in the hearts of his peers, and had, doubtless, contributed no little to bring about that remarkable conference.

When the parties had come within speaking distance, Lord
Gormanstown, on a sign from Lord Fingal, moved to the front, a
little in advance of the others, and O'Moore instantly following his
example, the chieftain of Leix and the Norman peer were brought
within a few feet of each other in sight of their respective friends
and followers. Then Gormanstown, with a grave and formal
bow,—to which O'Moore responded by raising his plumed hat

with that winning grace peculiar to himself,—thus addressed the Irish chieftain :

"As the *Custos Rotulorum* of this county of Meath, Mr. O'Moore, I desire to know wherefore it is that certain of your Irish troops have of late trespassed on this our territory of the Pale, which as loyal subjects we are bound to keep and to hold intact for our lord the king—further, I would know, most worthy sir, why you with your company appear in arms at this present, I and mine being here assembled with peaceful intent and no other ?"

"As regards your first question, my lord of Gormanstown," O'Moore replied with dignified composure, "we would have it known of all men that in taking up arms and calling on all true Catholics to aid us, we have but two undoubted objects in view, namely, the defence of our holy faith, unjustly and most cruelly proscribed, the vindication of our rights as citizens, and further-more, the assertion of our sovereign lord the king his righteous prerogative, traitorously assailed by certain of his rebellious lieges. These, my lord, be our ends in waging this war."

"As a Christian and a man of honor," said Gormanstown with impressive earnestness, "I ask you, Mr. Roger O'Moore, if these be the sole ends and objects which you have in view—behind these are there no narrower and more selfish objects, less worthy the appeal to arms?"

"As God liveth," said O'Moore solemnly, and he raised his right arm towards heaven, "as God liveth, my lord, I have specified truly unto you the grounds of our quarrel with the present government of this country—false and double-dealing men as we hold them to be, and traitors to the king their master as they are to God and to us over whom they are ap-pointed to rule in justice and in all righteousness. The God of all truth who hears my words, knows whether I speak according to truth this day !"

After a short consultation with the principal lords and gentle-men of his company, Lord Gormanstown advanced again to O'Moore, and extending his mailed hand, which the chieftain, it may be presumed, was not slow to take, he said slowly and distinctly :

" If that be so, Mr. O'Moore, we of the Pale will join heart ·
and hand in your loyal and commendable efforts on behalf of God
and the king's majesty."

This announcement, made with the calm precision and the
dignified composure so characteristic of the speaker, yet without
the slightest tinge of arrogance or affected condescension, was
instantly communicated by O'Moore's companions to their anxious followers at the base of the hill, while Rory himself hastened
to express in a few appropriate and well chosen words the pleasure he received from, and the importance he attached to, this
formal adhesion.

O'Byrne, less accustomed to control his feelings, and, perhaps, not quite so conversant with the etiquette of the day, rode
eagerly forward and shook Lord Gormanstown warmly by the
hand, while his whole face glowed with joyful animation.

" By St. Kevin !" he cried, "your words are right welcome to
our ears, my lord of Gormanstown ! Heretofore, we have been
fighting the battle single-handed, as one may say, but that could
only last awhile, do our best—and surely it will nerve our arms
with new strength when Clan-Saxon of the Pale arises in its
might to strike with us for homes and altars !"

" It was high time they should," said McMahon quickly, "an'
they held back much longer all the water in Lough Erne would
not wash out their disgrace. I give you joy, Lord Gormanstown,
for that you and these other noble gentlemen have taken it in
head to retrieve your character in the eyes of Catholic Europe
ere yet it be too late."

However nettled the Palesmen might have been by this characteristic allusion to their tardiness, they were not the men to
give way to unseemly ire, especially where they knew that no
actual insult was meant. A general introduction immediately
took place, and after some brief inquiries from those of the Pale
as to the present prospects and intentions of their new allies,
Lord Gormanstown requested the High Sheriff, who was present,
to convene another and larger meeting for that day week, to be
held on the hill of Tara.

" The place is favorable to our purpose," said his lordship aside
to O'Moore and the other Irish chieftains. " It is central for us

of the Pale counties, and as the seat of the ancient royalty of this kingdom it must needs be dear to you of the Milesian race, who will, I doubt not, deem it a fitting spot for the solemn consummation of our alliance!"

This graceful compliment to the national traditions of an unkinged people was both understood and appreciated by the chieftains of the old race, and when, the auspicious conference being closed, the parties separated to retrace their respective ways homeward, the friendly farewell clasp exchanged between the Irish chiefs and the Norman nobles was accompanied by a hearty cheer from their followers on either side, those amongst them who stood high enough on the sloping sides of the hill to have a view of what passed, telegraphing their friends and fellows who were not so fortunate.

While this auspicious alliance was being formed between the Catholic English of the Pale and the old Irish, as they were called, the national cause was rapidly gaining ground in other parts of the kingdom. The Kavanaghs of Carlow, with the O'Byrnes and O'Tooles of Wicklow, had marshalled their clans and raised their standards for God and the right. But the faithful tribes of Wicklow had already paid dear for their patriotic efforts to aid their brethren in the north. Sir Charles Coote, with his sanguinary bands, recalled from Meath for the express purpose, was sent amongst them, armed with plenary authority to burn, harry, and massacre all before him.

The Castle of Wicklow being closely besieged by the O'Byrnes, Coote was ordered to relieve its garrison, which he did with that wanton slaughter of the besiegers with which no other general would disgrace his arms. Being once in possession of the fortress, he took occasion to make daily excursions amongst the natives of the town and its vicinity, just by way, he jocularly said, of making their acquaintance. The nature of these visits may be easily understood, and *was* so well understood by the surrounding population that the gates of the old Castle were no sooner heard to turn on their hinges than mothers fled with their young children to the recesses of the neighboring mountains, while the men, with stern and desperate resolution, seized whatever weapons they could find, and, drawing together for mutual defence, awaited in silence the descent of Coote's murderous troops from the Castle. Scenes of horror were enacted on these occasions, the recital of which makes the blood run cold.

In Coote's first descent upon the town, the inhabitants taken by surprise, were wholly unprepared for the humorous pranks wherewith the soldiers under his command, and under his eyes, amused themselves. Babes were torn from the arms of their shrieking mothers and tossed on the points of spears or bayonets from one to another of the soldiers, amid shouts of laughter and yells of delight. And Coote himself stood by, enjoying the rare sport, and commending the dexterity of their performances.* How females were used in these pastimes, it becomes not us to tell, but in very many cases, they were ripped open by way of winding up. This, however, was not suffered to be of frequent occurrence, for, as I have said, after the first or second visit of these barbarians the women and children took refuge in the caves and fastnesses of the mountains on the least intimation of their approach. Even there they did not always escape, for, on one occasion, some of the soldiers having learned where a party of the helpless fugitives were concealed, swore with hellish glee that they would smoke them out. To work they went, made a fire of brushwood at the mouth of the cave, and then placing themselves in silence round with bayonets screwed on their muskets, they coolly awaited the result of their pleasant frolic.

They had not to wait long, for no sooner had the thick smoke penetrated to the interior of the cavern than groans and choking cries were heard, at first in the feeble voices of children, then came the half-suppressed shrieks of women, and a chorus of fiendish laughter burst from the savage listeners without. Presently the sounds from within were heard to approach the aperture, and through the flickering flames were seen fearful-looking female forms, some with infants in their arms, all blackened and begrimed with smoke, attempting to make their way through the fire. At this sight, compassion moved the heart of one of

* Unfortunately these Wicklow horrors are matter of history—even Protestant writers admit that Sir Charles Coote exercised all manner of cruelty amongst the Wicklow tribes.

the officers, and seeing the soldiers thrusting the unhappy creatures back into the fatal cave with their bayonets, he sternly rebuked them, and made an effort to have the fire extinguished.
Alas! he himself was reprimanded by his fierce superior from behind in a voice of thunder, and ordered immediately to his
quarters.

Captain Jameson bowed and walked away, well pleased at heart
to escape from such a scene. That was the last time he ever
went out with Coote, for next day he sent in his resignation and
retired from the army in disgust.

Before the gallant band of soldiers quitted that mountain-glen,
they made sure that no human being remained alive in the cave,
for they drove the fire farther and farther into its mouth, until at
last the groans, and cries, and piteous moans, all died away,
and the silence which followed assured them that their work
was finished.

CHAPTER XVI.

"But screw your courage to the sticking point,
And we'll not fail."
                                        SHAKESPEARE.

"The better part of valor is discretion."
                                        SHAKESPEARE.

THE middle of December had hardly arrived when Drogheda was in the condition of a closely-beleagured town. Some twelve thousand* of the allied Irish army occupied the villages for miles around. The meeting at Tara had been followed by immediate action on the part of the lords and gentry of the Pale. Each nobleman and gentleman undertook to raise a certain number of men within the limits of his own district. Lord Gormanstown was appointed commander-in-chief of the army, to be raised in the five counties, and Lord Fingal was commissioned to act as master of the horse. The Ulster forces were still, of course, under the command of Sir Phelim O'Neill, with Art Oge McMahon; Philip O'Reilly and Sir Con Magennis as subordinates in command. Roderick Maguire also commanded a troop of horse, and Lorcan a company of infantry. The junction with the Lords of the Pale and their adherents infused new life, with new hope into the easily-disheartened or easily-elated Irish, and when the siege of Drogheda commenced, and they found themselves undertaking it under auspices so favorable—provisions supplied in plenty by the fruitful territory of the Normans—they were quite sanguine of success, notwithstanding the well-known strength of the place and the numerous garrison which the voice of rumor assigned to it.

* D'Alton, in his *History of Drogheda*, says that the besieging army amounted to eighteen thousand before all was over.

9A

194 THE CONFEDERATE CHIEFTAINS.

Sir Phelim had his headquarters in Bewly House, within three miles or so of the town on the banks of the silvery Boyne. Parties of his troops were also in possession of Rathmullen Castle, with the villages of Bettystown, Mornington, Oldbridge, Tullyallen, and Ballymakenny.*

Any one at all acquainted with the geographical situation of Drogheda will see at a glance from this enumeration of the places held by the Irish, that they had the town invested on every side—seaward they had Bettystown and Mornington, landward, and commanding the river they had the heights of Rathmullen and the plains of Oldbridge, while back into the country in various directions, the other posts mentioned extended their control. But, alas! with all these advantages—including the possession of the harbor which they closely blockaded—there was one great want on the part of the besiegers, so great, indeed, that it left them with all but empty hands in the presence of the enemy. This was the old story—the almost total want of artillery or ordinance of any kind. Their arms and ammunition, too, were very insufficient for such an army—had they been even in a degree proportioned to the number of men, the siege of Drogheda would stand differently recorded on the page of history.

And so it happened that while the garrison was reduced to the most grievous straits by the unceasing watchfulness of the besiegers, while reinforcements and supplies were alike excluded by sea and land, and while a brave, and numerous, and vigilant force occupied every available position around the town, its strong walls were, week after week, unassailed, and its immediate precincts still uninvaded by hostile foot.

The governor of the town, a tough old Puritan soldier, Sir Henry Tichbourne by name, was a man who held all Papist recusants in holy horror, and thought them only to be treated with sword in one hand and Bible in the other, by way of a double exorcism. Still he had not the ferocious cruelty of Sir Charles Coote—at least the shedding of blood or the sight of human torture gave him no pleasure, although if the cause required it, he

* See D'Alton's *History of Drogheda*, p. 230.

could kill, and burn, and destroy as well as Coote or any other general of the time. He was, however, a brave and skilful officer, and his defence of Drogheda, under such adverse circumstances, raised him high in the estimation of his own party, as it made him feared and respected by the other.

The straits to which the garrison was reduced at that time, almost equal the hardest necessities of Derry or any other siege of modern times. And what most afflicted Sir Henry and his officers was the fact, that the shameful neglect of the government had quite as much share in producing their hardships and privations as the watchfulness of the besiegers. Letters addressed to Lord Ormond and the government were repeatedly intercepted, complaining in the bitterest and most moving terms of the wants of the garrison. But the wants continued, and the weather increased in severity, and the various parties sent out at different times under the pressure of necessity to seek provisions were, for the most part, either captured or slain by some of the numerous Irish detachments encircling the place. At last, famine and despair, made more excruciating by the stinging sense of neglect, brought about strange things. The soldiers of the garrison were frequently seen scaling the walls by night, at the imminent risk of discovery from within on account of the blazing warlights kept up at regular intervals along the walls and ramparts. On reaching the ground these men made their way directly to some Irish post, stating that they fled from salt herrings and bad water to which fare the provident and remunerative bounty of the Lords Justices had so long consigned them.

It was amusing to witness the surprise manifested by some of these men on finding themselves actually in the presence of Sir Phelim O'Neill, the great Irish ogre of their guard-room stories, the fierce warrior whom they looked upon and spoke of as half man, half demon, hideous in person as diabolical in spirit. The boisterous laughter wherewith the rough chieftain heard these ludicrous imaginings of their diseased fancy, both startled and amazed the semi-puritanical soldiers of Tichbourne; yet the blunt and unexpected good-nature with which their starving stomachs were relieved by his orders very soon reconciled them to his Papistical want of gravity.

Many a desperate struggle, without the walls, marked the passage of those long, long weeks, during which the Irish army kept watch and ward around the old town. Having no encampment, the severity of the weather forbade them to remain in the immediate vicinity of the town, where shelter was not to be found, so that the troops were posted here and there within the distance of a few miles, wherever they could be protected from the inclemency of that unusually rigorous season. The frequent sallies of those from the town, made in different directions, kept the besiegers constantly on the alert, from the continual uncertainty in which they were as to the point where the *sortie* was to be made.

In the midst of their hard and arduous duties, only a few days before St. Thomas's Day, which was that fixed on for a grand attack, the mercurial Celts of the north were elated beyond measure by the unlooked-for arrival of Miles O'Grady, one of the few great harpers remaining in Ireland, who had travelled all the way from the hills of Breffny to chant the war song for the O'Reillys, to the fortunes of whose chief he was for weal or woe attached, and had been so from early boyhood. It was at Oldbridge that the Clan O'Reilly lay, and thither Miles made his way, his small harp slung on one shoulder, and a wallet on the other containing his oaten cakes, with a little flask of usquebaugh. He was accompanied by a youth of some twenty summers, a tall and rather delicate stripling, with a mild and somewhat pensive aspect, and clustering brown curls, which would have given him a girlish look were it not for the dark hue of his complexion and the fire which gleamed in his large eyes. He was a stranger to all the Irish host, even the harper could give no other account of him than that he had found him wandering on the confines of Louth, inquiring the way to Drogheda. His name, he said, was Angus Dhu, at least he would give no other, and by that soubriquet he was ever after known amongst the soldiers.

Notwithstanding the attraction of Miles's music, his young travelling companion did not long remain at O'Reilly's quarters. Wandering about from one post to another, he at length reached Bewly House, and by some strange whim there took up his abode

amongst the martial clansmen of Tyr-Owen. The northern accent was on his Irish tongue, and many questions were, therefore,
put to him regarding the distant land of the O'Neills, but the
questions soon ceased, for he declared himself wholly unacquainted with that part of the country. Much curiosity was at
first excited by the singular reserve in which the youth chose to
enshroud himself; but after a few days the mystery was forgotten, and Angus Dhu came and went like any other individual of
that "varied host."

St. Thomas's Eve came on dark and dull as the days usually
are at that season—the few short hours of daylight were spent in
preparation for a general attack, too much time having been
already lost in useless delay, according to the opinion of the
most experienced officers. Silently, and as they fondly hoped,
unnoticed by those within the town, the Irish leaders prepared
their respective troops for the assault, too sanguine, most of
them, in their hopes of success to entertain the possibility of
failure. But Sir Henry Tichbourne was not the man to be taken
unawares, as the besiegers found to their cost. When under
cover of the darkness, they applied their scaling ladders to the
walls, and mounted with hearts full of hope and courage, nothing doubting of success, they found bristling bayonets and grim
faces behind them at every accessible point. Silent as the grave
was the watch of these stern veterans, the first intimation the assailants received of their presence being from the point of the bayonet, so that in very many cases those coming next on the ladders
were only apprised of the reception awaiting them by the death-
groan of their comrades above and their heavy fall to the ground,
too often dragging their fellows with them clutched in their dying
grasp. Courage and skill were alike useless: however it was
that Tichbourne had disposed of his forces there seemed not a
single point left unguarded, and, as the Irish officers understood
when too late, the cressets and other lights usually burning on
the walls were that night nowhere to be seen. It was a night of
darkness, silence and death, and the loss sustained by the besiegers
was so considerable as to stamp its horrors indelibly on their
minds. But although repulsed with heavy loss, and necessarily
thrown into confusion by a result so wholly unexpected, the

Irish soldiers, for the most part, exhibited such steady courage as to excite the surprise of the garrison. Many instances of hardy and persevering valor were displayed on that memorable occasion, and one of these came near to obtain possession of the West Gate from which a *sortie* had been made on the assailants, a party of the followers of O'Neill. The gate was, in fact, taken and retaken several times before the attention of the rest of the garrison was called to that particular point, the Irish being led on by a youth who seemed animated with more than mortal courage, and on whom defeat had no other effect than that of a spur to renewed action. Even in the breathless rush of that fell struggle, amid the gloom of the winter night and the silence of mutual caution, the neck-or-nothing bravery of that young Irish soldier attracted the attention of both parties, and although the arrival of a strong reinforcement from the Tholsel gave victory to the defenders of the gate, and left the brave assailants on the outside, still his feats of valor were not forgotten, and Sir Phelim himself on the following day made special inquiries concerning him. But whoever he was notoriety was not his object, for, the useless struggle of the night once over, his identity was not to be traced.

Next day Angus Dhu made his appearance in a block-house erected by the besiegers at the mouth of the river where Shamus Beg was left in command of a small party. The account which Angus gave of the night's disaster was gloomy enough, and the hearts of his hearers sank within them as they listened, but when the youth came to tell of the mysterious stranger who had so nearly taken West Gate, and of Sir Phelim's anxiety to find him out, dejection and despondency were swallowed up in curiosity and that eager thirst for the marvellous so common to all Celtic people.

"Who knows but it's one of the old ancient heroes mentioned in prophecy that's coming back to help us in our need," said Shamus thoughtfully. "We all know they're to come one day or another."

"Yes, but when they do," said Angus quickly, "they'll not go without their errand—they'll leave their mark behind them, Shamus, or where's the use of them coming at all. It isn't to be

beaten as we were last night that thev'd show their faces—no,
no, I'm thinking the young man—let him be who he might—had
a little business to settle with the cut-throats—a message to deliver or something that way.'

Angus started in some confusion and changed color, for he saw
Shamus's eyes fixed on him with a look of keen scrutiny that
made him wince. Muttering something about looking out for
squalls he darted to the door, and was soon apparently lost in
contemplating the wintry flood,—hardly to be recognized as the
silvery Boyne,—pouring down into the boiling waters of the Bay.
As for Shamus and the other soldiers of his party they were too
well accustomed to the lad's strange humors to feel or express
any surprise.

Christmas was more merrily spent amongst the Irish troops
than might be imagined under the circumstances. What with
the surpassing music of O'Grady's harp, the numerous pipes and
other instruments then called into requisition for other than martial purposes, what with the various assemblies of the officers
held at the different mansions in possession of the army, and the
solemn celebration of the joyous mystery of the time, the Christmas holidays passed cheerily away. For well nigh the first time
in their lives, the proud Normans of the Pale were brought into
close and constant communication with the native chiefs, and
the result was, as might be expected, a more cordial feeling between them.

It was on one of these festive occasions when Lord Fingal was
entertaining in military fashion the other leaders of the army,
with their respective officers, that Art McMahon was requested
to speak to a person outside the door who had just arrived from
Dublin.

" From Dublin!" the chief repeated aloud, and his words were
echoed with a start by many of the lords and gentlemen; "from
Dublin!—who *can* it be?—the bearer of some overtures, perchance, from my lord of Ormond."

Expecting some communication of great importance, McMahon
left the hall, and dead silence prevailed during his absence, each
gazing in his neighbor's face to learn the purport of his thoughts.

Only a few moments had elapsed when the chieftain's firm

tread was heard approaching, and all eyes were instantly fixed
on the door. His portly form was no sooner seen at the entrance
than the anxious cloud disappeared from every brow, for he was
laughing heartily. Advancing up the spacious hall to his place
at the table, he said to Lord Gormanstown who occupied the
presidential seat:

"Your lordship has doubtless heard of the mountain in labor
—a new version of that old story is what I have to tell. To save
you all the trouble of asking questions, you must know that the
new arrival is no other than an old follower of our house, Malachy McMahon by name, who has been to Dublin in search of the
reading for certain dreams of his."

"Is it Malachy na soggarth?" inquired O'Reilly; "I heard he
was gone to see your brother—poor simple man! how did he
fare?"

"As might be expected, Phil—he saw the outside of the
Castle walls—no more. But even that was a comfort to the poor
fellow——'

"If it was, I paid dear for it," said Malachy from the lower
end of the hall, he having followed his chieftain so far. The
general attention once attracted to him, his singular appearance
and abrupt speech called a smile to every face.

"How is that, Malachy?" inquired McMahon. "What went
wrong with you?"

"Not much with *me*, only what I heard. I fell in with a friar
—a Franciscan I think he was—and he told me all about what
the hell-hounds done to our noble Tanist and Lord Maguire——"

"And what was that?" cried his chief with a start. "What
has befallen Costelloe?"

Malachy groaned and covered his face with his hands while
his chief, approaching him with rapid step, urged him to speak.
"Tell me, in God's name, have they killed my brother?"

"If they didn't kill him all out," said poor Malachy, "it was
almost the same thing—they put him on the rack, and kept him
there till the life was most gone—they wanted to make him confess, the friar told me, about that commission Sir Phelim has from
the king."

"It is false!" cried Lord Netterville, starting from the table;

" there be no such commission—but what did Mr. McMahon confess—or did he confess anything ?"

" He had nothing to confess," said Art proudly, as he turned his ghastly face towards the company ; " the rack could force nothing from poor Costelloe !"

" Not a word," hastily put in Malachy, anxious for the honor of the house of Uriel ; " not a word they could get from either of the two—Lord's blessing be about them !"

" Lords and gentlemen—friends all!" said Art McMahon, in a choking voice, " how long is this to last ?—how long are these miscreants to exult in our sufferings ?—oh ! my brother !—my brave brother ! why was I not near with half a hundred of our faithful clan—when they *dared* to stretch your free-born limbs on their accursed rack !—oh, God ! why was I not there ?"

Without waiting for an answer, he rushed from the hall, followed closely by Malachy, anxious, doubtless, to inform his followers of what had happened.

Even the coldest of those who remained behind was roused to resentment by this new outrage, and a solemn vow was taken on the spot alike by Irish chief and Norman noble to wipe out the long score which they owed to the government if God spared them life.

The army from that night forward became restless and impatient. Anxious to do something, yet condemned to a state of inactivity almost in the presence of the hated foe, the hearts of young and old panted for an opportunity to grapple with the veteran soldiers of the garrison, who, by this time, they deemed well worn by continual famine.

Early in the month of January, one cold, frosty morning, the wildest excitement suddenly spread amongst besiegers and besieged. Sundry attempts had been made at various times lately to relieve the garrison, all proving ineffectual because of the unceasing watchfulness of the beleaguering forces. That morning, however, a sloop and a pinnace laden with provisions had boldly sailed up the bay, and, favored by a landward breeze, crossed the sand-bar at the mouth of the harbor, managed to get over the chain, which, for further security, had been laid across, and in safety reached the wharf at James's Bridge amid the cheers and

plaudits of a multitude, consisting of thousands of the half-
starved garrison and townspeople, who had been watching with
greedy eyes, ever since they hove in sight, the precious little
craft, which, at such fearful risk, brought life and hope to them.

The shouts of exultation from within the town brought increased dejection to those without, and so much time being already lost, some of the leaders began to talk seriously of raising
the siege, and turning their attention to some other place where
success was more probable. Towards evening, however, their
prevailing despondency seemed to vanish, and a more cheerful
spirit took possession of all. There was bustle and buoyant
excitement where late there had been dullness and dejection, and
the change was, under the circumstances, altogether inexplicable.
Divers mysterious meetings and hurried councils took place
during the latter part of the day, but as night came on all was
again quiet, and silence seemed to have settled down on the Irish
host.

In the mid-watches of the night, about five hundred chosen
men, chiefly from McMahon's and O'Neill's countries, marched
out in the direction of St. James's Gate, and having reached an
old door, sheltered from general observation by a projecting angle
of the wall, the officer in command—it was Eman Oge McMahon
—struck three times on the wood with the point of his sword.
The door was instantly opened, and, silent as spectres, the clansmen marched through in single file, finding themselves, as well
as the faint star-light would permit them to judge, treading the
alley of an old orchard.

"Now," whispered the person who admitted them, "now or
never—you have the game in your own hands, and there be many
within the town who will bless God if you succeed—forward in
His name!"

"Whither?" asked Eman, in the same tone; "we are but
strangers, as you know!"

"To the Mill-mount, an' you take a friend's advice—cross the
bridge, and make straight up the hill—the garrison there is
small, and you will have no trouble in surprising them—if you do,
you will find several pieces of ordinance which will ensure your
success—either that, or master the guard at the gate close by
here, and then let in as many as you will!"

Alas! by some fatal misapprehension, the party did neither. Making straight for the heart of the city, and, forgetting in the wild excitement of the moment, the extreme necessity of prudence and caution—confident, moreover, of having victory in their own hands, a thrilling shout burst from their ranks, meant at once to apprise their comrades without of their being fairly inside the walls, and, at the same time, to strike terror into the slumbering and apparently unconscious garrison.

"Great God!" cried Eman, "what have ye done?—we are lost —lost!"

It was too late to redeem the fatal error. The sound of horses' hoofs was heard approaching with headlong haste down Shop street towards the bridge. At the same moment the drums beat to arms, and the Irish, not knowing how many or how few were the assailants gathering around them in the darkness, made an effort to regain the orchard, and thence the door by which they had entered. About two hundred of them succeeded, but, alas! the enemy had already mustered in strength, and the stern voice of Tichbourne was heard commanding no quarter to be given.

"Hew them down," he said; "in God's name, let not one escape!"

Even while this pitiless order was given, doors were softly opened in the rear of the bewildered Irish, and many of them were drawn in by friendly hands unseen, undreamed of by the Puritan soldiers or their relentless commander. Others finding their retreat cut off, turned on the foe with their pikes and made what defence they could. These were almost to a man cut down by the swords and sabres of Tichbourne's troop, so that fully one-half of those who marched so proudly through the orchard some half an hour before, paid with their life the forfeit of their imprudence.

Amongst those who fell was the gallant young leader of the party, who, refusing to quit the place and leave any of his men exposed to danger, was cut down, sword in hand, by one of Tichbourne's officers.

Thus ended, in shame and humiliation, disappointment and death, an attempt which might and should have placed Drogheda in the hands of the Irish.

CHAPTER XVII.

" What tho' the field be lost ?
    All is not lost ; the ungovernable will,
    *   *   *   *
    And courage never to submit or yield,
    And what is else not to be overcome."
                        MILTON'S *Paradise Lost.*

" A tale more strange ne'er graced the poet's art,
    And ne'er did fiction play so wild a part."
                                        TICKELL.

WITH varying success the Irish army remained in the neighborhood of Drogheda all through the months of January and
February—at times there seemed every probability of the garrison being reduced by famine to surrender, for the supplies so
wonderfully introduced into the town in the beginning of January lasted but a very few weeks. Famine and sickness soon
began to produce the saddest effects amongst the hardy soldiers
of the garrison, and strong hopes were entertained by the leaders
of the besieging force that the town could not much longer hold
out, when towards the end of February a fearful storm came on,
which carried away the boom from the mouth of the river, together with various defences erected there for the greater security of the harbor. Before any of this mischief could be repaired, certain of the government cruisers, ever hanging around
the coasts in wait for an opportunity of approaching the town,
succeeded in making their way to the wharf, and plentifully supplied the wants of the garrison.

Thus strengthened, and invigorated with renewed hope, the besieged not only defended the town more vigorously, but issuing
forth, in considerable detachments, and at short intervals, they

attacked the various stations occupied by the Irish, sometimes
with success, but just as often to be driven back again to the
shelter of their strong walls. Many a hard struggle took place
between the contending parties for the possession of fords and
passes on the river. On one occasion, in which the Irish were
defeated, so obstinate was the contest that the Nanny-water at
Julianstown ran red with the blood of the slain. On nearly tho
same spot where they gained a complete and bloodless victory,
they were themselves, so soon after, vanquished with fearful loss.
One by one several of their strongest posts were taken, owing to
their fatal want of ordinance, and to crown all it was announced
that the Earl of Ormond was at length marching to the relief of
Drogheda with a strong force and with orders to burn, pillage,
and destroy the houses and possessions of all who had declared
for the rebels or in any way assisted them.

Hearing this, Sir Phelim O'Neill thought it high time to betake
himself again to the woods and fastnesses of Ulster, until such
time as Providence might send him a supply of arms and ammunition, with such artillery as might enable him to encounter a
regular army in the field. Reluctantly he came to this decision,
which his allies of the Pale, moreover, endeavored to combat
with a view to the protection of their own goods and chattels,
but Sir Phelim took it into his head that the preservation of his
entire force depended on effecting a speedy retreat, and retreat
into Ulster he would and did, to the great joy and exultation of
the garrison, which for three months and better he had kept so
closely straightened, with scarcely a piece of cannon in his possession, and other war-stores in such limited quantity as to be
wholly insufficient for such an undertaking.

With the exception of the miserable failure of that fatal night
—and Sir Phelim never forgave himself for not having entrusted
the enterprise to older and more experienced commanders—
everything was done that either courage or prudence could dictate, and if the siege of Drogheda was at length abortive, the
fault lay in the grievous wants already mentioned, wants which
should, from the first, have prevented an undertaking of such
magnitude and so great importance.

Philip O'Reilly had just returned for a brief season of rest to

his paternal halls, and the clansmen of Breffny were resting in
peace after the fatigues of the luckless Louth campaign, awaiting another summons from the north, when the chief was apprised of the death of old Dr. Beddell. Application had been
made to Bishop McSweeny for permission to bury him within
the precincts of his former cathedral, and after some hesitation
that prelate gave his consent.

On the day of the deceased bishop's interment, a sight was
seen which filled his friends and co-religionists with surprise. A
lonely funeral they expected to have of it, for the few Protestants who still remained in the neighborhood feared to make any
demonstration, or in fact to be seen abroad at all. Great, then,
was their astonishment when, on the morning fixed for the funeral, a hundred or so of the patriot-soldiers of Breffny marched
to the late prelate's house with soft and mournful music, and
announced their intention of accompanying his remains to the
grave.

At first the bishop's family and household were more alarmed
than pleased by the appearance of this martial band, but when
the officer in command—it was the former high sheriff, Miles
Mac Edmund O'Reilly—entering the house, assured them that
his men were only desirous of doing honor to the memory of the
lamented dead, they were all deeply touched by so public an
expression of kindly sympathy.   •

The Bishop, too, joined the funeral cortege, with many of the
chief men of the O'Reillys, and although the day was a stormy
one in the early spring, they followed the honored remains even
to the old diocesan graveyard of Kilmore where the vault of his
predecessors awaited him. And the solemn music of the Breffny
minstrels was the dirge of the good old prelate, and the clansmen
of Breffny paced with downcast eyes and arms reversed, after
the mourning friends and relatives, and when the body was laid
in the tomb, they insisted on firing a volley over it by way of a
parting salute, for they remembered that the good man there
consigned to earth had shown himself their friend when few of
his order or profession would have said a word or testified a
feeling in their behalf.

When, however, the vault was closed, and the echoing roll of the musketry had died away amongst the neighboring hills, Miles O'Reilly stepped forward, and, filled with thoughts of what had been and what was to be, he exclaimed in Latin:

"May the last of the English rest in peace!"

The musicians, catching his thought, struck up "O'Neill's March," one of the most popular tunes of the day, and to its enlivening notes they marched out of the graveyard and resumed their homeward way, satisfied that they had shown all proper respect to the memory of a generous foe, yet elated with the thought that no other should ever fill his office amongst them or usurp the rights of their lawful prelates.

"He was a good man," said they one to another, "for a Protestant, but there's few of them like *him*, and, only God to spare us our eyesight, we never want to lay eyes on a minister or a bishop of his sort——"

"It will not be our fault if ever one of them roosts in Kilmore, anyhow," rejoined another; "please the Lord their light is quenched for good,—and it's it was the unlucky light to us ever since it was first lit at the fire below!—glory and honor to Sir Phelim, only give him fair play,—him and the O'Reilly and the rest of them,—and they'll get us back our rights, or they'll know for what!"

The spirit thus expressed by the clansmen of Breffny, with the entire, perhaps exaggerated confidence they had in their hereditary leaders, was common amongst the lower classes of the soldiery, but in the minds of the chieftains and officers themselves, the conviction was every hour gaining ground that their real commander had not yet made his appearance on the scene of action. But to go back a little.

When Sir Phelim was about making his retreat from Drogheda, Shamus went to him one evening with a face of blank dismay, and told him that the youth Angus was missing since the previous day, and was neither to be found dead nor alive. Now, independent of all personal considerations, the lad's services had been of such a nature since his sudden appearance amongst the men, that even the rough nature of Sir Phelim was touched by this intelligence, and he gave Shamus orders to take ten or a dozen men and make a strict search everywhere around the neighborhood. However anxious they all were, for Angus was a general favorite, they might have searched long enough to little purpose, had not some prisoners been taken that day from a foraging party, and from them it was casually ascertained that a young man answering to the description of Angus had been caught prowling around that same old orchard which had proved so fatal to poor Eman and his party. He had managed to get in on the occasion of a *sortie* from St. James's Gate, but refused to confess what his intentions were.

Sir Phelim and others of the chieftains immediately surmised that the poor fellow had taken this bold and venturous step, hoping that by concealing himself till the fall of night, he might succeed in opening some gate or door unobserved, and thus to introduce a party of his friends, who, warned by former sad experience, might be able to surprise the garrison. Indeed, it was found that he had intimated some such design to his friend Shamus several days before, asking whether he thought it at all practicable, but Shamus having, as he thought, laughed him out of such a boyish notion, the affair was no more alluded to between them, and Shamus forgot all about it until the mysterious disappearance of Angus brought it again to his mind. He now bitterly reproached himself for not having acquainted some of his superiors at the time, with the romantic scheme which now, in all probability, had brought destruction on the brave youth.

Sir Phelim, after some deliberation, sent a herald with a flag of truce to Sir Henry Tichbourne, proposing an exchange of prisoners; this, at first, was refused, and O'Neill, in his wrath, swore that those in his possession, amounting to half a dozen or so—some of them subaltern officers—should be hung before sunset in sight of the town-walls.

The fatal preparations were already made, and the temporary gallows loomed up tall and spectral above surrounding objects —the sound of funeral music, and the measured discharge of musketry denoted the approach of the final moment, when the West Gate of the town rolled slowly back, and out came a small party of horse, the first man bearing aloft a white flag. On and on they came towards the place prepared for the execution, and as they drew near, the flag-bearer, detaching himself from the others, rode forward and announced that Sir Henry Tichbourne, having thought better of the matter, was willing to agree to Sir Phelim O'Neill's proposal in regard to the prisoners, and had sent his for exchange.

"Well for him he did," said the chieftain curtly; "you see our patience has no great stretch," and he grimly pointed to the gaunt, unsightly gallows. "Here you, O'Rourkes, bring out the Englishers—ha, Angus, my good lad! I am well content to see you again!"

The Irish prisoners were now handed over, but still there seemed some delay in regard to giving up the others. Sir Phelim blustered and swore, and threatened punishment—the prisoners were delivered up, with one exception—a young officer of dark, forbidding aspect, and a cynical expression of countenance. Him the Leitrim men held fast, looking at the same time as though no stretch of authority should induce them to give him up. Sir Phelim's ire began to rise, and some of the Norman lords who were present looked eagerly for the solution of so strange a proceeding. One or two of the Irish officers who chanced to be near whispered to each other a solution of the enigma.

"What the fien l is this?" cried Sir Phelim, angrily; "let the gentleman go, with the rest, ye stupid varlets!"

"If it's pleasing to you, Sir Phelim, we'd rather not," said Manus O'Rourke, stepping forward; "this prisoner is ours—it was we of Breffny-O'Rourke who took him, and we desire to await our chief's judgment in his regard——"

"Who is he, then?"

"The son and heir of Sir Frederick Hamilton, against whom every O'Rourke in Breffny has sworn revenge."

"Ha! Hamilton—I know!" The chieftain turned his scathing eye on the young ensign, who, on his part, looked as though he thought his situation somewhat perilous. Still he returned the glance with one of defiance rather than deprecation.

"By the soul of Heremon," said O'Neill slowly, "but it grieveth me to thwart you in this thing, Manus O'Rourke, for that brood of vipers were well cleared out of your fair country, but mine honor—*our* honor, Manus, will not permit us to keep the stripling now."

"How is that, Sir Phelim?" demanded O'Rourke sternly.

"Why, because it was from us the offer of exchange came, and we then made no exception. Had I known in time of this Hamilton being in your hands, by my faith he had gone to Drumahair for your chieftain's good pleasure—now when they have sent all our prisoners, at our request, we cannot for shame keep any of theirs in custody. No, no, Manus, *it cannot be*—you will have some other opportunity—justice can wait—soldiers of Breffny, I appeal to your honor in this matter, hoping that you will let this prisoner go with the others!"

"It is hard, it is very hard, Sir Phelim O'Neill," said the uncompromising Manus, "still I acknowledge your honor is at stake, an I I am sure there is not an O'Rourke here who will hold out against you!"

A sullen murmur was heard amongst the men of west Breffny, but still none of them gainsaid the words of Manus. Dark was the scowl, however, with which they regarded the son of their enemy as with a smile, half of contempt, half of triumph, he walked over to the party from town.

"Ye have done well, men of Breffny," said Sir Phelim, in a husky voice, "and by the sword of Nial it shall go hard with me, an' we bring not that savage Hamilton to justice ere the war comes to an end. If I aid ye not in this matter, be my name forgotten in the land where my fathers ruled!'

A loud cheer from the O'Rourkes attested their sense of Sir Phelim's kind dispositions in their regard, and as the other clans present caught up the sound it rolled far away into the distance, along the level borders of the Boyne.

While O'Neill turned to speak with Angus, who stood, cap in hand, awaiting speech of him, the Norman lords discoursed amongst themselves of the scene they had just witnessed, and more than one expressed his surprise at the unexpected gentleness displayed by the northern leader. The main features of the scene they were at a loss to understand, till, having applied to Manus O'Rourke, who was a lieutenant in their army, for explanation, he gave them, with no softened coloring, an ac-

count of the relative conduct of Sir Frederick Hamilton and the
O'Rourke of Breffny. Hearing this, the lords of the Pale could
not help expressing their admiration of the generous forbearance
shown by the Clan O'Rourke on this occasion, when revenge was
a second time in their own hands, and even justice might seem
to authorize their detention of their prisoner.

But another surprise awaited these noblemen, in common with
the chieftains, their allies. Angus Oge had a singular story to
tell, though his captivity had been but of three days' duration,
and as the night was closing in, with storm and darkness, Sir
Phelim invited all the officers present to go to his quarters to
hear what the youth had to say. Although Shamus had hitherto
kept in the background, he was not out of hearing, and, slily
availing himself of his privileged position in regard to his chieftain, he glided into the hall at Bewly amongst the crowd of lords
and gentlemen, and managed to hear every word of the story,
albeit that the narrator, overcome with the timidity natural in
such a presence, told his simple tale in low hesitating accents,
and with eyes that sought the ground.

"I think I was as near death since I left here," said Angus,
"as one could be and escape it. There's no more feeling in them
black-hearted soldiers of Tichbourne's than there is in a whin-stone,
and their general is worse than any of them, Christ save us! for
all you'd think to hear him talk he was a saint at the very least
—if he was cutting your throat, or blowing your brains out, he'd be
discoursing to you of the goodness of God, and the ways of righteousness, so that you'd think there was honey on his lips. When I
was taken before him in a condemned looking place they called the
Tholsel, he preached a sermon to me that Father O'Hanlon himself could hardly beat, but the last words spoiled all, for he told
me that I was to die that very day as a spy. 'And now,' said he,
knitting his black brows together, 'now go to the Lord Christ,
and beg of him to free your mind from the thick clouds of
Popish darkness. He will illumine you, and if you do but ask
Him. His light will conduct you through the dark valley.' 'Why,
then,' says I to myself, 'I wish you'd tell me something I didn't
know before.' Well! there I was Sir Phelim, sorrowful enough
you may be sure—especially in regard to having missed my

mark—and thinking that I must die like a dog without benefit
of clergy, and me shut up there in a dark hole without as
much as a glimpse of light. If it wasn't for a pair of beads I
had, and that I made good use of them, I don't know what on
earth I would have done, for I was falling into a kind of despair
with the fear and the dread that was on me—sure enough it
must have been the Blessed Mother of God that brought me
through, for myself thinks it was a miracle and nothing less."

"Well! well!" said Sir Phelim with manifest impatience, "how
was it, boy? let us hear!"

"I will, Sir Phelim, I'm just coming to it. The jailor was
just after telling me, for my comfort, that all the other Irish
prisoners were to be exchanged only me, and that I was to be
shot before sunset, when in comes another, and says he, 'no such
thing,—the fellow has better luck than honester folk!—his life
is saved for this time——'

"'Why, how is that?' says the jailor, and, though myself
didn't dare to open my lips, you may be sure I was on thorns to
hear more. 'Well,' says the turnkey to the jailor, 'if you were
guessing for ever you'd never light on it. What do you
think of Lady —— coming herself to Sir Henry to ask pardon
for the varlet?—he said the name in a whisper almost, so that I
couldn't hear it, and sorry enough I was for that same, for the jailor
himself cried out: 'Can it be possible?—well! after that, I'll
wonder at nothing—but I suppose Sir Henry couldn't refuse her.'
'So he said,' says the turnkey back again, 'for she asked it as a
favor that she'd never forget, and Sir Henry said as it was the first
she ever asked of him, he couldn't refuse though he didn't deny
but what it was sore against his will to spare the fellow's life. I
heard a whisper amongst some of the soldiers,' says he in a low
voice, 'that Sir Henry wouldn't give in so readily, only for a
notion he has in regard to her ladyship's daughter—a born
beauty, they say she is, and old as the general is, it seems he's
looking out for a wife still.' At this the two laughed, and the
jailor says winking at the other, 'I see—I see—that's all plain
enough, but what the d—l put it in the old lady's head to petition for a scurvy Irish traitor.'"

" That was just what myself wanted to know," said Angus, "so I got as near as I could and cocked my ear to listen, but I wasn't anything the wiser, for the other only shook his head and said it was a mystery to him."

Various names were suggested by the Norman lords and gentlemen, but their guessing threw no light on the subject, and Sir Phelim exclaimed in a snappish way :

" We be just as much in the dark now as we were before—is that all you can tell us regarding this dame of quality ?"

" Not so, Sir Phelim," returned Angus with a smile, and he glanced sideways at his friend Shamus ; " before I left Drogheda I had a visit from that same lady, a lady of noble presence she is, too, and with her was the fairest maiden these eyes ever beheld." The arch youth paused and looked around, enjoying, as it were, the surprise now depicted on every face, turning from one to the other as their various ejaculations reached his ear.

" Ay, marry," said he, " the lady came to see me, and she told me she felt herself much beholden to certain of the Irish chieftains, and she gave me a message for one in particular."

" And who might that be ?" demanded O'Neill.

" The O Rourke of Breffny !"

" The O'Rourke !" cried Manus, stepping eagerly forward. " Did she say O'Rourke ?"

" She did, and as your lord is absent, I may give it to you, for the lady said I might, in such case, deliver her words to any of his kinsmen. She commends herself to Owen O'Rourke, and sends him word by me, with kind and courteous greeting, that for his sake, and in virtue of his request, she saved my life, begging that noble gentleman to believe that she holds his debt as still standing, and will, with God's help, do much more in payment thereof if so be that these troubles last much longer!"

" I know now who it is," said Manus O'Rourke,—" it is——"

" Nay, speak not her name," said Angus quickly, " she charged me to keep it secret, from all who knew it not already."

" Humph !" cried Sir Phelim, " O'Rourke's smooth face and winning ways have made an impression on some soft-hearted dowager of the Pale—what think ye, my lords ?"

"Nay, I pray you, Sir Phelim, do not the noble lady injustice," said Manus eagerly; "the bottom of this affair is well known to me, and she were as inhuman as her husband—from whose hands God save us all—did she not feel grateful to Owen O'Rourke!"

"Well! well! have it your own way," said Sir Phelim; "your secret must be respected for the present, we have other matters to think of than ladies' whims!"

CHAPTER XVII.

"Those high-built hopes that crush us by their fall!"

CAMPBELL.

"The wise and active conquer difficulties,
By daring to attempt them; sloth and folly
Shiver and sink at sights of toil and hazard,
And make th' impossibility they fear."

ROWE.

THUS the hopes of taking Drogheda were for that time abandoned by the allied chieftains, much against the will of the Norman lords who were extremely disconcerted by this unlooked-for disappointment so soon after their coalition. The high expectations with which they had joined the army before Drogheda may be gathered from a letter which they addressed, even so late as the end of February, to Lord Clanrickarde. This letter was dated from "the Catholic camp near Drogheda," and explicitly informed the politic and time-serving Marquis that the nobles of the Pale had made common cause with the native Irish.

"And we now give your lordship to understand that by God's assistance the work is, by the help of our neighbors of Ulster, and by our own endeavors, in a fair way, we having already in the field, about Dublin and Drogheda, about 12,000 able men, and more expected daily, for the most part well armed; and besides we can assure ourselves of the good will and endeavors of the rest of our Catholic countrymen throughout the kingdom."*

It was painful, then, for these high-spirited noblemen, at length thoroughly interested in the great national movement, to be obliged to retreat before the first advance of Ormond. Still,

* See D'Alton's *History of Drogheda*, Vol. II., p. 243.

as they said, they felt strong in the confidence that their cause
enlisted the sympathies of all the Catholics of the kingdom (with
the exception, they might have added, of those under the fatal
control of Lord Clanrickarde and such as he) and that, in retiring
from the plains of Louth, they did but bend for a season to the
passing storm. In common with all the native Irish they looked
eagerly forward to foreign succor, and still more confidently than
even their allies, they believed in the secret sympathy of the king.
This last was a dream of their own sanguine imaginations, based,
at least then, on no solid foundation, yet to it they clung as the
principal anchor of their hopes and prospects.

But although King Charles had no real sympathy with the
heroic struggles of his Irish subjects, there was a power now
coming slowly and majestically into the field which was worth
a thousand times more to them than any influence the faithless
monarch could have exercised.

The persecuted Church of Ireland, subdued and spiritless to
all appearance, and timorous in public action, had as yet made
no demonstration in favor of her gallant defenders. Now this
apparent timidity, or indifference, or whatever it might be called,
had passed away, and a synod of the Bishops was held at Kells,
very soon after the retreat from Drogheda, presided over in person by the patriotic primate, Hugh O'Neill. Then and there the
undertaking of the confederates was first pronounced "just and
lawful," and a blessing solemnly invoked on their arms.

The spirit which animated that august assembly in the ancient
city of Columba, went forth within a few weeks to every corner
and extremity of the kingdom, infusing new life and the fresh-
ness of hope into hearts that were beginning to grow cold and
despondent.

Messengers, some of them priests, were sent abroad to the
different Catholic countries, and Father Luke Wadding was honored with a special embassy. The Pope and his Catholic Majesty of Spain, and Cardinal Richelieu, then the ruling spirit in
France, were each notified of the position of the patriot Catholics
of Ireland.

The government, on the other hand, were at length aroused
to action. Lord Ormond was sent northward, as we have seen,

with orders to burn and ravage all before him. Had the Earl
been allowed his own way he would have followed Sir Phelim's
army into Ulster, believing that, from their almost total want of
supplies, they would necessarily afford an easy victory to an
army such as that which was now at his command. The Lords
Justices, however, would not hear of his venturing beyond the
Boyne, being still governed by their selfish fears of leaving the
metropolis without sufficient protection. And yet to all men it
appeared that they might safely have permitted Ormond to carry
out his politic design, seeing that they had made Sir Charles
Coote governor of Dublin, with a large and efficient force at
his disposal, and that, under his able superintendence, the
defences of the city had been strengthened in every possible
way.

When summoned back from Wicklow to take command of the
garrison of Dublin, Coote had encountered the warlike clan of
the O'Tooles, assembled to bar his progress with such arms as
they could collect. To almost any other general, it would have
been a formidable sight to see these bold mountaineers ranged in
order of battle full on his path amid the wild fastnesses of their
native rocks. But to the ruthless and impetuous Coote nothing
presented any serious obstacle—fear and pity were alike strangers
to his bosom, and unfortunately his men were chosen from thousands
for qualities somewhat similar to his own, so that fearing neither
man nor devil, fire nor sword, they were never known to retreat
before any force, no matter how superior in numbers, and their
headlong charge was irresistible when their fiery old captain,
sword in hand, led them to the attack.

The Wicklow mountaineers, on that memorable occasion,

"—— fought like brave men long and well,"

and many a hardy veteran bit the dust beneath the weight of
their vengeful arms, but weapons and skill were against them, and
that courage which springs from desperation, for, in addition to
their usual ferocious valor, Coote's men were then inspired
by the sense of imminent peril. After a hard and bloody contest, then, they at last were forced to give way, or rather to open
a passage for the red-coats, for no account of this affair says that

10A

they retreated, but only that Coote and his bravos "cut their way through them." Nevertheless, Sir Charles made his way back to Dublin, and was there duly installed in the military government of the capital, to the terror and dismay of the Catholic inhabitants.

With their precious persons, then, under the guardian care of Coote, and the metropolis fortified on every side like a castle, Parsons and Borlase might have dispensed with the immediate presence of Ormond, but the terrific accounts of Sir Phelim O'Neill's doings met them at every turn, and filled their cowardly souls with the meanest and most servile fears. Well knowing what they deserved at the hands of Catholics, they could not but regard their armed bands as fierce avengers, ready to deal destruction on those who had driven them to rebellion.

The news of the coalition between the Catholics of the Pale and the native Irish, was, to outward appearance, a most unwelcome surprise to the Lords Justices, but in their hearts nothing could have given them greater satisfaction. Their first step was a key to their feelings in this matter. No sooner did they hear of the rising of the Pale than they wrote to the English Parliament, and got an act passed confiscating two millions and a half of the estates of the Confederate Catholics, and this was shamelessly held out as a certain means of remuneration for those who joined in putting down the rebellion. No stronger inducement could be offered than the fat lands of the Pale Counties, and hordes of greedy adventurers immediately flocked around the standard of the Justices—profuse in their professions of loyalty, but at heart caring little for any cause, except that which afforded a chance of amending their shattered fortunes.

Various rumors were at this time afloat with regard to the Catholic lords and gentlemen of Munster, where a second Coote, Sir William St. Leger by name, was goading the people on to rebellion by the cruellest pecuniary exactions and the fiercest religious persecution. Like the Normans of the Pale, however, with whom very many of them were closely connected, the Catholic gentry and nobility of the southern province were loath to relinquish their hopes of government favor. With the people the case was widely different—bound by no ties to any particular party, buoyed up with no delusive hopes, and in the actual endurance of all manner of oppression, they were only anxious to be led against their tyrants. But their natural leaders, the Catholic aristocracy of the land, having little real sympathy with them, feared nothing so much as an outbreak which might possibly compromise them with the Lords Justices. The threatening attitude of the people and the unmistakeable signs of revolt everywhere becoming visible, excited the selfish fears of the Anglo-Irish magnates of the province. At the head of these stood Lord Muskerry, the lineal representative of the great McCarthys of Desmond, but unhappily, also, the brother-in-law of the Earl of Ormond.

Even as Gormanstown and Fingal had been, was still McCarthy of Muskerry—a very loyal nobleman, indeed, anxious to keep the peace at any cost, and willing to do anything and everything rather than have his fair domains go in as a share of the forfeited *two and-a-half millions.*

So, very early in the month of December, just about the time when the lords of the Pale were forming their patriotic alliance with the Irish chieftains, away posted Donough McCarthy, with quite a large number of the first Catholics of Munster, to tell St. Leger how fearful they were of the rebellious dispositions of the people. There was no doubt, they said, that the hard usage to which they were subjected would eventually drive them to take up arms, if some immediate steps were not taken to keep them in order.

"And what the furies can I do?" cried St. Leger roughly, "other than I do?"

"It is true that you are doing your utmost," said Muskerry, "but not so with others—and that is just the object of our present visit. For my part, I am willing to raise a thousand men and maintain them at my own expense, if so be that the government will give them arms. Others of my friends here present are willing to do in like manner, according to their several ability, on similar conditions."

"What fools you take us to be, you hypocritical Papists!" was Sir William's answer; "do you think we would put arms in the hands of our deadly enemies?"

"Enemies!" repeated Muskerry, in a tone of surprise, only

slightly mingled with resentment; "enemies, did you say?—
surely you meant not the word, Sir William, and we giving the
best proofs of our loyalty that men *can* give!"

"Go to the —— Netherlands!" cried St. Leger, with brutal
vehemence, "you're all rebels at heart—ay, every cursed traitor
of your crew—go to! I'll none of your savage henchmen—send
them to him of the Red Hand!" And so saying, he walked into
an adjoining cabinet, slamming the door behind him, as though
to signify his utter dislike and contempt of his cringing visitors.

"By the holy faith of my fathers which these heretics perse-
cute!" exclaimed one of the noblemen present, with startling
energy, "I will do even as he says—never again shall my services stink in the nostrils of foreign tyrants, for, an' I send not
my people to O'Neill, they shall do his work here at home—so
help me the God whose Church I will henceforth serve and defend at my life's peril."

"Nay, be not so rash," interposed Muskerry, seeing that most
of those present appeared to be of the same mind, "do nothing
hastily——'

But his words were little heeded in the stern determination
which St. Leger's contemptuous treatment had evoked. The
half-slumbering spirit of patriotism, and the growing sympathy
with their struggling brethren in other parts of the country, till
then repressed by worldly prudence and expediency, burst forth
at that moment bright and vigorous, eager for action, and
ashamed of past tepidity. Even Muskerry himself caught the
genial flame, and resolved, at last, to take the stand which
his co-religionists had a right to expect from him. Thenceforward the proud banner of the McCarthys was seen where it
ought to be, in the van of the Catholic army of Munster, but,
unhappily, the day was far distant when its rich folds waved
over victorious bands.

In Connaught, the old heroic spirit of the native tribes awaited
but the spark to kindle it, and that was not long wanting. In the
Archbishop of Tuam of that day, the Connaught clans had a tower
of strength, for no truer patriot, no more fervent Christian than
Malachy O'Kelly, breathed Irish air at that troubled period.
His influence had early roused the people of Sligo, and those

parts, to follow the example of their friends in Leitrim, and thence on into Mayo, Roscommon and Galway, the healthful spirit of resistance to oppression made its way, strong in the twofold sense of right and might. But, alas! the gigantic shadow of De Burgo shed its blighting coldness over the fairest and most promising portions of Connaught. Inaccessible alike to religious enthusiasm and patriotic ardor, Clanrickarde, Catholic as he was, continued all through that long and changeful period the firm friend, and (not always) trusted confidant of the puritanical faction who held the land and the people in thrall.

A cold, calm, passionless man was this (so-called) great Earl of Clanrickarde—this head of the Norman tribes of Connaught—a man whose sympathies were in every instance with the oppressors of his country, and the persecutors of the faith he professed. Never was man more completely governed by prudence, more entirely politic and worldly-minded than Ulick Burke, who, like James Butler, constituted one of the great historical figures of that stirring drama. Like Ormond, too, Clanrickarde exercised a fatal influence on the action of the Confederate Catholics, but, of the two, the heaviest load of censure necessarily falls on the professing Catholic De Burgo rather than the renegade Butler, whose religion was after all kidnapped from him in his childish days ere yet his judgment could take cognizance of the truths of faith.

Had it not been for Clanrickarde, and his deleterious policy, Connaught alone would have effected great things for the national cause, for even as it was, deeds of heroism, the loftiest and most praiseworthy, were achieved in various parts of Clanrickarde's own country, during the really stirring times which followed, as will be seen in the sequel of this story. Meanwhile let us return to take a parting glance at the labors of our principal leaders.

In the midland counties of Leinster, the genius and varied accomplishments of Rory O'Moore were every day producing great results. With the Normans of the Pale, his influence was great and perceptible, while his hold on the native chieftains was still as strong as in the first days of the confederacy. The sentiment of "God, and our Lady, and Roger O'Moore" still retained much of its pristine warmth, notwithstanding the many reverses, and the grievous disappointments already encountered by those whom his sanguine spirit had at first buoyed up with delusive hopes.

Strange that with such favorable dispositions existing in every part of the kingdom—with the English of the Pale—dogged and stern in their resolves when once taken—armed in the cause—with Connaught and Munster stirred to their very depths, and great part of Ulster still in their own hands—with the blessing of the Synod of Kells still echoing in their ears, and fresh in all men's minds—was it not strange that just at that particular juncture—that is to say, towards the end of April,—the so-lately conquering army of Ulster—or rather the forces brought together by the northern chieftains—should be on the very verge of dissolution, and merely holding together as it were on suffrance, with little power for good to friends or harm to enemies. The sturdy spirit of Sir Phelim, even, had at length given way to the united pressure of disappointment, want of necessaries and protracted failure. The unsuccessful attempt on Drogheda rankled in his mind and depressed him more than he would willingly acknowledge—for his vanity had sustained a severe wound in being obliged to retreat before Ormond without striking even a blow, after losing so many weeks around the old borough.

It was long before the other northern chiefs began to imbibe Sir Phelim's desponding spirit—affairs grew desperate indeed when Sir Con Magennis, and Roderick Maguire, and Art McMahon gave up hopes of success.

A meeting was held about the middle of April, in one of the castles of Sir Phelim O'Neill, situated on the borders of Lough Foyle. Most of the principal chiefs were present, and the avowed object of their deliberations was the best means of extricating themselves from the difficulties of their position. At first various suggestions were made as to the raising of finances for carrying on the war, some proposing one expedient, some another.

Sir Phelim listened with ill-concealed impatience, turning from one to the other of the speakers with a lowering brow and a flashing eye as he strode the long hall to and fro, stopping ever and anon to hear some remark that struck him as forcible, or to make some curt reply.

At length he turned short on Lorcan Maguire who had said
something about Owen Roe : " In God's name," said he, " let me
hear nothing of ' our friends abroad'—I am sick of the very word.
They are all over-careful of their own safety, take my word for
it, to put their necks in danger by helping us.   They are all in
too good quarters where they are, depend upon it, to come hither
in search of poverty and hardship.   Know you, Lorcan ! the exact amount of our resources at this present moment while you all
talk of Father Luke Wadding and Owen Roe, and the people up
the country, and such like fustian ?   Do you know, I say, any
of ye, what we have of a certainty to count on ?"

One expressed total ignorance on the subject, another made a
random guess, evidently to satisfy the impatient chieftain as much
as anything else, while a third inquired to what particular supplies he had reference.

" To what particular one," cried Sir Phelim, in a tone half
fierce, half derisive ; " why, they be all about on a par with us.
Take, for instance, our ammunition—ha ! ha ! ha !   Of a surety,
your Catholic powers and ' our countrymen abroad' have done
well for us in regard to that article—we have just a little more
than one keg of powder remaining, so judge how far that would
go against a regular army well supplied with all things needful.
By mine honor, an' we ever take up arms again in this quarrel,
they must needs give us something else besides fair promises,
which, though very soothing to the ear, will do little in the way of
making head against a powerful enemy."

" What is to be done, then ?' demanded McMahon ; " are we
to stay here quietly awaiting the day when Ormond or perchance
Coote will be sent to visit us on our hearthstones ?"

" Not so," said Sir Phelim ; " rather than fall into the hands
of either—even the smooth-tongued Butler—I would hide my
head beneath yonder stream."

" Shame, shame, Sir Phelim !" cried Magennis warmly ; " let
no man hear such despairing words—all unmeet for warrior's
tongue to utter, much less a Christian."

" You who are both a warrior and a Christian, Con," said
O Neill with sneering emphasis ; " do you propose remaining here
to await a lucky turn in our affairs—help, for instance, from
abroad ?"

Magennis shook his head sadly. "Heaven direct us for the best!" said he, "it is a hard alternative, but I fear we must e'en seek some place of safety."

"Just so," cried Sir Phelim exultingly, while his brother Tirlogh laughed outright; "my notion is that we needs must place the sea between us and the bloodhounds who will speedily be out on our track."

"Sir Phelim!" said Roderick Maguire in a reproachful tone, "bethink you what you say!"

"I do, Rory, I do, and, before Heaven, it grieves my heart to speak in such wise, but what can we do, man! what can we do? Bethink *you* of our only keg of powder, our empty coffers, and our just as empty commissariat!"

Slowly and reluctantly, and with many a heart-rending sigh, the necessity of flight was generally admitted—at least until such times as the affairs of the insurgents assumed a more prosperous aspect —and even the sternest and bravest of the chiefs could no longer find any reasonable protest to enter against such a step. With heavy hearts and downcast eyes they were about to separate, sadly thinking that God only knew under what circumstances they might meet again, or if they ever should.

All at once the door was thrown open and in rushed the youth Angus, closely followed by Shamus Beg, the latter evidently remonstrating with his friend on the imprudent step he was taking. After them stepped softly in a third individual, a dark, silent young man, a soldier in O'Hanlon's company, between whom and Shamus an extraordinary friendship had been observed to exist from an early period of their military connection. This young man was named Donough, and his influence over the fiery clansman of Tyrone was by all remarked, but, like Angus Dhu, nothing more was known as to who he was, or whence he came.

On this occasion both Shamus and Donough seemed to be solely intent on restraining Angus within the bounds of prudence and decorum, but the youth, evidently laboring under some strange excitement, broke from their grasp and burst upon the astonished chieftains like some wild and beautiful vision.

"Sir Phelim O'Neill!" he cried, in Irish, the tartan on his breast heaving tumultuously with the force of his agitation, "is it true what I hear that the chiefs of Ulladh are giving up God's holy cause—the righteous cause of justice and *revenge*—giving it up like old *callioghs* at the very first back-set that comes on them. Is it true, Sir Phelim! or is it not?"

"Angus! Angus!" whispered Shamus, "for your life do not speak so! He will hang you as sure as death!—oh Angus! what's come over you?"

"Let me alone, Shamus," cried the excited youth, struggling to free himself from the other's friendly grasp, "he must and shall answer my question, *for it is the voice of God!*"

There was the fire of inspiration in his dark gleaming eyes, and his last words sounded strangely in the ears of the chieftains, most of whom were strongly susceptible of religious feeling. Even Sir Phelim, although less under the control of religion than many of the others, felt a strange emotion stirring within him at these singular words.

"Angus!" said he coming forward, and laying his hand on the youth's shoulder, "Angus, we cannot do otherwise—we have no means of continuing the war!"

"Say not so," cried Angus Dhu in a solemn tone; "the God for whom you do battle does but try your faith—the help so long delayed is even now at hand, and you will live to drive the enemy before you as chaff before the wind—fly not—desert not your post, as you fear the wrath of God—dare not one of you cross the water, at this time, for, an' you do, the land of Erin you shall never see again. Courage, chiefs of the Gael! this is the darkest hour, but the dawn is close at hand, and a day of glory and of brightness is rising over the mountains!" So saying, he turned and darted from the room, followed by his two friends silent and abashed. Strange to say, his words decided the chieftains to remain in the country and await the merciful designs of God in their favor. The result will be seen in our second part, when we hope to lay before the reader scenes and characters entirely new, yet still bearing on the fortunes of our "Confederate Chieftains," and the glorious work to which so many years of their lives were devoted.

END OF THE FIRST PART.

10*

THE

CONFEDERATE CHIEFTAINS.

CHAPTER I.

" A combination and a form indeed,
  Where every god did seem to set his seal,
  To give the world assurance of a man."

SHAKESPEARE.

THE burning sun of a July day was some hours' journey down
the western sky, and the shadows were beginning to lengthen
on moor and meadow in a pastoral district of Donegal County,
where the country assumes a less rugged aspect, and the mountains recede on either hand, leaving only a broken and undulating surface to mark their vicinity. In other years this so picturesque region, naturally one of great fertility, would have been
clothed at that season with the golden gifts of Ceres awaiting
the reaper's sickle, and the numerous orchards which nestled
away amongst its sunny knolls and swelling hills would have
groaned beneath the weight of heavily-laden branches, but now
nor waving crop, nor fruit, nor flower, graced the scene, for
war's desolating footprints were everywhere visible, and the
country, far as the eye could reach, was a dreary, dreary waste.
The labors of man were nowhere visible, save where shattered
walls, and garden flowers run wild, and shrubs and fruit-trees

bent and broken, gave evidence of former cultivation. Man had
been there, for his works were there in ruins, but man was there
no longer, an I after even a cursory glance, the traveller—they
were then passing few—came to the sorrowful conclusion that
the fair scene was a savage solitude, lifeless and voiceless all.
Even the road which wound in a sort of serpentine fashion over
and around the hills and hillocks was now so blocked up with
accumulated rubbish, so broken and indented with deep ruts as
to be hardly passable, especially for strangers.

And strangers they must have been, for all their Irish costume,
the two gentlemen who, mounted on the small, shaggy ponies
for which that region was then as now remarkable,* were slowly
and with difficulty making their way through the momentarily-
recurring obstacles which impeded their course. Both were arrayed in the picturesque costume of the native chiefs, with the
single exception that the *barradh* was replaced by a Spanish
hat, without feathers, descending in a point over the brows.
The cloak, which, as an indispensable part of the national costume, each wore, was of the shortest and lightest, so that even
the faint summer breeze lifted their folds, and left the richly-
ornamented jackets and embroidered leathern girdles of the
travellers full in view, with forms which, though cast in far different moulds, were both graceful in their symmetry, and indicative of much personal strength. The one who rode foremost
was a man of some five-and-thirty years, or thereabouts, tall
and commanding in stature, and of rather grave aspect, albeit
that his fresh and somewhat florid complexion, with the spark-
ling light of his clear blue eyes, gave a character of youthful
buoyancy to a face otherwise calm and composed in all its
lineaments. There was the slightest possible stiffness about the
whole face and figure, though the one was singularly prepossessing, if not handsome, and the other was, as I have said,
both graceful and athletic. Take him altogether, and he gave
you the idea of a man who had battled with the world, and had
come victorious from the struggle ; a man of earnest purpose, and

* I presume there are few of my Irish readers who have not seen,
or at least heard of, the Cushendall ponios.

stern resolve, yet full of the kindliest and most generous sympathies, lofty and pure in his aspirations, and having all his faculties under habitual control. His companion was a younger, and,
perhaps, a more attractive individual, with a slashing, dashing,
soldierly air, and a dark handsome set of features illumined
by a pair of brilliant black eyes, so wild, and, at the same time, so
piercing that you shrank from meeting their searching glance.
Yet was there an air of such carelesss gaiety about the jauntily-
attired youth that you loved to look on him, you knew not why,
and as you looked, you would perchance say within yourself
that he reminded one of the more warlike troubadours of old
Provence, or of the ambitious striplings, half boy, half man, who,
in chivalrous times, were wont either

"To follow to the field some warlike lord,
Or tune the lute in gentle lady's bower."

And truly the elder of these cavaliers might well have been a
"warlike lord," but nor page nor squire ever bore him with
such lightsome air in his master's company as did that handsome youth so richly attired withal, and so gracefully gay in
word and mien.

Yet graceful and captivating though he was, the younger gentleman seemed under a certain restraint in the garments which
at first sight so well became him, and as he glanced occasionally
at the truis and hose, and the somewhat clumsy buskins which
encased his lower limbs, a smile of mischievous meaning curled
his thin lip.

The two had been discoursing, as well as the frequent inter-
ruptions of the toilsome road permitted, and their theme was the
all-engrossing one of the strangely-complicated position of parties in the hapless land of the Gael, as the elder cavalier pathetically called green Erin. They both spoke in the Irish tongue,
the younger with the ease and fluency of a native, the elder with
a sort of hesitation and a slightly foreign accent, which told of a
protracted sojourn in other climes where the language of Ireland
was seldom, if ever, spoken. Good friends the two seemed to
be, however, and a perfect understanding appeared to exist

between them, judging by the cordial warmth with which they concurred in judging "men and measures." It was only at intervals and by brief snatches that they could carry on their conversation, but when a smooth patch of road made itself visible, they eagerly availed themselves of it to journey side by side and resume the thread of discourse so often broken.

"Then, by your showing," said the elder gentleman, as the other gained his side, after leaping his nag fairly over a pile of rubbish, " by your showing, gentle sir, the affairs of the Catholic party are not altogether desperate as yet."

"Desperate did you say?" cried the young cavalier impatiently, "I tell you no. So far, we have held our own—ay! marry, and more than that, balancing our loss and gain one against the other. Of a surety, those of the government faction —to wit, the secret abettors of the Parliament of England in this country—are in worse plight than we, and have less to boast of, and as for the king's party, of which I would fain speak in friendly terms, did truth allow (which woe is me! it doth not), as for them, their success, up to this time, is, as it were, a house of glass, which one stroke of ours would shiver to atoms. Had we but cannon and field pieces in any adequate number, we could bring even the proud Butler to his knee with marvellous quickness. You smile, sir stranger, but I tell you truly: Ormond could not stand before us had we but the things I mentioned."

"Nay, I know not that," said the tall stranger with grave emphasis, " I fear me much that you both underrate my lord of Ormond's talents, skill in war-craft, and the resources which he has at command. Moreover, there be others of the royal generals men of mark, and not unknown to fame. I have heard that Stewart and Montgomery have done wonders here in the north, with far inferior forces, against Sir Phelim O'Neill and his entire strength, while in the other province Coote and Ormond carried all before them, and every passing day, it would seem, strengthens the hands of our enemies; where in the onset we had but the two generals last named to dread, we have now many commanders of note to encounter. Inchiquin and Vavasour and Broghill, not to speak of others of lesser note, are a powerful strength to the enemy——"

"And what of that?" cried the other sharply; "if you come to speak of generals, we have those who need not fear to stand before the best of them. Think you, noble sir, that *we* have not gained of late even greater accessions of strength. A host of noble and distinguished names already adorn our muster-roll, and for every one *they* can boast, we can number ten."

The stranger shook his head sadly. "It is well," said he, "it is very well to see the noble and the brave enrolling themselves beneath the national standard, but of all those lords and honorable gentlemen, what one is known to fame by feats of arms or military skill? What have they done as yet, even in this matter, to give us hope of future success?"

"Much—much have they done," cried the young man eagerly; "were it not that you were a stranger in the country I would marvel at your asking a question so insulting to the brave men who have many times of late led the people on to victory—ay! and men of the Norman blood, too, for all the native chiefs were wont to deem them over-cold and indifferent!"

"Humph!" said the other, affecting an incredulity which he did not feel, "I should like to hear somewhat of these great achievements. Perchance the late battle of Kilrush, by some strange optical delusion, is set down by you hot-headed youngsters as a victory!—of that affair I have indeed heard, and my cheek burned as I listened. I was assured by those whose word I could not doubt, that Lord Ormond, with a force of barely three thousand men, put Lord Mountgarret and Rory O'More to flight at the pass of Mageny, with an army of eight thousand. Call you that a victory, young sir?"

"Twit us not with that disastrous affair, I pray you," said the young cavalier with undisguised emotion; "on that unhappy day we lost full many a brave comrade, some even of high standing amongst us, but as God liveth, sir stranger, it was no fault of our commanders, but was owing entirely to the want of proper discipline in our forces, with the old complaint of little or no artillery. I tell you our generals did what men could to arrest the course of victory, but, alas! the veteran, and well-trained soldiers of Ormond and Tichborne, armed at all points, were more than a match for our poor fellows, all unused to war as they were, and badly provided even with hand-arms. The fates would have it as it was, and we had only to give in for the time, but with God's good aid, the stain of that day shall not long rest upon our name—we shall not always be as bare as we now are in regard to the munitions of war. My word for it, Rory O'More, were there none other, will see that the disgrace which befel us at Mageny be redeemed to our country's credit."

"Now that you speak of him," said the elder gentleman, " know you where speech might be had of him? He escaped unhurt, I am told, from that famous battle"—this was said with a good-humored smile—"but can you tell me what he has been doing since? Surely, so much talent, and so many good parts, together with so much patriotism, cannot lie rusting in idleness at a time like this?"

"Wrong not O'More so far as to suppose it," said the youth with generous warmth, as, having paced his little steed carefully through the scattered fragments of a garden-wall which had fallen outward on the road, he once more took his station alongside of his companion; "Rory hath not been seen in public since that disastrous day, but he is not the man to give up a cause so lightly, and I warrant me he is working like a mole under the feet of our opponents. Silently and steadily O'More does his work, and to him, under God, is due the vast organization which even now embraces great part of the island. Many and many a Norman noble, now devoted heart and soul to our interests, would never have perilled life or fortune in the cause, were it not for that same Rory O'More of whom your words, and still more, your sneering tone, imply some doubt!"

It was with difficulty that the tall stranger suppressed a smile, as certain memories from the past floated up to the surface of his mind, but whatever his thoughts might have been, he chose to keep them to himself, saying only that he was glad to hear O'More had done so much.

"But I pray you, tell me, good youth," he said quickly, as if to change the subject, "what *has* been achieved by these commanders of whom you speak? Drogheda I have heard of, and Cork, Kilrush in like manner, ay! and the re-capture of many a northern stronghold by the royal generals, in so far that poor

Phelim Roe—excuse me," seeing that the other looked surprised
—" I mean Sir Phelim O'Neill—and his brother-chieftains here in
Ulster are all but in despair —failure, to speak in serious mood,
I have heard much of—but of success—at least to any extent—I
have *yet* to hear !"

" By the rood, sir stranger," cried the youth impetuously, " I
know not what to think of you. Where have you been that the
echo of our joyful shouts reached not your ear when Mountgarret took Kilkenny, and his brave son, Edmund Butler, compelled
Waterford to open its gates to him? Perchance you have not
heard, either, how Limerick hath been taken for us by Lord
Muskerry and Lord Skerrin——"

" Thank Heaven !" muttered the stranger, " the McCarthy spirit is at last aroused—it was well nigh time—but," raising his
voice, " what boots the taking of a few cities, when all the open
country is in the hands of the enemy. What though Waterford
and Limerick be ours, when St. Leger lords it still over that
province——"

" I cry you mercy, noble sir, he lords it no longer——"

" How ?—what mean you ?"

" I mean that the old firebrand is gone some weeks ago on a
voyage to the other world——"

" Dead, say you ? is Sir William St. Leger, then, dead ?——"

" Ay ! dead as a door-nail !"

An exclamation of pleasure was on the stranger's lips, but suppressing it, he asked very quietly : " Was he slain or what ?"

" Not he,—no arm of ours was so lucky as to execute vengeance on him—he died of—of *Limerick !*"

" How ?—what ?—he died of *Limerick*—what manner of
disease may that be ?"

" Ha! ha! ha !" laughed the arch youngster, exulting in the
thought that he had said a good thing, " I see even travelled
beaux may be puzzled at times by a simple word. St. Leger died
of Limerick just as Queen Mary is said by the scribes to have died
of *Calais*—the old blood-sucker took its loss so much to heart—
coming in the rear of ever so many other mishaps, that his heart
broke—or at least what served him for a heart—it was red-hot

iron, I rather think,—and off he went—to join Pluto's court below, most likely!"

"For shame, young sir," said his graver companion, "such
manner of speech befits not such a theme—death is ever a
solemn subject, and mortal man may not judge his fellow—
even though he be—a St. Leger. If the man be gone to his
account, leave him to the Sovereign Judge of all. How stands
the king affected, that is, what do our friends here believe the
royal mind to be?"

"The royal mind, quotha! By the mass, if there *be* a royal
mind, it is so enveloped in coatings of divers kinds that the art
of man may not penetrate its manifold disguise. Still there are
amongst us men who, deeming themselves wondrous wise, do pre-
tend to fathom that same royal mind, ay, marry! and to see amid
its tortuous windings a secret sympathy with our endeavors. For
myself, I have no faith in any such leaning of the king's majesty
towards us, albeit that Sir Phelim here in the north, and Lord
Muskerry in the south,* do profess to hold commissions from
him——"

"What say you?—commissions from the king!—can it be that
so wily a prince so far committed himself, at a time when his
enemies, the Puritans and Parliamentarians, had him encom-
passed round about?"

"I tell you, sir cavalier," said the young man earnestly,
"there is not a Puritan of them all who has less liking for us at
bottom than his grace's majesty. Why, it was but the other day,
as one might say, that, in his cringing address to the Parliament

---

* Warner tells a curious story, which I have never seen referred to
by any writer, to the effect that Lord Muskerry sent to Sir William St.
Leger by Mr. Walsh, an eminent lawyer of the national party, a
commission from the king duly stamped with the great seal, author-
izing him to collect forces, and to do whatever seemed expedient to
him, in support of the Catholic cause, thus identified with the cause
of royalty. Warner goes on to say that St. Leger was so convinced
of the authenticity of this document, that for that time he drew off
his forces and left Muskerry at liberty to follow out his plans. Warner's *Civil Wars*, Book III., p. 189.

of England, he demanded supplies to equip an army which he meant to lead himself into Ireland to punish his 'seditious Popish subjects.' Ha! ha! good for him that the Parliament refused to trust him. Neither men, money nor arms would they give him, so that he was fain to stay at home and leave others to chastise 'the pestilent Irish rebels;' another pet phrase of his when discoursing of us. Nay, nay, never tell me of King Charles being our secret friend. I question if even his queen, Catholic though she be, has much interest in our struggle, apart from its bearing on the position of her husband. Even Lord Gormanstown himself had, to my knowledge, conformed to that way of thinking before his death—slowly and unwillingly he came to own it——"

"Before his death!" repeated the stranger, with a start; "is Gormanstown then dead?"

"Dead! ay, marry, is he," replied the youth sadly, "he had staked all on the success of our cause, and his heart was fixed on the re-establishment of order and religion in this distracted land, but his hopes were too sanguine, and the brief series of disasters which followed the discomfiture at Drogheda, weighed down his heart with a load of sorrow which speedily brought him to the grave. Alas! yes! Gormanstown is gone from amongst us, and sorely do we miss him at the council-table, ay! and in the field, for, with the weight of fifty years upon him, he was still stout and active. But his prudence and his caution are our heaviest loss! God rest his soul in peace!"

"Amen!" said the other with solemn fervor, and both raised their hats from their brows, and then rode silently on for a short space, as though each were pursuing some train of thought suggested by the sad announcement just made.

"Heaven help us!" said the elder traveller at length, and he heaved a sigh; "what mournful traces doth not war leave behind it—ay! even on the soil! Truly this is a dreary road to travel—God forbid there be many such in Ulster!"

"And yet this is Phelim's work!" said the younger gentleman; "he vowed to have revenge for Island Magee, and, by St. Brendan! he hath kept his word—the enemy hath not had all the slaughtering to himself, I promise you, for all that the chieftains who commenced the work of revolution had no mind to shed blood—it was the hardest necessity that drove them to it. But one thing is certain, to wit, that the worst doings of our Ulster chiefs—even the fierce Phelim himself—do not equal in atrocity the cruelties exercised by some of the royal—or rather the Puritan captains——"

" Ay, marry," said the other, turning quickly in his saddle, " all Europe rings with the monstrous deeds of Coote and his colleagues——"

" Ha, the hell-hound, his name was as a spell-word of evil from which our bravest shrank in terror. I warrant me, the vault of hell re-echoes with the sound at this hour—he has fallen under the lash himself—ay! hath he, and of a surety, the infernal torturers have a long score to reckon with him—Christ save us! what a cloud!" and he pointed to a mass of dense black vapor which had been gradually gathering overhead and extending its wings like some huge bird of prey, until the sun itself was obscured, and seemed suddenly to withhold its light from the earth below, over which the shadow of the awful cloud settled down in darkness. What light remained was barely sufficient to guide the travellers on their devious and difficult way, and to make the scene still more ghastly, the forked lightning began to pierce the threatening mass of vapor, and the air became all at once so thick as to impede respiration.

" Now God and His holy angels shield us from harm!" said the elder cavalier, and raising his right hand he made the sign of the cross on his ample forehead ; " we are in for a thunder-storm, and most likely a tornado after it—look around, my young friend, and see if this wilderness contain no human dwelling. For me, I have been straining mine eyes in vain with the same intent since yonder ominous cloud began to obscure the heavens. Would that I had taken the guide—but then I deemed the way so short, and fancied I knew it so well—so I did, too, but alas ! it is not the same—changed—changed—all—Heaven save us ! Boy ! boy ! see you no dwelling ?"

" Boy !" repeated his companion with scornful emphasis, " methinks, sir stranger, you are over free ! One who has commanded a troop of horse, ay ! and (though he tell it himself) seen some service, must needs be other than a boy ! Mother of God .

what a scene!—what a ghastly glare, and heard you ever such thunder—it seems as though the end of things was at hand——"

"Ha! who comes there?" cried the other cavalier, as a third horseman dashed up at neck-or-nothing speed, apparently reckless of life and limb.

"Your guide," was the brief response, as the soldier, for such he was, passed the travellers at a gallop, and reined in his horse on reaching the front. "We at the castle knew what manner of road lay before you, and fearing some evil might befal you, thought it best to follow your footsteps, so as to be at hand in case your memory failed you."

"Thanks, good fellow," said the elder traveller, "thanks for your friendly forethought, but I see not now what you can do to aid us—place of shelter there seemeth none, and the rain will speedily pour down in torrents from yonder black cloud——"

"Follow me!" said the guide, "and we shall see—if my memory fail me not, there should be one dwelling inhabited somewhere hereabouts!"

The two gentlemen followed in silence, anxiously watching the motions of their guide, who kept a few paces in front, peering on either side through the gloom, down into the ground, as it seemed to them, hallooing through his closed hand ever and anon. Still no answer came, and still the storm increased, and the younger traveller waxed impatient.

"Man!" he called out angrily from behind, "what mummery is this? I tell you, no living soul is within hearing—he were worse than a fool who rested his hopes on such a chance! By my faith, Sir Phelim, I could wish your brawny self in my place this hour, an' you were, my good sir, you might perchance be more sparing of stone walls hereafter—holy St. John! we are in for another deluge!"

But just at that moment when the big drops began to patter against the faces of the travellers and the thunder growled behind them like a pack of wolves on their track, the wild halloo of the guide was faintly responded to, as though from the bowels of the earth, and in the midst of a pile of ruins a little back from the road, a light made itself dimly visible, a moving, twinkling light, too, seeming as though carried in the hand of a person not as yet visible.

"Thank God, they're here still," said the guide in a soliloquizing tone ; "I knew not but it's dead they might be by this time."

"Enter in God's name!" said a voice speaking the Irish tongue, from a yawning aperture in the wall, close to where the elder traveller stood—so close indeed that he started at the unexpected sound, and the equally unexpected sight of a female form holding aloft a piece of blazing bog-wood. "Shelter you can have, if nothing more!"

"Follow her!" whispered the guide, seeing the strangers hesitate, "within you have nought to fear—without, danger and mayhap destruction are abroad."

Nothing more was necessary, for the rain began to pour down in torrents. Leaping lightly from their nags, which the guide took in charge, the two gentlemen hastened after the unknown damsel through what seemed to have been a flagged passage leading, on the right, into a low chamber of narrow dimensions, the stone roof of which effectually excluded the pelting rain, while the total absence of anything like windows, although giving a tomb-like appearance to the place, served now to shut out the lightning, and conveyed a sense of security that was very acceptable to the travellers after their long exposure to the fury of the elements. A wide open chimney occupied one entire side of the little chamber, and on a low stool close to the hearth sat an aged woman, cowering, July evening as it was, with outstretched hands, over a few half-burned brambles. Her face, as she turned it towards the travellers, was ghastly pale, and old, and wrinkled, and misery was stamped on every feature, yet the silver-grey hair was deftly rolled back from her high forehead under a coif which, though of the coarsest texture, was scrupulously clean. Her skinny arms, bare from the elbows, were long, and lean, and yellow, but, what seemed strange to both travellers, and they noticed it at once, was an antique ring of the finest gold which glittered on the third finger of her left hand.

"Mother!" said the younger female, after placing the strangers on two rough blocks of wood which, except the stool before mentioned, were the only seats to be seen ; "mother, give the word of welcome to these noble gentlemen who have taken shelter here from the storm!" and so saying she placed her little torch in a clay-socket over the hob-stone. By its light, the aged crone carefully examined the faces of her guests, or rather that of the elder traveller, on whom her eyes first fell, nor spoke, nor even noticed his respectful salutation, till her scrutiny was accomplished. No emotion of any kind was visible on her withered features, neither joy, surprise, nor even curiosity, but slowly rising from her seat, she drew herself up to a height little to be expected from her previous crouching attitude, then bowing her head with an air of almost queenly dignity, she said:

"Welcome, son of the Hy-Nial! welcome to our miserable dwelling!—you come to us in storm and cloud as beseems one so long foretold. May your coming bring back the sunshine of prosperity to the mournful children of the Gael!"

"Son of the Hy-Nial!" repeated the younger traveller, turning in surprise to his companion who met his look with a grave smile, then rose and returned the old dame's salute with a reverence due to her age; "son of the Hy-Nial," said the young man still looking at him, "can it be that you are——"

"Owen O'Neill, commonly called in these parts, as I am told, *Owen Roe.*"

"I knew it," said the old woman in a voice now quivering with emotion; "I knew you were of the line of Con! Judith"—turning to her daughter—"said I not that the champion of the Red Hand was on his way to join the men of Erin?—I told you I saw him in my dream last night—ay! did I, and struggling with a huge wolf, which he will speedily have to do, and that not with one, but many—rejoice, my daughter, and smile as you were wont that your mother's heart may be gladdened!"

"Colonel O'Neill is welcome," said the young woman, coming a step or two forward from the dark corner into which she had retire1; "long hath his coming been looked for by the tribes of Ulster, and now is their hour of sorest need!"

The tone and manner of the speaker gave singular significance to her words, and were such as to attract the attention of both the cavaliers. The younger could hardly repress an exclamation of surprise, but O'Neill, habitually calm and cool, merely fixed his keen eye on the young woman, if young she could be called with the impression of some thirty years legibly stamped on her pale brow. There was little of youthfulness remaining in her face or figure, nor was she what could be called a beauty, but there was more than beauty, more than youth in the dark depths of her radiant eyes, and the exquisite delicacy of her fair Grecian features, expressive at once of mildness and candor, together with a certain amount of firmness seldom seen on so womanly a countenance. A heavy mass of rich brown hair was gathered in a soft twist to the back of her head, leaving its admirable conformation (as phrenologists would say) fully exposed to view. Her figure was tall and of perfect symmetry in its proportions, while every movement was marked by ease and grace. Sooth to say, it was hard to reconcile the air and bearing, the words and manner of either mother or daughter with the extreme poverty indicated by all around them. The dress of both was the coarse brown drugget, or "linsey-wool-sey" worn by the lowest classes of the peasantry, even that old and faded, although clean. Before any one had spoken another word, Judith had withdrawn into her obscure station, and the gentlemen were both too well bred to follow her thither with their eyes.

"Thanks, good ladies," said O'Neill after a moment's silence, "thanks for your kind and courteous welcome."

"Ladies, good ladies!" muttered the crone in a half-audible voice, as she slowly resumed her three-legged stool. "Ladies—ha! ha! ha!" and she croaked a sort of mocking laugh.

"Nay, I beg to be excused from tendering thanks," said the younger cavalier with an assumption of gaiety that did not conceal a feeling of bitterness lurking beneath. "The welcome was all for you—no word of kindness hath reached my ear, though I, too, am of the Gael—in outward show, at least!" he added in an under tone.

"Not so, Sir John Netterville," said the guide, who now appeared from the dark passage, "the feathers do not make the bird—you were not of the Gael, noble sir, when you rode with Dunboyne's troop to the luckless pass of Mageny!"

"Netterville! Netterville!" repeated the old woman slowly,

and turning, she fixed her still piercing eye on the now laughing, blushing face of the young nobleman, "methinks I should know that name—alas, yes! I once had a lover, a gallant Norman knight from within the Pale—Rufus Netterville was his name, a brother of my Lord Netterville."

"He was my grand sire, that Rufus," cried the young man, pale with astonishment, "but tell me, in Heaven's name, who are you?"

"You may well ask the question," the old woman replied, as she cast her eye around on her miserable abode; "young man, you see before you—the widow of O'Cahan, the daughter of Maguire!" Hearing this, even O'Neill was surprised out of his usual self-possession. "Alas, poor lady!" he exclaimed with emotion, "what a fall is yours!"

"Good Heavens!" cried Netterville, "can it be? How—how is it?"

"That my daughter will tell you, if perchance you tarry longer!"

A peal of thunder shook the old walls at that moment, and Netterville said with a gay laugh, "this storm is wondrous kind, you see, for it leaves us no choice!" O'Neill gave an anxious glance down the long passage, but the sky was still dark and threatening, and the heavy fall of the rain reached his ear even there. However great his hurry might be, he saw there was nothing for it but to stay and listen. Making a virtue of necessity, with grave politeness he expressed his wish to hear the story.

"But first I would wish to know of my young friend here," said O'Neill with much composure, "whether it be customary for the gentlemen of the Pale to assume the costume of the native chiefs in token of adhesion to their cause?"

"I understand you, Colonel," Sir John quickly replied, "and will answer your question by another: Is it customary with Irish gentlemen of foreign reputation landing hither from Spain or France to lay aside the uniform of the armies with whom their fame and laurels were won, in token that they hold no further connection with those friendly nations?"

"Aptly put, Sir John, but methinks a gentleman of such keen wit might further 'understand' that I, finding occasion to journey alone over a long tract of country whose condition I know not, may deem it more expedient to adopt the costume of the native gentry and nobility, as likely to attract less notice than the uniform of a foreign army!"

"Something similar is the case with me," said Netterville in a tone of levity that was clearly assumed, "the only difference being that *my* business is private and yours public. Are you satisfied?"

O'Neill answered with a slight bow. He was not *quite* satisfied, yet too polite to say so, he turned again to Judith and with a cheerful smile requested her to favor them with the promised recital.

CHAPTER II.

"And underneath that face, like summer's oceans,
  Its life as noiseless, and its cheek as clear,
Slumbers a whirlwind of the heart's emotions,
  Love—hatred—pride—hope—sorrow—all, save fear."
                                    FITZ-GREEN HALLECK.

JUDITH approached her allotted task with the air of one who
had but small liking for it. Without moving from her place in
the corner, she asked the guide if there was no likelihood of the
storm ceasing, and his reply in the negative appeared to give her
anything but pleasure.

"It is ill dallying in a vault like this, hearkening to old stories,"
said she, "when an oppressed country is groaning in sore tra-
vail. Nay, colonel, I meant no reproach," seeing that O'Neill
reddened to the eyes, "I do but lament the necessity which
keeps *you* here. As for your companion, neither time nor tide
awaits his going hence, and I see he burns to have the strange
enigma of my mother's fate solved. And yet the story is nowise strange or uncommon in these latter days, and will take
but brief space of time to tell."

"Child!" said her mother testily, "you mistake, the story is
of much interest."

"To us it is, mother," and Judith smiled sadly. "But not to
others."

The gentlemen both hastened to express their extreme desire
to hear it, such as it was, and Judith, without further remark,
complied. In a clear, calm, passionless voice she told how her
mother, although betrothed to young Netterville (with whom she
had become acquainted during a visit to her maternal relatives,
the O'Reillys of Breffny), was forced by her stern father to

fulfil a previous engagement made by him on her behalf with
the chieftain of Dungiven; how her husband, Brian O'Cahan, took
sides with the great Earl, and followed his fortunes all through
those disastrous wars which ended in ruin and defeat, leaving
Ulster a desert, and its noblest families beggars—"ay, starving
beggars," said Judith bitterly, "as we can tell to our sad misfortune. In the halls of Dungiven,* by the silver waters of the Roe,
my mother had long dwelt in such peace as the evil times would
allow, protected as well by the remoteness of her position as by
the strong arms of the clansmen left by my father, to guard his
home and the loved ones from whom cruel war kept him so
long absent. The years of the weary struggle passed—oh, how
tediously! and new sacrifices were demanded of my poor mother,
for the three brave boys whom my father left as children,
were no sooner able to wield a weapon than they quitted their
mother one by one, to take their places by their father's side
amongst the veteran warriors of the north. Alas! their career of
arms was short—it was the will of Heaven that they should see
their old home no more—their first campaign was their last, but
my mother knew not of her loss—it was carefully kept from her
—till, at the close of the long, long, bloody war, when the star
of Tyrone had set, to all appearance, for ever, and the victor of
so many battles had bent his knee before the upstart Mountjoy,

* The Castle of Dungiven, one of the principal strongholds of the
noble house of O'Cahan (O'Kane), is thus described by a writer in the
Dublin Penny Journal: "The house, which is one hundred and fifty
feet long and twenty feet wide, is seated on a gentle slope, and fronting the southwest, and having a fosse and mounds for a defence in
front, and, at either end of the building, round towers, projecting a
little, and furnished with loop-holes for musketry. On the northeast
are two courts, each fifty yards in length and forty in breadth, through
which is the principal entrance; the outer court is surrounded by a
low wall, having a reservoir of water within it; the inner court, which
is rectangular, is defended by a wall twenty feet high, with embra-
sures, &c., and at each angle are square towers as flankers: on the
inside this wall is strengthened by an arched rampart, and runs round
three sides of the rectangle. The situation is commanding, and the
views around it truly admirable."

when my father returned alone to his ancestral halls, foot-sore and weary, with garments soiled and torn, and his stalwart form bowed down with shame and sorrow, far more than years, then it was that my mother asked for her boys, and was told that they had fallen on the field of battle. Alas! it was little comfort for her to hear, from the lips of their father and their chief, that they had died as became their lineage, died, too, in the arms of victory, two of them at Benburb, and one at the Yellow Ford when Bagnall's haughty crest went down before the might of the Red-Hand."

"Woe is me!" muttered the old woman in a dreary, dreamy voice, as she sat apparently but half conscious, with her eyes fixed on the poor apology for a fire, which it seemed her business and her pleasure to keep alive; "woe is me! I deemed my loss a heavy one—alas! alas! I lved to be thankful that my boys were gone!"

Judith stopped and looked with tearful eyes on her mother, and Netterville was breaking out into an expression of sympathy, but the young woman, with grave dignity, motioned him to be silent.

"My mother loves not the language of pity," said she in a subdued tone, and she glanced furtively at O'Neill, whose eyes were moist, though he said nothing; "we of the old blood have pride in proportion to our poverty, Master Netterville—I mean, Sir John Netterville!—I told you, however, that my mother lost her children—they were all she had at that time. I have now to tell you that many months had not gone by, when my father lost lands and livings, houses, castles, and all, all that had been his, except the sorrowful partner of his life, and the few faithful followers whom neither hunger, nor cold, nor any other privation could detach from their lord and lady. Every foot of land he had was confiscated to the crown, in common with the domains of all the other chieftains, who had taken part with O'Neill in the late war, and at fifty, Brian O'Cahan found himself a houseless, homeless man, with a wife enfeebled by sorrow and suffering, looking to him for that support and protection which the stout warrior had no longer to give. Truly, it was a sad day when they turned their backs on

Dungiven Castle, and bade adieu for ever to the statelier halls of
Limavady,* and wandered forth in search of shelter, like unto
our first parents when driven from the shades of Eden."

"We *thought* we were leaving the Castle for ever—sure enough
we did," said the old woman with a ghastly smile on her withered
features, "for Brian said they'd be giving it and Limavady, too,
to some drummer or fifer of their army, to set him up for a lord.
But it seems they were afraid to leave the houses as they were,
for fear of O'Cahan taking them back some day or another—
which between ourselves was just what he meant to do,' she
added, nodding with a confidential air to O'Neill. "So they battered them down as well as they could, and woe is me! I was
fain to take shelter many a long day after in the old walls of
Dungiven with my daughter, poor Judith there. Child of my
heart!" and she turned her aged eyes on her daughter with a
look of ineffable affection, "child of my heart! she came to us in
our heavy sorrow; two years after we left our home, she was
born in a hut on the outskirts of our former territory, and she was
but a fortnight old when her father was arrested on a fresh charge
of stirring up the people to sedition. Heaven help us! that was a
black day to us, for the faithful few who had clung to us in our
poverty and destitution, fell before our eyes, one after another
in the vain and rash hope of saving their chief from falling a
second time into the hands of the king's soldiers. They fell one
by one, at the door of our hut, with a prayer for O'Cahan on
their dying lips, and over the pile made by their dead bodies on

*"Though the O'Cahans had a castle at Dungiven, yet the principal
residence of the chief was at Limavady (*Lim an madhah*), the dog's
leap, a delightful spot on the banks of the Roe, about four miles below
Dungiven, where the river has sought out a narrow way between
lofty and approaching rocks; the situation was happily chosen, and
affords no mean proof of the taste of these early chieftains. Nature
has there so assembled and disposed of her choicest features of
wood, and rock, and water, that they could derive or acquire but
little aid from art to heighten the charms of the scene. The last considerable chief of the O'Cahans, being implicated in treasonable practices with O'Neill and O'Donnell, early in the reign of James I., was
seized, and his estates forfeited in the year 1607."

our threshold, was Brian dragged forth with oaths and curses, himself bleeding you'd think to death, from a wound he got in the scuffle. My prayers, and tears, and cries were useless—they would not so much as give him time to bid myself and the babe farewell—he could only look at us and point to the blue sky above as they tore him away. . . . . . . That was the last we saw of him," she added after a short pause, during which all held their breath to listen—even Judith dwelt on her mother's words as though the tale she told was new to her ear. The old woman said not another word, but relapsing into her former stupor, sat gazing as before on the dull, cheerless fire.

"Like many another chieftain of our unhappy nation," said Judith, taking up the sad tale, " Brian O'Cahan died in prison—the wound he got on that fatal day was never dressed, and that, with the other miseries he endured, put an end to his life within a month. He died, and left my mother and myself—I was then, as she has told you, but a few weeks old—to buffet our way through the world as best we could. By that time, our ancient dwelling was a ruin, battered and broken down by the fierce, strong, Scottish soldiers who were left to work their wicked will on the poor conquered Catholics of Ulster——"

Here a fierce ejaculation from the guide drew all eyes on him. He had started to his feet, and stood with his right hand clenched, his cheek and brow glowing crimson red, and his eyes glaring like those of a tiger. With his strong muscular proportions, he certainly looked a formidable object, but while the gentlemen regarded him in utter amazement, Judith, approaching him, laid her hand on his shoulder, and said in a soothing tone:

" Donogh, my poor boy! what ails you?"

" What ails me?" he repeated in a fierce, wild way, still with eyes fixed on the opposite wall, as though some cause for his agitation was there visible. " Woman! woman! why ask me that?" Suddenly recollecting himself, however, he added with a strong effort at self-control, and a sort of hysterical laugh that was painful to hear: "Oh then, nothing at all ails me,—nothing only a kind of an inward cramp that I take now and then—God help me! isn't it sure to come on me at the wrong time. I ask your pardon, noble gentlemen, especially the colonel there, and yours, daughter of O'Cahan—for the start I took out of you, and the unseemly hole I made in your story."

By some strange impulse, O'Neill and Judith exchanged glances, but neither made any remark on Donogh's intrusive "cramp." Netterville, solely intent on the story, begged of Judith to go on, muttering something at the same time not very flattering to the guide. The latter, although the words were inaudible, appeared to understand their import, for he instantly said, in a tone half ironical, half respectful:

"It was just such another cramp, Sir John, as the one that seized *y u* at the battle of Kilrush, when that young friar appeared so suddenly before you, and was off again, like the shot of a gun, as I heard you tell Rory O'More."

"*You* heard!" exclaimed Netterville, turning quickly on his seat, his cheek blanched with emotion; "in God's name, who *are* you? stay—now that I look at you—do you not belong to Sir Phelim's army?"

"To Sir Phelim's army—O'Hanlon's company—your honor is right!"

"Ay! methinks I have seen you often in company with O'Neill's right hand man, Shamus Beg, I think they call him!"

"Very likely," said Donogh very coolly; "we often march together—but that's neither here nor there—the colonel wants to hear her ladyship's story!"

"And the storm begins to subside," said Judith, who had been to take a look at the weather, "when it ceases, my tale ceases, too, so that I must needs make short work of what remains. Dungiven Castle being in ruins, as I said before, the wife and daughter of its owner were suffered to dwell unmolested within its roofless walls; certain of our own people who had taken refuge from the fury of the soldiery in the woods around, came by night and formed a shelter for us, with the branches of trees, around one of the fireplaces in the former banqueting hall. These faithful followers, so long as they were suffered to remain in that neighborhood, took care that my poor mother was well provided with fire-wood, which they nightly placed within her reach, together with a share of such miserable food as they could procure for themselves. In fact, they watched over us with the tenderest care, and served us with even more devotion than if my mother were still mistress of Dungiven and Limavady."

"I *was* mistress of Dungiven!" said the mother, looking round as before with her strange smile, "I had it all to myself, and what more could I desire?"

"True for you, mother," observed Judith, "your power *was* absolute there, though you had only me, a little child, to rule. But the precious time is passing; such was the place, and such the circumstances in which my earliest years were passed, and you may well imagine that in a scene so wild, so strange, so lonely, I grew up just as wild, and strange, and lonely—the child of nature, of solitude, and of sorrow. I need not tell you that one of the first impressions stamped upon my heart was hatred of English tyranny——"

"It were strange an' it were otherwise," said O'Neill, speaking almost for the first time; "were it only your Rapparee* friends in the woods, they would teach you that. But how, or where, fair mistress, found you the stores of knowledge which, I see, so enrich your mind? where learned you to discourse in such wise as now you do?"

"Ah!" sighed Judith with a sudden change of manner, "that belongs to another portion of my story which were over long now to tell. Suffice it to say that for the little book-learning I

---

* Long before the war of 1641, the scattered remains of the broken clans of Ulster, driven after the wars of Elizabeth's and James's time, into the woods and bogs for refuge, were known by the names of Rapparees and Tories—outlawed and deprived, by the provident care of the British Government, of every means of support, they necessarily lived by plunder. Made desperate by want and inspired by the burning thirst of revenge, they became a bold and reckless race, being formidable to the well-fed foreigners who were snugly located in their former holdings, and even the proud legions of England were made full often to feel the vengeful power of the despised Rapparee. During the whole of the eleven years' war, which commenced in '41, the Rapparees did good service at times to the Catholic army, harassing the enemy by a sort of guerrilla warfare which they carried on on their own account, but generally in connection with the confederate forces.

possess, I owe it to a loved friend and cousin, now, alas! no
more—I mean the Lady O'Neill, wife of Sir Phelim. By chance,
she discovered us in our dismal dwelling, whose walls my mother affected so much as to prefer their shelter even to that of a
royal palace—and at first she would by no means consent to
leave them, but the persuasions of that true friend were so urgent, and above all her representations as regarded me and the
teaching I ought to have, that at last my poor mother gave her
consent, and we both were taken by the Lady Nora to Kinnard
Castle, where for twelve happy years we found a home. I was a
tall young damsel of eighteen or thereabouts, when we first
crossed the threshold of that house, knowing nothing of books,
and little of the world; I was thirty in years, and older still in
mind and heart, when cruel death deprived us of our best
friend and most dear benefactress—the Lady Nora died, and a
few weeks after her death, we were again without a home—
worse even than before," she said, after a pause, and with a
heightened color, she added, "for even the shelter of our old
ruin was no longer ours to enjoy."

"Why, how could that be?" demanded Netterville; "did the
government forbid you that, too?"

"Nay, nay," said Judith, "the government took but little note
of the existence of two poor helpless women such as we. Colonel
O'Neill," said she rising and pointing with a gesture of command
down the long passage; "yonder is the clear sky again—the
storm is past—need I remind you that time presses, and that
many eyes are strained looking for your coming? Depart in
God's name, though it ill becomes the daughter of O'Cahan to
speed the traveller from her mother's hearth!"

"You are right, lady." said Owen with that calm dignity which
belonged to him, "you are right, and I thank you. One thing
I would fain know, nevertheless, before I go hence——"

"And I," said Netterville, in his gay, thoughtless way, "will
not stir a step from here till I have learned whether Sir Phelim
turned you out of doors—or what—if he did, by the rood! he shall
answer for such black deed!"

O'Neill's deep, earnest eyes were on Judith at the moment, and
she felt that they looked what the **more reckless** Norman had

spoken in plain Irish. But Judith O'Cahan did not choose to afford further information. Drawing herself up with an air of dignity that made Netterville smile, whilst O'Neill thought it well became her, she said:

"I know not of any right you have, Sir John Netterville, to dive farther into our affairs than we choose to lay them open to you. I have told you all that I am willing to tell,—what remains could have no interest for you."

"Nay, Judith," said the old woman, "as you have told so much, I would have you tell all. What shame is it to you or me that you cannot listen to Sir Phelim's smooth speeches? This English gentleman asked if Sir Phelim turned us out of doors—not so, young sir, not so,—but rather would he have kept us in his home for life. I were well content to have staid on his terms, for surely even O'Cahan's daughter could not look higher than the lord of Tyr-Owen, but Judith closed her ears and her heart against him, and I besought her only to speak him fair for a while, and that mayhap either he would tire waiting, or she think better of the affair, but she told me she would rather die a thousand deaths than become Sir Phelim's wife. What could I say after that, for my child's happiness or misery is mine, too, so when the rough chieftain found she was in earnest in refusing to marry him, he stormed and swore, and said he *would* have her whether she liked it or not. We thought it was time to move, after that, so we left himself and his castle, and the ghost of my poor cousin Nora, Heaven be her bed! that people said was haunting him every night of his life, and out we went again on the wide world to hide our heads wherever we could. Our own old place we dared not go to, for there Sir Phelim would be sure to find us,—if Judith was willing, I would have gone with her to some of the chieftains of our kindred and craved protection, but Judith would hear of no such thing, for she said it would but breed dissension amongst the chiefs when it most behoved them to keep together. It were ill rousing the lion from his lair, Judith says, or thrusting others within reach of his claws——"

"Mother! mother!" cried Judith with sudden vehemence, "wherefore speak in such wise of matters that were better buried in oblivion? Donogh, my good lad, bring the horses to the road."

Donogh instantly vanished, and both the cavaliers standing up,
prepared to resume their journey. There was a cloud on O'Neill's
brow, and a flush on his cheek that showed some strong inward
emotion, but of what nature it was, none but himself might
know. As for Netterville, he swore a good round oath that one
day or another he would brand Sir Phelim with the disgrace of
such unmanly persecution.

"Nay, Sir John!" once more put in Judith, "I beseech you
that you never upbraid him with it. My mother and I can never
forget that his roof gave us shelter and protection when few
would dare to give us either,—for years long we eat his bread
and were welcome guests at his hospitable board—it would
shame me, too, to have my name so mentioned—and by stranger
tongue!—no! no!—if indeed you would befriend the friendless
daughter of O'Cahan forget that you ever saw her—ever heard
her hapless tale!'

"She is right, my friend," said O'Neill earnestly; "any interference of ours would but harm those we meant to serve. Come,
let us go!"

"Not till I have heard," said his mercurial companion, "by
what strange chance these ladies fixed on such a dwelling——"

"It was not chance," Judith replied, "we had often heard Sir
Phelim boast of the desert he had made of the English settlement, which he said had been a pestilent nest of Protestant
bigotry and all manner of injustice towards the natives of the
country for miles around who professed the old faith. Many a
time and oft did we shudder at the picture he was wont to draw
of its solitude and desolation, but we remembered it with joy and
hope when forced to flee from Kinnard Castle and the land of
Owen. Hither we came, like Noah's dove, seeking rest for our
wearied feet, and lo! having found it, here we abide—buried, as
it were, in a dreary tomb, yet still untrammeled by ties which
were chains of burning iron—to one of us at least!"

"As for *this* noble dwelling," said the mother, with a touch
of sly humor little to be expected, "it was not Sir Phelim that
left it as it is—it was a fire that broke out in it some three years
agone,—one fine summer's evening when all the Protestant
grandees for miles round were assembled in the large room

which those Englishers called the 'best parlor.' There was a
grand young English lady from somewhere within the Pale on a
visit here at the time——"

"Good God!" cried Netterville, pale with emotion, and gasping for breath, "who was the owner of the house?"

"It belonged to the Protestant minister," said Judith, regarding the young man with a surprised look; "it was what they call
the manse or glebe-house."

"And the young lady from the Pale?"

"She was, I believe, a beauty, and the daughter of a great
man——"

"Ay! great in wickedness, if in nothing else. I know all
about him,—but can this be the house of which I have heard so
much? If so," he added in an under tone, "I marvel not at its
desolation. But how say you, fair lady?—the noble damsel of
whom you speak was, then, the sister, or rather I think you said,
the niece, of Master Hatfield, the minister?"

"Nay, I said not that," said Judith with a quiet smile, "but
you say it, and of a surety you seem to know more about the
matter than do I. For us, we might have taken little note of
what fell out amongst the unneighborly Englishers, were it not
for a heroic deed performed, on that occasion, by one of our
own kin!"

"Who was that?" said Netterville, speaking in an abstracted
tone and manner.

"Our right noble kinsman, Maguire of Fermanagh. Passing
the house with a few retainers just when the fire was at its
height, and hearing the people crying on every side, that the
fairest maiden in Leinster was still somewhere within the house,
and must perish in the flames if not speedily rescued, Connor
did but wait to learn from some of the company the spot where
the lady was last seen, and, immediately darting in, he appeared
almost in the twinkling of an eye, bearing in his arms the motionless form of the English beauty wrapped in his heavy cloak.
Amid the cheers and joyous shouts of the crowd of spectators,
Maguire placed his fair burden in the arms of her rejoicing relatives. He had found her in that death-like swoon just within
the door, where she had fallen in a fright and remained unno-

ticed in the general confusion, when each thought only of self-preservation, and all who were so fortunate as to keep their senses, rushed in wild affright from the burning building. The brave chieftain had not himself escaped without some injury, but little recked he that the beauty of his brown silken tresses was gone, or that his face and neck were sadly scorched: so long as he had saved the lady from a cruel death he thought not of himself. To say the truth, the minister and all the rest were very thankful, and would have had Maguire go with them to one of the nearest houses to have dressing for his burns and other needful refreshment, but Connor had little liking for that company, and would not by any means consent to tarry when once he perceived the lady coming to herself."

Both the gentlemen were about to speak, but the old woman was beforehand with them. " You forgot to tell Judith that his uncle Lorcan, who was with Connor, hurried him away as soon as the damsel opened her mouth to thank him."

' And why so ?" demanded Netterville with strong emotion.

" Because he said there was that in her eyes that boded no good to one of his race. To make sure, he made the sign of the cross between Connor and the damsel, and after that, he had no more trouble; the Maguire did his bidding like a little child. Well for the Clan Maguire that its chief had Lorcan at his elbow that day, for it took one like him that has knowledge from the other world to see aught of evil in so fair a form as they say that lady had."

Netterville was strangely agitated, and muttered unintelligible words to himself, as he looked around the dreary habitation. " Thrice accursed walls !" were the only words that caught the ear, and even so much was not meant to be heard, for the young man, as if recollecting himself, glanced around with nervous trepidation, then broke into a wild, unmeaning laugh.

" By my faith, now, that is a pretty story," said he with boisterous gaiety; "'twas a good beginning for my Lord Maguire, and, as the old saw says, a good beginning maketh a good ending. Yet, methinks, the lord of Enniskillen (which proud title I hear he did assume) hath not as yet much to boast of. Pity the rack and the dungeon should follow on so fair a track,

Noble ladies, deign to accept my poor thanks for your hospitable entertainment——"

"Nay, speak not of it, Sir John!" said Judith with a lofty
grace that sat as well upon her as though a royal roof covered
her head; "an' you mean what you say, your thanks are not due
to us but rather to the friendly shelter of these walls—an' you
speak derisively, I have but to say, that the poverty of your entertainment is not our fault, but our misfortune. Farewell, Sir
John Netterville! I have heard much of you from your friend
and kinsman, Rory O'More, who hath much hope of you as
a true champion of freedom—see that his hopes be not misplaced, for, believe me, a dreary doom worse, Sir John, than
even the rack or the dungeon, awaits the recreant who is false to
his God! adieu, young sir, Heaven speed you on your way!"

So astonished was the Palesman at the singular words and the
still more singular manner of the speaker, that he left the place
without further speech to any one, though his pale lips were still
to be seen moving in commune with himself. His abrupt departure was not unobserved by the ancient lady, whose dignity was
sorely hurt by his omission of such parting salute as she deemed
requisite.

"Times are strangely altered," said she, " when the grandson
of Rufus Netterville deigns not to say farewell to Eveleen
Maguire—see what it is, Judith, to be old and poor!"

But her daughter was too much intent on other matters to
notice either the manner of the knight's departure or her mother's
offended dignity. The moment Netterville was out of sight,
O'Neill anxiously inquired whether the Maguire referred to was
the same who lay imprisoned in Dublin Castle.

"The very same," Judith replied; "you have heard, then,
Colonel O'Neill, of what befell him and McMahon?"

"Surely I did, fair mistress," and he smiled, "nay, even to
poor Costelloe's unlucky attempt at caricaturing in the Justice's
hall. I was told, too, of the torture inflicted on both those gentlemen," he added in a more serious tone, "the which was not
over pleasant to hear, but we of the conquered race are happily
well exercised in the virtue of patience, and must needs pocket

many things, which others would resent without a moment's
delay."

" Can nothing be done," said Judith anxiously, " on behalf
of those noble gentlemen—is there no way of effecting their
release ?"

" I know of none at the present moment," O'Neill replied
with habitual caution, " but the chances of war may perchance
turn in their favor when we least expect it."

" If *you* cannot assist them," said Judith, " their case is hopeless." Looking up at the moment she saw a smile on the colonel's face, which somehow brought a faint blush to her own pale
cheek, and she quickly added in a more reserved tone, drawing
back a step or two at the same time :

" This young Norman knight—pardon me, colonel, if I ask
where he joined your company, or what you know of him ?"

" Surely you may ask," said the colonel, regarding her with
increasing surprise, " although I be little used to be thus catechised
by ladies. I was journeying hither alone from Doe Castle where,
for the present, I have left my companions in arms—relying on
my memory for safe conduct to Charlemont Castle, and when
within a mile or so of entering this now desert region, I came
up with this Netterville, as he was making inquiries of a tall
peasant whom I took for an O'Dogherty, regarding the road
hitherward. Both being clad in this treasonable fashion, as you
see, we naturally exchanged a friendly greeting, followed by
some cursory remarks on the weather and other such common-
place matters, when, finding that our road lay in the same direction, we agreed to travel together, the more willingly when we
heard of the present state of this district. That was the first I
ever saw of Sir John Netterville, or he of me, so far as I know."

" Trust him not !" said Judith with startling vehemence ; " he
is fickle as the wind, or I much mistake, and there is a fearful
fountain of hate welling up within him that may one day work
evil to others besides its present object. See you not that he
now hates Maguire—no one can tell, then, how soon that hatred
may extend itself to all who are Maguire's friends. Believe me,
oh champion of the Gael ! no man of his blood ever yet espoused

in good faith the cause in which you are about to draw your sword."

"Heaven grant you be not a prophetess, fair lady!" said O'Neill thoughtfully, as he took her hand with an air of profound respect; "much depend on these Palesmen at this hour, an' they are but sincere in their present endeavors they may do good service—for me, I would fain believe them so—but—but—" he stopped and hesitated.

"Little said is soon mended," put in Judith with a smile that lit up her pensive features; "God be with you, colonel," she added still with the same bright look, as he shook her hand at parting, "an' we never meet again on earth, the memory of this hour shall be with us in our solitude,—that it was given us, poor and lonely women, to welcome *Owen O'Neill* to the land which, under God, he is commissioned to free. we shall ever esteem as a signal vouchsafement from on high—go your ways now, in God's name, and I pray you overlook the delay caused by my woman's prattle——"

"Nay," said the colonel gallantly, as he approached to take leave of the old lady; "nay, surely, I esteem not that delay unprofitable—much may it aid the cause hereafter—ay, marry, in more ways than one! Wife of O'Cahan, fare you well! In your prayers forget not Owen O'Neill or those who go up with him to battle for the right, and believe me your affairs shall not be unremembered by me. More I say not now!—farewell!' and he turned to leave the vault when the sound of loud and angry voices on the outside made him stop to listen.

"Merciful Heaven!" cried Judith, "it is *his* voice; oh! mother! mother! hear you that?"

"Child, I do," said the aged parent, "but I fear him not now—there be one present whom he must obey—fear not, daughter, for God himself taking pity on our misery, hath brought this meeting about."

Before the colonel could even ask what it all meant, a hoarse, mocking laugh re-echoed through the vault, the clank of heavily-ironed boots was heard approaching, and a man's voice cursing the obscurity of the place. "By my faith, Sir John Netterville," added the grumbler, "there be no Norman of the Pale fit to

stand between me and my liking! ha! ha! a stripling, with
scarce more than woman's strength, to tell Sir Phelim O'Neill
that he needs must do his bidding—an' I had no mind to enter,
foolish boy, I would see the matter out were it but to spite you."

"Sir Phelim, you shall answer for this!" cried Netterville,
behind him in the passage.

"Answer! to be sure I will, whensoever you choose." He suddenly stopped, and the mocking laugh died away in his throat,
for before him, full in the red torchlight, stood Owen O'Neill, his
tall form drawn to its fullest height, and an angry frown knitting
his brow. So unexpected was this apparition that the turbulent
knight of Kinnard was struck dumb for a moment. Not even the
sight of Judith and her mother, although his eye wandered to
both, could draw off his spell-bound attention from the figure
before him.

"Have I the honor of seeing Sir Phelim O'Neill?" said the colonel in a keenly sarcastic tone, after the pair had eyed each other
a few moments in silent scrutiny.

"Such is my name; what may yours be?"

"Somewhat like unto your own—I am *Owen* O'Neill."

"I thought as much, for smooth though your face be, the
seal of our race is on your brow, and its fiery spirit burning in
your eye. Be you welcome!"—and he reached out his hand
which Owen took with an air of condescension that must have
been galling to the pride of his overbearing kinsman—" my errand
abroad to-day was to give you a meeting, and conduct you to
the presence of the chiefs assembled at Charlemont Castle. Good
sooth, I little thought to find you like Achilles of old amongst
the petticoats! As for the ladies"—there was a sneering emphasis on the word—" I marvel not to see them so located or in
such a condition, for I know them to affect the company of owls
and bats. Save you, good mother, and you, fair Judith! I' faith,
a goodly dwelling you have chosen—the minister's, as I hope to
eat my supper—ho! ho! ho!"

"Better the company of owls and bats than that of recreant
knights," said Judith proudly, "and better a thousand times this
desolate ruin and freedom than castle or bower and servile
chains."

" Well said, Judith," quoth Sir Phelim, with another burst of
laughter; "you were ever glib with that tongue of yours—a
pretty hen old madam is, and a dainty chicken you—good sooth,
I much admire the flight you took and your wings cut so closely.
I wish you joy of your liberty!" The ironical tone in which he
spoke was not lost on his kinsman, nor yet the sinister look
wherewith he regarded both mother and daughter, the latter
especially.

" Sir Phelim O'Neill!" said Owen with the calm, mild dignity
of a master-spirit, "I much rejoice to meet you in this presence.
This young gentleman and I," pointing to Netterville, who stood
by in sullen silence, "being obliged by the storm to take shelter
here, heard with amazement, and, I must say, with indignation,
(towards whom you may guess!) the story of these ladies'
wrongs. I now wish you to understand that henceforward I will
have my eye on them—mark my words, Sir Phelim!—and the
man who dares insult their poverty, be he friend or foe, shall
answer to me for the outrage. Nay, no blustering, cousin mine,"
seeing that Sir Phelim was getting up a display of passion. "I
am not the man to be bullied—swaggering will not do with me.
I am willing to forget what is past, in this matter, but only on
condition that you leave these ladies free to do as they list."

" By the soul of Heremon!" said Sir Phelim, in a tone of
affected good humor, "you make over free for the length of our
acquaintance. Who made you the champion of these ladies?" .

" My knightly honor," rejoined Owen, "and the fame and
honor of our house—also my respect for the memory of a brave
and unfortunate chieftain. But here we may not longer tarry—
I have told you my mind on this head, and as you value my good
will see that you keep it in mind!"

Sir Phelim nodded a sort of assent, and glancing furtively at
Judith, said as he turned to lead the way out: "No need for all
this pother—the birds are not worth the trouble of catching
them. Good betide you, noble dames, for all Sir Phelim O'Neill
cares; ye may wed these two so valorous knights when ye list,
ay, the precious pair of you!"

" Lead on!" said Owen sternly; "no jesting at our expense—
nay, Sir John, heed not his idle words—lead on, Sir Phelim—

we follow." The knight saw fit to obey in silence, and the other
gentlemen having once more exchanged a parting salute with
the recluses, all three sallied forth into the clear sunlight, where
a party of Sir Phelim's followers were in waiting. The cheers
wherewith they greeted the appearance of Owen Roe O'Neill
made the desolate valley ring, and sent a thrill of joy through
the heart that seemed cold and passionless.

CHAPTER. III.

"No! when the battle rages dire,
And tho rouse 1 soul is all on fire,
Think'st thou a noble heart can stay
Hate's rancorous inpulse to obey ?"
        Mrs. Holford's *Margaret of Anjou.*

"What shall he be ere night? Perchance a thing
O'er which the raven flaps his funeral wing!"
        Byron's *Corsair.*

It was three months before the date of the events recorded in
our last chapter, when the long dreary season of winter had
passed away, and spring-time gladdened the earth, sending the
rills and rivulets laughing on their way, and making the woods
and meadows vocal with the song of birds. The cuckoo, "har-
binger of spring," made the woods of Carrick resound with her
one welcome note, and the lovely Suir was more radiant even
than its wont in silver sheen bedight. All without and around
the ancient castle of the Butlers was bright and balmy, fresh
and fragrant as the April day could make it, and the day was
the loveliest of the season, just such another as queer, quaint old
Herbert lovingly eulogizes :

"Swe t day, so cool, so calm, so bright,
The bridal of the earth and sky,"

yet, for all the beauty of the outward scene, there was little of
joy or "sweet content" within that lordly dwelling. The Countess sat with her infant daughter in her arms—in those good old
times even a Countess thought it nowise *vulgar* to be seen with
her children on her right honorable knee or even clasped in her

jewelle! arms—so the Countess sat with her infant on her knee at an open window, and although her eyes wandered at times over the fair scene without, it was not that she enjoyed its beauty, or dwelt upon its charms. Deep sadness was seated on her lofty brow, and albeit that Elizabeth of Ormond was not much given to the "melting mood," a close observer, had there been any such, might have noticed a tear now and then stealing down her cheek as she bent over the slumbering babe on whose face she gazed so fondly. And wherefore was the noble lady sad on that bright spring morning when all nature was glad? Alas! she deemed her dejection not without cause, for she knew that the dawn of that fair day had seen her lord set out from Dublin with a gallant army to wage war against the Confederate forces of Leinster. Whatever Ormond might be unto others, to her, at least, and to his children, he was all that a husband and father ought to be, and dreary was the void which his absence ever left in the domestic circle. But what was the tedium, the weariness of absence to the heart-wearing fears of a soldier's wife when her husband went forth

" ——To the wars, to the red field of fight,"

where death was certain to many and escape to none. What though helm and plume, and pennon gay, and the tramp of warlike men made a gallant show as Ormond's army moved along, or that Ormond himself waved the proudest plume and wore the noblest mien—it mattered not to the loving and pitying heart of Elizabeth, for her eyes were not gladdened by the proud array, while her soul was full of the bitter thought that the stately form of her husband might at any moment be struck down by the rude pike of some low-born hind. And to do the Countess justice we needs must tell that her sorrow was not altogether of a selfish nature. Her sympathies were still in great part with the Catholics struggling for their rights, and she wished that Ormond had not been sent on what she justly considered a mission of destruction.

"Alas! alas!" sighed the lady, "that a heart so generous as Ormond's to all besides should be so hard and pitiless in regard to the Catholics!—child! child!" and again her tears fell on the

infant's face, "to think that your father should be made to
play the part of a Coote, an Inchiquin, and a Broghill! Oh!
woe is me, that his children should inherit the curse of an oppressed nation!—what, Emmeline! are there tidings so soon?—
you seem excited."

"No tidings from the Earl, madam, that I know of," said the
person thus addressed, a pale but very lovely girl who had just
entered the room in what appeared no small trepidation.

"From whom, or where, then?" demanded the Countess with
a searching glance at her pallid face; "some news I read on
that tell-tale face—out with it, pretty one! be it what it may!—
stay—let me look at you—tell me, Emmeline! have you heard
from Dublin?"

"That have I not," the fair girl replied, "the news concerns
us all—not as your ladyship seems to suppose, only myself.
Prepare yourself, madam, to hear what I would that other lips
than mine had to tell."

Hearing this the Countess laughed. "Why, lady-bird, an' the
news affects not *my* absent lord, nor another whose name we
name not, how can it concern us all?"

"Think a moment, gracious madam! and your keen wit may
remind you of other dangers to be apprehended now even by
ourselves!"

"Great God! you cannot mean the approach of the—of the
rebels?—speak, Emmeline,—do you mean *that?*" and firm and
self-possessed as the Countess usually was, she turned pale and
actually trembled.

"Madam, I *do* mean that," the girl replied; "little as we
looked for their coming, it appears they are close at hand.
Hearing, I suppose, of your lord's departure from Dublin this
morning on the Leinster campaign, they have taken it into their
thick heads to be even with him, by revenging themselves on
his family and the walls of his castle. Truly, such a barbarous
device well becomes traitorous rebels! But your ladyship is
faint. I pray you summon up that high courage which I know
you to possess—let me summon your attendants—nay, madam
it may yet be possible to escape!"

"Not so, Emmeline, not so,—there is none—none—*none*—my

heart tells me we are all to perish—or worse—worse—and you,
too, daughter of my dearest friend! that you should be here to
share our wretched fate——"

"But, madam, they will not, perchance, dare——"

"I tell you they will dare all—too glad to revenge themselves
on James Butler whom they look upon with deadlier hate as a
renegade from their religion! Heavens above! they are in the
park—they surround the house even now! Emmeline! go you
to my children—gather them together, with all the women of
the household, and I will join you anon when I have conferred
with the captain of the guard."

Some half dozen of terrified female domestics, now rushed
unbidden to their lady's presence, bemoaning the sad fate which
awaited them, and refusing to believe that escape of any kind
was still possible. A few words of stern command from the
Countess had the effect of stopping their clamor, at least, and
with an assurance that all hope was not yet lost, she dismissed
them with the infant to join the general assembly of the household convoked by her orders. Emmeline still lingered, and the
Countess, forgetful of her previous request, seemed desirous to
have her remain.

"Could we but see any of their leaders," said the Countess
anxiously, as she moved somewhat nearer one of the windows,
"we might the better guess what awaits us; who, think you, are
they?"

"One of them I know, at least," said the fair Emmeline from
the recess of another window; "sees not your ladyship the Butler arms on yonder flag?"

"Child, you are right," said the Countess, and she drew a long
breath like one much relieved; "Mountgaret is there—oh! recreant scion of the Butlers!"

The door of the apartment just then opened, and a message
was delivered from the officer in command of the garrison requesting permission to speak with her ladyship.

"I was just going in search of you, Captain Jameson," said
the Countess with a condescending bow, "with a view to ascertain whether it were possible to hold the Castle against yonder
rebels. I fear me much that from an over sense of security,

still more than his frequent absence, my lord the Earl hath not
given due attention of late to the defences of the house. How
is it, Captain? Be the chances for or against us?"

"*Against* us, madam, as far as I am able to judge," returned the
gentlemanly officer, the same whom we have seen retiring from
the service in disgust because of the wanton cruelties of Coote.
"My good lord hath, as you say, somewhat neglected the affairs
of the garrison, notwithstanding that I made bold to remind him
by letter of the same more than once or twice. Having the defence of the kingdom in hand, it is little wonder if he forgot to
examine into the capabilities of this his noble Castle for sustaining a siege."

"He deemed it nowise likely," said the Countess, "that the
rebels should make such head here in Munster under the eye of
stout St. Leger, but, wo is me! that his wonted prudence should
fail in such wise, knowing that the chief lords of the country
are now in open rebellion—know you the strength of the enemy,
Captain?"

"That I have not been able as yet to ascertain, madam, but I
should judge it to be considerable since they make bold to attack this Castle of Carrick, and likewise from the officers of distinction whom I see with them."

Here the trumpet sounded for a parley, and Captain Jameson
hastened to the ramparts. During his short absence, Lady Ormond went to see her children, and calm their infant fears,
excited to agony by the senseless ravings of their English attendants, to whose terror-stricken fancy the clansmen of Munster
assumed the proportions and almost the propensities of the giants
of nursery lore. Leaving the Countess to reassure the frighten-
ened children, and equally frightened domestics, as best she
might, in the presence of the awful fact that "Mountgarret's
men" were in untold numbers round the house, let us return to
the fair Emmeline thus left alone.

During the brief colloquy between the Countess and Captain
Jameson the young lady had kept her station in the window,
watching intently the movements of the besiegers. All unnoticed
by her were the furtive glances of admiration sent in her direction by the Captain, who was not unknown to her, although it

happened that *she* was to him. Whatever her thoughts might
have been, she kept them to herself, but no sooner had Lady
Ormond left the room, than she began to commune with herself
in a half audible tone.

"Of a surety, an' the Castle be taken, as I much fear it will,
for I see they have no lack of cannon or aught that is needful
—an' the place be taken, my presence here might make it go
hard with the Countess and her dear children. Whatsoever treatment they may have a mind to give to Lord Ormond's family,
mercy I could not look for at their hands. And yet"—her beautiful face brightened for a moment, but the ray of light passed
quickly away—"few there are among their motley host like
unto *him*. No! no! I will not, cannot risk the chance of drawing deadlier vengeance on my honored friend and her helpless
children. But how—how—to escape unseen! Try it I must,
however, relying on God's assistance. Now for a disguise—God
direct me which to choose!"

Meanwhile the Castle had been summoned to surrender in the
name of the Catholic army of Munster, to which Jameson replied,
as a brave officer should, that if they desired to have it they
must *take* it, for given up willingly it never should be—so long
as a man remained to defend it.

"Then you are willing to expose Lady Ormond and her family
to the dangers of a siege?" said an officer, evidently of rank,
who, with a herald bearing a white flag, approached within ear-
shot.

"The Countess is much beholden to you, for your kind consideration," made answer Captain Jameson, with cool irony, "but
she prefers rather to run such risk, trusting to the strength of
these walls, than to——"

"To what?" demanded the Irish officer sternly; "I am ready
to pledge my word of honor that in case you give up the castle
quietly, her ladyship and every member of her household shall
have safe convoy to Dublin or wheresoever she may please to
appoint. An' you rashly resolve to hold out, the consequences
be on your own head. We are not ignorant, as you may
suppose, of your actual strength, and are, therefore, not to be
deceived by idle boasting. Our strength you see, or rather you

do *not* see its full extent, but, believe me, it is more than sufficient to take Carrick Castle—ay! even were Ormond himself of the garrison——"

Jameson's practised eye was not slow to perceive that *this* at least was no idle boast, for no one knew better than he that the strength of the building was more apparent than real. Had not the safety of Lady Ormond and her children been in question, he might have ventured to hold out in hopes of succor, but the stake was too heavy to be risked on his own responsibility, and he felt that under the circumstances, it was his painful duty to capitulate. The Countess was of the same opinion, notwithstanding her unwillingness to have it told that Ormond's Castle was in the hands of the rebels. Charged with full power to capitulate in the name of Lady Ormond, the captain returned to the ramparts. The herald still waited without, and the officer who had before spoken, immediately rode up, accompanied by two others.

"Before the noble Countess of Ormond can entertain any proposals," said Captain Jameson, "she desires to know whose word it is that she has to depend upon for safety and protection!"

"I had thought," returned the officer proudly, "that yonder heraldic device," pointing to the flag already noticed by those within the castle, "had sufficiently informed the wife of James Butler. An' she needs must have a name, tell her it is Colonel Edmund Butler who commands these forces—being so little informed on the subject," he added, in a sarcastic tone, "Lady Ormond may require to be told that Lord Mountgarret is *my* father —and—I am *his* son!—she will, I hope, deem my plighted word sufficient security—but, hark you! sir, we are somewhat pressed for time, and must be so far wanting in courtesy as to demand a speedy answer!"

In a very few minutes the Captain returned with a definitive answer that Elizabeth of Ormond was well content to trust in the honor and good faith of her much-esteemed cousin, Colonel Butler, whose proposal she would willingly accept, hoping that in his hands the castle should sustain as little injury as might be.

The Colonel was only too happy to take charge of the place on such terms, "although," as he jocularly remarked to Lord

Skerrin who was with him at the moment, " my fair kinswoman
may make her mind easy on that head, inasmuch as, with God's
help, the care of the house shall never more rest on *her* shoulders—her much-esteemed cousin!—ha! ha! truly, the noble Countess hath small cause to esteem any of our house at this present,
seeing that my father hath taken her castle of Kilkenny, and
his son her castle of Carrick! Fitzpatrick!" to a young lieutenant near him, " have the goodness to see what is going forward
around yonder postern! our men seem in a sort of commotion
there. Stay, I will e'en see for myself."

Before the Colonel had reached the sally port, he was met
by some of his own men with a prisoner whom they had taken
lurking in the shade of the walls, and who craved speech of the
Irish commander.

" He is a retainer of the house," said one of the soldiers in
Irish.

" So I perceive," said the Colonel," but what is your business
out, good fellow ?"

" That will I tell your noble lordship full quickly," replied the
Ormond servitor in a voice trembling either with fear or some
other emotion, " an' you grant me a private hearing—I like not
the looks of these followers of yours, and what I have to say
may not reach their ears!"

" A deserter, by St. Bridget's girdle!" said Fitzpatrick aloud to
a brother officer, and the word went round from man to man
with a boisterous roar of merriment, as the stout clansmen
of Munster and the equally stout Normans of the Pale eyed
with contempt the fragile and drooping form of the youthful
prisoner.

There was something in the tone and manner of the lad which
attracted the Colonel's attention, and perhaps excited his suspicions, so, telling the same party who had taken him to follow at
a little distance, he dismounted and led the way to where a
clump of trees screened them from observation.

" Speak on now—I listen!" said the Colonel, " but first I
would see your face."

" You would know me none the better, though you saw it.
You suspect some disguise, and you are right—I am not what I

seem, but rather a distressed damsel coming to claim the knight-ly protection of Colonel Butler !"

" An' you come from within the Castle," said the officer with a polite bow, trying at the same time to catch a glimpse of the face under the slouched hat, "an' you come from within the Castle, fair lady, you might surely have spared yourself this trouble, seeing that my ' knightly protection,' as you say, is already pledged for the safety of the female inmates——"

" It is well, and I joy to hear it, Colonel," said the lady, "but unhappily I have reason to fear that my presence, if known to your people, would endanger the safety of which you speak—hence it is that I am here.'

"Who, in God's name, are you then ?" cried the Colonel in surprise, "that you hold yourself beyond the pale of Irish honor or generosity ?"

Drawing a step or two nearer, so as to lessen the chances of being overheard, Emmeline—for she it was—gave her name and parentage in full.

Colonel Butler heard her with a blanched cheek and an ominous start. " By our Lady ! but that alters the matter !"—he said with a thoughtful air—" I marvel not that you feared to fall into the hands of Catholic soldiers. The knowledge of your lineage might tempt them sorely, but as God liveth, lady, they would not harm you—no, not even *your* father's daughter."

" Still I would rather not trust them, Colonel !"

" I tell you," said the chivalrous Butler, somewhat nettled at her want of confidence, " I tell you, fair mistress ! there is not a man in yonder force, that would harm a hair of your head, were I even to tell them who you are, if so be that they knew you had thrown yourself on us for protection."

" I implore you, Colonel Butler, put them not to what they might deem so hard a test——"

" How would you have me dispose of you," interrupted the Colonel—" I see my presence is again required—lady, speak your wishes !"

" An' it so please you, gallant sir, I would be sent to the nunnery in the town within, until such time as I can safely be conveyed to Dublin."

"That is just where I purpose placing the Countess and her family," said the Colonel, "until I have heard from my lord of Ormond. I pray you excuse me for a moment!" Calling to one of the men whom he had stationed near, he desired that Sir John Netterville might come to him. The message had hardly time to be delivered when that young officer made his appearance, with a gay : " What would you, Colonel ?"

" I am about to honor you with a mission of trust, Sir John," the Colonel replied with a good-humored smile. Lowering his voice almost to a whisper, he told him : " You are to convey this prisoner without loss of time to the convent in Carrick. Take a small party with you for escort—or stay—yourself will be quite sufficient with one attendant to bring back the horse we send with the prisoner—there be little danger of a rescue—ha! ha! ha!—you understand me, I hope !"

" Not over well, Colonel, but your bidding shall be done. By my faith, though, the errand is not so honorable as you would have me believe—at least, on the face of it!" And he glanced with a humorous eye at the somewhat shabby exterior of the serving-man of the house of Ormond whom he, a knight and a noble, was ordered to escort. A horse was quickly prepared for the prisoner, and, to the no small amusement of his brother offi- cers, Netterville trotted off as his guard to the town.

To say the truth the young noble was not altogether pleased at being selected for what seemed so ridiculous a mission, and, to the great satisfaction of his charge, he spoke not a word dur- ing their brief journey. When the old bridge was passed, and great part of the main street of the town, the knight drew up at the gate of the convent, on the corner of one of the cross streets, and then it was that his prisoner raised the slouched hat and disclosed to his astonished escort features indelibly engraved in his heart.

" Now, Sir John Netterville," said the lady with a bright blush on her delicate cheek, " now, you can claim admission for me. I own it did seem rather foolish, escorting a lacquey of the house of Ormond to a convent for protection, but now I hope you are satisfied that Colonel Butler really meant to pay you a compli- ment. For my own part, I am much beholden to you—indeed,

Sir John, I am—and would to God I might in any way contribute to make you happy—but that the fates have forbidden!—fare you well! Sir John Netterville! my father himself may one day thank you for this most signal service!"

"Great Heavens! is it you then—you, Emmeline—whom I have had near me so long!—cruel as you are, you will not go without telling me what this means—nay, I implore you, tell me!—alas! how little dreamed I that yonder castle of the Butlers held so rich a prize! But tell me why this secret departure—why this base disguise?"

In very few words Emmeline explained, and by that time the aged portress had hobbled to the door, asking through a small grating who waited without. Being told that a lady was there for whom Colonel Edmund Butler demanded shelter and protection, the venerable dame waddled away again, but returned in a few moments with a message that the reverend mother was only too happy to oblige Colonel Butler. The key grated in the rusty lock, and Emmeline threw herself lightly from the horse, and after exchanging a friendly farewell with the knight, stepped across the threshold, forgetful of her disguise. It was only when reminded of it by the old woman's exclamation of surprise, that she unbuckled her girdle with a smile, and the borrowed feathers falling off, she stood before the guardian of the gate in a rich but sober female costume. A grunt of satisfaction escaped the lips of the fat portress, as she closed the door on the young knight, and shut in, it might be, for ever from his eyes, the graceful form of Emmeline, the long and vainly loved.

Two hours after, Carrick Castle was delivered to the Confederate force, the Countess of Ormond, her children and servants, sent for the present to the Convent, over which a strong guard was placed, and the garrison permitted to march out in good order and betake themselves whither they listed.

Messengers were instantly dispatched by Colonel Butler to Lord Ormond acquainting him with what had taken place, and desiring to know whither he would have his family conveyed. It was the evening of the following day when Lieutenant Fitzpatrick returned with the answer to the Castle, now the headquarters of the Confederates in that section of the country.

Lord Ormond, he said, when he did, at length, overtake him, refused to receive Colonel Butler's epistle, alleging that he could hold no communication with rebels. Nettled at this, the reckless young officer told him very bluntly what had happened, asking in an ironical tone whether his lordship would condescend, after that, to read the Colonel's letter.

"Not on any account," was the answer, which the Earl took care should be heard by many of his officers; "my wife and family are in God's keeping, and even for *their* sakes, I may not encourage rebellion by holding written communication with them."

"This is your lordship's final answer?"

"It is, so help me Heaven!"

"Let me tell you, then, my lord earl," returned the hot-blooded young Ossory man, "you may reckon over much on Colonel Butler's generosity and forbearance. Sending such an answer you surely must forget the number of blackened walls and ruined homesteads which mark *your* track!"

"What said the Earl to that?" demanded the Colonel with ominous composure.

"He said I would do well to keep my tongue from wagging so glibly, and bade me to be thankful that I was suffered to escape with impunity; commanding me at the same time to quit his presence instantly, a command which I had no temptation to resist, knowing that you were anxiously awaiting an answer."

Colonel Butler, although some years younger than his kinsman, Ormond, was not without a share of Ormond's prudence, so that when questioned by Lord Skerrin and others of the officers as to what he purposed doing, he merely answered that his mind was not yet made up. Early next morning, however, he repaired in person to the Convent, and having told the Countess of her husband's heartless conduct, he ended by saying:

"Your ladyship and all those of your company, are, however, free,—free to go where and when you will. We, at least, war not against women and children."

"Colonel Butler," said the Countess with much emotion, "Elizabeth of Ormond thanks you, and will be mindful of your generosity while her heart continues to beat."

" Oh recreant scion of the Butlers !" said Emmeline softly at
her elbow, and the arch girl shook her finger playfully in the
face of her noble friend, " even recreants, you see, are at times
exceeding useful !" Then aloud, she, too, tendered her best
thanks to the Colonel.

Half an hour after that, Lady Ormond with her young friend,
her children and servants, were journeying rapidly towards
Dublin, escorted by a troop of Irish cavalry. What thoughts
coursed each other through the mind of those two Protestant ladies
as they travelled in safety under such protection the reader may
easily imagine.

Four weeks had barely passed away after the taking of Carrick Castle, when Emmeline and her mother were summoned
from a saloon of Dublin Castle, crowded with the beauty and
fashion of the metropolis, to receive, at their own gate, a mournful cortege, bearing home the body of the husband and father
from the scene of his tragic end—a tyrant even in his own
family, the man had not one fond heart to mourn his loss, yet
the manner of his death was so awfully sudden, and the tidings
came so unexpectedly, that all were filled with horror, if not
with grief. The pale sorrow-worn wife, however, who might
well have considered his death a boon, could not help remembering with a softening heart the thirty odd years they had past
together, and the sunny days of her early married life ere the
pursuit of arms had developed the latent cruelty of her consort,
and made his heart hard to all human pity. His two sons, men
of strong robust frame and iron will like their father, were too
fully imbued with his spirit not to feel a burning thirst for
revenge, and (if that were possible) a deadlier hatred of the
already detested Catholics. Such were the varied feelings of
the mother and her sons, but for Emmeline, the only daughter
of that house, what she felt was not so easily defined, and moreover it lay farther beneath the surface.

It was a strange sight to see the stately matron and her beautiful daughter receiving that grisly corpse; they radiant with
jewels and floating, as it were, in a mist of rich lace and gauzy
silk,* the dead wrapped in his bloody war-cloak, his grey locks

* We are told by Walker, quoting an English author, that the

13

matted with gore. His sons, too, in their brilliant court-uni-form, presented a strange contrast with him whom they had so often followed to victory, as they stood there side by side with folded arms and knitted brows looking sternly down on the unsightly form before them. Oh! it was a strange scene, a sad and solemn scene, its awful silence seldom broken by word or groan, or sigh. Passion was at work under various forms in the depth of every heart, but its workings were kept far down below the surface by the stern strong will that governed each.

It was night when the corpse was brought home, and accord-ing to the custom of those people then, as now, it was laid out in solemn lonely state in one of the principal apartments, with two great wax tapers at the head and two more at the feet. At the lonely hour of midnight, when the weary watchers in the ante-room were fast asleep, Emmeline stood like a white-robed spirit by the couch of death, her pale face looking paler still under the long tresses of fair silky hair which hung over her shoulders in wild disorder. Her eyes were stony and fixed as those of a statue, and her clasped hands rested against her bosom—the whole figure motionless and silent as though no breath of life warmed the heart within.

At last the beautiful lips parted and a sigh, a deep-drawn sigh, came forth, and another moment's pause, and Emmeline spoke in a low murmuring voice like the whisper of ocean-shells :

"Father, blame me not if my words *were* prophetic!—thou knowest, oh! author of my days! that it was a fiendish act, and the groans of *his* anguish rent my heart asunder—but still—still —I was wrong—oh! how wrong to speak such bitter words for a father's ear!—alas! alas! I deemed not then that the dark hour was so near at hand! God pity you, my father, as you lie there with a mountain weight of blood upon your soul and the curses of so many widows and orphans ringing on the midnight

---

Irish court-dress of that day was peculiarly rich and even splendid ! " Here," says Howell, the writer in question, " here is a most splendid court kept at the Castle, and except that of the Viceroy of Naples, I have not seen the like in Christendom.—Walker *on the dress of the Irish*, p. 60.

air around you! We loved not, oh father! thou wouldst not
have us love thee, but oh! my heart is breaking with the thought
that I—I thy only daughter—did as it were evoke this untimely
end! To my dying day I shall have this dismal sight before
mine eyes, as the heart-wrung groans of one too well beloved are
ever in my ear—oh! that eye could see or ear could hear no
more!—oh! that this heart were as cold and pulseless as thine
now is! But, great God, who visiteth the sins of the fathers on
their children, I must e'en wait till thy rigorous justice hath
been satisfied in my regard! Father! farewell! if it afford thy
vengeful spirit aught of consolation, know that the daughter who
gave thy paternal heart such a deadly wound is as miserable as
even thou couldst wish!"

Stooping down she kissed the ghastly brow of the sleeper,
and muttering to herself, "I might not, dare not, would not kiss
him thus, were he not dead—dead!" She glided again through
the ante-room, where the hired watchers still slumbered on, and
unseen, unheard, reached her own apartments just as a fierce gust
of wind shook the doors and windows of the old house. All that
night the wild storm howled without, moaning dismally in the
passages and wide chimneys, and making all within the house to
shudder. It seemed as if legions of tortured ghosts were keeping watch and ward over that lifeless body, shrieking for vengeance on the parted soul—and little wonder if they were in
shadowy crowds around, for it was SIR CHARLES COOTE that lay
there dead!*

---

* The ancient town of Trim was, as Carte quaintly observes, " the
tragic stage whereon he (Coote) acted his last part." Brewer, in his
Beauties of Ireland, gives the following account of the death of Coote :
" Whilst the town was possessed by the parliamentary party, in 1642,
it became the scene of a skirmish that proved fatal to Sir Charles
Coote, of ensanguined memory. The Irish beset the town, at the
break of day, in a tumultuous party, said to have been 3,000 strong.
Sir Charles, on the first alarm, issued from the gate, at the head of a
few horse soldiers, leaving others to follow as quickly as they could
muster. In the charge which he made upon the assailants, Coote was
shot dead, and it was thought that the ball was discharged by one of
his own troopers."

CHAPTER IV.

"Oh heaven! he cried, my bleeding country save!
Is there no arm on high to shield the brave ?
Yet, though destruction sweep those lovely plains,
Rise, follow-men! our country yet remains!
By that dread name, we wave the sword on high
And swear with her to live—with her to die!'
CAMPBELL's Pleasures of Hope.

On the 10th day of May, just three days after the tragical end of Sir Charles Coote, the patriot prelates of Ireland, with very few exceptions, came together by previous appointment in the ancient city of the Butlers, to deliberate with such of the lay-lords as could conveniently be present, on the affairs of the pending struggle. After many days of calm and prayerful deliberation, during which divers wise rules and regulations were devised and ordained, a solemn scene took place in the old Cathedral Church of St. Canice, when all the lords, temporal and spiritual, and all the Catholic knights and gentlemen then within the city, assembled by appointment to take the oath of association, drawn up by the bishops as a bond of union between the so-long conflicting races now embarking in the same glorious cause.

It was evening, and the last beams of the setting sun were reflected in all the colors of the rainbow in diagonal lines verging towards the high altar from the richly-stained windows facing westward. "The young May moon," dimly visible in the azure firmament, waited but the withdrawal of the more brilliant luminary to shed in her mild rays on the tesselated pavement and the time-worn walls, and the solemn assembly of the holy, the brave, and the noble.

Many tapers were burning on and around the grand altar, votive offerings from the knights and nobles present to Our Lady and good St. Canice; and their light fell on the calm, collected features of the bishops and other dignitaries of the Church as they occupied the stalls and benches of the chancel. Without the rood-screen in the spacious nave, stood a crowd of the noblest and bravest of the land, most of them men of Norman blood, for the summons to take the oath had not as yet reached the Irish country, whereas Kilkenny being one of the chief cities of the Pale, its Catholic lords and gentry were there in numbers. Almost the only noble of Irish extraction present was Lord Muskerry, but of the spiritual lords, the highest dignitaries were of the old blood, although very many of the inferior orders of the clergy were of English extraction. But there was one Irish chieftain present, who might well look with a swelling heart on that proud array, for the organization now at length assuming tangible shape had been first conceived in his fertile brain, and owed more of its present strength to him than to any other living man. That chieftain was Rory O'More, who, with his constant friend, Plunket, stood in a corner just behind where Lord Muskerry sat with the banner of MacCarthy hanging in heavy folds above him.

It were hard to describe O'More's thoughts when, just as the first ray of moonlight streamed in through a window opposite, Hugh O'Neill, the venerable primate, ascended the steps of the altar, and, after a short but touching prayer, gave utterance to the solemn words* which each one present repeated after him, holding up their right hands.

* The oath of association taken by the Confederate Catholics was as follows: "I ———— do profess, swear, and protest before God, and His saints and angels, that I will, during my life, bear true faith and allegiance to my Sovereign Lord, Charles, by the grace of God, King of Great Britain, France, and Ireland, and to his heirs and lawful successors; and that I will, to my power, during my life, defend, uphold, and maintain all his and their just prerogatives, estates, and rights, the power and privilege of the Parliament of this realm, the fundamental laws of Ireland, the free exercise of the Roman Catholic faith and religion throughout this land; and the lives, just liberties, possessions, estates, and rights of all those that have taken, or that shall take this oath, and perform the contents thereof; and that I will obey and ratify all the orders and decrees made and to be made by

"Thank God," exclaimed O'More, with that fervor which belonged to his character, as he and Plunket quitted the Church side by side, and turned in the direction of the river to enjoy a moonlight stroll on its verdant banks; "thank God, Plunket, things begin to stand on a more solid foundation—much hath been already done by this synod——"

"Truly yes," said Plunket, "this oath was happily devised—pray Heaven it answer the intent of its pious framers and clasp the *old* and *new* Irish together for so long as this struggle lasts! An' the vessel fall to pieces again, before our enemies are brought to terms, the condition of the people will be worse than it ever hath been."

"Marry, so think I, but, pri'thee, Richard, let us not give way to gloomy imaginings now when all seems bright and of good promise. I would there had been more of the old blood present, so that the voices of all blending in that solemn vow, the bond of union might be henceforward and for ever cemented with brotherly love. What thinkest thou, keen lawyer as thou art, of these rules already drawn up and the ordinances made?"*

the Supreme Council of the Confederate Catholics of this kingdom, concerning the said public cause; and I will not seek, directly or indirectly, any pardon or protection for any act done, or to be done, touching this general cause, without the consent of the major part of said council, and that I will not, directly or indirectly, do any act or acts that shall prejudice the said cause, but will, to the hazard of my life and estate, assist, prosecute, and maintain the same.

"Moreover, I do further swear that I will not accept of, or submit unto, any peace made, or to be made, with the said Confederate Catholics, without the consent and approbation of the general assembly of the said Confederate Catholics, and for the preservation and strengthening of the association and union of the kingdom. That upon any peace or accommodation to be made or concluded with the said Confederate Catholics as aforesaid, I will, to the utmost of my power, insist upon and maintain the ensuing propositions, until a peace, as aforesaid, be made, and the matters to be agreed upon in the articles of peace to be established, and secured by Parliament. So help me, God, and His holy Gospel."

"Such," says Rev. Mr. Meehan in his *Confederation of Kilkenny*, "such was this solemn oath, or 'fœdus,' which gave a distinct appellation to those who bound themselves by it, and whom we are henceforth to know as the Confederate Catholics of Ireland."

* The following enactments were made by this Council, "for the conservation and exercise of *this* union," viz.: between all "Irish

"It would ill become me to find fault with them," said Plunket with his humorous smile, "seeing that they be in part my own bantlings. However, such as they are, methinks no Capeers, magistrates, noblemen, cities, and provinces." Their wisdom, moderation, and entire fitness for the object in view, must strike all who read them :

I. Whereas, the war which now in Ireland the Catholics do maintain against sectaries, and chiefly against Puritans, for the defence of the Catholic religion,—for the maintenance of the prerogative and royal rights of our gracious King Charles,—for our gracious Queen, so unworthily abused by the Puritans,—for the honor, safety, and health of their royal issue,—for to avert and repair the injuries done to them,—for the conservation of the just and lawful safeguard, liberties, and rights of Ireland,—and, lastly, for the defence of their own lives, fortunes, lands, and possessions ;—whereas this war is undertaken for the aforesaid causes against unlawful usurpers, oppressors, and the enemies of the Catholics, chiefly Puritans, and that hereof we are informed, as well by divers and true remonstrances of divers provinces, counties, and noblemen, as also by the unanimous consent and agreement of almost the whole kingdom in this war and union,— we, therefore, declare that war, openly Catholic, to be lawful and just ; in which war, if some of the Catholics be found to proceed out of some particular and unjust title—covetousness, cruelty, revenge, or hatred, or any such unlawful private intentions—we declare them therein grievously to sin, and therefore worthy to be punished and restrained with ecclesiastical censures if, advised thereof, they do not amend.

II. Whereas the adversaries do spread divers rumors, do write divers letters, and, under the King's name, do print proclamations, which are not the King's, by which means divers plots and dangers may ensue unto our nation ; we, therefore, to stop the way of untruth, and forgeries of political adversaries, do will and command that no such rumors, letters, or proclamations, may have place or belief until it be known in a national council, whether they truly proceed from the King, left to his own freedom, and until agents of this kingdom, hereafter to be appointed by the National Council, have free passage to his Majesty, whereby the kingdom may be certainly informed of his Majesty's intention and will.

III. We straightly command all our inferiors, as well churchmen as laymen, to make no alienation, comparison, or difference between provinces, cities, towns, or families ; and lastly, not to begin or forward any emulations, or comparisons whatsoever.

IV. That in every province of Ireland there be a Council made up, both of clergy and nobility, in which council shall be so many persons, at least, as are counties in the province, and out of every city or notable town, two persons.

V. Let one general council of the whole kingdom be made, both of the clergy, nobility, cities, and notable towns, in which council there shall be three out of every province, and out of every city, one ; or

tholic can cavil at any of them.   The formation of the councils
is a grand stroke, a capital stroke, friend Roger, and as for the
other several ordinances, they serve, if other purpose they had
not, as a sort of creed for our National Confederation.   I tell
thee, Roger," said Plunket warming with his subject as he the
more considered it, " I tell thee, the work already done by this
assembly of lords, temporal and spiritual, will make amends to us
—ay! an hundred times over—for that unhappy affair of Mageny.   Nay, never look so downhearted, Roger! that was a heavy
blo⬤, God knows, but the wound it gave the nation happily
reached no vital part.   See you not how full of life we are—ay!
in truth, vigorous and lusty as the mountain roe, and as ready
to overleap all manner of obstacles that lie between us and
freedom.   Think no more of it, Roger, there was no blame attached to any who fought there——"

" Still, Richard, you must own it was discouraging, to say the
least of it.   Think of all the noble gentlemen whose names are
covered with the disgrace of that action.   There was Mountgarret himself, Dunboyne and Skerrin, Sir Morgan Cavanagh,
O'Byrne, and lastly, my humble self.   Such a show of men and
officers of note, and all for nothing—worse than nothing.   Ah!
Plunket, men may talk as they will of numerical strength, but,
after all, *discipline* is the main thing—we Irish were taught a
fearful lesson at that same bridge of Mageny, to wit, that vast

where cities are not, out of the chiefest towns   To this council the
provincial councils shall have subordination, and from thence to it
may be appealed, until this National Council shall have opportunity
to sit together.

VI. Let a faithful inventory be made, in every province, of the
murders, burnings, and other cruelties which are permitted by the
Puritan enemies, with a quotation of the place, day, cause, manner,
and persons, and other circumstances, subscribed by one of public
authority.

VII. We do declare and judge all and every such as do forsake
this union, fight for our enemies, accompany them in their war, defend, or in any way assist them, to be excommunicated, and, by these
presen's, do excommunicate them.

VIII. We will and declare all those that murder, dismember, or
grievously strike, all thieves, unlawful spoilers, robbers of any goods,
to be excommunicated, and so to remain till they completely amend
and satisfy, no less than if they were namely proclaimed excommunicated!"—Meehan's *Confederation of Kilkenny*, p. 30.

bodies of men are but an incumbrance on the field of battle if
they be not well trained and well accoutred."

"How, think you, will Clanrickarde and those of his party
take our ordinances?" said Plunket, partly with a view to
change what he knew was a painful subject.

"Not over well, I imagine, seeing that no alternative is left
them but excommunication, if so be they persevere in their
present abetment of the enemy's courses."

"Excommunication quotha!" repeated Plunket with that
caustic humor which ever characterized him; "methinks, Roger,
such Catholics as Ulick Burke take little heed of spiritual censures—so long as they be not debarred from government favor,
or the emoluments of office, the bishops may curse them ' bell,
book, and candle-light,' without troubling their digestion in the
least!—my God confound all such white-livered, time-serving
knaves, say I!"

"I do heartily admire your honest indignation, Richard!"
said O'More with his genial smile; "albeit that you may judge
my Lord Clanrickarde over harshly—I am told here that an
effort will shortly be made by some of the bishops to bring him
over to his rightful place in this struggle—let us wait to see
what effect their remonstrance will have before we judge the
Earl with such pitiless severity! But hark! is not that the ninth
hour sounding from the old clock of St. Canice? By my word,
Richard, it is,—we have tarried over long, you see, beguiled by
the beauty of earth and sky, and the Nore's tremulous reflection
of yonder planet's silvery beams—Muskerry and Mountgarret
and the rest will deem us somewhat indifferent counsellors, an'
we try their patience in this wise!"

"The fault is yours, good friend mine," rejoined Plunket with
a laugh; "sooth to say Madam Luna hath no such charms for
me, that for her dear sake I would take to wandering, ghost-
like, amongst the night-shadows. A soul full of poetry like
yours must needs do homage to the queen of night, but a man
of prose such as I, hath more fondness for the busy, bustling,
matter-of-fact daylight, when all the world is up and doing.
However, Roger, my good fellow, an' you quicken your steps,
so as to reach the Swan before our noble friends' patience be

exhausted, we may e'en have business of some import on hands to-night, touching matters to be brought before the synod to-morrow."

O'More was no less anxious than his friend to reach the place of appointment, whither they were invited to meet the lay-lords of the council at a supper given by Lord Mountgarret, for the avowed purpose of conferring together on the further proceedings of the deliberative body. Yet still the brave chieftain could not repress a heavy sigh as the old tavern* broke on his view at the turn of one of the abrupt angles in which Kilkenny, like most ancient cities, abounds. He was thinking, as Plunket rightly guessed, of that other such preliminary night-meeting which ended in the capture of McGuire and McMahon.

"Forgive me, Richard, if I appear gloomy and despondent— it is not from any fears anent the success of our cause that I now heave the sigh, but my heart is ever heavy when I bethink me of those two gallant friends of ours cooped up within the four walls of a dungeon at such time as this when most the country needs the swords and strong arms of her sons—nothing knowing, nothing hearing of what passeth amongst us their friends and comrades, other than what their jailers may see fit to tell them—oh, friends! friends! brave and generous and true-hearted! shall these eyes ever behold ye again? shall your long-shackled limbs ever bear ye again in freedom over the green fields where ye sported but few short months ago, lightsome and swift as the red deer of the mountains?"

They had just reached the door of the Swan, and Plunket who was himself catching the infection of his friend's melancholy, was not sorry to exchange his sole companionship for the cheerful, animated, and somewhat noisy crowd already occupying the Swan's best apartment. Happily for all concerned, no untoward occurrence came to mar the social enjoyment of that

---

* Lest our readers should be in any degree scandalized at the place chosen for such an entertainment by such a company, it may be well to observe that the word *hotel* had no place in the vocabulary of our ancestors, nor had the word *tavern* the same signification that it now has. *Inn* and *tavern* were the common names applied to all houses of entertainment.

evening, which was long looked back upon by the gallant gentlemen there assembled as a pleasant oasis in the desert of long-protracted warfare. Few such festive evenings fell to the lot of many there in after times!

Before the synod broke up towards the end of that month of May, another grand and more general assembly, both lay and clerical, was called for the following October, in the same good old city of Kilkenny. Agents were immediately despatched anew to the different Catholic Courts of Europe, soliciting assistance; foreign merchants were invited to export munitions of war to Ireland, and artizans skilled in the manufacture of arms were likewise offered every encouragement to induce them to take up their abode in the districts occupied by the Confederate forces.* Copies of the rules and regulations so far made were sent to all the Catholic noblemen and gentlemen throughout the kingdom, with a manifesto declaratory of the ends and objects of the Confederation just formed.

It was about the end of that same month of May that two gentlemen of noble mien might have been seen one evening pacing to and fro the length of the flagged way leading through the Upper Castle Yard in Dublin City. The massive gates opening on Cork Hill were not yet closed for the night, but there was none the greater bustle in the narrow old court lying so darkly in the evening shades between the massive walls of the Castle, for, during that stormy time of civil commotion, the citizens were not permitted, as they were before, and are since, to make the Castle Yards, Upper and Lower, a short cut to the streets below. The few straggling soldiers visible in the Yard were evidently careful not to come within hearing of the earnest discourse carried on in a low voice between the two individuals just mentioned, and even the sentries pacing their weary rounds on either hand, appeared equally willing to keep as far from them as their appointed limits would permit. Both gentlemen had that about them which denoted military as well as civil rank, although but one had anything distinctive in the costume which so well b.came his lofty mien and graceful form. His

* See Mechan's *Confederation of Kilkenny*, pp. 30, 31.

dark handsome features are not unknown to us, nor yet the
bland smile of condescension wherewith he listens—*deigns* to
listen, as it were, to the deep, full, measured tones of his companion. Such a smile was never seen, save on Ormond's face,
and Ormond it surely was. But who, then, was he who walked
so long by the proud Earl's side in friendly converse, nor seemed
in anywise overpowered by that nobleman's stretch of condescension in granting him so long an audience? Quite at his
ease he appeared to be, with his plumed hat thrown back somewhat from his broad, massive brow, and his mail-gloved hand
laid at times on the Earl's shoulder, as though to enforce conviction. There was a quiet consciousness of equality in the gentleman's whole demeanor towards Ormond, although he had
neither the exquisite polish, nor the insinuating address of that
accomplished courtier. Yet he, too, was a tactitian in his way,
and as a statesman was even then considered as not inferior to
Ormond himself, while in social rank he was fully his equal.
Indeed the British empire at that day contained not any nobleman of greater account, for he was no other than Ulick Burke,
Earl of Clanrickarde, the great Palatine of the West, the cautious,
calm, wily politician, who, belonging to the Catholics by religious profession, still adhered to the cause of their enemies, and
managed to maintain a high repute amongst them by his utter
detachment from his natural friends, and entire devotion to the
views and wishes of their oppressors. He it was who thus accompanied Ormond in his evening walk, and it was hard to say
which was the more astute politician, which the keener observer
of men and things. Still there were some essential points of difference between their characters, for while Ormond was entirely
devoted to his own interests, and made all others subservient to
them, Clanrickarde was honestly and heartily devoted to the service of the king his master, and what he considered the cause
of order—more sincere than Ormond, he was also much less skilled
in the art of dissembling, and could by no means descend to
intrigue or flattery to carry out his honest, though fatally erroneous views. In person, Clanrickarde was like Ormond, tall and
commanding, but the Connaught magnate was of larger proportions and more robust frame than he of Ormond, and although his

features were regular and well formed, they wanted the chiselled smoothness which belonged so peculiarly to the other. Take them as they stood, those two great Anglo-Irish lords, Clanrickarde was the larger and more athletic, perhaps the more imposing, while Ormond was immeasurably his superior in grace and elegance, and all manner of personal attraction.

Clanrickarde had been giving an account of his recent success in bringing the refractory town of Galway into subjection, and the manifold troubles arising to him from the want of proper supplies, which latter business had brought him to Dublin, although, as he said, he could ill spare even one day from the arduous cares of his government.

"Truly your lordship hath no enviable post there," said Ormond at the close of the narrative ; " you have a turbulent crew to deal with in that same Galway of yours. Much did we hear of the good and peaceable dispositions existing amongst all classes in your lordship's country, but, by my halidome, I was never deceived by those rumors, knowing well the stuff whereof those old Norman tribes are made—they are at heart both proud and Papistical, opposed to all authority but their own, and well content to let the Irishry spoil and harry all the country round so long as they leave them masters within their fourteen gates and towers !"

"They are in truth what you say," rejoined Clanrickarde, " yet I hold that Willoughby* is not without his share of blame in regard to the recent disturbances. He is as fierce and cruel as a tiger, and as obstinate withal as a donkey, so that a man can no more bring him to reason than he could teach yonder post to walk. It is little short of madness, as I take it, to fix such overgrown boys as he in places of trust. Truly yes, the townsmen of Galway are, as you say, proud and hard to manage, but an' I were left to deal with them as in former years, I warrant me they had never made common cause with the Irish

---

* Captain Willoughby, who then commanded the fort of Galway, was the son of Sir Francis of that name, who was appointed Governor of Dublin Castle very soon after that meeting of the Privy Council at which we introduced him to the reader.

enemy whom they hate as they do the Evil One. Many a
pretty piece of negotiation hath been spoiled for me of late by
the hot-blooded rashness of that same spawn of the Parliament,
for no sooner would the slightest difficulty arise between any of
his soldiers and the townspeople, than, bang into the town, came
down shell and shot, whereupon the citizens would at once
break off all communication with me, send my messengers back
in disgrace, and take to starving and otherwise annoying the
garrison in the fort. I tell you, my lord of Ormond"—and stopping in his walk, he made Ormond do the same by placing his
large hand like a grasp of iron on his shoulder—" I tell you,
an' the city and fort of Galway be now in the hands of the
government, small thanks are due to their pet Willoughby, for
all that they kept him so well supplied with things needful
while Clanrickarde was left to shift for himself and his poor
people as best he might."

"Nay, my good lord," said Ormond in his soft, soothing
way, " methinks you are over hard upon the government——"

" Hard!" repeated Clanrickarde with unwonted vehemence;
" before God I say it, James Butler, it hath seemed to me at
times that the Lords Justices desired nothing more than to
drive me from the king's service, and force me into the ranks of
rebellion—otherwise, had they never treated my poor services
with such base ingratitude, or taken so little pains to provide me
with munitions of war and other such matters as I stood in need
of for his Majesty's behoof. You know not, my lord, the straits
whereto I have been reduced in order to hold that western
country for the king, or the insults I have been forced to pocket
from the disaffected. Why, it was but last week that my Castle
of Aughanure, situate in a wild district of Connemara, was
coolly taken possession of by a party of the O'Flahertys, num-
bering no more than fifty or thereabouts."

" The O'Flahertys are up, then?" questioned Ormond.

" Up! ay, marry, are they, and for the matter of that they
were never *down*, save in so far or so long as authority and
strength could keep them so. Arrant traitors are they every soul
of them, and it needeth but a spark at any time to set their

whole country* in a blaze. I would the Castle had been burned
to the ground rather than fall into their hands."

"Methinks," said Ormond with his equivocal smile, "that
wish is unbecoming in the mouth of so loyal a nobleman. The
Castle may yet be retaken from the Papist enemy, and stand us
in good stead, whereas an' it were burned, there were an end
of it!"

"Humph! talk is cheap," observed the western Earl rather
testily; "your lordship knows little of these O'Flahertys. An'
the worshipful Lords Justices supply me not in far other fashion
they have yet done, it will be long ere I or mine set foot within
the walls of Aughanure. Young Murrough na Dhu O'Flaherty,
who led the party against it, and in one hour's fighting took the
Castle and made prisoners of its garrison, in the name, forsooth,
' of the Catholic army'—he, I tell you, Earl, will hold it against
all comers, unless, as I said, God moveth the hearts of those in
power to set me on a proper footing for war. Though young
in years, Murrough na Dhu hath the courage of a lion, and the
arm of a blacksmith—a youthful Hercules he is, I wot me well,
with a soul all on fire for what he deemeth the cause of religion
and country. Take Aughanure back from *his* hands!—by my
knightly word, it might try the skill of Ormond himself to do it
in that wild, unapproachable region!"

"Good my lord," said Ormond, without appearing to notice
the mention made of his own name; "good my lord, there seemeth to be an evil spirit at work amongst the young men of your
country. Not to speak of this fierce O'Flaherty, there hath been
wild work going on amongst them of late, as we have heard here
in Dublin!"

"Oh! your lordship hath reference to that mad prank played
some weeks since, by certain young men of Galway City, in regard to the taking of an English ship!—truly that *was* a feat, all
things considered. But as I told you before, it was all the work
of Willoughby. His idle threats and violent aggressions drove

---

* Nearly the whole of Jar-Connaught belonged of old, and consequently of right, to this princely sept, whose chiefs were dispossessed
to make room for the De Burgos.

the townspeople to desperation, and fearing that all who professed the old faith might any day be turned out of the city, like unto the Catholics of Cork and Youghal, if not slaughtered in cold blood, a number of bold, reckless, crack-brained youths did attack and finally capture a ship laden chiefly with arms and ammunition, which had been lying some days in the harbor waiting to land her stores for the use of the fort.* By that means these desperadoes got possession of firearms and other war-stores in plenty, which things they had not in any quantity before. '

" And then——"

" And then, my lord, they went in a body to the Church of St. Nicholas and vowed all manner of loyalty—lip-loyalty, we needs must think—towards his gracious Majesty, with entire devotion, however, to the cause of rebellion. Truly God and St. Nicholas must have turned a deaf ear to such orisons as they put up!—whosoever rebels against lawful authority, the Lord will not surely hold him guiltless!"

It was well for Ormond that Clanrickarde saw not the mocking smile which played around his finely-curved lip at the moment, else had the western autocrat never again laid bare his thoughts before the keen scrutiny of that wily lord. Having his eyes fixed at the moment in another direction, he saw not the face of his companion, and went on quickly with what he had been saying.

" Issuing from the Church, those rebels, with the mayor, I grieve to say it, at their head, took possession speedily of all the gates, declaring that they would hold the town for King Charles and the Catholic army until such time as God sent them relief. Knaves and hypocrites——"

" Shame, shame, shame, Clanrickarde!—traitor to God and His holy faith, dost thou dare thus to stigmatize the faithful and the true ?"

Thus spoke a deep, stern voice, almost, it would seem, at the Earl's elbow, and turning fiercely he demanded :

" My lord of Ormond, was it thou that spoke ?"

" By my life, it was not!" the Earl replied with very sincere astonishment, and both peered into the deep shade whence the

---

* This fact is historically true, to the immortal honor of old Galway.

voice appeared to have issued. Not a living soul was there visible, and Clanrickarde exclaimed with a shudder:

"The devil himself, then, must be in it, for the voice was close to my ear!"

"What ho, there!—close the gates instantly!—secure the traitor, whoever he be!"

Lord Ormond's command was quickly obeyed, but not before an aged mendicant presented himself at the gate nearest to the two noblemen, soliciting charity in the professional whine that marked his class then as now.

"Get you gone, old scare-crow," cried the proud Earl, raising his mailed hand, "or I strike you as you may not relish. Get you gone, I say, this be no place for beggars!'

"True for you, my noble master," the old man whined again as the massive gate was closed against him; "God reward you —as you deserve,—for sure it's your own good-looking face that covers the black heart!"

"What is the scoundrel muttering?' exclaimed Ormond.

"He is complimenting your lordship on your goodness of heart!" Clanrickarde replied with such a laugh as was seldom heard from his lips. "Nay, man, waste no time looking after *him*,—let us rather seek my invisible friend, an' he be within these limits!"

A burst of merriment from without the gate caused the two lords to start, and the voice of the mendicant was heard to say :

"A comical sight it surely is to see my lord of Ormond and the Papist Earl of Clanrickarde playing hide-and-seek together this bright May evening?"

The heavy gate was thrown open again, and Ormond himself, for once forgetful of his dignity, rushed out followed at slower pace by Clanrickarde, but the beggar had disappeared, and it were worse than useless to seek him amongst the crowd of citizens whom the beauty of the night had tempted abroad.

Before twelve o'clock that night messengers from within the city were far on their way to Kilkenny with an account of all that could interest the Confederate leaders in the foregoing conversation.

During the following week a very strong remonstrance was

addressed to Lord Clanrickarde, bearing the honored signatures of three illustrious bishops belonging to his own section of the country.* Malachy of Tuam, Francis of Elphin, and John of Clonfert were the names affixed to the eloquent and forcible appeal in which nought was left unsaid that might touch the heart, or awaken the slumbering conscience of the Earl. But Clanrickarde was not to be moved from his strange and anomalous position, and thenceforward the Confederates, both lay and clerical, gave him up in despair.

* In the West, three bishops . . . . addressed a remonstrance to the Earl of Clanrickarde, importuning him to join the national cause, "which was," in his opinion, "grounded upon wrong and bad foundations" In vain did Mountgarret and the bishops endeavor to convince him that he was helping to ruin his country. "No argument," said they, "though you should write it in our very blood, will ever persuade the Justices your affections are sincere, while you bear about you those marks by which they distinguish such as they have appointed for perdition. Let it not come to you to sprinkle your ancestors' graves with the blood of such as will sacrifice themselves in the justifiable cause."—*Clanrickarde's Memoirs*, 117, quoted by Meehan.

CHAPTER V.

"O, he sits high in all the people's hearts;
And that, which would appear offence in us,
His countenance, like richest alchymy,
Will change to virtue, and to worthiness."
                                        SHAKESPEARE.

THE day succeeding Owen Roe's arrival was a busy, bustling
day in and around Charlemont Castle. The chiefs who had been
there some days awaiting his coming were now engaged with
him in earnest deliberation on the measures to be taken in order
to co-operate effectively with the Confederate forces of the other
provinces. By common consent Colonel O'Neill was placed in
the seat of honor as president of the council, and near him sat
Sir John Netterville with a smile half serious, half playful, curling his thin lip. Opposite Owen, at the further end of the long
table which served as a council-board, the burly form of Sir
Phelim occupied the other "seat of honor," as Sir Phelim's air
of official arrogance plainly expressed. Yet the swaggering air
of consequence was but assumed at that particular time, for
poor Phelim was sadly sensible that the sceptre was departing
from him and for ever. Little as he had seen of his kinsman, it
had sufficed to show him that factious opposition to his authority—if supreme authority were given him—would be worse than
useless, and Sir Phelim, with all his violence of temper, and im-
periousness of manner, when inferiors or even equals were in
question, was not at all the man to resist the influence of a master mind placed by the will of the chiefs in authority over all.
    Glancing around the table from end to end we recognize many
an old acquaintance, old but unforgotten. Familiar they are to
us as the first actors in the great rebellion, but they were not so
to Owen O'Neill, whose keen eye scanned the features of each

in turn with the rapid, scrutinizing glance of one accustomed to read such books. Happily his own face brightened as he looked, for, whatever else he saw in the faces around him, he read in all the same fixed and settled purpose, the same longing to be up and doing, now that there was once more hope of something to do.

Amongst the many chiefs there assembled, there were but two of those who had been guests at McGuire's board on that fatal night when he and McMahon had fallen into the toils of the enemy. Philip O'Reilly and Tirlogh O'Neill were these two, and heavy were the hearts of both as the joyous hilarity of that scene arose before them. A shade of sadness was on O'Reilly's calm face, and as he turned involuntarily to speak his thoughts to Art McMahon who sat next him, his voice trembled with emotion as memory brought back the young, buoyant, jovial countenance of poor Costelloe—the last sight he had of him. What O'Reilly said to McMahon Owen Roe O'Neill heard not, but guessing from the expression on the face of either chieftain the thoughts which filled the soul of each, he addressed himself to McMahon:

"Chieftain of Uriel," said he, "be not cast down with mournful recollections—there is still hope for your brother, and even were there none, you have cause to rejoice in that the first sacrifice of propitiation was demanded and accepted from your noble and ever faithful house."

"Alas! Colonel," replied the chief sadly, "you speak as one who never had a brother—you know not, cannot know how I loved that light-hearted brother of mine, and oh God! to think what torments he hath undergone since last mine eyes beheld him—had he fallen in honorable warfare, ay! though it were but in the Spanish wars,* methinks I could resign him into the hands of Providence without a sigh, but this living death to which he is doomed—nay, talk not to me of being resigned"—this to O'Rourke who was seated near him—"I cannot, will not be resigned while my only brother languishes in a noisome vault of Dublin Castle. Oh! the heavy, heavy sorrow!"

* Costelloe McMahon had served with distinction in the Spanish army.

"Heavy it may be, Art," said the princely O'Rourke with a deep-drawn sigh, "but—but—the load is not all your own to carry—others have had brothers—oh, how dear!—and lost them, too, since this war began!"

The touching sadness of O'Rourke's tone was well understood by all, and many a hand was raised to dash away the trickling tear from eyes little used to weep. O'Neill had heard, since his arrival, the story of O'Rourke's wrongs, and now seeing the subdued anguish so visible on the chieftain's noble features, with his stern repression of all outward emotion, his heart warmed to him, and he said within himself:

"Ay! there is a man fit to lead others, for surely he well doth govern himself," and involuntarily he bowed his head before the majesty of sorrow so plainly stamped on the chieftain's brow.

"You speak truly, Owen O'Rourke," cried Roderick Maguire with that impetuosity which, unlike his brother, ever distinguished his words and actions; "we all have our crows to pluck with the truculent Lord Justices, and their minions—for me I cannot think of these things without feeling for my trusty skene—had I mine own way, Colonel O'Neill, we should long ere now have marched straightways to Dublin and burned the city over the heads of our cowardly tyrants an' they gave us not back our brothers safe and sound——"

"Ay, marry," said his uncle Lorcan with the solemn dignity which he thought became his age, "were it not for the warnings received from the guardian spirits of our house, methinks Rory would have led his own followers on that rash enterprize—is it not so, nephew?"

"Nonsense, uncle," was the irreverent and somewhat indecorous answer, "what care I for the spirits or their warnings, and *that* I have told you full many a time!"

"Have a care, nephew, have a care," and the old man shook his white head with a warning gesture; "your speech is far other than becoming—the spirits who have care of us are not to be lightly spoken of, as you may one day be brought to confess. Heed not his rash words, Colonel O'Neill,—he is young and hot-headed, but a brave fellow withal, as the Englishers in these parts can tell to their cost—a child he is in wisdom, honored sir, but, take an old man's word for it, he can do a good man's work when the falchion is in his hand and the Puritan enemy before him !"

"That were easy to believe," said O Neill, courteously, " even though the testimony were less worthy of credence—it is but to look at Roderick Maguire and we see the noble courage of his race stamped on every feature !"

"Courage alone is little worth," observed Rory with a reproving look at his uncle; "an ounce of your experience, Colonel, is worth a pound of it; however, *that* will come in time, an' the enemy.hold out."

During this incidental conversation many of the chiefs had been discussing in a low, suppressed voice the relative merits of the different commanders already in the field. Some made honorable mention of Mountgarret, others thought Muskerry the better officer, while others still were inclined to give General Barry the first place, as being, they maintained, the most successful captain who had yet appeared on the side of the Confederates. "Witness," said McMahon, "his recent capture of Liscarroll Castle.* That I take to be the noblest achievement of this war as far as it hath gone yet. Nay, nay, O'Hanlon, I understand your gesture—you would remind me of the taking of Newry by our friend here present—the which I have not forgotten. That, however, was partly a surprise, as Iveagh himself will own, but this new feat of Barry's——"

"Is, as you say, McMahon, the greatest thing done yet," said the generous chieftain of Iveagh, "and I am free to admit that Barry is a brave and skilful officer, but I am much mistaken if a greater than he hath not come amongst us—ay, and one of.our own race, too."

A murmur of applause greeted this speech, and Netterville laid his hand on Owen O'Neill's shoulder, as though he would

* Belonging to Sir Philip Percival. Lord Inchiquin declared it the strongest castle he had seen in Ireland. General Barry took it after a siege of thirteen days, although the ground around was so marshy that, in order to bring his guns within range, he was forced to dismount them.

have said: "Thou art the man!" But O'Neill little heeded the act, for his eyes were at that time rivetted on a tall, dignified personage who had just made his appearance at one of the side doors, and stood there looking on with a sort of paternal smile on his thin dark features. Before any movement on his part had revealed his presence, several of the chiefs called out simultaneously: "Bishop M'Sweeny of Kilmore!" and instantly all were on their feet, bowing reverentially to the smiling prelate as he greeted them collectively with the sign of the cross.

"Welcome to Charlemont, my lord," said Sir Phelim advancing with a surly attempt at condescension, "albeit that I know we are indebted for the favor to the arrival of my honorable kinsman."

"I deny it not, fair sir," said the lordly prelate, as his eye, running round the stately circle, rested on Owen Roe; "I am, as thou knowest, a man of peace, and am out of my element in the company of warrior-men. If I am here now, it is with serious intent affecting the country's and the church's weal. I need not ask which is Colonel O'Neill," that officer was already bending low before him, and when he at length raised his head, the good bishop stood a moment looking fixedly on his face, then laying his hand on his shoulder, he said with much emotion:

"Bless you, my son, bless you, soldier of the cross!" and with his thumb he made the sacred sign on the high, smooth forehead of the chief.

"Will your lordship honor us by taking a seat at our board?" said O'Neill respectfully; "if so, mine is at your service!" and leading him up the room he would have placed him in the presidential chair which honor the bishop declined,

"I pray you excuse me, Colonel, but my right reverend brother of Clogher must needs be here ere long, and——"

"Your right reverend brother of Clogher is much beholden to your lordship," said a cheerful voice from the still open door, "but, on the old principle of *first come, first served*, the seat is yours beyond all doubt. I might have got the start of you, my lord, were it not for a mishap which befel Malachy——"

"How! what?" exclaimed the chieftain of Uriel, advancing

with a flushed and anxious countenance; " no evil, I trust, hath
come unto him—how is it, my lord ?"

" Nay, cousin, the matter is not so serious that you need bo
disturbed in mind"—and the prelate smiled with that good humor
which made him so generally popular—" it was but that having
met a red-haired woman at our starting this morning, the which,
you know, Art, he deemeth to denote ill luck,* and being unable
to persuade me to return with him and commence the journey
anew, the poor fellow betook himself home again in much distress of mind for that I, a bishop, should be obstinate in running
the risk of some mishap. Neither could I, by any means, reason
him out of his own notion, and so home he went, notwithstanding his unwillingness to see me depart without attendance."

" And I say it here in presence of all these noble chiefs, and
I ask McMahon an' it be not so,—that your lordship is no more
fit to journey alone in these perilous times than a child of a year
old. If you weren't as *simple* as a child with all your learning, you'd be as feared of meeting a red-haired woman the first
thing in the morning as myself or any one else."

When the chieftains had enjoyed their hearty laugh at Malachy's expense, for Malachy himself was the speaker—that grave
individual bowed all round with a most deferential air; and
again his solemn voice was heard:

" Save you kindly, noble Chiefs of Ulladh, it isn't among the
likes of you the likes of me should open his mouth, and I
wouldn't set foot in the room with you all to the fore, no, not for
a mint of money, only when once I got sight of his lordship
there, I kept him in view till he came in here, and then I thought
I might as well take a peep at what was going on, and see if I
could get a sight of the great O'Neill that was so long spoken of
in prophecy."

With the condescending grace of a polished gentleman, O'Neill
advanced and reached his hand to Malachy, to the no small surprise of the simple follower of McMahon who looked as if he
doubted the reality of so glorious a vision. A few kind words

---

* This superstition is common amongst the peasantry of the northern
province.

from the colonel, however, and a smile of encouragement from
the bishop and the chief whose eyes he sought for confirmation
of his doubts, set the poor fellow at rest on that head, and with
a gesture expressive of wonder and delight he bowed himself
out of what he considered the most august presence in the land
of Ireland.

The presence of the Bishop of Clogher did not appear to
excite quite the same enthusiasm amongst the chiefs as in former times it did, and it might be that the prelate felt that, for
his manner indicate l the slightest possible degree of reserve, a
thing all unusual with him, and, as people thought, foreign to
his frank and hearty character. In the bearing of the chiefs
towards him there was now nothing more than the respect due
to his high office, but whatever it was that had brought this
change about, no one appeared willing to have it observed by
Owen O'Neill, or Sir John Netterville. Bishop McMahon, as the
senior of his right reverend brother was, therefore, placed in the
chair of authority, and then the council was formally opened by
Sir Con Magennis, who, rising from his seat with much dignity,
requested Colonel O'Neill to state what his hopes were with regard to present and future succor from abroad.

Owen Roe O'Neill was no orator—few military leaders are—
but his views, clearly conceived, were clearly expressed in a
concise and forcible manner, which, together with the calm dignity of his mien and his perfect self-possession, was sure to
impress favorably all those who heard him. Being thus called
upon, he arose, and, bowing to the bishops, then around to the
chiefs, he stated, in as few words as possible, what his expectations were with regard to foreign aid.

"I myself," said he, "have with me one hundred officers of good
standing, whose experience will profit us much—also arms and
ammunition for a force of a thousand men or thereabouts—these
await my orders at Doe Castle, in Donegal, which we succeeded
in taking from those who held it for the enemy."

As soon as he could make his voice heard above the loud
chorus of applause which greeted his ears on every side, O'Neill
resumed his discourse with the same composure as before:

"Cardinal Richelieu," said he, "as I learn from under his own
14

hand, is at present fitting out some ten or twelve vessels for our support, the which will reach our waters, if nothing adverse happen to them, early in the coming autumn—his Catholic Majesty of Spain gives me his royal word that the ship which he hath given to convey us hither, shall speedily be followed by others laden with all things needful for our uses, and I have it from the mouth of one whose word none of you will, methinks, doubt, that is Father Luke Wadding—that the Holy Father, out of his small means, is about to send to his children of Ireland such subsidies of money and arms as will surprise them."

This announcement, with the mention of Wadding's name, called forth another burst of applause, louder and more prolonged than before, and, by the time it was ended, Sir Phelim O'Neill was on his legs, and scowling with one of his blackest looks on the assembly.

" This, or something like it, have we heard full often ere now," said he, " ay ! before ever a sword was drawn or a pike raised against the enemy.   Strange to say, not one of these fine promises was ever fulfilled, and we were none the better that ever I could see, for our foreign expectations—pshaw ! far-off cows have long horns, and it may well be that the great Richelieu and Philip of Spain, not to speak of the Pope of Rome, have their hands so full at this present moment as to leave little room for our affairs. Methinks, with all respect for potentates and people beyond seas, that every chief here present hath in his own proper person done more for the cause than we can ever reasonably expect from *them*."

"That no one will gainsay, cousin mine," said Owen kindly, "and may Heaven forget me when I forget what hath been done by you all !   Still the war hath now reached a stage when foreign aid is necessary to us—how otherwise could we think to cope with Ormond, Inchiquin, Broghill, Vavasour, young Coote, and other captains of high renown in the south, east and west, with Stewart, Cole, and Montgomery here at your very doors—all more or less provided now with the means of continuing the war ?   Of Monroe's force in Carrick I speak not now, for, whatever be the object of the Parliament of England in sending them thither, they appear at present little disposed for active service.

With the generals I have mentioned already in the field, and every prospect of speedy aid from England for our enemies, what could we do without officers to train our raw and undisciplined forces, and arms and ammunition to put in their hands when they are taught to use them ?"

Some cutting remark of Sir Phelim's was stopt short by Philip O'Reilly, who hastened to prevent what he knew might breed discord.

"That we stand in sore need of help from abroad, Colonel O'Neill, no one here doubts, that we shall have it in due time, is, I think, well nigh as certain—we came not hither to discuss that point, but rather, it appears to me, to choose a leader for our future operations. How is it, friends and brother chieftains, and ye, our reverend lords! are we come together with that intent, or are we not ?"

" Surely yes," was the simultaneous answer.

" Let my lord of Clogher, then, of his goodness, put it to the council whether we have found the man to whom all will cheerfully yield obedience,"

" Chieftains of Ulster," said the bishop rising with the dignity which became his office, " the war which you were the first to undertake for the sacred cause of religion and liberty has, with the blessing of God, become general throughout the nation. Like the mustard-seed spoken of in the Gospel your attempt has been followed by so great results that we may liken it to a mighty tree overshadowing all the land. The whole country is astir; the princes and chiefs, and tribes of the old blood are not less active or less zealous in the cause than the chivalrous sons of the stranger"—and turning his head, the prelate bowed slightly to Sir John Netterville. who, rising from his seat, returned the graceful and welcome compliment with a profound reverence. " The enemy, too, is putting forth all his powers," resumed the bishop, " for a last desperate effort. It behoveth us, then, to place a man at our head—we of this northern province—who may turn our resources to good account, and do credit to us before friends and foes. Such a one stands now before you in the person of Colonel Owen O'Neill, a man who hath the skill and the prudence to marshal our clans and lead them on to victory. His veins are filled, moreover, with the blood of Cox, and the glory of the Hy-Nials is his by birthright."

"In the name of our holy mother, the church," said Bishop McSweeny with that impressive solemnity which ever characterized him, "I do hereby nominate Colonel O'Neill as the chief captain of our northern army."

"And I, too, my good lord," said he of Clogher, "well knowing, as doth your lordship, the opinion of our reverend brethren of the episcopate on this head."

"Chieftains of the North!" said Sir Con Magennis, rising in his turn, "it is now for you to confirm, as I know you will, the appointment just made in the name of that church for whose freedom still more than our own we draw the sword."

"Before we proceed farther in this matter," said Owen Roe with his usual calmness and self-possession, "I would know of my honored and valorous cousin here present whether he is willing to resign in my favor that command which he hath held in your army—it is surely not under *this* roof," and he pointed upwards, "that the services of Sir Phelim O'Neill can be overlooked!"

"Well said, Owen," cried Tirlogh, taking the word from his brother's mouth; "there was a day when but to speak of Charlemont or Dungannon in these parts made men cheer till their throats were hoarse for Sir Phelim O'Neill. Forsooth! times are changed, and though tongues can wag glibly in praise of the Norman Barry and other such mongrel whelps, there be none to say a word for Phelim O'Neill, or the towns and castles *he* was wont to take."

Many of the chiefs started up at the same moment, eager to protest against Tirlogh's ill-mannered allusion to their brethren of the Pale, but Sir John Netterville was already on his feet, his fine face covered with a crimson glow, and an angry frown knitting his usually sunny brow.

"Chieftains and noble gentlemen," said he, "I have listened with much interest to the several speakers, and looked forward to the result of your deliberations with unmixed satisfaction, knowing as I do that this gallant officer will be in himself an accession of strength to our common cause. Had a thunderbolt fallen in our midst I could not have been more astounded than I was by the speech of the gentleman from Tyrone. It is my pride and privilege to know General Barry, and I beg to assure Master Tirlogh O'Neill that Norman though he be his heart is centred in this cause—ay, truly, to the full as much as though all the blood of the Hy-Nials were in his veins—he is my cousin, I am proud to say, and the term 'mongrel whelp' I cast back in the face of him who spoke it. Purer blood is not within the Pale than that which courseth through the veins of Robert Barry."

"I know not an' there be *any* pure blood within the Pale," retorted the fiery Ulsterman, but before he could add another word, both the bishops enjoined him to keep silent, and with the air of a surly, disappointed mastiff, he was fain to take his seat, but Sir Phelim was up in an instant.

"I would know," said he, "before we go farther in this matter, by what right Sir John Netterville is here present. But seldom do we see those of his race in these northern wilds of ours. I demand his business whatsoever it be—for without business he came not here!"

"Business I have, Sir Phelim," replied Netterville proudly, "but other tongue than yours must needs put the question ere I answer it"—and turning he bowed to Colonel O'Neill

"An' your coming," said Owen, "have, as I opine, aught to do with the affairs of the Confederation, we will hold ourselves obliged, fair sir, an' you name it."

"There is at once my errand and my credentials," said Netterville, as he handed an unsealed document to O'Neill, requesting him to read it aloud. It was a letter from Lord Mountgarret, president of the Supreme Council, to Sir John Netterville, requesting that young knight to ascertain by a journey into the northern territories in what state of preparation the chieftains were, what aid might be expected from them, and whether Colonel O'Neill, so long looked for, had as yet arrived to take command of the northern army.

Sir Phelim was about to speak, but Bishop McMahon arose and with a dignified gesture motioned him to keep his seat.

"Here, then, Colonel, is another appointment," said the Bishop with a cordial **smile**; "the Supreme Council, you see, hath already fixed on you for the northern leader.—Chieftains of Ulster, I need not ask if you be of the same mind—the Church hath spoken by two of her prelates, the National Council by its President—for you the final decision is reserved—I pray you stand up, and whosoever is willing to have Owen Roe O'Neill for general of the Ulster forces, will hold up his right hand."

Instantly all were on their feet, and of all the chieftains present not one refused to hold up his hand save Tirlogh O'Neill, for Phelim himself did as all the others, although there was a scowl on his brow that portended no good. All eyes were turned on the fierce Tanist of Tyrone, but before any one could speak, his brother approached him behind and whispered in his ear, " For *my* sake do it, Tirlogh!" when all at once the sinewy hand shot upwards, but the effort was too much for poor Tirlogh, and covering his face with his left hand he fairly burst into tears, and the stout man sobbed like a petted child.

More than one of the chieftains manifested a wish to speak to the brothers, but the bishop made a sign for them to take no notice, and after a moment's pause he spoke again :

" Chieftains, it is well," said he, " we are now to consider Colonel Owen O'Neill as commander-in-chief of all the forces to be raised in this province. Duly appointed we hold him to be——"

" Not yet, my lord," said a deep voice from the door just behind the bishop's ; " another word remains to be spoken and by me!"

" And who are *you?*" demanded the prelate, turning quickly round to where all eyes were already fixed on a good looking young man who had just entered. He was clothed in a truis and jacket of grass-green hue, with a leather belt encircling his finely moulded form, and a glittering skene thrust in behind its clasp. On his head was the graceful and becoming *barradh*, but strangely enough his right arm was encircled above the elbow by a broad fillet of the coarsest brown drugget, with a large patch right on the front of the arm.

A shout of welcome recognition from many of the chiefs greeted the apparition, while Netterville, approaching Owen Roe,

whispered in his ear: " Good heavens! it is our guide of yesterday, but how metamorphised!"

" I know it," said O'Neill, "but, hist! he speaks!"

" In the name of the Rapparee force of Ulster, whose unworthy Captain I am, I do hereby give to General Owen Roo
O'Neill the full and entire command of that body—though I say
it, he may find their aid most effective, as Sir Con Magennis, Sir
Phelim, and others of the chiefs will bear witness!"

To the surprise of all, O'Neill—stranger to the country as he
might be considered—instead of slighting or mocking at this
new appointment, advanced to Donogh and took his hand, saying in all sincerity:

" I accept the offer, friend, and will look to your force as one
of the main supports of our future action! Acting in conjunction
with our disciplined forces, you may and will do us good service!"

Netterville felt much inclined to laugh, but there was that in
the bearing of the young Rapparee leader, for such Donogh was,
that, coupled with the respectful manner of O'Neill and the
chiefs, sobered down even his levity, and placed him on his guard.
Having said what he deemed necessary, Donogh bowed with an
air of dignity that surprised Netterville, and quietly resumed the
place whence he had stepped forward.

CHAPTER VI.

" The fiery soul abhorr'd in Catiline,
    In Decius charms, in Curtius is divine :
    The same ambition can destroy or save,
    And make a patriot, as it makes a knave."
                                POPE'S *Essay on Man.*

" Tho' thy slumbers may be deep,
    Yet thy spirit shall not sleep ;
    There are shades that will not vanish,
    There are thoughts thou canst not banish."
                                BYRON'S *Manfred.*

THE Council, or rather the meeting, had not yet broken up,
when by the side of the Rapparee Captain, where he stood leaning on the handle of his pike leisurely watching the proceedings,
there appeared another individual similarly dressed and accoutred, with the single exception of the head-gear which, instead
of the hanging cap worn by Donogh, was a small round cap of
scarlet cloth, tastefully ornamented with a black feather which,
as the young Rapparee was wont to boast, had not long before
shaded the haughty brow of an English officer, slain by his hand
in the battle of Kilrush. Having exchanged a silent nod with
his captain the new-comer calmly waited, as it would seem, the
close of the deliberations. Silent they both stood, until Sir Phelim
had been forced into resigning his authority to his kinsman,
when the younger of the Rapparees spoke out in a voice so clear
and distinct that it rang through the vaulted chamber like a
trumpet :

" More than that must you do, Sir Phelim O'Neill !—the sword
of the great Hugh rests in your gift—it belongs to OWEN ROE in
the high decrees of heaven !"

All eyes were instantly turned on the speaker, and Sir Phelim

exclaimed with a burst of indignation : " Before God, it is Angus
Dhu, whom I did heretofore so highly favor—I see he hath a
knack of feigning madness at times—beware, rash youth! how
you anger me now,—beware, I tell you!—for, by the Book! fallen as you deem me, I will speedily have that dainty head of
yours hoisted on a pike an' you address me in such wise—ay,
though fifty *Owen Roes* were to the fore!"

" You shall do as I bid you," said Angus solemnly, " and that
within the hour, or the Green Lady* shall walk under a thick
veil this night——"

" Angus! Angus! this to my chief?" cried a reproachful voice
from behind, and Shamus Beg rushing in breathless caught his
friend by the neck as though he meant to strangle him. It was
in love, however, not in anger, as his words proved: " I told
you to have nothing to say in it," said Shamus, while the big
tears of anguish streamed down his rough cheek ; " you often
said you'd do anything in the world for *me*, and still you wouldn't
do *this*—oh Angus! brother of my heart!" and he grasped his
two hands and looked steadily in his face, " how could you forget that what you say to *him* is said to Shamus ?"

" I did not forget, Shamus!" the youth replied with deep feeling, " but what Heaven *wills* man must *do*—that sword was
never meant for the hand of Phelim the cruel——"

" Angus!" cried Shamus with rising anger, " I cannot stand
this—we must fight, an' the one mother had borne us, if you
dare to say such words again !"

" Let the boy alone, Shamus," said Donogh with the quiet
consciousness of high authority ; " he hath told us things to come
many times ere now, and I will not that you cross him in this
matter, for he knows well what he says, take my word for it!"
Shamus grumbled a little, but for some reason known to himself
thought fit to retire without more ado.

---

* The Green Lady of the O'Neills is, or at least was, a generation
or so back, well known in the ancient territory of the Hy-Nial. Like
all the great families of Celtic origin both in Scotland and Ireland,
the O'Neills had, or were supposed to have, this guardian spirit to
preside over their destinies.

All eyes had been attracted by this strange scene, and many of the chiefs smiled to each other as they remembered the former meeting which Angus had in like manner interrupted, stemming with his single voice the fast-rolling current of their faint-hearted fears. Even the bishops looked the anxious curiosity which they did not care to express.

Owen Roe alone manifested neither surprise nor curiosity, whatever his inward emotions might have been, although an attentive observer might have noticed a heightened color on his check.

Tirlogh O'Neill, almost beside himself with anger, called upon his brother to have the daring intruder committed to the dungeon immediately, but Angus only smiled.

" Sir Phelim will do no such thing," said he ; " he knows my words are not of wind—answer me, Phelim MacHenry! will you, or will you not, do as I say ?"

"Now, by my mother's honor, boy !" said Sir Phelim with passionate warmth, "you are either mad or something worse. How could I give up the sword of Hugh to one who hath the bend sinister on his coat of arms ?"

" What does he say ?" inquired Angus, whose skill in heraldry was evidently but small, yet seeing the alarm which these words had excited amongst the chiefs, the uproarious applause wherewith Tirlogh greeted them, and the perturbation visible for the first time on the face of Owen Roe, the youth knew full well that their import was of the most serious nature.

" He says," whispered Donogh, guessing the meaning of the words from Sir Phelim's manner, " he says, what we all know for truth, and more's the pity, that there's a cross in Owen's blood, and for that reason he couldn't give him the great Earl's sword !"

" Heed him not, chiefs and nobles !" cried Angus darting forward, just as Owen had placed himself in front of his kinsman with a kindling eye and a blushing cheek ; "heed him not—I tell you again Owen Roe must have the sword of Hugh, ay ! must he, and the holy bishops here present shall bless it for his use. Sir Phelim, go fetch the sword hither !"

" I will not—may not—must not !"

"You shall, and may, and must, as I will prove to you in half a dozen words, an' you will give me private audience for so long as I may speak them!"

There was that in the eye, the dark, flashing eye of the young Rapparee, as he fixed it full upon him, which made Sir Phelim somehow sensible that it was his own interest to give the required audience, especially as Donogh said in his calm, impressive way :

"An' you take my advice, Sir Phelim, you will do as the lad wishes !"

"Sir Phelim," said Owen, stepping before him as he rose to leave the room, "Sir Phelim, you have insulted me in a way that, according to the usages of men of honor, blood only could expiate—still, as no one here, methinks, will doubt my courage, I will not so far forget the sacred precepts of Him whom first of all I serve as to bear you ill-will on account thereof; neither would I willingly commence this war, which I consider a holy one, by giving an example of dissension, that, too, with one of my own blood. It was, however, an unkind cut, Sir Phelim, as little honorable to you as to me—go now, cousin. if it so please you !"

Sir Phelim withdrew in some confusion, and during his absence little was said, all being equally interested in the result of the mysterious interview going on. Ten minutes had scarcely elapsed when Sir Phelim returned alone, with the fateful sword in his hand, the rich jewels on its hilt flashing up a ghastly light on a face from which every tinge of color had vanished. Tirlogh jumped from his seat with an exclamation of indignant surprise, and reaching his brother with a bound that made his long sword clatter in its sheath, he laid his hand heavily on his shoulder.

"Phelim! you shall not do it," he said vehemently ; "you dare not do it !"

"Tirlogh! I *must*," his brother replied in an under tone; "trouble me not farther, an' you love me !" And on he marched towards the head of the table where he placed the sword before the bishops with a poor attempt at a smile. With a heart-breaking sigh poor Tirlogh threw himself on his seat once more ; he saw that his brother's fiery spirit was governed by some stern law of necessity, but his fierce, impetuous nature could not brook what he deemed such abject submission, while his strong fraternal affection dipped the barbed arrow in deadliest poison. Still, as he murmured to himself, his chieftain's will was law, ay ! more binding than law could ever be.

It was a solemn sight to see when the bishops standing, as all the chieftains did likewise, Bishop MacMahon called Owen Roe before them and delivered to him the sword of Hugh O'Neill.

" Take this sword," said the prelate, " and use it as becometh a Christian soldier, in fair and legitimate warfare against the oppressors of God's faithful people, never in any selfish or private quarrel, nor to do the bidding of passion. Take it and use it even as the sword of Gideon was used of old, but see that it be with Christian prudence and Christian forbearance, not in anger or in malice, lest you sin before God !"

" It may be," observed Bishop M'Sweeney, " that the great leader who wielded that weapon so valiantly, was not always as mindful as he ought of the jealous God in whose interests he fought, and hence his fall, when all the Catholic world deemed him to stand most securely. Profit by that awful warning, Owen O'Neill, so that to you it may be given to steer our bark to the port of safety, which is civil and religious liberty in this realm! Bless you, my son, bless you !" and again he laid his hand on the noble head bent before him, for Owen had knelt to receive the sword. The Bishop of Clogher imitated the example of his reverend brother, and after some further consultation on the military movements to be undertaken, the meeting broke up, and the chiefs (due honor being first done to Sir Phelim's hospitality) betook themselves to their respective territories to forward what men they could for Owen's new army, the head-quarters of which were for the present fixed at Charlemont.

By that evening's waning light, Owen Roe and Sir John Netterville were pacing together the lofty battlements of the Castle, discoursing of many things, and pausing often to enjoy the beauty of the evening, both being unconsciously soothed and calmed by the hushed repose of the scene around, and the deep shadows settling down on the dark-rolling river below. Much was O'Neill interested in the military operations of the

Southern and Eastern Confederates with whom Netterville had so long been acting, and he listened with a soldier's ear to the tales which the young Norman knight loved to tell concerning the heroic deeds of Dillons and Cusacks, Aylmers* and Barrys, and many another fine old family of the English Pale. As the moon rose over the towers of the old fortress, throwing their shadows far out over the Blackwater, and giving grace and beauty to the homely old town of Charlemont, lying just beneath the Castle, on its opposite banks, the Irish general and the Norman knight leaning over the parapet, beguiled the hour with this so pleasant converse. The deep silence of the hour was nowise broken by the measured tramp of the sentries on the ramparts, and no sound was heard from the town beneath save that of

" The watch-dog's voice that bay'd the list'ning moon."

Many a tale of horror young Netterville had told relating to the savage butcheries of the miscreant Coote, and O'Neill listened with a sickening heart, not always able to repress the natural expression of indignation and disgust, although habitually guarded in all his words and actions.

" For all Sir Phelim's poor opinion of us, Anglo-Irish," said Netterville, "and though he have no better name for us than 'mongrel hounds,' we have, putting one thing with another, done our fair share of the work since the day of our covenant with Roger O'Moore and the other Irish on the hill of Crofty."

" Who doubts it, my friend ?" said O'Neill frankly, and he laid his hand on the knight's arm; "no, not even my kinsman, Phelim, though he do snarl and snap at times. He is at heart too much devoted to the cause not to feel the full value of our indebtedness to our gallant brethren of the Pale !"

" However that be," replied Netterville, "we ourselves know full well that we have had the brunt to bear in many a trying hour of peril, when Sir Phelim and his Northmen were far away,

---

* Sir Andrew Aylmer, who did good service to the Catholic cause during these long wars, was the brother-in-law of the Earl of Ormond, having married one of his sisters, as Lord Muskerry did another. The other two were consecrated to God in holy religion.

little thinking of our need. Spanish bred as you are, general, you must have heard of Lough Ree of the Shannon."

" Surely yes, Sir John, I know it well by name."

" Well, the islands in the lake, and the Kilkenny* shore adjoining, were, and are still, subject to the powerful house of Dillon, who have dotted the land with religious institutions of various kinds wheresover their sway extended. Not to speak of the noble Abbey on Hare-Island, around whose now mouldering walls the departed Dillons sleep in peace, there is, or was, till lately, on Saint's or Nun's Island, almost within hail of the other, a Convent of Poor Clares also founded and protected by the same noble family. It was a house of refuge to all the poor and distressed for miles around on mainland and island, and all men deemed it safe from the incursions of any of the contending parties. So little danger was apprehended, indeed, that even the hereditary protectors of the house thought it nowise necessary to burden or disturb the good Sisters by placing a garrison in or near the convent, and lulled in false security the saintly daughters of St. Clare pursued their works of mercy, and dreamed away their meditative hours in the still seclusion of their insular dwelling. Alas! that so blissful a calm should be so rudely broken! The good religious were in their chapel chanting the Vesper service when a party of English soldiers from the garrison of Ballinacloffy, on the adjoining shore, burst into the Church, and—oh, my God! shut out from mine eyes the scene that followed," and starting from his half-recumbent posture the young nobleman began to pace the rampart to and fro in a fit of unconquerable emotion.

" What!" said Owen O'Neill in a choking voice, " they dared to——"

" Dared!" cried Netterville, " dared! I tell you, General O'Neill, they dared to do the work of devils—sooner could I tear the tongue from my head than say what they *did*, but you may guess it from my silence. Having glutted their demoniac rage in every possible way, the wretches set fire to the convent and

---

* This place is situated in the county of Westmeath, and on the eastern borders of Lough Ree.

marched away, little thinking what was to follow. Oh, virgins of the Lord! they deemed ye unprotected, and as having none to avenge your wrongs——"

A deep groan from Owen Roe made Netterville look towards him. His head had sunk between his hands, and his whole frame trembled with suppressed emotion, yet he spoke no word, perchance could not speak. Before the knight could utter another word, a rough voice spoke out almost at his elbow, and Sir Phelim stepped forth from the shade of a buttress into the clear moonlight.

"It is a piteous tale, Sir John," he said with the vehemence which belonged to his character; "would to God I had been there with a score or so of my O'Neills—methinks, an' we came not in time to save the poor nuns, we would settle accounts with the devil-begotten Puritans——"

"The account *was* settled," said Netterville coldly.

"How was that?" asked Owen Roe, roused from his painful reverie as well by the abrupt appearance of his kinsman as by the announcement just made.

"By whom?" cried Sir Phelim; "prithee, man, tell us all about it ere we lose patience."

"It were ill losing what you never had," muttered Netterville to himself, and glancing with a half contemptuous air at Sir Phelim, he turned to Owen Roe.

"You will be glad to hear, General, that although your valiant kinsman here was not within a hundred miles or so of the bleak Shannon shore when this black deed was done, Bertie and his troopers* escaped punishment none the less. Returning to the shelter of their fortress, and being already intoxicated with the mad indulgence of their brute passions, the ruffians must needs quaff potations deep and long after their day's work. The usual precautions for the safety of the fort were, of course, neglected on that night; even the warder on the walls and the sentry at

---

* This fiendish act was perpetrated by a party of soldiers from the neighboring castle of Ballynacloffy, under the command of Captain Bertie, brother to the Earl of Lindsay. See Brower's *Beauties of Ireland*, vol. II., p. 246.

the gate were heavy-headed with much drink and kept their posts unheedingly. It was just when the orgies within were loudest and highest that Hubert Dillon rushed in with some eighty or a hundred of his followers, and falling on the ruffianly crew of revellers, cut them down without mercy, so that, as chronicles tell, hardly a man of them escaped. 'The mongrel whelps,' Sir Phelim, proved themselves of true blood in that hour of retributive justice!"

"Marry they did," quoth Sir Phelim gleefully, "and for the sake of those same Dillons I am content to crave your pardon, Sir John Netterville, for any unseemly words that may have escaped me. I am a rough spoken man, young sir, and somewhat hot-blooded, but, i' faith, I am not the man to keep malice, let my enemies say as they will. How now, cousin?"

But his cousin made no answer, being in fact out of hearing of the question, though still within sight. He had followed to the other end of the rampart a figure which he had observed in the shade behind Phelim's back, beckoning him to go thither. Having reached the extreme end, at a spot where no sentry was within sight or hearing, the figure approached for an instant, and whispered softly but distinctly:

"Be not surprised if you see a ghost this night, and be sure, sure that you note well its actions. Keep a light burning in your chamber all night. Farewell and God be with you!"

The speaker was no other than Angus, whose mysterious influence over Sir Phelim Owen had witnessed with surprise. Fain would he have detained him a moment, but his faint and low "stay, young man!" was apparently unheard, for Angus came no more. He had glided round a projecting angle, and was nowhere to be seen. Nor did Owen Roe see him again during his stay at the Castle, which was necessarily of some weeks' duration.

The entertainment provided by Sir Phelim that evening for those whom he regarded as his guests, was worthy of his far-famed hospitality. A few of the neighboring chiefs, amongst whom was O'Hanlon, had accepted Sir Phelim's invitation to remain for the night, and altogether there were some ten or twelve assembled at supper. A jovial party they were, too, and well inclined to do honor to the feast before them, with the single exception of Owen Roe who, at all times temperate and even abstemious, was on that night graver and more thoughtful even than his wont, to the no small surprise of the other guests who naturally expected to see him somewhat elated by the flattering reception given him, and the auspicious opening of his career in Ireland.

Tirlogh O'Neill, too, was more silent than living man had ever seen him, and there was a sullen frown knitting his shaggy brows that made one shrink from looking twice at him. More than once during the evening, he took occasion to renew the subject of Sir Phelim's superseded command in a way that gave infinite alarm to the sage O'Hanlon and others of the guests. But they little knew the stuff that Owen Roe was made of when they deemed him capable of being provoked to anger by the petulant taunts or scoffs of Tirlogh O'Neill.

"Here's to you, Phelimy Roe,"* said Tirlogh, as he raised a brimming bumper of the wine of Bordeaux; "you'll still be general-in-chief amongst us of Tyr-Owen, any how—and wherefore not, I want to know, when King Charles himself, God bless him! gave you full authority in these parts, not to speak of what belongs to *the O'Neill*"—a triumphant glance at Owen Roe gave point to the words, but, to Tirlogh's great surprise, Owen was smiling and composed, Phelim abashed and disconcerted. The look which the knight gave his brother was expressive of anything but gratitude or satisfaction, and poor Tirlogh cut but a sorry figure as he glanced uneasily from Owen to Phelim and from Phelim back to Owen.

Netterville noting well the relative effect of the words, thought it a good joke, although he knew not for his part what it all meant. With the natural buoyancy of youth, he exclaimed gaily: "I would that same commission of Sir Phelim's was more extensively published. We, of the Pale, have heard much con-

---

* Sir Phelim O'Neill had also the soubriquet of *Roe* or red, in allusion to his florid complexion, bestowed on him by his own and neighboring clans. By the name of *Phelimy Roe* he is still spoken of in the north country.

cerning it, but, I grieve to say, there be many so skeptical as to doubt its existence. Nay, be not wroth, Sir Phelim, for, by mine honor, I mean no ill—I do but say what I have many times heard."

"They lie in their throats," cried the knight of Kinard leaping to his feet, his face all on fire with fierce, ungovernable passion; "I say they lie in their throats who say I have no commission from the king. As well might they say there be no king to give one."

"Alas! the day," said Owen Roe in a dreamy, abstracted tone, "they may *have* that to say with truth ere long, an' things go on as they *do* in England. God protect the royal Stuart, for surely he is in the hands of the Philistines, though mayhap he know not of his danger!"

"Let him look to it then," said O'Hanlon gruffly; "he hath been playing a double game, and deserves to fall between two stools, as the saying is. Double dealing seldom serveth for much good, and that same King Charles is full master of that art, or Teague O'Hanlon is no true man!"

"I like not your speech, fair sir," said Netterville tartly; "the faults of a sovereign, an' he have them like other men, rest between him and his God. We Catholic knights and nobles might well leave abuse of our liege lord to the cropped-ear'd prigs of the Scotch Covenant, whose detestation of '*the man, Charles Stuart*,' must needs point him out as the friend of Papists. Nay, never look so cold on me, friend Teague," he gaily added, seeing the chieftain's face darken, "I have seen you too often at the head of your clan fighting 'for God and King Charles' lightly to suspect you of disloyal thoughts. Forgive me, O'Hanlon, I did but jest!"

"More fool he or we to peril life for so faithless a prince," Owen muttered to himself, and then rising he craved Sir Phelim's leave to retire on the plea that his health permitted not late vigils.

"But the commission, General!" cried Netterville as he shook hands across the table with the good-natured O'Hanlon whose anger was never either very violent or of long duration, "let us have a sight of it ere you go!"

Sir Phelim expressed his willingness to show it, at the same time muttering a curse between his teeth, but Owen begged to be excused, saying that another time would do as well for the gratification of their common curiosity.

"An' you be advised by me, Sir John," the general added as he past his seat, "you will follow my example and retire immediately. Proposing, as you do, to set out betimes in the morning, you will need a long night's rest."

With a ready perception of his friend's motive, the young Norman gracefully declared his willingness, and, after some faint objections from their host, both were shown to their respective apartments, Netterville by Tirlogh, Owen O'Neill by Sir Phelim himself.

It was the best sleeping-room in the Castle that in which Owen was lodged, and albeit that curiosity had but a very small share in his composition, he certainly did make a brief inspection of the spacious chamber with its old-fashioned furniture, even before he knelt to perform his nightly devotions. The room was curiously wainscotted with Irish oak, black and polished as ebony; the large mirror, surmounting an antique toilet-table, was framed in the same, and the narrow, high-backed chairs and the four-posted bed with its canopy of rich crimson velvet, all were in perfect keeping one with the other, so that the chamber, rich and tasteful as it was, had a gloomy and somewhat ghostly look. Still the bed looked so tempting, with its cool, fresh, snowy linen, that the general gave himself little trouble about the sombre character of the place, and, leaving the lamp burning on the table, according to the mysterious instructions of the young Rapparee, he lost no time in seeking repose. Much he wondered at the singular warning given him by Angus, although so far was he from attaching any importance to it that he laughed at the bare idea of a ghostly visitation.

He had been some hours asleep, and the night was already far spent, when his light slumbers were broken by the door creaking on its rusty hinges, and starting up on his elbow, he saw crossing the floor a tall figure in a short white garment barely reaching below the knee. The lower limbs were bare, and brawny limbs they were, to be sure; no wonder that they should, gentle reader, for the sinewy limbs and the thick head of reddish, curling hair and the massive features were those of the real, substantial Pheliny Roe, the knight of Kinard himself, walking in his sleep, and no spirit, as Owen saw at a glance, and seeing, he smiled.

The eyes of the figure were wide open, and, at first sight, would appear fixed on the opposite corner of the room, whither the naked feet were turning their steps. But no, there was no consciousness, all the motions were mechanical.

Owen, as may well be imagined, watched the figure with curious eyes. Not that he remembered Angus's injunction at the moment, but from the natural impulse of curiosity. Walking slowly to that corner of the room which was concealed from Owen's view by the foot-hangings of the bed, Sir Phelim approached a tall, old-fashioned escrutoire which had hitherto escaped the general's notice. The latter, leaning from his bed, now eagerly watched the motions of the somnambulist, who, having slowly raised the lid of the antique desk, began groping and fumbling through the secret drawers and shelves within, muttering drearily to himself as he did so, and shaking his head as one grievously disappointed.

"Gone! gone!" he said in a voice loud enough for Owen to hear, "gone to the grave and the worms, mayhap, with old Toby Caulfield. I would I had it to convince these prying churls—they say I forged it, but they lie,—they lie—I forged it not—thou canst bear me witness, old lord, an' thy spirit be anywhere here—but stay—let me whisper—tell not that hypocritical, long-faced kinsman of mine—tell him not the cunning device whereby I tricked the chiefs and people into belief. Ay! it *was* a pretty conceit—thou sayest well—an' what if I did borrow that old deed of thine, or rather the seal, for mine own use—the end was a good one, and thou, stern old royalist as thou ever wert, could not anywise object to it, seeing that we *be* the king's liege subjects, deny it who may!—go to, old man, name not the *murder* to me—of that I am guiltless, anyhow,—as God liveth I am. For the other, it is done, and cannot be undone—only keep it from Owen Roe—the secret of this unlucky commission, and all will go well—it *were* a thick veil surely on the face of the Green Lady, the disgrace which that disclosure would bring on our house. The boy is right—it must be avoided—come what may!"

So saying, he closed the desk with a heavy sigh or rather groan, and crossing the floor without turning to the right hand or the left, glided from the room as noiselessly as a spirit.

What Owen learned from all this we can but guess, for his thoughts on the subject he kept to himself then and ever after.

CHAPTER VII.

" Love will find its way
Thro' paths where wolves would fear to prey."
                                        BYRON'S *Giaour*

" How little do they see what is, who give
Their hasty judgments upon that which *seems*."
                                        SOUTHEY.

NEARLY the same July sun that gilded the green pennon of
Owen Roe when its folds first rustled in the sea-breeze over the
keep of Doe Castle, saw the long-imprisoned chieftains of Fermanagh and Uriel brought forth from the cells where their eyes
had almost forgotten how to look and their limbs how to walk.
Silently, and, as it were, stealthily, their prison-doors were
opened, and guarded on either side by a soldier, each was led
forth bound and manacled. Again, after the lapse of nine
weary months, the friends looked upon each other, and oh! the
thousand, thousand thoughts to which that glance gave utterance. It was but for a moment, however, that this mute inter-
change of feeling lasted, for a troop of cavalry and a whole bat-
talion of infantry were in waiting to receive the prisoners from
the Constable of the Castle, whose duty it was to give them up.

" By my faith," said McMahon with a melancholy smile as he
noted the imposing array, " by my faith, Connor, we be no such
pitiful wights after all. This guard of honor surely befitteth
rather our birth and former estate than the beggarly rags of our
present livery. What think you, brother in misfortune? Doth
it not seem over much respect for two ragged jail-birds like ourselves?" And casting his eyes down over the tattered remains
of his once gay costume, he laughed lightly and scornfully.
Maguire acknowledged the witticism of his friend by a faint smile

and an admonitory gesture, but word spoke he none. His more
pliant, and (it might be) more susceptible mind, had lost its
former spring and assumed the gloomy cast of surrounding objects; dull and spiritless, and, to all appearance, dead to hope
was the once haughty chieftain of Fermanagh, his fine countenance pale, and wan, and haggard, his long brown hair.matted
and dishevelled. It were hard, indeed, to recognize in him the
gay, good-humored, and ever-attractive Lord Maguire of our
earlier acquaintance, the proud and sensitive, yet warm-hearted.
Oh! it was a sad sight to look upon that wreck of manly beauty
and high estate, and to think of the cause for which he suffered,
the cause of eternal truth and justice. McMahon, more robust
in body and more stubborn in mind, had also a mercurial lightness of heart which no amount of suffering could altogether
subdue, and with these peculiar characteristics he had borne up
like a giant under the pressure of his hard lot. True, his cheek
had lost its roundness, and with it the fresh color borrowed from
the "breezy heath" of his native Uriel; neither had his clear
blue eye the same mirthful twinkle as in former days, though its
light was still unquenched, and its bold, free look ever the same.
The garments of both were, as poor McMahon's jest indicated,
sadly the worse for wear, being identically the same in which
they were captured so many months before.

Sir Francis Willoughby, Governor of the Castle, quickly made
his appearance on a balcony, and gave the stern order to
"march!"

"March!" repeated McMahon, "where to, I pray you, good
sir? That question have we asked full often since the order
reached us, but as yet no man hath made us the wiser."

"It boots ye little to know," replied the stern governor, "the
knowledge may come over soon. Captain Hardy, the hour hath
struck—move on, sir!"

"Not yet, Sir Francis, an' it please you," said a voice unheard before; it was that of one of Coote's troopers, who, dashing into the court-yard at full speed, delivered a message from
Sir William Parsons, then on a visit at Blackrock, to the effect
that the prisoners were to be remanded to their cells for half
an hour's space, or an hour, if needful.

" For what purpose, knowest thou ?" demanded Willoughby.

" It hath pleased the Lord Justice to impart so much knowledge unto me," the young soldier replied, touching his morion at the same time in military style; " rumors have reached him that the Lord Maguire here present hath of late manifested more loyal sentiments, and, desirous of encouraging any such laudable dispositions on the part of these pestilent rebels, he, of his great wisdom and clemency, sendeth hither the worshipful and godly gentleman, Master Osee Judkins, with intent to learn by private converse, from either or both prisoners, in what way they stand affected now towards the righteous cause."

At this McMahon laughed outright, and Maguire was just on the point of uttering an indignant denial of any such *change* as that ascribed to him, when a voice, barely audible to himself, whispered at his side in Irish: " Let them think so—say nothing"—and passing him like a shadow swept the dark-robed, Dutch-built figure of Master Osee Judkins, for whom the soldiers made way right and left, till, arrived opposite the balcony, he posted himself in front of the Governor, and thus delivered himself :

" May it please you, Francis Willoughby, to send back these recusants to their respective places for one hour, or less, as the case may be, until such time as I have ascertained to the satisfaction of that righteous ruler, William Parsons, what change may have taken place in their traitorous and bloody dispositions. It hath pleased the Lord to afflict him this morning with a grievous flux, by reason of which he may not venture abroad."

Hearing this McMahon laughed heartily: " Pray Heaven," said he, "all the evil humors of the man may find vent in that same flux !"

A stern rebuke from Judkins only made the reckless Ulsterman laugh the more, and he was about to say something not very complimentary to any concerned, when the harsh, loud voice of Willoughby arrested his attention :

" Remand the prisoners for an hour—give Master Judkins access to them separately in their cells. Captain Hardy will send a messenger to delay the ship for the time specified."

"Ship!" repeated McMahon; "are you sending us, then, beyond seas—mayhap it be to England!"

"I see you are as good at guessing as at portrait-painting, Master Irishman," said Hardy advancing, "but no more talk, an' you are a wise man,—soldiers, take them in, but remain here under arms!"

If any one looked around at that moment for the trooper who had brought Sir William's message, it would have seemed as though he vanished into thin air, although the presence of his horse fastened to a post at the rear of a sentry-box might, had he been observed, have suggested the idea that the rider must be still about the premises.

Little recked the bold trooper though his horse *were* seen, for in attendance on Master Judkins he had passed on to the interior of the Castle, on and on, even to the cells wherein the friends were again lodged, heavily ironed as they were.

What passed between Master Judkins and Maguire is not ours to tell, but the success of the embassy may be inferred from the fact that after a conference of some fifteen or twenty minutes, carried on in so low a tone that the trooper listening without could not catch a word of it, Maguire all at once burst forth into what appeared a perfect frenzy of indignation, and the worshipful and godly Osee Judkins called loudly for help. The turnkey, also waiting without, hastened to open the door, none too soon, it appeared, for the bodily safety of Sir William's ambassador, threatened with a blow from the chained hands of Maguire which might, as he justly feared, have sent him to the shades below.

"Secure this madman," said Judkins in breathless trepidation; "he will hear nothing from me—nothing, nothing—the other may be more reasonable—him will I try as in duty bound, —but, alas!"—and he sighed heavily—"I much fear the result will be the same—perverse and unregenerate are they all—all— alack! alack! for the sinful bonds that hold them fast in the evil way!"

"Out, out upon you, canting knave!" cried the wrathful chieftain; "an' I had you within reach of my arm, your prating were cut short, I tell you!—ay, marry, go to McMahon, with

15

your pious twaddle,—he will teach you to go errands for Parsons—and to *us!*—off with you!"

"I pray you, good fellow," quoth the agitated Judkins, "show me with speed to the lodging of the other—an' he be not more tractable than this individual, my mission will profit William Parsons but little. O Rome! Rome! Babylon the new! how fearful are the spells of thy foul magic!"

And groaning piteously the good man betook himself to the cell occupied by McMahon at no great distance, the turnkey walking before. By some curious oversight that functionary forgot to turn the key on Maguire, or perchance he deemed the presence of the fierce-looking soldier better than bolt or bar. It so happened that Coote's terrible troopers were at that particular time a portion of the city garrison, so that they were often on guard about the Castle, and might, therefore, be almost individually known to the officials. However it was, the young soldier was left alone at the door of Maguire's cell, and, to that nobleman's great surprise, the footsteps of the others had hardly died away when he addressed him in a low, tremulous voice, drawing his sword at the same time so as to deceive prying eyes:

"Connor Maguire, they are taking you to England, fearing a rescue."

"Ha, then, an' such be their fear," said the chieftain, a flush of joy suffusing his pale face, "it denotes strength and success on our part—accept my thanks, oh Heaven!"

Much affected by this utter forgetfulness of self, the soldier's voice trembled still more when he spoke again: "But you ask not who *I* am that come to you in friendship under such guise as this," pointing to the ball-coots* curiously emblazoned on his scarlet doublet. "Ay, look well at me—look into mine eyes—is their language that of a foe?"

Maguire started and drew back a pace: "What—the lady Emmeline here, and in such wise bedight!"

"Heed not the fashion of my garments, Connor Maguire, but hearken to the words which I have perilled all to speak. Hast

---

* The well-known cognizance of the Coote family.

heard from the gentleman just gone how matters stand with the Confederates, which name I hear hath been assumed by those of your party ?"

" Little or nothing did that gentleman tell me of what I so much desire to know—other business brought him here."

" Ay, marry, I guessed as much," said the disguised fair one with a strange smile ; " well, then, hear me : the Catholics are everywhere up in arms, save only in Galway, where Lord Clanrickarde had power to hold them to their good behavior."

" God confound him !" Maguire exclaimed through his closed teeth.

" For shame, my lord, to speak so of so honorable a nobleman !—but let it pass ; your Church hath at last declared openly for the Confederates."

" That is well !"

" And, as I hear, blessed their arms——"

" Better still—what more—what of this Council of Kilkenny that I have heard derided and scoffed at by the jailors ?"

" It consisted of the bishops and many lay-lords—they appointed local and provincial councils all over the land, with one Chief, or Supreme Council, as they term it, to which all the others are subject. Many other laws and regulations were enacted, but I know them not, or could take time to tell them an' I did. One thing I know : Lord Mountgarret is President of the Supreme Council——"

" Humph !"

"And a general assembly of the estates—so the phrase goes— is to meet again in October in the same city——"

" It is very well ! The Normans of the Pale are heartily into the matter ?"

" Heartily !—good sooth they are, as I could testify, did time permit—suffice it to say, they are, as it would seem, almost to a man, head and ears implicated in the rebellion—between them and the old Irish much hath been done for the cause which you affect—the greater part of Munster is in their hands, so, too, with Connaught——"

" But what of the North ?"

" Rebellion begins to raise its head again——'

" Ay, I was duly informed here," said Maguire bitterly, "that the great Ulster army was broken up and the chiefs hiding in holes and corners—what hath wrought such a change ?"

" The arrival of a certain Colonel O'Neill from Flanders or somewhere there—at least so they say here in Dublin !"

" What! Owen Roe ?" cried Maguire with joyful eagerness.

" I believe they call him so."

" Now, God be praised for that news," ejaculated the chieftain fervently—and he raised his tearful eyes to heaven. " Phelim, I know, would do his best," he murmured to himself, " but he *was* not—*is* not the man to marshal a host and keep men together,"—then raising his voice he said, "accept my thanks, fair Emmeline !"

" I admire your patriotism," said the lady with a faint blush on her delicate cheek ; " and your thanks are valued as they ought, but in this last sad hour—*moment* I should say—when discovery may be my death, and yours may be nearer than you think—are we to part as ever before ?'

" Emmeline," said the chieftain with a quivering lip and a downcast eye, " daughter of our enemy ! what wouldst thou have me say ?"

" Alas ! Connor, that parent of mine who *was* thine enemy is beneath the sod, the other is *thy* friend, and the *enemy* of no living creature."

" Your father dead !—Sir Charles Coote dead ! How ?—when ?"

" I may not, cannot tell thee now—moments are too precious —say only, ere we part, most likely, for ever, dost thou still regard Emmeline Coote in no other light than as the daughter of a foeman ?"

Maguire bit his lip till it was colorless as his cheek, but no word of answer came.

" Say !" resumed the lady with that startling vehemence which now and then marked her manner, " say, Connor Maguire, *am* I still an enemy ?—I who, with intent to serve thee, have laid aside full many and many a time the garments of my maidenhood and donned such unwomanly vesture as to make my cheek burn with shame—I who have braved danger, ay ! and death, even on the field where death was rifest, watching and waiting for some turn of affairs favorable to your chance of escape—I who have closed mine ears to the voice of love and looked coldly on the best and bravest when they bent before me—I who am here—*here*—within these fated walls to look once more upon your face and win a word of kindness from your lips before they take you hence——"

"But whither do they take us, Emmeline?—tell me that, I implore thee!"

"Whither but to England, to London, most like to the Tower to await a trial."

"It is well," said the chief, drawing himself up proudly, "it is well they deem us of so great importance, but as for trying us in England, that they may not, dare not do—such trial were mockery!"

"I tell thee, Connor, they will do and dare all things—law is as nought in their hands, for their *will* is the law in this land, this party of the Parliament—but answer my question while time permits—already in the distance I hear heavy footsteps—an' they have time to return from Blackrock, whither, I know, they have sent, we are all lost. *Is* thy heart still hardened towards her who hath watched at the door of this thy dungeon, ay! the long night through, sharing thine anguish though all unknown to thee—dost thou still regard *her* as an enemy, the daughter of a hated race, who hath never regarded thee but as the preserver of her life?"

It seemed as though a sudden pang here seized upon the lady's heart for all at once she stopped and turned ghastly pale. Maguire saw the change with alarm—he knew not that it was the sting of conscience which quivered in her heart, as hateful memory recalled the night of his arrest and the part which the unbridled spirit of revenge had made her play. But the generous heart of Maguire was never prone to suspicion, and her ominous threat on that fatal night, and the scathing mockery of her greeting subsequent to his capture were at that moment forgotten—her love, wild, passionate, and unquenchable, was alone remembered.

For a moment he stood irresolute in accordance with the usual indecision of his character, but a glance at the beautiful eyes so

intently fixed upon him, and the trembling eagerness expressed
in every perfect feature of the face before him, at once unsealed
his lips and sent a warm glow to his sunken cheek.

"Emmeline," said he, "this is neither the hour nor the place
to make professions which in my case were but empty sounds.
This only will I say"—he paused—glanced again at the bright-
ening orbs to whose witchery he had never been insensible, and
went on in quick, hurried accents : "This only will I say—I am
not—nor ever was—ungrateful, and were I still Chieftain of Fermanagh—ruling as a prince the broad domains of my fathers,
instead of a poor, despised, ragged captive far from home and
friends—then should the Lady Emmeline hear from me, what
now were shame to speak—go, too lovely and too loving !—fairest of Saxon maidens! go—leave me—forget Maguire, and be
happy !"

"Oh Heaven! I thank thee," murmured the lady with passionate fervor, and the tears, so long pent-up, streamed unheeded
down her peachy cheeks ; "for this moment have I lived, and
even death were welcome now, could we but die together. But
no—*he* shall be saved, come what may. Connor Maguire, this
moment repays me for all—all I have suffered, all I have done.
But enough hath been said. We must *act* now. Here, divest
thyself quickly of those garments and don these !"—and tearing
off her doublet and trunk hose she flung them into the cell,
without changing her own costume in aught, for duplicates of
the articles aforesaid appeared underneath. "Leave your tattered vesture in the cell," whispered Emmeline, "and come
forth as quick as may be!" So saying she retired some paces
from the door, and drawing her long sabre anew, took to pacing
to and fro in the passage as though on guard.

"Emmeline," whispered the chief, "what is thy purpose ?—
explain, if thou wouldst have me do thy bidding !"

"I would save thee—or die with thee—haste—haste !"

"But how ? What wouldst thou do ?"

"Clothe myself in thy cast-off garments and remain in thy
place !"

"And I ?"

"Will escape as Coote's trooper an' thou delay not too long !"

" Never, never," cried the generous chieftain, with the air of one not to be moved from his purpose; "never, and leave thee for a victim. Begone, Emmeline, this moment begone—for me there is no hope—but thou—oh, fly ! fly ! an' thou lovest me !"

" It is too late—oh, Connor ! Connor !"

" Hast said thy say to the prisoner, young sir ?" demanded the deep, authoritative voice of the turnkey, who at that moment appeared with the respectable Judkins, the latter crest-fallen and silent, doubtless the effect of his double disappointment ; " hast said thy say, for the hour is all but expired, and both must be given up on the instant——"

With a heavy sigh and a despairing look at the object of her romantic passion, ere the door was closed upon him, the fair Emmeline sheathed her sword, and followed the official. Master Osee Judkins brought up the rear, muttering to himself words that to a practised ear would have sounded strangely like Latin, with this interpretation :

" Give them help, O Lord, from Thy holy place, and from Sion protect them !"

Reaching the courtyard, and questioned by Willoughby himself as to the success of his mission, the grave gentleman shook his head sadly, observing that the great clemency of his patron, William Parsons, was, in the case of these recreants, thrown away —literally pearls thrown before swine, " the which, thou knowest, Francis, is set down as folly in the Book of books."

But Willoughby was in no mood to descant on Scriptural philosophy, and he roughly admonished the "reverend seignor" to betake him whence he came, without more ado.

" I'll warrant me thou art some newly-arrived place-hunter from beyond the Channel," said he, "arraying thyself in the solemn garb of the covenant the better to hunt down a good fat quarry here amongst the Irishry—go to, old meddler,—or rather, look to him, soldiers, till my messenger return. Meanwhile, bring forth the prisoners once more, waiting the Lord Justice's will in their regard !"

Great was the consternation of all present when the messenger returning stated that Sir William Parsons had entered into no negotiations with the prisoners, nor had sent any message to them whatsoever, but was, on the contrary, exceedingly wroth that their shipment had been delayed on such pretence. He, moreover, commanded Willoughby to look closely after the audacious impostors, who must have had some treasonable motive for such an act.

Orders were instantly issued for the gates to be closed and the traitors secured, but alas! Judkins was gone—the place that knew him late, knew him now no more, and equally vain was the search for "Coote's trooper," horse and man had both vanished, none could tell how.

In the utmost trepidation, Sir Francis sent once more for the prisoners, doubtless fearing that their mysterious visitors had kidnapped both of them, by means of some Popish glamoury or other. To his great relief they were speedily brought forth, and without further delay were placed in the centre of the column and marched to the Bridge-foot, where the good ship Royal Charles waited to receive them.

"Fare thee well, Sir Francis!" cried McMahon at parting; "I commend to thy favor the worshipful and godly Osee Judkins —an' thou takest a friend's advice, thou wilt send him on an embassy to the Council of Kilkenny.'

"Sirrah, dost thou dare to mock me?" vociferated Willoughby.

"Sirrah in thy teeth, Willoughby! I defy thee!"

These were the last words poor McMahon spoke on Irish soil, for the armed minions of the government tore him away, and when the final moment came he was dragged with his friend on board the ship; his heart was too full for parting speech.

CHAPTER VIII.

"Shout for the mighty men,
    Who died along this shore—
    Who died within this mountain's glen!
    For never nobler chieftain's head
    Was laid on valor's crimson bed,
      Nor ever prouder gore
    Sprang forth than theirs who won the day
    Upon thy strand, Thermopylæ!"

REV. GEORGE CROLY.

"Tho' gentle in her bearing, yet, of all the rude crew there,
    Not one would dare uncourteously to treat that lady fair."

OWEN ROE was at all times an early riser, and on the morning
following the ghostly visitation related in a preceding chapter
he was out reconnoitering the vicinity of the Castle, and the
town of Charlemont, long before the roseate glow of the dawn
had faded from the eastern sky. With the practised eye of a
military leader he had noted every brake, and bush, and knoll on
either side of the river, in anticipation of some future occasion,
and having traversed the narrow limits of the town, making
observations as he went, he was hurrying along through the deserted little main street, anxious to reach the Castle before the
inhabitants began to stir, when a blithe voice hailed him from the
river side with a gay "God save you, General!"

"And you, too," O'Neill responded with right good will as the
young Rapparee Captain gained his side from the bank whose
hawthorn bushes had concealed him.

"You're early out, I'm proud to see," observed Donogh;
"Commanders like you and me," he added with an arch smile,
"should never let the sun catch them a-bed. Now that's one
thing Sir Phelim had need to learn if he ever means to do much

for king or country. He's entirely too fond of the bed, General, not to speak of something else that's just as bad—or worse"— and he made a motion of his hand as though draining a goblet.

Although convinced in his heart that there was but too much truth in what the young man said, still Owen O'Neill was not the man to encourage such discourse from a mere stranger.

"Excuse me, friend," he said in a firm but very gentle tone; "Sir Phelim, thou knowest, is my kinsman, and being so, I would rather not hear of his faults—if faults he have. This Castle is a place of some strength, but I perceive it stands in need of some repairs."

"Ay, for the reasons I told you of," replied Donogh, "your honorable kinsman hath not done much to strengthen it."

"Knowest thou the exact strength of the Scotch in these parts?" O'Neill asked abruptly.

"It were hard to say," the Rapparee replied in a voice so unsteady that the General looked at him with surprise, and was amazed to see every feature of his comely face in convulsive motion; "pardon me, General," he said, or tried to say, but further he could not go.

"But why this agitation, young friend?" O'Neill anxiously inquired.

"One day thou shalt know all," was the faint reply, "ay! and mayhap before long, but ask no farther now. General," he said with a sudden change of manner as a new idea struck him; "General, wouldst wish to see our lodgment in the woods, and make acquaintance with my comrades?"

"Methinks I would," O'Neill replied after a short pause, "provided they knew not of my coming—I would see them in their ordinary life."

"Thou shalt see them, then."

"What, now? Is your encampment, then, so near?"

"I said not now," said Donogh with recovered composure; "night will best show you what manner of men they be who follow my banner"—again he smiled—"so an' it pleaseth thee, noble sir, to come with me for some hours when the shades of night cover the earth, I will show thee what knight or noble never saw save those of our own blood!"

" Thanks, good friend," said the General; "I will gladly take thee at thy word. We part here, I think, or art bound like myself for the Castle ?"

" Truly yes," laughed the Rapparee; " I mean to break my fast at Sir Phelim's expense—this musket of mine"—pointing to the one which hung over his shoulder—"hath brought down nothing this morning yet. But, tell me, General, and excuse me, an' I make over free—what thinkest thou of that gay Norman knight who left here yester-morn ?"

" Marry, he seemeth a gallant gentleman, and well affected towards the good cause. More I know not of him. But thou, Donogh, if such be thy name," the Rapparee nodded, "thou and he had met before—what of him ?"

" In sooth I know but little," the young man replied, "but that little would make me fearful of trusting him too far. Not that I would doubt him now, for he is, as thou sayest, a gallant gentleman, and his father, the old Lord Netterville, I have seen dealing heavy blows with his own good sword on some of Ormond's fellows at that unlucky pass of Mageny ; but still, General, I would not trust the son while he turned on his heel——"

" And wherefore not, Donogh ?"

" Why, an' it please you, General, there's a lady in the way, and hard fortune to them for ladies! but it's they that keep the world in hot water, anyhow! Now, this Sir John Netterville suspects—and, between you and me, I think he's not far wrong— that the beautiful lady he has an eye on, thinks more of Lord Maguire than she does of him—didn't you see how the venom was spewing out of him when the O'Cahan ladies told how the young chief saved her life ?"

O'Neill nodded assent. " Well, then," resumed Donogh, " when the black drop is in him that way, it will show itself maybe when you least think it. If ever the Lord of Fermanagh gets out of prison, an' that lady and he come together—which God in Heaven forbid,—for she comes of a rascally breed—then I wouldn't give a snap of my finger for Sir John Netterville's good will towards us Irish."

" There may be something in what you say, friend," said O'Neill with a thoughtful brow, for he was thinking how Judith,

too, had warned him on this head; "in any case, this young
knight is not, or never may be, subject to my command—our
paths are widely different, Donogh. But hark! the trumpet
from the walls—to rouse the garrison, most like."

The lady-moon had not yet showed her silver disk above the
horizon that night when Owen Roe O'Neill and his trusty guide,
having crossed the bridge at Charlemont, and traversed the then
scarcely formed village of Moy, sped on their way with lightsome step through the heathy moors of Tyrone, in the direction
of Benburb, following the course of the river. Little conversation
had passed between the two, for O'Neill was busy with his own
thoughts and speculations, and Donogh, through respect, kept
some paces in advance. Reaching the old Castle of Benburb, even
then a gray ruin lone and unlovely, untenanted save by the
bird of night, Owen Roe suddenly stopped and fixed his eyes
on the old fortalice. Grand and commanding it looked, seated
high on its rocky throne, with its solitary tower and its shattered
outworks clearly reflected in the winding stream, while the
moonlight brought out in strong relief the Cyclopean structure
of the time-worn and war-worn edifice.*

"What building is this?" demanded the General.

"That—oh! that is Benburb Castle," the guide carelessly replied; "I thought you knew it, General."

"I *guessed* as much," said O'Neill, his eyes wandering eagerly
over the storied scene. "In dreams," he murmured as if to
himself, "I have visited ere now the Blackwater's banks—Benburb, and Portmore, and the Yellow Ford are as places I have
often seen. Ay! surely that is Benburb Castle, even such as
I saw it in a vision of the night when the great Hugh stood before me and uttered words concerning this nation which mortal
lips may not speak again."

"Good Lord!" said Donogh to himself, and he moved some
steps away; "good Lord! he's talking to the ghost of Hugh

* This ancient stronghold of the O'Neills is composed entirely of
huge boulders, apparently from the river's bed, joined by no cement
of any kind. This peculiarity of construction gives Benburb Castle
a look of still greater antiquity than it really possesses.

O'Neill,—and may be it isn't right for me to stay so near. In God's name I will, though, for sure I promised to take him to the wood, and I'm bound to keep my word. Blessed Mary! what a tongue he has when he comes to use it! Now I'm sure Phelimy Roe could no more discourse that way than he could fly. I'll move a little farther, anyhow, for sure if I heard the spirit's voice it was all over with me. Still, if I could only catch one word from the great O'Neill of all—even if he *be* a ghost—but no—no—if *the voice* froze my blood and the heart in my body, who would do what *I* have to do—what *must* be done? Sure it isn't a poor *gersha* that would do it?"

Thus soliloquizing, Donogh leaned his arm on a broken wall, and, keeping his eye on the General, to see that no harm befel him, he sank into a train of thought, very bitter and very painful, judging by the contortions of his usually mild face, and the lurid light which flashed at times from under his darkly frowning brow.

Meanwhile, O'Neill stood contemplating the Castle and the river, and the river's banks. Lost in the thick-coming memories of the past, the glories of his warlike ancestors, the tales of their noble achievements, drank in his earlier years from the lips of his exiled father, these, with the old, old story of the nation's wrongs and the people's sufferings, all came rushing on his mind, and, bowing his stately head, as though under the influence of some mighty presence, he stood motionless as a statue.

"And this is the Blackwater?" he said within himself, "the frontier-line of the land of Owen, the impassable barrier against southern raid, the boundary which Saxon might not cross and live!—the river which hath witnessed, above all others, the heroic deeds of the sons of Nial—thou—thou—old stream, the god-made threshold of their broad domains—thou reflectest to my mind, as clear as in a mirror, the martial exploits of Hugh, and Shane, and Donald of illustrious memory,* and many an-

---

* The valorous exploits of poor Shane O'Neill against the myrmidons of English oppression are well known to most readers, and the Donald here mentioned was the same who, in a preceding reign, treated as a royal sovereign with the Spanish monarch, soliciting aid for Ireland.

other princely chief of my race who upheld in his day the cause
of country and religion. Oh river, now so bright in the fair
moon's ray, well have the Saxons named thee *Black*,* for a black
stream hast thou been to them. Ha! ha! thou art not yet so
black as thou shalt be, an' God spare me life. An' it be given
me to rule this land and this people, there remain yet other
pages of thy story to be turned over, oh stream so fateful to the
children of Nial! And thou, crumbling relic of our house's
greatness, weird witness from the past, I greet thee with respect.
Should success attend mine efforts, thy age shall be renewed—
thou shalt grow young again like the eagle, and thy now defenceless walls bristling with the captured cannon of the enemy,
thou shalt, as of old, keep watch and ward over the passes of
the river. Fare thee well, Benburb! my heart is stirred within
me, I know not why, as I look upon thee, and my soul is on fire
for high emprise—shades of my fathers! I follow in your footsteps——"

"I knew it," muttered the Rapparee leader who had heard
distinctly these latter words; "I knew he wouldn't talk so without the best of company. I would he were safe away from here,
for the icy breath of the dead will pierce the marrow of his bones
—but what am I saying—sure he isn't like other men at all—
him that was so long foretold in prophecy—isn't it half a spirit
he is himself? The ne'er a matter, he's flesh and blood, anyhow,
so I needn't fear him!" And with that he advanced towards
O'Neill with a determined air, as one who felt proud of a victory
over himself.

Dexterously and discreetly avoiding all allusion to what he
had seen or heard, Donogh met the General with an encomium
on the beauty of the night as though he had been lost in admiration.

"Isn't that the beautiful moon all out, General? and did you
ever see so many stars? myself was trying to count them there,
but it's what they seemed to be making their game of me for

---

* O'Sullivan, as quoted by Mitchel, says that the English gave
the name of *Blackwater* to this fine river on account of the many defeats sustained by them along its banks or in its vicinity.

the ne'er a one of them would stand still a minute but winking
and blinking at me up there and popping their bright heads in
and out till I was fairly bothered and had to give it up entirely.
Are we for the Brantree now?"

"The Brantree!* the Brantree!" O'Neill repeated like one in
a dream; "methinks I should know that name—it was of evil
repute, was it not, in the olden time?—the Brantree Wood! yes,
yes, a place of shelter for the robbers and outlaws of the country——"

"Have a care, General, what thou sayest," whispered Donogh;
"hedges and ditches have ears at times, and the Brantree is not
to be meddled with lightly—still, I see the place is not unknown
to thee, and this I tell thee that there be those hereabouts who
even now give it no better name."

They were passing at the moment an old, old graveyard, with
a church in the midst seemingly as old, and O'Neill somehow felt
a desire to linger a moment at the gate. Not so with Donogh, who
was passing rapidly on, having, it would seem, no sort of fancy for
the lone dwellings of the dead. Just as they passed the gate,
however, a cracked female voice was heard to issue from the
shadow of its deep archway.

"Why, then, Donogh, is it to pass Eglish† you'd be doing, with
the great O'Neill from abroad, and not stop a minute to show
him where so many of the children of Nial rest? For shame,
Donogh! I thought you had more gumshin in you. It's an ill
compliment you'd be paying the spirits that have waited long
for him to revenge their wrongs."

"Who can that be?" cried O'Neill in surprise.

"Hush, hush," Donogh whispered again, then raising his voice
he said in a soothing tone:

---

* The Brantree Wood is, or was, even in the last generation, an ex-
tensive woodland tract not many miles from Benburb—most probably
a remnant of the wide-spreading forests for which Tyrone was once
famous. Many wild traditions concerning it were common amongst
the people.

† I have slightly changed the topographical position of old Eglish,
but the other facts are correct.

"Sure you couldn't suspect me of the like of that, Granny? I was for taking the General to the brow of the hill above where he'd have a good look at the place."

"Bring him hither, I tell thee, that *I* may have a good look at *him!*"

"We must do as she bids us, General," said Donogh to his wondering companion; "no one thinks of gainsaying granny."

"I am quite willing," said Owen Roe, and the two approached the gate.

"Stop there," said the cracked voice, "there where the moonlight is full on his face—there now—that will do!"

Owen Roe stood still as directed, and looked curiously into the arch, now partially illumined by the moon's rays shining through the thick oaken bars of the gate. At first he could see only a dark crouching thing in the farther corner. Slowly, slowly, it began to move, and raising itself up a foot or two higher, it appeared a little old woman leaning on a stick, with the hood of her red cloak thrown over her head so that only occasional glimpses could be had of the withered face beneath. Yet O'Neill did not fail to note that there was something more than ordinary in the bold, firm lines of that wrinkled visage, and the small dark eyes that gleamed out so wildly from under the red hood.

"Stand back there, Donogh," said the weird hag, "keep your own place, my boy, in this presence." The Rapparee did as he was bid, and O'Neill, who had braved death on many a field and in many a shape, felt a strange awe creeping over him, for he knew that the keen old eyes were reading his soul through the features of his face. Silent they all three were for a brief space, and then the strange old woman drew a long breath and spoke, as though to herself:

"He will do," she said, nodding her aged head as though the fate of the nation rested on her nod; "*he* will do, anyhow—Phelimy Roe may go—shake himself—I see the brightness on *his* brow,—that is the blessing of God,—and there's the quietness, too—that is the good conscience—ay! and there's the grandeur and the loftiness of the high blood of Nial—and the strong arm and the fleet limbs—surely, yes, there is the man to

bring the past and the future together and make the sad days of
bondage and mourning like unto the bright days of old—ay!
that is the man for whose coming I waited, and now I care not
how soon I go to my fathers here within! Long have I watched
the sleep of the sleepers in the dark hours when only *themselves*
were near me, waiting for *the man* that was promised—now, I'll
go home—home—home!"—and so saying, out she stept into the
clear moonlight on the road, supporting herself on her knotted
oaken staff. "There now," she hoarsely muttered, "there's the
gate to *you*—son of my race, take old Mabel's blessing, ere she
go hence forever! These eyes have seen the great Hugh in the
height of his splendor, and alas! in the depth of his sorrow, too
—I lived to see Owen Roe, *the O'Neill* of God's making, and so
my race is run."

Owen Roe would have gladly questioned the old woman who
had "seen the great Hugh," but his first attempt was unsuccessful, for she waved him off with the air of one who must be
obeyed, and tottered down the road, muttering gloomily to herself. She had not gone many paces, however, when a new
thought seemed to strike her, and she turned her head half
round.

"Donogh," said she, "I need not tell you to obey *him* in all
things, and to fight till death against the enemies of God's people—but this I want to tell you: Keep close watch over them
you know—the lamb can't be safe while the wolf is near the fold
—so to God and you I leave them!"

"Granny! Granny!" cried Donogh in some trepidation, "they
are not depending now on poor fellows like me and mine; the
General here has taken them in charge from the very first—so
there's no fear of them with God's help and *his*—there's a muz-
zle on the wolf already!"

"Praised be the Lord, that makes my mind easy!" and turning again to the road, the aged crone moved away with an unsteady faltering step. O'Neill stood looking after her for longer
time than he was conscious of, spell-bound, as it were, by her
strange, weird look, and ways not less strange. He was roused
by the respectful voice of Donogh at his side:

"General," said he, "for all granny was so wishful that you'd

see it, I don't know if you'll care much about the place. When
you saw herself, you saw the greatest curiosity I ever knew
about Eglish—barring the bell——"

" The bell ! what bell !"

" Why, a bell that rings underground in it whenever one of
your name of the real old stock without any mixture is brought
for burial.* The minute the corpse is carried inside the gate,
the bell begins tinkle, tinkle, but as if it was away ever so far,
and there it keeps ringing with a silvery sound till the grave is
closed.

" Did you ever hear it yourself, Donogh ?" O'Neill interrupted
with a most incredulous smile playing about his mouth.

" Well ! I can't say I did, General, but there's them living in
the neighborhood that *did* hear it."

" I wish I could hear it myself," said Owen Roe, as he turned
from the gate after a hasty survey of the old cemetery ; " hearing, like seeing, is believing, thou knowest, Donogh. However,
an' we mean to visit the Brantree *this* night, I would we were
on our way. Not but what I could stand longer," he said within
himself, " contemplating yonder quiet scene where so many of my
kindred sleep in peace under the moonlit sod." And he looked
back with a parting sigh.

The word was all that Donogh needed, and again the pair addressed themselves to the road. Few words passed beetwen them
until, having ascended the steep hill, they found themselves on the
outskirts of the forest ; dark and mysterious it lay before them,
with the moonbeams flickering here and there through the open-
ings in the thick foliage above.

" Welcome to the Brantree, General !" said Donogh, as they
stepped into the deep shade ; " there's a path here that will take
us some distance, if you will just follow me, or—give me your
hand, and I'll lead you on !"

" Thanks, friend," said O'Neill, " but I will not trouble thee
so far—now that my eyes are accustomed to the gloom, I can
perceive the pathway by the help of those occasional glimpses
of light from above."

* This story is current with regard to more than one graveyard in
the old Celtic parts of Ulster.

"In former times," observed Donogh, as they made their way slowly through the bushwood, "we had not come even so far in without a challenge. From the time that the chieftains raised their banners and the power of the stranger was broken in the land, the dwellers in the woods gave themselves but little trouble keeping sentry, for indeed it's roaming abroad they used to be through the fields—but of late since things began to go against us, and Sir Phelim and the other chiefs weren't able to hold their own, we were forced to take to our old quarters— with God's help, though, the tables will soon turn again——"

"Who goes there?" said a rough voice almost close to them.

"The best of friends, Murtagh," replied Donogh; "are you all alive here?"

"Ay, ay, Captain, alive and kicking." "Kick away, then, and good luck to you!"

The path which had hitherto guided the progress of our travellers now disappeared, or rather they turned away from it in a diagonal direction into a a deeper and still darker portion of the wood where rocks piled on rocks at times rose up before them.

"Who comes here?" demanded another voice from behind a projecting fragment of rock.

"The pike's point," was the answer.

"Sharp as ever—pass on!"

"Now, most noble sir," whispered Donogh, "we're near our journey's end. I hope you'll not be disappointed in regard of what you came to see; at any rate, it will be something new!"

As yet there was no sign of any living being, nor a glimpse of light, for there the moonlight never made its way, and Owen Roe began to wonder how he could be so near an encampment when all at once his guide stopped short, and said in a loud cheerful tone that woke the echoes of the woods:

"General Owen Roe O'Neill, welcome to the Rapparee Camp!"

At the same moment a sight burst on the General that in all his experience of camps he had never seen—a sight both new and startling. A glade of the forest was before him, or rather a rocky woodland dell, into which the unclouded moon, now high in the heavens, shed down her floods of silvery light. A

mighty rustling, as of a forest shook by the storm, followed
upon Donogh's greeting, and from out the dark shades all
around, and down from the shelves of the rocks, men, strong,
stout, stalwart men, came bounding together on the green
sward, while others who had been lying sprang to their feet,
so that the place was literally alive with men. Some were attired in the saffron-dyed garments distinctive of the Irish kern of
that and former days, a garment the voluminous folds of which*
gave formidable breadth to the figure of the wearer ; others wore
the national *truis* and *cochal* formed of various materials, but
in general of showy and mixed colors ; while some again were
scantily clad in the coarsest cloth wrapped around them somewhat after the Indian fashion. Most of the heads had no other
covering than their thick *glibbe* of long hair, others had high
round caps made of the skin of various animals, while not a few
were seen with silken or velvet *barradhs*, and even plumes were
not wanting to catch the moon's ray as their owners stood in
conscious superiority amid the strange associates which oppression and the wild thirst for revenge had given them.

"Shoulder your pikes!" cried Donogh, and instantly a forest of those formidable weapons shot up gleaming in the moonlight air. That was the Rapparee's salute.

"Behold our General—Owen Roe O'Neill!" said their Captain again ; "he has come to visit us in our wild-wood home,
desiring to do us honor!"

"He is welcome!—*Cead mille failthe !*" went forth from every
tongue, and the sound was like the ocean-surge rumbling amid
the rocks.

What O'Neill felt at that moment it were not easy to describe,
but a few burning words he spoke, words of strength, and hope,
and power, which made the Rapparees forget their usual and
not unnecessary caution, and a wild and long-continued cheer
awoke the startled echoes of the place, and roused the red deer
from their midnight lair.

"I have given him command over you in your own name !"

* We are told that from twenty to thirty ells of this dyed linen
were sometimes employed in the fabrication of one of these garments.

said Donogh; "are you content to do his bidding in all things—sons of the Gael, say?"

"We are content," spoke the deep many-toned voice again. "By our father's wrongs and ours, we will faithfully serve him!"

"For God and holy Ireland!" said Owen Roe in a tone of deep feeling.

"For God and holy Ireland!" the homeless multitude responded.

"It is well said," spoke a voice from the farther side of the glade, a voice which made Owen O'Neill start, for soft and feminine it was, although clear and distinct, and moreover it sounded strangely familiar to his ear.

"Comrades, fall back right and left," said the Captain. The wood-kern instantly obeyed, and a still stranger scene was presented to the eyes of the foreign bred descendant of the Hy-Nials. Under a sort of awning, skilfully and neatly formed by the interlaced branches of the forest trees, seated in rustic state on a primitive-looking chair well adapted to support her feeble frame, the aged Lady O'Cahan occupied the most prominent position. By her side stood her daughter, whose voice it was, as O'Neill rightly judged, that had so lately fallen on his ear. A score or two of women, wild, gypsey-like figures, yet many of them worthy studies for the painter, or the sculptor, were grouped around the aged lady, all, however, at a respectful distance, the moonlight giving to the whole scene a rich and picturesque character.

"Do mine eyes deceive me," said O'Neill, "or are those the ladies of Dungiven?"

"Even so," replied the Rapparee Captain; "we found that ever since their hiding-place was discovered they were watched day and night, and the fear began to come over them again, so I thought, and so did themselves, that it was not safe to be there any longer, and the boys here went to work and made the finest litter ever you saw of the branches of the trees, and brought their ladyships home."

"And it is to the Rapparees they come for protection?"

" Why, to be sure it is, General, and where else would they go—there's not a man you see there that wouldn't lose a thousand lives, if he had so many, to save them from hurt or harm."

And truer words were never spoken, for *there*, at least, Judith and her mother reigned as queens.

CHAPTER IX.

"And many an old man's sigh, and many a widow's,
And many an orphan's water-standing eye—
Men for their sons', wives for their husbands' fate,
And orphans for their parents' timeless death——"
SHAKESPEARE.

- "To trample on all human feelings, all
Ties which bind man to man, to emulate
The fiends, who will one day requite them in
Variety of torturing."
BYRON's *Two Foscari*.

IT was a pleasant renewal of acquaintance when Owen Roe was conducted by Donogh to a seat near the Lady O'Cahan, who rose with dignity to receive him, and extended her hand with as lofty an air as though she stood under the silken canopy as of old on the dais in Dungiven hall. To O'Neill's respectful salutation, Judith only bowed and said: "Welcome to the Rapparee camp, son of the Hy-Nial!"

"Chieftain of Tyr-Owen!" added the old woman.

"Nay, madam, not so," said O'Neill quickly; "such proud title belongeth not to me—I am simply, Owen Mac Art, endowed by the favor of the good people of these parts with the style of *General*—however unworthy I be to bear it! But chieftain of Tyr-Owen I am not—never can be!"

"Chieftain of Tyr-Owen I say thou art—or soon shall be." The aged lady repeated with solemn emphasis: "Before yonder moon puts forth her horns again the sept shall have a new ruler, and one shall sit in the chair of Royalty* whose feet have never

* The ancient coronation-chair of the O'Neill's on the Rath of Tulloghoge. The seat of it was, in former times, the famous *Lia Fail*,

yet pressed the grass of Tulloghoge! Believe my word, for the
voices of the night have made it known unto me!"

"*Dominus Vobiscum, fratres!*" said a voice from behind one
of the rocks, and Malachy na Soggarth stept out just in time to
prevent the commotion following on the unexpected sound. He
was accompanied by a nephew of his whom all recognized as
one of the holy confraternity of Rapparees. The fame of Malachy had long ago reached beyond the limits of McMahon's country, and no sooner was his name whispered around than a murmur
of kindly greeting was heard on every side.

"Welcome, Malachy," said the Captain advancing with a
smile to shake him by the hand; "in good hour thou camest
hither, but what wind bore thee to the Brantree?'

"By my word, good sir," said the panting follower of McMahon,
"I had hard work to get here, as Looney there can tell you.
But still I wanted to see what the place looked like when you'd
be all at home, the which I had often heard the boy say was a
fine sight entirely. When the bishop and myself came down to
Charlemont to the great meeting, I thought as I was so near I'd
go to Lough Derg* before I went home. So I just let his

or Stone of Destiny, afterwards removed to the royal abbey of Scone,
in Scotland, and now, it is believed, in Westminster Abbey.

* There are few of our readers unfamiliar with the name of this
famous little lake—a very small one it is, too—situate amongst dreary
hills in the county of Donegal. As containing the island which enjoys
the possession of St. Patrick's Purgatory, the Lough is and has been
for many centuries an object of veneration, not only in Ireland, but in
other Catholic countries. Speaking of Lough Derg a modern tourist
observes: "On the ridge where I stood, I had leisure to look around.
To the southwest lay Lough Erne, with all its isles and cultivated
shores; to the northwest Lough Derg—and truly never did I mark
such a contrast. Lough Derg under my feet—the lake, the shores,
the mountains, the accompaniments of all sorts, presented the very
landscape of desolation; its waters expanding in their highland solitude, amidst a wide waste of moors, without one green spot to refresh
the eye, without a house or tree—all mournful in the brown hue of
its far-stretching bogs, and the grey uniformity of its rocks; the surrounding mountains even partook of the sombre character of the place,

lordship go back his lone for this once, especially as the chief
was with him. I mean to start for the Island* now, by the peep
of day the morrow, but first I thought I'd see how matters stood
here, now that we're in a fair way for another brush with the
enemy."

Casting his slow glance around, Malachy's eye now lit on Lady
O'Cahan, and off went his cap at once with a " God and the
Virgin save you, lady !" Neither she nor her daughter was
known to him, but he well knew by the rough respect paid to
them that they were branches of some fallen tree that had tow-
ered high in its day.

O'Neill next came under Malachy's observation, and then his
surprise was at the height. Bowing down as low as he could
without losing his equilibrium, he drew himself up again to his
full perpendicular, and, for once, lost the use of his tongue.

" What, Malachy McMahon here ?" said O'Neill with a pleasant smile; " are you a Rapparee, too, Malachy ?"

" A Rapparee! your lordship!" Malachy exclaimed in no
small trepidation ; " me a Rapparee! me that wouldn't have
the heart to kill a chicken! a poor Rapparee *I'd* make !"

" No, General, said Donogh advancing, " Malachy isn't so
unlucky as to have any title to *that* name."

" Unlucky! how is that, Captain ?"

" Why, you see, there's ne'er a one of us here that hasn't a
commission from the enemy."

" A commission from the enemy—what may that mean ?"

" Well! it's a word that doesn't sound well," said the young

their forms without grandeur, their ranges continuous and without
elevation. The lake itself was certainly as fine as rocky shores and
numerous islands could make it. . . . ."

* THE ISLAND, so called by way of distinction, is the largest of
those which dot the reddish surface of Lough Derg (i. e. *the red lake*).
It is called the Station Island, as most of the stations are performed
there. In a cave of this world-famed island is the renowned Purgatory of St. Patrick, the scene of Calderon's great poem. On this
island are situate the chapel, priest's house, &c. On the Saint's Island,
one of lesser extent, are the ruins of an ancient priory.

16

Captain, "but still it's true—there's not a man here that hasn't his license to fight from one or other of the Puritan generals!"

O'Neill was at a loss to understand his meaning, and Donogh hastened to explain with a bitter laugh. "Now," said he, "General O'Neill, what I mean is this: there is not one of us pikemen here who hath not a dismal score to settle with these accursed strangers, a debt as binding on our consciences as one of red gold—ay! and a thousand times more so. Stand forward, Florry Muldoon! and tell the General what hath made you a Rapparee!"

The person addressed, a tall and venerable-looking man of some sixty odd years, advanced, with his pike on his shoulder, and spoke in a deep, husky voice:

"The wife of my bosom and the children of my love—my two fine sons and three daughters, the flower of the country side, were butchered by a party of Montgomery's soldiers before mine eyes—" he stopped—he could say no more.

"Did they *only* butcher them all, Florry?" said another veteran pikesman by his side,—a fierce-looking man of stalwart frame, still erect and firm.

"Wasn't that enough?" said the other, turning short on him.

"It *was*, Florry, sure it was, enough to make you a sworn Rapparee, but it wasn't so bad but what it might be worse. Now I had only one daughter—only one—and there's many here can tell you what Nora O'Boyle was—it wouldn't become me to say it anyhow,—me that *was* her father—well! that darling of the world—the best child that ever broke the bread of life—one of their officers laid an eye on her as she was washing clothes at the river with some neighbor women, and—and—they took her, so they did, and they threw her over one of their cruppers all as one as a bag of oats, and they put a gag on her mouth, and carried her off, and hilt or hair of her we never seen till after her poor mother died of a broken heart, and then she dropped into us one black day without knowing where she was going, for—for—the wits had left my *lanna* entirely. Och, boys, boys, wasn't it a wonder I kept my own—wasn't it?—nor I suppose I wouldn't either, only that I tried to keep myself cool and quiet on account of the work that was before me. And I did part of it already—

faith I did so, for that devil's limb of an officer was pointed out to me not long after by one who had seen him taking the gersha away, and I gave him his oats—ha! ha! ha! I'll go bail he'l be as quiet as a lamb for the time to come."

"Why, wh t did you do, Pete ?" said his Captain much interested, as were all who heard the sad recital.

"Do!—oh, then, I did plenty!—I clove him to the belt with this brave hatchet of mine—do you see it, Captain?—it's my companion ever since by night and by day, and will, as long as there's a hell-hound of them Puritans on Irish soil to be hunted —oh faith, yes, Nora O'Boylo was well revenged, and shall be better, if I am spared !"

"And you, Diarmid!" said the Captain to a tall, athletic young man, with a frank, good-natured countenance, on which no trace of strong passion was visible, "what brought you here ?"

"It's easy told, Captain," the young Rapparee replied with a sudden change of manner—a ruffling, as it were, of the smooth surface; "I had two young brothers, as promising boys as you'd see in a summer's day, and Stewart's soldiers hung them like dogs from one of the trees in our own haggard——"

"Hung them!" repeated O'Neill in horror; "and why, good friend, I pray thee ?"

"Why, General, the soldiers stopped to water their horses near our house where the poor fellows were fishing,—for fun for themselves the *Sassum dergs* began to poke at the boys with their bayonets, calling them 'Papist brats' and all such hard names. At last one of my brothers—poor Connor—told them they had better leave off their tricks, or Sir Phelim might have a word to say to them—with that they made at the two, though one of them never opened his lips to say them ill, and they tore the clothes in flitters off their backs and made ropes of them to hang them!"

"And where were *you*, Diarmid, when that was done ?' said Judith from behind.

"Your ladyship may well ask the question," said the young man turning quickly and bowing very low; "my father and myself were at the bog a mile or so off, cutting turf—if we had been on the spot, it's like we couldn't have saved the gorsoons,

and it's like, too, that I wouldn't be here now to tell the tale—
but—" he paused to take breath, and a dark scowl settled on
his brow—"but, we'd have done for *the hangmen*, anyhow, if
nothing more. Still and all, I have one comfort," he added
with a ghastly smile, "if *they* escaped us, others of the murdering crew *did not*—we've brought down some of their highest
heads since then, and though I am alone now,—for the old
father is at rest long ago in Tynan mould,—there's strength
enough in this arm"—and he held up his brawny right arm—"to
do the work of two!"

"Your story is bad enough, Diarmid," said another young fellow, a strapping Tyrone mountaineer, coming forward, "but
wait till you hear mine."

"Ay! ay!" said many voices, "hear what Denny has to tell.
His is the worst of all."

"I had a kind loving mother once," said the tall Rapparee in
a gloomy voice, "and I had but her—we two were alone in the
world, and it's little either of us *cared* for the world, so long as
we had one another. Well! my poor mother was very fond of
her beads and her prayers, and when I used to be away from
home she'd spend most of her time in a sort of a cave in the
hill-side where there was an altar made of clay with a big flag
over the top, where Mass was said of an odd time before daylight in the morning when any priest came the way. There was
an old wooden cross up over the altar, you see, and my mother
and some others of the neighbors would go there when they
could to say their prayers on account of the cross and the altar
and Mass being said in it at times. But that didn't last long,
for one of the black nebs* that lived almost in the door with us,
happened to find out the secret, and doesn't he watch his opportunity till Mass was a-saying the next time, and then off he goes
to Castle-Stewart and brings a party of the red-coats and—and
they made a fire at the mouth of the cave—and smothered every
soul in it—ay! priest, people, and all!"

He got over the last part of his recital with much difficulty,

* This name was often given by the Catholics of Ulster to the stern
Puritans their neighbors.

for the words were choking him, and when he had ended, he clenched his ponderous fist and ground his teeth like a tiger athirst for blood, then, as if unable to endure the sight of mortal man, he turned and rushed into the depth of the forest.

"Poor fellow!" said one of his comrades looking after him, "he was away at the time with Sir Phelim's army near Drogheda."

"Great God! how terrible—how piteous are these tales!" cried Owen O'Neill, his features betraying the extent of that emotion which he cared not to express; "was ever people so wronged, so outraged as this?"

"And remember what I told you at the start, General," said Donogh in a husky voice, "that every one of us here has credentials from the enemy. You see now what kind they be, and may guess from that what manner of soldiers the wood-kern are, and why it is that they hate us as they do. We stink in their nostrils, and no wonder. However, General, I think you have heard enough to convince you that you may trust a Rapparee at any hour or in any place. Slieve Gullian there beyond will move from its old stand before one of us betrays the cause."

A deep murmur of applause now ran through the assembly, and the very pikes on the men's shoulders made a clatter by way of accompaniment.

"You have spoken only for the men, Captain," said Judith O'Cahan from her place beside her mother; "let *me* remind the General that all these helpless females have similar tales to tell. The daughters of the land are, it may be, the most aggrieved, in that they must perish, these woful days, when deprived of their natural protectors, and turned out on a bare, desolate country, where those who would befriend them have not the power or the means."

"Ay," said the old man Florry Muldoon, "just look at the old madam, and think of what she was!"

"Let that pass, I pray you," said Judith haughtily; "*our* wrongs are known to General O'Neill, and we love not to hear them told over!"

The pride of her princely lineage tinged the pale cheek of O'Cahan's daughter, and made her averse to have the dark pages of her house's latter fortunes held up for the inspection of a multitude.

This O'Neill saw, and he well understood the feeling. "Friend Donogh," he said, hastily addressing the Captain, "I am anxious to learn what score you have against the Sassenach. You told me but lately that I should one day know it all—is the time yet come?"

This question produced a startling effect on Donogh. The blood rushed to his face, then back again to his heart, and left him pale and livid as a corpse. A sudden faintness came over him, too, and he grasped the arm of Angus Dhu who stood near him at the moment.

"Poor boy! poor boy!" ejaculated Malachy, "there's a weakness coming over him—is there any water at hand?"

"Ay, oceans of it," said Donogh, mastering himself by a violent effort, and no little amused by Malachy's compassionate demand for water; "were you wanting any?" Turning to O'Neill before the slow organs of Malachy had prepared an answer, the young man said:

"Although I'd a'most as soon take the earth from over them and leave all comers to look upon their mouldering remains as to tell over the black, horrid murder of my nearest and dearest, still, I'll do it at your bidding, General O'Neill, to let you see what devils in human form you have to deal with. You have heard surely of Island Magee?"

"Heard of it, Donogh! ay, marry, have I—all Europe hath rung with the name, and the horror of that massacre hath made the blood in even royal veins to run cold—it moved the inmost heart of Christendom."

"Well! General, on that night of woe, I lost father and mother, sisters and brothers—well nigh all I had in the world——"

"Except one little bit of a *gersha*," said a voice from the outskirts of the crowd, "and no thanks to the *Sassum dergs* if you didn't lose her, too."

"True for you, Shamus!" cried Donogh quickly, for the voice was well known to him; "God knows, and I know, and Aileen knows, too, who it was that saved her. That's Sir Phelim's foster-brother, General," dropping his voice to an under tone.

"And is *he* one of you?"

"Well, no, General, he never took the oath, nor nobody asked him, but he comes and goes as he lists amongst us, for a truer comrade or a braver soldier never shouldered a pike. You might depend your life to him, though I don't say but he has a little coolness towards you on account of your stepping into Sir Phelim's shoes. You might as well touch the apple of his eye as touch his chief in aught."

"No blame to him for that," said Owen in the same low tone, "but," raising his voice, "you said most of your family were slaughtered on that fatal night."

"I did, General, and though I say it myself, there wasn't a happier or a more united family from here to there, nor one more comfortably situated—that is, for poor people—than *Corny Magee's!*" He stopped—his voice was lost in choking sobs, but any further words of his were superfluous at the moment, for, at the mention of that name, so often told over in the sad story of the massacre, a wild shout, a yell of execration for the perpetrators of the black deed, burst from the war-like Rapparees, making the rocks and the old woods ring again. Before the sound had died away, Donogh sprang on a ledge of rock near him, where the moonbeams shone full upon his light yet athletic figure and his now strongly agitated countenance. Tearing off the stripe of brown drugget from his arm, he held it up to the view of all.

"And there," said he, "mark those stains—they are the mingled blood of my parents—this was a piece of my mother's kirtle—it is now, and shall be to my latest breath, the badge of my office as avenger of my race! General, I pray you, excuse me," he said in a faint voice, as he reached his side again, amid the oft-renewed groans of the fierce multitude, "my heart is oppressed, and my brain throbs as though it would burst my head—I must e'en lay me down a brief space or the senses may go from me entirely! Angus, good boy, see if you can't find somewhat to offer the General in the way of eating or drinking!"

So saying, and leaning on the arm of Shamus, who had darted through the crowd for the purpose, the young Captain withdrew into the neighboring thicket, where his couch of heather had

been spread by careful hands. After a few moments, Shamus
came back, with the Captain's orders for the men to betake
themselves to rest. A few minutes more and the moonlight
glade was as silent and lonely as though the Rapparees were
miles away. The women quickly followed the example of the
men, and betook themselves to the place set apart for their accommodation, viz., a sort of sylvan saloon inclosed, where the
rocks and trees left it open, by a rude screen of wicker-work.

Before they retired, these amazons of the woods did not fail to
compliment the so-long expected leader, whose personal appearance and general demeanor they had been criticising amongst
themselves, "after the manner of women," to his decided advantage.

General O'Neill was much too polite, and, we must add, too
devoted an admirer of the sex, to receive such a manifestation
with even a show of indifference, and the smiling condescension
wherewith he thanked his fair friends for the expression of
their good opinion quite won their hearts. There was not one
of them, matrons or maids, who would not have sworn on the
Book that fine summer night that Owen Roe would have the
country cleared of the foreigners in "less than no time."

But there were those who spoke or stirred not whose opinions
would have carried more weight, and when, last of all, Judith
offered her arm to her mother, without even a word of encouragement, he felt disappointed he scarce knew why.

"Lady O'Cahan," said he, approaching her with the most
profound respect, "it grieves me more than I can say to leave
you and fair Mistress Judith in such unsafe quarters."

"Say not unsafe, I pray you," said Judith with the earnestness which belonged to her character; "I tell you, we deem
ourselves as safe here, surrounded by these wild, outlawed men,
as we would under cover of my father's ramparts in the days
when they were high and strong. There is not one of these
brave poor fellows that would not die to save us!"

"They have been the best of friends to us," muttered the aged
lady in her strange dreamy voice, "an' we ever come to have a
home, none of them shall want a shelter were they baun'd an
hundred times over."

" Heaven bless you, madam," said Donogh coming forward, " it's well we know what's in your heart for us, and sure you needn't make so much of the little we ever did for you—the black stranger couldn't do less, if he had e'er a heart within him! Well, General, I suppose you'd be wishful to get back now—it will be broad day before we get to the Castle."

" I want to lie down, daughter," said the old woman faintly, "the old bones of me are tired—tired—oh! age—old age, when thou and poverty come together, ye are poor, poor mates— poor, poor mates! Fare thee well, Owen O Neill, and take an old woman's blessing."

" God and the saints protect thee," whispered Judith, as she led her mother back into the woods. " Let me hear full soon of the inauguration on Tulloghoge—an' the clan will have it so, see that you oppose it not. _The O Neill_, thou knowest, ever holdeth the balance here in Ulster !"

CHAPTER X.

"To the common people,
How he did seem to dive into their hearts,
With humble and familiar courtesy!"
SHAKESPEARE.

"What fate imposes, men must needs abide;
It boots not to resist both wind and tide."
SHAKESPEARE.

A WEEK or so after Owen Roe's visit to the Brantree, a funeral train was seen wending its way amongst the hills and hillocks of that undulating district contiguous to old Eglish. The cortege was long and imposing in its character, for the clansmen of Tyr-Owen who bore the honored name of O'Neill were there in large numbers, and the martial regularity of their step and the gay costume so well known in the northern wars, gave a military air to the procession; but for the crowd of wailing women that followed next to the bier, (a sort of two-wheeled car commonly used then and long after by the peasantry,) one might have supposed that the dead was one of the warriors. Few would have guessed that it was the half-crazed "Granny the gate"* whom the O'Neills were bearing to her last resting-place amongst the dust of her progenitors. Yet so it was, and the death of that lonely old woman was sincerely mourned by the kind-hearted and unsophisticated children of the soil who had done all that her demented state would allow to make her last days comfortable.

* This custom of giving *soubriquets* from personal habits or pursuits has come down even to the present generation in the rural districts of Ireland. It is clearly borrowed from our own "Celtic Tongue," and has a strange sound in that imported from beyond the Channel.

And soon the procession was largely increased by many of the outlawed tenants of the Brantree, anxious to pay their tribute of respect to the blood that had filled the veins of Granny. Their captain, however, was not to be seen, for, long before the hour appointed for the funeral, he had gone in the train of Owen Roe miles away on an exploring expedition. It so happened that they reached the churchyard wall just as the gate was thrown open to admit her who had so long kept watch and ward thereat. Alighting from their horses, they followed the funeral into the graveyard, and strangely enough, from the moment the gate was opened, the low tinkling of a bell was heard distinctly, falling soft and silvery on the ear like the voices of long-departed friends heard in dreams of night. The cry of the keeners was instantly hushed, and the clansmen bowed their heads to listen.

"Now, General," whispered the Rapparee Captain, "what did I tell you—you believe my word now, do you not?"

"It is very strange," replied O'Neill, musingly. "But," he added, speaking to himself in an under tone, "supernatural agency is out of the question—a mystery there must be in it, and I would I might fathom it.* It sounds like a church-bell," he said to Donogh ; "hark !"

"It is even so, noble sir, and we simple country folk take it for a warning to be mindful of God's service. In days when there were no priests to be had here—even worse times than our own—they tell me that that was the meaning the people took from the sound of these-churchyard bells, and hearing them they thought of the Church and the Holy Mass and the Priest in his robes, and they promised to be always faithful to religion, and to do what it taught them, and they looked forward to better days to come.† God knows where the sound comes from !" he added, with the simple earnestness of a believer.

---

* Let no proud skeptic scoff at these innocent traditions and soul-soothing superstitions, peculiar to a faithful, unsophisticated people, circumstanced as our pious forefathers were. They are the superstitions of a Christian nation, long ground down by the persecuting arm of heresy.

† The story current amongst the peasantry is that some venturous

Meanwhile the interment proceeded, and while the nearest relations of the deceased were filling up the grave, the solemn and sweet tinkling of the invisible bell formed a strange accompaniment to the dull, heavy sound of the earth falling on the rough coffin.

Superstition had but little hold on the mind of Owen Roe, and yet the tinkling of that churchyard bell made no slight impression upon him, and came often on his ear in after years amid the roar of battle and the deafening crash of artillery.

When the last shovelful of earth was laid on the grave the knell ceased, and each having breathed a short prayer for the eternal repose of poor Granny, quitted the churchyard in silence, leaving the lone old watcher of the gate to sleep her last sleep in peace. Once outside the gate, the presence of Owen Roe was noticed by a wild cheer of joyous recognition, and the clansmen, supposing him to be there through respect for the old blood, pressed eagerly forward to shake hands and express their unbounded satisfaction. And the new-made general, the foreign officer of rank, exchanged a courteous greeting with each, and received their gratulations with evident pleasure, well pleased, as he said, to shake the hands that were to aid in working out the deliverance of their country. He was glad to make the acquaintance of so many of his "kith and kin," as he adroitly phrased it.

When Sir Phelim heard of his kinsman's appearance at, what would now be considered a *pauper* funeral, he burst into a loud laugh, and declared that Red Owen must be mad—mad as a March hare. When a few days had past, and Shamus came to tell him that he heard of nothing wherever he went but the g odness of Owen Roe and the *gra* he had for the old stock, and how he showed it more in the little time he was among them than *others* that were bred and born on the spot and *had a better right* to look after the people.

persons in after times, seeking to find out the secret of "the underground bell," dug up the consecrated earth till they came upon it, and lo! what should it be but the bell of a neighboring monastery, buried there ages before, during the spoliation following on the Reformation.

" Didn't I tell you now," added Shamus with a sagacious and exulting nod, " didn't I tell you the gentleman from abroad wasn't so mad as you thought in regard to the funeral? Take my word for it, Sir Phelim, he's as sharp and as cute a man as ever stepped in shoe leather. He never does anything without knowing well, well what he's about."

" I wish he was in Flanders back again!" said Sir Phelim in a petulant tone, which made his foster-brother laugh.

" He's not, then, nor won't be, so we must only make the best of it, and not be fretting about what can't be helped. But listen hither, chief!" and Shamus drawing near, stood up on his toes (for his stature, as his sobriquet of *beg* implied, was somewhat of the shortest) to whisper in Sir Phelim's ear: " I'm afeard they'll be for making him the O'Neill!"

" They dare not!" cried the chief with one of those sudden fits or bursts of anger to which he was subject; " they dare not, ingrates as they are!"

" I tell you they *will* dare, and that before long!"

" By the shrine of Ardmacha an' they do, I will—I will—"

" You will—what?"

" Kill all before me—I will, by the holy rood!"

" Ha! ha! ha! that sounds well, my chief," said the privileged foster-brother, and, were this foreign O'Neill not to the fore, you might get the better of them, but what do you think he and all the others would be doing while you'd be *killing?* No, no, Sir Phelim dear, think better of it, and you will see that the only way for you to hold your own is to keep cool and quiet— as quiet as a cat watching a mouse, and rub people down as smoothly as Owen Roe does. Humor them in little things, and they'll give you your own way in great things."

" I'd scorn it, Shamus," said Sir Phelim vehemently; " I'd scorn to make so little of myself. Even to keep the power and *the name* I wouldn't do it—I leave such tricks to this Spanish-Irish cousin of mine. But in the matter of the chieftainship, I tell you, Shamus O'Hagan, that I'd sooner they'd cut off this right arm of mine than give *him* that title—him a foreigner and—a bastard!"

" Whisht, whisht, Sir Phelim, darling," said Shamus anxiously,

and in a whisper; "for the love of God don't say the like of that
—they'll—they'll—oh, **Mother of God!** they'll do everything—
they'll have your life!"

"My life!" repeated the chief scornfully; "let them try it—
I should like to see them!—but an' they did seek my life, in
the foulness of their ingratitude, they might, perchance, have it
—but the title of O'Neill—the headship of the clan—never, never,
nerer—so help me Heaven and this strong right arm!—let the
spawn of a bastard breed look to it! Low, indeed, were the
chieftainship of Tyr-Owen fallen when it rested on the shoulders
of Owen Mac Art!"

"God and the Kinel-Owen will decide that!"

"Eh, what?—did you speak, Shamus?" cried Sir Phelim
with a start.

"Is it I, Sir Phelim?—why, no, I didn't—the Lord save us!"
and Shamus stood with open mouth, and a comical expression
of wonder on his broad face, looking hither and thither and all
around, but no human being save themselves two was visible in
the close paddock where Shamus was training a promising young
colt as a war-steed for his chief. The place was surrounded by
a high stone wall, here and there overhung by hawthorn and
elder bushes, and Sir Phelim darted off in one direction to see
whether the bushes contained an eaves-dropper, while Shamus,
letting go the halter, left *Brian Boromhe* to kick up his heels
and enjoy a canter round the paddock, while he scrambled to
the top of the wall to make a survey of the premises. But nor
man nor woman, beast or bird was discovered by either, save
only a solitary magpie sitting far up on the topmost bough of a
tall beech-tree, which in beauty and in breadth graced a corner
of the enclosure.

"I'll tell you what it is, Sir Phelim," said the foster-brother, as
the two stood together again, panting and sweating after their
fruitless chase, "if I had a gun loaded with a piece of silver, I'd
shoot that devil of a mag, for I'd almost swear it was it that
spoke, and you know"—lowering his voice—"the witches are
as plenty as blackberries round here. I'll go bail now if one
could only bring down that unlucky bird, it would turn into an
ill-favored old hag. There's plenty of them, between ourselves,

that have no liking for your four bones, God forgive them! But think no more about it, Sir Phelim dear! just watch now how beautifully I'll bring this fellow to his knees—when he gets the word you'll see he'll pop down all as one as a Christian!"

" You'll do what all the Danes in Ireland weren't able to do, then," observed Sir Phelim, with an attempt at pleasantry all unusual with him.

" What is that, Sir Phelim?" asked honest Shamus, whose faculties were never of the sharpest.

" Why, you say you can bring *Brian Boromhe* to his knee, and that's more than *they* could do with all the power they had —but there's Thorlogh making signs to me from the gate—now look to it, Shamus, that you go not blabbing amongst the neighbors in regard to what has passed."

" I'll make no promise of the kind," said Shamus gruffly as he turned away; "I'd thank people to keep their advice for them that needs it."

But Sir Phelim was already out of hearing, and Shamus was alone with *Brian Boromhe* and the magpie, who indubitably kept her perch for no good, as Shamus thought, and her persevering chatter gave him no little annoyance, as might be seen by the uneasy glances which he threw in her direction from time to time, muttering to himself certain objurgations not very complimentary either to magpies or old women, between whom Shamus had established a connection in his own mind, based on the supposition already hinted at.

From his brother Sir Phelim learned that a tumult had arisen amongst the soldiers in his Castle of Dungannon which only his own presence could quell. Carefully keeping the secret from Owen Roe, to whose arrival he at once attributed this commotion, the impetuous knight set out in a towering passion for Dungannon, with Shamus and some score or two of his followers.

The waning moon was near her setting and the dawn close at hand when the trumpet announced the chief's return to Charlemont. It was remarked by those who gave him admission that there was a ghastly paleness on his usually florid countenance, and a nervous tremor in his voice and manner, all of which led to the supposition that things had not gone well with the sturdy

knight at Dungannon. On questioning his attendants, however,
this notion was found erroneous, for, on the contrary, Shamus
and his fellows gave a most satisfactory account of their lord's
demeanor—unusually firm and self-possessed, his passion at the
start notwithstanding—and of the little trouble he had had in
bringing the men to subjection. What, then, must have caused
the unaccountable change in Sir Phelim's manner, the strange
depression, the wild restlessness of look and gesture? Many a
question was put to Shamus on the subject, but Shamus either
knew, or affected to know nothing of it.

The surprise of the garrison was at its height when it became
known that Sir Phelim had sent messengers out the first thing
in the morning to summon the clansmen to a meeting within the
week at Tulloghoge, on a day and hour specified, to transfer the
chief power of the sept to Owen Roe O'Neill. The latter had
hardly completed his brief soldierly toilet when he was invited
to walk abroad with the chief, and could scarce believe his ears
when Sir Phelim, with that grim courtesy which he well knew
how to assume at times, addressed him in this wise :

"I wish to inform you, General O'Neill, that before the week
is out you may expect a change here of some importance—to all
of us!"

"Of what nature, may I ask?"

"Of a nature, General Owen, to elevate *your* social standing
by more than a cubit's length, and lower mine in a like measure." This was said with a bitterness that could not escape the
other's penetration. He probably suspected what it meant, but
chose to affect ignorance.

"An' you favor me no with some further enlightenment,
cousin mine, I can by no means fathom your meaning."

"I did not think you had been so dull, you Spanish-Flemish-
Irishmen."

"Nay, Sir Phelim," said Owen somewhat haughtily, "I came
hither at your request, apparently to receive some intelligence
at your hands, an' you choose to keep it to yourself, do so in
God's name, but spare your taunts—they are unworthy a chieftain and a gentleman."

The lofty air with which Owen spoke was not without its effect on Sir Phelim, and his own weaker, although more blustering, nature involuntarily gave way before it.

"When you are called upon, General O'Neill," he said in a subdued tone, "to receive, a few days hence, the highest honor in Clan Owen's gift, say not that Phelim O'Neill kept you in the dark concerning it!"

Without another word he walked away, leaving his kinsman at a loss to understand what powerful agency it was, that had brought him to such a frame of mind.

During the next three days Owen had little opportunity of observing the workings of his kinsman's mind, and at the end of that time half a dozen gentlemen of the O'Neills came in form to the Castle to announce the sovereign will of the Clan Owen in regard to this new and stately branch of the family tree. He was to repair, on the following day at high noon, to the royal rath of Tulloghoge, there to receive the insignia of power and the homage of the sons of Nial. Sir Phelim, too, was summoned, but he flatly refused to go, saying that he washed his hands of them and their affairs from that day out. Tirlogh, on the contrary, intimated in his usual gruff way his intention of being present.

"I'll break your neck an' you do," cried Phelim, with sudden passion, and he shook his clenched fist at him.

"That would be no so easy matter, Phelim," replied the younger brother with a grim smile; "however, an' you wish me not to go, then go I won't, for, let who may have the white wand, you'll still be *my* chief, anyhow—interlopers may come with their treacherous smiles and undermine you in the love and affection of your people, but, by the shield of Eoghan More, there shall be one man of your clan who will never bow to another *O'Neill* while the pulse beats in your heart, old fellow!"

These bursts of fraternal affection were so strong on the part of Tirlogh, that when circumstances brought one out, all present were more or less touched, and the fierce clansman himself was so moved on the present occasion that he arose, kicked his seat out of the way, and rushed from the room, leaving Sir Phelim with a countenance of comical distress, as though he could hardly restrain his tears, but fain would appear to laugh, and treat the matter as a joke. Genuine, unsophisticated feeling is ever sure

to command respect, and notwithstanding the ludicrous gestures
of the rough chieftain in trying to conceal his emotion there was
not one of the spectators disposed to laugh. As for Owen he
arose from his seat with a face expressive of the kindliest feeling, and crossing the floor to where his kinsman sat, he grasped
his hand in silence. Nor was honest Phelim insensible to this
delicate expression of sympathy, for he returned the friendly
pressure and with a quivering lip articulated some words of
gratitude.

At last the hour arrived when Owen Roe attired for the occasion in the full costume of a Celtic chieftain, such as we saw
him wear on his journey from the coast, but that now the Spanish hat was replaced by the national *barradh*—was conducted by
the chief men of the clan to the seat of royalty on the rath
of Tulloghoge, and the Kinel-Owen, the stout gallowglass and
the hardy kern, were ranged around in a vast circle, the inner
ring of which was composed of the old men of the sept, fathers
in their generation. Behind and on either side the newly-elect-
ed chief, were grouped the various chiefs tributary to the house
of Nial, some of them, however, represented by their proxies;
and O'Hanlon, the hereditary marshal of the Hy-Nial princes,
stepped forth and placed in the hand of Owen the white wand of
power and laid upon his shoulders the scarlet cloak of royalty,
and the princes and the warriors and the aged men bowed down
before him, and hailed him as chief of the Kinel-Owen. Strange
to say, amongst the chiefs was seen Sir Phelim of Kinard, but
he bowed not with the rest, nor did homage at all, other than
by advancing when the ceremony was over and shaking the new
chief by the hand. At this sight a wild, enthusiastic cheer burst
from the multitude, and rang through the grand old forest—that
cheer was for Sir Phelim O'Neill, and such a cheer had his name
never before drawn forth even in the hey-day of his power. It
was the expression of popular admiration for this unexpected
and graceful display of generosity. Truly it *was* marvellous, all
things considered.

Of all the sons of the Kinel-Owen there assembled, not one
knew the secret of Sir Phelim's abdication, as it might be called.
Shamus Beg was the only mortal to whom it had ever been re-

vealed, and that with an injunction of inviolable secrecy. Little did any of the clansmen think that it was the Green Lady who had wrought the wondrous change when, on his moonlight journey from Dungannon, she met him at a cross-road where he stopped to await his followers who had fallen a little behind, and charged him in her deep sepulchral voice to resign the chief power immediately in favor of Owen Roe, under pain of the most fearful penalty.

CHAPTER XI.

"Shall we resign
Our hopes, renounce our rights, forget our wrongs,
Because an impotent lip beneath a crown
Cries, ' Be it so ?' "

SIR A HUNT.

" All that the mind would shrink from of excesses,
    All that the body perpetrates of bad,
All that we read, hear, dream, of man's distresses,
    All that the devil would do, if run stark mad—
Was here let loose."

BYRON'S *Don Juan.*

LEAVING Owen Roe for a brief space to the arduous duties of his new office, and the great work of organizing such an army as he wished to have out of the raw levies sent by the different chiefs, we will, with the reader's good leave, take a passing glance at the ancient City of the Tribes, the grand old Queen of the West. In all Ireland there was neither town nor city which had borne more or done more for the national cause than Galway of the Normans during the short time which had elapsed since her brave people were driven into open rebellion. What with the cold temporizing policy of their powerful neighbor Clanrickarde, who was governor of the city and county, and the ruthless persecution of young Willoughby, the commander of the fort, the tribes of Galway, thoroughly Catholic as they were, had no easy card to play. The insurrection had made considerable progress in almost every other part of the kingdom before Galway raised the standard of revolt, and this backwardness was owing, not to any indifference on the part of the inhabitants, or any want of sympathy with their brethren in other parts, but solely because of the wily machinations and insidious policy of

" the great Earl," as those of his vicinity were wont to call him. The almost canine ferocity of Willoughby, and his diabolical hatred of everything Catholic, rendered him the scourge of the city, and placed him in open antagonism with the people even when the influence of Lord Clanrickarde maintained a superficial peace. But fierce passions and strong prejudices (not to speak of righteous desires or fixed principles) were at work beneath the upper surface, and Galway was, as Clanrickarde well knew, in the condition of a mine which needed but a match to blow it into combustion. Every few days, or at most, every few weeks, little explosions were taking place in various parts of the city and its vicinity, which, though amounting to little in themselves, were quite sufficient to alarm the ever-watchful loyalty of Clanrickarde. In fact that nobleman was kept in a most unenviable state of excitement, ever fearing, and with reason, a tremendous outbreak on the part of the citizens, and never able to rely upon Willoughby who only kept faith with Papists for just so long as it suited his purpose. In the endless difficulties which arose between the city and the fort, Clanrickarde was of course the umpire, and it often happened that he was hardly settled within the strong walls of Oranmore or Clare-Galway,* after bringing these unmanageable neighbors to terms, when presto! came a message from the city complaining of some new insult on the part of the governor, or *vice versa*. Now it was that the soldiers in the fort above had been amusing themselves throwing shell and shot into the city to the great danger and serious detriment of the citizens ; St. Nicholas' Church, or St. Francis', or St. Augustine's had been grievously injured by the wanton fire from the fort, or perchance some of the wives or daughters of the townsmen had been kidnapped and otherwise ill-treated by the soldiers. Again it was Willoughby who lodged the complaint that the turbulent townsmen had cut off his supplies and refused to let his men pass through their limits. Sorely puzzled was Ulick Burke, with all his skill in strategy, to preserve even a

* Two of the principal fortresses of the De Burgos. Oranmore is situate on a peninsula, or rather promontory, stretching far out into the beautiful bay of Galway.

show of peace between such refractory neighbors, and there were
times when he was strongly tempted to throw up his office in
disgust. But, alas! who then would keep the sturdy Galway men
to their good behavior, and with bit and bridle bind their jaws
for the safety of the king's lieges? Who but he could in any
way control them, and in case he withdrew from his onerous post
what was to keep them from joining the rebels? So reasoned
Ulick Burke, and with the spirit of a martyr he resolved to bear
all things rather than yield such a triumph to the enemy. So
long as Willoughby had the best of the quarrel, and that they
could, between them, keep the bold spirit of the townspeople
within bounds, all was well, but the bare possibility of seeing the
Confederate colors flying from the high places of the old town
was gall and wormwood to " the white-livered De Burgo," as his
fellow-Catholics were wont to style him. Not his the heart to
glory in the noble spirit oozing out day by day from the pores of
the fair city, the patriotism which not all his power, backed by
the tyranny of Willoughby, could entirely repress, and the chivalrous deeds achieved within and about the city for the sacred
cause of liberty and religion. With Clanrickarde, the gallant
band of young men who boarded and captured that English ship
in Galway Bay to the great advantage of their party were nothing better than marauders, the O'Flaherties, and the Condons, and
many another warlike sept who were up in arms for God and
the right were " pestilent rebels" well worth a hempen cord
every man of them. Oh! Ulick Burke! great wert thou and
esteemed wise of men in thy generation, yet fool that thou wert,
in thy mistaken loyalty, thou didst lick the hand that smote thee,
and fawn on those who thirsted for the blood of thy best and
truest friends, the priests and prelates of that Church which thou
didst wrongfully call mother! Ulick Burke of Clanrickarde! a
fearful load hast thou on thy soul against the great day of reckoning, oh thou! who might have done much to succor those who
struggled to the death against oppression and intolerance, but
instead thereof didst lend thy powerful aid to the tyrant and the
persecutor! The Church, thy poor outraged suffering mother,
judged thee in thy day, and Christ her spouse judged thee beyond
the grave according to thy deserts, let us then spare our indig-

nation, and endeavor to wri'e and read thine acts with patience. Pity we may not afford to such a man for he chose his path with his eyes open and walked his tortuous way regardless alike of admonition, threat or censure, ay! even the dread censures of the Church!

On a certain night about the end of July of that year of 1642, a stranger of noble presence arrived at the Castle of Oranmore in the questionable disguise of a boatman from the Claddagh shore opposite. Some half dozen of those brave fellows had ferried him over, and woe betide the "covenanting carl" who dared to question the identity of any one in their company. Fortunately, however, none such were to be found in that vicinity, and Clanrickarde's followers were too well accustomed to the unceremonious visits of the Claddagh men to refuse free ingress to any of their number. Assuming the rough and somewhat discourteous manner of the fishermen, the stranger in question told his comrades to remain in the courtyard "till he'd give his message to the great *Earla*."

"By the shield of Clanrickarde!" said a burly Connemara man, who, with a score or so others of the Earl's retainers, was lounging about the courtyard, "by the shield of Clanrickarde, boys, that comrade of yours is more of a land-lubber than I ever thought to see a Claddagh man. I wouldn't give a *traneen* for all the fish *he* ever took."

"Husht!" said another, "maybe it's the admiral he'd be!"

"*You're* no conjurer anyhow," observed one of the fishermen

"Why not, ma bouchal?" laughed the good-humored mountaineer.

"Why, because if you were, you'd never make such a guess as that. Our admiral's face tells its own story wherever he goes, and with God's help *he'll* never be taken for a land-lubber. No, no"—and approaching closer to the group of soldiers, he. lowered his voice almost to a whisper—"there's one in *his* coat,' pointing over his shoulder to the door by which the stranger had entered the Castle, "that's far above the admiral."

Sundry exclamations of surprise followed this speech. "What! above the admiral!" cried the man who had first spoken, "and a Claddagh boy says it?"

" He must be a priest," observed a wiseacre, whose word was law amongst his comrades.

" Higher than that," the fisherman replied, shaking his head.

" Good Lord! can he be a bishop?"

" Have a care what you say, Ewen!" whispered one of his comrades to him who had last spoken.

" Never mind," cried several of the others, " if there's a place in Ireland's ground these evil days where that name is sacred, it is here—*here*"—and he stamped his foot on the old pavement; " the De Burgo may join hands with the bloody *sassum* an' it lists him, but those who follow his banner have a spirit above such meanness, as he may find some day to his cost!"

" Well said, Terence," responded a gigantic halberdier from Joyce's country; " so long as we're only teaching manners to the proud Normans of the town abroad Phil Joyce is both ready and willing, for God sees we owe them many a grudge—but when it comes to pointing as much as a finger at the Catholic army, God's blessing be with it! oh! faith, I'd as soon turn on the old mother at home—I'm thinking it's backwards our arms would work—awow!"

" An' he *be* a bishop," said one of the soldiers, " you've a right to let us know, Shan!" addressing one of the boatmen, " for sure you know well enough it's not often we have the chance of seeing one here—that is, of late days, since Ulick More began his colloguing with the devil's chickens!"

" Sure we knew you'd be overjoyed to hear it," the Claddagh man made answer, " an' that *he'd* be as safe among you as——"

" As he'd be in the Claddagh, Shan," put in the tall Joyce countryman, " an' that's as much as I could say."

Meanwhile an interview of a far different kind was going on within the Castle. In a circular chamber occupying the second floor of one of the turrets, Clanrickarde stood with reverent mien in the presence of that mysterious boatman who occupied a seat near the centre of the room. It was strange to see the haughty Palatine in scarlet doublet and silken hose, bowing down before the wild-looking fisherman in the brown linsey-woolsey tunic and truis of the same rude texture, as the latter raised his hand with a menacing air and knit his shaggy brows till the fiery orbs they shaded were only visible by their light.

"Curse me not, good my lord!" said De Burgo soothingly; "bethink thee enough of that hath been done ere now!"

"I would curse the father who begot me, did he stand in thy shoes, Ulick Burke," the visitor replied with stern emphasis, rising to his feet at the same time; "yea, were that father whom I loved and honored to play into the hands of God's enemies as thou dost, and lend them help to trample down still lower those of his own faith, nay, to *crush* them as vile worms, I would hold him as an enemy, and avoid speech of him as I will henceforth do in regard to thee—an' there come not a change in thy words and a.tions!"

"That may never be, then, my Lord Archbishop," said Clanrickarde proudly; "no power on earth could draw me aside from the allegiance due to my lawful prince——"

"Fool! fool!" cried the excited prelate, "what of the allegiance thou owest to God—the King of kings?"

"I serve Him when I serve the ruler He hath placed over me," Clanrickarde replied coldly.

"But who is to judge how that matter stands? Tell me, Lord of Clanrickarde, is it not the spiritual rulers of God's people— the ministers of His altars—the expounders of His will?——"

"I know not that—in this case."

"I tell thee, my lord earl, it is so in every case—ay, marry, and thou knowest it, too!—woe—woe unspeakable to the man who, professing the Catholic faith, wilfully closes his ears to the counsels and admonitions of the Church! But time is precious and other duties call me hence! We may meet no more on earth, Earl of Clanrickarde, but I would not willingly give thee up as lost—thou on whom we so much relied—thou who hast the power to lend a hand to thy oppressed fellow-Catholics—say, oh say, wilt thou not aid us in our struggle for liberty—for liberty, nay! for *life*—wilt thou not, oh chief of the Clan Rickard?—nay, nay, thou wilt not refuse a prince of the Church suing to thee thus lowly on behalf of an oppressed people—nay, nay, thou canst not!" And seizing both the Earl's hands the prelate leaned forward and peered with his keen dark eyes into

17

the half-averted face of De Burgo, as though seeking to read the answer there.

Coldly, and with little or no emotion, Clanrickarde made answer: " I have sworn allegiance to King Charles, and while breath is in my body I mean to keep it inviolate. I pray you, good my lord, trouble me no more, but take this as my final answer."

" And thou still persistest in keeping aloof from our Confederation, and taking counsel of our enemies ?"

" I do, so help me God! and in my poor judgment even your grace might do well to follow my example. It ill becometh the prelates or pastors of the Church to preach rebellion !"

" Silence, man !" said the prelate suddenly, and with such vehemence that Clanrickarde started and drew back a pace ; " silence, I say ! dare not to utter such words in my presence !— traitor to God and His holy Church, faithless, cold-blooded, time-serving Christian, dare not to dictate to the hierarchy of this martyr-nation. I tell thee, proud minion of a deceitful prince, friend and ally of the murderer Willoughby, that the rudest kerne who follows the standard of the Catholic army is worth a thousand such as thee for all thy pompous titles, and the God whom he serves, and for whom he sheds his blood, will exalt him in the latter day, when thou shalt be like Judas ' in thy appointed place.' I say not where that place will be—it is for thee to look to it. Fare thee well, lord, when next we meet it may be on the field of battle——"

" Good Heavens, your grace cannot mean that you would personally take up arms ?" cried Clanrickarde following to the door.

" That do I mean and nought else. When such as thou desertest thy rightful post, even such as I must advance into the gap. Pray Heaven it be my lot to fall in a cause so holy and so just—but, alas ! I am not worthy of the martyr's crown—poor, frail, sinful man that I am !"

Mastering himself with that facility which grew out of long habit, Clanrickarde hastened after the prelate, praying him to partake of some refreshment.

" Not a mouthful," he replied, " not a mouthful of meat or drink that belongs to thee shall ever cross my lips—no, no ; I will sup at the Clad lagh on fish and oaten cake with a draught

of water—thy wines and viands were poison to me—and, moreover, Ulick! no Christian may eat or drink within thy walls from
this time forward—by a statute of the Council of Kilkenny, as
thou knowest, any one aiding or abetting the enemy doth by
his own act incur the penalty of excommunication. Mayhap
thou knowest not that?" he added with bitter irony.

"I knew it," the Earl replied, "and am much surprised at
the uncharitable rashness of those who deal so freely in anethe-
mas—shining lights they are truly!——"

"May God enlighten *your* eyes, anyhow," said the Archbishop
as he stepped into the court and beckoned to his trusty Claddagh men—"blinder art thou than the bat that wings his cir-
cling flight at eve around these towers!"

"God help me!" muttered the Earl to himself as he saw his
men bowing down on either side to crave the blessing which
the good prelate, seeing himself discovered, was not slow
in bestowing; "God help me, even mine own retainers have
little heart for the service put upon them in these evil times.
See how reverently they bow to that seditious prelate—a plague
on them for sea-bears that brought him thither, they must be
pretty sure of these fellows of mine when they let them so easily
into the secret—still I know not but it may be as well. Oh! that
I could weed such noxious plants out of our hierarchy, then
would the flame of rebellion soon die out in the land!"

Of this there was little likelihood so long as the agents of the
turbulent and intolerant English Parliament were sent in the
king's name into Ireland with ample powers to do what mischief
they could, in short to kill and destroy indiscriminately not only
all that bore the name of Irish, but such of the English as did
not immediately attach themselves to them. In accordance with
the policy carried out by the Lords Justices from the very beginning, all manner of cruelty and injustice was exercised towards
the people of the country, evidently with the intention of fomenting a rebellion so lucrative to those righteous rulers. Thus
Monroe, Stewart, Montgomery, and their confreres in the north,
Coote and Inchiquin, Cork and Broghill in the other provinces,
and, though last not least, Willoughby in Galway, carried on the
war in the true spirit of extermination, sparing neither age, sex,

nor condition. Now the sole object Clanrickarde had in view
was what he called "putting down the rebellion and restoring
peace to the country," and in this he was foiled at every turn
by the (to him) unaccountable aggressions of Willoughby. No
sooner had he, with infinite trouble, patched up some venomous
quarrel between Willoughby and the incensed Catholics, than
the former, without any known reason, issued out upon the adjacent country, robbing and murdering all before him, and spreading ruin and desolation wherever he went, or, perchance, on the
most trivial pretext, discharging fire and shot into the town
below, sometimes for a whole day without intermission, until
the burghers were roused to fury and ready to risk all in an
attack on the fort. News of these things reaching the Earl at
Oranmore (for he was fain to keep near the city), post haste
he went to accommodate mat'ers once again, cursing in his
heart the brutal ally whom the fates had given him in his government, and Willoughby, in return, hated Clanrickarde as he
hated all who bore the name of Catholic, and slily laughed in
his sleeve at the notion of the great De Burgo being his henchman to command, and a right useful tool for all purposes. Not
content, however, with thwarting the wily statesman in his
pacific endeavors, good Captain Willoughby sent off a secret
dispatch to the Parliament in London to have an auxiliary sent
him on whose aid he knew he could well rely in forcing the
" over-patient asses of Galway to gallop off into open rebellion,
the which would better agree with the malice of their hearts
than this sneaking hang-dog pace at which they were kept,
forsooth, by Clanrickarde's bridle."

With this laudable intent, then, Willoughby's "familiar" summoned came, in the person of an English admiral, Lord Forbes
by name, with an entire fleet at his command. Early in the
month of August the good people of Galway town, the bay
shores and the islands were astounded by this unlooked-for and
most unwelcome apparition, and none more so than Lord Clanrickarde, who felt hurt and offended that such a step had been
taken without consulting him as governor of the county. He
immediately sent to ascertain the admiral's intentions and received such an answer as made him more incensed than ever;

in fact, plainly intimating that he, as a Papist, had no right to put such questions, and that he should learn, perchance, sooner than was pleasing what brought him there.

The gentle measures employed by this new agent to bring the Galway burghers to a proper state of subjection may be found in the next chapter.

CHAPTER XII.

" Where, where, for shelter shall the guilty fly,
    When consternation turns the good man pale ?"
                                        YOUNG's *Night Thoughts.*

" He saw—and, maddening at the sight,
    Gave his bold bosom to the fight ;
    To tiger rage his soul was driven ;
    *   *   *   *   *
    The pale man from his land must fly,
    He would be free—or he would die."

IT was the seventh day of August when Lord Forbes with
his squadron made his appearance in Galway Bay to the great
satisfaction of Willoughby and his Puritan garrison in the fort,
with whom he immediately exchanged signals. The terror and
consternation with which the people bordering on the coast
beheld the approach of this English fleet were but too well
grounded, as the result showed. Without the slightest provocation of any kind, or any hostile demonstration whatsoever, the
admiral dispatched a number of boats to the Clare coast filled
with armed men, who, landing, burned and destroyed several
villages, slaying the defenceless inhabitants without mercy
wherever they came in their way.

This sort of exercise, although, doubtless, very pleasing to the
ruthless strangers, and productive of much amusement to the garrison of the fort as they watched the work of destruction from
their elevated po t, was not at all to the liking of the natives,
who, Irish and Papists as they were, had no fancy for such en-
tertainments got up at the expense of their lives and properties.
Even **Lord Clanrickarde** was not over well pleased when mes-

senger after messenger arrived at the Castle in quick succession with news of the devastation going on. There was one little reason that made the great and wise Ulick peculiarly averse to Forbes's mode of pacification, and that was that the villages destroyed, and, indeed, most of the country thus laid waste, belonged, as it happened, to himself. In a state of commotion very unusual with him he ordered out a yacht and proceeded in all haste to visit the admiral, supposing that half a dozen words of advice from him would be amply sufficient. Great was his surprise, and greater still his indignation when Forbes cut his dignified remonstrance very short, with a rough assurance that the work he complained of was but beginning, for that, "with God's good aid, it was his intention, as it was also his instructions, to slay as many of the children of wrath and perdition as avenging justice sent in his way."

"Is Lord Forbes aware that *I* am a Catholic?" demanded the Earl sternly.

"I have heard as much," replied the ungracious admiral with something like a smile on his vinegar face. "I will give you the benefit of the doubt arising from your well-known *loyalty*—I will judge you by your *acts* rather than your *profession*—and do, therefore, consider you as entitled to certain immunities."

"Immunities! what immunities, I pray your lordship?"

"Why, immunity from detention, for instance," replied the Scotch lord with the same sinister smile as before; "think you I would suffer an *undoubted* Papist—any other, in fact, but my Lord Clanrickarde"—and he bowed with ironical respect— "to quit this ship—alive?"

"My Lord Forbes!" said the Earl haughtily, "an' such be your manner of jesting I like it not, nor do I deem it becoming in your circumstances. An' you knew it not before, or otherwise are oblivious of the fact, I would remind you that I am ruler in these parts, appointed by the king's majesty."

"And I would remind you, my Lord of Clanrickarde," repl'ed the caustic Admiral, "that *I* am ruler in these waters—for so long as it listeth me to remain—holding from a higher power still——"

"I pray your lordship to explain that latter phrase," said the self-possessed Clanrickarde; "I know of no higher power in this realm than that which I have named—to wit, Charles, King of England," and he reverently raised his plumed hat from off his brow.

"I hold from *the Parliament* of England," Forbes returned with an ironical smile at the graceful gesture which at once expressed the other's loyalty and his high court breeding.

"You shall answer for this, my Lord Forbes," said Clanrickarde angrily; "such an insinuation as your words convey no subject of King Charles may or ought to hear."

"Better the Parliament surely than the Pope," retorted the Scotchman, bitterly.

'I came not here to bandy words," said the Earl coldly, "but rather to give you an advice which you will do well to follow. In case you persist in your insane course, I wish you to understand that you do it at a risk, seeing that the people of these parts are now peaceably inclined and disposed to live as good and loyal subjects, forgetful of all that hath been done to them by Captain Willoughby and his men here of late; this is owing, I tell you plainly, to my humble endeavors, the which hath cost me infinite trouble and much cost—an' you now, with the aid of Master Willoughby, disturb this so happy state of things by provoking the king's lieges to break the peace, I say, you will be responsible for all the consequences—are you willing to run this risk?"

"I will do as I please," replied Forbes very shortly; "I know the work before me and I will do it, with Heaven's aid. What ho! there, my Lord of Clanrickarde's yacht!—I pray your lordship to excuse me," he said with mock courtesy, "but your visit hath already outstript your welcome."

"Suffer him not to depart," said a harsh, stern voice from behind the admiral; "accursed be thou an' thou sparest even one of these Ammonites—smite him, Henry Forbes! ay, even with the edge of the sword!" And the speaker advancing, broke upon the astonished vision of Clanrickarde in the guise of a Puritan preacher, fierce, wild, gaunt, and enthusiastic, with a fire something akin to insanity gleaming or rather shooting from his large, angular-shaped eyes.

"Softly, softly, Mr. Peters," said Forbes in the most persuasive tone he knew how to assume, and he placed his hand before his strange chaplain to bar his farther progress in the direction of the Papist lord,—"softly," he repeated, lowering his voice to a whisper, "it were unsafe to harm him. An' thou lovest me, keep thy mouth closed till he be out of hearing. Nay, I will have it so—I will explain when he is gone hence."

Lord Clanrickarde could not catch the words, but he guessed their import, and it amused him no little to see the rampant fanaticism of Peters so far outstripping the wily caution of his no less intolerant patron. As he descended the ship's side, he heard the chaplain pronounce a stern anathema on the sinful "compliance," as he phrased it, of the Admiral.

"A heavy judgment will fall upon thee, Henry Forbes," said the meek Christian minister, "for as much as thou couldst have cut off one of the heads of this monster, even Popery, and did not,—yea, when he was delivered unto thee, this double-faced minion, that thou mightest execute judgment upon him—in that thou didst not smite him with the edge of the sword, I say unto thee thou hast sinned grievously, and incurred the sentence of wrath! So, he goeth hence in his pride, that man of evil ways, goeth hence to do the will of the tyrant Charles Stuart—yea, verily, he laughs—laughs at thy wicked compliance to the enemy—avaunt, servant of the evil one"—and he shook his clenched fist at the Earl now speeding over the water in his graceful little bark—"I spit upon thee," he called out in a still louder voice, "and will bear testimony against thee with all the strength of my body as a whited sepulchre full of all uncleanness. Avaunt, son of the scarlet woman who sitteth on the seven hills!"

Clanrickarde only smiled at this rhapsody, the more so as he saw Forbes endeavoring, with all his might, to keep the furious preacher within some bounds of decency, but the threatening gestures of the man did not escape the keen eyes of the Earl's retainers in the boat, and their indignation was so strongly excited, that it required the positive commands of their lord to keep them from shooting him.

"Not so, friends," said the politic Earl, "not so—I hold the man as of unsound mind, and esteem him more an object of pity than of anger. Lower your muskets, I charge ye!"

It was not without reluctance that the Connaught men obeyed, but when de Burgo declared his will it was not to be disputed with impunity, and so the rabid chaplain of the fleet escaped for that time.

Whether the Earl's surmise as to Peters' saneness of mind was correct or not, that worthy had so fast a hold on the understanding of his patron that in most cases he moulded him to his own purposes. Hence it was, and under such guidance, that the good citizens of Galway and the people of the adjoining country were hunted to death as enemies, nay, rather as outlaws, by the horde of merciless fanatics who manned the fleet, men to whose breasts compassion was a stranger, and charity a word unknown. Willoughby and his garrison troopers were a scourge to the old city, but Forbes and his Scotch fanatics were as fiends incarnate, inventing in their monstrous cruelty and detestation of the Irish such works of horror as make the flesh creep on one's bones to think of.

Who can imagine the horror and dismay of the Catholic people of Galway when news came into the city that St. Mary's Church, situate in the west suburbs,* was in the hands of the Puritans. From its peculiar situation, on the crown of a hill sloping downwards to the bay, and commanding the whole of the west suburbs, with a portion of the city proper, this edifice attracted the notice of the Scotch admiral, who, perceiving at a glance its importance as a military post, without loss of time threw a garrison into it, and mounting his guns on every available point, opened a cannonade on the city. At the same moment, as though they acted in full concert, the cannon from the fort raked the streets of the devoted city, whose people were guilty of no other offence than a too close adherence to the pacific counsels of Lord Clanrickarde. They professed loyalty and prac-

---

* Those who have read MAUREEN DHU will remember the situation of this Church, being identical with that of the Dominican Priory, so often referred to in that story. It still bears the name of St. Mary's, and is the parish Church of the Claddagh.

THE CONFEDERATE CHIEFTAINS.

tised neutrality ever since the noble effort of the young men
had been quashed by the machiavelian policy of that most wily
statesman and cold-hearted politician. The guns of Willoughby
and Forbes spoke the thanks of their Puritan rulers for the
humble submission of the Galway tribes.

How the proud Lynches, and Browns, and Blakes, the merchant
nobles of Galway, cursed the easy credulity which had made
them the dupes of Clanrickarde, as the shell and shot from the
opposite extremities raked the city from end to end, the cross-
fire from the fort and, oh wo of woes! from St. Mary's holy hill,
sweeping the streets and avenues of the old town! How the
women and the old men and little children crept, under cover
of projecting walls and archways, and through by-lanes, to the
shelter of the churches where they had worshipped God in
peace in days not long past, and how fervently they prayed to
the good St. Nicholas, St. Francis or St. Augustine, as the case
might be, to hear their sorrowful supplications, and protect them
from the fury of those who were athirst 'for their blood! For
many days their prayers seemed to avail not, and heavier
grew the hearts of these helpless petitioners as time rolled on
and succor came not, and the ear of heaven seemed closed
against them. As for the stout burghers of Galway, little recked
they that bomb and mortar were dealing death around;—fear was
unknown to their brave hearts, and every shot that re-echoed
through their streets, every one of their fellow-citizens stricken
to death, did but add new fuel to the flame kindled in their souls
by recent events. The fighting men of the city were one and all
filled with the spirit of those who captured the English ships in
their harbor, and the gallant young men who accomplished that
feat were now in the changed circumstances of the city, almost
deified by the populace, who before had regarded them, through
the loyal medium of Clanrickarde's judgment, as "dangerous
and seditious." Now things were all changed, and the City of
the Tribes was at last thoroughly identified with the national
cause, thanks to the laudable exertions of Willoughby and his
new naval auxiliary.

The municipal council of the city was sitting one day in earnest
deliberation, with the patriotic mayor, Richard Martin, at their

head. All at once a tremendous commotion was heard outside, and the aldermen starting to their feet looked each other in the face, as though fearing what they dared not utter, that the Puritans had broken into the town. While they stood deliberating what course they should take for the protection of life and property, if so be any chance of protection remained to them, the door was flung wide open, and in rushed a wild, yet warlike figure, arrayed in the ancient Celtic costume. Surprise made those men of Galway pale, as the warrior stood panting before them, for seldom indeed were Galway stones pressed by the foot of the dispossessed chieftain of Ir-Connaught, the bold, impetuous young leader, Murrough *na Dhu*. All knew his dark, handsome face, but no one cared to speak his recognition, for had they put their thoughts in words it would have been in the phrase of fair Eleanor's father addressed to young Lochinvar :

"Oh com'st thou in peace, or com'st thou in war,"

for sooth to say the warlike O'Flaherties were deemed no safe neighbors by the Norman burghers of Galway town. Nor was the chief's appearance, or his gestures on the occasion, by any means calculated to re-assure them.

Before any one else had spoken he spoke himself. "Men of Galway!" said he in his own rich and musical tongue,* "why sit ye here in idle parley when the foul fiend is working his will at your very doors by the hands of yonder Scotch imps of his?"

"We know it, brave chief!" said the mayor dejectedly, "but what can we do with such overwhelming odds against us? Even now are we met to consult together if perchance anything could be done on behalf of our poor city, but as yet God hath not enlightened us on that head. Alack! alack! we know full well what is going on on either side of us!"

"Still I tell you," cried the chieftain, "you know it not—ha! hear ye those shouts of wrath and vengeance? Ay! ay! they may shout till their throats are hoarse but avail it will not—come hither, Richard Martin"—and seizing the astonished mayor by

* The Connemara Irish is said to be about the purest vernacular of that tongue.

the arm he drew him to the still open door, the others following as though by instinct—" there—look towards the west!—see you that flame ?"

"Great God! I do, what may it mean? Are they burning the Claddagh ?—the fire seemeth in that direction! Alas! alas! for our brave poor fishermen! that surely is *their* village!"

"Not so," replied O'Flaherty in a strange hoarse voice; " not so, Richard Martin! Wouldst know what food it be that feedeth yonder lurid flame, I will tell thee. It is the bones of the dead and their mouldering coffins and the flesh that the worm hath spared in the earth below——"

" Merciful Heaven! what mean you ?"

"I mean that these earth-born devils, finding themselves unable to come at you or me, or such other wild animals, did dig up the dead from their graves in St. Mary's churchyard, and having first enjoyed to their hearts' content the pleasant recreation of kicking and smashing the poor remains of mortality, they have e'en made a bonfire of them,* the which, Mayor of Galway! your eyes may see. Ha! ha! that smoke is black, and thick, and heavy,—little wonder, for methinks it cometh from hell's fire !"

Various exclamations of horror escaped the listeners, then more numerous than at first, as people were coming from all directions to the Town Hall hoping to have their curiosity gratified as to the cause of this new commotion, forgetting the danger to which they were exposed. O'Flaherty was not slow to fan the flame which his tidings had enkindled, and his burning words roused the men of Galway into sudden and vigorous life. The lethargy into which they had of late fallen vanished at the touch of this new magician, and the hot old blood of Galway arose in fury, ready to do and dare all things whatsoever the so-lately dreaded O'Flaherty advised. Elated at the thought of having

---

* This hideous fact is historically true. All the historians of that period, as well Protestant as Catholic. mention this sacrilegious deed of Forbes. See Hardiman's *Hist Galway*, Warner's *Civil Wars*, &c., &c. Would any but a Puritan commander ever devise such an act of sacrilege, so horrible, so useless to the perpetrators ?

so gallant a chieftain for their leader, the citizens cried out that
the fort must be taken. To this, however, the mayor objected
as a rash and unsafe step, and Murrough *na Dhu*, after a moment's thought, took the same view of it.

"It were but to ensure the destruction of your city and a fearful loss of life," said he, "to attack the fort now—while that
devil-begotten Forbes is in front of us with his fleet—but wait,
my friends, *wait* till he departs hence and, my life for it, Willoughby and his hornet's nest shall be scattered to the winds—
leave the matter to me, friends and fellow-Catholics, as ye have
so far honored me, and, by the bones of the outraged dead on
yonder hill, this plague-spot shall be taken from your midst—
ay! were Clanrickarde himself within it!"

"But bethink thee, good youth," said the mayor, laying his
hand on the chieftain's shoulder, "that ere Forbes move hence
the greater part of our poor citizens may meet their death! were
it not better to stir at once? An' the fort were silenced, we
could easier defend ourselves against the fire from St. Mary's
Hill."

"We may not do it, Richard Martin!" the chief replied as he
glanced upwards at the commanding fortress; "an' we did, it
would but draw on your city a terrible vengeance from yonder
accursed fleet—wait, I tell you, we shall have our opportunity
an' we be not rash. Fare ye well! I must home to my own
people to prepare them for giving that support which you may
need."

He was moving away regardless of the discontented murmurs
of the populace, when the mayor again addressed him.

"Murrough O'Flaherty, you are brave and generous or report
belieth you—much have you done in your own person for the
righteous cause—may we depend upon your assistance or rather
your guidance?—you will not fail us in our need?"

"I have said it," Murrough made answer, drawing himself up
to the full height of his lofty stature; "when did a prince of the
O'Flahertys fail to redeem his plighted word? Brave hearts
have ye here within your city, and with God's good aid, we shall
take the fort as easily as they took a ship of war, against odds

still greater! Once more, farewell, and God be with ye till we meet again."

For two whole weeks after that was Galway exposed to the double cannonade, and her harassed inhabitants already began to think of capitulating, for Lord Clanrickarde, as usual, was negotiating for what he called "peace." Anxiously the citizens looked towards the far mountains of Jar-Connaught, but no war-like band was seen to issue thence, nor did Murrough appear to redeem his promise. Despair was taking possession of the mayor and the aldermen, and they had all but determined on following the Earl's advice on his promise of obtaining favorable terms for them; but better things were in store for the suffering townspeople. All at once the prayers so long offered up in vain, as it would seem, were heard above. Without any apparent reason for so doing, Lord Forbes moved off with his fleet one fine day, making no one the wiser as to why he went, and before Willoughby had recovered the shock of his ally's unaccountable disappearance, Murrough na Dhu was again in the city, this time with a company of his chosen men, and being immediately joined by the bravest and most experienced of the citizen soldiers, they took the fort by storm, put its garrison to the sword, and demolished the walls that they might never again harbor an English garrison. Strange, and not less creditable than strange, is the fact that Willoughby was included in the terms of capitulation and suffered to escape to England.

How different were the conduct of the people's enemies had they a popular leader in their hands, even less obnoxious than Willoughby!

CHAPTER XIII.

" The keen spirit
Seizes the prompt occasion,—makes the thoughts
Start into instant action, and at once
Plans and performs, resolves and executes !"

HANNAH MORE.

" Night closed around the Conqueror's way
And lightnings show'd the distant hill,
Where those who lost that fatal day
Stood few and faint, but fearless still."

MOORE's *Irish Melodies.*

WHILST the Puritan admiral was wreaking his impotent fury, as we have described, on the mouldering bones of the Claddagh villagers in St. Mary's churchyard, General Barry was advancing with a large army into the county of Cork, where the principal places of strength were in the hands of the enemy, foremost amongst whom was the Earl of Cork with his seven warlike sons, all officers of some note. Lord Broghill, the third in age, is already known to the reader as one of the best captains of that day, and of the others, Lord Kinalmeaky, although young in years, was already noted for his savage ferocity* which appears to have endeared him to his amiable parent, for we find that illustrious and most successful adventurer writing to the Earl of Warwick after one of the engagements which had proved fatal to the Confederates :

" And now that the boy hath blooded himself upon them, I hope that God will bless him ; that as I now write but of the killing of an hundred, I shall shortly write of the killing of thousands."*

* Smith's *History of Cork.*

Such was the spirit which actuated the Puritan generals of that day, and such were the men, bold, brave, cruel and unprincipled, with whom the Confederate leaders had to deal. The seaports of the noble county of Cork were chiefly in the hands of the Puritan generals, as was also the greater portion of the interior, but Robert Barry was not the man to shrink from difficulties which his own valor and prudence might surmount, and thus in a hopeful spirit he undertook this Cork campaign. Passing rapidly through the country, and dexterously avoiding the various detachments of the enemy's forces scattered over the district, he took many of the strongest castles from the hands of the Puritans, amongst others Sir Philip Percival's famous Castle of Liscarroll, as the reader has already seen. Although the capture of this fortress was justly esteemed a great triumph for the Confederates, still there were those amongst Barry's officers who considered it a loss of time, especially as Annagh Castle, another of Percival's, with some other fortresses in that county, were besieged at the same time, which necessarily weakened the Catholic forces. But Barry would not hear of passing so much as one stronghold that could or did shelter a Puritan band, and notwithstanding the singular dispatch wherewith he took them one after the other, weeks of very precious time were lost. Flushed with conquest, Barry unhappily forgot to attend to what was passing around him.

The last day of August had arrived, and the victorious general was still projecting the seizure of other castles. At evening he stood with one of his officers, surveying from a distance the fine old fortalice of Cloghleigh, seated on a commanding eminence, and he said to his companion that with God's blessing they should call it theirs before the week ended——

"An' you do, General Barry, you will rue it all the days you have to live," said a quiet-looking gentleman of middle age, who under favor of his Celtic costume had approached the outskirts of the army unperceived, and dismounting from a smooth nag, whose bridle hung carelessly over his arm, he joined the two officers with the air of one who felt himself their equal.

"How is that, friend?" said Barry with a start.

"Why, your scouts are not worth much or you would know

ere now that Inchiquin is within a few hours' journey with a force far superior to yours."

"Say you so, good sir?" exclaimed Barry cheerfully, his thin pale lip curved with a scornful smile. "By St. Brendan the Mariner, I am right glad to hear it. I have been long desirous to have a tilt with Murrough. But were he within a mile, yonder castle must be ours—it sits so gracefully looking down on those two fair streams,* queen and mistress of both."

"Heed not the castle," said the quiet stranger, "you have castles enough in these parts to protect your friends. Rather collect your scattered forces and advance to meet Inchiquin, ere he have time to bring more troops together."

"You are more of a soldier, friend, than one would take you for," observed the other officer, as he glanced with a smile over the heavy frame and placid countenance of the stranger. "His advice is good, General Barry, and we might do worse than follow it."

"But the castle," said the general with his eyes still fixed on it, "surely a few hours would suffice to take it with such a force as ours."

"I tell you let the castle be," said the stranger testily; "one would think you were the disinherited Condon himself that you make so much ado about the old rookery! An' you stay to take it, I swear you shall never set foot within its walls."

"Do you threaten me, sir?" said Barry haughtily.

"I threaten you not," the other calmly replied; "I do but tell you what I know will come to pass. I take my leave of you, General Barry! and you, Lord Skerrin"—that officer started on hearing his name pronounced so unexpectedly—"an' I had yonder force at my command, Murrough of the Burnings should be brought to a stand before he were a day older!"

The strange adviser leisurely mounted his nag, and was turning away down a bridle road, in the direction leading from the

* This old fortress of the Condons occupies a commanding site near the confluence of the Funcheon and the Araglin. See *Parliam. Gazetteer of Ireland.*

camp, when Lord Skerrin hastened after him, and laying his hand on his saddle looked inquiringly up into his face :

"Are you a soldier, friend?" he asked; "hast ever fought these Puritans?"

"I have *seen* fighting," was the curt reply, and, clapping spurs to his little steed, the stranger and it bounded off at a light gallop, away and away—

"———————— over brake, brush and scraur,"

turning his head once to make a warning gesture ere he plunged into the depth of a narrow defile lying some hundreds of yards off between two steep banks of earth.

Whatever effect this singular visit had on Barry he chose not to declare even to Lord Skerrin, but a council of war was summoned by him that very night, and by the light of the camp fire orders were issued to call in all the scattered detachments of the army. By the morning's dawn the troops were under march, in the direction of Inchiquin's supposed position. As the general, with Lords Skerrin and Dunboyne, and some other officers of rank were about to hasten after the rear division, he turned his eyes in the direction of Cloghleigh Castle, behind whose battlements the sun was just appearing. 'Great Heavens! what sight was there that he looked and looked again, then rubbed his eyes, and finally turning to his friends asked what flag was that floating from the keep.

An exclamation of surprise and pleasure escaped from every mouth.

"Our own colors, by the rood!" cried Skerrin joyfully; "see an' they be not!"

"Surely yes," said the more phlegmatic Dunboyne, "that is beyond a doubt, methinks, but how came they there?"

"God alone knows," Barry replied with a thoughtful air.

"And our demure friend of yesternight, general," said Skerrin with a smile, "quiet and cool as he seemed, methinks he hath moved in this matter. He told me he had seen fighting in his time, but I would wager this new casque of mine against yonder kern's deer-skin"—pointing to an individual in the saffron-dyed doublet of the Irish foot-soldiers who stood surveying their

party at his leisure leaning against the trunk of an aged beech
—"I would make that bet, I say, that the drowsy-looking personage I have named fought and fought well last night while we
slept. What think you, Barry?"

Before the general could answer a wild cheer broke from
the long lines of the advancing army, and the glittering pikes
and shining blades and waving banners suddenly came to a stop.
The amazing sight of their own colors floating over a castle
which they had never summoned to surrender had likewise
attracted the eyes of the soldiers, and cheer after cheer rent
the skies in joyful recognition.

"You guess well, my Lord Skerrin," said he of the saffron
doublet, without moving an inch;" your friend of yesternight
knoweth full well how your colors came on yonder flag-staff,
seeing that he placed them there himself."

"I knew it," said Skerrin with an exulting smile; "I knew
there was more in that man than met the eye. But who may
he be, good fellow, and how came he to take the castle?"

"He is the lord of Condon's country," said the kern advancing from under the tree with a heightened color on his sallow
cheek, "that is to say the rightful lord, for all that he owneth
not a foot of land at this hour."

"And his name?" questioned Barry.

"The English call him Arthur Condon, by the sept he is still
known as *the Condon*, lord of Cloghleigh and all the land for
miles around."

"We have heard the story of his wrongs, but, I say again,
how did he come to take the castle, well garrisoned and well
provided as it was?"

"The stout arms of the Condons took it," the man replied with
sudden animation, "their stout arms and their trusty pikes."

"Had they nought else but pikes?"

"A few muskets they had—some of them little use from rust
—but such arms as they had they made the most of."

Various expressions of admiration escaped the officers present
and Barry suddenly asked: "Were you there, good friend,
when the castle was taken?"

A roguish smile beamed out on the quiet face of the kern like sunlight from forth a heavy cloud: "Well! general, as you put the question, I suppose it's no treason to say I was looking on."

"By my patron St. George," cried Skerrin, as stepping forward he looked into the stranger's face, "an' I mistake not, you are our informant of yesternight—yes, yes, I see it now."

"I admit the fact," said the other, still smiling.

"Ha! and your name?" asked Barry and Skerrin in a breath.

"Arthur Condon, the chief man of that name, although a very poor one, but such as he is, very much at the service of General Barry and subject to his order"—and he bowed with the easy self-possession of a gentleman.

"I am much beholden to you, sir," said the general, and he warmly shook him by the hand; "your achievement of last night shows the value of your co-operation. But methinks your present habiliments belie your condition—wherefore that disguise?"

"You ask me frankly, general, and I will tell you: from an itching I had to see how the surprise I planned would affect you all, myself noticed by none. But I see the army is again in motion—pardon me, lords and gentlemen, in that I have detained you over long when moments are so precious."

"One moment more, Master Condon," said Barry, as he placed his foot in the stirrup ready to mount the charger which a horse-boy held by the bridle; "you that can take such strongholds as that"—pointing to the castle—"must needs have valiant men at your command—could you not spare us some?"

"Not a man, general,' said Condon with a blunt determination which surprised all and made the courtly Norman nobles who surrounded Barry look at each other with wondering eyes.

"Not a man!" the general repeated in blank surprise, "and wherefore not, you who but now offered your services so freely?"

"Why, because, general, we can serve you better here at home —this is *Condon's country*, you know, so called in past times, now only in name, but with God and Our Lady's aid we mean to make it so at this juncture, were it but for religion's dear sake, that our altars may once more arise from the dust, and our priests stand before them vested as of old. We would see yonder flag streaming from every fort within our ancient borders,

and to that end we follow not the army as our hearts would desire, but rather do your work here as we of the soil only can.
Fare ye well, noble gentlemen, and God speed ye! when next
you come this way you will find the country all your own, or
learn that Arthur Condon hath found a grave in the land he loved.
—in any case, my heart is with you, and my life devoted to your
sacred cause! Hark! your trumpets call!—would that I too
might obey the summons, but here my lot is cast—here—at least
for a time—is my sphere of action—retributive justice will have
it so!"

As if inspired by reason his nag approached him at this moment from the gap of a neighboring fence, and leaping on its
back with the lightness of five-and-twenty, the chieftain waved
a parting salute and disappeared by the same opening, leaving
Barry and his officers filled with admiration as well as surprise.

The gallant Condon well redeemed his pledge, as the chronicles of those days bear witness,* and his brave spirit infused life
and vigor into many who before were weak and wavering.

But, alas! for the fine army led by Barry to meet the foe that
morning. Had he advanced a week sooner, before Lord Inchiquin had had time to collect his scattered forces, he might have
obtained such a victory as would strike terror into the enemy,
but unfortunately it turned out as Condon had feared that the
time spent by the Confederates in taking castles had been turned
to still better account by Inchiquin, and enabled him to retrieve
the series of minor defeats which had left him well nigh without
an army and badly furnished with provisions for what he had.
This state of things was well known to Barry and others of the
Confederate leaders, and relying on it, they had been tempted
to secure as much of the country as they possibly could. Hearing now that Inchiquin was somewhere in the neighborhood of
Liscarroll they marched thither with all haste, and learning from
their scouts that he was advancing towards them, they took up
a position on the third day of September on an eminence not far
from the castle.

---

* "The sept of the Condons were giving the Confederate leaders
the most effectual assistance in another part of the country."—Meehan's *Confed.*, *Kilk.*, chap. I.

Great was the surprise of the Confederate generals when the enemy came in sight, to find him some thousands strong in foot with several troops of horse. Lord Inchiquin himself commanded the centre of three divisions, and with him as a volunteer was Lord Kinalmeaky. Other officers of experience led on the other divisions, and the men, as it happened, had far the advantage of Barry's in point of discipline. This the Confederate leaders saw, and they prudently resolved to allow the enemy to exhaust his strength in a charge. And bravely the men of Munster withstood the fierce onslaught, their serried pikes forming, as it were, an iron rampart which no force of the enemy could break through. The Puritans fell back in some confusion, for Inchiquin had received a dangerous wound and many other officers had sustained more or less injury at the hands of the formidable pikemen. The Irish charged in turn, and their charge was also bravely resisted; orders were then given on both sides for a general attack, and when it came to close quarters the training and discipline and greater experience of the enemy became apparent. Fighting hand to hand the officers were seen engaged in mortal combat, and many a chivalrous deed of valor marked that fatal scene; Inchiquin removed to a place of safety, watched the fight with eyes starting from their sockets, and a whirlwind of passion sweeping athwart his impetuous soul. One after one he beheld his officers disappearing, either carried wounded from the field or sinking amid the slain, but still his forces kept their ground, and his flinty heart little recked who fell so long as victory forsook not his banners. Vavasour was there and Kinalmeaky, and their waving plumes were security against defeat. All at once a wild shout of exultation arose from the ranks of the Confederates, and rang far over hill and dell:

"Kinalmeaky is down! Kinalmeaky is down!—death to the Puritans!' and as though the fall of that destroying fiend had inspired the Catholics with fresh courage, and their enemies with despair, the serried ranks of the latter began suddenly to waver, and Inchiquin, forgetful of his wound, raised himself from the ground with a mighty effort and waved his arm with frantic energy:

" Vavasour! Percival!—we are *lost*, an' they force you down
the hill! Heavens! what are you about? Ha! they waver
now! Now, Vavasour! on them—on them—slay them without
mercy—no quarter—no quarter, I say!—they fly—by the great
Immortal, they fly! After them and the day is ours!"

And so it was. Sir Charles Vavasour, an aged and experienced
officer, on whom the command devolved, seeing the discouragement of his troops after Kinalmeaky's fall, and the corresponding
exultation of the Confederates, applied his whole energy and
skill to rally his despairing battalions and bring them up for
another charge. He succeeded, and the desperate courage
which his words had infused into his men so nerved their arms
and edged their swords that their attack was irresistible. Rushing with headlong force against the line of the Confederates now
sadly thinned, their bayonets and sabres did fearful execution, and
their cavalry dashing in on the wavering ranks trampled down
all before them. The Irish, seized with a sudden panic, broke
and fled in disorder towards a bog which lay at a little distance.
After them like blood-hounds rushed the Puritans, urged on by
the cries of their ruthless commanders.

" Cut them down! down! every man of them!"

" No quarter, as you fear the righteous God!"

" Death to the brood of the scarlet woman!"

Wounded as he was, the sight of the flying Catholics and the
cries of the pursuers so inflamed the natural ferocity of Inchiquin that, despite the entreaties of his attendants, he sprang on
his horse and darted off to join the chase, looking like the ghost
of some hideous murderer, with his ghastly haggard face and
blood-stained garments. Before the main body of the Irish army
had been formed into order for retreat by the exertions of its
brave but (on that occasion) unfortunate commanders, several
hundreds had already perished in that fatal morass by the
merciless swords and bayonets of the Puritans. Just as the rear
guard was formed, almost in the face of the enemy, night suddenly closed in dark and moonless, and the victors, still unsa-
tiated with blood, were stopped in full pursuit.

Better acquainted with the locality than their enemies, the
Confederates continued their march all night, and long before

the dawn had placed a wide stretch of country between them and their pursuers. Saddened and discouraged they were, but still unsubdued, and burning for an opportunity to retrieve their losses and efface the stain of that day's disgrace from the banners they had saved with so much blood. Heavy as was their loss, moreover, they had still the poor consolation of knowing that the enemy counted well nigh as much, and, above all, they thought with the stern joy of avengers that if there was sorrow in their camp that night there should be wailing on the morrow in the princely halls of Lismore* over one of the cruellest of their oppressors.

* Lismore Castle was then and long after the dwelling of the Boyles, Earls of Cork.

18

CHAPTER XIV.

" I pray thee, cease thy counsel,
Which falls into mine ear as profitless
As water in a sieve."

SHAKESPEARE

" And extreme fear can neither fight nor fly,
But, coward-like, with trembling terror die."

SHAKESPEARE.

" To make the cunning artless, tame the rude,
Subdue the haughty, shake the undaunted soul—
These are the triumphs of all powerful beauty "

JOANNA BAILLIE.

WHILE Barry and his brave associates were sustaining with
varying fortune in Munster and Leinster the cause of religion and
liberty, Owen Roe was quietly and cautiously biding his time,
training his army according to the newer and more approved
modes of warfare practised on the continent, so that when the
time came for his taking the field he might meet his opponents
on, at least, equal terms. He was busily engaged one day
towards the end of August directing the evolutions of a body of
cavalry on a common outside the town of Charlemont, when
Shamus Beg and some half dozen of his fellows who had been
sent on a commission some miles northward, arrived in company
with just another such party, arrayed in the costume of Monroe's
soldiers, and accompanied by a trumpeter. A shout of execration burst from the clansmen at the sight, whereat Shamus
waxed wroth.

" Can't you have manners, now, you great ghomerils," said he,
" and let the men alone, when it's only doing an errand they

are? Don't you see the decent boy with the trumpet here waiting to have a parley with the general?"

"With me," said Owen Roe riding up at the moment.

"With you and no other, máy it please your generalship. Do
you think we'd have brought them safe here if it wasn't for
that? Speak up now, Sassums!" turning to them with a ludicrous air of authority. Here's *the O'Neill* now. Humph! I
mean General O'Neill. Speak up and don't be afraid. Devils
an' all as you are, you'll go back with whole bones *this* time."

"Don't promise too much now, Shamus aroon," said a stalwart O'Neill from the cavalry ranks; "they never show us
mercy, when they have us in their power."

"I know that as well as you," said Shamus, "maybe I don't,
to my heavy, heavy sorrow, but that's neither here nor there—I
gave them my word I'd see them safe over the county march
again, and the first man that says 'boo' to them must have a
bout with me. Do you mind, now, Rody?"

Rody, notwithstanding his bluster, *did* mind, for the weight
of Shamus's fists was sufficiently well known to make the threat
effective. The good-humored laughter which greeted Shamus's
assumption of authority gave that privileged person no offence,
for his sense of dignity was too deep-seated to be easily disturbed.

Meanwhile the trumpeter had advanced at the general's invitation, and staring the latter full in the face, he said without any
the slightest military salute:

"Be you the man whom the rebels call General O'Neill?"

It was fortunate for the presumptuous speaker that none but
the general fully understood what he said.

"I *am* the man so called," O'Neill replied drily, but without
any show of resentment; "what is your business with me, good
fellow?"

"I have got a bit paper here somewhere," said the ill-mannered Puritan, fumbling awkwardly in a pouch fastened inside
the breast of his doublet, whence he at length drew forth a letter
which he handed to the general, saying, "cur new general sends
you that, and wants an answer by return!"

"And who may your new general be?"

"I opine you'll see it in the letter," said the fellow curtly, having evidently no relish for discoursing with Popish recusants.

Smiling at the boorishness, so characteristic of all the man's tribe, O Neill turned aside to read the letter, after warning his men to take no notice of the strangers.

Breaking the seal with no small curiosity, Owen Roe glanced at the signature, and perceived that his strange and unexpected correspondent was no other than Lord Leven, whose arrival at Carrickfergus with reinforcements for Monroe was already noised abroad throughout the country. "It is rather odd," thought O'Neill, "that he should take to writing letters to me of all men —let us see what he has to say."

Any one watching his countenance would have seen that the contents of the letter amused him mightily, for ever as he read the smile on his lip became more humorous and his eyes twinkled with a merrier light.

"Well," said Shamus Beg to one of his comrades, "I'd give a trifle to know what's written down there that it makes the general look so droll. An' it was Sir Phelim, now, I'd have a chance of hearing the secret before long, but, ochone! sure this man keeps his mind to himself so close that no one's the wiser for what he thinks or what he knows. Sure enough he's a wise man!"

"Shamus!" said the general, "I leave these men in your charge while I prepare an answer for the letter they have brought me. See that no accident befal them!"

"Oh! the sorrow an accident, general, will befal *them*," said the foster-brother of Sir Phelim; "they're under *my* protection already, but *your* bidding goes beyond that again."

The cavalry were then dismissed for that day, but still most of them lounged behind, anxious to see the *Sussum dergs* started again before they left the ground.

O'Neill, alone in his chamber, read Lord Leven's letter again, and again the arch smile curled his thin lip. "He wonders, forsooth," said he half aloud, "that a man of my rank and reputation should come to Ireland to support so bad a cause, and very civilly intimates that I would do well to return whence I came. Truly the man hath an over great opinion of his powers of persuasion when he taketh it upon him to offer me advice. Plague on him for a Puritanical coxcomb, what a fool he must e'en take me for. Methinks I were hard run for counsel when I would seek it or take it of mine enemy. A plausible knave he is, moreover, with his fair, soft speech—well, I will answer him in such wise that he will never volunteer advice to me again."

And thereupon Owen Roe took up his pen and indited such an epistle to Lord Leven as must have given him a distaste for advising Irish chieftains generally, and the toparch of Tyrone in particular.

Amongst other cutting remarks there committed to paper, Owen Roe told the new Scotch general very plainly that he thought he had a better right to defend his own country than his lordship had to march into England against his lawful sovereign.* This Leven had done, as O'Neill well knew.

The answer written and dispatched was duly delivered in Carrickfergus, Shamus himself seeing the Scotchmen, as he had promised, to the county march. His task, nevertheless, was not so easy as he had expected, for while still on the Tyrone side of the border he fell in with a party of Rapparees who had been out on a foraging expedition. Who should be leader of the band but Angus Dhu, and the young man was riding up with his usual cordiality to greet Shamus, when his eye falling on the sergeant in command of the Puritans, he turned ghastly pale, and putting his right hand across his eyes he said, or rather shrieked:

"Mother of God, Shamus, know you with whom you are keeping company?"

"That do I all too well," said O'Hagan, "but they brought a letter from Carrick to the general—I met them on the way by chance and conducted them to Charlemont, and now they have the general's answer back with them, and he gave them in charge to *me*, Angus, to see them safe over the border."

"Shamus O'Hagan," said the young Rapparee withdrawing his hand from his face but still averting his eyes from the hated Sassums, "Shamus, friend of my heart, hast thou for-

* Rinuccini's Memoirs.

gotten that awful night when, from amid smoke, and fire, and
death, thou didst bear thy beloved with the swiftness of the wind
in the vain search for safety ?"

" I remember it well," said Shamus, lowering his eyes before
the fiery orbs that were flashing upon him.

" Hast forgotten the hell-hounds who pursued thee in that
fearful chase seeking to tear the defenceless one from thee—hast
forgotten *Lindsay !*"

" Forgotten Lindsay ! no, never while life beats in my heart !"

" There he stands, then," and the young man pointed to the
dark-vi aged sergeant who, although not understanding a
word of what was said, could not avoid hearing his own name
and the tremendous emphasis laid upon it. Conscience filled up
the blank, and the livid countenance of the wretch betrayed at
once his consciousness and his fears. Instinctively he drew
back among his comrades as Shamus, turning, fixed his eyes
searchingly upon him.

" Queen of Heaven ! but I believe you're right, Angus—it is
Lindsay himself, and no other. Ah ! you curse of God villain
you drove me into the salt sea that night with the pulse of my
heart that you'd fain have taken from me."

" Ha ! it was your ain sel that leaped yon gulf, then," cried
the Scotchman all aghast, and forgetting his fears for the moment, he darted forward and grasping O'Hagan's arm looked
him in the face, " I thought you jist drowned yoursel with that
bonnie lassie—you'd pleasure me much an' you'd tell me how
you got awa' frae ahint yon awsome black rocks."

" The d—l give you knowledge, you ill-conditioned vagabond,"
was Shamus's answer, accompanied by a thrust with the butt end
of his musket that made the Scotchman reel in his saddle—" an'
you open your lips again, I'll—I'll—but, ochone, sure I can't—I
can't—my hands are tied, more's the pity."

" Shamus," said the young Rapparee in a very decided way,
"that man is our prisoner—the captain has us all on our oath,
as you well know, never to let one of Monroe's hell-hounds escape us—wherever we meet them, by day or by night, we're
either to cut them down or bring them alive to *him*. Now, I
know he'd like to settle accounts himself with this murdering

villain. I claim him, then, in Donogh's name—the others I know not—if they were at work *that night* I saw them not—they may go, therefore, but Lindsay we must and will have!"

"It must not be, Angus," said O'Hagan resolutely, and he moved in front of the obnoxious Scotchman who was now again trembling like an aspen. "I owe him no more good will than yourself, but he is in my charge, and came here on my word—I tell you, boy! the man that lays hand on him is my enemy, were he the son of my own mother! Back! every man of you!" for the fierce-looking Rapparees were closing in around, obedient to a sign from Angus. "Back! or dread the vengeance of Tyr-Owen!"

"Shamus O'Hagan!" said the old man, Florry Muldoon, as he brandished his formidable pike nearer the Scotchmen than any of them liked; "Shamus! ma bouchal! it's a folly to talk that way—you ought to know by this time that we of the woods fear no living man—if Angus here says that black neb must be taken to the Brantree, taken he'll be, depend upon it, so get out of the way or you may be sorry, were you Pheliny Roe himself, instead of his foster-brother."

"Florry, I don't want to fight with you," said Shamus, "that and hang myself is the last thing I'd do, but I tell you again I must leave these villains safe over the march; after that the old de'il may take them for me, and sure he has the best right to them!"

Now the Rapparees far outnumbered Shamus's party and the Scotchmen put together, and Shamus well knew the reckless bravery which made them the terror of their foes. He knew that if it came to close quarters he and his were pretty sure to have the worst of it, but even that would not deter him from doing his duty. It was the sight of Angus whom he loved with more than a brother's love, and the thought that he might perchance fall in the scuffle—that was what troubled poor Shamus and made his heart sink within him. Angus on his part was just as unwilling to meet Shamus in mortal strife, but come what will he was resolved to take Lindsay dead or alive. His followers waited but the word to fall on, and their eager eyes watched every turn of his expressive countenance while their fingers clutched their pikes with a restless itching for the onslaught.

"Boys," said the fiery young leader at length, "I see there's no help for it—if Shamus *will* go between us and our revenge, his blood be on his head—if they give us that man quietly"—pointing to the miserable Lindsay where he cowered in his saddle behind his reluctant protector—"well and good—the rest of the black nebs may go in peace for us—but *him* we must have! Shamus! will you, or will you not, give him up?"

"I couldn't do it, Angus, and you ought to know that—for the love of God—let us pass on, and wait *you* some other opportunity—you'll have it, and revenge will keep till then—oh, don't —don't, Angus, or we *must* fire——"

"Stand aside, Shamus O'Hagan, or—" and the young man grasping his pike half way down the handle, prepared to aim a deadly thrust at Lindsay.

"Leave it to your captain, Angus!" cried Shamus, driven to the last extremity; "I'll appeal to him, for he promised to do the general's bidding!"

"You're a greater fool than I took you for, Shamus Beg!" said Angus; "how will the Captain decide the matter when he's not within miles of us——"

"The captain is here," said a deep voice from behind a bushy hawthorn which there overhung the road; "Shamus's word and the general's will must be respected—let them go *for this time*, and quickly, so that I see not the accursed face of Lindsay—an' I did, I must do a deed which belongeth to a future hour—pass on, Shamus, and remember it is for your sake and Owen Roe's that I do what by right I should *not* do—pass on!"

"God's blessing and mine be with you, Donogh," said Shamus with deep feeling; "we were friends before, we'll be brothers now!"

"And I, Shamus," said Angus as he drew his party to one side, to let the others pass; "will you ever forgive *me?*"

"I forgive you now, Angus, my fine fellow"—and Shamus as he passed him shook his hand lustily—"*you* were right in your own way—so was I—let us be none the worse friends for what has happened. Get along here before me, you devil's limb !" addressing the sergeant who was far from being as yet re-assured, " your carcass is not worth fighting for, God knows, but no matter—ride on, I tell you !"

The Scotchmen were only too happy to obey, and as the whole party rode off at a brisk canter, Donogh leaped the low fence and, looking cautiously around, gave a short whistle, whereupon two of his men appeared at an opening in the hedge a few yards distant, bearing between them a sort of rustic litter on which sat the aged widow of O'Cahan, followed closely by her daughter on foot with two more of the Rapparees, the latter keeping some paces behind through respect for the lady. The whole cavalcade set out at once on the road to Charlemont, escorted now by the party under Angus, to whom Donogh had whispered some directions.

It so happened that they had proceeded but a little way when Sir Phelim O'Neill was seen approaching by a bridle road followed by some six or eight of his own retainers.

" What ho ! who goes there?" cried the knight as he pushed his horse to a gallop to meet the party ; " why, the Rapparees, as I hope to be saved—and well mounted, too ! But the captain on foot—how is that, good fellow ?"

Just at this moment he caught sight of the ladies, and a change came over his bold visage.

" Ha ! by the sword of Nial, this is a sight !—I wish you joy, madam, of your elevated seat," bowing with mock respect to the mother, while to the daughter he said, " strolling tinkers, or what ?—mayhap gypsies?" and he burst into a loud laugh that was more forced than natural.

Judith answered only by a scornful look, but Donogh advancing to her side, took upon him to reply—" Sir Phelim O'Neill, I d have you to know that these ladies are under our protection—he who does them ill, ay ! or says them ill, is no friend of ours."

" And who the fiend cares for that?" said Sir Phelim contemptuously ; " oh, I beg pardon," correcting himself, as it were, " I forgot Owen Roe, your great friend and patron. But, answer me this, young man : whither do you take those Rapparee ladies in such state ? Have they tired of forest life ?"

Before Donogh could answer, Judith herself replied: "We are on our way to Charlemont, and are not tired of forest life, thanks to the generous care of these brave fellows."

"Why leave them, then, in God's name, since you like so well their entertainment?"

"Because, Sir Phelim," replied Donogh, "there are rumors abroad that the Puritan generals do purpose making an attack on the Brantree, and although for ourselves we fear them not, we must place these ladies beyond their reach, for fear of the worst!"

"Ay, for fear of the worst," muttered the aged lady, looking down with a moistened eye on the wild-looking fellows who formed her guard; "it were an evil hour for us when the enemy prevailed over our faithful Rapparees—poor fellows! they and we are alike—hunted from post to pillar, without roof to cover us, or means of support, other than charity gives us—or force can take!" she added with her dreary smile.

"And you go to Charlemont to take shelter under the wing of Owen Roe?" said Sir Phelim, endeavoring to conceal the emotion which he really felt under an appearance of spiteful levity.

"Even so, Sir Phelim," said Judith again, "he hath promised us protection—he hath power to make his word good—he hath strong walls around him, and there is room enow within them for the widow and daughter of O'Cahan. I pray you let us pass without further discourse."

"Judith O'Cahan," said Sir Phelim, now thoroughly in earnest and lowering his voice, for he had contrived to get near her, "Judith O'Cahan, there is no need for this humbling yourself, an' you have one grain of prudence. There is a safe and honorable asylum still open for you and your mother, as you well know!"

"Name it not, Sir Phelim," exclaimed the lady, her pale cheek reddening with indignation; "I have told you my mind on that head—it hath undergone no change!"

"Fool! fool!" muttered the knight with a sudden movement of anger, which, however, glancing around, he saw fit to repress.

"Take my horse, then, Mistress Judith," he said, making a mo-

tion as if so alight, then added in a jocular way in English, and in
an under tone, "since you will not take myself—I beseech you
lady, be not obstinate—so long a journey on foot ill beseemeth
your sex and quality——"

"Urge me no farther, Sir Phelim," said Judith still more
decided than before; "I may not pleasure myself with aught
that is yours."

"And wherefore, thou flinty charmer?"

"Ask thine own heart—the blood of Coey-na-gall* runs in
my veins, *and my memory is good*, oh! son of the Hy-Nial!——'

"But my mother will be glad to receive you and *yours*," persisted Sir Phelim; "you know she liveth apart from me with
her son, Hovenden—surely with her you will be safe—even
from *me!*" and he smiled.

"I know not that," said Judith shaking her head doubtfully,
"but even were it as thou sayest, Charlemont is our present
destination, for there we are sure of safety!"

"Have *I* not admission there?" asked Phelim with bitter
emphasis—"I who took it from the enemy when Owen Roe was
tilting it in Arras beyond?"

"I say not but you have," said the lady calmly, "but once
there I fear you not—move on, men, my mother is a-weary and
needeth rest!"

There was so stern a dignity in Judith's demeanor as she
spoke these words that Sir Phelim himself dare not resist, and
Donogh was not slow in giving the necessary order to his men
when once the imperious knight manifested no further opposition.

With a gruff salute from Sir Phelim, courteously returned by
Judith and her mother, the parties separated, and half an hour
more saw the homeless pair safely housed in Charlemont Castle,
where apartments were allotted them by Owen Roe. Few words
of welcome escaped his lips as he received them, but few as they
were they satisfied the mother and daughter.

---

* Coen-na-gall (the Scourge of the Stranger) was a famous chieftain
of the O'Cahans in earlier times; he was celebrated, as his name implies, for his successful resistance to foreign tyranny.

CHAPTER XV.

"But slaves, that once conceive the glowing thought
Of freedom, in that hope itself possess
All that the contest calls for;—spirit, strength,
The scorn of danger, and united hearts,
The surest presage of the good they seek."

                                        COWPER'S *Task.*

"Who, all unbribed, on Freedom's ramparts stand,
Faithful and true, bright wardens of the land."

                                        CHARLES SPRAGUE.

THE middle days of October were past, and the ancient city of Kilkenny (to which we would now conduct our readers) was a scene of gay and joyous bustle. Hostelries were crowded with the military retainers of the great chiefs and nobles, while private houses of all classes were filled with guests, and the stately mansions of the rich and noble were honored with the sojourn of knights, and lords, and priests and prelates. Never in her palmiest days, not even when Lionel, Duke of Clarence, called the estates together there for consultation, had the old city seen a grander display, or a greater number of distinguished personages assembled within its walls. Men of noble stature and lofty bearing were there from the Irish country clad in the graceful costume of their race. Chiefs from the far hills of Ulster, and the mountains of Connaught, from the fertile plains of Leinster and the golden vein of Munster, were there with their followers, and clansmen from the north and from the south, from the east and from the west—O'Reillys, and McMahons, and Maguires, and Magennises from the hills and vales of Ulster, were seen in familiar converse with McCarthys, and O'Connors, and O'Rourkes, and twenty other O's and Macs from the other Celtic districts,

while, distinct alike in language and in dress, the retainers of
the Norman nobles and gentlemen walked apart, discoursing
after their own fashion, rarely or never mingling with the Irish
of the same class. Not so, however, with their masters: for
them the distinction between the old and new blood seemed no
longer to exist—most of them spoke both Irish and English,
which was not the case with their followers, and many subjects of
interest were common to both as warrior knights and nobles.
Grouped together might be seen a tall, robust, Celtic chief in
truis, *cochal*, and *barradh*, with long flowing locks (the well-
prized *coolin*), a Norman noble from the Pale in dark-colored tunic
and knee-breeches with a long cloak of the same sober hue fastened close around his neck, his strongly-marked features
shaded by a broad-leaved, low-crowned hat, his slighter form
and generally shorter stature contrasting rather unfavorably
with the muscular proportions of his Celtic neighbor. With
these perchance was a marshal-looking gentleman whose foreign
aspect and sun-browned features, and French or Spanish costume would seem to point him out as of different origin from
either of the others. His speech, too, was marked by a foreign
accent, although he spoke both English and Irish, the latter
better and more fluently than the former. About these strangers
the chief interest seemed to gather, and their " tales of distant
lands" were greedily swallowed alike by Gael and Norman, few
of whom had ever crossed any of Ireland's four seas. Ecclesias-
tics of various grades were mingled with the groups, clad in
cloak and cassock, and, stranger still, monks and friars were
there in the habits of their several orders, the white robe of the
Dominican, and the brown habit of the Franciscan, and the gray
gown of the Augustinian contrasting chastely with the gay and
many-colored garments of the Celtic chiefs. Such sights as
this were for ages unseen in the good city of Kilkenny, and the
people were almost wild with joy, and full of the hope that the
dark evil day was passed away for ever, and that their clergy were
thenceforward to walk as other men in open day and in
their proper garments, not as thieves under cover of the night
and in all manner of strange disguises. From end to end the
old city was in commotion, Irishtown and Englishtown all

the same ; the very boats on the river seemed suddenly instinct
with life, so gaily and so cheerily, and with so much bustle did
they keep shooting hither and thither, along the Nore and up
the Bregah,* hither and thither, to and fro, so that a looker-on
would wonder what they were all about, or what maggot had
got into their crazy timbers. Colors were floating, too, from
every tiny mast, the gay white and green of the Confederates,
a·d the same colors met the eye in all directions waving in
plumes over noble brows, in drapery suspended from the upper
windows of houses, and in flags flaunting in the autumn breeze
on the highest elevations in and around the city. It was only
on the Castle, Ormond's Castle, that the royal flag of England
floated in solitary state. At the opposite extremity of the city,
on the rival hill, the national colors waved defiance from the
flag-staff of old St. Canice, and the bells of that stately pile
chimed forth at times a right merry peal for joy that religion
was again paramount in the good old city of the Butlers.

And wherefore all this joy and all this bustle ? why was the
city in its gala dress, and the citizens all in a state of pleasurable
excitement ? why, because the grand Assembly of the Confederates was to take place there within the week, and all was in a
state of preparation for the greatest event that had occurred in
Ireland, perhaps since the days of Brian Boromhe.

It was joy to hear the names that were on the people's lips as
they cheerily chatted on the streets and in the houses, in the
workshops and the hostelries, and wherever men came together for
business or amusement. The house chosen for the meeting of
what might truly be called the National Assembly was situate
in what is still called the Coal Market, a portion of the long line
of street which under one name or another intersects the entire
length of the city from the Cathedral to the Castle. The building was an ancient one and no wise imposing in its character,
although it was the residence of Sir Robert Shea, who appears

        The Bregah, a small tributary of the Nore, separates the new
and old parts of the city commonly known as Englishtown and
Irishtown.

to have lent or given it for the purpose.* It contained on the first floor a spacious hall, the farther end of which was slightly raised above the rest, and that was apportioned to the lords lay and spiritual, who had also a small room overhead for their private consultation. The remainder of the hall was for the use of the Commoners. The whole was lit by rows of high, narrow, arched windows, and its general character was rather gloomy, all the better adapted, perhaps, for purposes of deliberation. It had a reverend look, that old hall, and although without any pretensions to grandeur or state, when fitted up on that memorable occasion and decorated with national devices in the florid style of that age, it presented no mean appearance.

For many days previous to the opening of the Assembly, the citizens of all classes were watching the arrivals with all-absorbing interest. The name and title of each was duly noted, together with the style and quality of his apparel, the number and equipment of his followers, with the comparative rank and wealth of all shrewdly guessed at from these appendages.. By the Norman craftsmen and burgesses of the Englishtown of Kilkenny, the lords and gentlemen of the Pale were rated far above even the highest chieftains of Gaelic blood, the great toparchs of the north and south. Of these, Lord Muskerry, the MacCarthy of former days, stood the highest in the esteem of the townspeople from the fact of his being the brother-in-law of Lord Ormond, while Mountgarret on the other hand, notwithstanding his being a Butler, lost considerably in their estimation, because he had had the great Earl of Tyrone for his father-in-law Not all the glory of the Butlers could efface, in the minds of those supercilious Normans, the deep disgrace of being allied to an Irish family.

Exactly the reverse was the case beyond the Bregah where, in the narrow streets, and lanes and alleys of Irishtown, dwelt those of the old blood, whose hatred and contempt for the stranger and "the upstart" were as great as his for them. In that section of the town, it was Owen Roe and Sir Phelim

* For a further account of this venerable edifice and its present condition, see Hall's *Ireland*, Vol II., p 15.

O'Neill, O'Reilly, McMahon, McGennis, O'Connor, O'Sullivan and
all such, whose arrival was most carefully noted, and all that
appertained to them and their followers discussed and comment-
ed on with affectionate pride.   The fame of Owen Roe had penetrated even there and all were anxious to have a look at " the
chieftain of the Red Hand," the hero of so many battles, and
the successor, it was hoped, of the great Hugh who had all but
effected the liberation of Ireland.

With the clergy of all classes Owen O'Neill seemed just as
popular as with the people of the old blood.   There were, however, a few exceptions, and amongst these was conspicuous, however it happened, Bishop McMahon of Clogher with a certain
Franciscan friar more distinguished for worldly wisdom than for
any virtue commended in the Gospel.   The latter individual,
Father Peter Walsh by name, manifested from the first a singular coldness towards O'Neill, though why or wherefore few but
himself could tell.

The days preceding the opening of the Assembly passed
quickly and pleasantly with most of the Confederates in friendly
consultation, in visits to the numerous antiquities and places of
historic note so profusely scattered through the dingy lanes and
alleys of the old city, and most pleasing of all, in the renewal of
old acquaintance and the making of new, between men drawn
together for a common object and bound together for weal or
for woe by a solemn oath.   Those who had grown up side by
side in the dear old land and parted as boys to seek abroad that
instruction which the laws denied them at home, met again in
Kilkenny, one perhaps a soldier of fortune, the other a distinguished ecclesiastic.   Officers were there not a few who had
risen together step by step in the service of some foreign prince,
and others who had drawn the sword on opposite sides in the
wars which then convulsed the continent.   In Kilkenny all that
was forgotten : all were there as Irishmen, to give the mother
country and her sacred cause the benefit of their dear-bought
experience, and to place at her service the swords that had
carved out fame and mayhap fortune in more favored lands.
Priests, too, were there who had pored over the same ponderous volumes in early boyhood in the classic halls of St. Omers,

Salamanca or Louvain, but who, parting midway in their course, went to enrich far distant lands with the sacred lore and the priestly virtues drawn from those venerable founts. But wherever their lot was cast, whatsoever their position or the nature of their calling in foreign climes, the news of the great revolution going on in Ireland had stirred the pulses of their hearts, and the light of freedom blazing on the hill-tops of the Green Island had reached alike the soldier in his tent, the priest in his sanctuary, and the monk in his cloister. All Europe resounded with accounts more or less exaggerated of what was going forward in the Holy Island of the West, and the news of the great national assembly to be held in October drew the sons of Ireland and *their* sons home from every point of the compass.

From the black marble steps by which the front of St. Canice is reached a gallery runs along one side of the building, commanding a fair view of the city, and the river, and the noble castle of the Butlers, making altogether a picture of rare scenic beauty. On the evening immediately preceding the solemn opening of the Council, or (more properly speaking) Parliament, four notable persons stood together in earnest conversation on matters appertaining to the great business in hand.

One of these was no less a person than Malachy O'Kelly, Archbishop of Tuam, the same zealous and patriotic prelate who, a few weeks before, had denounced the powerful de Burgo in the midst of his armed retainers. Near him stood a Franciscan friar, whose somewhat unmeaning countenance had a look of dogged determination that might be set down as obstinacy, with more than a little cunning. Altogether the man was far from pleasing in his exterior, presenting in face and form a marked contrast to the portly and frank-looking Archbishop, with his quick, earnest glance and animated countenance.

One of the others was Owen Roe O'Neill, in his Celtic costume, looking as calm and cool as though nothing of moment were under discussion—hearing much but saying little—and watching through his half-closed eyes the faces of those around him. Near him, leaning carelessly against the buttress of the old Cathedral, stood a gentleman of soldierly bearing, whose fine oval countenance lost somewhat of its easy, good natured expression by reason of the large whiskers and moustache, which, although no improvement in point of beauty, gave a more martial character to the wearer. His stout and rather square-built figure was handsomely attired in the uniform of a French officer of that day, slashed doublet and truncated hose, with a cocked hat and a plume of snow white feathers. This was Thomas Preston, a brother of the late Lord Gormanstown, who had been many years serving in the French army to the great advancement of his name and fame, if not fortune. Like O'Neill he had gathered together a large number of Irish officers, his brothers-in-arms during his career in France, and through the munificence of the great Richelieu, then holding the helm of state in that country, he had sailed for his native country with two ships of war, bearing a good supply of arms and ammunition for the use of the Confederate Catholics. About the middle of the preceding month of September, Thomas Preston had given the good people of Wexford a glad surprise when he sailed into their harbor one fine day with his French ships and his goodly company of Irish officers and the colors of the Confederates hoisted so briskly the moment the vessels neared the shore. That cheering event had been the subject of conversation, and Preston, after enlarging on the favorable dispositions of the great Cardinal, as evinced by this first magnificent contribution, turned to O'Neill with a smile of affected candor:

"I would that his Catholic Majesty had been so liberal. Methinks it was a paltry trick he played you, after so many fine promises, to send you home with one poor brig—out upon so great a sovereign so to reward so valiant a servant, were higher motive wanting for his generosity!"

"There spoke the French prejudice," said O'Neill calmly; "you little know the royal Philip, an' you deem that 'one poor brig' the sum total of his bounty to us. Fair and soft, you know, Master Preston, go far in a day, and my royal master is by nature cautious and circumspective."

"And his servant is like unto him," muttered Preston in a half audible tone, as turning away he affected to admire the prospect before him, albeit that nature's charms had few or no attractions at any time for him wanting the

—— files arrayed with helm and blade
And plumes in the gay wind dancing,"

which alone have beauty for the soldier's eye. Preston had a soldier's heart and a soldier's spirit, for most of his life had been a soldier's life, and his joys and pleasures were all of a martial character.

O'Neill eyed him a moment from the elevation of his superior height, and it seemed as though a biting retort rose to his lips, but it came not forth, for seldom indeed was it that passion betrayed him, and he was determined that no petulance of his should throw a shade on the brightness of the path, where he trusted that Preston and he should walk hand in hand to victory. The Archbishop's keen eye had been observing both, and, laying his hand on O'Neill's shoulder, he said in Irish:

" Honor and glory to him who overcometh self."

Now it so happened that Preston had no knowledge whatever of the native tongue, but, seeing the glow of satisfaction on O'Neill's cheek, he was at no loss to comprehend the meaning of what was said, and his hasty temper took fire at what he considered the slight put upon him.

" I need hardly inform you," said he, " my Lord Archbishop, that your language is a stranger to my tongue—as I am, I perceive, to your counsels. My presence is a burthen that must needs be removed. Give your Grace good evening !"

He was turning away when the Archbishop, with a significant glance at O'Neill, tendered his apology for speaking in Irish, assuring Master Preston that he never dreamed of his being unacquainted with that tongue.

" It is passing strange an' he be," said the Franciscan, speaking for the first time ; " why, my Lord of Ormond doth affect that tongue and speaketh it as a true Milesian lord. Even my lady the Countess hath a full knowledge of it. and I know not but their children all speak it." ·

The prelate smiled, and his smile was full of arch meaning, while O'Neill fixed a wondering glance on the heavy features of the friar.

" I would it were otherwise, Father Peter Walsh," said the

Archbishop: "if Master Preston had more knowledge of our tongue, and what concerneth us, and Lord Ormond less, it were all the better for us."

He is a dangerous enemy, that same Ormond," said Preston abruptly, "more so, as I take it, than Inchiquin or Broghill, seeing that he carrieth a double face, whereas the others show themselves such as they are."

"Your opinion is mine," Master Preston, said the prelate warmly, "and I rejoice to find you so much alive to that lord's duplicity. You will be the better able to cope with him—he is the serpent in the grass, take my word for it!"

"My lord! my lord!" said the Franciscan, roused to sudden energy by this stricture on the man whom he strangely enough had chosen for a patron, "my Lord Archbishop, it grieveth me to hear you speak in such wise of the only powerful friend we have amongst the Protestants! Surely, it is ungrateful. Surely, surely it is. Now, General O'Neill, you and Master Preston being in a manner strangers in this land, are, as it were, in the dark concerning many things that ye ought to know. As a priest of the Catholic Church I solemnly assure you that were this unhappy disturbance left to my Lord of Ormond and my Lord of Clanrickarde, they would make all things smooth and pleasant for us, ay, marry! and we should soon have all we want—but, woe is me! woe is me! their pacific counsels are unheeded, their warning voices unheard, and rash men are hurrying the nation into the vortex of rebellion, unknowing how to draw it forth again or quell the storm themselves have raised!"

"Father Peter Walsh," said the Archbishop sternly, "your infatuation with regard to Lord Ormond becometh intolerable, and hath even now carried you beyond the bounds of Christian decency. I hereby pronounce what you have said untrue in every particular, and do solemnly assever that the two men you have named are the direst enemies of our sacred cause."

"What! Clanrickarde as bad as the renegade Ormond?" said O'Neill in surprise; "hath your Grace then no hope of his final co-operation?"

"No more than I have of Ormond's—he hath made unto himself an idol, the which is Charles of England, and whosoever boweth not with him before that shrine is a rebel and a traitor in his esteem, be his standing in God's Church what it may—nay, Father Walsh, I charge you say no more—before God, I am sick of your twaddle——"

"And *I* take God to witness," said the pertinacious friar, "that your Grace and all who hold your opinions do these honorable lords foul injustice in that——!"

"You are either a fool or a knave, Peter Walsh," said a dark-visaged man who just then joined the party.

"A Franciscan could expect no better from one of your order," replied Walsh with a disdainful glance at the black robe of the Jesuit, for such the other was. "What do you know of this matter?"

"As much as you—or it may be more," said the son of Ignatius pointedly; "that which I know I say, and I tell you, in the presence of his Grace of Tuam and these gallant gentlemen, what I would tell Ulick Burke were he within reach of my voice, to wit, that his heart is as hard against us as Murrough O'Brien's, and the enemies of our faith have no more zealous supporter than he. Would to Heaven he would cease to profane the name of Catholic whereto he hath no other title than an empty sound——"

"Ha! I know you now!" cried Walsh; "methought your face was familiar—you are——"

"It matters little who I am," said the Jesuit waving his hand authoritatively; "*I* know you, too, Peter Walsh, and so, I trust, do most of the Confederates."

A messenger here arrived from the Bishop requesting his Grace of Tuam, General O'Neill, and Colonel Preston to repair immediately to his house where their presence was urgently needed.

CHAPTER XVI.

" Were his eyes open ? Yes, and his mouth, too ; —
Surprise has this effect, to make one dumb,
Yet leave the gate, which eloquence slips through,
As wide as if a long speech were to come."

BYRON.

" He who would free from malice pass his days
Must live obscure, and never merit praise."

GAY's *Epistles.*

ON reaching the Bishop's house* our party found a number
of the Confederate chiefs assembled, and all eagerly engaged discussing some event apparently of great importance. In a large
arm-chair, near one of the high, narrow windows, sat the aged
Bishop of the diocese, an old, old man with a worn and wasted
countenance, and a form bowed down beneath the double
weight of age and sorrow, for the episcopal office was an entail
of misery in the dark days on which David Rothe's episcopate
had fallen. There was energy and spirit, nevertheless, in the
fine old eyes which had once been bright, and there was firm
determination about the sunken mouth and the thin colorless lips.
By the side of the Bishop stood a tall, dignified personage with
a strongly marked Norman countenance and that unmistakeable
something in his air and bearing which indicates rank and h gh
position. Something there was about the gentleman's appearance
which reminded one of poor Maguire as we first saw him, although
he who now stands before us is older evidently by several years.
There is a firmness, too, and a certain military boldness about
the face and figure which never characterized the chieftain of
Fermanagh, and which give you the impression of a self-relying,

* The family mansion of the Rothes is situate in the Coal market,
exactly opposite the house in which the Confederates met.

independent spirit, capable of high and daring enterprize. On the other side of the Bishop's chair, and leaning familiarly on its arm, stood Bishop McMahon, while in front of him stood Lord Fingal, his thin sharp features cold and calm as though nothing could ever stir the heart within him. By his side stood Sir Phelim O'Neill, looking as fierce as if he meant to attack somebody on the instant.

"My Lord of Tuam," said Bishop Rothe as soon as he caught sight of that dignitary, "we have good news for you—come hither! General O Neill, and Colonel Preston, here is my lord of Castlehaven come to join us——"

"Nay, my lord," said the tall gentleman by his side after exchanging a courtly bow with the newly arrived prelate and the two officers, "nay, my lord, I, as yet, hold myself free to pronounce on that matter—I would fain ——"

"Keep the middle course," put in Sir Phelim O'Neill; "methinks your lordship hath pursued it over long for all you have made of it. Had you come out boldly as we did at the start," Castlehaven smiled, "you would have laid us under obligations—your thanks from Ormond and the Justices being but small in any case—whereas now, albeit that we are glad to see you here, we know full well that you come because you cannot help it!"

"Truly it must be a hard necessity," said the archbishop, "that threw so loyal a nobleman as Lord Castlehaven into our rebellious ranks."

There was the slightest possible touch of irony in these words which the peer well understood, and with a heightened color he replied : "I acknowledge it, my lord archbishop! I am a loyal man, and desirous above all of upholding my sovereign's authority in this realm."

"So are we all," said Archbishop O'Kelly promptly, "so are we all loyal men—God forbid we were not—an' the king's majesty were only as loyal to us as we are to him, our differences were but small."

"And yet, my reverend lord, there was no lack of haste in flying to arms!"

"Pardon me, Lord Castlehaven," said Owen Roe, speaking

for the first time, and with his usual calmness of demeanor, " pardon me in that I cannot think as you do concerning that matter. In my poor judgment, no nation under heaven hath shown so much endurance as this of ours in regard to those Stuart princes—before God this day I have thought many a time that patience amongst the poor oppressed Catholics of Ireland did overstep the bounds of virtue—had they kept the peace much longer, I had turned my back on them as a cowardly and pusillanimous race with no heart to help themselves, and therefore unworthy of help from God or man !"

Castlehaven made no answer, but he fixed his eyes on O'Neill's face with a keen and searching look, as though anxious to see farther into a book so well covered.

" Be it as it may," said Bishop McMahon in his quick way, " we rejoice to see Lord Castlehaven here, and do bid him heartily welcome in the name of the Confederate Catholics——"

" Much cause have we to thank the worshipful Justices," said the incorrigible knight of Kinnard; " had they given his honorable lordship a better return for his loyal service we might e'en have whistled for him, and danced to our own music—ho ! ho ! ho ! a pretty reward truly !—he spoke them fair and bowed himself in and out of their presence, and used many hard words doubtless in regard to us poor Popish recusants and rebels, and lo ! they send their minions and burn his houses and lay waste his lands—but kicking doth agree well with some dogs, and straightway my lord of Castlehaven, finding himself accused of treasonable practices (bless the mark !), hurries off post-haste to Dublin to justify himself in the sight of Parsons and Borlase— by my knighthood, Castlehaven ! they served you right to clap you in prison as a traitor*—you were a traitor——"

" How, Sir Phelim ! what meaneth this language ?" said the Earl haughtily.

" I say again you _were_ a traitor, my lord earl ! a traitor to your God and to your country ! They served you right, I tell you !"

* For an account of Lord Castlehaven's case, and the means whereby he was driven into rebellion, see his own *Memoirs*, pp. 20-30.

"Sir Phelim! Sir Phelim!" said Bishop Rothe, raising his finger by way of rebuke——

"I crave your lordship's pardon, an' I speak too warmly," said Sir Phelim; "it is a way we have amongst the hills of Tyr-Owen."

"Such fashion of speech is not to my liking," said Castlehaven coldly; "methinks it is out of place on this occasion!"

"Surely it is, my lord," said Owen Roe; "we are here to deliberate for the common good, not to twit each other on things past. I pray you excuse my worthy kinsman in that he cracks his jokes so as to leave the edges oversharp!"

"I pray you let your kinsman speak for himself, Master Spaniard," said Phelim shortly; "an' he choose to tell his thoughts more freely than others it is no business of yours. I but meant to make known to my lord of Castlehaven and these other lords and gentl.men who are not of our blood, that we of the Irishry can see as far into the mill-stone as he that picks it. No offence, I hope, to the noble earl who, an' he is pleased to lend us a hand, may find Phelim O'Neill as true a friend as though his speech were framed in more courtly fashion!"

The frown vanished quickly from the lordly brow of Castlehaven, and he said with a bland smile: "I will frankly own, my lords and gallant gentlemen, that the Justices have left no stone unturned to drive me to this step, the which I take it was their purpose throughout."

"So it was with all of us, my lord," observed Fingal; "we of the Pale were, as you well know, right loyally disposed, and did make advances towards the Lords Justices——"

"Advances!" repeated Sir Phelim in a contemptuous tone, while Owen Roe and the two prelates of Irish blood could not help smiling; "we all know what manner of advances they were, soliciting arms to use against us wild Irishry—the which were no great benefit to you when you got them——"

"Sir Phelim O'Neill, I protest against this insulting language," said Fingal angrily, while the bishops strove by signs to close the knight's mouth; "an' we petitioned for arms it was for our own defence, as God he knoweth!"

"For your own defence!—truly, my Lord Fingal, you must

19

take us for fools!—was it in his own defence that Talbot of
Malahide marched forth against the brave clans of Wicklow, as
it were, to finish Coote's work? Bah! such Catholics are as so
many festering sores in the body—I would to heaven I might
deal with them! I vow to God I would sooner measure swords
with one of your Clanrickardes or Talbots, or such like men,
than the blackest Puritan in the English Parliament!"

"Hear you that, Father Walsh?" said Preston, who had not yet
spoken; "but what! the Franciscan hath vanished—and the
Jesuit, too!"

"Not so, colonel," said Owen Roe, pointing to another group
of which the dark-visaged son of Loyola was the centre; "he
is enlightening Philip O'Reilly and Owen O'Rourke on the
atrocities perpetrated in Dublin prisons—by my life he speaks
as one who had seen it all—what manner of man may he be,
for I heard him half an hour since bearing testimony against the
Galway Earl in the same oracular fashion. How cometh he to
know all these things and to speak of them as an eye-witness?"

He had addressed himself to the Bishop and the latter replied
with a careless glance at the Jesuit: "He is, in sooth, a far-
seeing man, and a clear-headed—otherwise, I see or know nothing worth remarking. But where is Father Walsh? Came
he not hither with your Grace?" addressing the archbishop.

"Of a surety, my lord, he followed us in, but I see him not
anywhere present!"—and the prelate stretched himself to his
full height to look around the room—"no, truly, I see him not!"

"An' your Grace seeketh Father Peter Walsh," said a bene-
volent-looking prelate of middle age, who had been engaged in
a quiet conference with Sir Morgan Cavanagh and Bishop
McSweeny of Kilmore; "I saw him but late busily engaged
writing as I passed through one of the Bishop's parlors."

"Writing!—humph!" and the two prelates exchanged glances,
and both looked significantly at Castlehaven. None of the Confederates who knew the friar were surprised to hear that a dispatch was sent off that same evening to Lord Ormond from the
gate of the Franciscan Abbey. Indeed Father Peter took little
pains to conceal his devotion to that lord, deeming it rather a
proof of his religion and patriotism than otherwise.

Whilst the scene just described was passing at one end of the room, one of a different kind was going on at the other. Alone, in the midst of that animated crowd, old Lorcan Maguire stood like the spirit of the past gazing around him with eyes of wonder, a pleased expression on his wrinkled, yet still commanding countenance. His nephew, Roderick, who was also in the room, had just left him to speak with Colonel Preston and Sir John Burke at a neighboring window, and the old man looked so lonely that Hugh Byrne was crossing the room to engage him in conversation, when all of a sudden he started off with the lightness of early youth and disappeared through an opposite doorway, where a dark narrow passage led to the main hall of the building.

A hearty laugh from the good-humored colonel attracted general attention, as he in turn stood alone in the centre of the room gazing down the passage.

" By Our Lady, Rory," said he addressing Maguire, " that venerable uncle of yours hath a flea in his bonnet—never saw I man of his age tramp so lightly as he hath done but now from this room. Here did I cross the room to have a talk with him on matters appertaining to the other world, and in the twinkling of an eye he flew—ay! faith, *flew*—through yonder door—think you he saw a spirit ?"

" I pray you heed him not," said the attached nephew ; " he hath odd ways at times and doeth things that perchance no one else would do, but an' you knew him as I do, Hugh, you would respect even his oddities ;" and the terror of Enniskillen, the fierce young avenger of Maguire's wrongs, shamed not to raise his hand and wipe away a tear. Anxious to attract attention from his uncle's movements, whatever their object might be, he hastily resumed the thread of discourse, inviting O'Byrne to listen to Preston's account of Father Wadding's reception on a late occasion at the Court of Versailles, when the great Cardinal pledged himself before all the diplomatic corps to see justice done to Ireland. This interesting recital drew a crowd of the deputies around Preston, Lord Castlehaven among the rest, and, by the time it was ended, he had all but made up his mind to join the Confederates.

"You will do well, my lord earl," said Nicholas French, the wise and learned Bishop of Ferns, to whom he had specially addressed himself, "Look around this room—note well the lords and gentlemen and priests and prelates in it assembled—yet of a surety they be but a third or so of those whom the morrow will bring together for solemn deliberation—bethink you if the cause upheld by all the chief men of the Irish Catholics, as well clerical as lay, ay! even at the point of the sword and to their grievous and unspeakable privation of worldly goods, can be a bad one? The bare idea is absurd, and unworthy a moment's entertainment. Make up your mind at once, then, my lord of Castlehaven, leave worldly considerations behind as so many of your friends have done even now, and girding on your armor for God and poor bleeding Ireland, win fame and honor, and, above all, the approval of your own conscience! In God's name, my dear son, do as I tell you, to the end that at the great accounting day this my admonition may not rise against you in judgment!"

"I will take the rules, then, and the written oath to my lodgings," said the Earl, "and consider them over night, begging the favor of your lordship's prayers that I may be directed from on high what course to take."

Whilst this was passing within the room, Lorcan Maguire had darted down the passage in the wake of a muffled figure whose attire, as well as he could judge from the dim light, was the coarse frieze of a Franciscan, with the high narrow hood drawn over the face. This was the apparition whose beck had drawn the old man from the room so inopportunely for the Wicklow chief.

It was a youthful face, although a haggard one, that looked up at the old man from under the hood when, panting after his race, Lorcan came to a stand. The light was dim, so that objects were barely discernible, and yet it seemed to him as though he had seen the face before and the glance of the upturned eye made him quail he knew not why.

"Father," said he after a moment's awkward silence, "I would know your pleasure."

A wan smile flitted across the face in the hood at the word "father," but it vanished in an instant, and a soft musical voice spoke : " Doth Master Lorcan Maguire forget the head of his house, or hath he no bowels for the son of his brother languishing in a foreign land ?"

" Friar, I do not !" said the aged chief with a convulsive start ; " by my right hand, I would give my life an hundred times over to see Connor Maguire chase the roe as of old on Fermanagh hills—or better still, to see his youthful valor wielded against the foe—forget Connor ! my poor Connor, whom I first taught to cast a javelin or bend a bow—stranger, as soon would I forget my own heart."

" It is well—I knew it. I will tell you, then, mine errand hither. Brave and wise old man, I have thought of a plan by which your nephew and mayhap his companion may be set at liberty."

" You have ? Mother of God ! let me hear it !"

" Come farther this way, then—indeed I think it were best seek a place of greater privacy before my lips utter the words which, heard by other ears than yours, might do evil rather than good. Follow me, an' you would hear more !"

Gliding out into the open air, the monk, as he appeared to be, moved swiftly along the street, closely followed by Lorcan, till reaching the gaping arch of a once stately castellated building, then in ruins, he entered what had been the hall and Lorcan after him.

" Uncle of Connor Maguire," said the muffled figure, " would you, for his sake, venture into the great English capital ?"

" Why, truly, stranger, it doth seem like thrusting one's head into the lion's mouth, but, natheless, could I thereby do aught towards Connor's liberation—marry, my old blood runs merrily at the thought. Monk !—boy !—or whatsoever thou art"—and the impulsive old man seized his companion's hand and bent eagerly forward—" tell me only how I can serve poor Connor, and see if I shrink from any peril !"

" The peril will not be yours alone," said the stranger quietly ; " peril there will be, I deny it not, but another will bear the brunt of it. It is but for your company and the protection of your reverend age I ask you !"

"How! what am I to think?" said the old man drawing back.

"The spirits will tell you what to think before the time of starting," said the monk in a half-serious, half-jesting tone; "I have heard that Lord Maguire hath creatures of air to watch over him, so trusting in their good offices, and those of the wise seer of Enniskillen, I will dare all things, yea, even the bolts and bars of the terrible Tower of London! Fare you well, more than friend, Heaven have you in its keeping till we meet again."

He was gone before Lorcan could question him farther, and the old man returned like one in a dream to the Bishop's house pondering deeply on what had past.

Meanwhile the foundation of much evil had been laid unwittingly by those most devoted to the national cause. Many of the Confederates had dropped off singly or in groups, some for the dispatch of business, some in search of amusement. Lord Muskerry and Lord Mountgarret, having only then heard of Castlehaven's arrival, had just made their appearance, and it was clear from the manner in which the peer received their enthusiastic welcome, that, being of his own order, he placed the greater value on their friendship. When the room was thinned, as we have said, it so happened that most of those who remained were either prelates or distinguished laymen, and when the shades of evening began to gather around Bishop Rothe invited all present to partake of his evening meal:

"Frugal ye will find it," he said, "my lords and noble gentlemen, but with such good company it will pass pleasantly."

He rose as he spoke, leaning heavily on a gold-headed stick which had been resting by the side of his chair. The two gentlemen nearest to him at the moment immediately stepped forward to offer their support, and as ill fortune would have it, who should they be but Owen Roe O'Neill and Thomas Preston. Although the latter was the first to offer his arm, the aged bishop turned to O'Neill, and with a paternal smile placed his arm within his, and looked up in his face with beaming eyes. The apologetic bow with which he acknowledged Preston's civility was far from satisfying that officer, although he turned away with an air of assumed indifference. There was wounded pride and more than that in the look which he cast on O'Neill, and Owen said within himself: "I much fear there is mischief in that glance. Surely he cannot owe me a grudge because the bishop took my arm instead of his. That were mean indeed and all unworthy so gallant a soldier."

Yet so it was. From that hour, the irrascible scion of the house of Gormanstown never failed to cherish a secret dislike towards O'Neill, a dislike which all through the pending struggle showed itself in various ways to the serious injury of the cause for which both fought so well.

"What could have induced his lordship to give so marked a preference to the northern leader?" inquired Castlehaven of the venerable Bishop of Ferns as they left the room together.

"Truly I know not, my lord earl," replied the prelate; "an' it were as thou sayest, the which I saw not, I could give no other reason than this, that my right reverend brother had the happiness of administering the Bread of Life to General O'Neill this morning, whilst Colonel Preston and many of the other lords and gentlemen were a-strolling through Ormond's grounds."

"Humph!" said the soldierly peer with a smile of dubious meaning, "then O'Neill is somewhat of a devotee—and it would seem that character is in favor here—perchance more so than high estate or military experience."

"So should it be, my lord," responded the calm and ever-prudent Nicholas French; "in an assembly of Catholics, met for such a purpose as ours, and trusting not in our own might but in the justice of our cause, it is surely expedient for all, as well lay as spiritual persons, to invoke the God of battles by constant prayer, and the frequent reception of the Sacraments!"

Castlehaven said no more, for they just then entered the bishop's homely eating-room, where the frugal repast was already spread, awaiting their coming.

CHAPTER XVII.

" We have cherish'd fair hopes, we have plotted brave schemes,
   We have lived till we find them illusive as dreams;
   *   *   *   *   *   *   *
   And the steps we have climb'd have departed like sand.'
                                        EPES SARGENT.

" This leader was of knowledge great
   Either for charge or for retreat ;
   He knew when to fall on, pell mell,
   To fall back and retreat as well."
                              BUTLER'S *Hudibras.*

THE twenty-fourth day of October, 1642, is one of the few in
the latter ages of Ireland's history on which the eye loves to
dwell. It was on that day that the grand assembly of the
Confederate Catholics of Ireland first sat as a legislative body,
and we may be pardoned surely if we look back with melancholy pride on that vision of departed glory, suggestive as it is
of what Ireland might be and may yet be. The Confederation
may be renewed and fixed on a more permanent basis in some
fortunate contingency of the national affairs, and a future generation may see that sight, perhaps within the walls of the metropolis itself, but never again may be seen in Ireland another
assembly like that whose remembrance invests Kilkenny with
such varied and profound interest. The distinctive features of
that scene belonged to that age, and with it have passed away
for ever. The time and the circumstances were such as to give
that national assembly a character of peculiar interest as well
as importance. The Normans of the Pale and the ancient Irish
were still two distinct races, distinct alike in appearance, costume, manners and language. The chieftains of the old blood
still retained their ancient and most picturesque costume, while

the lords and gentlemen of the Pale were clad in the sober and rather stiff, yet not ungraceful habiliments usually worn by the same class in England. Those again who came from abroad were as yet clad in the costume they had been wont to wear in the countries of their adoption, many of them glittering in the brilliant uniform of the Spanish, Austrian, or French armies, for the principal officers all took their seats at the council-board. The bishops were there in their episcopal garments, and the mitred abbots each in the distinctive habit of his order. These, with the lay-lords, formed the upper house, while the second order of the clergy, both secular and regular, sat with the gentlemen who were delegates from the several towns and cities, and with them constituted the lower house answering to the House of Commons. The lawyers again wore the grave and dignified costume of their office, so that each of the classes composing the assembly was easily distinguished from the others, and all together conspired to form one of the most imposing arrays ever witness d on Irish ground. Looking back now through the vista of two hundred odd years, how the heart swells with mingled pride and sorrow as we contemplate that picture: eleven bishops and archbishops, fourteen lords, and two hundred and twenty-six commoners,* many of the latter chiefs of high standing, all assembled in the sacred name of civil and religious freedom, to take the government of the country into their own hands and frame laws for the wants and requirements of their people in the true spirit of paternal legislation. Oh! it was a grand, a glorious scene, one that Ireland may well be proud of, for on that day, at least, all was peace and harmony, and brotherly love, all distinctions of race, all hereditary and personal feuds seemed buried, it was fondly hoped for ever. Few, few such bright spots adorn our annals!

A happy man was David Rothe, Bishop of Ossory, that day,†

---

* Meehan's *Conf. Kilk.*

† Moore tells us on the authority of Dr O'Connor that it was this learned and most estimable prelate who first suggested the idea of a general Confederacy, and also that he gave up his Cathedral for the first Session of the Assembly.

when, prior to the opening of the session, the Confederates once
more filled his Cathedral, and he stood at the high altar which
he had recently erected and in the sight of that vast assemblage
offered up the great Sacrifice of the New Law. And when Mass
was over, and those present who had not as yet taken the oath
came forward to repeat the solemn words before St. Canice's
altar, how fervently did the old bishop raise his hands and eyes
to heaven and invoke a blessing on themselves and their undertaking.

Amongst those who there took the oath of association was
Owen Roe O'Neill, with the officers he had brought from Spain,
and Preston with his Franco-Irish companions in arms. As
these two distinguished officers stood side by side with right
hand uplifted, repeating the solemn words, the Irish chief in his
Celtic garb and the Norman gentleman in his French uniform,
they were a fine picture to look upon, and many hearts amongst
the highest and noblest and wisest there beat high with hope in
the accession of two such leaders. Could any one present have
foreseen the petty jealousy, the heart-burnings and the ruinous
strife that grew up between those two, he could have wept tears
of blood for the curse that was to blight so fair a prospect. But
no one there happened to have the gift of prophecy, and so the
brightness of hope was unclouded.

Before the last words of Owen Roe's oath had died away in
echoes amongst the arches of the roof, another of noble mien
and scarcely less martial bearing stepped forth and declared
himself willing to take the same pledge. It was Lord Castlehaven, and a murmur of applause and satisfaction ran through
the assembly, for that Earl was highly esteemed of all, and a
man of undoubted bravery; connected, moreover, with many of
the first families of the kingdom, and hitherto so remarkable for
his staunch adherence to the government party. .

"I desire to take the oath," said the Earl, and he drew himself up with a look that seemed to say: "I trust you are all
sensible of the favor I confer on you by joining your ranks."

"Bless you, my son, bless you," said the old bishop when the
Earl had taken the oath; "you have done well, and I hope God
will crown our joint efforts with success. General O'Neill and

Colonel Preston, you will rejoice as I do to see my lord of Castlehaven by your side at this hour—be ye henceforth as brothers working together as one man for the common good !"

Those who looked at Nicholas French of Ferns, or Malachy O'Kelly of Tuam, at that moment might have detected a certain quiet smile expressive of some doubt on the subject of the union, and down amongst the commoners certain significant looks were exchanged—but no one spoke with the exception of Lorcan Maguire, who said very gravely to Art McMahon near him :

" I fear, Art, the chain is not made that will bind the Palesmen and the sons of the Gael together !—there are rivers of blood between us, hard, hard to bridge across !"

" My lord of Ossory," said the aged nobleman, Mountgarret, in his place at the chancel railing, " your words do remind us of a work that must needs be done this morning before other duties are taken in hand : I mean the appointment of general officers for the several divisions of our army."

" It is well thought of, my Lord Viscount," said the prelate with a benignant smile, " but that you will do in our Parliament House, an' I may so call it—be it your first act within those walls."

" I object to the term *parliament* as applied to this assembly," said Lord Castlehaven quickly ; " our proceedings must have no such character, unless, indeed, you desire to become what the enemy would have you, rebels against the king's majesty."

" Loyalty again !" said Sir Phelim O'Neill to Miles O'Reilly his next neighbor; " very loyal gentlemen have a way of throwing cold water on everything. An' we wait till their fire do boil our pottage, we may wait longer than will suit our stomachs. Rebels, forsooth! how the word sticks in his loyal throat! faugh!"—and honest Phelim drew up his large nose as though something of an ill odor *had* touched his olfactory nerve. O'Reilly laughed and shook his head but made no reply. He was thinking of the day when after burying Bishop Beddell with all the honors, he had apostrophized his memory as " the last of the English," and he said within himself: " they are and will be an English colony—churchman and soldier, peer and yeoman, they are all alike—English hearts have they and none

other—natheless, their own interest may bind them to us now.
An' it be so, it is well."

From St. Canice's the Confederates adjourned to the hall prepared for their deliberations, where the lords (spiritual and temporal) and the commoners having taken their respective places
in the upper and lower sections of the hall, they proceeded to
the election of their speaker, and with little opposition, Master
Nicholas Plunket, a distinguished lawyer, a "grave and reverend seignor," was duly installed in that office, and took possession of the black oak chair prepared for his speakership behind
a table of the same beautiful wood.* Corresponding to Master Plunket's office in the Lower House, although of a different
nature, was that whereto another eminent lawyer, Patrick
D'Arcy by name, was appointed in the Upper House. Seated
on a high bench of antique form—historians will have it "a
stool"—this learned gentleman in wig and gown represented the
Lord Chancellor, as it were to decide on the legal points mooted
during the session.

These preliminaries settled, with Master Nicholas Plunket on
his chair behind his high table, and Master Patrick D'Arcy on
his "stool" of office, the assembly proceeded to business, and
first of all to define its exact nature and the objects it had in
view.† Like all the other acts of this legislative body, that de-

* The chair and table used by Master Plunket during that memorable session were to be seen until a few years ago, when their pro-
prietor, to avoid the trouble of showing them to visitors, had them
broken up and burned. So, at least, says Mrs. Hall, and I suppose
we must accept the statement, although it is hard to believe that so
much vandalism is to be found in Kilkenny. Could not the man
have sent such precious relics of the past to the Royal Irish Acad-
emy if he found their ownership too great a burden ?

† The assembly had all the appearance of a parliament, although
the first act of the lay-lords, prelates and commons, was to declare
that they did not intend it as such, fearing to infringe on the prerogative of the Crown, to which belonged the privilege of calling,
proroguing and dissolving the Senate. It was, however, a provisional
government, "to consult of an order for their own affairs till his
Majesty's wisdom had settled the present troubles."—*Meehan's Confederation*, p. 43.

claration was moderate, calm and earnest, firm and dignified withal, and calculated to win universal respect.

The next step was the appointment of the generals for the respective provinces, and when Lord Mountgarret stood up for that purpose, as President of the Supreme Council, a general stir was visible amongst the members of both houses.

"This question," said the veteran peer, "hath already been considered in the Council, but we would fain submit our choice to the General Assembly. First of all we have named Colonel Owen Mac Art O'Neill general of the Ulster forces. Is it your will that he be so appointed?"

An affirmative response came from all parts of the hall, in fact from every member of both houses, save only Sir Phelim O'Neill, who bit his lip and remained silent, to the great satisfaction of the chiefs near him, who had feared an explosion that would startle the house.

"For Leinster," resumed Mountgarret, "we have thought of another officer of rank, and, like General O'Neill, of high repute abroad. You all, doubtless, know who I mean."

"My Lord President," said Sir James Dillon, from his place in the Lower House, rising and bowing to the chair, "as this is a matter foreign to our legislative functions, I conceive myself at liberty to address you directly. I object to that appointment before the name be publicly mentioned—there be one here present who hath, I conceive, a prior claim to the command of that army."

Hearing this, a murmur of surprise ran through the assembly, and each looked inquiringly at his neighbor, then every eye was turned on Preston, who sat motionless in his seat with a countenance of assumed composure, while his rapidly changing color and the angry frown on his broad brow showed him ill at ease and much disturbed in mind.

"You surprise me, Sir James Dillon," said the President, "and I needs must say that I regret to hear what I have heard from you. Union is, of all things, the most important to us, and I had hoped that these appointments would have been made without one dissentient voice. Do you still persist in your design of proposing another general for Leinster?"

" I do, my lord, and I think the majority of the assembly will approve of the nomination I am about to make."

" In God's name let us have it, then," said the old lord with the slightest possible show of displeasure; " who would *you* have to command the army of Leinster ?"

" He is here, my lord! to speak for himself," and turning he bowed to a cavalier in a costume half-Spanish, half-Irish, who had been sitting for some time near him partially concealed by the tall form of Owen O'Neill. In the general bustle attending on the opening of the assembly this personage passed unnoticed, but when he rose and stepped to the front and bowed around with a smiling countenance as to a gathering of old familiar friends, a cry of joyful recognition arose from lords and commons :

" It is Roger O'Moore!' exclaimed the Norman knights; " it is Rory O'More," echoed the Celtic chiefs, and all seemed alike rejoiced to see the accomplished chieftain of Leix once more in their midst.

" Why, then, a hundred thousand welcomes, Rory !" cried Sir Phelim O'Neill, as he crossed the hall to have a shake hands ; " where have you hid yourself since——"

" Since Kilrush," said O'Moore in an under tone, as he warmly shook the proffered hand, at the same time making a sign for the impulsive northman to resume his seat. " This is no place or time for explanations !"

Meanwhile a conference was going on in the upper part of the hall between Lords Mountgarret, Muskerry, Castlehaven, and one or two of the bishops. A difference of opinion seemed to prevail amongst them, judging by their jestures and the earnest manner in which they spoke. Lord Gormanstown, from his near relationship to Preston, thought it indecorous to give an opinion, but, while he affected to converse on some other subject with Lord Fingal, who sat next him, there was a restless, anxious look on his face, and he glanced furtively from time to time at the group of peers before-mentioned.

O'Moore and his friends manifested no such anxiety ; they were evidently confident of success.

At length the other peers took their seats again, and Lord

Mountgarret addressed the assembly with the air of a man who had an unpleasant task before him.

" No one here," said he, " doth entertain a higher opinion of Mr. O'Moore than I do myself—as a man, a gentleman, a Christian, and a patriot, we are all prepared to admit his rare merit—but, lords and gentlemen, what experience hath he had of military affairs ?—war is a trade which, like all others, must needs .be duly learned ; ay ! and well-practised to give promise of success. What apprenticeship hath our honored friend made to that trade to entitle him to set up in business ? And, bethink you, it is the business of the whole nation ?"

" But this have I to say, my Lord Mountgarret," said O'Moore with that lordly air which he well knew how to assume, " to wit, that your lordship's memory must needs be somewhat shortened of late, else would you remember that the whole of this business, now so flourishing, was first started by me. Surely the man that set the wheel a-moving has the best right to keep it in motion, and, moreover, though I say it myself, the people are all well affected towards me, and will follow my standard sooner than that of a stranger—craving Colonel Preston's pardon !"

Lord Mountgarret shook his head. " I am myself somewhat of a soldier," said he, " as you all know, and, with the best intentions, I confess I have found myself often at fault for want of skill in strategy. I know full well, Mr. O'Moore, what we all owe to your untiring zeal and patriotism—I know, too—we all know that you might raise an army in less time than any one here present, but, being raised, what would you do with it ?"

"What other men do—I promise no more," said O'Moore carelessly.

"What Mountgarret did at Kilrush and Barry at Liscarroll," said Castlehaven with a malicious smile to Lord Dunboyne near him ; " methinks we have had enough of such generalship."

Mountgarret heard not the words, but the same thought was his own.

" My lords and gentlemen," said he addressing the assembly, " I will refer this matter to your decision, reminding you only that much time hath already been spent without any profit

worth speaking of. Castles and towns have been taken and retaken, skirmishes beyond number have been fought with various
success, and, I grieve to say it, the more important actions have
all gone against us, to the great discouragement of our followers, and the great waste of our supplies, begged all over Europe
—why is this, brethren of the Confederation?—I hardly know
myself, you may not choose to answer in such wise as your
judgment would suggest, but this we must all acknowledge, that .
it behoveth us to seize the greater and more certain advantage
offered us for the furtherance of our cause. For the command
of the Leinster army you have now to choose between Colonel
Thomas Preston, a gentleman of tried valor, and of long and
honorable experience in the art of war, and our much esteemed
friend, Master Roger O'Moore, who, with high blood in his veins
and all manner of accomplishments, not to speak of the part he
took in setting this work a-going, is yet wanting, as all must
know, in that experience which is the first thing to be looked
for in a general——"

From a half-open door, behind Master D'Arcy's elevated seat,
came the voice of one singing, loud, clear and bold :

> " The taunt and the sneer let the coward endure,
>   Our trust is in God and in Rory O'Moore."

" Close that door !" cried the President angrily, as he marked
the smile on the faces of the Irish chieftains. " It is for you
now to decide, my lords and noble gentlemen, who shall be commander-in-chief of the Leinster forces."

" There be out-door machinery at work, I perceive," observed
Preston in a tone of affected indifference ; " Master Rory O'Moore
must needs have his heart set on the office when he employs
the ballad-mongers of the city to sing him into it. Truly he
may have it, for all I——!"

" Have a care what you say, Colonel Preston," said Sir John
Netterville who sat next him ; " we may deem it inexpedient to
place O'Moore at the head of an army, but, natheless, the
man steps not in shoe leather who may speak lightly of him in
this company. His day will come, for nought is wanting to him

but military service—he hath a good head and a strong arm and courage to dare all things——"

"I thank you for your good opinion, Sir John," said O'Moore who had overheard what passed between them; "but my day, as you call it, will never come, an' it come not now!"

Much talking and debating followed, most of the old Irish present being inclined to appoint O Moore, but even they were, after some consultation, convinced that the step would be unwise, not only on account of the inexperience of that chieftain as a military leader, but also because of the offence it would give to Preston, after the unanimous appointment of Owen O'Neill. O'Moore, it was thought, could and would waive his claim in view of the common good. Dillon, Netterville and Sir Phelim O'Neill, all stood up to protest against the appointment of any other than O'Moore, but with a majestic wave of his hand Mountgarret silenced them all, and then proceeded to declare Colonel Thomas Preston duly commissioned to the supreme command of the army of Leinster.

"It is well," said O'Moore, standing up once more with that graceful self-possession which he never lost, "it is well, and the assembly hath doubtless shown its wisdom in its choice. It was the dream of many a weary month to me that I should have the command of the army to be raised in that province—where of old the O'Moores fought much and well—with that expectation I did apply myself to study the art of war hoping that the time for action was not far distant. The dream was presumptuous, it may be, and I am free to admit that you have done well in securing the military talents of Colonel Preston. With such a commander all must needs go well, and I need not say that no heart will rejoice more in his success than he who now addresses you—for the last time."

"For the last time, Rory! say not so, I beseech you!" said Owen Roe advancing towards him with more emotion than he usually manifested, while many others followed his example, all eager to testify their respect and esteem. "What were the Confederation without Rory O'Moore?"

"What it hath been for months past, when my name was unnamed and my absence unnoticed by any. For your sake, Owen,

I am sorry, for it *was* my hope, I may confess it, that as brothers-in-arms we should uphold together the glorious banner which Sir Phelim here and O'Reilly and McMahon uplifted on your Ulster hills just one twelvemonth since." And in turn he grasped the hand of each chieftain as he named his name. Owen's hand he held the longest and looked into his eyes with the fond affection of a brother. "Fare you well, friend of my heart," he said with a fervent pressure of his hand which O'Neill returned with deep emotion; "neither of us foresaw this hour when by the Manzanares' banks in sunny Spain we talked of home and freedom, and what things we must needs accomplish for the oppressed children of the Gael. Your aid is gladly accepted, Owen, but mine hath been rejected—they have cast me out, and I go forth to seek a new sphere of action!"

"Mr. O'Moore," said Lord Mountgarret, "I grieve that you should deem us so ungrateful. There will be many offices of high trust in our gift, the which you can fill with profit to the nation."

"I thank your lordship," said the chieftain coldly; "you had but one office which I desired to have, and that you have given to another."

"But surely," said Archbishop O'Kelly from his place in the upper hall, "surely you will not abandon the cause for that you cannot have things your own way. Nay, you will not, dare not ?"

"God forbid that I should do as your grace saith," returned O'Moore with a reverential salutation; "I can serve you abroad if not at home, and so, with the divine blessing, I mean to do. For myself, you shall see me no more, but my heart shall ever be with you, and what I can do to raise subsidies abroad shall be be freely done. It hath been said that I am more of a diplomatist than a soldier, and it may be true. Since you will not have my service in one capacity, I must e'en render it in the other. I humbly salute your grace and all this illustrious assembly— may heaven direct your councils to a good end!"

"Will you not shake hands with me, Master O'Moore ?" said a strong, sonorous voice near him, and Preston elbowed his way through the crowd of chiefs.

" With all my heart, *general!* and may success attend you!"

" Hear you that?" said Sir James Dillon to those around him ; "poor Roger is the first to give him that title."

" Could we not prevail upon you to remain with us?" said the new general.

" It cannot be, Master Preston! my path of duty began beyond seas, and there I see it is to end. It matters not, good friends!"—and he turned to each with a moistened eye and a flushed cheek—" we shall all work to the same end, and if we meet no more on earth we shall meet, I trust, where our reward awaits us. Friends! kind friends—true friends—remember me as I shall ever remember you!"

And grasping again each offered hand, he cast a parting glance around the room, bowed with all his wonted grace to the lords and prelates, many of whom stood up to receive his farewell, and then walked with a princely mien to the door, where, turning, he bowed to the entire assembly, and withdrew in silence.

Although many an eye was wet amongst the Irish chiefs, and even amongst the Norman Palesmen, few ventured to give expression to their thoughts, whatever they might be. Sir Phelim O'Neill, indeed, was almost the only one.

" Well! I thought Rory would have overlooked it," said he, as though speaking to himself; "an' it had been me, now, no one would have wondered, but Rory O'Moore to leave us in anger that way—I wouldn't have wished it for half of Tyr-Owen, even on his own account!"

CHAPTER XVIII.

"And though he posted e'er so fast,
His fear was greater than his haste ;
For fear, though fleeter than the wind,
Believes 'tis always left behind "
BUTLER'S *Hudibras.*

" I will believe
Thou wilt not utter what thou dost not know ;
And so far will I trust thee."
SHAKESPEARE.

THE Leinster affair once settled, the other appointments occupied but little time. Barry, as might be expected, was unanimously chosen to command the army of Munster, or rather
continue l in that office. As for Connaught, the name was no
sooner mentioned than Lord Castlehaven and Bishop McMahon
and half a dozen others were on their feet in an instant to name
the Earl of Clanrickarde.

" I object to that appointment," said the Archbishop of Tuam.

" On what grounds, my lord ?" inquired Castlehaven.

" On the grounds that that lord is not only no friend of our
cause but a bitter and determined enemy."

" But suppose he should one day see through his error, and
take his place amongst us ?"

" It will be time enough, then, to nominate him for any office."

" But could we not name him now as commander-in-chief ?"
persisted the Earl; " he may decline, and probably will, but,
natheless, the compliment might please him."

" I tell you no !" repeated the prelate sternly ; " he would not
thank us for the compliment, and, moreover, the man deserveth
no respect at our hands. I will never consent to send our offices
of trust and honor a-begging after renegades—pass him over, I
say !—we will none of him !"

"But, I pray your grace to consider—" chimed in Lord Howth, who seldom volunteered an opinion.

"I *have* considered—we have, or ought to have—*all* considered that we might as well appoint Lord Ormond as Lord Clanrickarde! It were the act of fools, and I say again I will have no more of it. My Lord Mountgarret, I pray you close this matter! Sir John Burke hath been spoken of for this command, an' I mistake not!"

"Ay, hath he," said the Bishop of Clonfert, himself one of the De Burgos, "a Burke worth a dozen of Ulick, at least for us, and a chief man in that province, too; one, moreover, who hath seen good service and stands well approved!"

"So let it be, then," said Lord Mountgarret, and immediately he declared Sir John Burke general of the Connaught army, no dissentient voice being raised against him. These four generals, then, duly appointed, were empowered to levy forces at need in their respective provinces, and otherwise to take such measures as might be found expedient for the interests of the service. Lord Castlehaven, having so lately joined the Confederates, received no special appointment, but agreed, nevertheless, to serve in any of the provinces in a sort of general way, as he tells us in his Memoirs.

That done, Mr. Patrick D'Arcy arose and begged to remind the Supreme Council and the honorable Assembly of a certain matter of much legal importance. All eyes were instantly turned on the grave lawyer, who, after sundry " ahems," of a professional nature, went on :

"The Council will, I presume, find it necessary to issue writs and documents of divers kinds from time to time?"

"Assuredly, Master D'Arcy," said Lord Mountgarret; "that is understood."

"And you will seal them, doubtless?"

"Of a surety, Master D'Arcy! Wherefore not?"

"I said not against it, my lord, but would simply ask where is your seal of office?"

"I protest I never thought of that," said the aged nobleman looking around, while a glow of pleasure suffused every face at the thought of having a " great seal," for their Supreme Council.

" What say ye, lords and gentlemen, who will furnish a device
for our sign manual ?"

Many devices were furnished and many opinions offered on
the subject.   Some were for having the Celtic and the Norman
emblems associated, others for only one national device, and
others again for a union of religious and national emblems.   The
latter thought, which was that of the bishops, prevailed, and a
beautiful design was speedily adopted: " In the centre was a
large cross, the base of which rested on a flaming heart, while
its apex was overlapped by the wings of a dove, on the left of
the cross was the harp, and on the right the crown."*

A goodly device it was, and the motto was no less happily
conceived : PRO DEO, REGE, ET PATRIA, HIBERNI UNANIMES.
Thus the legend ran, and coupled with so fair a device, it happily expressed the objects which the united Catholics of Ireland
had in view.   Their hopes, their plans, their aspirations, were all
condensed into that one admirable sentence, and when the seal
was struck and first presented to the assembly it gave satisfaction to all.   When first used in the name of the Confederation on
an order to raise men and money in the wealthy province of
Leinster, the document was handed round for inspection, and we
may imagine the feelings of Owen Roe, and many others scarcely
less devoted to the national cause, as they gazed on the precious
memento.

" The great seal of Ireland," murmured Owen partly to himself, partly to O'Reilly of Breffny, at his side ; "now that
sight was worth living for.   *Pro Deo, Rege, et Patria,*—for God,
our king, and our country—surely yes—*Hiberni Unanimes.*
Heaven grant, friend Philip, we be always *Unanimes*—on that
point doth our success turn."

" Come, come, general ! no doubts, no fears with that seal before us, the grand assembly sitting in council, our colors flying
over tower and town, and our vessels scouring the seas."†

* Meehan, quoting Harold's *Life of Wadding.*

† Independent of the ships sent from the Continent, letters of
marque were given to many others by the Supreme Council to serve
as privateers.   These were, even at the time we write of, numerous
on all the coasts.

" Ay, marry, and Father Luke Wadding scouring the lands,"
put in Sir Phelim whose bulky form just then intercepted the
light from a window behind Owen. "That man is worth a dozen
privateers—no disrespect to *them*, either."

" Poor Rory!" sighed Owen still following the train of his own
thoughts, with his eyes fixed on the seal, " you were the first to
set this union on foot, and now when it waxeth strong and taketh
shape and form you have cast it from you as a worthless thing.
Oh, Rory! friend and faithful councillor! is this your example
for our *Hiberni Unanimes?* Shall we see you no more, oh!
gifted son of the ancient race? Excuse me, friends! but my
heart is heavy when I think of Rory O'Moore, going forth as he
does, with the barb of ingratitude rankling in his heart!"

" Pooh! pooh! man," said Sir Phelim carelessly ; " an' he be
so easily separated from us he is scarce worth the having.
Others have lost what they had as good a right to as Rory had
to the Leinster army. But who cares for a home-spun native
like Philip O'Reilly or Phelim O'Neill—what say you, Philip?"
and he slapped O'Reilly lustily on the shoulder.

" I cry you mercy, Sir Phelim," said the Breffny chief somewhat chafed ; " I would rather have your word than your blow
any time. Of your affairs or mine there is no question now, but
as for O'Moore, I cannot think, general"—addressing Owen Roe—
" that he means what he says: he will not leave us at such a
juncture !"

" I fear he has left, and for ever," said Owen sadly ; " I have
sought him in vain since his appearance before the assembly,
and I am told he hath actually sailed for Spain." And so he had,

" And the land of his heart's hope he saw never more."

A great stir was made at first about his disappearance, and
little else was talked of for many days, but the surmises and
conjectures, the regrets and complaints all came at last to an end,
and were swallowed up in the whirl of passing events, and the
name of Rory O'Moore gradually died away on both sides the
Brogah, and was forgotten, save by Owen O'Neill, and Dillon, and
Netterville, and a few others who had been his early associates
in the great work.

Whilst all Kilkenny was ringing with the unaccountable retirement of O'Moore from the Confederation, the young Tanist
of Fermanagh and the friends of his family were thrown into
strange confusion by the mysterious disappearance of Lorcan.
The old man had bade his nephew good night with unusual emotion one evening late, after the breaking up of the assembly, and
Roderick laughed as he shook his hand, saying : "Uncle, what
is amiss with you ? One would think you were going a long
journey !"

The old man shook his head and sighed. "The doom of our
race is dark and heavy, Roderick, my son, and it weighs down
the head of age at times."

"Ha! ha! the spirits are at work again, I see. Have they
followed us all the way to Kilkenny ?"

"Nay, Roderick, scoff not at 'the things which thou knowest
not," said the old man solemnly ; "all places are alike to the
creatures of air. They *have* been with me, son of my brother,
since I came to this city of memories, and they have told me
things which my lips may not utter or your ears hear."

"Said they aught of Connor ?' inquired Roderick with more
earnestness than he was aware of.

"Even that I may not answer, nephew ! *Their* words are not
to be repeated unto mortal ear. This only will I tell you : the
oak of Fermanagh shivers in the blast—the storm is in its
branches—the voice of the winds is loud, and wild, it may be
mournful—the hour of fate draws nigh—how it will pass—how
the storm will end—what the wind-spirit discourseth unto us, is
hidden from me, as yet. Farewell, son of Maguire! farewell,
Roderick of the spears! pleasant dreams be yours this night,
pleasanter than those of your old uncle!"

Do as he would, all that night bold Roderick could not get
rid of the strange impression left by his uncle's words and manner. Accustomed as he was to his eccentric ways, he could not
but feel that there was something more than usual in his
thoughts, and in vain, and, indeed, involuntary speculation on
what it might be, the Tanist spent his night. Next morning
brought the astounding news that Lorcan was not to be found—
he had been seen at early dawn passing out through one of the

gates in company with a young Franciscan friar. The sentry at
the gate who chanced to be acquainted with the personal appearance of the old northern warrior, gave a ludicrous account
of the singular figure he made in a surcoat, hose and jack-
boots, with a small steel morion on his head, and the long grey
locks, the growth of seventy summers, which had streamed on
the breeze in Milesian glory, all carefully shorn away. It was
a picture to excite the risible faculties of those who knew the
old man, and at first his nephew did laugh heartily, supposing some strange conceit, some passing whim, had induced Lorcan to don that garb, so odious in his eyes, and that
evening, or, at farthest, the ensuing day would bring him back
to his anxious friends. But when evening came, and morning
came, and the next day passed away without any tidings of
him, then Roderick began to couple his disappearance with his
mysterious inuendos of the previous night, and something smote
him with a sad presentiment of evil. Who could the friar be
who held secret communings with the simple old man, and finally carried him off on some errand known only to themselves,
for that Lorcan's disappearance was owing to this stranger's influence Roderick was quick enough to perceive.

"What the mischief," cried Hugh Byrne when his friend un-
bosomed himself of his fears and misgivings; "could it be the
same friar at whose beck Lorcan quitted me so hastily some
days since at the bishop's?"

"How is that, Hugh?—I heard not of it—I pray you tell me
how it was!"

O'Byrne then related the incident which, of course, went to
confirm Maguire's suspicions. That the friar was somewhat
other than he seemed there was every reason to suppose, but
as no clue was left to trace the mystery, Roderick was forced
to leave the matter as it was, hoping that time would ere long
throw light upon it.

On the night following Lorcan's disappearance, there stood by
the old market-cross of Kilkenny two men arrayed in the Celtic
garb as usually worn by the clansmen, with coarse woollen scarfs
of variegated colors wrapped in many folds around their chest
and shoulders instead of the short cloak or cape worn by the

20

chiefs over the tight-fitting jacket. One of these was tall, and lank, and slightly bent forward, while the other was short and thick, and well planted on his limbs. They were talking in the native language concerning what they had seen since they came to Kilkenny, and as the hour was late and the streets well nigh deserted, they conversed in a louder tone than they would otherwise have used in such a place. Moreover, they were neither of them accustomed to the restraints of city life, for their days had all past amid the woods and in the fields under the free canopy of heaven far away in "the north countrie." So they chatted away on that night in the market-place of Kilkenny as fearlessly and freely as though they stood on their native heath within Ulladh's borders.

It was no other than Malachy McMahon and Shamus Beg O'Hagan who had chosen so drear an hour and so strange a place for their confabulation. It appeared from what they had been saying that Malachy was in attendance on Bishop Heber who had come forth by appointment in that silent hour to meet Father Peter Walsh, with whom he was then engaged in earnest conversation under the deep arch of a building some way up the street.

"He told me," said Malachy, "to walk up and down the street till he'd be ready to come. Between you and me, Shamus! I don't think much of that same friar he has taken up with since we came here. God forgive me for passing an opinion on one of his cloth, but to tell you God's truth, Shamus dear, there's something in that man's eyes, and in the sound of his voice that makes me that I can't warm to him. But that's neither here nor there—they say he's a very pious man and a great scholar all out—at least the bishop says so, and what would bring him here now if he wasn't the right stamp."

"What sort of a stamp, do you think, was that other friar that kidnapped poor old Lorcan Maguire?"—Shamus asked this in a tone half serious, half jocular—"there's one thing I can say myself about him and that is that he has the fairest and the comeliest face I ever saw under a hood. I'm thinking there must have been some eyes red, ay, and hearts sore the day he was ordained."

"Do you tell me so, Shamus," replied Malachy drawing nearer and speaking in a more confidential tone; "I never got a sight of him myself, but as sure as I'm here it came into my head that it might be ne'er a monk at all but just a spirit or something that way that inveigled the old man away on account of the dealings he had with things of the kind all his life. Eh, Shamus? Lord save us, did you hear anything?"

"Why no, then, did you?"

"Well upon my veracity I did, Shamus! if I didn't hear like somebody laughing I'll never trust my ears again."

"Nonsense, Malachy, you're ever and always imagining things," said Shamus slapping him on the shoulder, "and even if somebody did laugh, what of it? I'm sure there's plenty of people hereabouts not in bed yet these stirring times."

"True, true, Shamus!—God bless you, but it's you has the brave heart—it was God sent you across me the night, sure enough. How did *you* happen out at all?"

"Oh! I was just taking a bit of a walk with some boys from our own place," said Shamus evasively, "and as we turned a corner over there beyond, I caught sight of you walking up and down like a sentry, so I knew you'd be all the better pleased to have company whatever you were about, and I just let the others walk on till I'd come and see what you were at."

"It was God sent you," said Malachy with simple earnestness, "for, to tell you the truth, I was beginning to feel mighty queer —there's a ghostly look about the old buildings round here that I don't like at all, at all."

"You would like the place less an' you knew it better, honest fellow," said a gaily-dressed cavalier advancing from under the shade of the neighboring doorway.

"The Lord save us, sir! what is it you mean?" cried Malachy with a sudden start, as much at the stranger's abrupt appearance as the intimation his words conveyed.

"Have a care, Malachy!" whispered Shamus, "it's Sir John Netterville, no less!"

"I mean," said the knight carelessly, "that the cross of Kilkenny hath not the best of names. He were a bold man here in the city who would keep it company at this lone hour."

"Ah then, why so, an' it please you, Sir John?" inquired Shamus, for Malachy was suddenly struck dumb with fear and bewilderment.

"You know me, then?" said the young knight turning quickly.

"Indeed then I do, honored sir, there be few amongst us to whom the heir of Netterville is unbeknown, and sure didn't I see you down at Charlemont not long ago? But if it wouldn't be making too free, would you condescend to tell us what's amiss with the place about here?"

"Maybe it's a gentle place it is?"* ventured to put in Malachy.

"Worse than that," and Netterville shook his head with a most doleful air. "Know you that there was a woman burned on this very spot for witchcraft some three hundred years ago?"

"Mother of God!" cried Malachy, "a woman burned—a witch—on this spot—come, come, *come*, Shamus!" raising his voice each time till it reached a scream, and clutching him at the same time by the shoulder. But Shamus had no mind to go without having his curiosity satisfied, and he would not stir an inch.

"Ah then, how was it at all, Sir John? or is it in earnest you'd be?"

"In sooth it is, Shamus—(you see I know *you*, too)—there was a witch burned here as sure as you and I have life in us—just on that spot where your friend is standing——"

"Oh, holy St. Malachy!" cried the man of Uriel, "I'm done for now!" and with a spring little to be expected from his sober gait and mature years he reached the steps of a door some yards distant. Even that did not seem a place of security, for looking back, and seeing the old spectral cross still so near, he darted off in the direction of the bishop, nor stopped till he gained his side, puffing and blowing like a whale.

The burst of merry laughter which echoed through the silent street behind him sounded on Malachy's startled ear like the

* Any place supposed to be frequented by the fairies or good people was set down in common parlance as *gentle*, just as those sprightly elves were collectively styled "the gentry '

unholy mirth of a company of witches—even Shamus's voice, familiar as it was, gave Malachy no security.

In reply to the bishop's anxious inquiry as to what had happened, poor Malachy, as soon as he could speak, related in a faltering voice the cause of his fright.

"My poor Malachy!" said the bishop with affected commiseration, "it was truly an unlucky chance which brought you thither."

"It was all along of your lordship," said the spoiled favorite testily; "had you and his reverence here been in your beds it isn't wandering about. like a ghost I'd have been—oh, wirra! wirra! what came over me at all ?—as sure as I'm a living man it was on the very spot I stood on she was burned, for I feel ever since a kind of a weakness on me and a meagrim in my head that I never had before in all my born days. I'll tell you what it is now, my lord, you must read an office for me the first thing you do to-morrow morning, or I'll never be worth a pin!"

"That is the least I can do, Malachy," said the bishop with a sly glance at Father Peter, who found it hard to keep from laughing, "since you say it is my fault, and, in sooth, I think Father Walsh might do something that way, too, seeing that he is to blame as well as I for keeping you out of your bed."

"One is enough," said Malachy with unusual gruffness; "I'll not trouble his reverence at *this* time. But might I make bold to ask will you stand here much longer? Dear knows," he added in a half audible voice, "if you were as wise as you're old, it isn't here you'd be or in such like company. But, ochone! isn't it like a child he is with all his learning!"

Malachy's abrupt appearance put a speedy end to the conversation, whatever might have been its nature, and the friar and the bishop moved quickly away in opposite directions, the latter followed as close as might be by his faithful attendant.

By the time Sir John Netterville had enjoyed the hearty laugh afforded him by Malachy's ludicrous terror, that important personage was fully out of hearing, and the knight instantly approached Shamus with an entire change of manner.

"Now that I have frightened away that grave simpleton," said he, "I would know from you, Shamus, all that you know yourself concerning the friar who, as you said a while ago, kid-napped Lorcan Maguire."

"Lord, sir, I know no more about him than just what I told Malachy," Shamus replied, somewhat startled by the sudden vehemence of the other's manner; "I did but say that he was young and well-favored—and that is all I *could* say inasmuch as I never laid eyes on him till yester morn—you needn't look so hard at me, Sir John, for as true as if I was on my knees to the priest it's the truth I'm telling you."

"And you never saw that friar till yester morn?—bethink you, Shamus!"

"Never, Sir John, never, as I'm a living man!"

"Hath Sir Phelim any knowledge of him, think you?"

"I would you might ask himself that question," the clansman replied somewhat sharply, for he liked not such questioning; "it would ill-become me to speak for my noble master."

"You are right, honest fellow," said Netterville musingly; "it were well an' all servitors acted in like manner. Fare you well, and commend me to your master."

"Before you go, Sir John," said Shamus timidly, "maybe you'd be kind and condescending enough to tell me was it in earnest you were about the witch?"

"Surely yes, Shamus," the knight laughingly replied; "there be few in Kilkenny town who cannot tell you the story of the Lady Alice Kelter, her two waiting-maids and accomplices, Basilia and Petronilla, and her wizard son William Utlaw, with a certain imp whom they named Robert Artisson, and who did the bidding of the powerful witch Lady Alice."*

"Christ in heaven save us!" ejaculated Shamus, and raising his right hand he made with the thumb thereof the sacred sign on his forehead; "and was it *her* they burnt?"

"Not so, Shamus, it was the woman Basilia. The lady's rank saved her, I know not how, and the other waiting-maid managed to escape from the country. It is a strange tale, Shamus, and

---

* For a curious account of this strange episode in the local history of Kilkenny, see *Dublin Penny Journal*, Vol. I., p. 74, and Hall's *Ireland*, Vol. II.

overlong for me to tell, but ask any of the people hereabouts
and you will hear it all. Hark! the cock proclaimeth midnight
—it is a dreary hour and a lonesome place—methinks you and
I were better housed than shivering here in the cold moon's ray."

So thought Shamus, too, and as he hurried away in search of
"the boys from his own place," he muttered: "There's no luck
with their underhand work, that's the truth. Now there's Bishop McMahon and that tricky friar above yonder, Sir John Netterville here, and Sir Phelim and General Preston down there
below with their heads together—what it all means I'm sure *I*
can't tell, but there's something in it—that's plain."

CHAPTER XIX.

" A prison is in all things like a grave,
  Where we no better privileges have
  Than dead men ; nor so good "

                                        BISHOP KING.

      " Oh ! give me liberty !
  For were even Paradise my prison,
  Still I should long to leap the crystal walls."

                                        DRYDEN.

WHILST the Confederates were wielding supreme power in
Kilkenny, appointing generals, framing laws, issuing letters of
marque, and even coining money on their own authority, and
astonishing all Europe by the boldness and promptness of their
measures, Maguire and McMahon lay immured in their English
prison far from home and friends, and a prey to the nameless
horrors of suspense in such a state as theirs. The roll of Irish
drums came not to them over the waters, or the echo of their
nation's voice from the halls of St. Canice's city. They knew
nothing, heard nothing of what was passing in their own land,
and had not even the poor happiness of bearing their misery
together. They were separated, and their life was a dreary
blank—an intolerable burden it would have been were it not for
the faith that was strong within them and kept them from yield-
ing to despair. But their hearts were growing cold and heavy,
for it seemed to them as though all the world had forgotten
them and left them to their hard fate. This saddening conviction came slowly on Maguire's mind ; the experience of his prison-
life had shown him that a spirit of love kept watch over him,
and the wonders he had seen accomplished by its agency buoyed
him up with delusive hope, against reason and probability.
Long he looked for the re-appearance under one shape or another of her who had promised never to forget him, and this

gleam of hope threw a faint sunshine athwart the gloom of his
mournful existence; but as time wore on, as day succeeded day,
and week followed week, and still no change, no ripple on the
sluggish stream, the solitary star faded in the dim obscure, and
a deeper dejection settled down on Connor's heart. It was not
the dark gulf yawning before him, all the more terrible for its
dim uncertainty, neither was it the utter privation of all comfort
that weighed the heaviest on that proud, sensitive heart, but the
thought of being utterly forgotten in his dungeon while so many
of his kindred breathed the free air of heaven, not to speak of
the friends whose dangerous counsels had, as he bitterly thought,
hurried him into the pitfall.

"An' we had but struck even one blow for our country and
our God, or been sharers in one glorious action, this so drear
blank were not within us," he said within himself full many a
time; "we would then have had at least one bright spot to look
back upon, one thought to cheer us, but caught like a brace of
bag-foxes, branded as traitors to the king without having drawn
a sword or struck a blow in our country's cause, and here left to
pine in a foreign land, while at home the work we helped to plan
is done by other hands, and the men of our race, mayhap, smiting the oppressor and rending their chains for ever,—oh! God!
what a fate is ours—poor lone scape-goats pining in the desert
of this accursed land!"

Nevertheless, forgotten as the prisoners supposed themselves
to be, there were those who never lost sight of them, and were
sorely troubled about their spiritual welfare. Of this number
was Mr. Conyers, the Lieutenant of the Tower, a worthy man in
his own way but somewhat thick-headed and a fanatic withal.

Great was the surprise and not small the indignation of Lord
Maguire when this godly gentleman one day paid him a visit for
the purpose of introducing a gifted divine, a recent acquaintance
of his, whom he declared endued with more than mortal powers
of persuasion, assuredly for the advancement of Christ's kingdom
on earth.

Is he a priest?" said Maguire coldly and without looking at
the preacher.

"Young man," said Conyers, "beware how you insult the

children of light by so much as naming in their presence the
doers of dark deeds?"

"An' he be not what I said, I'll none of him," said the Baron
resolutely.

"Son of Belial, thou *shalt* hear him," said the official personage with rising anger; "thou and thine accomplice in guilt, blinded
as ye both are, shall open your ears to the words of life from
the mouth of this evangelical man—if willingly the better for
yourselves, but hear him ye shall!"

"Yea, verily," said the minister, a thin and somewhat emaciated young man, with a most woe-begone expresssion of countenance; "yea, verily, Master Conyers, we will even sow our
seed, be the soil as it may, and leave the fructifying thereof to
Him who giveth the increase. My lord of Essex hath, as you
know, a strong and merciful desire to snatch these poor brands
from the burning."

"An' your lord of Essex would but take heed of his own
spiritual affairs," said Maguire sharply, "he might find enough
to do."

"Did I ever tell you, Master Conyers," said the melancholy
preacher, without appearing to notice the prisoner's remark,
"how a godly friend of mine in Dublin was moved by the spirit
to attempt the conversion of these hardened sinners?"

At this Maguire opened his eyes and tried to catch a glimpse
of the minister's face, but it was turned from him. Conyers
answered in the negative.

"I marvel at my forgetfulness, for verily the deeds of Osee
Judkins were in all men's mouths."

Hearing this name, so well remembered, a light suddenly
broke on Maguire, who with difficulty repressed the exclamation
that rose to his lips. The preacher half turned at the moment
and glanced furtively in his direction.

"Were his gifts equal to those of your learned companion?"
demanded Conyers.

"Say not *learned*," exclaimed the divine, as if somewhat
offended by the term; "that wonderful man is *not* learned according to the ways of men—of books he knoweth nothing—his
knowledge is from above, and his discourse with powers unseen

by mortal eye. Verily he is a powerful man, and for that reason I named him unto you as one fit to deal with the traitor McMahon, whom men speak of as more'obdurate than his fellow here present."

"Truly, master preacher," said Maguire laughingly, "I am much beholden to you for your good opinion. Methinks it were pity to baulk such a fair-spoken man in his godly purpose of expounding unto me. Since your gifted friend hath been given a hearing by McMahon, *I* will not refuse to hear *you*, apprising you beforehand, however, that my faith is not to be shaken by the breath of living man."

"We shall see," returned the minister calmly, "and Master Conyers will perchance favor me with his company while I unfold the high mysteries of Revelation before these eyes now darkened and unable to bear the Gospel light ?"

"I pray you excuse me, reverend sir," said Conyers hastily ; "I have a multiplicity of business on hands this morning, and must, therefore, decline. I will now look in to see how it fareth with Master Seagrave—that McMahon is a reckless desperado, and the man is old—though, to say the truth, he looketh as though he were well able to defend himself—ay! even by the carnal weapon! I will see to it, natheless, and return hither anon."

He had hardly closed the door after him, locking and double-locking as usual, when the preacher commenced his polemical attack after a strange fashion. From beneath the folds of his long black cloak he drew forth—not a Bible—but a file, pointing at the same time to the straw which served the Baron for a couch. The suggestion was instantly acted on, and the instrument once out of sight, the minister next pointed to the small grated window which, at a height of several feet, gave light to the room.

"*Here* is death—all but certain," whispered the stranger; "*beyond* is freedom—it may and *must* be—in the dead of night make your file acquainted with that grating, but be sure you leave one bar uncut, and thereto, on the third night from this, you will fasten the end of that rope," producing a small coil from under the clerical cloak.

"But who—who are you?" demanded Maguire in the same whispered accents. "Mother of Mercy! now I see your face,

I know full well—ah! I knew it—there is but one alive who would run such risk for Connor Maguire."

"In that you err," said the strange visitor; "your uncle Lorcan hath willingly shared the danger—for your dear sake."

"Ha! he is, then, the powerful wrestler with the Evil One—the man who by means of his unearthly gifts is to bring over Costelloe McMahon?"

"Even so, but hearken to what yet remains. Having fastened the rope to the uncut bar, you must e'en let yourself down, trusting your life to Providence ; and, oh Connor! be careful—remembering that another life is bound up with yours! One thing I forgot—on no account descend till you hear me say twice over, ' Babylon the mighty hath fallen !' Note you well what I say?"

"Ay, Emmeline, and I will do it, with God's good aid, were it but for thy sweet sake—life hath grown precious to me of late since thou, beloved, taught me its value."

The look of unutterable affection which accompanied these words sent a thrill of joy to Emmeline's heart, and she felt as though death itself were a light evil when balanced against Maguire's love. She extended her hand—a beautiful hand it was too—and the Baron seizing it pressed it to his lips and to his heart, then dropped it, and, sighing, turned away. The disguised fair one eyed him with a conscious, exulting smile, then drawing forth from her loose hanging sleeve a small Bible, she gave a peculiar set to the wig of long black hair which covered her head, and composed her fair, chiselled features into the look they had worn in Conyers' presence.

"I will e'en commence now," said she, "the godly task set before me, lest perchance we be taken by surprise." Raising her voice, then, with a warning motion of the finger, she spoke:

"Verily that power which you call the Church hath made compact with the Evil One to hand over to him the souls of men —an' you come not forth from her, Lord of Enniskillen! you shall perish with her !"

The laugh which he could not repress died away on Maguire's lips, for Mr. Conyers at the moment opened the door, and asked what progress had been made.

"But little, I fear," was the preacher's answer. "Heard you not the mocking laugh wherewith the reprobate greeted my poor attempt at exhortation ?"

"He shall laugh the other way ere long," said the lieutenant sternly, "but your friend hath better hopes of the other. An' you pay them another visit, when opportunity offers, you may find both better disposed."

"They will but lose their time," said Maguire in a surly tone as the pair withdrew, the preacher promising to return in a few days.

He did return but only to find Conyers and all his understrappers in an agony of fear and the Tower one scene of confusion. In answer to his urgent inquiries oft repeated, the divine was informed that the two Irish prisoners had made their escape on the previous night.

"Made their escape ?—how is that ?"

"We have no time for giving explanations," said Conyers who just then made his appearance. "Were it not for the recommendation of my lord of Essex, master what's your name, I would e'en suspect that you know more about this thing than any here."

"Truly I know not your meaning, Master Conyers," said the minister with perfect composure, "but I know you have spoiled by your unaccountable neglect the most promising case of conversion I have yet had. It would have made my fortune with Lord Essex and other godly noblemen now at the head of affairs, had I but won over that pestilent rebel and recusant. Hath his lordship — hath the honorable House knowledge of this event ?"

Conyers was so angry that he literally could not speak. seeing which the minister quietly made his exit, saying with a formal bow that he would go on the instant to the Earl of Essex to acquaint him with the gross insult which had been put upon him.

"Who brought the files ?—answer me that !" cried the perturbed lieutenant, following him to the door.

"Files !—what files ?"

"Why, the files that cut the prison-bars of these recusants !"

"Come with me before Lord Essex and I will answer you—

madman as you are!" returned the preacher in a contemptuous
tone, still moving on towards the street.

But that did not suit Conyers' purpose. He, in common with
many others, dreaded Essex more than he did the king, so go
he would not. All that day he had a new cause of terror expecting an angry visit from that powerful nobleman, but Essex
never came, and when Conyers went himself some days after to
see how the land lay, he was astounded to hear that the preacher
had never made his appearance there since the escape of the
prisoners.

"Surely that knave hath outwitted us both," said the grim
Parliamentarian general in a low voice, "and what is worse, I
see not how we can remedy the evil he hath wrought, so, I
think, Master Conyers, the best we can do is to keep our own
secret and say nothing of this wolf who came upon us in sheep's
clothing. For this time we can but set a watch on the various
outlets of the city, so that, if the varlets are not already gone,
they must needs fall into our hands—but an' we catch them,
Master Conyers——"

"Ay! my good lord! you will make sure of them!"

"Sure! ay, marry, *sure!* Verily, I tell you, Master Conyers,
their next prison shall be more secure than the White Tower."
And he smiled a grim smile.

Whilst all London was ringing with the escape of the Irish
traitors, and Conyers, protected by the powerful influence of
Essex, was enabled to ward off the storm of anger which would
otherwise have been his destruction, Maguire and McMahon
were safely lodged in the house of a faithful Englishman, a
Catholic, who had once been a servant of the former in Dublin.
This man had all along been in the secret of the projected
escape, had provided the files and ropes necessary to effect it,
and it was to his house, at his own request, that the two friends
were conveyed by their liberators.

It was a raw cold night in dark November and the flickering
flame of the oil-lamps did but little to dispel the gloom which
enveloped the great city. All around the town was dark and
silent as the tomb, save ever and anon when the voice of the
warders was heard proclaiming how the night went from the

several divisions of the old fortress. It was a bold venture for
Maguire and his friend to swing themselves down from the
height of the White Tower trusting to the frail support of a rope.
Yet they did so—even Maguire nerved with a strong and trusting spirit by the faith that was his support throughout, and also,
it might be, by the tenacious love of life, strongest and most
intense as the prospect of death draws near. They had both
worked steadily at filing the bars during the long dark nights,
and on the third morning all was in readiness agreeable to the
instructions they had received. How long that day seemed, and
how the night-hours when they came weighed like lead on the
hearts of the poor solitary "jail-birds," as they bitterly styled
themselves. How anxiously they noted the sounds of life gradually dying away in the vicinity of the Tower, and how many
fears and hopes chased each other through their minds concerning the welfare of the devoted friends who were running such
risk to effect their liberation. Fervently did they pray that,
whatever became of themselves, no harm might befal those loved
and loving ones on whom, next to God, their hopes rested.

The night was far advanced and in all probability the warders
were cozily taking a nap, sheltered in some wise from the piercing wintry air, when all at once rose a cry beyond the moat,
faint and subdued, yet distinctly audible to the two anxious
listeners :

" Rejoice, ye just, Babylon the mighty hath fallen !"

Immediately Maguire and McMahon removed the bars, already
cut asunder, fastened the rope securely to the one in each window left uncut, listening anxiously the while to ascertain whether
the signal cry had attracted attention. After waiting for some
time until they were perfectly satisfied that the slumbering
guards of the Tower had paid no attention to the sound, they
recommended themselves to God, the Blessed Virgin and the
Saints, and at the same moment both let themselves down, and
although their heads were dizzy with the swift descent from such
a tremendous height, with the agonizing fear which only faith
and prayer could enable them to bear and live when they found
themselves suspended in mid-air, yet on reaching the ground
they speedily and, as it were, miraculously recovered their breath

and the power of volition, and, by God's great mercy, succeeded in swimming across the moat. Once on the other side they breathed more freely and ejaculated a fervent thanksgiving as, for the first time, they exchanged a hasty shake-hands. The outer wall was still before them, but whilst they stood deliberating in whispers how they should surmount that last obstacle, a ladder of ropes was thrown across it, and after a brief but generous strife as to who should first ascend, McMahon, stouter and more active than his friend, seized the Baron and fairly lifted him to the first step of the ladder, whispering in his ear a characteristic joke on his slowness of motion.

In a few seconds, the two stood together safe and sound on the outside, where Lorcan and the faithful Smithson awaited them in the disguise of oystermen. The ladder was hastily removed, and stowed away under Smithson's great jacket, then, without pausing to ask or answer questions, the four marched off, two by two, in the direction of Drury Lane, where Smithson's domicile was situate.

"Maguire," said his friend as they trudged along, "how do you feel?"

"Like one in a dream," Connor replied; "I cannot get convinced, do as I will, that I am once more at large, and I have dreamed that so often that I know not but this, too, may turn out a delusion."

"Let me wake you up, then," said the mercurial Tanist, and drawing his fist he gave him a smart box on the side of the head; "is that a delusion, think you?"

Before Maguire could answer a watchman from behind grasped McMahon by the shoulder. "What meaneth this, my masters,—brawling on the street at an untimeous hour? Who be ye?"

Startled by this apparition and the abrupt inquiry which it behoved them not to answer, the friends exchanged looks of alarm, and began to meditate flight, but a low, cautious laugh from old Lorcan made them cast their eyes on the supposed guardian of the night, and the next moment Maguire had clasped a small white hand that came suddenly out from beneath the loose sleeve of the watchman's coat.

"Thank God!" murmured a soft voice from under the Charley's clumsy cap, "thank God! you are so far safe—but much caution is yet requisite. Hasten your steps."

"But whither have you been?" said Maguire anxiously as the two fell a pace or so behind; "my escape seemed but half certain when I looked for you in vain."

"Shall I tell the whole truth?" said the soft voice, and it slightly trembled; "I was on my knees under a projecting arch, within sight of the Tower but seeing it not, for I dared not raise mine eyes—oh Connor! what I felt during those moments!—and I prayed—ay! even to Mary the Virgin Mother—for the first time in my life—I begged of her who had herself known human agony, to look with pity on mine, and bring you safe through that awful moment—nay, do not laugh."

"Laugh, Emmeline! not for ten thousand worlds!" said the chief with thrilling earnestness; "your words are as balm to my sorrow-worn heart—ay! precious as the honey-dew of eastern story. But where are you lodged?"

"At the house of this good man," meaning Smithson; "your uncle and I have been well accommodated, but now methinks it were well for us to go elsewhere—I, at least—until such time as you are all enabled to embark for Ireland, the which may not be for some weeks to come."

"But whither—whither would you go?" Maguire anxiously inquired.

"Nay, fear not for me—there be relatives of my mother here in town to whom I will go in my own proper semblance. There, your uncle is looking back—fearing, perchance, that some supernatural agency—whereof I know not but he suspecteth me the possessor—may spirit you away beyond his ken! Being a watchman, I must fall far behind, moreover, lest some prying eye might detect our companionship! Fare you well!"

"Be that *your* spiritual counsellor?" said McMahon, finding his friend again alongside; "an' it be, I begin to incline to your uncle's notions concerning the guardian spirits of your race. I have not yet heard from you who or what this benefactor is, but, feeling that we owe our lives to him, her, or it, I desire to tender my share of the thanks due, at the next appearance of the

gracious vision! I pray you bear that in mind, Connor! lucky
fellow as you needs must be!"

Whilst these things were going on in the English metropolis,
the belligerent parties in Ireland were pushing on the war with
increasing vigor and activity. Ormond, with the comparatively
small army at his command, was rapidly overrunning Leinster,
while Preston's levies were being raised and prepared for effective
service. Lord Inchiquin and Lord Broghill, with Coote, Vavasour and other generals of note, were keeping their ground, and,
more than that, in Munster, notwithstanding that the Confederates
were masters of the greater portion of that province. Muskerry
and Mountgarret had gathered some laurels, and Colonel Butler
had taken many a castle since the day he so chivalrously sent
Lady Ormond in safety from Carrick's walls. O'Byrne had distinguished himself in many a skirmish with the enemy amongst
his native mountains, and Sir John Netterville, with Richard
Butler, a younger brother of Ormond, had also gained some advantages for the Confederates. The former had defended Netterville Castle during a protracted siege until relieved by a brigade
under the command of Lord Dunboyne, another brave and efficient officer. Sir James Dillon and Sir Morgan Cavanagh had
proved their prowess in various engagements with Ormond's
forces on the fertile plains of Leinster. One and all they had
gone forth from the Council Chamber in Kilkenny (where the
Supreme Council still sat) filled with new ardor and a more intense devotion to the sacred cause they had espoused.

When Owen Roe and the other Ulster chiefs turned their steps
homeward from Kilkenny, they found on approaching their own
borders that some new impetus had been given to the motions
of the clans, especially those of Tyrone and Armagh. The
whole country was in motion, and everywhere groups of men
were seen with lowering brows and moody looks discussing some
subject that seemed strangely to excite them. Weapons, too,
were being whetted, and bows were newly strung, and the long
javelins of tough mountain ash used with such tremendous effect
by the Irish spearmen were everywhere seen in a forward state
of preparation. The strangest thing of all was that there was
no information to be got as to the cause of this sudden commo-

tion. In the border countries, on the outskirts of Ulster, the people seemed not to know : they had heard of a great rising to take place when Owen Roe got back from Kilkenny ; nearer home, there was word of some strange event that had come like a thunderbolt on the half-awakened clans and roused them to sudden fury. What had taken place no one could exactly tell, but it was something very terrible, as every one said, and at last it assumed the vague, though palpable form of " another black deed of the Sassums or Albinachs.*"

" But what—what is it ?"

" Oh! the sorra one of me knows—aren't they always at some devilment or another—but they say this was past the common, and the men are all on for a great battle as soon as the general comes home—Lord send him safe to us !—I don't know what they're about up the country, but we want him badly here!"

Owen Roe smiled at those who were with him on hearing this from an ancient dame but a few miles from Charlemont. "Methinks," said he, " they are all bent on keeping us in the dark— but hark ! is not that the distant sound of wailing ?—ay ! is it— loud and many-voiced !—ride on, my men, for my heart tells me that some evil thing hath befallen our poor people !"

The same excitement was visible all through the country as the travellers now dashed along at full speed, but Owen Roe asked no further questions, till, reaching the banks of the Blackwater, a short distance from the castle, where he intended to cross, he encountered a party of the Rapparees with Florry Muldoon at their head, marching on foot in the direction of old Benburb. A hearty cheer of welcome burst from the brave fellows as they recognized the general.

" Now, at least, we shall hear all," said Owen, and accosting Florry, he demanded what it was that had set the country all in a blaze.

" The old story, general," said the old Rapparee with a kindling eye ; " the Scotch devils, finding you and Sir Phelim and most of the chiefs away. broke in on us and carried off the cattle and—and——"

* The Gaelic name for the Scotch.

" And what else ?   Did they kill any one ?"

" Well! and to be sure they did—the murdering villians, to be sure they did—when did they ever come and go among us without shedding blood—och wirra! wirra! wirra!"

" But did they do much harm this time ?" asked Owen with some strange presentiment knocking at his heart.

" It's as well for you ask no more questions, general dear," said the well-known voice of Donogh, " you'll know it all before long, and sorrow is time enough when it comes. Away with you, Florry, and get them pikes from O'Flanagan if he has them ready. We'll be wanting them now, please God, when once the general's home again. Don't come back without them, and tell him I said so!"

" Revenge! revenge!" shouted the woodsmen; "blood for blood!"

" I tell you it's at hand now," said their young leader; " be off and do as I bid you, and you'll have it all the sooner."

" In God's name what is the meaning of all this ?" said O'Neill, as the Rapparees marched away obedient to the last stern command. " Here I find the country all astir—I am told darkly of cruel murders and robbery and what not, yet no man seemeth willing to give me much knowledge anent the mishap whatever it be!"

" Why, the short and the long of it is, general," said the young man in a perturbed voice, " Stewart came in at one side on us and Cole at the other, about ten days agone, and, thinking they'd have it all their own way, they killed and destroyed whatever came under their hands, and although we poor wood-kern peppered them well at times when we got them in detachments here or there, or wherever their numbers were of no use to them, still the devils made good their point and fleeced the country right and left—ay! and took some precious lives, too—but they did one deed at last that brought vengeance on them swift and sure, and drove them back to their lair again."

" And what was that ?"

" Come with me to Benburb. an' you be not over tired, and you will know all!"

" Tired!" said Owen, " why, an' I were hardly able to sit my horse I would go to have this mystery solved. What say you friends and comrades ?"

Most of those with him were followers or adherents, and all declared themselves willing to go, so turning their horses' heads, on they dashed in the wake of Donogh, who had jumped on a horse that was grazing by the river side, and, without saddle or bridle, kept his place in the van of the flying cavalcade.

The wintry day was drawing to a close when they reached Benburb, and the deepening gloom of evening was settling cold and cheerless around the old castle, but as Owen glanced upwards at its frowning walls, a light suddenly appeared through one of the narrow loop-holes, and the chieftain rubbed his eyes and looked again, for, to his knowledge, no living thing was within the ruined fortress.

" Donogh !" said he, " do mine eyes deceive me, or is that a light in the castle up yonder ?"

" Indeed, then, it is, general, and look if there be not a green flag on the top. Well ! myself didn't see *that* before—they got some of the boys to put it up, expecting the general's return," he musingly said, partly to himself, " but, come in, General O'Neill ! and you'll find one to read your riddle !"

The old stone staircase leading upwards from the hall was still, if not perfect, at least passable ; and a stream of faint, flickering light from above made its rugged steps dimly visible through the yawning darkness of the hall beneath. A stillness like that of death brooded over the dreary spot, and many a stout heart would have feared—

" To tempt the dangerous gloom,"

but Owen Roe, und. terred by the utter wildness and desolation of the scene, was only the more anxious to penetrate the mystery so suddenly connected with the old castle of his ancestors.

" Whither now ?" said he in a whisper to Donogh, but the whisper, low as it was. awoke the echoes of the long-deserted hall.

" Up—up, general !—only yourself, though, and me to show you the way."

" By my father's grave, Captain Donogh," said a fiery young

follower of the chief, "you do take us coolly—think you we came
so far from our road to see or hear nothing, and stand shivering,
moreover, in the cold frosty air, among ghosts and goblins, and
all such things, till mayhap it's enchanted we'd be ourselves?"

"Never mind, Shane, my boy," whispered the Rapparee in a
soothing tone, for he heard most of the others grumbling in like
manner, though not so loudly, "we'll give you the front rank
some of these days, and that will be more pleasing to you than
what you'd see up yonder, for, God he knoweth, it is a pitiful
sight!"

Meanwhile Owen had made his way up the rough, moss-grown
staircase, his long sword clattering as he went, and the plume
on his hat dancing with every step. Reaching the top, he stood
still transfixed, as it were, with wonder, we may not say affright.
A scene was before him which he never forgot, never *could* forget, till his dying day. At the farther end of the large square
chamber on a couch made of straw and mountain heather piled
to some height, lay a sheeted corpse, stiff, and wan, and ghastly
in the light of three small tapers placed at the head. Close by
knelt a female figure wrapped in a dark-colored mantle, the
folds of which could not conceal the exquisite symmetry and
graceful outline of the form within. There was beauty, too, and
grace in the bowed head and the clasped hands and the statue-
like repose of the whole figure. Around, like so many enchanted
beings, were a dozen or so of women of all ages, some kneeling,
some squatted on the flagged floor, but all rocking to and fro
after the manner of Irish mourners, and each telling her beads
devoutly. At the foot of the death-couch stood Angus Dhu, his
arms folded and his tearful eyes fixed on the corpse. No sound
from below had disturbed the mourners, and Owen's exclamation
of wonder was the first intimation they got of other presence
than their own.

"Mary. Mother!" cried the chieftain, "who have we here?"
—and his voice trembled with a nameless fear.

"The general!" said Angus joyfully—the women clapped
their hands, and all but shouted for joy—the kneeling figure
stood up and turned towards O'Neill—it was Judith O'Cahan!

CHAPTER XX.

. " Murder itself is past all expiation,
The greatest crime that nature doth abhor."
GOFFE.

"Treason and murder ever kept together,
As two yoke-devils sworn to each other's purpose "
SHAKESPEARE.

THERE was no stormy outburst of grief, no outward sign of
emotion on the part of Judith as she and O'Neill stood again
face to face. Indeed Owen of the two betrayed the most agitation, as, pointing to the corpse, he said : " She is gone, then,
Judith ?"

" Even so, general! the hunted hare hath found rest at last,
and I am motherless."

" But how—when ? what caused her death ?"

" The bayonets of Stewart's soldiers," said Judith with pre-
ternatural calmness, and a stern compression of the lips that
showed a gush of feeling welling up within ; " eight days ago they
gave her her death, but the breath was in her till yesternoon——"

" Queen of Heaven! Judith O'Cahan," cried Owen O'Neill
starting and changing color, " how is this ? Did the Sassums
murder your mother ?"

" I have said it !"

" But where—how ?"

Judith made an effort to speak, then raised her hand to her
forehead and pressed it hard, hard.

" An' your ladyship will give me leave," said Angus Dhu,
" I will tell the general how it was"—Judith nodded and he went
on : " You were only a day or two gone, general, when the old
lady, Heavens be her bed ! took a notion that her end wasn't far
off, and nothing would please her till we went and brought her

the priest.   She got going to her duty, thank God, and so
did every one in the Castle when they had the chance, not knowing in these days when their hour might come—after that her
ladyship got the greatest strength ever you seen for a start, and
what did she take into her head but that she must go and die
in her own old Castle of Dungiven. Well, sure, nobody would
make so free as to laugh at her, but the lady Judith here did
all she could to get her persuaded not to leave Charlemont where
she was safe and well cared for. But she might as well talk to
the winds, go to Dungiven the old madam would, for she hadn't
many days to live, she said, and she couldn't die in peace anywhere else. Well! after that, general, no one could say again
her, so Manus O'Neill that you left in charge at the Castle, got
a kind of a litter made for the two ladies, and sent a score or so
of horsemen with them—*our* captain wanted to send a party of
his own boys with them but Manus wouldn't hear of it, and away
they all went—vo! vo! they did, but—but they never reached
Dungiven, for before they had crossed the county march—with
Tyrone heather still under their horses' feet—they fell in with a
troop of Stewart's cavalry and—and——"

"And what?"

"And your brave clansmen were most all cut to pieces trying
to keep the ladies from falling into the hands of the scarlet devils,
and old madam was stabbed in two or three places, and if her
ladyship here to the fore wasn't murdered, too, it was because
the officer kept telling his bloody crew to take her alive, and not
to harm her or he'd have their lives——"

"And because, Angus, the Rapparees were upon them before
they could finish their work—you forgot that, my good lad—but
I have not forgotten that I owe you and Donogh, and the other
brave fellows who were with you, more, a thousand times more,
than my life."

"Speak not of it, lady!" said the youth modestly; "our captain did but keep on your track, fearing lest your escort might
not be sufficient—it was God that brought us there and your
good angel!"

"And what did you, Angus?" said O'Neill turning quickly.

"Well, general! if we weren't in time to save the old madam,

we did the next best, I'm thinking. We sent the villains home
with a dead officer instead of a live one, and made them less by
a dozen or so——"

"And yourselves?" The youth's countenance fell, and he
remained silent.

"Alas! general," said Judith sorrowfully, "they paid dearly
enough for their victory—they laid O'Boyle and two more of
their best men in Eglish mould next day, side by side with the
brave O'Neills who like them fell in our defence!—oh! mother!
mother!" she said, turning passionately to the corpse, "what a
heavy woe came of your wayward wish!"

"But why, why came you hither?" demanded Owen. "Why
not return to Charlemont?"

"Because," said Judith, "I saw that the hand of death was
on my mother, and I took her here to die where solitude and
desolation were around us like unto mine own heart."

There was another reason which Judith kept to herself, but
which the keen glance of Owen Roe read in her downcast eye
and the faint flush on her worn cheek. She could not with propriety have remained alone in the garrison, so she conveyed her
dying parent to the tenantless mansion of Benburb, and the
Brantree women came to keep her company and "do what they
could for the old madam." Their services were not long required on behalf of the aged widow of O'Cahan. Death released
her from her sufferings, and they had but to render the last solemn
duties to her corpse, and watch and pray with the mourner
whom her death left alone in the world.

There was a burning glow on O'Neill's cheek as he listened to
this piteous tale, but he made no show of anger. When all was
told he turned and looked at the corpse, lying there so calm and
still after such a life of storm, with the nobleness of her origin
clearly stamped on her marble-like features, and the ring that
had bound her to O'Cahan still glittering on the shrunken hand
stretched by her side in the rigidity of death; he thought of the
wild July storm, and the ruined dwelling, and the strange meeting; he remembered that the lips now cold in death before him
had pronounced his first welcome to his fatherland, and a whirl-

21

wind of feeling rushed upon his soul, and, sinking on one knee, he bowed his head on his hand and murmured:

"May Heaven be propitious to you, noble daughter of Maguire, sorrowful widow of O'Cahan!—dark were your latter years on earth, and mournful was your end! What things I had planned for your behoof it boots not now to tell—you are better, I trust, than I could make you, and with that hope I must needs rest content, since nought remaineth for me to do. As a Christian man I may not think of revenge—the arm that is raised to smite your murderers must do it from other, holier motives. Oh! would that you had known how I longed to right your wrongs! would that I had done aught to serve you!"

"An' that be your wish," said Judith, "be consoled—my mother, feeble as her mind had grown, knew well what were your intentions in her regard—the hope of seeing you before life departed from her did keep her spirit, I verily believe, some days in the flesh, and her last wish is for you to carry out——"

"Name it!"   •

"It relates to the disposal of her remains," said Judith, and lowering her voice almost to a whisper she repeated the solemn charge which, as it happened, involved both trouble and danger, and so Judith remarked.

"It shall be done," said the chieftain in a faltering voice, for he was touched by the trust reposed in him by the honored dead.

"Those of her own kin," resumed Judith, "she might not ask to do this thing, seeing that it is not her will to rest amongst them."

Before any more had passed a great commotion was heard on the stairs, and Sir Phelim O'Neill suddenly appeared at the top. Some of his followers, seeking to force their way after him, were seized on the stairs by those below and set on their feet outside the door, "forsooth when *we* were kept down here freezing in the dark, *you* shall not mount without our master's leave."

Being fewer they had to submit, and Sir Phelim, at the moment, took little note of what was passing behind him. Striding across the room, he looked first at the corpse, then at Judith, then at Owen Roe, and some mighty torrent of passion seemed gathering to burst forth.

" I heard of this," said he, " many miles from here, but I could not enter my house until I had seen it with my own eyes. And so they killed her, Judith ?—they killed that old, venerable woman with the snows of seventy winters on her head, and the grandeur of her princely line stamped on her aged face. They killed her—did they not ?"

" Sir Phelim, they did !"

The hot blood rushed to the knight's face and his whole frame shook with stormy anger. Grasping the hilt of his sword with a sort of convulsive motion, he made as though he would sheath it in some one's flesh on the instant, but quickly withdrawing his hand, he turned suddenly and seized his kinsman by the shoulder.

" Owen Mac Art !" he cried, " can you stand this ?"

" No better, it may be, than you," said Owen with forced composure.

" I have been your enemy, Owen, I tell you plainly," said the impetuous knight, " but for the dear sake of revenge—revenge for this foul murder, not to speak of all the others—I will join you heart and hand—by the Great——"

" Hush ! hush !" said Owen eagerly, " swear not at all—an' your word be not sufficient, your oath would give me no greater security. I believe you, and will gladly accept your aid !"

" By the Mass, then, Owen, we'll not leave an old hag of their sort in the seven parishes with whole bones in her skin !"

" For shame, Sir Phelim ! for shame," said Owen sternly ; " what had their old women to do with the death of Lady O'Cahan ?—I never yet harmed woman or child, nor will I begin now when I battle for God and the right !"

" Well ! well ! no need to quarrel about it—you'll have your way, and I mine, but we'll pull together anyhow."

" I accept your alliance on no such terms," said Owen ; " there hath been over much of this bloody retaliation even on our side since the war commenced, and I tell you I will never stain my sword with such foul murder, nor will I connive at it in others."

" By the—ahem ! by the boot, Owen, you are too squeamish by half—these bloody-minded foreigners will have the best of it, take my word, an' you make war in that fashion. Let us be

friends, nevertheless, for the sake of her who lieth there stiff
and stark—united we can do much, divided less than nothing."

"It is well, Sir Phelim!" said Owen with emotion, and he
reached his hand to his kinsman, who gave it such a shake as
though he meant to wrench it from the arm.

"Now, Judith," said the knight, "seeing that matter settled,
I would know what is to be done in regard to your mother's
interment."

"Nought have I to say on that head," she replied coldly; "it
is already provided for.'

"Ay, it is ever thus," said Sir Phelim, bitterly, "whatsoever
I do is displeasing to you, and even death itself cannot win a
civil word for me—I shame to see the widow of O'Cahan laid
out in this ruinous place, long tenanted only by bats and owls,
and such like, and I marvel at you, her daughter, that you do
take the matter so coolly—I call God to witness that the fault
resteth on your own shoulders, and no ways on mine, seeing
that my Castle of Kinnard, or any other house whereof I am
master, hath been at your disposal."

"Sir Phelim, I am a-weary of your presence," said Judith
haughtily; "this house is mine, in that I have borrowed it of the
O'Neill," bowing to Owen, "for my present necessity—I pray
you leave me alone with my dead and her mourners!"

The thunder-cloud that instantly gathered on Phelim's brow
was dispelled by the calm good sense of Owen, who, although
well aware that Judith's uncivil hint was not meant for him,
nevertheless appeared to take it so, and, seizing his kinsman by
the arm, he said:

"The Lady Judith is right, Sir Phelim!—this be no place for
rough soldiers—men such as we—let us go hence—there is a certain matter whereof I would treat with you in private!"

"I will bury her as becometh her blood, were it but to spite
you," said Phelim shaking his fist at Judith with as much vehemence as though he meant to strike her; "see that you play
me no trick in this matter, or, by the soul of Heremon! I will
make you rue it!"

A smile of defiance was Judith's sole answer, and, taking
leave of her only by a look, Owen drew the angry knight away,

not, however, until both had knelt and offered up a silent *Pater*
and *Ave* for the repose of the parted soul. As the two chieftains retired, the wild death-song of the women, interrupted by
their appearance, was again renewed.

On the second day after that, a funeral procession, grand and
solemn as the chieftains of Tyr-Owen could make it, set forth
from the Castle of Benburb. Owen and Phelim were both there
with their respective followers, all well mounted and armed to
the teeth, in preparation for any sudden assault. It was a
goodly array of the Kinel-Owen, and the hero of Arras might
well be pardoned if he looked on them with eyes of pride. The
corpse of the Lady O'Cahan was placed on a sort of bier with
wheels, drawn by four coal-black horses. Eight women in dark-
colored cloaks and hoods sat on either side of the coffin keening
their low mournful strain, descriptive of the nobleness and virtue of the dead, the long line of chieftains from whom she
sprang, and the woes that had made her latter days evil. Then
changing their tone they would tell how the fierce *Albinach*
shed her blood, and how many curses would fall on his seven
generations for that foul deed. Now low, and sad, and tender,
now loud, and wild, and stirring as a trumpet's voice, that wail resounded along the hill-sides, and through the valleys of Tyr-
Owen, and the people, as they heard it, came forth on the road
sides to see who it was that was thus passing to "the lone place
of tombs," and, seeing the two chieftains, and the mounted cavalcade, and the lady so pale and so beautiful borne by four stout
gallowglasses on a litter close behind the corpse, they said to
each other, "some great one of the old blood is departed," and
falling on their knees, they offered up a fervent prayer for that
soul's welfare. And Judith cast a gracious look on these pious
supplicants, for dearly did she prize their orisons on behalf of
the dead.

At length the mournful procession approached the confines of
Derry, and soon from the ancient country of O'Cahan crowds of
stalwart mountaineers came hurrying down, eager to assist at
the funeral of the so-lately forlorn widow of their chief. Word
had been sent thither by Owen Roe, apprising the O'Cahans of
the mournful event, and, knowing the manner of their aged

lady's death, they approached with a wild and vengeful cry, each bearing on his right arm some band of a reddish color, the well-known symbol of revenge.

"Peace to her soul," they cried, "the white-handed daughter of Maguire, Eveleen of the silver cords, beloved of the valiant O'Cahan! Welcome, daughter of Brian! sorrowful daughter of princes! Welcome to the land that in right is yours!" and Judith bowed her stately head in token of her thanks.

There is not on Irish ground a scene of more solemn or romantic interest than the old Abbey Church of Dungiven—seated on a bold projecting rock full two hundred feet above the beautiful Roe, which there rushes down with the force of a cataract. "Here everything disposes to seriousness and meditation; the grandeur of the mountains, the ascending sound of the torrent beneath, the repose of the place, its seclusion from little things, and the awful monuments of mortality around it—it is a scene which contemplation must love, and devotion may claim as peculiarly her own."*

Honor to the memory of "the monks of old," whose admirable taste selected such sites for religious seclusion, and honor to the chiefs who established and maintained them there.† The splendor of Dungiven Abbey has passed away, and the old Augustinians who peopled its cloisters, and the chieftains who wielded the sword in their defence, lie mingled in the dust of the tomb around the sacred walls, but the memories of both are clustering like shadows amid the old arches, and long after the last vestiges of the building shall have passed away, their faith and their piety, and their munificent charity shall continue to shed a halo round the beautiful but lonely spot.

To this old Abbey Church it was that the remains of the aged Lady O'Cahan were conveyed on that bleak wintry day amid the spears and battle-axes of the bold clansmen of the north, and the mournful sound of the pipes, and the wailing of the *keeners.*

Who that knows aught of the O'Cahans has not heard of

* Rev. Mr. Ross's *Statistical Survey.*
† The Abbey of Dungiven was founded for Augustinian monks, about the year 1100, by a chief of the O'Cahans.

Cooey-na-gall, the greatest that ever bore that name, and the
terror of the invader, as his surname implies?"   Well! in the
chancel-wall of old Dungiven Church there is a tomb of rare
beauty, a grand old Gothic monument, erected by his clan to the
memory of that illustrious chief, and there it was that Eveleen
Maguire, the destitute widow of the last O'Cahan, had commanded her mortal part to be deposited.   It was a strange
thought of the old woman, but her daughter and the chieftain
who carried out her wish were at no less to understand it, and
so they laid her with honor in the most honored grave of her
adopted people, even the tomb of Cooey-na-gll.   For ages long
it had not been opened, and the six grim warriors sculptured on
its front had kept watch undisturbed over the death sleep of
the chief.   Now when the secrets of the venerated tomb were
again laid bare, and the day-beam penetrated for a few brief
moments to that dark recess within the chancel-wall, a strange
feeling of awe crept over the beholders, and men peered, curiously yet fearfully, too, over each other's shoulders, hoping to catch
a glimpse of the bones of the renowned hero.   Owen Roe and
Sir Phelim stood in front, and by an involuntary impulse the
former sank on his knee the moment the tomb was laid open.
All present followed his example, and his fervent ejaculation of
"Peace to the honored dead!" was responded to by the multitude in an "Amen," like the voice of the torrent beneath.

At this moment an old, gray-haired man made his way through
the crowd, and a cry of joy escaped the O'Cahans.

"It is Father Phelimy!   It is Father Phelimy—glory be to
God, he's just in time!"

The old man approached the coffin where it was laid in front
of the tomb ready to be lifted in, and Judith, when she saw him,

* *Cooey,* or *Cumaighe,* (in English Quintin) *na-gall O'Cahan,* the
chieftain above referred to, was so named on account of his valiant
exploits against the early English invaders—the words *Cooey-na-gall*
signifying "the greyhound of the plain, hunter of the foreigner."
The death of this renowned warrior is recorded in the Annals of the
Four Masters thus : "1365. Cumaighe O'Kane, Lord of Oireacht-na-
Cathain, died at the pinnacle of wealth and celebrity."

arose from her knees beside it, and extending her hand to him, burst into tears—they were tears of joy, and murmured, "Thanks be to God!"

A blessing was on the old man's lips as he drew from an inner pocket a sadly dilapidated volume, and commenced reciting the burial-service of the Church.

"I will say some Masses for her when I can." he whispered to Judith as he closed the book; "and now, my children, give dust to dust, and lay Eveleen·Maguire in that tomb which no man again shall open from this day ever. 'Blessed are the dead who die in the Lord,' and, furthermore, 'Blessed are they that mourn for they shall be comforted,' and again, 'Blessed are they who suffer persecution for justice' sake,' and even so didst thou, widow of Brian O'Cahan! Even to the death wert thou persecuted, O woman of heavy sorrows, but assuredly great is thy reward in heaven, yea, even the reward which awaiteth those who suffer and are sorrowful for Christ's dear name! *Requiescat in pace!* daughter and wife of the noble! well hast thou chosen thy resting-place with the glory of my hapless race!"

The coffin was placed within the tomb, the quaintly-carved stones were again replaced, no sigh or sob from Judith giving token of what she felt, the crowd left the Church, and only the two chiefs, the old priest, and the bereaved daughter remained.

"Now," said Judith, drawing herself to the full height of her tall stature, and gathering her cloak around her with statue-like grace, "now I am alone in the world, I shall henceforth live for my country and my creed!—revenge I name not, but my mother's murderers are also my country's tyrants—to compass their fall shall be the end and object of my life! Uncle of my father!" addressing the priest, "for the present I claim an asylum of you!"

"Alas! poor child," the old man murmured with a heavy sigh, "would that I had a fitting one to offer thee!—thou knowest I am myself on keeping amongst the faithful clansmen of our house!"

"I know it, my reverend father," said Judith in her decided way, "but, where thou findest shelter, I will not be rejected, and so I say unto thee as Ruth said to Noemi in the days of old:

'Whithersoever thou shalt go, I will go, and where thou shalt dwell, I also will dwell.' God sent you hither when least I hoped to see you, and your presence is protection for the lonely daughter of your nephew!'

"Be it so, then," said the aged priest with a wan smile, and he took her hand within his own; "my dwelling is on the hills amongst the faithful wood-kern, but, woe is me! I know that kind of life is nothing new to thee. Poor, poor child!" he fondly murmured, "hapless daughter of princes!—homeless, houseless lady of the land!"

"Thou wilt not then harbor with my mother?" demanded Sir Phelim, in a rougher tone even than his wont, for the heart within him was softened by the pitiful scene, and he would fain conceal his emotion.

Judith shook her head, and the knight muttering some wrathful words between his teeth, turned on his heel and strode away.

What passed between the three thus left together is not for us to tell; suffice it, that during their brief colloquy, things of high import to the national cause were treated of, and it may be that Judith did not conceal from the great leader the plans which she had formed for her future guidance, for when, at length, she quitted the old Church, supporting her aged relative rather than receiving support from him, Owen O'Neill murmured to himself as he stood looking after their retiring figures:

"There be more in that maiden's head than some of our wisest could fathom—I would we had a score or so of men with heart and brain like hers to head our columns!"

He turned to take a parting look at the tomb which now contained his staunch old friend, and as the tumultuous cheers which greeted the appearance of Judith and the priest fell on his ear from without, he sighed as his eye rested on the stony figure of Cooey-na-gall lying so still and motionless on the tomb where it had lain for centuries; he thought of the mouldering bones he had seen within, and he said in a half audible voice:

"Such is earthly glory!—great wert thou in thy generation, oh! warrior of the hills, O'Cahan of many steeds! but what art thou now—what remaineth of all thy glory? Alas! alas! *sic transit gloria mundi!*"

His brief soliloquy was suddenly interrupted by a wild and
vengeful cry from without the churchyard where Sir Phelim and
those of the Kinel-Owen awaited his coming. Hastening to see
what the matter was, Owen found Donogh and a small party of
his Rapparees newly arrived, their smoking steeds showing how
hard they had ridden. Sir Phelim stood with his hand on the
neck of Donogh's horse, looking eagerly up in the young man's
face, while as near as the presence of that dreaded chief permitted, crowded the clansmen around—listening to the news the
Rapparees brought. And little wonder that their faces grew
dark as they listened, and that Phelim's broad chest heaved
tumultuously, for Owen himself, with all his long-practised self-
control could scarcely repress his indignation.

The tale, when told over for the general's ear, gave another
pretty picture of Scottish treachery, only less revolting in its
way, than the massacre of Island Magee.

Leaving Donogh to tell the tale in his own way, we may as
well give the reader an idea of what had taken place.

At the extreme northern point of the Irish coast on an insular
rock, separated from the mainland by a yawning chasm, through
which the ocean wave dashes with fearful violence, stood the
ancient Castle of Dunluce, at the time of which we write, owned
by the Marquis of Antrim, a Catholic nobleman, who had married a short time before the widow of the notorious Villiers,
Duke of Buckingham. This Marquis of Antrim, Randal McDonnell by name, being a Catholic, and somewhat of a favorite
with King Charles, was an object of dislike and suspicion
to the Lords Justices and the Puritan leaders in Ireland, but
Randal had hitherto given them no handle for compassing his
ruin, living quietly at home in his castle on the rock well content, it would seem, to let others alone if they let him alone.
He was himself what is called a pleasant fellow, his wife a right
merry and witty dame, and being such they generally contrived
to have a pleasant company gathered about them. Their household was, accordingly, a gay and racketing one, and in a round
of amusement passed the days and the nights cheerily over the
inmates of Dunluce Castle. The echo of the strife raging
through the island was spent before it reached that wild north-

ern shore, and to the shame of Randal McDonnell be it said, he gave himself little concern as to which of the contending parties had the best of it so long as he and his were free to "eat, drink, and be merry" in far Dunluce.

It happened on a day that Monroe the Scottish general sent word to the Marquis of Antrim, "whose loyalty," he said, "stood well approved," that having been scouring the neighborhood for some days in search of the rebels, the which had cunningly evaded his pursuit, so that he could not by any means come upon them, he would, with the noble lord's permission, stop for refreshment at his Castle of Dunluce, nothing fearing of treachery from a nobleman so highly esteemed for loyalty and all good behavior as my lord of Antrim.

Well pleased was "my lord of Antrim" and his gay Dowager Duchess by this distinguished compliment, and to work they went with right good will to make all things agreeable to the Scotch general and his officers during their stay, and provide them with suitable entertainment.

The numerous retainers of the Marquis were drawn up in imposing array in the courtyard to receive the military visitors, and it may be that the smiling host began to feel somewhat uncomfortable to see that the latter far outnumbered his own people, and were altogether as grim-looking a set as ever his eyes looked on. As he stood observing them while they crossed the narrow drawbridge two and two, he wished in his heart that he had manfully declined receiving Monroe's visit, but the wish came all too late if danger was really to be apprehended, which as yet Randal was slow to believe.

The fears and misgivings were of short duration when once the light-hearted Marquis entered upon his duties as a host, and, to all appearance, his cordial welcome was duly appreciated by his guests. The banquet was spread, and ample justice done to the good things prepared, and even the black-visaged Puritans seemed to have lost somewhat of their gloomy moroseness in the genial influence of the hour, when, all at once, Monroe stood up and slapped one hand against the other with a sound that rang through the large hall. His men were on their feet in an instant.

"Arrest that man and all his household!" said Monroe pointing to the Marquis, and notwithstanding threats, promises, and persuasions, it was done instantaneously. Within an hour the Marquis and his family were sent prisoners to Carrickfergus, and the castle rifled by the Puritan soldiers was immediately taken possession of for a garrison.

Monroe never laughed, but the capture of McDonnel and his impregnable Castle was ever after related in his grave style as a capital joke, and one of the most notable acts of his life.

Such was the tale told by Donogh, who had been up in those parts, as he said himself, "on a little business of his own." The effect of the narrative on the hearers may easily be conceived, coupled with the brutal murder which had so lately convulsed the country with rage and horror.

CHAPTER XXI.

" And when the cannon mouthings loud
  Heave in wide wreaths the battle-shroud,
  And gory sabres rise and fall,
  Like sheets of flame in midnight pall."

DRAKE

" True fortitude is seen in great exploits
  That justice warrants, and that wisdom guides;
  All else is towering frenzy and distraction."

ADDISON'S Cato.

AFTER the stirring events recorded in our last chapter, it was
confidently expected that General O'Neill would gather his forces
together, and, availing himself of the popular excitement, make
one grand effort to clear the province of the hated Scotch
marauders, who were preying on its very vitals. But, to the
surprise, and, indeed, disappointment of all, he quietly went on
mustering and drilling and exercising his battalions, with the
aid of the officers who had accompanied him from Flanders. In
vain did Sir Phelim storm and rage, and pitch the "drilling" to
the d——l, as he did full fifty times a day—in vain did the
chieftains of Breffny and Uriel, and the young Tanist of Fermanagh, urge him to more active measures, alleging that if they
were gathering strength by delay, so also were the Puritans.
Owen was still immovable, close and dark with regard to his
own views, yet not unwilling to hear what others had to say.
And yet the news from the other provinces was of the most
stirring kind; skirmishing was going on in every quarter, with
varying success, but on the whole the Confederate armies were
gaining on their adversaries. In Connaught, Sir John Burke
had striven so successfully since his appointment that, in the
face of Clanrickarde's covert opposition, and the utmost exer-

tions of the whole government party, he had reduced the Lord
President Ranelagh, with Coote and some other generals, to fly
the province, and make for the capital in search of the supplies
wherewith the dilatory Lords Justices had failed to provide them
in time.   Preston in Leinster had taken the strong town of
Birr, not to speak of lesser conquests, while Barry in Munster
had driven Inchiquin to take refuge with his forces, and what
provisions they could secure on the way, within the walls of
Cork, Kinsale and Youghal.   Lord Broghill, too, was shut up
with a small force in Cappoquin, so that the affairs of the enemy
seemed in a desperate condition in the three provinces.   Why
was it, then, that Ulster alone was backward, and, to all appearance, inactive, when such a golden opportunity seemed to present
itself?

    "Why is it, I ask you again?" said Sir Phelim, angrily strik-
ing the table around which Owen had gathered a few of the
chiefs in Charlemont Castle.

    "Because," said Owen, speaking somewhat more freely than
was his wont, "because Ulster hath suffered overmuch already
from rash, ill-considered measures.   Ay! even to become the
laughing-stock of the sister provinces, for the great flourish made
at the start, and the little wool gathered after so much noise.
When the Ulster army takes the field again, I would have it such
as to turn the scale of victory.   I mean to give it the title of the
Catholic army, the which, being a proud distinction, must needs
be proudly sustained.   Let our good friends in the upper provinces stand their ground a little longer, as it seems they are
well able to do, and when we come to their succor we can deal
the enemy such a blow as he may not recover!"

    Some of the chieftains present were convinced by Owen's
reasoning, marvelling the while at his consummate coolness,
but Sir Phelim was only the more incensed, and could hardly
keep from expressing his contempt.

    "Truly," said he with much bitterness, "the Lady Judith hath
cause to be proud of her champion—an' she had taken *me* for
her liege-man, her mother's murder were bloodily avenged before now.   If O'Cahan's blood be in her veins she will spurn
you like a dog."

"Have a care what you say, Phelim," said Owen hastily; "you may stretch endurance so far that even I may have patience no longer. As for the lady on whom your tongue doth run so glibly, I am well assured that she hath more understanding of this matter than you, and albeit that I am not 'the liege-man' of any woman breathing, I respect *her* too much to hear her name bandied at will—*even* by my valorous cousin. I pray you, therefore, to discourse in such wise as becometh a soldier, without dragging in names or things foreign to our subject.'

"Ho! ho!" laughed the incorrigible knight; "I warrant me, you will hear more of it than you relish from the respected lady herself.'

Owen thought of the Church of Dungiven and Judith's masterly counsel, and he smiled. His smile was gall and wormwood to Phelim, and he bit his lip till the blood almost showed. The fierce sarcasm hovering on his lip was choked in its birth by the arrival of a courier with dispatches for the general from Sir John Netterville.

With eager haste Owen broke the seal and read, the others watching his countenance with painful anxiety. He had not read far when his brow darkened and his ruddy cheek grew pale.

"Ill news, my friends," he said, looking up with a troubled expression, " Preston hath encountered a heavy mishap."

" How ?—where ?—when ?" cried the listeners all in a breath.

"At Rathconnell, in the county of Westmeath. As ill luck would have it, he met Ranelagh and Coote on their retreat to Dublin, and must needs have a tilt with them, after the manner of your fighting cocks"—and he glanced maliciously at Phelim— " I *thought* Preston was over fond of making a stir, the which hath cost him full dear on this last occasion, for the Puritans with a much smaller force cut their way through his army drawn up to bar their progress—that comes, Sir Phelim, of over combativeness——"

" Said you *Rathconnell* was the place?" inquired O'Reilly of Breffny in an agitated voice.

" Ay, surely!" said Owen, referring again to the document in his hand, " but what of that, friend Philip ?"

At first the chieftain declined answering, and would fain have laughed the matter off, but curiosity once aroused was not so easily allayed, and there was no evading the keen scrutiny of Owen's eye.

"Were Malachy na Soggarth here," said the Breffny chief, "ye would, doubtless, have known before this. My knowledge of the prophecies is but small, compared with Malachy's, yet unluckily I have heard from my childhood that a great battle was to be fought at Rathconnell——"

"And what further sayeth the prophecy?"

"It sayeth, General O'Neill," said O'Reilly slowly and with emphasis, "that whichever party wins that battle wins all Ireland!"

A scornful laugh burst from Phelim O'Neill; McMahon cried "pooh! pooh!" and Roderick Maguire shook back his long tresses with a smile of disdain. Not so Owen Roe, between whom and O'Reilly uneasy glances were exchanged, and notwithstanding their evident desire to appear unconcerned, neither could entirely succeed. Although Owen O'Neill was the last man to be influenced by superstition, this, he conceived, was far removed from superstition. The gift of prophecy had never been entirely withdrawn from the faithful; one portion of this prediction was already fulfilled, might not the other be fatally true? "God in Heaven forefend!" murmured Owen to himself, and then with a significant glance at O'Reilly, he forced a laugh and affected to make light of the prophecy as an old wife's tale.

But little recked Preston and his bold Leinstermen for what they considered a trifling defeat. For every loss they sustained they gained half a dozen minor advantages, which, taken together, were rapidly giving them possession of the Province. Lord Castlehaven was rendering effective aid, chiefly to Preston, and some of the most chivalrous deeds of that tedious war were achieved by that gallant nobleman.

Whilst the Puritans, according to their custom, were butchering without mercy such as fell into their hands, without distinction of age, sex, or rank, it was the proud distinction of the Catholic leaders that they showed mercy to hundreds of the feeble and defenceless in every part of the country. About the same time that Stewart's marauders were perpetrating such atrocities in Ulster, Lord Castlehaven was escorting " a number of men and women of quality," whom he found cooped up " in a great room" in Birr (when General Preston took that strong town) to the friendly garrison of Athy. When the Catholic troops took possession of the town, this numerous company of the chief persons flocked together for shelter, naturally fearing the dread retaliation of the Irish for the horrible cruelties exercised upon them by the Puritan generals, and when Lord Castlehaven made his appearance they fell on their knees and besought him with piteous cries to save their lives. With the spirit of a Catholic soldier he complied, and obtaining his general's consent to take command of the convoy, he took with him a strong force,* and conducted them in safety to their friends at Athy after a toilsome march of two or three days through woods and bogs.

Again at Ballenakill, a strong castle taken by Preston, after much hard fighting, the garrison, having at length surrendered, was conveyed to a place of safety by the same nobleman. Such chivalrous acts as these are amongst our proudest recollections of that disastrous time, and as Owen Roe told them over for Sir Phelim's special benefit, his cheek glowed and his eye glistened, and he said :

" That is what I call Christian warfare, becoming knights and gentlemen——"

" Thou shalt do no murder," saith the Lord of Hosts, interrupted Phelim with unusual solemnity, " to the which I would add as regardeth these canting varlets, if thou dost thou shalt surely suffer, for as God liveth we will show you no mercy an' you show us none. That black-livered crew will thank you none the more for fair dealing, and take my word for it, neither you nor Castlehaven would fare any better in their hands than the monster Sir Phelim O'Neill, who giveth them as good as they

* Lord Castlehaven tells us in his Memoirs that the number of people whom he thus conveyed to Athy was about 800, amongst whom were many " men and women of quality."

bring, and lashes them like hounds when he gets his hands on them !"

Owen smiled and shook his head but said no more. He had little time to waste in idle conversation, for there was hardly a day but detachments from some of the enemy's quarters were making foraging excursions into the country of Tyr-Owen or the adjacent county of Armagh. Many of these freebooting parties were met and defeated by his people led on by their respective chiefs, but still the evil increased and became intolerable, so that with any other general but Owen Roe, in whose wisdom they had unbounded confidence, the tribes of Ulster would have risen in a body to drive out the foreigners as they did once before. As it was, it required all Owen's powers of persuasion to keep them quiet under such provocation, and his most effective argument was that the day was rapidly approaching when his army could take the field, and then it would be *his* turn to clear the province, once, he trusted, and for all. And then the preparations he was seen making—the rare and novel training he was giving to his soldiers, teaching them such warlike exercises and manœuvres as made the simple clansmen stare. It was the greatest sight their eyes had seen, the squares and columns of Owen Roe's army, the marching and countermarching, and the skilful handling of weapons new to the northern clans. Under the teaching of such a master as Owen Roe, the warlike followers of the Ulster chiefs rapidly acquired the discipline they had never known before, and learned to unite their strength for a common effort.

At length Owen began to feel satisfied with the proficiency of his troops and a change was gradually perceptible in his tactics. As a preliminary step he cleared the country of cattle and other provisions that might fall into the hands of the enemy, sending the inhabitants back into the woods and mountains with a fair share for their sustenance. This was a capital stroke of policy, for the enemy were thereby reduced to the greatest straits in their garrison towns and in the wild border districts to which they had latterly retired for the convenience of making incursions.

The long winter had passed away in these preliminary operations, and the wise policy pursued by O'Neil! was manifest in its results. Monroe and Stewart were driven to the utmost extremity for want of provisions, and menaced by the presence of O'Neill's army, remained cooped up, as it were, in the more northern parts of the province, while all the central portions were occupied by the Catholic forces on, on to the borders of the Pale—where Preston and Castlehaven were masters of all the principal strongholds.

Things were at such a pass when, one bright May day, Owen Roe, with some of his staff and a score or so of his followers, was out hunting, providing for the hospitable board at Charlemont while indulging in his favorite amusement. He chanced to be on the Charlemont side of the river, and at no great distance from the castle, when all at once the well known signal cry of the Rapparees was heard loud, wild and impatient. The general suddenly pulled in his horse, saying, "Friends, the Rapparees are abroad—what meaneth that cry?" Eagerly his eye scanned the horizon but nothing unusual was to be seen.

Again the cry rang out over hill and valley: "The Albinachs are on you!—fly!"

"Great God!" said the general, "that is Donogh's voice—where can the enemy be?—ha! yonder they come!—Saints of Heaven! they are in force, too—mark yon forest of spears!" And he pointed to a gleaming, glittering line too clearly visible between him and the horizon. "Haste ye, friends! haste ye for liberty's dear sake!"

"I' faith we have much need, general!" cried a dashing young captain, Con Oge O'Neill by name, who was one of his kinsman's aid-de-camps; "that is a host—we are scarce a handful!—pity 'tis to fly, but fly we must an' we would do aught to leave a name behind us!" And suiting the action to the word he leaped his steed over a quick-set hedge and made off at a gallop for the castle.

All the party followed his example, and the towers of Charlemont were already in sight when a troop of Monroe's light cavalry, detached for the purpose of pursuit, gained upon them, and came cantering up behind.

"Ride for your lives, men!" cried Owen Roe; "yonder is safety," pointing to the still distant walls. "Our lives are worth

something to the cause! On! on! on!" and on they all dashed
with lightning speed.

But vain their speed—behind them fast and near came the
Scots urged on by Monroe himself, who in person brought up the
rear.

Near and nearer came the foe, and, for some time, fast and
faster flew on the O'Neills—on and on over hedge, ditch, moss,
and moor sped the chase, the pursued having much the advantage in leading the enemy such a dance as they pleased—a few
hundred yards would have brought them to the castle, when,
all at once, the thought flashed on Owen's mind, "an' they
reach the castle so close at our heels, Charlemont is lost—now
God direct me for the best!"

A narrow lane or *boreen* lay right before him, fenced in on
either side by a close hawthorn hedge, and as Owen's practised
eye glanced along it, he suddenly called to his companions to
halt:

"We will give them battle," said he, "in God's name, when
we get them once fairly wedged—so stand your ground, my
men! an' you would save Charlemont!"

"God bless you for the word, general," said Con Oge as he
reined back his prancing steed abreast with Owen's; "they'd
be into the gates, the born devils, neck and heels with ourselves,
and by St. Columb! that must not be! But, holy Saints! general! fly *you*—your loss would be worse than fifty Charlemonts
—we'll keep them here, at any rate, till you're safe housed!—
oh God! fly—here they are!" And seizing the general's horse
he would have backed him out through the little band, but
Owen commanded him sternly to desist.

"It is too late," said he, "and were it not, I would e'en stay!
—there, Con! there—defend yourself—boys! stand fast together—if one fall, let another take his place—they cannot pass,
an' you keep close!—now—now, for God and country!"

Great was the surprise of Monroe and Monroe's troopers when
they saw such a handful of men form in order of battle thinking
to obstruct their way, and if Puritans ever *could* laugh they
would have laughed then. Unluckily, they found it no fun
when once they came to blows, for, blocked up as they were on

either side, their numbers were of no use to them, the front ranks only being able to act. The conflict was fierce and yet tedious—many hard blows were exchanged, and some five or six of the Scots fell beneath the stalwart arms of the O'Neills. All at once Monroe, still in the rear, thought of detaching a portion of his troop for the purpose of making a circuit through the fields to take the little band in the rear. He succeeded, but hardly had they made their way into the adjacent field, when a cry of "Death to the Scots!—Island Magee!" was heard —then the sounds of fight—cries and imprecations from Monroe's men—shouts of vengeance from their assailants, and thus the conflict raged on both sides of the fence. Owen Roe and his little band knew that the Rapparees had come to their aid, but see they could not what was going on so near, for their own lives were in imminent peril, and it required a superhuman effort to keep the enemy at bay. Every sense was strained to the utmost, for skill and attention were more needed even than strength, in order to parry the deadly thrusts of swords and bayonets. Still in the van fought Owen Roe, and still by his side was Con Oge, while their brave companions pressed close behind, and by God's great mercy, not one of the devoted band had fallen—no sound escaped from any of them, while the Scots cursed, and reviled, and threatened at every blow. Long, long did the unequal conquest last—the sounds of fight died away behi.d the hedge, and nought but groans were heard breaking drearily on the din of battle in the lane. Suddenly the trumpets sounded on Charlemont walls, and Owen and his followers thanked God, for their strength was beginning to fail. At the same moment a clattering of horses' hoofs was heard in the field beyond the scene of the late conflict, and Monroe's shrill voice rose high above the tumult :

"Come awa' frae awheen rebels !"

Those in front were not slow in obeying, for the brunt of that battle was more than they could well bear, and the sight of their dead comrades down amongst the horses' feet was not at all to their liking, nor yet calculated to steady their hands—a backward movement was quickly perceptible amongst them, and Owen Roe had no mind to stop their retreat, but Con Oge,

with the mercurial recklessness of a young soldier, called out
after them as they backed their horses down the lane:

"What the d——l, Monroe! will you leave Owen behind you?
Here he is—can you not take him?"

"We'll hae him yet!" said the grim veteran officer who had
kept the front all through the fray; "we'll hae him yet, laddie!
where the lonan winna save him—an' maybe your ainsel to
boot!"

"There's luck in leisure, comrade—you'll take your time,
will you not?" laughed Con over his shoulder, and the Scot
looking back shook his fist at him as they rode each his way,
Monroe still calling on his men to ride faster, faster, to rejoin
the army, whose banners and glittering arms made a formidable
show in the distance.*

Owen Roe, with his wonted coolness, chided Con for thus
bandying words with an enemy, whose unaccountable retreat
was a rare God-send, deliberately wiping his sword as he talked,
riding the while at full speed towards the castle, as though to
show his equestrian skill. All at once, at a turn of the broad
road on which the party were now caracolling, a strange and
ghastly sight presented itself, and Owen Roe himself, stout as
his heart was, quailed before it. Some fifteen or twenty of the
Rapparees were there, mounted as usual on good horses, (pressed
into the service,) but without saddle or bridle, either, other than
a hempen rope, which they made to serve the purpose. Wilder
and more haggard even than their wont, and scantily covered
from the winter's cold, with matted locks and thin, wasted features, their eyes withal burning like living coals, and the pikes
they carried crimson with gore. Donogh, himself, rode first,
but little better equipped than the others, and his usually mild
face wearing a ferocious expression, while ever and anon he
shook at arm's length a piece of cloth dabbled in blood, and
laughed with maniac glee, and his comrades chorused his
hideous mirth.

"See there, general!" cried the excited young leader, and he

---

* This poor attempt and pusillanimous retreat of Monroe are strictly
historical.

shook the bloody rag closer to O'Neill's face than was at all pleasing; "see, there, Owen na lamh dearg! we came to help *you*, and it's we that helped *ourselves* finely! Ha! ha! ha! ha! do you know what that is ?—do you know ?"

Owen shook his head, and he shuddered, too—the other went on: "You have seen it before, for all that—you remember that night in the Brantree—ay! I see you do—well! here it is again for you, the pretty ornament I have worn on my arm for so many weary months—I promised to wear it till the blood that was on it would be washed out in the heart's blood of the murderer—and—and—ha! ha! ha! that's what I'm after doing now—do you hear me, general ?—the strip may go to the flames now, for, by the right arm that did that deed of justice, it was well soaked and washed in that same muddy puddle——"

"Then you chanced on your mother's murderer in that field beyond ?"

"Chanced! ay, faith, that did I—I knew him by the marks and tokens I had in my mind ever since that bloody night—but that wasn't all, general! that wasn't all—we settled with Lindsay, too——"

"Lindsay! who is he ?"

"Ha! I thought you knew—Lamh dearg aboo! there they come!" meaning the troop of cavalry now cantering across the plain from the draw-bridge of the castle. "Why, Lindsay—Lindsay was—it's too long to tell, general! but we of Island Magee had a crow to pluck with him, and—we plucked it—that's all—sure they had made an officer of him, the hang-dog villain—they had—and it's him was at the head of the party Monroe sent round to steal a march on you—there was twenty or thereabouts, General O'Neill! and would you guess how many went back alive ?—just two—two, as I'm a living man, and even them have our mark on them—they have!"

"Poor fellows! brave fellows!" said Owen with a pitying glance at the half-naked limbs of his trusty auxiliaries, "you have probably saved our lives by cutting off that party. Accept my thanks for your timely aid. I must see that your equipment be somewhat better—come with us to the castle—you need refreshment!"

" God bless you, general! we're well used to cold and hunger, anyhow—pull out, comrades! there's fire and food in Charlemont——!"

The party from the castle by this time were close at hand, and no words can express their joy on finding their general safe and sound after such an encounter. Hearing how the matter was, all eyes were turned on the Rapparees, and every heart throbbed with gratitude for their timely interposition.

It so happened that Shamus Beg was at the castle that day on business of Sir Phelim's, and as the Rapparees crowded into the wide hall, where the blazing fire at either end invited their approach, Donogh felt his hand lovingly squeezed, and the voice of that true friend spoke at his side, wishing him joy of the great luck he had in regard to saving the general.

" And I paid my mother, Shamus! what I owed her!" cried the young man eagerly ; " see there's my piece of drugget—ay ! look—there's fresh blood on it, Shamus aroon! and you know what sign that is—and Lindsay, too, my boy! *you* hadn't passed your word for him this time—ha! ha! ha!——"

" Donogh!" said Shamus catching him by the arm, " is it truth you tell me?—is he dead?——"

" As dead as ever you or I'll be—why, Shamus! you look as if you were sorry!"

" Well! I'm glad and I'm sorry both—I'm glad he got his earning at your hands, but I'm sorry I missed him myself—I always had a look-out for him—still, it can't be helped—it's well enough as it is—where is Angus from you the day ?"

" He went off Derry side this morning, himself and Florry, on an errand for the general here—I'm as well pleased he wasn't with us a while ago, for, between you and me, Shamus! he can't bear the sight of blood, though as brave a gossoon as ever drew a pike! Thanks be to God, Shamus! I'm thinking it's a good morning's work we made of it one way with another !"

Although the wine-cup was, for the most part, a stranger to the lips of Owen Roe, he emptied a goblet that day with Con Oge and his other officers to the health of Donogh and his Rapparees— who had borne so large a share in the dangers and successes of the day.

But O'Neill was not the man to sit quietly at home within his Castle walls with the enemy almost at his threshold. "He waxeth over bold, Con!" said he to his young kinsman; "we will clip his wings for him before long, an' there be strength in the Red Hand."

And they did, too—on the following day, Owen Roe marched from Charlemont long before dawn with a whole brigade of his army under the immediate command of Colonel Sandford, and taking a short-cut through the mountains, guided by some of the clansmen from that neighborhood, they pounced upon Monroe when he least expected it, and their fierce onset was irresistible. Rejoiced to have, at length, the so-long wished-for opportunity, the Irish soldiers rushed like lightning on the astonished foe, bearing down all before them. No time was given the Scots to recover from their confusion—O'Neill's horse were trampling them down in headlong charge, while the heavy axes of the gallowglasses rang on their steel morions, cleaving them through and through, and the pikes and bayonets of the kerns skewering them like wild-fowl. And down from the mountains in another direction dashed the wild wood-kern with their fearful shout: "Island Magee!" and their pikes finished the work so well begun. Monroe bewildered and dismayed—for his wits were never of the clearest—owed it to the steady and cool bravery of a few of his officers if he escaped that day to Carrickfergus with his thinned and shattered forces.

This victory, while it served to encourage the natives, and infuse new life into the sluggish clansmen, whose martial ardor had begun to yield to procrastination and disappointment, had also the effect of stirring up the Scotch generals from their winter lairs around the borders. Cole was up with his northern Protestants on the Fermanagh side. Monroe began to bestir himself in Antrim—Stewart, ever active, quitted O'Donnell's country and advanced cautiously into Tyr-Owen. Montgomery and Chicester, uniting what men they had, suddenly approached O'Neill's district, and word was brought the General in Charlemont Castle that they were foraging the country round.

"Let them," said Owen Roe, "let them—much good may they get of their plunder!" The wily general had sent the

22

cattle to the hills where no Scot in all Ireland would venture in search of them, guarded as they were by the entire strength of the Rapparees.

A few days more and Owen Roe was on his march to Leitrim, where he meant to co-operate with the O'Rourkes, O'Reillys and others of the border clans, still harassed by the lawless barbarians under Hamilton's command. It was a curious sight, or would be now, to see Owen Roe's army in motion, wending its tortuous way amongst the green hills of Ulster. Gallant and bold was the clansmen's bearing, and right proudly they marched in the van, with their spears and battle-axes flashing in the summer sun, and the new banner of the Confederate Catholics, with its sacred emblems, floating side by side with the ancient flag of Tyr-Owen, the Red Hand blazoned on a white ground. Gallowglasses and kerns, enveloped in their saffron-colored garments, loose and large, but confined at the waist with a leathern girdle; chiefs in their national costume, too, looking stately and bold and elate with hope; but, strangest of all to modern eyes would have been the herds of cattle and the troops of women and children, forming what was called the *creaghts*.* These were the families of the clansmen, whom they dared not leave behind.

* These *creaghts* are often mentioned by Castlehaven in his Memoirs as "Owen Roe's Creaghts."

CHAPTER XXII.

"With grave
Aspect he rose, and in his rising seem'd
A pillar of state : deep on his front engr. ven
Deliberation sat, and public care."

MILTON.

"On, on to the just and glorious strife,
    With your swords your freedom shielding ;
Nay resign, if it must be so, even life,
    But die, at least, unyielding !"

SOME weeks before the events just related, when the stormy winds of March were blustering through the streets of the old town of Trim, and whirling in eddies around the towers of De Lacy's Castle, there was such a stir within the walls of the old fortress as though another General Assembly of some kind were taking place there. But no such thing : of a far different nature was the event which had for the time quickened the pulses of the old borough. Lords and knights of high renown were there with their troops of followers, but none of the old blood were amongst them. In the great hall of the castle some ten or twelve nobles of high degree were assembled, not for purposes of deliberation, nor as delegates from the people, but in accordance with the will of King Charles and in obedience to his command. In his sore need, he began to look to the Confederate Catholics of Ireland (whose successes were well known to him) for that succor which might strengthen his hands against the rebellious Parliament of England and the Puritan faction in both countries. All at once the monarch pretended to discover that his Catholic subjects of Ireland really *had* some grievances, and he sent pressing orders to Ormond and the Lords Justices to treat with them on the subject, hear their complaints,

and so forth, and forward them to him. To this end he further
appointed a commission, consisting, with Ormond, of the Earls
of Clanrickarde and Roscommon, Sir Maurice Eustace, and one
or two others of lesser note. These noblemen and gentlemen
were to confer, on the part of his Majesty, with other commissioners appointed by the Confederates, and with hearts buoyed
up with hope of an amicable settlement, the Supreme Council
deputed a corresponding number to repair to Trim in accordance with the royal command.

In that stately hall, then, of Trim Castle, Lord Gormanstown,
Sir Lucas Dillon, Sir Robert Talbot, and a few others met the
king's commissioners, and both parties looked anxiously for the
coming of Lord Ormond. Long they looked, but looked in vain,
for the king's lieutenant-general knew better than to forward
the king's views in effecting an accommodation. Accordingly,
whilst Ulick of Clanrickarde and his friend of Roscommon were
treating, in all sincerity, with the Catholic commissioners regarding the grievances which had compelled the Confederates to
take up arms, and declaring the benign intentions of their royal
master in their regard, James Butler of Ormond, true to his
utterly selfish character, was acting on the instructions of the
Lords Justices and with his army ravaging and laying waste the
country *in the king's name*, a day's march or so from the walls
of Trim.

It was a grievous disappointment to Gormanstown and Talbot,
and, indeed, to all the Catholic commissioners, that Ormond was
not present. Their faith in him was great, those Norman nobles
of the Pale, whereas Clanrickarde, although of their own faith,
had little of their confidence. In that they erred, fatally, blindly
erred, for Clanrickarde, disloyal Catholic as he was, was yet
true to his king, and, utterly forgetful of his own interests,
labored in earnest and with all his might to effect an accommodation which he knew could not fail to serve his royal master
materially at that critical juncture of his affairs. For the interests of his fellow-Catholics, he cared not a straw—let *them* take
things as they found them, just as he did, but the fortunes of
the Royal Stuart were of primary importance to Ulick Burke,
and to them all else must needs give way. With Ormond the

case was far, far different, and of that Clanrickarde had strong
suspicions, but he was not the man to speak rashly on any subject, least of all in what concerned the most powerful lord in
Ireland, the king's trusted lieutenant, and the hope of Irish
royalists.

The deputies sent by the Supreme Council were just the sort
of plastic materials whereon the sage Ulick might work to his
satisfaction. They were all of the class even then known as
"moderate men," that is to say, men moderately attached to
any party, but strongly attached to their own interests—men
who were scandalized by the more impulsive patriotism of their
Celtic associates, and more anxious in reality to stand well with
Lord Ormond and his party than with the Supreme Council of
the nation. Had any chieftain of Irish blood formed part of that
deputation, he would have scowled darkly, perchance, on that
Talbot of Malahide who had served the Justices against faithful
Wicklow, and who now made his obeisance before Clanrickarde
and his brother commissioners as a deputy from—the Confederate Catholics. But neither Mac nor O was on the commission,
for the very good reason that the magnates of the Pale had even
then a preponderance in the Supreme Council.

With characteristic coolness and tact, Lord Clanrickarde expressed his surprise at Lord Ormond's absence, " seeing that his
lordship's name stood first on the commission. Doubtless he is
detained by some lawful cause appertaining to his Majesty's
service."

" I hope it be not of such a nature, then," observed Lord
Gormanstown, "as that matter of Timolin ?"

" Of what nature was that, I pray your lordship ?" inquired
the Galway earl.

" Methought it had reached your lordship's ears, for it hath
been much talked of. It fell out in this wise——"

"Nay, good my lord," quoth Sir Robert Talbot, " seeing that
the matter hath no bearing on this question, it is but loss of
time telling it over."

" Pardon me, Sir Robert," said the less accommodating head
of the house of Preston, " I think it *hath* some affinity to the
present business!"

" I would hear it," said Clanrickarde curtly.

"About a fortnight since, when my lord of Ormond was ordered by the Lords Justices to advance upon Wexford and Ross by way of Carlow, having occasion to pass by Fitz-Richard's old fortress of Timolin, garrisoned for us by fourscore men or thereabouts, the Earl summoned them to surrender, the which demand they answered by hoisting our colors, which his lordship seeing waxed wroth and did begin to batter the castle, and for many hours kept up such a fire that the place was no longer tenable—still the brave fellows refused to yield, until at length the building took fire, and the rafters were blazing over their heads—then the garrison capitulated, and were suffered to march out——"

" And then ?" demanded Clanrickarde with a strange smile, for he had heard all this before, notwithstanding his seeming ignorance.

" And then, my good lord," resumed the peer, " they were all cut to pieces, I suppose by some unlucky mistake, albeit that the Earl himself was present——"*

" Very strange, truly," observed the Earl.

" Ay, marry, my lord, strange is it, in sooth," said Sir Lucas Dillon; "and the more so when we consider how my lord of Castlehaven did himself convoy the garrison of Birr all the way to Athy—so with my Lord Mountgarret's castle of Ballenakill, and many others taken by our generals—it is passing strange, and I marvel much at my lord of Ormond, above all men, giving in to such bloody and treacherous deeds—at a time, too, when he cannot but know that our lord the king much desireth peace with us !"

" I can no wise account for it, indeed," was still Clanrickarde's cautious answer, and then, changing the subject, he urged the necessity of dispatch in preparing the statement of grievances intended for the king.† But little remained to be done, the

---

* This massacre at Timolin is unfortunately historical. It is one of the blackest stains on Ormond's memory.

† One of the requests put forth in this famous remonstrance goes to prove beyond all doubt that the alleged massacres and murders of

document having been carefully drawn up for the Supreme Council, subject to such alterations or amendments as their commissioners might find expedient. It was presented in due form to Lord Clanrickarde, Mr. Walsh, one of the Catholic commissioners, observing with a smile:

"An' the old saying hold good, this remonstrance of ours must needs be of excellent account—an' *the better day make the better deed*, we could desire none better than *St. Patrick's Day*. May our good patron bless the work that its fruit may be a lasting peace, honorable and advantageous to all!"

And all the commissioners said "Amen," and Lord Clanrickarde, with his usual gravity of demeanor, expressed his conviction that there could be no doubt of the result, seeing that the king, of his paternal goodness, had nothing more at heart than the contentment of his lieges in Ireland. Whether the politic earl really believed this himself or not, his so solemn asseveration was greedily swallowed by the Norman lords and gentlemen to whom it was addressed, and they parted in all courtesy and kindness from their fellow-commissioners, and went back to assure the Supreme Council that things were in a fair way.

Good easy men they doubtless imagined that the petition from which they hoped so much was transmitted "by the first post" to "their gracious sovereign" for his just and equitable consi-

the Catholics throughout this civil war were neither more nor less than base fabrications of the enemy. "The leading men among the Irish have this to say for themselves," says Lord Castlehaven, "that they were all along so far from favoring any of the murderers, that not only by their agents (soon after the king's restoration) but even in their remonstrance, presented by the Lord Viscount Gormanstown and Sir Robert Talbot, on the 17th of March, 1642, the nobility and gentry of the nation desired that the murders on both sides committed should be strictly examined, and the authors of them punished according to the utmost severity of the law, which proposal, certainly, their adversaries could never have rejected, but that they were conscious to themselves of being deeper in the mire than they would have the world believe."—CASTLEHAVEN'S *Memoirs*, p. 17.

deration, never dreaming that it was destined to raise a tempest
in the Parliament House in Dublin before it left the kingdom.
Yet so it was, and before ever it reached the hands of Charles
Stuart, it was discussed and dissected before "the Commons
House" in Dublin, and, so hotly discussed, too, that the worshipful body of lawgivers came to loggerheads on account of it,
and the parliament was prorogued till the beginning of May.*
Thus, whatever effect the unlucky Remonstrance might have
had on the king's mind, the intentions of its framers were
wholly frustrated, and the ill-starred monarch was deprived by
his traitorous servants in Dublin of the means of judging for
himself how matters stood between him and his discontented
Irish subjects.

It is probable that the king, crippled as he was, resented the
detention of this Remonstrance, and blamed Sir William Parsons, for, before that prorogued parliament came together
again, that crafty and perfidious governor was superseded in
his command, and Sir Henry Tichbourne (notable for his defence of Drogheda against Sir Phelim O'Neill) appointed in his
stead.

Great was the joy and exultation of the Confederates when
the news of Parsons' recall was spread throughout the country.
His rapacity and cold-blooded cruelty had done much to foment
the rebellion, and taking place at such a juncture, his removal
from office was accepted by the ever-hopeful Catholics as a
concession, and a very important one, to their just demands.
There is little reason to think that the king or his advisers had
any such object in view in taking this step, but some pains were
taken by Lord Clanrickarde and men of his stamp to give the
affair that turn in the eyes of the Catholic party, well knowing
that their hearts were ever well disposed towards the king, and
anxious to see his acts in the best light. "Hope on, hope ever"
was truly their motto as regarded the faithless Stuarts, and it
required the saddest experience to tear from their eyes the
bandage they had themselves put on.

All this time the Confederate arms were in the ascendant in

* Borlase's *Irish Rebellion*, p. 155.

almost every part of the country. Preston and (especially) Castlehaven were more than holding their own in Leinster—in Connaught, affairs were no less prosperous. Lieutenant-General Burke, well supported by the Catholic nobility and gentry, had done wonders during that long winter. With him were acting, amongst others, the heads of the brave Galway tribes, Sir Roebuck Lynch and Sir Valentine Blake, with the son and grandson of Lord Athenry. Amongst his chief officers were also three valiant gentlemen of the ancient house of Kelly, known in that day as "the three Teige Kellys," and, in fact, most of the chief men of the province professing the old faith.* It was a sore grief to Lord Clanrickarde—recently made a Marquis—to see the Confederate armies triumphing all over the province, and at last besieging his town of Galway, without his being able to afford any relief to his ancient ally, Willoughby, once more and for the last time cooped up in the fort. Truly, Ulick de Burgo was a sorrowful man that day when, amid the solitary grandeur of Oranmore, his ears were stunned by the cannon of the Catholic army battering away at the gates and walls of Galway, and he forced to reply to Willoughby's distressed prayer for succor that he had none to give. His new coronet. would he gladly have bartered for the power of serving "the Puritan enemy" that hour, but alas! neither men, money, nor arms remained at the great Ulick's disposal, and, what was still more grievous, had he had supplies of any kind to give, it would have profited the garrison but little, for, sad to tell, the unreasonable Confederates had cut off all access between him and the fort, placing a chain right across the bay so as to blockade the city by water as well as by land. What a pass were things come to in that western country!

"An' this matter be not brought to a speedy end by the king's royal clemency and wisdom," sighed the new made Marquis, as he stood looking out from his castle-keep on the wintry waters of the bay, and, drearier sight to him, the ships of war riding at anchor, with the green flag of the Confederates floating from their topmasts; "an' it be not, I fear for the English dominion

* Meehan's *Confed. Kilk.*, p. 66.

in this realm, and if the Irishry have once their own way, they will overturn many a fair holding by way, forsooth! of demanding restitution.* May God confound their treacherous courses!"

Whilst matters were in this position in the western province, the Catholic army of the south, under Barry and Purcell, was no less successful. Inchiquin, Vavasour and Broghill, with all their bravery and military skill, and long experience in the art of war, were, for want of the necessary supplies, unable to cope with the Confederate generals, and finally reduced to the sorest straits.†

The Catholic armies were, on the other hand, well provided with the chief necessaries for carrying on the war, for money and arms were pouring in from the various courts of Europe. Friendly governments who had waited to see what the Irish would do for themselves, beholding the gallant and pertinacious efforts now at length likely to succeed, began all at once to take a lively interest in the Irish war, and, in fact, to regard the nation as all but free. Envoys were sent accordingly from the courts of France and Spain‡ to the General Assembly when it met again in Kilkenny in the month of May, while letters arrived

---

* There was a lurking suspicion amongst all the Anglo-Irish, even those who took side with those of the old blood, that, in the event of success, the latter might turn on them and exact the restoration of the lands wrested from their forefathers.

† "The condition," says Mr Meehan, "of Inchiquin in the south may readily be imagined from a letter which he sent in the early part of May to the Earl of Cork: ' Our present state,' wrote the Earl, ' falls out now to be more desperately miserable than ever: in regard we have no manner of help or relief amongst ourselves, and the provisions we depended on out of England doth fail us, which will put us to a terrible extremity, here being nothing to deliver forth on the next pay day. I request your lordship to lend or borrow £300, for victualling those in Youghal. To-morrow, with a heavy heart, I shall march forth, to linger out a few days in the field where I am not likely to continue so long as to enterprize anything of advantage, for want of provisions for the men and money for the officers.' "

‡ The envoy from France was M. De la Monerie; from Spain, M. Fusyot, a Burgundian.

from the ever-active Father Wadding from the capital of the
Christian world, announcing that his Holiness Urban VIII. was
also about to send an agent to the Confederate Catholics of Ireland with fresh supplies of arms and money.

And these things were told Charles Stuart, cooped up within
the walls of Oxford, and daily expecting to be besieged by his
rebellious subjects, the Puritans of England. And then he
thought of " the Graces," and the Defective Titles, and the Court
of Wards, and all the many edicts he had published against
" Popish Recusants," and he groaned in spirit. He said
within himself: " Had I but dealt fairly and justly with those
poor Catholics of Ireland they would now be my best and most
trusty friends. Nay, these canting knaves of England and Scotland would not dare push me to the wall as they do, had I the
strong arm of faithful Ireland whereon to lean. Alas! they
know I have not—they know it well—they know how I have
dealt with that people—when I might have done them justice,
even in a measure, I did not, and now their success, which might
also have been mine, doth but straiten me the more—all Europe
begins to respect them as a nation—help is coming to them from
all quarters—so Clanrickarde writes me, and him do I believe
beyond most others—they have ships, and arms, and money
—I would we could say as much for our royal self—and
men enough for the training! Surely it were our interest
to speak them fair, and act fairly by them, too—natheless, that
were as much as our crown were worth, by reason of the intolerance of these Puritans! I would we had not given in so much
to them in that matter in times past—it is now too late to draw
back—natheless, something must be done, and that full quickly!
—we cannot keep that war on foot with a worse rebellion—ay,
marry, a veritable rebellion—staring us in the face here at home
—rebellion!—ha!—ARE our Irish subjects, indeed, rebels? Is
it our authority they resist, or the oppressions of our ministers?
Before God, I cannot but hold them well affected to our person
as, in times past, they have ever been to the princes of our
house!"

In pursuance of this train of thought, certain instructions of a peremptory nature were forthwith sent to Lord Ormond, the nature of which will presently appear.

Little dreaming of what was passing in the royal mind of England, and perchance caring little if he did, Owen Roe O'Neill was marching with his gallant little army of Ulstermen, such as we have described them, to join the friendly clans of Leitrim. Such a junction was too much to be dreaded by the Puritans of Ulster for them not to make an effort to prevent it. Accordingly, the Catholic army had barely reached the confines of Fermanagh, where the ancient town of Clones stands just within the county of Monaghan, when the scouts brought in the startling intelligence that Sir Robert Stewart was in hot pursuit with a much larger force.

"An' that be his fancy, we must e'en humor him," said Owen Roe; "better now than when our march hath been longer."

"By my faith, general, we have been over long resting on our oars," cried light-hearted Captain Con, as he tried the temper of his bright blade by bending it till hilt and point almost came together; "it is time to pull up now an' we ever mean to do it. Lamh dearg aboo! sons of Owen, our turn is come at last!"

"Be not so eager for the fray, Con," said Owen with a kindly smile, for he loved the impetuous young soldier; "mortal strife ever cometh too soon! Saints and angels! what a host!" The Scottish force was just visible crowning the summit of a gentle acclivity some half a mile distant.

Sir Con Magennis here advanced to Owen's side, and begged him in a low, cautious tone not to wait for such a force as that commanded by such a captain as Stewart.

"Nay, Sir Con," said the chieftain somewhat indignantly, "you would not have us run away before their very eyes—bethink you of what the antients tell us: 'Never seek the battle, nor shun it when it comes!'"

Magennis shook his head, but he answered: "Be it as you will, O'Neill!" and then hastened off to see that all was right amongst the men of Iveagh.

It so happened that a long and narrow pass lay between the two armies, and of this Owen Roe hastened to take possession, lining it on either side with double rows of his light kerns armed with guns and bayonets. Hardly were the troops disposed in order of battle when the heads of Stewart's columns were seen approaching the farther end of the defile, commanded by Sir William Balfour and Colonel Mervyn, two officers of established reputation.

"Sons of Owen, the odds are against us this time," cried O'Neill, "but your fathers have routed the foe ere now with a worse chance than ours. Remember the lane at Charlemont wherein a score of us kept Monroe's army at bay for a full hour—be firm and fear not—we may give these proud Scots a story to tell an' they reach their quarters! Fix bayonets, men!"

The clicking sound of this motion had hardly died away when the whole body of Stewart's cavalry came up at a gallop, and, without time for deliberation, were ordered by their general to force the pass. Had they paused even a moment the sternest of those grim veterans might have shrunk from the task, but, accustomed to implicit obedience, on they dashed, on through the bristling rows of bayonets, cutting and hacking on either side with their long sabres—not unscathed they passed, for at every step some of their number bit the dust, and the riderless horses kicked and plunged, and made sore confusion in their ranks. Yet maddened by the fall of their comrades, and determined to cut their way through, on, and still on they dashed, the brave kerns on either side standing their ground right manfully, yet still unable to stem the rushing torrent—on, on swept the death-dealing Puritans, flushed now with the certainty of success, and the shouts of exultation from behind.

"Babylon is fallen!—death to the recusants!"

"The Red Hand for ever!—Lamh dearg aboo!" made answer the Kinel Owen, as their cavalry dashed into the narrow defile, meeting the enemy with a force so overwhelming that men and horses rolled over and fell back on those behind, throwing all into confusion. On and over the prostrate foe swept the fierce horsemen of Tyr-Owen, with Con Oge in their foremost rank, driving all before them, till the pass was cleared of the enemy, save only the dead and dying, whose groans

mingled dolefully with the shouts of exultation and defiance exchanged between the combatants. The Irish, believing the day
their own, set up a cry of exultation, as their cavalry retreated
through the pass, to resume their stations in the rear—hardly
was the movement effected, when Stewart himself advanced at
the head of his cavalry to try the pass again, pointing with his
sword to the Irish lines beyond. This time O'Neill's musketeers
closed their ranks obedient to the voice of their general, discharging their pieces in the face of men and horses, with such
stunning effect that the cavalry were forced once more to retire,
leaving several of their comrades dead or wounded as before.
As a last resource, Stewart commanded a party of infantry to
seize the pass at all hazards. This was done, after a desperate
struggle, during which many of the brave Irish defenders of the
pass were cut to pieces. The engagement now became more
general, and Owen Roe, advancing to the front, was attacked
by a nephew of the Scottish commander, ambitious, no doubt, of
fleshing his sword on the greatest of all the Irish.

"Yield, rebel and traitor! yield!" cried the excited young
officer; "yield or die!"

"I will do neither," said O'Neill, smiling at the boyish impetuosity of his opponent; "defend yourself, young sir!" and drawing his sword he prepared for the combat, with as much coolness as though no enemy were within sight.

"Spawn of perdition, this to your heart, then!" cried his
fierce assailant, aiming a deadly thrust at his heart, which Owen
parried, and was preparing to close with his antagonist, when a
piercing cry arose from the ranks of the Kinel Owen: "God in
heaven! see to the general," and quick as thought a well aimed
ball made its way to the heart of Stewart, while a dozen pikes
pinned his horse to the ground.*

"So perish all your enemies, Owen!" said Con Oge at his
kinsman's back; "he was bent on slaying you, the Puritan
hound!"

* Meehan's *Confederation. Ibid*, note to p. 69, quoting *O'Neill's
Journal.*

"Nay, Con, were he the devil himself, he was a brave fellow——"

No time was left for further parley, for by this time the battle raged on all sides, and Owen, seeing the greatly superior numbers of the enemy, began to think of effecting a retreat while it was yet time. To accomplish this object, he ordered up a reserved body of cavalry commanded by Captain Shane O'Neill. No sooner was this perceived by the enemy than yells of savage execration burst from the Puritans, and the fanatic preachers of wrath and blood were seen goading them on to yet more desperate efforts.

By a series of admirable manœuvres the Irish cavalry made their way between their own foot and that of the enemy, beating down the Scotch bayonets with their broad-swords, and keeping up a show of attack in order to cover the retreat of the infantry.

"Sons of Owen! death or victory!" cried Con Oge O'Neill, whirling his sabre high in air—they were his last words, for the next moment the gallant young leader fell backwards on his horse pierced by a mortal wound. In the heat of the contest his fall was for a moment unnoticed, and that one moment was fatal to him. Darting with maniac fury through the thick of the fight, a man in a semi-clerical habit threw himself on the half-dead officer and stabbed him again and again. One long agonized groan, a gurgle in the throat, and poor Con was senseless clay. His assassin might perchance have escaped unnoticed as he came, but his bloody exultation could not be concealed. Holding up the crimsoned falchion to the view of all, he uttered a yell of savage triumph, crying: "Wo—wo, to the worshippers of idols—lo! I have slain a strong man of the Ammonites!"

The words were hardly uttered when the minister (for such he was) fell pierced by many wounds, the steel corslet which he wore under his short black cloak, shattered by the blow of a ponderous battle-axe, and his scull cloven through a morion of the same metal.

"The light of heaven may he never see that cut your thread of life, Con Oge!"

It was Shane O'Neill that spoke, and after charging some of his troopers to convey the body to the van of the infantry, he made another vigorous attack on the enemy, whose line was still unbroken, then began slowly to retreat, with his face to the foe, his gallant troop beating back the advance of the Puritan cavalry with the determined courage of well-tried veterans. The trumpets in the rear kept sounding the retreat, and Stewart, after a short conference with Balfour and Mervyn, came to the conclusion that it was as well to let the Irish go their way. Having forced the pass, they were so far victorious, and from what they had seen of Owen Roe and his little army they judged it best to be content with what they had gained, rather than risk all by a further contest.   Their loss was already considerable, much exceeding that of the Irish, so that their measure of success was dearly purchased, and gave bitter foretaste of what was to come.

On these terms they parted, the Puritans gloomily discontented that their prey should escape so easily, the Catholics thankful that matters were no worse with them, and little grudging the foe his doubtful victory for which they had made him pay so dear.   Not unrevenged was Lady O'Cahan that day, and if Con O'Neill fell, an hundred dark-browed Puritans paid the penalty.   .

Well satisfied to escape so easily, yet sad and sorrowful for the loss of his favorite young kinsman, whose remains he consigned to consecrated earth within the friendly territory of the O'Rourkes, O'Neill rapidly pursued his march to Leitrim, where, according to his expectations, his army received considerable additions from the chiefs of that country, whom he found well prepared for war.

It was within the hospitable walls of Drumahair, where Owen was the guest of the O'Rourke, that a dispatch was brought him, bearing the well-known seal of the Supreme Council. Hastily tearing it open he glanced over its contents, but before he reached the end his hand trembled, his cheek was suffused with crimson, and his eyes glowed with unwonted fire.

" Heavens above, O'Neill ! what has happened ?" cried

O'Rourke, whose eye was on him at the moment. "What news from Kilkenny can stir you so?"

"Read for yourself," said Owen Roe, handing the document to his friend, while he himself arose and commenced pacing the hall to and fro with a disturbed and angry aspect, ever and anon repeating to himself, "Fools! dolts! What spirit can possess them? Where be their wits?"

CHAPTER XXIII.

"Let the ancient hills of Scotland
  Hear once more the battle-song,
Swell within their glens and valleys
  As the clansmen march along!"
            AYTON'S *Lays of the Scottish Cavaliers.*

'His words seem'd oracles
That pierced their bosoms;—'
            REV. GEORGE CROLY.

"WHAT think you of that, O'Rourke?" said Owen Roe as his friend handed back the document.

"I think, Owen," the chieftain replied with noble indignation, "I think there be traitors within our camp, else why listen to such terms at such a moment. For myself, so long as the towers of Manor Hamilton cumber the ground, or the monster who owneth them breathes the air of heaven, so long do I mean to war against that pestilent crew by all fair and honorable means——"

"Your hand, Owen O'Rourke!" said O'Neill stopping suddenly in front of him, and the two exchanged a clasp of more than brotherly agreement, "pray Heaven and our dear Lady there be enough of us of that mind in the Assembly to overrule this mischievous motion—an' there be not—then God be our aid, for I much fear what is gained will come to nought."

"But what—what is your intent, Owen?"

"I will send off a messenger this very hour with my strongest protest against this wily device of the enemy——"

"And what then?"

"Why, make the best use of our time pending the negotiations: you know what I mean?"

"That do I, and, by my father's shield! you shall have what little aid we can give you. Where left you O'Reilly?"

"He and McMahon were to join me here on the eighth day from my leaving Charlemont. They promise large reinforcements."

"It is well," said O'Rourke, and calling to him his faithful kinsman, Manus, he ordered him to send trusty messengers to Cavan to hasten the movements of its chief, requesting him to speed the message on into Uriel.

"Let the chiefs know that we await them here, Manus, and that minutes are hours till we see their banners advancing."

Leaving the northern chiefs to commence that grand campaign for which their astute leader had been so long preparing, let us see what was passing in Kilkenny that had so disturbed the calm mind of Owen O'Neill.

Pursuant to the king's command, Ormond had sent proposals to the Confederates for one year's cessation of arms, and notwithstanding the firm and strenuous opposition of the bishops and most of the old Irish who were of the council, the lukewarm Normans of the Pale, with the aid of Muskerry, Mountgarret, and one or two others of those half-English "trimmers," had succeeded in appointing a commission to treat with the Marquis.* The question, however, was still an open one in the Assembly, where all the genius and eloquence of Nicholas French,† the fervid enthusiasm of Archbishop O'Kelly, and the united influence of all the prelates were brought to bear against the Cessation.

"What!" said the venerable Bishop of Ferns, in reply to Lord Mountgarret's announcement that the commissioners had been named, "what! will your lordships, then, play into the hands of Ormond who, with his colleagues, can alone benefit by this measure?"

"My lord!" said Mountgarret, "I marvel much to hear a

---

* Ormond and Clanrickarde were raised to the rank of *Marquis* in or about the same time.

† The illustrious Bishop of Ferns, one of the most eminent prelates that ever adorned the Irish Church.

man of your order raising his voice against peace—of the which our poor country hath so great need!"

"Peace is a good thing, my Lord Mountgarret," returned the prelate drily, "but like many other good things it may be bought too dear. 'Our poor country' hath often had more need of your lordship's pity than at this juncture when the valor of her sons hath brought the enemy to sue for peace. Truly, this nation hath never stood so near her deliverance, never made the oppressor quail as now he doth—wherefore draw back now when a few steps onward may bring PERMANENT peace made on equal terms?"

"My reverend lord," said Muskerry in a tone of great excitement, "you who have not the brunt to bear have little feeling for our necessities. Rest is needful unto us, and time not less so. A year's peace will enable us to recruit our shattered forces, and otherwise supply our wants"

"Talk not of wants, I beseech your lordship," the prelate warmly rejoined; "what are our wants now compared to those of the enemy? Wants, forsooth! Is it the Catholic soldiers whose feet are tracking the road with blood for want of covering to their feet? Is it the Catholic soldiers who are forced to fight with empty stomachs?*—not so, my lords, not so—it is the Puritan bowels that make a rumbling now for food—our armies in all the provinces are passably well fed, clothed and cared for, thanks to the Giver of good things——"

"Here, surely, is some mistake, my lord of Ferns," put in Mountgarret hastily; "we are assured by Lord Ormond that his army is in fair condition, and wants for nothing——"

"Believe him not, for the truth is not in him—we have wit-

---

* Sir Philip Percival, an actor in the scenes he describes, thus pictures the condition of the government forces: "The state and the army," he says, "were in the greatest distress. The streets of Dublin had no manner of victuals many times for one day, so that the soldiers would not move without money, shoes, and stockings; for want of which many had marched barefooted, and had bled much on the road; and others, through unwholesome food, had become diseased and died." See Meehan's *Confederation.*

ness within call more credible than he were he fifty Marquises—
I pray you summon hither the Rev. Father Quin, of the order
of Jesuits."

Marvelling much what this might mean, the necessary orders
were given, and speedily appeared before the lords spiritual and
temporal, the dark-visaged son of Loyola, whose shadow has
more than once crossed our pages.

"Father Thomas Quin," said the Bishop of Ferns, "no man
here present knoweth so well as thou the state of Ormond's
army. Our friends of the council have it on his lordship's authority that his men want for nothing—ahem! only the cessation of arms, would his lordship admit it—of that they be in
sore need. How say you, Father Quin?"

"I say," returned the Jesuit, "that, for all his lordship's
boasting, there be no more miserable wights in this realm than
the men who fight his battles—an' they be not reduced to the
last extremity ere this, never men were so near it."

"Father Quin," said Lord Mountgarret testily, "we all know
the coloring which your party would fain give to this matter——"

"My party!" repeated the Jesuit coldly, "my party, Lord
Mountgarret, is the Catholic body entire—the son of Ignatius
hath no party within the Church:—eyes have I to see, and ears
to hear, and as your lordship knows full well, I see and hear
what few Catholics in this land may know and live!"

"I deny it not, Father Quin!—God forbid!—I did but mean
to insinuate——"

"That which your lordship did *not* insinuate when one of our
order—I say not whom—did risk his life, with your lordship's
knowledge, to administer the last rites to young Aylmer and
Lysaght O'Connor, when Ormond's friends, if not with Ormond's
consent, had them treacherously executed.* Your lordship
would have, doubtless, esteemed that Jesuit a reliable witness—
were Ormond himself at the bar!"

* "At the battle of Rathconnell, Lysaght O'Connor and the son of
Garret Aylmer had been made prisoners by Sir Richard Grenville;
in order to exasperate the Catholics, Parsons and his colleagues wrote
to Sir H. Tichbourne to have them executed by martial law."—Meehan's *Confederation*.

"Well said, friend Thomas!" said Dr. Kirwan, Bishop of
Killala, who sat near his brother of Ferns. "You speak as becometh your habit—ay! truly, even as one who feared them
not——"

"*I* fear them!" repeated the Jesuit scornfully, "I who have
so often braved death, to their knowing, in the most hideous
forms that Puritan rage could devise—*I* fear a set of pusillanimous Catholics who are ready to barter away on hollow, deceitful
promises, the hard-won measure of freedom wrested from the
enemy—*I* fear them!—nay, my good lord, an' they give in to
that double-faced plotter, Ormond, in this thing, the day will
speedily arrive when no man will fear them—when all good
Catholics will spit upon and execrate them! I crave pardon of
your lordships"—bowing humbly to the Bishops—"and to this
honorable council, if I have spoken with overmuch warmth,
but, were my life the forfeit, I could not help it!"

"Father Thomas Quin," said Mountgarret—and he rose from
his seat, but his whole frame trembled so that he was forced to
rest his right hand on the arm of his chair—"Father Thomas
Quin, no man is more willing to admit the value of your services
than I am myself, but—but—this language is intolerable. It is
a foul slur to cast upon so many honorable lords and gentlemen
of degree——"

"Very indifferent Catholics are they, natheless," said the
uncompromising Jesuit, "else would they reject with scorn
such overtures coming at such a moment from such a quarter."

"You speak strongly, Master Jesuit."

"None too strongly, Master President! *I* know Ormond—
you do not—any of you who signed in favor of this Cessation
—else had you sooner cut off your right hands than do it to pleasure him.' *I* know him, and therefore do I speak in this
wise."

"Have a care what you say, Father Quin," said Lord Muskerry rising in great agitation, "Ormond's name is above reproach
as above suspicion!"

"It is neither one nor the other, my Lord Muskerry, as far
as Catholics are concerned, and to your face I say it, spouse of

Eleanor Butler*—if any man here or elsewhere will deny that
James Butler, Marquis of Ormond, is the worst enemy we have
to deal with, here stand I, Thomas Quin, prepared to maintain
the proposition by evidence clear and incontestible. What say
you, my lords?"—and he turned slowly round the semicircle
formed by the Norman nobles—" be there any man here who
will assert in *my* presence that James Butler of Ormond stands
well disposed towards Catholics? What, silent all?—it is well!
With your lordships' leave, I will now retire. I must be in
Dublin Castle before high noon to-morrow, an' God spareth my
life!"

After exchanging a friendly shake-hands with Archbishop
O'Kelly, Bishop French and Bishop Kirwan, the sturdy disciple
of Ignatius strode down the hall, greeted as he passed with
many a fervent blessing from those of the old blood, while most
of the Anglo-Irish looked somewhat coldly upon him. But
little cared the Jesuit for cold looks—no man, perchance, on
Irish ground, had braved death oftener than he, and his bold
spirit seemed to soar to yet more daring heights whenever danger
became more imminent—where duty or charity called him,
there he went, deterred by no obstacle, his inventive genius
surmounting all, as his great personal courage and iron will
raised him above all. In those days of terrible persecution,
many a poor Catholic would have gone to his account " una-
nointed, unanneal'd," were it not for the ubiquitous and all-pene-
trating Jesuit who, under one disguise or another, contrived to
find his way full often to the gloomiest dungeons in search of his
suffering brethren, the victims of Parsons' insatiate cruelty.†
His valuable services were known and fully appreciated by all

* Lord Muskerry had espoused the Lady Eleanor Butler, sister of
the Marquis.

† Thomas Quin, a Jesuit. stationed at Dublin in 1642, was untiring
in his religious exertions and used occasionally to attire himself as a
soldier, a gentleman. or a peasant, to elude the vigilance of the Puritans, in order to gain access to the houses of the Catholics.—Gilbert's *Dublin*, p 221.

The adventures of this remarkable man would of themselves furnish an interesting volume.

classes of the Confederates, but being himself of the old blood,
the English of the Pale were at times somewhat shy of him on
account of his great influence—when Bishop French summoned
him as a witness against Ormond, he well knew that no one present
would dare controvert his assertions openly, and that if the fatal
policy of the Ormond party prevailed, as, from their numbers
in the council, he feared it would, they would have to carry it
out in the face of such testimony as even they could not reject.

A few days more and Nicholas French rose again in the
council-chamber to renew the subject of " the cessation." Dispatches had that morning arrived from Owen Roe O'Neill, dated
from the borders of Westmeath, and stating that the country
up to that point was all in the hands of the Confederates—with
the exception of Carrickfergus and a few other garrison towns in
the far north. This announcement excited no small surprise,
especially amongst the Norman lords present.   .

" Truly," said Lord Gormanstown, " it was about time for
O'Neill to bestir himself. An' he lay on his oars much longer
the battle would have been well nigh over. He is a slow man
and over-cautious, I opine.'

" The more like the tortoise in the fable, my lord," said Bishop
French with sly emphasis, " you begin to see now what he can
do when he deemeth his weapons tempered for use. Scarce two
weeks have passed since he took the field in good earnest, and,
with the single exception of that affair at Clones, his course
hath been marked by brilliant success. A good beginning,
surely!"

" Well enough for the time," said the peer coldly, " but somewhat early in his career to count on."

" My Lord Gormanstown," said the Bishop, " I would have
you take notice that General O'Neill hath done more in the two
weeks last past than any of our commanders hath done in as
many months—no disrespect to them, either—but——"

" Does your lordship mean to cast a slur on the others," put
in Gormanstown abruptly, " to exalt O'Neill's prowess and what
not, at the expense of those who have borne the burden and
heat of the day ?"

" An' it go to that," returned the prelate, " your lordship cannot but know that there be many who think those generals of whom you speak might have done more with the time and opportunities they had——"

"My lord of Ferns," said Gormanstown, pale with anger, "this language of yours were better explained. You would not have us think——"

"I crave your lordship's pardon," said the Bishop, with that mild yet firm gravity which ever belonged to him, "I crave your lordship's pardon, an' my speech be not to your liking. Truth must be told, nevertheless, and since you put it to me, I do say, speaking in the interests of our Confederation, that with the forces at his command, and the great abundance of all needful things which he hath had from the first beginning, I do say before this honorable council, that which thousands say elsewhere, to wit, that General Thomas Preston hath not pressed Ormond as he might have done. An' he met that false lord face to face, now that his army is so greatly weakened and ours in such fair condition, our colors were flying ere this on Dublin Castle."*

"So little being done, then," said Gormanstown, in a sarcastic tone, "wherefore doth your lordship object to a cessation of hostilities?"

"Far be it from me, lord of Gormanstown, to say that little hath been done; it is because much hath been done, Divine Providence assisting, that I hold the cessation inexpedient—had less been done on our side, no such proposition would ever have come from the enemy, and the very fact of their making it, proves to a certainty their weakness and our strength."

"But, admitting that, my reverend lord," said Muskerry, "in what way will the cessation injure us?—an' it give the enemy twelve months' rest, it will give us the same—we shall be, at least, nothing worse than we are now."

---

* Ormond, who had left Dublin at the head of 6 000 men, accompanied by Lord Lambert, failed to bring Preston to an action; nor did the conduct of this general fail to engender suspicion, for he had an army which was well supplied, whilst that of the Marquis was, according to the testimony of Carte, "ready to starve for want of provisions."—Meehan's *Confederation*, p. 70.

13

"That I deny, my lord," said the far-seeing prelate, "that I deny *in toto*. We, having the advantage, ought to follow it up. *Strike while the iron is hot*, said the wise men of old. Our armies are now elated with success, agree to the Cessation and you cool them down, ay, marry, as much as Ormond himself could desire. Push on the war now, and, as God liveth, the Cross will be triumphant in this land, and the wiles of the oppressor brought to nought before the year is out. Make a truce with the enemy and you stop the victorious career of our genera's and damp the courage o₁ their troops. Here hath Sir John Burke brought well nigh the whole of Connaught into subjection, so that even Clanrick-arde's Galway hath had to capitulate.* Castlehaven and Preston are far ahead of the enemy in Leinster—our old friend Barry, with the aid of my Lord Castlehaven, hath humbled the pride of Inchiquin and Vavasour in Munster, and we know that Owen Roe and the northern chieftains hold Ulster in safe keeping for us. My lords, an' you make a truce now you arrest the uplifted arms of your warriors and leave them standing as fools face to face with the enemy. It were madness, I say, madness"—he paused and looked around on the pale faces and contracted brows of the nobles, then rapidly added, "either madness or something worse!"

The vehemence with which the prelate spoke was not without its effect on those who heard him. Be their sympathies as they might, the lay-lords had no arguments to bring forward in op-position to those of Dr. French, and, hoping to gain time, they

---

* The siege of Galway was pressed with vigor ; and so straitened was Willoughby, that he offered to surrender the fort to the Marquis of Clanrickarde, after Rear-Admiral Brooke had failed to throw in supplies. Burke would not hear of such an overture, unless the Mar-quis consented to take the Confederate oath, which he sternly re-fused, and the parliamentary general surrendered the fortresses of Galway and Oranmore to the heroic Burke on the 20th of June. Three days afterwards a squadron entered the bay, but the colors of the Confederates were streaming from the flag-staff. The Archbishop of Tuam was one of the parties who drew up the articles with Wil-loughby ; and this infamous murderer was permitted to depart in peace.—*Confederation*, p. 71.

appeared to give in somewhat, especially as they saw that the prelates were all ranged against them.

Leaving the lords of the Pale to digest at leisure the unanswerable reasoning of the Bishop of Ferns, let us glance for a moment at Castlehaven's proceedings in Munster, whither, as the Bishop intimated, he had been sent to assist General Barry, then pressed rather hard by the united forces of Inchiquin and Vavasour.

Kilmallock was besieged by a strong force under Lord Inchiquin himself, and to raise the siege was the first and most pressing duty of Castlehaven. It is true he had been somewhat unwilling to undertake that expedition, but, once fairly into it, his spirit rose with the occasion, and he marched from Kilkenny in gallant style, with that military parade of which he was fonder than most men. He had with him as aid-de-camp, Captain Fitzgerald, better known as Garret-Garrough, an officer who stood high in his estimation. Learning that Barry and Purcell were in the neighborhood of Cashel, thither Castlehaven bent his course, and in the shadow of the old Rock, flung far and wide by the summer-day's sun, the two generals formed a junction, their united forces amounting to about 3,000, well trained and well provided. In addition to this regular force of horse and foot, Castlehaven had at his command a novel appendage to an army in the shape of a numerous troop of boys, mounted on light, fleet horses. Doubtless the grim veterans who followed Inchiquin's banner would have smiled in scorn at sight of these puny warriors, with their slight, boyish figures and fair unsunned faces, and javelins as light as if meant for pastime. And yet they were not to be despised, as their general well knew, for within those boyish forms were the spirits of grown men, hearts undaunted, and souls of fire, prompt to do and dare what their seniors well might shrink from.

Moving rapidly on Kilmallock, Lord Castlehaven was met by scouts with the surprising intelligence that Inchiquin had raised the siege and marched away by night towards the K·rry mountains,* detaching Vavasour with some 1700 men on an expedition to Castle-Lyons, it was thought, in the county Cork.

---

* This circumstance alone is sufficient to prove the high reputation

Castle-Lyons, however, was not the object of that forced
march of Vavasour, nor would Inchiquin have detached such a
force from his own for the capture of any village. But in the
neighborhood was the Castle of Cloghleigh, so gallantly taken
by the Condons, as the reader will remember, and held ever
since by our old acquaintance, Arthur, for the Confederates.
Dear to the vengeful heart of Inchiquin was the thought of
wholesale massacre, and he had sworn a fearful oath that the
sept of the Condons should be extinguished in blood ere the war
was over.

Now Barry well remembered brave Arthur Condon, and his
taking of the castle with such masterly skill and heroic valor,
and he started in terror when he heard of the direction taken
by Vavasour.   Going at once to Castlehaven, he urged him to
set forth in pursuit without a moment's delay.

"Haste, haste, my lord," said the chivalrous veteran ; "haste,
I charge you for Christ's dear sake. Haste an' you would save
some four score odd of the bravest fellows on Irish ground—by
Our Lady, we cannot go fast enough, let us ride our best !"

Castlehaven had heard the tale ere then, and, truth to tell, he
was fain to succor the gallant Condon as man could be. Starting, then, in pursuit of Vavasour, the army marched night and
day till a mountain only separated them from the enemy. It
was Condon's Country, and beyond that mountain lay Cloghleigh
Castle. It was evening, Saturday evening, and a troop of horse
was dispatched to watch the motions of the enemy. The cavalry
officer to whom that charge was entrusted was a tall, stately
man, in the prime of life, with a strongly marked, yet rather
handsome countenance, reminding you of some one you had
seen, and once seen never forgotten. It was a startling thing to
find the living likeness of Ormond in the Confederate camp, and
yet it was easily explained—that captain of dragoons was Richard
Butler, brother to the great Marquis, and brother-in-law of Lord

which the Confederate armies had by this time gained, seeing that
Lord Inchiquin had at the siege of Kilmallock a force of 7,000 men,
as Castlehaven positively states in his Memoirs, whereas the Confederates, as we have seen, numbered no more than 3,000 regular
soldiers.

Castlehaven, a staunch adherent of the national cause, and as true a Catholic as ever bent knee before an altar. Like many another of the Norman nobles engaged in that struggle, Richard Butler embarked therein in all sincerity, and fought on the side of truth and justice as became a Christian knight, until the poison from his brother's lips gradually diffused itself into Richard's heart, and he learned to distrust his fellow-Catholics of the old blood. At the time of which we write, however, there was not one of the Confederates more heartily devoted to the cause than Richard Butler, of Kilcash, and it pleased him well to be sent on such an errand that fair summer's eve.

The hours of the short midsummer night passed slowly and heavily in the Confederate camp, just three miles from the castle. Every soul, from the generals down to the horse-boys who cared their steeds, was anxious for the fate of the brave Condons; yet it was thought unsafe to proceed further till the enemy's motions were ascertained with certainty. All that night the Confederates kept watching and listening, but no sounds of strife came on the breeze, and they hoped that the Puritans, like themselves, were awaiting the morning light for action.

Fatal security; fatal delay! With the earliest dawn came the far-off roll of musketry and the heavy booming of the cannonade. Instantly the drums beat to arms, and the army was in motion without a moment's delay—alas! too late. Before the last man had quitted the place of encampment, word was brought to Lord Castlehaven that Cloghleigh Castle had been taken by Vavasour, and the heroic garrison cut to pieces, when marching out on honorable terms.* Butler had only arrived in time to witness the sad catastrophe, and small as his force was, he immediately attacked the base cut-throats, without pausing to consider the fearful odds against him.

With the vengeful cry of "Butler Aboo!" his followers rushed headlong on the enemy, and before he had recovered the confusion following that fierce onslaught, the Irish trumpets gave note of the army's rapid approach.

* See Castlehaven's *Memoirs*, p. 40.

"Now, Vavasour," cried Richard Butler, "accounting-time
is near; so sure as God is in heaven, you shall rue this cruel
outcbery—keep your ground, my men, and fix bayonets—let
them charge our bristling steel!—for God and our murdered
friends this day!"

Whilst Vavasour and his officers were vainly endeavoring to
surround the gallant little troop so as to cut off their retreat, the
heads of the Confederate columns were seen crossing the mountain's brow—it was but the cavalry, however, under Lord
Castlehaven, Barry with the infantry being left far behind, and
flying in squadrons on either side like winged messengers of
wrath, came the boy-horsemen, blithe and active as mountain
goats.

Vavasour, knowing the Confederate army at hand, had sent
off his cannon and baggage towards Fermoy, fearing their capture by the enemy, and now he had to encounter the avenging
army of the Confederates without as much as a piece of ord-
nance. Seeing the large body of cavalry approaching, the
Puritans made another desperate effort to cut off Butler's troop,
but with incredible dexterity they kept hovering on the flank,
acting only on the defensive till the loud huzzas of their comrades told them that succor was at hand, and then in on the
enemy they dashed at one side just as Castlehaven's men did at
the other. Their joint attack was so overwhelming that Vavasour gave orders for his foot to move slowly on towards the
river, hoping that the cavalry might be able to cover their retreat by keeping the Confederates engaged. He reckoned without his host, however, for while the two divisions of the Irish
cavalry pressed furiously on his flanks, the rear was harassed by
the pertinacious attack of the boy-cavaliers, who, with their
light, sharp lances, did much execution, goading on both men
and horses, caracolling around with strange velocity as they
darted their javelins, yelling and hooting the while after their
boyish fashion.* The Confederate cavalry fought well that day,

* "That troop of boys, mounted on fleet horses, was pressing on the
forlorn hope, not after the fashion of drilled and disciplined men,
but rather like 'the Moorish and Getulian horsemen,' says Borlase,
'mentioned by Sallust in Jugarth's war.'"—Meehan's *Confederation*.

and the Puritans fell beneath their blows like forest-trees when the storm sweeps through their midst, but the brilliant victory they gained was due as much to that youthful band of heroes with their wild, untrained valor, as to the more systematic attack of their seniors-in-arms. Almost surrounded as they were, and maddened by the strange annoyance from behind, which their horses felt still more than themselves, the Puritan cavalry at last gave way, and were driven forward on their own infantry, trampling them down with fearful slaughter. The whole fell into confusion, and horse and foot broke and fled before the avenging arms of the Confederates. But after them dashed Castlehaven and Butler with their valiant dragoons, and around and before them hovered "the boys;" to crown their misfortune Vavasour himself was taken prisoner, and after that the rout became general. Many officers were taken prisoners, and 600 of Vavasour's best soldiers "were killed between the Manning-water and Fermoy." Even their cannon was overtaken and captured, and their colors all fell into the hands of the Confederates.

Bloodily was the murder of the gallant Condons avenged that day, and the rumor of that great victory gave new life and hope to the Confederates all over the kingdom.

CHAPTER XXIV.

"The death-shot hissing from afar,
    The shock, the shout, the groan of war."
                                    BYRON's *Giaour.*

"I know the action was extremely wrong;
    I own it, I deplore it, I condemn it;
But I detest all fiction, even in song,
    And so must tell the truth, howe'er you blame it!"
                                    BYRON's *Don Juan.*

SCARCE had Castlehaven's splendid victory over Vavasour been reported in Kilkenny when other couriers came dashing in from the border county of Meath with as stirring tidings from Owen Roe. That chieftain had taken up a strong position at Portlester, a few miles from Trim, where Sir James Dillon had joined him with a small but effective force. All was likely to be needed, for the clansmen had little more than time to exchange a friendly greeting with the stout Palesmen who marched under Dillon's banner when news came in that Lord Moore was approaching at the head of a strong force.

"Let him come," said O'Neill quietly; "with the help of God and our good neighbors of the Pale here we are well able for him."

Just as Moore's cavalry came in sight, another messenger came riding in, his horse all covered with foam and himself panting for breath.

"In God's name, what tidings bring you?" said the general with some anxiety.

"Colonel Moncke is advancing from Wicklow——"

"Cometh he this way?"

"Even so, general, and fast enough, too, as poor Mullingar

here—that's my horse, please your nobleness!—can tell to
his cost, the creature! Dear knows, we had a nard ride of it,
himself and me, to give you the word in time!"

"You have done well, my brave fellow," said Owen, unable
to repress a smile even at that critical moment; "take Mullingar
and yourself to the rear and refresh yourselves."

"But Colonel Moncke will be here in no time, general, and
the other villains are close at hand yonder. I'm afeard—I'm
afeard it will go hard with you!"

"Never you mind that, honest fellow, but do as I told yon!"
and away rode Owen to where he had a breastwork thrown up
over night—behind it now lay the choicest marksmen of his
army.

"God's blessing be about him every day he rises," ejaculated
the sturdy scout, looking after him with admiring eyes, "see
how well he doesn't forget Mullingar or me in all the stir. Lord
save us all this day, what a mighty great army there is of them—
the black-hearted villains. Holy Mother! save our fine brave
Catholics from them, for it's you that can, and I'm sure you
will, too—well, come along, Mullingar! you or me couldn't do
much till we get something in our bellies—if we once had that,
my good fellow, we'll have a chance at the murdering crew
yonder—it will go hard with us or this good pike of mine makes
them one the less, anyhow!"

Meanwhile Owen Roe paid a visit to his grand stronghold, to
wit, an old mill which he had found there in good condition, and
in which he had posted threescore men, with some pieces of
cannon mounted on the walls. Standing on the crown of a
gentle acclivity, and rearing itself to a considerable height,
the building commanded no small portion of the level country
a ound, and O'Neill's skilful eye was not slow to discover the
advantage it afforded. He no sooner heard of Moore's approach
than he placed the great body of his troops in a position which
concealed them from the advancing enemy; the mill and the
elevation on which it stood being flanked by a grove of ancient
beech and sycamore furnished an effectual screen.

The preparations were hardly completed when up, at a gallop, came Lord Moore and his cavalry, hastening on in advance

298 THE CONFEDERATE CHIEFTAINS.

of the foot with the eagerness of men sure of victory. The
mill and the wood were before them, and O'Neill's defences, but
O'Neill's men were only visible in such numbers as their wily
general chose to show.

" Victory will have small merit here," said Moore contemptuously, " a mere handful of Irish kern. They have garrisoned
yonder mill, I see! and breastworks, forsooth!—on, on, men,
on!—we can take *that* with our broad-swords!"—and he pointed
with his own—" be sure you let not a man of them escape——"

Still no sign of life amongst the Irish, and on rode the fierce
Puritan soldiers, all elate with the thought of the utter extermination commanded by their chief, when all at once from the old
mill came the thundering peal of artillery, and a dense volume
of smoke—a cry of horror from the Puritans, and the lifeless
body of their leader rolled from his horse to the ground. A
cannon-ball had pierced his stony heart; the Catholics had lost
an inveterate foe, and the oppressor a willing and powerful agent.

Following up their advantage, the Irish rushed from their
cover, and darted, horse and foot, on the panic-stricken enemy
with their terrible war-cry : "Lamh dearg aboo!" headed by
Owen Roe himself, while Dillon and O'Rourke made a detour on
either hand in order to cut off the enemy's retreat. Disheartened by the fall of their general, and bewildered by the unexpected appearance of such a force, the Puritans were easily
thrown into confusion, and turning the rein attempted to fly.
But the broad-swords and battle-axes of the Irish were whirling
around them, and the wild death-shout rang ever in their ears :
" Death to the black-hearted stranger!" and to crown their
misfortune, their own infantry, unknowing what had happened,
now met them in the way, barring their onward progress.

Lord Moore and his troopers had long been the terror of the
border-country, and the memory of many a bloody contest, and
many a dismal scene of slaughter, whetted the Confederates'
swords that day. Like a whirlwind they rushed on the retreat-
ing foe, dealing death and justice at every blow, until the enemy
were forced to cry for quarter, and then Owen Roe's sonorous
voice was heard above the roar of battle commanding his people

to desist. The work of death was suddenly stopped, and each applied himself to secure his prisoners.

"Now God be praised!" cried Owen O'Neill, "such a victory I did not dare to hope for."

"Something was telling me all the time," said the owner of Mullingar as he leisurely wiped his mouth on h's jacket sleeve and mounted his four-footed friend, "something was telling me we were to have the best of it this time."

"And now for Moncke!" said Owen Roe in a cheerful voice to Dillon on his right, "I would he were here while our fellows' blood is up!"

But Moncke came not then or again—he had heard of Lord Moore's death and the total route of his forces, and he wisely turned aside from O'Neill's path, the more willingly as his regiment was literally in a starving condition.*

In much the same state was the whole Munster army under Lord Inchiquin, then Vice-President of that Province. "He had received no supplies from England, except a regiment without arms, which he thought were sent only to accelerate his ruin; bringing neither money, nor provision, nor even the hopes of either . . . . . thinking, then, the loss of the Province to be inevitable, and fearing the ruin of many thousand Protestants, it was resolved in a council of war to cause the ships of Lord Forbes' squadron, in the harbor of Kinsale, to be stayed and drawn ashore, that they might be ready

---

* It was about this time that the officers of the English army in Ireland, being unable to obtain the means of subsistence from the Lords Justices and the Irish Government, were reduced to the last extremity of want; wherefore, says Warner, they made a second application to the Justices and Council: and despairing of relief from them, they drew up at the same time an address to the king; representing that their case was now become so desperate, through their fruitless applications to the English Parliament, "that unless his majesty should interpose they could not discover anything that might stand betwixt them and absolute destruction."—*Civil Wars*, Book IV., p. 244.

to receive and transport those people to England, who must otherwise have been exposed either to the sword or famine."[*]

The Confederates, on the other hand, were well supplied with all things needful for carrying on the war; the booming of O'Neill's cannon all along the borders of the Pale was echoed back by Castlehaven's and Barry's from the walls of Munster, while the distant shores of Lough Corrib and Galway Bay resounded with the joyous cheers of Burke's all-conquering army.

Things were at this pass, and the truce postponed for one month, when, towards the end of July, there appeared before the Supreme Council in Kilkenny an Italian ecclesiastic, Scarampi by name, an humble priest of the Oratory, a thin spare man, of a mild yet penetrating countenance, and a small well-formed head, bent slightly forward, as it were, from the habit of subjection. There was little to distinguish Father Pietro Francisco from any other member of a religious order, nor was there in his bearing aught that savored of arrogant pretension, and yet the proud nobles of the Pale bowed reverently before him, and the stateliest prelate there addressed him in a tone of deference. And why was this? Why, because that humble Oratorian came to them from the Court of Rome, bearing bulls according a jubilee and many other spiritual privileges to those who had taken up arms for the faith in Ireland.

"And furthermore," said the reverend ambassador, "our Holy Father, knowing that your valiant soldiers have also much need of carnal weapons wherewith to combat the enemy, hath, of his goodness, and of his own resources, sent you what he could, at this present, of arms and ammunition, the which, being landed at Wexford, will be here anon, to be distributed as seemeth good to you."

The expression of gratitude on the part of the council, by its venerable president, was abruptly broken in on by our old acquaintance, Tirlogh O'Neill, who was one of the members.

"May it please your reverence," said he in his blunt way,

---

[*] *Ibid.*, p. 253. Here we see from unexceptionable Protestant authority to what straits the Puritans were reduced.

"there is no need to hurry—the valiant soldiers aforesaid have grown tired, it seems, of hard knocks, and must needs patch up a peace, come what will o't."

"What sayeth the noble Signor?" demanded Scarampi of the Archbishop of Dublin.

The prelate explained in Latin, whereupon Father Scarampi was much amazed.

"In that case," said he, "our reverend friend, Luke Wadding, must have deceived his Holiness, in that he hath represented your affairs as being in such flourishing condition that but little more was needed to secure the nation's independence and the full rights of our Holy Church in this realm of Ireland. I marvel much an' it be so, for Luke hath been ever esteemed among us a man of rare probity and great wisdom."

There was a sly undercurrent of humor in this speech, which did not escape the Irish members of the council, such of them, at least, as understood the pure Roman Latin, in which it was spoken. The truth was the good Padre had heard of the proposed cessation on his way from Wexford to Kilkenny, but he knew too little of the state of parties to comprehend the selfish motives of its advocates in the council.

"Padre Scarampi," said the uncompromising Archbishop of Tuam, "Father Wadding's veracity standeth unimpeached in this matter. God hath been pleased to bless our arms in such wise as, for the time, may be deemed little short of a miracle. Our armies are at this hour in possession of three provinces, with no small share of the fourth—we have men, money and arms, with provisions almost at will, and have so cornered the enemy everywhere that they scarce know which way to turn them, the while they have grown so lean from sheer hunger that one man of ours is equal to two or three of them. I know not if Ormond himself hath had a full meal of late."

"My Lord Archbishop," said Muskerry sharply, "you forget of whom you speak!"

"Surely no, my lord, surely no," said the prelate with some severity; "I am not oblivious of the respect due from me—from all of us—to James Butler of Ormond—and to his friends in this council!" he added significantly. Tirlogh O'Neill rubbed his hands and chuckled right gleefully while Mountgarret and Muskerry, Gormanstown, and the rest of that set, looked the daggers which they did not choose to put in words.

"But the peace?" inquired the Oratorian—"what of the peace? Your affairs being in such fair condition—you having the best of the battle, as you say, wherefore, in God's name, consent to a peace which must needs be of advantage to your enemies, seeing that it is they who seek it?"

The Archbishop turned with a smile and bowed to Lord Mountgarret who had been talking in a low earnest tone with some of the other lay peers. Mustering as much composure as he could assume, the President hastened to explain that the country was well nigh exhausted by a two years' war, and the brave soldiers of the Catholic armies stood in need of rest——

"I crave your lordship's pardon," said Philip O'Reilly, "but I knew not before that our soldiers were tired of the war. An' they had a voice in this matter, there should be no peace till we had gained our ends at the sword's point. Methinks Ormond himself could not wheedle them into laying down their arms at this present, without good security for the payment of some, at least, of the old debt. I pray your lordship, therefore, not to drag ' our brave soldiers' through the mire which hath gathered around this question. Say rather that the bond of confederation hath been found irksome, and that some amongst us do esteem the favor of my Lord Ormond, and that thing which they call loyalty to the king's majesty, far above the interests of our common faith and the re-establishment of our long-lost rights."

This speech, bold, and manly, and straightforward as became the O'Reilly, caused the Ormondists to wince, and, being interpreted to the Pope's ambassador, elicited from him a smile of approbation. Stranger as he was, he quickly observed the shirking, temporizing way in which the question of the truce was treated by the large majority of the council, and before he quitted their presence that day, he gave them plainly to understand what he thought of the matter.

"In the name of his Holiness Urban VIII.," said he, "I do protest against this peace, unless, indeed, it be a lasting peace, honorable to yourselves as soldiers of the Cross, and of solid advantage to your Holy Mother the Church, on whose behalf you took up arms. An' your grievances be not at once remedied, and your rights as Christians and as freemen placed on a firm basis, no peace—no truce, say I—follow up your successes by yet greater efforts—Catholic Europe will aid you, so that you shall want for nothing—the more you do, the more will be done for you—so sayeth the Father of the faithful, so sayeth your trusty and approved friend, Luke Wadding—so say the great and the noble of my own land, and in proof thereof, my Lord Mountgarret, there is the sum of 30,000 dollars received by Father Wadding from certain of our Italian nobles towards defraying the expenses of this righteous war."

And he placed on the table the munificent contribution worthy the nobleness and generosity of those from whom it came. Due acknowledgments being made on the part of the Confederated Catholics, Archbishop O'Kelly requested the Padre to state precisely the purpose for which the money was intended.

" Otherwise," said he, " reverend father, we may have it expended for the purchase of a peace—money is a rare commodity amongst our enemies in these days, and even the lordly palm of Ormond might not shrink from being greased with Italian gold —an' he cajole our lords into a cessation of arms with such odds in our favor, he might e'en persuade them that our money were as well vested in his hands—I pray you see to that, good Father!"

" Most reverend lord," said Scarampi in reply, " there can be no mistake regarding the intentions of the donors. We in Italy heard much of the extraordinary efforts made by a brave and faithful but impoverished nation to avenge its wrongs and recover its rights—we heard of the puissant valor of Owen O'Neill, and Burke, and Barry, and many more, and what things they had done on behalf of God's people—of Ormond, too, we heard, and Inch'quin, and Broghill, and other great captains of the enemy's host, but as God liveth, my lords and gentlemen, we heard not that any of the gallant Confederate Chieftains had opened their ears—or hearts—to the poisonous breath of the enemy. We heard not, in the halls of the Vatican, of truce or treaty spoken of here in Ireland—we heard only of battles and

sieges, and the noise of a fierce struggle, and our hearts did
burn, yea! even the paternal heart of Urban, to send timely
succor to those who battled for the right—had we heard of parleying, and truce-making, and such like, methinks yonder gold
were still in the coffers of those who sent it so freely. Pardon
me, lords and gentlemen, if I, a stranger, speak so plainly in
this matter, but standing here, as I do, to represent the Sovereign
Pontiff, I would ill discharge my duty did I not enter my solemn
protest against a measure which I know would, if carried out,
undo much of the glorious work already done."

Mountgarret and his friends excused themselves in the best
way they could, with many asseverations of devotion to the
cause, assuring the Padre at the same time that there were two
sides to the question, whereas he saw but one. They labored
hard to make him understand the friendly dispositions of Lord
Ormond.

"As evinced by the massacre at Timolin," interrupted Colonel McMahon, who was also a member of the Council.

This sharp retort, duly interpreted to the Italian by one of
the bishops, so disconcerted the "peace-cabal" (as his Grace of
Tuam aptly called them in a whisper), that they knew not well
what subterfuge to have recourse to, and were fain to adjourn
till the following day. A severe rebuke was first administered
to McMahon for his contumacious language. The chieftain of
Uriel bowed and smiled, and expressed his regret that he had
not sooner known the close sympathy between the Marquis and
the honorable Council. It was worth something, however, to
know it even then.

The strenuous opposition of the Pope's ambassador, the biting
sarcasms of the Irish chieftains, and the avowed displeasure of
the bishops, had all and each their effect on the time-serving
lords of the Pale and their adherents in the council. Anxious
to oblige Lord Ormond, and to obtain peace on any terms, they
yet shrank from the formidable array of the opposition, strengthened by the earnest expostulation of Owen Roe, who, unable to
leave his post on the borders, forwarded his views to the council,
couched in language rather strong for their liking. It was at
this juncture that Lord Castlehaven arrived in Kilkenny, post-

haste from the South. He had heard of the proposed truce while enjoying a brief interval of rest at his brother's house, and lost no time in appearing before the council with all the leading members of the Ormond party whom he could find in town.* Brave soldier as he was, and successful general, Castlehaven was already tired of the war, and that because his heart had never been with the Confederates. He was driven into their ranks by the cruel injustice of the government affecting himself personally, and, strongly imbued with a contemptuous dislike of the old Irish, he never could, or never did, completely identify himself with them in the quarrel. If he fought, it was for his own reputation, and to gratify the inordinate self-conceit which was one of his most prominent characteristics. Cherishing a profound respect for Ormond, it was never with his will he had drawn the sword against him, and looked eagerly for an opportunity of ingratiating himself once more with that powerful nobleman.

Taking with him, then, Sir Richard Barnewell, Sir Robert Talbot, Colonel Bagnell, "and such others as were in town well affected, and leading men in the Assembly, though not of the Council," his volatile lordship entered the hall where the council was sitting, having first agreed with his "well-affected" friends that "if they would stick to him he would give the matter such a turn" as would serve them all,† to wit, carry out Ormond's politic designs to the satisfaction of that nobleman, and thus secure his favor.

This unexpected reinforcement so strengthened the hands of Mountgarret, Muskerry, and the other Ormondists, that they immediately assumed a high tone and frowned down all attempts at opposition. Even the honest and conscientious efforts of Scarampi, backed by the expressed wishes of the Pope, sank into insignificance before the supercilious airs of Castlehaven with the prestige of victory around him.

It was not without a hard struggle that Scarampi, the bishops and the chiefs, were defeated. Defeated, however, they were, owing to the overwhelming majority of Ormond's friends (many

* See his *Memoirs*, p. 41.   † *Memoirs*, p 41.

of them his near relations) in the council. In the last stormy
debate, Castlehaven, irritated by the firm resistance of the clergy
and their adherents, was heard to mutter between his teeth a
bitter invective against "such turbulent and factious opposition."

This roused the ire of the native chieftains, several of whom
were on their feet in a moment.

"Ah, Touchet! Touchet!* it's in you for the taking out!"
cried Tirlogh O'Neill, shaking his clenched fist at him; "this
comes of your underhand dealings with—you know who!"

"Master Tirlogh O'Neill," said the haughty peer with a
withering smile, "I must decline noticing such scurrilous remarks applied to myself—it may not be amiss to inform you,
natheless, that there be some of our noisiest patriots—mayhap
near akin to yourself—whose 'underhand dealings' are none
the safer to the Confederates that they be with one of your own
generals—nor spite nor envy hath aught to do with *my* relations to the cause—hear you that, Tirlogh O'Neill?"

The brother of Sir Phelim could not but feel this home-
thrust, for the fact of that chieftain's intriguing with Preston
against Owen Roe was patent to all the army. As a match to
a mine was the effect of Castlehaven's taunt on his irascible
temper, and he flew at once into such a passion that nothing
but the interference of the venerable primate, his own kinsman,
could have kept him from drawing his sword on the spot to
chastise the insolent offender whose provoking coolness and
indifference exasperated him still the more. Finding that Tirlogh would not listen to reason even from him, the Archbishop
took him gently by the arm and led him from the hall, under
pretence of saying a word to him in private. The "word" kept
him all that day to say, for neither Tirlogh nor his Grace of
Armagh again appeared.

Little did Castlehaven heed poor Tirlogh's honest, blustering
anger: he and his "well-affected" friends had carried, or were
about to carry, their point, the clergy and the "turbulent *old*
Irish," notwithstanding. O'Neills and O'Reillys, McMahons and
O Rourkes, and all the other "outside barbarians," might storm

---

* The family name of the Earl.

and rage for all *he* cared—Ormond's good-will once secured,
and peace established for a whole year, there was no knowing
what lucky chance might turn up in the interim to put a total stop
to the war. Truly "a consummation devoutly to be wished."
As for the money sent by the Pope and other friendly princes,
it would, in the event of a lasting peace, be found extremely
useful in defraying the expenses of the king's struggle with his
rebellious subjects of England and Scotland. Little knew the
learned Oratorian what was passing beneath the smiling exterior of the lay lords and councillors, least of all what speculations they had with regard to the money and other supplies
brought by him. He could not approve of the men's acts, but
neither could he suspect the extent of their selfishness, or how
devoted they were at heart to the most dangerous enemy of
their sacred cause.

What little effect the presence and the remonstrances of the
Pope's agent had on the narrow, selfish policy of the Anglo-Irish
councillors, will be best understood by what we are about to
relate.

About the middle of September, that is to say, some weeks
after the arrival of Padre Scarampi in Kilkenny, Lord Ormond
sat in his tent one day where his army was encamped in the
vicinity of Naas. The curtains of the tent were drawn back,
giving a view of the ancient town, and Stafford's unfinished
Castle of Jigginstown, even then falling into decay,* with many
a mile of rich champaign country, all gilt and beautified by the
mellow rays of the autumnal sun shining down in midday glory.
But dearer than all this to Ormond's eye was the group of gentlemen, some of them of right noble mien, standing, hat in hand,
before the tent with a most submissive and deferential air, not
unlike to that usually seen on the faces of juvenile offenders,
when, smarting from parental blows, they present themselves
for pardon, with a promise "never to do the like again."

* "Jigginstown Castle," says the Parliamentary Gazetteer of
Ireland, "situate in the southwestern environs of the town of Naas,
was commenced on an enormous scale by the unfortunate Earl of
Strafford, Lord Lieutenant of Ireland in the reign of Charles I ; its
ruins now form a singular and striking object."

As though to mark his insolent contempt of the supplicants,
the Marquis, forgetful of that high-bred courtesy for which he
was famed, kept his seat while the others all stood, and, like
Fitz-James in Scottish song, he

"———— alone wore hat and plume."

Grander and prouder even than his wont, he seemed to look
down from a lofty eminence on those who stood there waiting
his pleasure, and well he might, for the realm of Ireland contained not any men that day more worthy of contempt than
they, although one of them was Lord Muskerry, the Marquis'
own brother-in-law, and the others were all of rank only second
to his own.   They were there as commissioners from the Supreme Council of the Confederates, to sign the articles of peace,
and Ormond treated them in every respect as abject petitioners.
    There was Muskerry—alas! how fallen from the position he
occupied on that memorable day when he took the oath of confederation before the altar of old St. Canice, with the banner of
the MacCarthys waving above him—there was Dillon—*not* Sir
James, the friend of O'More, but a very different man, Sir Lucas
of that name—there was Talbot of Malahide, just where he
ought to be, bartering away the proud independence which
O'Neill, and Burke, and Barry had won for his fellow-Catholics—
there was Barnewell, and Neale, and Brown, and Walsh, and
Plunket, and, shame to tell! there was *Magennis*—happily not
the Lord of Iveagh, the gallant Sir Con, but a certain *Heber
Magennis*, a kinsman of that chieftain.   The half English
McCarthy,* and this degenerate scion of the house of Iveagh
were the only men of the nine commissioners who had Irish
blood in their veins, and assuredly though their blood was Irish
their hearts were not.
    With an air of supreme condescension the stately Marquis
complimented the commissioners on the loyal and commendable
act just consummated, the which indicated a returning sense of
duty on the part of " the rebels."

* This time-serving Lord Muskerry was afterwards rewarded for
his betrayal of Catholic interests with the title of Earl of Clancarthy.

"Rebels, my lord?" said Muskerry with some warmth; "I pray you recall the word, for you cannot but know that the King's highness hath no truer subjects than the Confederate Catholics of Ireland!"

"Well, well!" said Ormond with a satirical smile, "an' it please your lordship better we will say *Confederates*—good men and true no doubt are ye all"—and he laughed a strange inward laugh—"in this thing have ye done well, and no doubt his Grace will make all things so smooth during this year's cessation of arms that even the pestilent rebel, O'Neill, and the rest of the Irishry, will have no rag of pretence for renewing hostilities."

"Irishry, my Lord Marquis!" repeated Muskerry again with a heightened color, while Magennis made a step in advance as though half resolved to venture on a word of expostulation—his courage, however, failed him as he glanced timidly at the frowning brow of Ormond, and he quietly slunk back into his place.

"Another slip of the tongue," said the Marquis in a jeering tone; "I pray you, good Donogh! be not so sharp—between friends such mistakes go for nothing. This cessation which I have yielded to your necessities, ought, more than all, to convince you of my good will."

"Pardon me, my lord," put in Dillon, "our necessities are not so great—an' necessities be in the way, they are not on our side."

"Pooh! pooh!" said the Marquis with a well-feigned air of incredulity, "tell that to others knowing less than I do of your affairs——"

"I do assure your lordship," began Muskerry, but Ormond stopped him with a majestic wave of the hand, and a smile that was half pity, half scorn. Rising from his seat he summoned some officers of his staff who stood backwards in the tent, and bowed the Confederate delegates out with much apparent courtesy but real disdain.

"But, my lord," said Muskerry, sorely nettled by such cavalier treatment, "my lord, we would have a word with you concerning that matter of the dissolution, seeing that we of the Confederation do hold the present parliament illegal, as you well know, and that point hath not been settled to our liking."*

"An' it be not in the articles, brother mine, it is beyond my power to arrange it now."

"But we understood——"

"It matters little, Donogh, what you or I *understood*—the articles of treaty are now signed and otherwise perfected—leave that matter of the parliament to the king's majesty, as becometh loyal and well-affected subjects."

So saying he withdrew with his officers into the inner compartment of his tent, and the commissioners were fain to take their way back to Kilkenny, more dissatisfied, all of them, than they were willing to own to each other.

---

* "Before the ink in which it (the treaty) was written dried the Confederate commissioners discovered that Ormond had no notion of calling a new parliament, although he knew that the present one was irregular and illegal."—Meehan, quoting CARTE, iii., 430.

CHAPTER XXV.

" Ah, God ! that ghastly gibbet!
    How dismal 'tis to see
The great tall spectral skeleton
    The ladder and the tree!'
*   *   *   *

" He is coming! he is coming !
    Like a bridegroom from his room,
Came the hero from his prison
    To the scaffold and the doom."
*   *   *   *

" There was color in his visage,
    Tho' the cheeks of all were wan,
And they marvell'd as they saw him pass,
    That great and goodly man."

" The grim Geneva ministers,
    With anxious scowl drew near,
As you have seen the ravens flock
    Around the dying deer.
He would not deign them word nor sign,
    But alone he bent the knee !
And veil'd his face for Christ's dear grace
    Beneath the gallows-tree."
                    AYTON'S *Lays of the Scottish Cavaliers—*
                            Execution of Montrose.

WHEN the Catholic Commissioners were, after many week's detention of their Remonstrance in Dublin, permitted at length to proceed to England to lay it before the King, his Majesty received them graciously, and after hearing what they had to say, and promising to consider the statement of grievances put forth in the Trim document, he sent them back with an urgent request to Ormond to settle the difficulty with the Confederate Catholics as soon as might be. Sorely pressed even then by the rebellious armies of his Puritan parliament, he turned with long- ing eyes to the victorious Catholics of Ireland, who could alone give him permanent and effective succor. This he represented to Ormond again and again in his private dispatches, although publicly he was still constrained to censure their acts, and speak of them in the cant phraseology of the day as "pestiferous rebels."

When the Commissioners returned to Ireland their party was increased by a young Protestant lady of rank, who had been staying with some relations in London, and was now going back to her Irish home furnished with a pass for herself and her servant, an aged man who looked as though he might have served the lady's grandsire in a by-gone age. It was not with the consent of her English friends that our adventurous fair one placed herself under the protection of the Catholic gentlemen, but having known Sir Robert Talbot and one or two others of their number in former days in Dublin, she declared herself quite willing to travel in their company. Such opportunities being few at that day, and her mother at home being impatient for her return, she would not hear of postponing her departure.

The displeasure of the young lady's godly relatives would have been much increased had they known that on the day preceding their departure, she was closeted with Lord Muskerry, the head of the deputation, for full half an hour. What the nature of their conference was may be gathered from the parting words which passed between the Viscount and Emmeline Coote, for she it was, as the reader has probably guessed.

"Fair Mistress Coote," said he, "I fear you will bring grievous trouble on yourself by journeying homewards in our company. Your brothers will by no means overlook such an offence against Puritan notions of fitness."

"Nay, my good lord, after what I have disclosed to you, wherefore speak to me of such matters? One who hath devoted her life to the attainment of an object, can think of no danger, no inconvenience that regardeth only herself. But you really deem it unsafe for *them* to join your retinue?"

"It were certain destruction to them, my good young lady, and most like to us, one and all."

"Then you refuse giving them this chance?"

"With reluctance I *must*—we have passports but for a certain number——"

"Leave two of your servants behind."

Muskerry shook his head. "It were useless, fair mistress,

worse than useless—the personal description of your friends is too well known—they could not escape in broad day."

" *My* friends!" repeated Emmeline with rising anger, for she saw and despised the pusillanimous fears of Muskerry. " Methinks, Lord Muskerry, they might well be *your* friends. However, I will press you no more—the God who released them from their dungeon will provide them with the means of escape. I will go to Ireland, as I purposed, but solely with a view to their interest—to apprise their true friends of how they be situated, and move them to devise some plan for their deliverance."

It was a sorrowful parting when Emmeline and old Lorcan came to take leave of the two poor captives, virtually as much so as when the walls of the Tower lay between them and freedom. Bitter was their indignation when they heard of Muskerry's cold indifference, so little to be expected from a chief of the Confederates. Had they been better acquainted with the respective attitudes of the " old" and " new Irish" at that time, their surprise and disappointment would have been less, but knowing nothing of the internal workings of the Confederation, they had thought in their simplicity that no sworn member of that body could fail to sympathize with them, or to lay hold of even the slightest chance of forwarding their escape. McMahon, as usual, tried to laugh it off, saying that they would be even with his lordship ere long, but Maguire could not conceal his dejection, and when the final moment came he trembled like an aspen leaf. In vain did Emmeline conceal her own emotion to speak to him of bright days to come—in vain did his brave old uncle assure him that it would go hard with the Maguires and McMahons (were there none but they) an' they devised not some plan to convey the two safely to Ireland—" and then, Connor, my son," said the veteran warrior, " and then—you and Costelloe here will be in for the best of the sport—the best is all to come, and you'll meet the bloody villains with the red sword of vengeance in your hand—son of my heart, you will !" Poor Connor shook his head sadly, and then in silence they all parted—some in hope, some in fear, all in sorrow.

For some days after the departure of their best friends, Ma-

14

guire and McMahon were more or less buoyed up with the hope
of a speedy opportunity of returning to Ireland. Days past
away, however, and weeks, too, and still no nearer prospect of
escape, no message, no word of hope from home. Shifting about
from place to place amongst the few faithful Catholics who were
cognizant of their condition, continually in dread of detection,
and lamenting the risk incurred by those who sheltered them,
their life was as wretched as could well be imagined. The only
comfort they had was in being together, for the load of misery
shared between them was less intolerable, and when they talked
of the glorious. struggle going on at home, and cheered each
other with the hope of yet girding on the sword and taking their
rightful place in the van of Ulster's chivalry, then the grim,
ugly *present* faded from their view and they lived for a while in
a brilliant, stirring, dashing *future*—alas! never, never to·be
theirs!

One dark October night, as the story goes, when our fugitives
were once more a-hide in Smithson's house in Drury lane, Mc-
Mahon, contrary to the advice of his more timorous friend, put
his head out of the window to hail an oyster-wench whose sten-
torian lungs were waking the echoes of the half-deserted streets
in the vicinity. Responsive to the call, the woman approached
the window, the oysters were bought and paid for, and still no
appearance of Maguire's fears being justified. No look of surprise, no word of recognition escaped the dame as she stood
without in the dim light of a flickering oil-lamp a few yards distant. She even cracked a rude joke, as her money was told out,
touching the *fattening* nature of her oysters, in allusion to poor
Costelloe's haggard face, looking the while as stolid as a circus-
clown.

No sooner, however, was the pale handsome face withdrawn,
and the window closed, than the Englishwoman planted her dis-
engaged arm a-kimbo, and said to herself with a low exulting
laugh : " My fortune is made now anyhow—as sure as my name
is Betsy Brigg that 'ere chap is one of them Irish traitors as
escaped from the Tower. Step out now, Betsy, lass! an' it be
so, thou may'st fling thy basket into the moat !"

Hours before the wintry sun shone out through the fogs of

London, Connor Maguire and Costelloe McMahon were again
in the hands of the pious Master Conyers, and Betsy Brigg was
the richer for that night's work by a thousand marks.

"Now, God have mercy on our souls!" whispered McMahon
in Irish, as the officers dragged the luckless prisoners down the
narrow stair-way; "it is all over with us, friend of my heart!"

"Don't say that, Costelloe!" returned Maguire in a voice of
terror; "don't say it is all over—God is good!"

"I know that, Connor,—I know He *will* be good to our poor
souls,—but, depend on it, He hath delivered our bodies to the
will of the enemy! Ha! you base-born churl!"—in English to
one of the constables who had given him a crack over the
shoulders to hurry him on—"you had not dared to do so were it
not for these fetters! Ay! do your worst—the nobleness of our
blood though it move not your pity, doth raise us above complaint! Have courage, my poor friend, my more than brother!"

Maguire could not answer: stunned by the crushing blow
which had in an instant, as it were, annihilated all their hopes,
he gave himself up to despair. Just as they were parting, however, at the inner gate of the Tower, he called out, as if by a
spasmodic effort:

"Pray for me, McMahon, as I will for you!"

"I will, Connor, I will!—if we meet no more in *this* world,
farewell!—God be with you! By our Lady, our death wil
make somewhat of a stir at home—methinks Uriel and Fermanagh will be in the van when the red day of vengeance cometh!"
He was silenced by a blow on the mouth from the mailed hand
of an official. Oh! the torture of that moment when the proud
McMahon could only chastise the wretch by a look, hand and
foot were both fettered! But such a look was that, so scathing
in its concentrated fire, that the cowardly caitiff slunk away
behind his fellows, unwilling to encounter that withering eye
again.

A few weeks after that, the prisoners were brought to trial,
and poor McMahon, convicted of the deadly crime of "Papistry"
and with the lesser one of "wickedly conspiring against the
peace of the realm," was sentenced to be "hanged, drawn, and
quartered" on the hill of Tyburn.

316 THE CONFEDERATE CHIEFTAINS.

Right nobly did the Tanist of Uriel bear himself during the mockery of a trial, and when the judge asked him as usual what he had to say why sentence of death should not be passed upon him, he smiled with bitter scorn and replied:

"Nought have I to say to you!—to the Judge of judges I answer for my acts! He knoweth and seeth all, and He will avenge me and mine in the latter day—I am, by God's mercy, a Roman Catholic, unworthy though I be of the name, and I *did* desire to see my country freed—these be my offences—of these I am guilty—proceed then to judgment!"

"Had you, or had you not, a commission to levy war against the lawful authority of these realms?—answer truly as you hope for mercy!"

Again the scornful smile lit up the shrunken features of poor Costelloe: "Mercy! I look not for mercy at the hands of English judges other than the mercy shown to my fathers in times past, but on the faith of an Irish gentleman I know of no commission—heard of no commission save in your questioning. This I said on the rack in Dublin, this say I now before a hostile court. Though King Charles hath not dealt fairly by us Catholics, yet will I not wrong him—God save the king from the hands of his enemies—we owe him no thanks, but we know him for our true and lawful sovereign, and will not belie him —God forbid! I say again, proceed to judgment—I would know the worst at once."

The worst was soon known, and McMahon heard the iniquitous sentence without the slightest change of countenance. A shade paler he might have grown as he listened, but nor look nor word betrayed any emotion of fear. Cold and calm he was, and his blue eyes wandered with a strangely indifferent look over the grim array of scowling faces before, and above, and around him.

"Hanged, drawn, and quartered!" he repeated slowly, as though to himself. "It is well—the *manner* of my death surely is not over creditable—but the shame is with *them*—not with me! My soul to God," he said in a loud clear voice, "my cause to the Confederate Catholics of Ireland!—Heaven prosper their righteous efforts!—May I have a priest to prepare me for death?"

"Surely no—it were the worst cruelty to grant you such a boon."

"Then God himself will be my priest!" and nothing more did McMahon say. He was taken some days after to Tyburn and executed according to the sentence, maintaining to the last the same bold and fearless spirit that had marked him through life —the hand that had made grotesque sketches on Borlase's walls, while awaiting his first trial, never trembled on the gallows when the hangman stood by McMahon's side, and a brutal, pitiless mob gazed up with eager eyes, curious to see how an Irish rebel died.

Poor Costelloe McMahon! bold, brave, light-hearted Costelloe McMahon! he died as became his high lineage and the noble cause for which he so freely gave his life. He died as became a Catholic cavalier, rejecting with scorn the offer of a minister to pray with him—

> "A beam of light fell o'er him,
> Like a glory round he shriven,
> And he climb'd the lofty ladder,
> As it were the path to heaven!"

Signing himself with the cross on forehead, lip and breast, he bent his head a moment and clasped his hands, then made a sign to the hangman and was speedily launched into eternity, while the crowd below, wondering at such marvellous fortitude and resignation, forbore to hoot or revile, as was their wont when Papists were executed.

And how was it with Lord Maguire while his companion in misfortune was thus expiating on the gallows the enormous crime of being a Catholic and a lover of his country?

Maguire, after all, was not so easily disposed of as his friend, notwithstanding his want of that physical energy, and that exuberant flow of spirits which were characteristic of poor McMahon. It so happened, then, that Connor Maguire, Lord Enniskillen, being placed at the bar, did most unreasonably and unexpectedly protest against any such trial, demanding to be tried by his peers in Ireland, inasmuch as a baron of that kingdom could not lawfully be tried in an English court of law.

Great was the surprise of the judges, and great, too, was their

disappointment, for they had humanely counted on making short
work of the two "pestiferous Papists," never thinking, in their
sweet simplicity, that an Irish peer would dare to claim the
prerogative due to his class. The plea was, however, unanswerable, at least for the time, and so the judges were forced to
remand the prisoner to his dungeon. Poor Connor! he naturally
supposed he had gained an advantage, seeing that a trial in Dublin might give him some chance for life, and straightway hope
began to revive, and gleams, faint and far, shed a dim light on
the dreary darkness of his soul. The fate of his companion was
well known to him, for his tyrants took care that he *should* know
it, and knowing, see in it the consummation of his own sufferings. Under other circumstances he would have been inconsol-
able for Costelloe's melancholy end, for the friendship from
boyhood existing between them had been fostered by commu-
nity of suffering and misfortune into more than brotherly love:
now he almost envied his fate, in that the ghastly death-scene
was over, and all the horrors of suspense and bodily fear, and
the thousand, thousand tortures of their hard captivity. And
then he thought of Emmeline, and how she would feel on hearing of his being re-captured, and he wondered whether there
was still any possibility of her being able to assist him, and hope
whispered faint and low that there *was* still a chance, and Connor listened to the beguiling voice until he half believed its
"flattering tale." If he could only have his trial take place in
Dublin before the peers, many of whom had been his own friends
and associates in former days—surely—surely he might expect
a measure of justice at their hands which in that Puritan English court was beyond the range of probability.

In the most fearful of all suspense, with the fate of McMahon
staring him in the face, haunting his feverish slumbers by night,
and oppressing his heart by day, Maguire lay in his noisome
cell, buoyed up with the one solitary hope of being removed to
Dublin for trial. As time rolled on, and the dark, dreary days
of a London winter grew into weeks and they into months,
without any change in his affairs, poor Connor took it as a favorable sign, and the gleam of hope grew stronger from day to

day. He little knew the doggedness (so to say) of English hate. The Puritans had not forgotten him in his cell.

The spring time came on, and a certain Mr. Justice Bacon took it upon him to decide that "a Baron of Ireland was triable by a jury in England!" Oh, wise Mr. Justice Bacon! learned in the law wert thou and well instructed in the ways of persecution!—and thy *dictum* was of course received as law and a special act passed by the Parliament to make it so. Alas! poor Connor Maguire! his enemies had no mind to give him the chance which a trial by his peers on Irish soil might afford him.

On the 10th day of February, Lord Maguire was again arraigned before an English judge and jury. His case had been so long before the public that it had come to excite more interest than most others of the kind,—common as they were in those evil days;—and so the court was densely crowded. And there in the dock, before that curious multitude of strangers, stood the young chieftain of Fermanagh, tall, and thin, and very pale, his long auburn locks parted in the middle and hanging down at either side almost to his shoulders, after the manner of the old Irish. Whether through derision, or in order to excite the anti-Irish prejudices of the spectators more and more, he was clothed in the habiliments wherein he was first captured, carefully preserved, it would seem, for the purpose, though worn almost to tatters during his year's imprisonment in Dublin. It was the intention of his persecutors, doubtless, to make him ridiculous, but in that they failed, for never had Connor Maguire looked more noble than he did standing at the bar, with his old faded cloak wrapped around his tall slender form, and a calm self-possession visible in his manner that gave him an air of true dignity. Not without a shudder did he find himself *again* at the bar with neither counsel to defend him, nor, as he had reason to believe, one friendly soul amongst the vast crowd that filled the court. He looked up to the judges—dark stern men they were, with unmistakeably Puritan faces—he looked to the jury-box—what he saw there was not more encouraging—then fear came upon his soul, and hope well nigh vanished, and cold sweat oozed from every pore, and Connor

felt as though his limbs were suddenly failing him, and the
sight of his eyes growing dim.

> " The fear of death was on him,
> And despair was in his soul—"

It was but for a moment—he prayed for strength and strength
was given him, and the love of life prompted him to struggle
even then against the fate which he so much dreaded. Shaking
off by an almost superhuman effort the weakness inherent in
his nature, he bestirred himself to note what was going forward,
condensing all his faculties into observation. God and himself,
he thought, were all he had to depend upon, and he rallied all
his powers to meet the terrible exigency. Nerved and excited
by this stern necessity, Connor Maguire displayed during his
trial an amount of ingenuity surprising to behold, together with
a knowledge of the English law little to be expected from an
Irish chieftain of that day. Every objection that a skilful lawyer
could make was made by him; every turn and twist of the law
was successively employed; every handle it offered, eagerly laid
hold of—alas! in vain, in vain, those safeguards of British justice were never meant to benefit a "pestilent Irish Papist!" they
were no protection to Connor Maguire.

Being arraigned, as we have said, he first demanded time to
have his witnesses brought from Ireland.

"What can your witnesses say for you?" was the strange
reply, and the demand was sternly refused.

"I humbly desire to have a formal trial," said the chieftain——

"In what respect do you mean?" responded the judge with
sweet simplicity. "You are now arraigned—evidence will be
brought against you—I conceive that is a formal trial——"

What could the prisoner say to such reasoning as this?

The jury was then called, and Lord Maguire challenged the
whole panel, "for causes best known to himself." No other
answer could be got from him, and so for that day the trial was
postponed.

It was only for a day. On the following day his lordship was
again brought up for trial. Another jury was summoned, and

this time the chieftain's indignation could not be concealed under legal forms. He again challenged the jury, and being asked his reasons, replied:

"Under favor, I conceive, that my lands being sequestered, those men that have bought my lands should not pass upon my trial; and, therefore, I desire that they make answer to it, upon oath, whether any of them have adventured or not."

It was not without reason that the wronged and plundered nobleman spoke thus—he saw, doubtless, impanneled on his jury, some of the very men who were most interested in putting him out of the way, and hence his honest indignation. His object was overruled, however, on the shallow pretence that a general challenge such as that was not admissible. Still Connor persevered, unwilling to submit to such outrageous mockery of justice when his life was at stake.

"I beseech you hear me in it," he said with touching earnestness.

But hear him they would not—the jury was impanneled, such as it was—the trial went on—evidence was not wanting to prove Lord Maguire an arrant Papist and a noted rebel—the latter being a necessary consequence of the former.

Amongst the witnesses brought over from Ireland were Sir William Cole, late governor of Enniskillen, Sir Arthur Loftus,* and Lord Blayney. What manner of evidence these loyal planters gave it is easy to imagine, but lone and desolate as poor Connor felt, and withal burning with indignation, he could not refrain from smiling as he heard Cole gravely relate how Captain Roderick Maguire had expelled him from his post with small ceremony, and "taken upon him the managing of all business."

"Heaven bless you, my gallant brother!" he said within himself, "you were thinking of your poor Connor then—was I within your reach it would take strong walls to keep you from me, oh, Rory! bravest of Fermanagh's sons! Should I perish now, it is something to know that there is one to revenge the wrongs of all our race!"

* It has been aptly said that amongst the present possessors of "the land of the waters" are men with these very same names

Lord Blayney, examined on the treasonable religion of the prisoner, not only established his guilt in that particular but also that of his supposed friends in Ireland.

" Lord Fingal," said he, " is a Papist, and Clanmorris a pestiferous Papist."

" What! all Papists!" exclaimed Sergeant Whitfield in holy horror; " good Lord deliver us !"   .

The evidence was, of course, conclusive.   Touching the matter of " the conspiracy," the judges deliberately stated that Lord Maguire had acknowledged it on his first examination.   This he positively denied, whereupon the written deposition was brought forward, and Whitfield said :

" There it is under my Lord Maguire's own hand."

" Truly my name is thereto appended," said the unfortunate nobleman, "but *not* in my own hand."

On this Lord Blayney was again called to prove the handwriting.   "Beyond a doubt," said he, " that is my lord's hand—I have had many letters from him."

"I crave your lordship's pardon," said poor Connor ; " I know not that you have had many letters from me."   The confusion visible on Blayney's face went, of course, for nothing.   What though he dared not meet the eye of the astonished prisoner, and slunk from the box with the hang-dog expression of conscious guilt visible on every feature !

" I would not exchange places with that man," said Maguire in an audible voice ; " no, not for what he holdeth of McMahon's country !"

Alas! *truth* was not expedient in that court—the evidence was, of course, inco: testible (so said the judges!), and on that evidence "Connor, *alias* Cornelius Maguire, commonly called Lord Enniskillen," was found *guilty*, and summoned to receive his sentence.

Sentence !—sentence of death ! oh ! the agony of that thought.   The blow so long delayed was then about to fall— death in its most hideous form was close at hand—a death of public shame.   For a moment Maguire was overcome—his faculties were benumbed and speech forsook his lips.   Was there, then, no hope ?   Raising his eyes to the bench of judges he marked the cold, contemptuous stony look on every face, and somehow the sight roused him from his stupor.

"I desire to know," said he, "by what law I am condemned."

"The law is well enough known," was the judge's answer.

"I was not tried by my peers," persisted the Irish lord.

"You put in that plea before, the which was overruled."

"I desire counsel to advise me thereon."

This was shortly refused. "Your time is past for counsel. You must have none assigned to pick holes in the indictment."

Other legal objections poor Connor made, displaying a degree of tact and ingenuity that must have astonished even his judges, but all were met in the same spirit—dry, cold, peremptory. Every point was "overruled," and "said Connor, *alias* Cornelius Maguire, commonly called Lord Enniskillen," was sentenced to be hanged, drawn, and quartered, as his companion had been before.

Hearing this, a mortal paleness overspread Maguire's face. "This, then, is the end of all my hopes," he murmured, and bowing his head on his chest, he remained for a moment motionless. What passed within his soul during that moment was only known to God and himself, but suddenly he stood erect and glanced silently up at the judges with a calm and earnest look.

Seeing that the prisoner remained silent, the question was then put to him whether he would have any ministers to pray with him, "and advise him for the good of his soul."

"I desire none of them," made answer the prisoner, "but I desire I may be sent prisoner to Newgate."

"Ay," said the King's Counsel, "his reason is, because there are some Popish priests there."

"It cannot be," said the Judge, "your sentence is to return to the Tower, where you may have ministers, if you will, to advise you on your soul."

"I desire the attendance of a priest of my own religion."

Quite impossible! He was told to prepare for death on the following Saturday.

"I desire a fortnight's time to prepare."

"You cannot have a fortnight."

" I desire three days' notice."

That as a special favor was granted, and Maguire, perchance, a little encouraged by the concession, ventured to request that he might be executed in some other way than hanging, " the which," said he, " is unbecoming my rank as a peer of Ireland."

But no! this was too great a favor—the high-born chief of the Clan Maguire, the accomplished " peer of Ireland," must needs be executed like a common felon—the more degrading his end, the better it pleased his remorseless enemies.

He was removed from the bar, and then a fresh attack was made on his religion. He was advised to confer speedily with some godly minister " for the good and comfort of his soul."

" I say I'll none of them," replied the chieftain ; " an' I be not allowed a priest of the Catholic Church, I will have no minister !"

" Think better of it, my lord," said a certain Mr. Prynne, one of the leading functionaries who had before enlightened the court with the information that the prisoner had neither lands nor livings in Ireland! " Think better of it—these Popish priests are they whose counsels have led you to this shameful end which you so much appear to dread. Since they have been such destructive counsellors to you in your lifetime, you would do well to discard them and their bloody religion, and to seek better advisers at your death, lest you eternally lose your soul."

Without a moment's hesitation, Maguire replied, " My mind is made up. I am resolved in my own way."

" My lord," said another of the lawyers present, " you were best to hear both sides."

" I have told you," said the chieftain haughtily, " that I am settled in my own faith—I desire no speech of any minister."

He was then conveyed once more to the Tower, and during the nine days that elapsed before the closing scene, he resolutely drove away all worldly thoughts and affections. Even of Emmeline he did not dare to think, although at times the question would protrude itself between him and his devotions. " Hath she, at last, given me up ?—doth she shrink from the condemned

felon? It matters not now who holdeth me in remembrance or
who doth not! My God to me and I to Him!"

His petition to be executed as became a nobleman having
been forwarded to parliament, was by that body disdainfully
rejected, and on the 20th day of February the noble chief of
the Maguires was drawn on a sledge through London to the
fatal hill of Tyburn, so often stained with the blood of the brave
and good. Arrived there, the prisoner was placed in a cart,
where he knelt " and prayed a while."

Having so often declared his intention to have no minister at
his death-hour, it might be supposed that his enemies would
have ceased their importunities on that head. Not so, however,
not so. The Sheriff, good pious man! must needs try his hand
on the Popish lord.

" Do you believe you did well," said he, " in those wicked
actions ?"

" I have but a short time—do not trouble me !"

" Sir, it is but just I should trouble you, that you may not be
troubled for ever !" oh! zealous and most charitable Mr. Sheriff
Gibbs!

"I beseech you, sir, trouble me not," said the poor prisoner
again; " I have but little time to spend."

But the Sheriff insisting, would have had him acknowledge
himself in the wrong in what he did, for the satisfaction, as he
said, of the people.

" I beseech you do not trouble me !" still said the persecuted
sufferer; " I am not disposed to give you an account. Pray
give me leave to pray !"*

Oh! the grandeur, the majesty of Maguire's mien as he
uttered those words—" Pray give me leave to pray !" Surely
more touching words were never spoken by human lip. There
was all the humility of the Christian mingled with supreme
contempt of his persecutors and their impotent assaults.

A new tack was then taken—the Commission again ?—had he,

* In this short account of the trial, I have given the noble-hearted
chief's exact words. They are too sublime in their lofty simplicity
to be lightly altered. I give them verbatim from the published account of his trial.

or knew he of others having any commission—"who were actors or plotters with you, or gave you any commission?"

"For God's sake give me leave to depart in peace."

All this while Maguire had been looking intently on a piece of paper which had been thrust into his hand as he left the Tower Gate. As he looked, his eye brightened and his whole aspect changed. What was in the paper? There was a short selection of thoughts and reflections befitting that awful moment, together with some brief ejaculatory prayers suitable for the occasion. But there was more, oh! far more than these, there was a brief note from a priest, who signed himself his "friend William," to the effect that as he was deprived of the opportunity of confessing his sins, he should not want the consolations of religion. On a sign specified, this good priest who had ridden many a weary mile for that purpose, was to give him absolution from his place amongst the spectators. To encourage him the more the appearance of the priest was clearly indicated. He was to sit "on a red horse, in a white hat and a grey jacket," and lest this good "friend William" should meet with any mischance, the presence of two or three other priests was intimated, so that the prisoner could not fail to secure the "plenary physic" for his soul at his departure on his last journey. The sign agreed upon was that Maguire was to raise his hand to his face and bow down his head. "I beseech you, dear sir," said the letter, "be of good courage, for you shall not want anything for that happy journey, and offer you yourself wholly for Him, who did the same for you."

And so Maguire did, and hence the nobleness of his end.

Mr. Sheriff Gibbs, thwarted in his pious designs, ordered the prisoner's pockets to be searched. They contained nothing but his beads and crucifix, which Connor eagerly took hold of.

"Come, my lord!" said one of the officials, pointing to these sacred objects, "leave these and acknowledge your offence to God and the world. It is not your *Ave Marias* nor those things will do you any good."

Maguire heeded not his impertinence, but calmly turning to the people who were present in crowds to see the spectacle, he spoke these memorable words:

"Since I am here to die, I desire to depart with a quiet mind, and with the marks of a good Christian, that is, asking forgiveness first of God, and next of the world. And I do forgive (from .the bottom of my heart) all my enemies and offenders, even those that have an hand in my death. I die a Roman Catholic, and although I have been a great sinner, yet am I now, by God's grace, heartily sorry for all my sins, and I do most confidently trust to be saved (not by my own works), but only by the passion, merits, and mercy of my dear Saviour Jesus Christ, into whose hand I commend my soul."

"Prepare for death!" said the harsh voice of Sheriff Gibbs.

Connor Maguire bent his stately head a moment and closed his eyes while he made his act of contrition, then slowly raised his right hand to his face and murmured, "Absolve me, O Lord, from my sins—cleanse my soul with Thy precious blood!"

"The moment is come!" said Sheriff Gibbs.

Lord Maguire turned for the last time to the people: "I do beseech," said he, "all the Catholics that are here to pray for me—I beseech God to have mercy on my soul!"

They were his last words. The fatal noose was on his neck. A few minutes more and his half-dead body was cut down and quartered, and another bright name was added to the glorious list of Irish martyrs.

Comment on such a death were superfluous, but who can help remarking the wondrous change wrought by Divine grace in the character of this truly noble son of the Maguires? Who could recognize in that stern confessor of the faith the timid and vacillating guest of O'Moore, whose extreme caution and (as it seemed) pusillanimous fears would have crushed in its infancy the great struggle for freedom?

Before that Puritan English Court his character assumed another development, he was there the subtle disputant, pleading his own cause with marvellous skill—fighting the enemy with his own weapons, and struggling like a drowning man for life.

He perished in the flower of his years—a martyr to the sacred cause of civil and religious freedom, and surely the proud ancestral tree of "the Maguires, sons of the waters," has given no name to Irish history so dear as that of Connor.

CHAPTER XXVI.

"Who on his staff is this? who is this whose head is white with
age; whose eyes are red with tears; who quakes at every step."

*   *   *   *   *   *

"Who comes from Strumon," they said, "amid her wandering
locks? She is mournful in her steps, and lifts her blue eyes towards
Erin? Why art thou sad, Evir-Choma? who is like thy chief in
renown?"   MacPherson's *Poems of Ossian.*

MEANWHILE great events were going on in Ireland. The
fatal truce was scrupulously observed by the Confederates as
regarded the armies of the king, but Monroe, with an army of
17,000 men, held for the Parliament in Ulster. The double-
dyed traitor, Inchiquin, had also declared for the same cause in
Munster, moved thereto by anger for the king's bestowing the
Presidency of that Province on the Earl of Portland, whereas
he had gone over to England for the special purpose of soliciting that office from his Majesty at Oxford. Here, then,
were two powerful armies of "Covenanting carls" to be encountered by the Confederates during the period of the Cessation
with Ormond. As regarded the latter nobleman, the king had
shown his satisfaction at the successful issue of the negotiations,
by appointing him to the office of Lord Lieutenant, in room of
the Earl of Leicester, who had discharged none of its functions,
having never gone over to Ireland. There was Ormond, then,
at the head of the Irish government, uniting in his own person
the civil and military command, and, shame to tell! many of
the Anglo-Irish Confederates were seen creeping once more into
the capital and hanging about the Court, a fitting sequel to the
degrading scene at Jigginstown.* Still did the chieftains of the

---

* The advantages derived by Ormond from his able diplomacy may old blood keep jealously aloof, maintaining that independence so honorable to them, and mourning in secret over the blind infatuation which allowed Ormond to bring about that unlucky Cessation. As regarded the Confederates the pernicious effects of that measure were every day becoming more apparent The generals had found themselves unable to keep their soldiers from taking leave of absence and rambling about the country hither and thither under one pretence or another, to the no small detriment of their clothes, and other equipments, their horses, and all the rest. The armies were, therefore, more or less broken up, and when corps were got together again, they were, in some instances, hardly fit for service. The ships, too, that had been chartered by the Council, and done such good service in protecting the coasts, landing men and ammunition from foreign countries, and in various ways contributed largely to the success of the Confederates, now betook themselves whence they came, their services being, as it were, no longer needed. Their place was immediately supplied by shoals of the Parliamentary cruisers of every size (sailing under orders to spare neither man nor woman of the Irish), so that the coast was completely bombarded, and all communication with the Continent well nigh cut off.

These were serious misfortunes in themselves, but to make matters worse, the Supreme Council must needs send off 3,000 of its best men, together with considerable store of arms and provisions to Scotland, to aid the gallant Montrose in his chivalrous efforts to maintain the royal authority. Little as the faithless Charles deserved it from them, and albeit that the Council acted unwisely in sending them abroad at such a time on such an errand, the career of those brave Irish regiments in Scotland undoubtedly added a glorious page to the military history of our race. They were commanded by a Catholic Ilesman

---

be collected from the fact, that hitherto the Confederate ships intercepted all supplies, and left Dublin in such a state, that upon search being made in the city and suburbs there could not be found fourteen days' provisions for the inhabitants and soldiers.— Sir P. Percival's *Statement*, quoted by Meehan.

named Alexander McDonnell, the Colkitto of Scottish story,
under whose guidance they performed prodigies of valor during
that disastrous war in Scotland—

> " What time the plaided clans came down
>   To battle with Montrose."

The heroic devotion wherewith these chivalrous Irish soldiers
fought for a king to whom they, as Catholics, owed so little gratitude, must have touched the unhappy monarch, and opened his
eyes as to who were his true friends.

About the same time the Supreme Council, with a just appreciation of the services of Father Luke Wadding, sent an
agent to Rome to solicit his Holiness to elevate that eminent ecclesiastic to the rank of cardinal.* There is little doubt that
Urban VIII. would have conferred that high dignity on a man
for whom he had ever manifested the highest esteem, but if
such were his intention death prevented him from carrying it
out—that great and good Pontiff died during that disastrous
year†—the Confederate Catholics of Ireland lost one of their
best and truest friends, and, in all probability, the Irish nation
missed the opportunity of having a Prince of the Church to
boast of.

The memorial sent to Rome on behalf of Luke Wadding contained also a most interesting account of the state of Catholicity
in Ireland at that precise period, which must have given no
small contentment to the closing days of Urban. From that
document we will give an extract without other apology for so
doing than the cheering picture it presents of what the Confederates had achieved :

"It is now manifest to the whole Christian world with what
fidelity the Catholics of Ireland have clung to their ancient
faith, and how they braved death, and exile, and the confisca-
tion of their substance, rather than renounce the religion of

---

* See McGee's *Gallery of Irish Writers*—Life of Luke Wadding.
† Urban VIII. died in July, 1644, and was succeeded by Innocent
X., on the 15th of September.

their ancestors. To you, most holy Father, it is particularly known how heroically the Irish people, without arms or munitions of war, have struggled against the phalanxes of those who, sworn enemies of the Holy See, had vowed and sworn to pluck up our religion by the very roots. Our holy war has had a glorious result. The Lord God is now publicly worshipped in our temples, after the manner of our fathers; most of the cathedrals have been restored to our bishops; the religious orders possess the monasteries, and seminaries have been opened for the education of our youth. This great work has been accomplished through the goodness of God, and the many favors bestowed on us by you; verily in future times the brightest page in the history of your pontificate shall be, that you found the Catholic religion despised and prostrate in our island, and ere that pontificate closed beheld it raised up in splendor, and magnificently attired, even as a bride for her spouse."

All this had been effected by the Catholic soldiers of Ireland during the three or four years which had elapsed since that memorable 23d of October when the war-fires first blazed on the hills of Ulster. Alas! that Ormond's insidious diplomacy could undo by slow degrees what Catholic valor had so brilliantly won, and that dissensions should arise amongst men united for the holiest of purposes. By union, all this marvellous success had been gained, by the disunion which Ormond succeeded in introducing into their ranks, we shall see how it fared with the Confederates.

Towards the close of the year's truce, the Supreme Council being then sitting at Waterford began to discuss the propriety of pawning that portion of the kingdom which the Confederates held in order to obtain money for carrying on the war.‡ Owen Roe, being then in Waterford on business with the Council, was summoned before it to give his opinion, a proof that his character for wisdom was at least equal to his military fame. He heard the proposal with his usual calmness, but a frown gathered on his brow.

"What!" said he, "pawn the land which our swords have

‡ Meehan's *Confederation*

won! The soil that is watered with our soldiers' blood!—my lords and gentlemen, I will never consent to it——"

" But how are we to carry on the war?" demanded the Archbishop of Dublin.

" How have we carried it on up to the present?—pardon me, my lord, an' I speak over sharply—but I thought all this honorable council must needs feel as I do that help hath been sent us from Sion, and that He who hath given is still powerful to give. No, my lords and brother Confederates, I for one will never consent to give any foreign power an interest in Ireland. Beg and even borrow, an' ye will, but *pawn*—faugh! I like not the word! it savors of such distress as hath not yet fallen to our lot, nor *shall*, with Heaven's good aid!"

Most of the bishops being of the same mind the proposal was finally rejected, and soon after, the Council returned to Kilkenny. By that time the news of the execution of Maguire and McMahon had arrived, and the most lukewarm of the Anglo-Irish were roused for a season into something like fervor, and half regretted the Cessation. The northern clans, especially those of Fermanagh and Uriel, could with difficulty be restrained from bursting simultaneously on the enemy, and by one bold stroke securing victory and revenge.

The vengeful fury of McMahon and Maguire was shared, as might be expected, by Sir Phelim O'Neill, ever opposed to his kinsman's systematic and cautious mode of warfare, and when Owen Roe, as usual, employed his supreme authority on the side of order and deliberation, the chieftains, so terribly aggrieved, could not help accusing him of coldness and want of feeling. Their dissatisfaction was well known to Owen, and he summoned them all to meet him at Charlemont where he explained at some length his plans for the future, whereby their wrongs would be more effectually revenged than by a wild, disorderly onslaught which might well end in their own destruction and the ruin of their cause.

" Before God this day," said he, " I feel your wrongs as my own. Costelloe McMahon I knew abroad, and held in high esteem ; Maguire, by his heroic death, hath covered himself with glory (as indeed they both did), and made his name dear

to all of us. Death was gain to them, but, natheless, friends
and brothers, they have left us a debt to pay, and it will go
hard with us an' we pay it not. The day of vengeance will
come, so sure as my name is Owen O'Neill, and it will come all
the surer and mayhap all the sooner, will you but restrain your
lawful anger until I give you the word—then—then, chieftains
of Ulster, I swear you may work your will and revenge your
wrongs with one crushing blow! Nay, Sir Phelim!"—and rising,
he waved his hand majestically—"nay, thus shall it be—seek
not, I charge you, to stir up strife—there be enough of it, and
too much, in the Confederate camp, thanks to Ormond's trick-
ery—let us of the old blood—here in Ulster—have peace
amongst us that a blessing may rest on our arms. What say
you, McMahon? and you, my young friend?" to Rory Maguire.
"Shall we dishonor ourselves by violating this Cessation, agreed
on in our name, though without our consent—or suffer it to ex-
pire, after the manner of honorable men, and then settle our
account in our own way and at our own time?"

Whilst Maguire and McMahon, but half convinced, withdrew
into a corner to confer together, the trumpet at the gate announced an arrival, and very soon after a singular apparition
greeted the eyes of the assembled chieftains. Grim and ghastly
as a warrior of old arisen from the tomb, with his grizzled elf-
locks hanging in wild disorder from under the rim of his *bor-
radh*, and his eyes glittering with unnatural brightness, Lorcan
Maguire strode up the hall wrapped in his war-cloak, and leading by the hand a lady of rare beauty, attired in the deepest
mourning of that day. The palor of death was on her face, and
in her eyes a settled look of despair that was pitiful to behold
in one so lovely and so young.

Involuntarily all the chieftains rose as this vision of beauty
and of woe appeared before them. The sight of Lorcan was no
great surprise of itself, for the old man, since his return from
London, had been going about amongst the chiefs endeavoring
to stir them up.

"Rory Maguire!" said the old man as his quick eye sought
out his nephew, "come hither, Rory! and welcome the beloved
of Connor—her story is not unknown to thee!"

In an instant Roderick Maguire was by the lady's side, and he took her offered hand with the reverence due to a superior being, the while tears rushed unbidden to his eyes, and the color mounted to his cheek.

"Welcome!" he murmured in a faltering voice; "welcome! fair Emmeline—more than sister!"

"Thanks, Roderick!' spoke the pale fair mourner after a moment's pause; "thanks, brother of Maguire! I am here to speak with Owen Roe and the northern leaders—which, I pray you, is Owen Roe?"

"Lady, he stands before you!" said O'Neill stepping forward, and bowing with that grave courtesy which became a gentleman of rank. "Deign to honor me with your commands!"

"Courteous chief," said Emmeline, raising her heavy eyes to his, then glancing timidly around on the stately circle, "I come to seek for justice and revenge at your hands. Justice mocked and outraged in an English Court—revenge for the blood of MAGUIRE and his friend! I have carried my sorrows to Kilkenny, and told my dismal tale before the grand Assembly of the Confederates; the proud Norman lords listened with cold indifference, or faintly spoke of 'submission to the law,' 'Cessation,' and I wot not what—the murder of those innocent men under the guise of justice moved them not at all, or so little that I lost all hope of redress from them, and so I turned my weary steps northward, sure of finding amongst Maguires and McMahons, and the other valiant septs of Ulster, the ear to hear and the arm to right their kinsmen's wrongs! Chiefs! I stand before you the betrothed of Connor Maguire—have I journeyed hither in vain?"

Most of those present had heard in one way or another the story of Emmeline's ill-fated love and her more than womanly devotion, and now when she appeared before them in the majesty of her beauty and her sorrow to plead the cause of one whom they had all loved, their hearts swelled with pity and with admiration.

"By the sword of Heber, no!" said McMahon, with a reproachful glance at Owen Roe; "foul shame it is that no move is taken in that matter, and, on the word of a chieftain, gentle lady! the fault rests not with us of Uriel or Fermanagh. Had we our way you should have heard ere now of a terrible revenge, and as God liveth, no human power can keep us in much longer——"

"Art! Art! have patience!" said Owen Roe, "nurse your wrath yet awhile as I have told you, and for every drop of Costelloe's blood you shall have satisfaction! Lady!" turning to Emmeline, "I crave your pardon, an' my speech be over free but I would know how your brother, Sir Charles Coote, doth regard your passages with our friend deceased——"

"My *brother!*" repeated the lady with startling vehemence, "speak not of him I charge you! he is henceforth no brother of mine!—were it not for him I might, as I purposed, have made yet another attempt to save the life that was dearer far than my own—my inventive powers were not exhausted, and I *might* have succeeded—but—but—" here she raised her hand to her head, made an effort to continue and failed, then turning to Lorcan, motioned for him to speak.

"When the Lady Emmeline reached Dublin," said the old man, " she went to visit her mother, and although she wanted none of her brothers to know she was there, and begged her mother to keep the secret, they found it out somehow, and before she knew what they were about, Sir Charles had her taken and put in the mad-house."

' In the mad-house!" cried many of the chiefs simultaneously in a voice of horror.

"Even so, noble gentlemen!" said Emmeline, with flashing eyes and burning cheeks. "An' ye doubt it—see here!" and raising the silken riding-hood from off her head, there was seen a close-fitting velvet cap which being, in its turn, removed not a vestige of hair was there. The head was closely shaved, and while the chieftains exchanged looks of wonder and compassion, Emmeline burst into a wild hysterical laugh.

"Ay! ye may stare!" she cried; "there is a sight to look upon. There was a day when the loss of the tresses so dearly prized would have well nigh driven me mad, but I miss them not at all now since *he* is dead, whom alone I wished to please. I care not, then, for my fair tresses—let them go and welcome—

but, oh! the maddening thought that the man who immured me
in a mad-house, and told them I was raving mad—that *that* man
should be my father's son!—oh! chiefs! and gallant gentlemen!
think of it!"

All hearts were moved by this sad appeal, and by a common
impulse every hand sought the sword or skene, while a low, deep
murmur ran through the assembly like the angry surge that
predicts the storm.

Owen O'Neill enjoined silence by a motion of his hand, then
calmly addressed the fair petitioner.

" Lady, suffice it to say, we are men and have hearts to feel"—
and suiting the action to the word he laid his hand on his own
heart—"Maguire and McMahon died for our cause—their memory
is dear to us—we will revenge their sufferings and death when
we can do it to our satisfaction, and believe me, fair daughter
of the Sassenach! the doleful tale we have heard but now will
nerve our arms with deadlier force in the hour of retribution."

"Thanks, most noble chieftain, thanks!" said Emmeline in a
voice half choked with sobs; "for myself I have renounced
kith and kin—my mother alone excepted, and as remaining with
her in Charles Coote's house were impossible, I demand a safe
and honorable asylum from the chivalrous sons of the Gael!"

Several of the chieftains stepped eagerly forward—Sir Phelim
to offer his mother's house, McMahon and O'Reilly the protection of their respective wives, and Magennis that of a maiden
sister, who kept house by herself at Dromore-Iveagh.   Owen
Roe fixed his thoughtful eyes on the lady, while Lorcan at one
side and Roderick at the other seized her hand.

"I would to Heaven, lady!" said Owen Roe, "that I could
promise you an asylum befitting your station and safe at the
same time as we could wish——"

"I pray you, general, heed not my rank—think only of my
necessities!"

"An' you are willing to endure hardship, sweet lady, and
shift your dwelling at the approach of danger, you shall not
want a fitting companion—you shall share the hard lot of O'Cahan's daughter!" This last was rather addressed to the chiefs,
and Lorcan Maguire exclaimed with some petulance:

" A pretty asylum that will be, lurking in holes and corners with poor old Father Phelimy—an obstinate piece of woman's flesh that same Judith always was !

" And still is," chimed in Sir Phelim, " or it isn't as she is she'd be now !"

" The general is right, natheless," said Roderick Maguire ; " Judith O'Cahan is of all women in Ulster the one to take charge of the Lady Emmeline——"

" Take charge of her !" repeated Owen O'Neill with a grave smile.

" Keep her company, I mean," said the young chieftain hastily.

" What ye judge best, that will I do," said Emmeline meekly. " Keep me amongst you, friends and kinsmen of Maguire, loyal knights and gentlemen, and I ask no more. *His* people are henceforth my people !"

" God bless you, my child, God bless you !" said old Lorean, pressing her hand with deep emotion; " I would go myself and protect you and Judith but the spirits of my race say otherwise. My place is evermore in the ranks of Owen's army, waiting, waiting for the day that will wipe out all our score against the Puritans, and then, Emmeline, my daughter, then old Lorean will go to his long home where the young and the brave are gone before him !"

Meanwhile Owen had sent for Donogh and Angus whom he knew were in the neighborhood of the Castle, and when they arrived he demanded if they knew where the Lady Judith was to be found.

" That we do full well, general," said the Rapparee captain, " herself and his reverence were with Captain Con's mother, poor lady! at Strabane, but yestermorn—I know not how long they may sojourn with her but there they be now."

" Better place could we not desire," said Owen cheerfully ; then turning to Emmeline: " Lady, you shall have a home such as I did not dare to hope for—one of the noblest matrons of the O'Neills—a mourner, too, like yourself—hath a house well garrisoned at Strabane, and with her is now the lady I spoke of as your fittest companion. An aged priest is of their company,

15

it is true"—he smiled sadly—" but that inconvenience we cannot remedy."

" Say not inconvenience, General O'Neill," said the lady earnestly ; " had Maguire lived I meant to embrace his religion—his martyrdom—as I needs must call it—hath but given me a new motive. I esteem it a signal favor from on high to obtain thus easily the needful instruction."

" In that case, lady, these faithful fellows"—pointing to the Rapparees—" will convey you thither in safety before the night falls. Nay, fear them not, though they bear the dreaded name of Rapparees. I have trusted them ere now with the keeping of some not inferior in nobleness or beauty even to the Lady Emmeline !" and he bowed with a smile all his own.

" Say it out, man !" cried the rough voice of Sir Phelim ; " we all know who you mean."

" I have said enough for my purpose, cousin mine," said Owen coldly ; " Donogh, to your care I confide this noble lady —take a party of your own, and escort her with all speed to the Castle of Strabane, greeting good Mistress Una from me, and—and—the Lady Judith—say I commend—all the chiefs commend—this noblest of English maidens to their good offices——"

" With your leave, general," said Roderick Maguire, "my uncle and I will be of the party—it behoves us to see the Lady Emmeline safe housed."

This new proposition gave general satisfaction, and before an hour had elapsed the strangely-assorted party set out for Strabane, the lady mounted on a handsome palfrey, the gift of Sir Phelim O'Neill.

Before the chiefs had come to any decision the news of Inchiquin's going over to the Parliament came with stunning effect, followed, as it soon after was, by the account of his horrible massacre at Cashel, where in one day he slew some thousands of the inhabitants who had betaken themselves to the Rock and its sacred buildings for safety when they heard of his approach. But to " Murrough of the burnings" no place was sacred, and so the shrine at which his fathers had worshipped—the Royal Cathedral of Thomond was desecrated that day by the blood of thousands of victims, amongst them some twenty priests who had taken refuge behind the high altar—and there were in humanly butchered.

About the same time fresh reinforcements arrived from Scotland to swell the army of General Monroe, who had publicly taken the covenant in Carrickfergus at the bidding of the English Parliament.* The forces under his command now numbered full twenty thousand, and the whole country was thrown into a state of consternation, knowing by experience that the war carried on under Puritan auspices was a war of utter extermination.

Owen Roe's army, like most of the others belonging to the Confederation, was in great part scattered and disorganized by the truce with Ormond, and when any number were brought together their discipline, their arms and accoutrements were all in bad repair. Whilst O'Neill was turning in his mind what he had best do under such discouraging circumstances, he was summoned to Kilkenny in all haste.

Arrived there he found the General Assembly in full session and all in a state of trepidation, because of the inundation of rebel Scots into various parts of the kingdom, and Inchiquin's desertion to that party with the army at his command. "He was bad and very bad as a Royalist, what will he be as a covenanting rebel?"

"Could *you* but deal with Monroe in Ulster," said some of the lords to Owen Roe, "so that he may not league with Inchiquin and Broghill in the south for our destruction!"

"I know not that I could meet him single-handed at the present time," said Owen; "thanks to your Cessation, my army is not what it was a year ago—very far from it."

"What is to be done, then?" said Lord Netterville curtly.

"Can you think of nothing, general?" inquired Mountgarret anxiously.

O'Neill paused a moment, then said with some hesitation, "could you spare me some assistance now?"

"How much would you think needful?"

* Meehan's *Confederation*, p. 90.

" Say four or five thousand foot, and as many hundreds of cavalry."

" You shall have it !" was the prompt reply, and orders were immediately issued for the equipment of such a force for Ulster.

Owen Roe, with all his calmness and indifference to selfish objects, was no little pleased with the thought that he should return to his own Province at the head of a trained and disciplined force, which, united with what he could muster at home, would place him in a position to advance against Monroe without further delay. Dispatches from home urged his return, one of them from Judith O'Cahan, who saw with alarm the daily-increasing power of the Scots, and feared, not without reason, a general massacre at their hands. Yet day after day Owen lingered in Kilkenny, hoping that the next would see him under orders for the north with his Leinster auxiliaries.

At length the wished-for summons came to appear before the Council, and with a beating heart Owen Roe obeyed. He stood before the lords and gentlemen in their hall, and heard from the lips of Lord Mountgarret the grave announcement that Lord Castlehaven had kindly consented to take the command of the Ulster army. Tirlogh O'Neill started quickly from his seat, anxious to explain that the appointment was not made with his will, or that of " any gentleman of the Council, of Irish blood."

Owen Roe silenced his friend by a gesture full of dignity, then turning, he bowed to the Assembly.

" It is well, lords and gentlemen of the Council !—far be it from me to say otherwise, seeing that my lord of Castlehaven hath won such good repute in this war. If he be but one-half as successful in Ulster as elsewhere I shall be well content. An' the Council have any commands for me I would have them, by nightfall, as I leave town early to-morrow. Master Tirlogh O'Neill, I would see you this evening at my lodgings in Patrick street—till then, God be with you."

Significant looks were exchanged amongst the Norman lords as the chieftain strode with a stately step down the hall. Many amongst them feared for the result of this ill-advised step, and

some were even for recalling O'Neill, and cancelling the appointment in his favor.

A heavy load was, therefore, taken from their hearts when
they heard that from the Council-hall, General O'Neill had
repaired to the lodgings of Castlehaven, and frankly congratu-
lated the peer on his new appointment.*

---

* Castlehaven's *Memoirs*, p. 46.

CHAPTER XXVII.

Now one's the better—then the other best,
Both tugging to be victor, breast to breast;
Yet neither conqueror or is conquer'd,
So is the equal pulse of this fell war."

SHAKESPEARE.

" Thou need'st not tell it ; he is dead.
God help us all this day !"

AYNTON.

THE appointment of Castlehaven to the command of the Ulster
auxiliaries took place early in May, 1615, and the two following
months of that summer were stirring and eventful ones for the
Confederate Catholics.   Owen Roe returned immediately to his
camp at Portlester awaiting the arrival of the Leinster troops,
but their coming was more tardy than he expected, for the
Supreme Council had found it necessary to dispatch Castlehaven
to Connaught, in the first place, to reduce some refractory
parties who would not submit to the Cessation.   It was July
before the Earl was at liberty to turn his attention to the northern Province, and then he marched to Granard, in the county
of Longford, with what forces he had at his command, the remaining portion of the army destined for Ulster being ordered to
meet him there.   He had hardly reached Granard, however,
when the news of Monroe's advance at the head of a powerful
army caused him to fall back hastily on Portlester, where he
formed a junction with O'Neill.

Monroe was not so near as Castlehaven had been informed,
and the army was preparing to march northward in order to
check, if possible, his devastating course, when all at once it
was found that detachments of his force were approaching in
different directions, stripping the country as they advanced of
everything in the shape of provisions.   The Confederates imme-

diately sent out parties to watch the motions of the enemy, and
so it happened that a line was formed by the advanced posts of
either army—while the main body, of the Scots especially, was
far behind. They at length approached each other so closely
that continual skirmishing was going on with varying success,
whilst the two Confederate generals were concerting means to
check the progress of Monroe. Still there was far from being that
cordial unanimity between them that might have been expected
from such close identity of interests.

It so happened that Owen Roe was attacked by a sudden indisposition on the very eve of a rather serious engagement, in
which the Confederates suffered severely. When the news
reached Owen on his sick-bed, and the particulars were made
known to him, he started to his feet, and though still far from
being well, he hastened to Lord Castlehaven's quarters.

"What is this I hear, my lord?" said O'Neill in an agitated
voice.

"That you ought to know best, General O'Neill!" said the
peer coldly. He was engaged at the moment in conversation
with some of his officers.

"Most likely your lordship knows it, too," said Owen with increasing agitation; "how came it to pass, I ask you, that in
this late affair, your officers stood by—ay! even yon cowardly
cock with the feather," pointing to a certain Colonel Fennell
who had been in command of the party, "whilst my kinsmen
were cut to pieces by the enemy? How was it, I ask you, Lord
Castlehaven?"

"Verily I cannot say," replied the Earl with the coolest indifference; "your people might have been somewhat rash,
or——"

"Not so, my lord, not so," said the Ulster general with more
anger than he was ever known to manifest; "not so, but your
people—or rather your officers—were cowards—base, skulking,
heartless cowards, else had they not looked coldly on whilst my
brave O'Neills were butchered—as for that Fennell——"

"Cowards, General O'Neill! have a care what you say—Colonel Fennell is an officer well esteemed——"

"I tell you, my lord, he is an *arrant* coward, and since you refuse to censure his conduct, he shall answer for it to the Supreme Council in whose service we are all engaged—let him stand forward here and deny, if he dare, the truth of what I have stated."

But Fennell had disappeared, and Castlehaven, to cover his retreat, muttered something about having given him a commission.

"It is very well, my lord," said O Neill sternly; "I am then to understand that there is no redress to be expected from you —as I have said, it must be sought elsewhere. Fennell and even your lordship may find out that the life of a Tyr-Owen clansman is worth as much as that of a Leinsterman. O'Neills have good memories, too, my fine friend, and they cannot but see now what value you set on their lives, and in what account you hold their friendship. Depend upon it, James Touchet, we will keep this day's work in mind."

"With all my heart, O'Neill," said the peer with a disdainful smile. "An' your clansmen be not able to take care of themselves, they are ill worth fighting for."

Such being the spirit in which the two generals entered upon that Ulster campaign, it is easy to understand that their chances of success were much diminished. Still they bore it bravely, one and the other, in presence of the enemy, and although their forces were far inferior to those of the Scottish general in point of numbers, the latter was fain to retreat back to the far north without coming to any decisive engagement. Owen Roe had his head-quarters at Belturbet, and Castlehaven his at Charlemont, they had also a strong fort and a magazine at Tanderagee, so that their lines extended over the greater portion of central Ulster. Their chief force was, however, concentrated in the neighborhood of Charlemont, Monroe's army hovering like a dark storm-cloud on the northern horizon.

At length the Scottish general advanced to the very banks of the Blackwater, and there he lay full in sight of the Confederates with the main body of his army far outnumbering theirs. It was a curious sight to see the rival hosts reposing on the opposite sides of the old historic stream, watching each other's movements like two surly mastiffs, each one fearful of disturbing the

other by the slightest motion. As regarded Castlehaven this
caution was no more than what prudence required, seeing that
his numbers were so far inferior, but that Monroe, with his vast
army, should hesitate about risking a battle showed a craven
and cowardly spirit—quite consistent with the man's love of
carnage. Monroe, it is plain, had a special vocation for cutting up
detached parties, but none whatever for meeting the Confederate
soldiers in pitched battles. Castlehaven's officers made merry
over the matter for some days, and then the soldiers becoming
impatient at the delay, the general resolved to cross the river
and attack the enemy's quarters. All that night the Irish army
was in gay commotion expecting that the morrow would
bring the long wished-for day of vengeance. The morrow
came, the summer dawn crimsoned the wooded shores of
the Blackwater; the far-spreading plains and the distant mountains of Tyrone were gradually revealed in the early sunbeam,
but Castlehaven's soldiers looked in vain for the Scotch battalions whose dark outline had for days lain motionless before
them. Unseen were their grazing steeds by the river, unheard
the roll of their morning drums; they had vanished during
the night, Monroe and his *seventeen thousand*, and the Confederates were left to keep watch alone over the passes of the
Blackwater! Monroe had merely waited to collect what provisions he could on his own side the river, and then made the
best of his way back to his old quarters at Carrickfergus.

This was esteemed a great triumph by Castlehaven, who,
with characteristic self-conceit, took the whole credit to himself, and boasted that Monroe had feared to .encounter him.
Owen Roe listened with a contemptuous smile, and said in a
tone of good-humored raillery:

"Whether was it from our united army, or your lordship's
puissant arm, that the Scotch earl made his escape? I think
my Rapparees even had somewhat to do with it, they have
kept buzzing like angry wasps on the outskirts of his army,
stinging where they saw an opening, so that the thick hides of
the Scotch must be well blistered ere now. As for you
and me, my lord, it be time enough to boast when we have
done something. We must follow Monroe."

"When you have furnished your promised supplies, O'Neill, not sooner."

"Hath not my army done its share of the fighting since you came into Ulster?" demanded Owen. "Have not my men borne the brunt?"

"Truly they have fought well for their numbers," said the Earl carelessly, "but what with your *creaghts* and herds of cattle, and such like, your men have had their hands full——"

"My herds of cattle are small in number, surely," said Owen with his calm smile, "an' my men did no more than keep yours fed—it was not amiss. As for the creaghts, you would not have us leave our women and children to the tender mercies of the Puritans?"

"Not so, but surely there be more men in your country than those we see in your ranks. An' there be not, I have small hopes of making head against the Scotch."

But O'Neill had small hopes of immediate success—he saw clearly that if the Puritans were ever to be driven from Ulster it was not Castlehaven or the soldiers of the Pale that were likely to do it, and he made up his mind to husband his own resources and apply himself once more to gather together the scattered clans and prepare them for one desperate struggle.

Events, meanwhile, were transpiring which gave a new turn to the affairs of the Confederates, and made Castlehaven draw off his forces with all haste from Ulster while he himself repaired to Kilkenny much disturbed in mind. The Council was sitting at the time, and as the Earl's quick eye glanced around the room he speedily detected the presence of a stranger, a man of noble mien and courtly manners, who occupied a seat near the President.

"Give us joy, my lord," said Mountgarret, "we are at last in a fair way of having peace—the king's most gracious majesty hath been pleased to move in the matter, and here is my lord of Glamorgan duly accredited from him to treat with us thereupon."

"How! Lord Herbert of Glamorgan, son of the loyal and valiant Marquis of Worcester, who hath done such good service to the king?"

"The same," said Glamorgan, rising and bowing with a gratified smile.

"Then am I well pleased to see you here," said the peer;
"there be no man in all England, an' report speak truly, more
fit to treat between his grace's highness and his Catholic subjects of Ireland."

"It is Lord Castlehaven who speaks," said Mountgarret, turning to the English lord, "the Earl of Castlehaven, a brave and
noble gentleman, right well affected towards the peace."

"It were strange an' I had not heard of his lordship," said
Glamorgan, and thereupon the two noblemen exchanged bows,
and the most perfect understanding from that moment existed
between them.

"I would ask your lordship," said the aged primate, Hugh
O'Neill, "hath his majesty lost his confidence in the great marquis that he deemed it expedient to send an envoy extraordinary?"

"Not so, most reverend lord," said Glamorgan hastily, "my
lord of Ormond is still one of the foremost in the king's favor,
but being a staunch Protestant he cannot have that sympathy
with the Confederates which would move him to consider their
claims with intent to give satisfaction. He desires peace on
certain conditions not at all favorable to the Catholics—whereas
the king my master desires it on any terms. The good service
done in Scotland by your men sent over to Montrose hath been
most acceptable to his grace——"

"It had much need, my lord earl," quoth Tirlogh O'Neill,
"seeing that it hath drawn upon us the full fury of the Parliamentary rebels. Had Colkitto and my lord of Antrim left the
Graham to make shift with his Highlanders, Monroe had not
been roused from his lair and set upon us, nor Inchiquin bought
over to betray his king. Marry, my Lord Glamorgan, it was a
stretch of generosity on the part of this honorable Council to
send some of its best regiments to serve a king who—ahem! I
respect him and will say no more."

It appeared on further examination that Lord Glamorgan was
vested with the most ample power to treat with the Confederates, and to make peace with them, as he said, "on any
terms." His royal master was at length fully sensible that

instead of being rebels to his authority the Catholics of Ireland were his only hope after the loyal cavaliers of England. He had found to his heavy cost that the Irish Protestants, even those who had been serving in Ormond's army, were far from being devoted to his interest,* whilst the Catholics, notwithstanding their many grievances, were true as the steel of their bayonets. Whatever might have been the king's secret sentiments with regard to his Catholic subjects, his necessities were too urgent to allow him any further indulgence of bigotry in his dealings with them, and he was forced to throw himself, as it were, on their generosity, counting largely, it must be confessed, on their Christian forgiveness.

It was stern necessity that drew from Charles Stuart such articles of peace as those submitted that day in his name to the Confederate Catholics of Ireland who were but too willing to meet his advances. They had been just discussing the terms of a permanent treaty proposed by Ormond, in which that wily statesman was fain to withhold from them those rights which their swords had for the present secured to them, how great then was their joy when they found the so much wished-for peace placed within their reach by their sovereign himself on such terms as they hardly dared propose to his Protestant viceroy.

These were the terms agreed to by Lord Glamorgan on the part of the king:

"I. That all the professors of the Roman Catholic religion in Ireland shall enjoy the free and public use and exercise of their religion.

"II. That they shall hold and enjoy all the churches by them enjoyed, or by them possessed, at any time since the 23d of

---

* Of the regiments sent over to Chester by Ormond during the Cessation, Borlase, in his History of the Irish Insurrection, says: "Such was the reluctancy of the common soldiers that the sharpest proclamations hardly restrained them from flying their colors, both before and after their arrival in England." The Irish Catholics, on the contrary, who enlisted in the king's service, were faithful and true to the very last.

October, 1641, and all other churches in the said kingdom, other than such as are now actually enjoyed by his Majesty's Protestant subjects.

"III. That all the Roman Catholics shall be exempted from the jurisdiction of the Protestant clergy, and that the Catholic clergy shall not be punished or molested for the exercise of their jurisdiction over their respective flocks. And, also, that an act shall be passed in the next parliament for securing to them all the king's concessions.

"IV. That the Marquis of Ormond, or any others, shall not disturb the professors of the Roman Catholic religion in possession of the articles above specified.

"V. The Earl of Glamorgan engages his majesty's word for the performance of these articles.

"VI. That the public faith of the kingdom shall be engaged unto the said Earl by the commissioners of the Confederate Catholics, for sending 10,000 men by order and declaration of the General Assembly at Kilkenny, armed, the one-half with muskets, and the other half with pikes, to serve his majesty in England, Wales, or Scotland, under the command of the said Glamorgan, as lord general of the said army; which army is to be kept together in one entire body, and all other the officers and commanders of the said army are to be named by the Supreme Council of the said Confederate Catholics, or by such others as the General Assembly of the said Confederate Catholics of Ireland shall entrust therewith."

Such was the treaty signed on the part of the Confederates by their commissioners, Richard, Lord Viscount Mountgarret, and Donogh, Lord Muskerry. A copy of its articles had previously been submitted to each of the leading members of the Council. The hopes it held out were bright and beautiful, but they vanished, like the roseate blush of dawn. For very specious reasons advanced by the Earl the treaty was not made public, and the Confederates went on fighting the rebellious Puritans, and religiously observing the Cessation with Ormond, further extended to the December following.

News had by this time arrived of the death of the good Pope Urban VIII., and the accession of Innocent X. to the papal

throne. Anxious to pay their respects to the new Pontiff, and
enlist his sympathies in their cause, the Supreme Council dispatched their secretary, Richard Belling, to Rome to congratu-
late his Holiness, and at the same time to report the progress
of affairs to their faithful agent, Father Luke Wadding. That
Innocent X. took no less interest in the struggle going on in
Ireland than his predecessor, succeeding events will show.

Meanwhile, the Confederates were alarmed, and not without
reason, by the threatening aspect of the Parliamentary forces
in Ireland. They had hoped that Ormond would unite with
them during the Cessation in resisting the progress of these
worse than rebels, from whose fanatical fury neither age, sex,
nor condition was safe. Where they conquered, indiscriminate
slaughter followed, for the extermination of the Papists was
their avowed object. Ruthless, gaunt, and terrible as hungry
wolves, the Puritans rushed on their prey, intent only on destruction. Such were the soldiers of the Covenant, and Ormond
knew it well—he knew they were bent on uprooting that mon-
archy which he professed to uphold, and yet so far from assisting the Confederates to oppose them, he secretly abetted their
designs as far, at least, as Catholics were concerned. Thus it
was that while Mountgarret and Muskerry, and Father Peter
Walsh, and all the rest of that faction were blindly playing into
the hands of the new Lord Lieutenant, he was coquetting at the
same time with Broghill and Inchiquin. Whilst his royal master
was urging him by every means to conciliate the Confederate
Catholics, and conclude a permanent peace with them, he was
raising objections to their just demands, and excusing himself
under one pretence and another from joining them against the
Puritans. Many fine promises were made by him, and to
believe Father Peter Walsh, nothing was so near his heart as
the overthrow of the Puritans; but, nevertheless, things went
on as they were, the Parliamentarians steadily gaining ground,
the Confederates scrupulously observing the Cessation with the
king's troops,* and maintaining the war against the king's enemies and their own.

---

* So strict were they in the observance of the truce that Lieuten-

Whilst the Council was still rejoicing over the concessions
made by the king, word was brought that Sligo had been taken
by the northern Scotch under Stewart, and was by him held for
the Parliament. No news could be more unwelcome at that
moment, for Sligo was on the direct road to Galway, and Galway
was one of the principal strongholds in possession of the Confederates. All was fear and consternation in Kilkenny, for the safety
of all Connaught was now at stake. The altars so lately recovered, the temples so carefully adorned and beautified, all, all
were exposed to the fury of the fanatic, and must be protected
at any cost.

Sir James Dillon was ordered to proceed immediately to the
relief of Sligo with what forces were available in the neighborhood of Kilkenny, but, alas! they were far short of the numbers
necessary for that perilous enterprize. What they lacked in
numbers, however, they made up in courage and resolution, and
their enthusiasm knew no bounds when the venerable and patriotic Archbishop of Tuam placed himself at their head.

In vain did his brethren of the episcopacy and even the laylords seek to dissuade him from risking a life so precious.

"Think you, my lords," said the heroic prelate, "I could
leave my poor people under the hoof of Stewart and Hamilton—
no, no, Sligo must be relieved, come what may, that is to say,
we must make the attempt, and should it please God that we
fail, Malachy O'Kelly you will see no more. Would to Heaven
that the sacrifice of so poor a life could deliver Sligo, or stop the
murderous career of the Puritans—oh! freely, freely were it
given!"

What could be said to such a man at such a moment—his
brother bishops could only breathe a silent prayer for his
safety and watch his departure with beating hearts. So he
girded on his sword to do battle for the faith, and took his
place by Dillon's side amid the cheers and prayers and tears of
those who remained behind. His example was eagerly followed by several clergymen belonging to his archdiocese, who
were proud of taking up arms in so holy a cause.

ant-General Purcell was sent to chastise some of their own number
who had violated its articles.

Not many of those who marched from Kilkenny that day ever returned within its walls. A few days after, whilst the whole city was in a fever of anxiety to know the result of the expedition, a small party of cavalry approached the walls with Sir James Dillon at their head, almost every man bearing more or less the marks of bloody conflict. Nor banner, nor music had they, nor baggage of any kind, and it needed not words to declare what their wan, dejected faces and doleful plight told all too well.

> News of battle! who hath brought it?
> All are thronging to the gate;
> " Warder—warder! open quickly
> Man—is this a time to wait?"
> And the heavy gates are opened
> Then a murmur long and loud,
> And a cry of fear and wonder
> Bursts from out the bending crowd.

" Silence!" cried the stern voice of Mountgarret as he and Lord Glamorgan, with some other lords and gentlemen, dashed up at a gallop; " Sir James Dillon, this is a dreary sight—where have you left the Archbishop?"

" He hath won the martyr's crown, my lord," was the sad reply, " cut to pieces was he by the swords of Hamilton's troopers —a little way from the walls of Sligo—with his priests around him faithful to the last."

> Wo, wo, and lamentation!
> What a piteous cry was there!
> Widows, maidens, mothers, children,
> Shrieking, sobbing in despair!*

" Good Heavens! Sir James, and you shame not to tell that you left him there—left his consecrated body a prey to the rage of the fanatic?"

" You would not reproach us, Lord Mountgarret," said Dillon mournfully, " an' you knew but all. We had made our way into

* Aynton's *Lays of the Scottish Cavaliers.*

the town over heaps of the dead and dying. His Grace of Tuam fighting like a hero in the van, and the townspeople thronging to our assistance, Sligo would soon have been ours, when, probably, by a sharp device of the enemy, drums and fifes were heard in the distance, and the terrible cry of 'Coote to the rescue!' resounded through the streets above the din of battle. Fearful of seeing our brave fellows attacked front and rear by the Puritans, in which case their destruction was inevitable, the Archbishop commanded a retreat—we retired accordingly with our face to the foe, fighting every inch of the way, but, alas! the terror of Coote had taken possession of our soldiers, and, thinking every moment that he was on their rear with his fierce bloodhounds, a panic ran through the ranks, the stout arms lost their strength—horse and foot began to waver, the enemy saw it and pressed us more closely, the cry of 'Coote! Coote!' ringing in our ears from behind—back, back to the gates—out through them in wild disorder, and by the time the outside was gained, all authority was at an end. A general rout followed, and our heroic Archbishop, disdaining to fly, was cut to pieces with his priests who gathered around him in the vain hope of saving his life. For us, my lords," he said proudly, as soon as the cries of the multitude permitted his voice to be heard, "For us—the sad survivors of that fatal fray—I say not what we did—suffice it that our numbers had not been so few were it not for the repeated efforts made to recover the Archbishop's body."

"Heaven help us all this day!" said Mountgarret with a heavy sigh; "who can wonder, my Lord Glamorgan, that we of the Council long for peace. *He* was ever opposed to it, and see what thing hath come upon him."

Of course it was Lord Glamorgan's interest to coincide fully with the aged President, and to represent the calamitous death of the Archbishop as a judgment from Heaven on those who kept the people from returning to their allegiance. There was none present there to gainsay so foul a calumny on the dead.

Far different were the feelings of O'Neill and McMahon, and the other Irish members of the Council, when the doleful tidings reached them. Not to speak of the loss of that powerful and influential prelate whose strong and vigorous mind had exercised a salutary control over the temporizing Norman lords, as his fervent piety and sterling patriotism commanded the respect of all, there was the maddening thought that he had fallen by the hands of the Puritan butchers, his consecrated remains hacked and mutilated to glut their diabolical hatred. He that was ever first to feel for their wrongs—he that had been so moved but late by the judicial murder of Maguire and McMahon, he that had never spared himself to advance the common weal, that he should have been abandoned in his last moments to the fury of the murdering Scotch, while so many thousands of his faithful people were in arms the country over—oh! it was torture to think of it, and the hot-headed chiefs of the Gael, few as they were in that assembly, raised such a commotion that Glamorgan and the Ormondists were alarmed for the peace. The bishops were less noisy in the manifestation of their grief, but they felt their loss most sensibly. They, nevertheless, regarded the fate of their departed brother as enviable, now that the bitterness of death was past, and the palm of martyrdom gloriously won. So they celebrated his obsequies with all the solemn pomp befitting the occasion, in the old Cathedral of St. Canice, the aged bishop of Ossory presiding at the altar, while bishops and archbishops, and stoled priests without number, joined in the funeral chant, and the armed Confederates who thronged nave and aisle made the responses sound like the growl of distant thunder.

Such was the end of Malachy O'Kelly, Archbishop of Tuam, one of the leading spirits of the Confederation—another martyr to the cause of truth and justice!

CHAPTER XXVIII.

"Oh! names like his bright beacons are
    To realms that kings oppress,
Hailing with radiant light from far
    Their signals of distress."

Spirit of the Nation.

It was the thirteenth day of November, 1645, and the old city of Kilkenny was again in motion. The gloom and horror of the Archbishop's death had passed away—its memory uneffaced, but covered over by newer impressions—and the citizens were again crowding the streets with eager, expectant faces, and the sounds of joy were heard on every side. The city once more wore its holyday garb, and even the glories of that day, four years gone by, when the Confederation took life and form, were eclipsed by the splendor of this new occasion. From the earliest hours of the morning crowds were hurrying from all directions within and without the walls towards St. Patrick's Gate, and there they patiently stood regardless of the drizzling rain which all day long streamed down incessantly.

Just outside the wall, close by St. Patrick's Gate, was then situate the old Church of St. Patrick, where a new one of the same name now "rears the cross on high." The hour of noon was not far off, when on a sudden the bell of the Black Abbey rung out a joyous peal, answered quickly by the Church of St. Francis. Forth at once from the gray old Church outside the gate issued in long procession the regular and secular clergy of the city, heading towards the gate, and preceded by the gorgeous banners of their respective orders. A joyous stir was visible amongst the multitude, and cries of "he comes! he comes!" rang through the crowded streets, caught up from mouth to mouth. All eyes were turned on the old gate, and presently appeared from under its arch a sight that made every heart thrill, and brought tears of joy from many an eye. Sur-

rounded by the noblest gentlemen of the country, amongst whom
was conspicuous Richard Butler, Lord Netterville, and Richard Belling,* and followed by a dense multitude of people from
the adjacent counties, who had joined the cortege as it passed
along, came a noble-looking man of middle age, and of foreign
aspect, robed as a high dignitary of the Church, and mounted
on a horse richly caparisoned. This horse had been led out
from the city to meet the exalted personage, who had journeyed till then in "a rude litter." The rain poured down fast and
faster, but it could not damp the ardor of the citizens at that
moment, nor dull the sound of the merry peal chiming out from
every belfry of the town. The deep-mouthed cannon on the
walls lent their thundering voice to swell the chorus of welcome;
and so it was amid the joyous shouts of thousands and tens of
thousands, the pealing of bells and the booming of cannon that
the stately priest entered the city of the Confederation. A
costly canopy was held over him by four of the principal
townsmen, their heads uncovered, regardless of the pelting rain,
and no sooner had he emerged from beneath the arch than he
was met by the Vicar-General of the diocese of Ossory, the
mayor and aldermen of the city, and the chief magistrates of
the county. Having welcomed the illustrious stranger to the
ancient city of St. Canice, these dignitaries took their place in
the procession amid the loud plaudits of the people.

On then moved the brilliant cortege and the mighty multitude, faster and louder pealed the bells, and heavier boomed
the cannon; on and on, following the line of Patrick street, till
the old market cross stood in its antique beauty before the admiring eyes of the stranger, and he paused a moment to look
more closely at that interesting monument of medieval taste
and piety. Just then issued from the bishop's house nearly
opposite, a company of fifty students clad in their collegiate
costume. At their head was one whose noble proportions well
became the Roman *toga* which fell in ample folds around him

---

* The Secretary Belling had accompanied the Nuncio from Rome.
Butler, Netterville, and some other gentleman of rank had been sent
by the Supreme Council to meet him as soon as they heard of his
landing on the southern coast.

and the laurel wreath which encircled his brows. No sooner
had the foreign prelate paused before the ancient cross than
this young man stepped forward, and with lowly reverence recited a Latin oration which appeared to give the stranger no
ordinary pleasure for he turned to Lord Netterville at his side
and smiled his approbation. When he had responded by a few
graceful words in the same language, thanking the young gentlemen for their courtesy and delicately alluding to their class-
ical attainments, they, in their turn, joined the procession, and
the canopy was again in motion, nor stopped till it reached St.
Canice's holy hill. The crowd immediately fell back on either
side, and the procession moved slowly up the hill amid the
deafening cheers of the multitude.

Under the deep arch of the grand portal of St. Canice's stood
the venerable figure of Bishop Rothe, bowed down with age as
we have elsewhere described him, yet noble and commanding
even in decay. His numerous infirmities had prevented him
from joining the procession, so he stood at the door of his Cathedral awaiting its approach with a cheerful, benignant smile
lighting up his shrunken features, while ever and anon he
turned to express his satisfaction to the few priests whom he
had kept with him, amongst whom was conspicuous the lank
figure and pale face of the Italian Scarampi!

At length the canopy was set down in front of the Church,
and the stately stranger alighting from his horse advanced
towards the bishop. Surely it was the proudest moment in
David Rothe's life* when he welcomed to the city of Kilkenny
and the old Church of St. Canice the Archbishop of Fermo,
Nuncio of his Holiness Innocent X., sent by that good Pontiff
to promote the cause of religious freedom in Ireland, and to

---

* Three years before the occurrences here narrated, David, Bishop
of Ossory, had erected a monument to commemorate the restoration
of St. Canice's Cathedral to the ancient worship, and it needs no
flight of fancy to suppose that on this memorable occasion he may
have echoed the words of the Canticle: "Now dismiss thy servant,
because my eyes have seen salvation, and the glory of thy people,
Israel "—*Confederation*, chap. V., p. 109.

second by every means in his power the efforts of the Confederate Catholics! Such was the style and dignity of the stranger,
John Baptist Rinuccini, name dear to every Irish heart.

Old and infirm as he was, Bishop Rothe would have knelt
before the representative of the Holy Father, but that the
Nuncio would not permit. Raising the old man with an air of
filial reverence he tenderly embraced him, and then both
together entered the Cathedral, followed by bishops and priests,
lords and gentlemen, and as much of the dense multitude as
could possibly obtain admission.

Oh! it was a grand, a glorious scene, the interior of St. Canice's
at that moment, when the Nuncio ascending the steps of the high
altar intoned the *Te Deum,* the vast multitude catching up the
sacred strain till the vaulted roof echoed with the exulting
sounds. Never was that noblest of psalms sung on a loftier
inspiration, never with more thrilling enthusiasm, as the voice of
priest and prelate, knight and noble, blended in one harmonious
volume of sound.

Truly it was a grand occasion. Will Ireland ever see such
another sight? Why was not Owen Roe there to witness it, or
Rory O'More! Alas! poor O'More! how his heart would have
thrilled to those glorious sounds, how that vision of light and
splendor would have charmed his poetic mind! But it might
not be—it might not be—far in his Flemish exile he heard but
the echo of his country's voices, and saw its joys or sorrows but
in dreams.

" Oh! joyously, triumphantly, sweet sounds ye swell and float!"†

Even now after the lapse of over two hundred years we can
feel the gushing joy that was " borne on every note," but to
those who sang there was an under-tone of sorrow running
throughout the gladsome strain; even that stately Italian prelate thought of the martyred dead—how was it then with the
kinsmen of Maguire and McMahon, and the episcopal brethren
of O'Kelly?

As if reading the thoughts of many there, the Nuncio, after
giving his blessing to the multitude from the steps of the altar,

† Mrs. Hemans.

demanded of Bishop Rothe whether the Archbishop's obsequies
had yet been celebrated. Being answered in the affirmative he
expressed his satisfaction.

" For my own part," said he in Latin, " I celebrated them in
Limerick on my way hither. Oh! may Heaven receive thy soul
in glory!" he added, looking upwards with characteristic fervor,
" faithful guide of these faithful people,—pastor who gave thy
life for thy sheep, a high place in heaven, sure, is thine! Pray
thou for us as we for thee—pray for us that it be given us to
accomplish the deliverance of thy people!"

After an hour or two given to rest and refreshment in the
house prepared for the Nuncio's reception, during which interval
Lord Muskerry, General Preston and others of the Confederate
Chiefs paid their respects to him,—he set out on foot accompanied by his Italian retinue, Bishop McMahon, Belling, Netterville, Butler and many others to visit the aged President of the
Council—who had not as yet made his appearance.

Strangely enough, as it appears to us, it was in the Castle of
Kilkenny that Lord Mountgarret received the Pope's Ambassador, and we may hope that Richard Butler's heart swelled with
joy and pride as he welcomed the Nuncio to the lordly dwelling
of his fathers. Bitter, however, must have been the thought
that the present head of his house was a renegade from the
faith of the stern old Catholic Butlers.

Those who have seen the Castle of Kilkenny need no description of that stately pile, yet even they can hardly realize what
it was when the Nuncio Rinuccini honored it with a visit on that
memorable occasion. The many additions made to the original
edifice by the dukes and marquises of Ormond have added
little to its beauty, how much soever they may have increased
its splendor. The baronial grandeur is still there, more striking, perhaps, than ever, but the architectural harmony and
completeness is gone. Nevertheless, it was then, as it is now,
a dwelling not unworthy the Butlers of Ormond, towering in its
pride over the rapid waters of the Nore and looking down with
an air of protection on the fair city resting at its feet.

When the Nuncio reached the Castle hall with his retinue, he
was received at the foot of the grand staircase by the Arch-

bishops of Dublin and Cashel, by whom he was conducted to the great gallery, at the farther end of which Lord Mountgarret awaited his arrival. The stately old nobleman was seated on a chair richly adorned, whilst near him was the seat intended for the Nuncio covered with damask and gold, with the pontifical arms magnificently emblazoned on the back.

Mountgarret arose as the Nuncio approached, but instead of going forward to meet him, as etiquette would have required, he stood awaiting his approach. Without appearing to notice this want of courtesy (to say the least of it) Rinuccini at once addressed the President in the Latin language :

" My Lord President," said he with that lofty air of command which was natural to him, " my Lord President, it is hardly necessary to inform you that his Holiness Pope Innocent X. (successor to Urban VIII. of happy memory) hath deputed me with the fullest authority to take part in the struggle so nobly maintained by the pious Confederate Catholics of Ireland. Your cause he esteems as the cause of Catholicity, and he well commendeth the patience and constancy shown by you in carrying on this thrice-bles ed war."

Here the President's countenance fell, and he seemed for a moment as though about to interrupt the speaker, but he probably thought better of it and kept silent.

" His Holiness," went on the Nuncio, " hath it also much at heart that the king of England's cause should prosper to the confusion of the evil-minded men who have manifested their disloyal sentiments towards him. It would give our common Father much contentment were his faithful children of Ireland in a position to aid their king in his struggle with his rebellious Parliament." Mountgarret's face brightened up again, whilst he and the other leading Ormondists exchanged significant glances.

" Our desire is to support the king," repeated Rinuccini, whose keen eye had not failed to detect the meaning looks of those around him, although their full signification was not as yet known to him. " Truly that is one great object to be kept in view, but the first and greatest duty of you and me and of every Catholic, is to battle for the right—for the free untrammeled exercise of our holy religion, aye ! to the shedding of all our blood. No compromise, no treaty, no tampering with the enemy until the Catholic faith be re-established in this realm as it was at the time of the Reformation, or in the earlier part of the reign of Henry VIII. That, gentlemen Confederates, is the main and primary object of our endeavors, and with less than that I, John Baptist Rinuccini, will never rest contented, nor yet will his Holiness Innocent X., who is fully resolved to uphold you in your struggle to the utmost extent of his resources. Oh! soldiers of the Cross!" he added, turning with enthusiastic fervor to the crowd of lords and gentlemen by that time assembled in the gallery, "dauntless sons of Catholic Ireland, be not deceived in this matter. Hearken not to those who would cool your zeal or incite you to give up mid-way in your path—treachery is abroad—the enemy is gnawing at the roots of the stately tree whose branches now cover the land—as ye love your own souls—as ye love that faith for which your fathers lost lands, and livings, and life itself, go on with the good work now so far advanced—an' the tempter lure ye from the path, our cause is lost, Catholic Europe will blush for shame, and the paternal heart of Innocent will bleed for your infatuation. But no! you will not thus tamely yield what your valor hath won! By the bones of your slaughtered kin, by the bitter pains of persecution, by all the memories of your wrongs, it shall not be! you will follow up your advantage, and grasp that glorious victory which is even now within your reach."

"Most reverend lord," put in Mountgarret, "you seem in ignorance of the peace which for wise and lawful ends we are negotiating,"

"The which is much needed in this distracted country," echoed Muskerry.

"Peace! peace! who talks of peace?" said the Nuncio sharply; "what manner of peace would you gain now with the enemy still in full strength? I have brought you, my lords and gentlemen, from our Most Holy Father, and other friends of the cause, that which will help you to win real peace, lasting peace—I have brought you such supplies of arms and ammunition as never crossed the seas to you before; money, too, hath his Holiness sent you from his own treasury, and my

16

valued friend, Father Luke Wadding, hath also forwarded by
me some 36,000 crowns, all which I have and do hold for your
use in red Spanish gold. By using these to advantage you can
make peace, on your own terms, such peace as alone is worth
having, that is to say, peace based on full and entire freedom."

" To what extent would your grace have us demand freedom ?"
said Mountgarret coldly.

" To the extent, my Lord President, of placing the Catholic
religion on an equality with all others—freedom for your homes,
freedom for your altars, freedom for your clergy; also that restitution be made the church for the robberies of these latter ages,
which is to say that her property be restored to her intact.
This is the freedom which will secure *peace*, this is the freedom which the Father of the faithful desires to see established
amongst you, and for which end he hath sent me hither, not to
make treaties for the convenience and contentment of a Protestant viceroy."

" My Lord Nuncio," said a smooth oily voice from behind the
President's chair, " I pray you suspend your opinion of this
matter till such time——"

" And who are *you*?" demanded the Nuncio, breaking in
abruptly.

" An humble son of St. Francis," said the smooth voice
again.

" And a devoted servant of Ormond," whispered Bishop
French, at the Nuncio's side.

" Advance and show yourself," said Rinuccini with some sternness, and forthwith Father Peter Walsh made himself visible in
the brown habit of his order. The Nuncio returned his lowly
reverence with a slight bend of his stately head, and then eyed
him for a moment with that keen scrutiny which reads men's
hearts, then waved him back with a motion of his hand, as
though desiring no further acquaintance. A crest-fallen man was
Father Peter, but his troubles were not yet over.

" There now," said another voice from the depth of an adjoining doorway; " there now, Father Peter Walsh! take that
for your pains, and it's you that well deserves it. It isn't the
poor simple Bishop of Clogher you have now !"

Not even the presence of the Nuncio could repress the burst of laughter that ran around the room, whilst the grave Italians wondered what it all meant, and looked from one to the other in blank amazement. The Nuncio himself, however, could not repress a smile when the matter was explained to him. But no one enjoyed the joke more than Bishop McMahon, albeit that it touched him on a sore spot which he would now fain conceal.

"Malachy, my dear man," said he with a good-humored smile, "this is not the place for you, *soggarth* and all as you are."

"I know that, my lord," said the quaint appendage to the see of Clogher, "and it isn't the place I'd be in either only for a letter that came for you there a while ago from a place called Flanders, wherever that may be, dear knows! It's a priest that came with it, and he says it's from Master Rory O'More, and that there's a power of money in it for paying the men, and everything that way."

An exclamation of surprise and pleasure escaped many even of the Ormond faction on hearing this announcement, and all forgot that there was anything ludicrous in the medium through which it was conveyed. The name of Roger O'More was still dear to all the Confederates, and they rejoiced to hear that he yet took an interest in their affairs, and was working for them beyond the sea.

"When it rains it pours," muttered the old President to himself in a querulous tone; "an' we wanted their supplies we might not have them in such plenty."

"They will stand us in good stead for the king's service," suggested Nicholas Plunket in a low voice at his elbow as if reading his thoughts.

Bishop McMahon, having dismissed Malachy to see after the entertainment of O'More's reverend messenger, addressed the President and the assembled Confederates with that overpowering energy which distinguished him from most others. He declared himself entirely opposed to any further negotiations with the enemy until such time as they could command their own terms.

" War! war! war!" said he, "war unceasing!—no more
truce-making, no more parleying—Rome hath spoken, we have
but to obey. My lords and gentlemen and brother Confederates, there is but one way for us, and that is the way that
leads to victory. How can we fail to look forward with hope
when the Head of the Church has sent his representative to
aid us in the contest? when money, and arms, and all things
needful are showering on us like dew from heaven? God is
with us, brethren! that is plain—wherefore, then, lay down
the sword that hath gained *so much* until *all* is gained? Let it
not be said of us that we lacked the courage or the perseverance
to finish the work so well begun! Freedom is more than
half won, shall we not win it? Ay, truly, though we die for
it—what is death in such a cause?"

Bishop McMahon's address was heard with alarm by the
Ormondists present who had of late been reckoning on that en-
terprizing prelate as a friend to the peace. They were fain, however, to conceal their chagrin, but it did not escape the piercing
eyes of the Nuncio, who took leave of Mountgarret that day
with a feeling of contempt for the pitiful weakness that made
so many of the Confederate chiefs actually subservient to Lord
Ormond, in whom the astute prelate already saw the arch enemy
of the Catholic cause.

He was accompanied on his return by Lords Muskerry and
Netterville, and on leaving the Castle he found General Preston
waiting with his troops under arms to conduct him to his domicile. The Nuncio seemed pleased with this attention, although
it was no more than he had a right to expect.

Returning to his home he found the Earl of Glamorgan in
anxious expectation of his coming. Being introduced by Lord
Muskerry, Glamorgan proceeded at once to business, and informed
the Nuncio of his royal master's willingness to do all that lay
in his power to ameliorate the condition of his Catholic subjects
in Ireland. But, in order to enable him to carry out his benefi-
cent designs, the Earl said, he must have good help from them
without any delay for the prosecution of the war in England,
where the rebels were fast gaining ground.

"Thus your grace cannot but see," added Glamorgan, " that

the king's cause and that of the Confederate **Catholics are at
this** moment identically the same. To sustain his highness
against the rebellious Puritans is in reality to **sustain yourselves
—ourselves, I would say!"**

The Nuncio smiled at some passing thought, but he said
gravely: "What security have we, my Lord Earl, that such be
his Majesty of England's gracious intentions in our regard?
Here we have his trusted friend Ormond, standing out against our
just demands in regard to religion, and protesting that he will
never consent to the public re-establishment of the ancient faith,
no, not even to secure the peace so necessary to his master's interest. How is it, my Lord Glamorgan?"

"An' your grace will condescend to read these documents,"
said the Earl, "one of them a letter to yourself under his
highness' own hand, you will see that my powers in this matter
are no less ample than those of my Lord Ormond."

As the Nuncio read his dark face gradually brightened, and
by the time he reached the end of the last epistle his doubts
seemed *almost* to have vanished.

"I am much beholden to your royal master," said he, "in
that he hath been-pleased to write me what I take to be a solemn
promise to do justice to the Catholics of this realm as soon as
his present difficulties will permit. He commends you to me in
the highest terms of praise, and assures me on the word of a
prince that whatsoever engagements you contract in his name
he will see duly ratified—on condition that we will afford him
and I esteem it a favorable augury as regards the success of my
mission. For the rest, your lordship's instructions are of the
mission. For the rest, your lordship's instructions are of the
most satisfactory nature. Were the Marquis of Ormond less prejudiced against our cause all would go well."

Glamorgan made an attempt to defend the marquis on the
score of "expediency," but the Nuncio shook his head and looked
incredulous. Preston just then made his appearance and Rinuc-

---

* This letter of Charles the First to the Nuncio Rinuccini is beyond
all doubt authentic. Its authenticity indeed is hardly ever called in
question.

cini abruptly asked for General O'Neill, "whose bravery and prudence," said he, "I have heard much extolled in Rome."

"Humph!" said the Leinster general with a supercilious smile, "he keeps, for the most part, with his half-naked kern in his own province;—mayhap fame hath blown his trumpet over loudly. But late he hath had to get help here against the Scots, and the Council being of no such opinion as your grace, with regard to his bravery or prudence, gave the command to my Lord Castlehaven, who is, indeed, far beyond O'Neill in military skill."

Rinuccini listened with a sad misgiving, too surely justified by succeeding events.

CHAPTER XXIX.

"Nay, Father, tell us not of help from Leinster's Norman Peers,
If we shall shape our holy cause to match their selfish fears—
Helpless and hopeless be their cause, who brook a vain delay,
Our ship is launched, our flag's afloat, whether they come or stay.

"Let silken Howth and savage Slane still kiss their tyrant's rod,
And pale Dunsany still prefer his monarch to his God,
Little we lack their fathers' sons, the marchmen of the Pale,
While Irish hearts and Irish hands have Spanish blades and mail.

"Then let them stay to bow and fawn, or fight with cunning words ;
I fear me more their courtly arts than England's hireling swords ;
Natheless their creed they hate us still, as the Despoiler hates,
Would God they loved their prey no more, our kinsmen's lost estates!"
                                        C. G. DUFFY.

A FEW weeks after the Nuncio's arrival in Kilkenny, a meeting of the General Assembly took place at his request. He was naturally anxious to see what materials he had to work upon, and the various leaders brought face to face so that he might judge for himself how they stood affected towards each other. It was the first time he had seen the two races brought into immediate contact, and he looked anxiously for the result. The meeting was a full one as might be supposed. Castlehaven was there full of the idea that he had been the salvation of the Confederate forces in Ulster, endangered, as he basely insinuated, by supineness, " or something worse,"* on the part of Owen Roe. Preston was there, too, looking fierce and warlike as ever, and Owen Roe was there with his cold, calm smile and collected mien, and his keen observing glance. There, too, was Sir Phelim, determined to put in his claim for a share in the command of the northern army. Most of the Ulster chiefs were, indeed, present, as were also the great Irish toparchs of the south and west,

* See his *Memoirs*.

whilst the Palesmen were there in full muster anxious to conclude the peace with Ormond and fearing the opposition of the
Chieftains, now more formidable than ever from the presence
and declared sentiments of the Nuncio.

The question of the peace was, of course, the first that came
up for discussion, and Rinuccini had soon the desired opportunity of fathoming the hearts of the Confederate Chiefs.

Mountgarret and Muskerry, Netterville and Gormanstown,
Fingal and Howth, and many another name in high esteem
amongst the Confederates, were all urgent for peace—peace on
any terms, so as to leave the king at liberty to oppose the English rebels.

"Truly, yes," said Castlehaven, "it devolves on us as loyal
gentlemen to waive all other matters for the present—our treaty
with my lord of Ormond doth secure us against religious
persecution——"

"Until such time," said Owen Roe, "as the enemy recovers his
strength—no longer. See you not, my lords and gentlemen,
that we gain nothing by this treaty but bare toleration for our
religion—scarcely even that—whereas we bind ourselves to aid
the king with men, money, arms, and even provisions; his
majesty, after all, reserving to himself the consideration of our
claims? What manner of bargain is that, lords and gentlemen?
They have the substance, we the shadow."

The Nuncio looked at Owen Roe with a smile of approbation,
which did not escape the Norman lords.

"Such language well becomes you, General O'Neill," Castlehaven replied quickly; "an' his highness had no more loyal
subjects here in Ireland than they of the old blood, small aid
might he hope for in his sore need. Shame on the Catholic
who at such a moment presses him for concessions beyond his
power to grant!"

"Your pardon, my lord!" said Bishop French, "he did not
grant them when he had the power. Far be it from me, however, to make light of his majesty's distresses—may Heaven
confound his enemies—but I am entirely of General O'Neill's
opinion—the king and his deceitful lieutenant, Ormond, are
driven by hard necessity to seek our aid—what are they giving

us in exchange ? Nothing, that I can see, only empty promises, and even they far from meeting our just expectations."

"You do his majesty much injustice, my reverend lord," said Glamorgan, who occupied a seat near the Nuncio ; "what more can you desire, or in reason demand, than he hath empowered me to promise 'you in his name ?"

"I deny it not," said the prelate curtly, "but I much fear for the performance thereof. An' your articles, my Lord Glamorgan, were likely to be carried out, I would be the first to urge a peace, but to my thinking, as matters stand, it were best not to lay down the arms which have brought the proud Ormond to treat us with some show of respect."

"An' my advice be taken," said Owen Roe, "there would be no peace made with any king or any party that could not or would not guarantee the free exercise of our religion, the restoration of Church property, and for our bishops the right of sitting as spiritual peers—in short, that *all* penal restrictions be removed—we have the power, lords and gentlemen, to bring this about, wherefore stop short ?—wherefore throw away the golden fruit within our reach—the fruit of our four years' heavy toil—the fruit of our martyrs' blood ? King Charles' cause is not without our sympathy, but the ancient faith of our fathers— the sufferings of our own kith and kin on account of their fidelity have the first claim on our attention. My lords and gentlemen, I will never consent to any such peace as this of Ormond's !"

"You speak as though the treaty were in your pocket!" said Castlehaven in a tone of contempt.

"Or rather he thinks Hugh O'Neill's sword sharp enough to cut it !" said Preston with bitter irony. "Not that I am much in favor of the treaty myself, but——"

"General Preston," exclaimed Sir Phelim with his usual impetuosity, "Owen and myself are not often of the same mind, but by the Red Hand of Tyr-Owen we *are* this time. One battle gained is worth all the treaties you could make in a year. The sword and not the pen must secure our rights."

"With all respect," said Philip O'Reilly, "I humbly submit that his Majesty of England hath no such claim to our grati-

tude as that we serve *him* rather than our Holy Mother the
Church, for whose honor and well-being we first commenced
this war."

In an instant Mountgarret, Muskerry, and Castlehaven were
on their feet, all eager to protest against what they were
pleased to call this "seditious language." Sir Lucas Dillon, too,
smoothly expressed his horror, and Nicholas Plunket declared
himself much amazed.

"Most reverend lord," said Owen Roe, addressing the Nuncio
in the Spanish language, "I humbly pray that you be not scandalized at our warmth of speech. We of the old blood are apt
to speak our thoughts over freely, but as for 'sedition' we hold
ourselves as loyal men as those who stood hat in hand but late
in front of Ormond's tent bowing before him like——".

"Like hungry dogs begging for bones!" suggested Sir Phelim, whereupon the Irish chieftains laughed and the Normans
waxed wroth.

"We appeal to the Nuncio," said Muskerry pale with anger.

"So do we," said Owen Roe, "let his grace decide between
us—you for peace and *toleration*, we for war and *independence*,
as regards religion!"

The Nuncio rose and all were silent, while every eye was
turned upon him. For a moment his eagle glance scanned the
assembly as though taking in its numbers and general character, then, gradually narrowing its range, it rested on the faces
of those who had taken the lead in the discussion. The sternly
knitted brow and the keen searching eye that gleamed from
beneath it gave no indication as to which party had his sympathies, but his words speedily removed all doubt.

"General O'Neill," said he, "I think as you do." He paused
and looked around as though challenging opposition. No one
at first ventured to speak—and Rinuccini proceeded.

"I say now in public that which I have said to many of you
in private, that I came hither on the part of the Sovereign Pontiff to aid you in your struggle for freedom—whatsoever diverges
from that object is beyond my province. I deeply feel for the
cruel position wherein your monarch is placed—so does the
Holy Father, as witness the sums by him advanced for the sus-

tainment of the king of England, but nearer and dearer to *my* heart, yea, and to that of the Holy Father Innocent, is the cause of the long-suffering, ever faithful Catholics of Ireland. My lords and gentlemen of the Confederation, your cause is a sacred cause—it is *our own*"—and he pressed his bosom with both hands with the impassioned energy of an Italian—" it is an affair of life or death, not only to you but to millions yet unborn. Either to worship God as freemen in the stately temples erected by your pious fathers, now happily again in your own possession, or to run once more into the holes and caverns of the earth with the divine mysteries which are man's proudest heritage. Like this noble chief, this worthy son of the great O'Neills"—turning to Owen—" I do not choose to accept mere toleration, when we can command the fullest measure of freedom."

" Then," said Mountgarret with ill-concealed vexation, " we are to understand that your grace opposes the peace now pending between us and my Lord of Ormond ?"

" Assuredly I do," was the prompt reply, " unless that lord will consent to our just demands—on *his* terms, no peace—no peace for me—death a thousand times sooner—ay, even the bloody grave of Malachy O'Kelly, whose soul may Christ crown with glory !"

" It is well, my Lord Archbishop !" said Mountgarret haughtily ; " it is well to know this so soon. Permit me to say, natheless, that the treaty hath already proceeded too far to be lightly broken off—ay ! even by a Nuncio—for which good thing our Lord be praised."

" Are you a Catholic, my Lord Mountgarret ?" was the Nuncio's stern rebuke.

" Truly, yes, most reverend lord ! at least, I hope so."

" Nay, nay—say not a Catholic—an Ormondist rather—Ormondists are ye all who tamper with the freedom of the Church to please that man—*these be the Catholics*"—and he pointed to the O'Neills and the other chiefs who had so warmly protested against negotiating with Ormond. " An' you would deserve that proud title, do the will of God and His vicegerent on earth, even as *they* do—rather than the will of a Protestant governor, yea, a man who hates your religion as renegades only can !"

Brows were knitted amongst the haughty Palesmen, and faces grew red and then pale with anger, but it was only Mountgarret that spoke, and his whole frame trembled and his thin lips were firmly compressed.

"Truly, my lord," said he in a voice that he vainly strove to keep steady, "truly it is our misfortune—we of the English race —to have fallen so soon under your grace's displeasure—I say it is our misfortune, but—but"—he paused and looked around as if to gather the suffrages of his own party—"but I see not that our mishap is like to be soon remedied. We must live without your favor—since we may not have it on other terms than disloyalty to our lawful prince—for *those*," and he in his turn pointed to the chieftains of Irish blood, "for those, they live and breathe in disaffection—loyalty they hardly know by name—but for us, my Lord Nuncio! we are proud to acknowledge our subjection to his gracious majesty Charles the First— we are British subjects—proud of the name—glorying in our allegiance!"

"I tell you again, my Lord Mountgarret," said Owen Roe more sternly than was his wont, "we fling the word disloyalty back in your teeth—loyal men are we, but more loyal to God than to any earthly ruler—an' your patron, Ormond, will not ratify my Lord Glamorgan's treaty, he may make cartridges of his own —*we'll none of it*, so help us, Heaven!"

"How can you help it?" said Preston in a taunting tone.

"Ways or means are not wanting to us, Master Preston," O'Neill replied with lofty self-reliance; "our motives are known to God—He will not abandon those who fight for the glory of His name."

"Thank God!" said Rinuccini, "there is still such faith to be found in Ireland!"

The upshot of this stormy debate was that the Nuncio caused all the arms and ammunition he brought from Italy to be conveyed to Kilkenny, and declared his intention of giving the whole to Owen O'Neill, together with the greater part of the money in his possession. This, of course, raised another storm in the Council. The Norman lords and gentlemen were furious, and threatened to withdraw immediately from the Confederation if a portion of the supplies were not given to Preston. After some deliberation, Rinuccini at length agreed, but the share he assigned to the Leinster general was so small compared with that given to O'Neill that the former could hardly be persuaded to accept it.

"He may or may not," said the uncompromising prelate, "no more shall he have. Ulster, I see plainly, must be the scene of a grand campaign, so as to clear it, if possibly we can, of those fanatical Scotsmen. There must our strength be concentrated, and, for the present, General Preston must make shift with what he has."

Owen Roe, then, was at length approaching the consummation of his cherished wish; he was to have at his command the chief army of the Confederation, with supplies of every kind necessary for carrying on a determined and energetic war, such as might in a short time clear his own Ulster of the ruthless Puritans who had so long kept it in thrall. Stout Phelim, too, was by his side eager for the coming opportunity as a leashed hound for the chase. Surely, then, the day so long looked for was not far distant.

Whilst the northern chieftains, inspired with fresh enthusiasm, hastened home to aid in the preparations for the opening campaign, the Confederates in Kilkenny were startled by the intelligence that Lord Glamorgan who had set out for Dublin with two Commissioners from the Council some days before had been arrested by order of the Lord Lieutenant on a charge of high treason.

"And how was it?" Mountgarret asked, in amazement of a gentleman who had accompanied the Commissioners from town; "what was there, I pray you, to substantiate such a charge against a well-known favorite of the king, whose house hath all along been distinguished for devotion to the royal cause?"*

* The Marquis of Worcester, Glamorgan's father, was one of the most trusted and efficient of the royal Generals throughout that Puritan rebellion—it is said that he and his son, the Glamorgan of our story, between them advanced the almost incredible sum of £220,000 from their own private resources for the sustainment of the king.

"It seems the Marquis thinks there is cause sufficient," replied Sir John Netterville, for he it was; "much did I hear at the Castle concerning a certain secret treaty of that Earl's, a copy of which was found on the body of the Archbishop of Tuam —know you, my lords, anything of it ?"

The malicious glance of Netterville's dark eye was not lost on Owen Roe who could hardly believe his own eyes that what he saw was real. Turning to the old Lord Netterville who chanced to be near him at the moment, he asked in utter amazement:

" Do mine eyes deceive me, or is yonder gay cavalier your lordship's son ?"

" Surely, yes—methought Sir John Netterville was well known to you."

" So I thought, too, my lord, but the Sir John Netterville who *was* well known to me was a brave adventurous knight of the Confederation—the gentleman before us weareth Ormond's colors, and cometh hither, moreover, an' I mistake not, on Ormond's errand. I pray your lordship read me this riddle !"

" It is easy of solution," quoth the Palesman with icy coldness; " to serve Lord Ormond at the present time is to serve the Confederation."

" Ha ! lieth the land that way ?" said O'Neill musingly, yet so loud that his words reached the ear of the young knight. For a moment his bold careless glance sank before the piercing eye of Owen Roe, but quickly he recovered his self-possession, and making his way behind the high-backed oaken seats of the hall to the place where O'Neill sat, he extended his hand with a smile which he meant for a cordial one.

" It is some time since we met, General !"

" The longer the better it would seem," interrupted Owen, drawing himself up with a freezing air of contempt, and thrusting one hand into the breast of his jacket, whilst the other rested on his knee. "An' I were in your boots with those colors topping my head, I would not stand where you do—no, not for the broad lands of Netterville !"

Lord Netterville's brow darkened and his hollow cheek turned ghastly pale. He was fain to speak, but could not, and sat with his eye fixed on O'Neill as though spell-bound by the

extent of his audacity. His son was less surprised, but his
anger, restrained by the place and the presence in which he
found himself, was the deeper and the more concentrated.

Approaching close to O'Neill, he stooped down and leaning
over his shoulder whispered in a hissing tone: "The favor of
the fair Emmeline will surely make up for my defection—I
sought her out but late in the sorry habitation your bounty
hath given her—sought her, I own it in shame, to renew my
suit, and——"

"And?" inquired Owen, interested beyond concealment.

"And she spurned me from her as though I were a dog!—
ay, marry, did she!" and the unhappy young man ground his
teeth in impotent rage, while the livid hue of his wasted cheek
touched Owen's heart with pity. "She spoke such harsh and
bitter words concerning our common ancestry—her own and
mine—that madness itself could hardly excuse her. She *hath*
gone mad, it is said within the Pale, since Maguire's death;
ha! ha! ha! a fitting end he made of it—for my part, I think
you Irishry have bewitched her, and I swore an oath which I
mean to keep, that henceforth we meet as foemen should!"

"But what of the oath of Confederation?"

"As for that," said Netterville with a light laugh, "let one
cancel the other. I have sworn, I tell you, to thwart your
views, and, mark me, the Macs' and O's shall rue the day they
stepped between me and Emmeline!

"Young man, you are my prisoner!" said O'Neill aloud, and
he grasped him by the shoulder. In an instant all was confusion; astonishment was depicted on every face, for no one had
overheard the whispered dialogue, and that Sir John Netterville
should have been employed by Ormond to treat with his own
friends seemed no way strange to the Norman lords.

"At your peril, arrest me!" said young Netterville fiercely,
and he laid his hand on his sword. "You dare not, Owen
O'Neill! whilst your truce with Lord Ormond lasts—I came
hither on the plighted word of your commissioners who might
perchance share Glamorgan's prison by now were it not for
me!"

At this moment the Nuncio entered, and the scene that met

his eye was anything but encouraging, for it seemed as though the old and the new Irish were about to spring on each other with murderous intent.

Several of the bishops were already gathered around Owen Roe and the handsome young knight—to Rinuccini a stranger —who still writhed in his iron grasp. There was a deep hush as the Nuncio approached and demanded in Latin of Bishop French what this scene meant. Being informed he smiled sadly and shook his head, muttering to himself: "It is as I feared— these Ormondists are but one step from the enemy—their oath is the only tie that now binds them to us. May God change their hearts!"

With a heavy sigh he motioned to O'Neill to let the young man go, and Owen obeyed without a murmur, but he whispered in Netterville's ear as he flung him back to the wall: "We meet again at Phillippi!—go now in peace!"

With a black scowl of hate which made Owen wince with all his courage, Netterville took his father's arm and both proceeded down the hall. Another trial awaited the renegade. Sir Phelim O'Neill had made his way into the Council-room, and hearing from Tirlogh what had taken place, he grasped Sir John's arm as he passed him by.

"What! turned traitor so soon? Doing Ormond's dirty work? Blood of the Nettervilles! what a fall!"

"I have not taken to *forgery* yet, Sir Phelim," said Netterville with a bitter sneer, "when I do, say I have fallen, not before!"

The effect of these words was so stunning that before Sir Phelim had recovered the shock, the Nettervilles, father and son, had left the hall. Looking round with a ghastly smile, the knight of Kinnard tried to pass the matter off as a jest:

"Truly he is a pleasant knave," said he, "that young Netterville—ever ready with his answer. I would he were honest as he is witty!"

Whatever importance Sir Phelim or Owen might attach to Sir John's desertion, the matter weighed but little in the mind of Rinuccini compared with the treacherous arrest of Glamorgan, which justified all his previous suspicions of Ormond.

Even the most devoted adherents of the Lord Lieutenant dared not in the face of such a fact defend him before the Council, and for the time, Rinuccini had it all his own way. For himself he manifested no surprise, declaring such an act in perfect accordance with the view he had taken of the Viceroy's character and his real sentiments towards Catholics.

His private devotions were interrupted that evening by a late visit from some four or five of the Confederates, and the Nuncio wondered very much what urgent affair had brought them at such an hour. Bishop French was happily one of the party, and through him the others explained the nature of their visit.

"In case they made up their minds to attack Dublin without delay, what support could the Nuncio give them?"

Rinuccini's heart swelled with joy at the bare suggestion of a step so bold and so decisive. Still he was not in a position to answer them.

"I would I might tell you on the instant, my lords and gentlemen," he said with an air of satisfaction, "but I know not myself what amount of money will remain at my disposal till I have learned how much will be expended on those frigates, which, as you know, I have sent to Flanders to purchase. We have much need of them now, seeing that your privateers have all departed from your coasts since the first commencement of the truce."

This uncertainty was not what the Council had expected, and the Nuncio's answer, reported to them, threw a damp on the fitful flash of their ardor evoked by Glamorgan's arrest. O'Neill, on the contrary, was roused to more active exertion, and, encouraged by the Nuncio's undisguised approval, and his promise of speedy succor, he prepared to set out for the north in company with Sir Phelim O'Neill, McMahon of Uriel, and O'Reilly of Breffny.

It was a gratifying sight to the Nuncio when, the northern chieftains going to crave his blessing prior to their departure, Owen Roe and his fiery kinsman knelt side by side with bowed heads and clasped hands. Strong, firm man as Rinuccini was, his voice trembled with emotion as he blessed each noble head, and when they arose he said with a moistened eye:

"Sons of the Gael, my hope is in *you*. As God liveth, you must fight the battle for Him and yourselves. What aid I have to give shall be yours, and your fair Ulster shall be first cleared of the tyrant foe !"

He then took the hands of Sir Phelim and Owen O'Neill, and joining them said : " Be you as brothers henceforth—in union ye conquer. In wars of this nature, self must be forgotten, and only the common good and the holy cause kept in view."

At this moment Sir John Netterville was announced, and the Nuncio, fearing the result of such a meeting after what he had witnessed in the Council Hall, requested the chieftains to withdraw into another apartment till the new visitor had retired. On the threshold they met Netterville. He would have passed them in contemptuous silence, but Sir Phelim could not refrain from giving him a piece of his mind.

" An' your face were not made of brass," said he, " you would not dare show it here. After all, you're more to be pitied than anything else. Pass on !"

The fierce retort on Netterville's lip was changed for a gesture of defiance, for through the open door the young man caught the stern glance of Rinuccini fixed full upon him, and with a strange feeling of embarrassment he entered the room whilst Owen Roe turned and looked after him a moment with a heavy sigh.

" Poor fellow !" he said within himself, " I had better hopes of him through all my dark forebodings !"

CHAPTER XXX.

"Give praise to the Virgin Mother! O'Neill is at Benburb.
The chieftain of the martial soul, who scorns the Saxon curb;
Between the hills his camp is pitch'd, and in its front upthrown,
The Red Hand points to victory from the standard of Tyrone;
Behind him rise the ancient woods, while on his flank anear him,
The deep Blackwater calmly glides and seems to greet and cheer him.

"By all the Saints they're welcome! across the crested wave,
For few who left Kinnad this morn ere night shall lack a grave.
The hour—the man, await them now, and retribution dire
Shall sweep their ranks from front to rear, by our avenging fire;
Yet on they march in pride of heart—the hell-engender'd gloom
Of the grim, predestined Puritan impels them to their doom."
HAYES' Irish Ballads.

PASSING over the spring months of that memorable year of
1646, fruitful as they were in stirring events, we will convey the
reader once again to those scenes of old renown where the ancient keep of Benburb overhangs "the Avon Dhu of the north"
—Avon Dhu of the O'Neills.

It is a radiant night in early June and

"Beneath a bright and bonny moon,"

shining high in mid heaven, two great armies are again encamped. Again Monroe is there with his whole force; no less
than ten regiments of foot and fifteen troops of horse lie along
the Blackwater under his command this summer night. And
the Irish army, beyond the river, looked wondrous small compared with that Scottish host; so well it might for it numbered
scarce five thousand foot, with eight companies of horse.* But
that little army was a host in itself, a mighty host, for not Castlehaven with his Norman auxiliaries from the Pale was there,
but Owen Roe O'Neill with the clans of Ulster, the impetuous

* Rinuccini's *Memoirs.*

sons of the soil, burning to wreak revenge on the Scots, who
for six long years had been working their wicked will on man,
woman and child, till they had made the fair land a desert.
Few were the Catholics as compared with their foes, but for
every man that was wanting the ghosts of slaughtered friends
and kindred were there in scores; their shadowy presence pervaded all the ranks, for each man there had his share of the dismal memories of those bloody years, and every arm was nerved
with superhuman strength, now that the cherished hopes of
years were approaching their consummation. Owen Roe, with
the sanction and advice of the Nuncio, was, at last, confronting
the Scots, determined to drive them from Ulster if there was
strength in him or his. The clans of Ulster were well represented
on that battle-eve, for though few or none were there entire,
hardly one was wanting. O'Neills and Maguires, McMahons
and O'Hanlons, O'Reillys and O'Rourkes from the two Breffnys,
O'Boyles and McSweenys, and O'Muldoons from the north, and
O'Donnells and O'Cahans from the farthest north of all where
the Foyle and the Roe wind their silvery way through the
mountain-glens of Donegal and Derry. O'Dogbertys were not
wanting from wild Innishowen, from the banks of " the bountiful Culdaff"—ay! they were there, a stalwart band, those song-
famed " tall peasants of fair Innishowen," well prepared to read
the riddle† of Ireland's fate at the bidding of Owen Roe.

And how were the clansmen employed during those moonlit
hours within sight of the enemy whom they had hurried from
the border country to meet? Who were the men in black cassocks—few they were in number, not more than three or four—
who glided hither and thither amongst them, or, seated on ar-
tillery-wagons on either slope of the two hills between which
the army lay, raised their right hand over the head of every

† " When they tell us the tale of a spell-stricken band,
  All entranced, with their bridles and broadswords in hand,
  Who await but the word to give Erin her own,
  They can read you that riddle in proud Innishowen.
    Hurrah for the spearmen of proud Innishowen !—
    Long live the wild seers of stout Innishowen !—
    May Mary our Mother be deaf to their moan
    Who love not the promise of proud Innishowen."
                                        C. G. Duffy.

soldier there as he knelt in turn before them ?   Reader, the men
were confessing their sins, in preparation for a still more solemn
rite, and of the priests who heard them one was Father Eugene, an
eminent Franciscan, who had been appointed by the Nuncio
Chaplain to the Ulster forces, and another, our old friend, Father
Phelimy O'Cahan.   On the skirt of a wood in the rear of the army
sat Heber of Clogher, on the stump of a fallen tree, engaged in the
same pious work, albeit that the stole which marked his priestly
office was in stern and strange contrast with the stuffed jerkin
which encased his brawny shoulders and the steel morion which
lay beside him on the grass.   Yes, the patriotic prelate had
clearly girded on the sword, ambitious, it might be, of sharing
Archbishop Malachy's glorious fate.   Near and around where
the bishop sat the men of Uriel were encamped, McMahons and
McKennas, and the stout borderers of Farney, and whilst some
were on their knees preparing for confession, others were engaged in the construction of an altar under the skilful direction
of Malachy *na soggarth*.   If ever man was in his element it was
Malachy that night, and the usual gravity of his demeanor was
deepened into a solemn dignity befitting his high office, for
Malachy esteemed himself on that occasion second to no other in
importance.   His claims were tacitly acknowledged by the bold
clansmen around, who came and went, and fetched and carried
at Malachy's high behest, all well pleased to have a hand in so
great a work—under the direction of " Bishop McMahon's right
hand man."

Yes! Malachy was in his glory, and by a curious coincidence,
Shamus Beg O'Hagan was again his companion, as on that other
night five years gone by when the long unused chapel of Kinnard Castle was the scene of his pious labors.   But Shamus was
no idle spectator at this time listening to old-world stories, for
with Donogh the Rapparee, and one or two others, he was busily
engaged forming a canopy of flags to protect the altar from
wind and weather.   The manner in which this task was performed had given Malachy entire satisfaction, till, stepping back
a few paces to ascertain the general effect, he cried out all
aghast:

"Good Lord! Shamus, isn't that the Red Hand you have on the top above?"

"An' to be sure it is, Malachy!—what else would it be?"

"Why, my soul to God, Shamus! but you're a bit of a ghomeril after all—isn't it *our* flag that ought to be there, not *yours?*——'

"Ha! ha! Malachy! wise as you are, I have you this time"—and Shamus indulged in a low chuckling laugh. "Sure *you* needn't object to have the Red Hand uppermost when your chief will fight under it to-morrow?"

Malachy gave in with a heavy sigh, muttering, "I suppose it's to be or it *wouldn't* be."

"Don't sigh so heavily, old friend," said the deep voice of Donogh, or rather Phelim McGee. "They're not on Irish ground this night that need be ashamed to follow the beck of the Red Hand. Owen Roe is the man for us!"

"Who says he isn't?" questioned Malachy in a snappish tone all unusual with him. "My lord!" said he, approaching the bishop who had just dismissed from his knee a gigantic follower of Rory Maguire, "my lord! if you don't take a few hours' rest you'll not be able to lift your head in the morning!"

"No need to lift it surely when I don't lay it down," said the good-humored prelate, "and besides, Malachy, it matters little when to-morrow's sunset may find that same head stiff and cold —let me alone, I pray you! for much remains to be done, and the time is short. Kneel!" he said to a stout gallowglass who had been waiting patiently for his turn—"bestir yourself, Malachy! —and see that the vestments be all in order—Mass will commence ere long." Away started Malachy to one of the baggage wagons in quest of his vestments and altar linen, whilst Shamus Beg stood looking at the altar and the banners all clearly revealed in the moonlight, and somehow a feeling of sadness stole over him. It was not fear—for Shamus never feared "man or devil," as he often boasted, but rather a heavy weight as of sorrow. Angry with himself for being so "down-hearted" he muttered between his teeth: "Ah, then, Shamus boy, what's coming over you at all?—sure it wouldn't be fear that's on you, after all the bloody battles you've had a hand in! Come, come, rouse yourself now, and be a man!"

Turning quickly to regain Sir Phelim's tent whence he had issued some half an hour before, he met the deep earnest eyes of Angus Dhu fixed full upon him. The young Rapparee was leaning on the handle of his pike immovable as a statue. His face was paler than usual and his garments covered with dust, for Angus had ridden hard and fast since the night fell to be present at the expected battle. He had but just arrived and exchanged a brotherly greeting with his captain who expressed his joy that he came in time with the little party under his command. Shamus and Angus were ever glad to meet, and it was some time since they had met before.

"Well! if that isn't queer," said the foster-brother with a start; "you're the very one I was thinking of, Angus! When did you get in, or how are you at all?"

"I got in about ten minutes ago, and I'm well enough only a little tired, but I mean to take an hour's sleep or two, if the enemy lets us alone that long, and then, please God, I'll be able for any Scotch devil amongst them! But how is yourself, Shamus? I don't know whether it's on my eyes it is, but I think you're not in the best of health." And the young man's voice trembled slightly.

"Health! Angus!" cried Shamus, cutting one of the frolicsome capers of *Auld lang syne.* "Is it me not in good health! —never was better in all my born days—an' sure if I wasn't even, the very thoughts of to-morrow would make me a new man. But listen, Angus, to what I'm going to tell you, for we don't know the minute the alarm may come, and I wouldn't miss the chance of saying what I *have* to say—no, not for broad Tyr-Owen. In the first place, then, I'm overjoyed to see you, Angus."

"No need to tell me that, anyhow," the Rapparee replied with sly emphasis.

"Well, well, what I mean is that I'm doubly glad to see you now for a reason I have."

"And what is it?"

"If anything happens me to-morrow, I want you to take this

broken ring to a *gersha* down in the County Antrim. She has
the other half, and you will give her this, and tell her it's the
only ring she'll ever get from Shamus O'Hagan. Tell her it isn't
his fault, but he did what he promised to do when the war was
over and our rights gained. If I live, please God, I'll get back
the ring from you, Angus, and take it down there myself, but if
I don't—you'll be sure to do it."

"But supposing I fall myself—" suggested Angus, smiling
through tears. "How then?"

"Pooh, pooh, you'll not fall—there's no danger in life! Keep
the ring, and do as I bid you!"

Angus laughed, yet there was little mirth in his laugh. He
suddenly took hold of his friend's hand and clasped it with convulsive energy.

"Shamus!" said he, "you don't know all the love that's in my
heart for you. You don't, Shamus, but maybe you will soon.
Anyhow, I'll do your bidding—Aileen Magee shall have the
ring—that's if anything happens you."

"Aileen Magee!" repeated Shamus in amazement, "why,
sure I never mentioned her name—or did I—for, indeed, there's
such a load on my heart that it makes me dull and heavy like
—Did I tell you the girleen's name?"

"Well, no!"—and Angus smiled faintly—"but if you didn't,
maybe some one else did. Move a little this way, for there's
the General going to confession——"

"The general! which general?—oh! I see, it's Owen Roe you
mean! I thought it might be Sir Phelim, but sure, no matter,
it's all in the family. Well, the Lord be with you, Angus—but
stay, stay"—and approaching him, he lowered his voice to a
whisper—"I forgot to tell you where you'd light on Aileen."

"Oh, never mind!" replied Angus, with a careless toss of his
head; "when I want to find her, I'll know where to go. She'll
be little worth, anyhow, by the time your message reaches
her."

"What's that you say?"

"I say it's not far from daylight now—ahem! so I'll off and
help Phelim—oh, bother! Donogh I mean—to get the boys in
readiness. Hillo! there's his whistle, I must be off."

"But Angus—stay one minute!—where—when will I see you again?"

"God knows," said Angus with emotion, "God knows, Shamus aroon!—why, the captain is in a hurry!" Putting his hand to his mouth he returned the signal call, then wrung Shamus by both hands, and darted off into the wood, where, for the present, the Rapparees were placed. An hour later and they were sent by the general to aid in the defence of the bridge already held by a detachment from Sir Con Magennis's regiment.

The day was just dawning when Sir Phelim O'Neill stood at the door of his kinsman's tent and peered cautiously in expecting to find Owen asleep. Not so, however, for the latter was on his knees in full equipment, whilst his two aide-de-camps, also drest, lay sleeping soundly with their heads resting on the side of the heathery couch that had been prepared for the general.

"Humph!" said Phelim as Owen rose and came forward, "at your devotions so early?—what with the squalling of psalms *yonder*, and the praying and so forth *here*, so pious a battle was never fought as this is like to be. But that is not what I came to say. They tell me you sent off Colonel Bernard McMahon and Colonel Patrick McAneny over night with their whole regiments—up Monaghan side. Is it true, Owen, or is it not?"

"It *is* true?—but what then?"

"Why, I'd like to know what put that in your head, and we scarce half the number of the enemy at our best? Come, now, Fabius of your country!* answer me that!" He spoke in a tone half jeering, half friendly, and Owen was not the man to resent a joke, however surly, from a brother-general at such a moment.

"I will answer you, Phelim, and truly," said Owen with perfect good humor; "nay, more, to your satisfaction. I have learned that Monroe had sent to his brother Robert to join him without delay with all the forces at his command, and as the latter would come on us from the rear we should find ourselves between two fires, either of which is enough for our numbers

---

* Owen Roe was from an early period of the war distinguished by this proud and honorable title.

17

to cope with. How think you, cousin! was I not right in sparing those two regiments, if happily they can keep Colonel Robert back until we have settled with Covenanting George?"†

"Forgive me, Eoghain!" said honest Phelim with some emotion; "I know you are a wiser man than I, and have a longer head by a great deal. You are the *shield*, I know well, but let blustering Phelim be the *sword* and you shall have the planning of all. Tell me, do you mean to attack, or wait Monroe's onset—which? See the sun is already peeping on us from behind the hill!"

"Hark! is not that the low tinkle of a bell?" said Owen with a start.

"Bell, indeed!" answered Phelim with a laugh; "sure it's dreaming you are, Owen Roe! I hear a sound like the measured clash of steel, but no bell."

"Anyhow, it is the signal for Mass, I know that!" said Owen, and he muttered to himself as he proceeded to rouse his drowsy aide-de-camps!

"When, oh! when shall I hear thee no more, bell of old Eglish! Art thou a knell for me or mine this day? Not so, for I feel within me the assurance of victory!"

The sun had but just raised his broad disk above the horizon when Bishop McMahon in his loud clear tones was reciting the *Introibo ad altare Dei* at the foot of the military altar, with Father Hartegan, one of the chaplains of the army, serving Mass, and Malachy, of course, in official attendance. On one side knelt Father Phelimy O'Cahan, his aged face beaming with the light of hope, on the other the tall dignified form of the Franciscan, Father Eugene, the Nuncio's special representative. In a semicircle fronting the altar were Owen Roe and Sir Phelim O'Neill, Sir Con Magennis, Owen O'Rourke, Philip O'Reilly and Art McMahon, the principal chiefs of the army; the colonels and other officers remained with their regiments for fear of surprise. A few yards back knelt Roderick Maguire at the head

† General Monroe had a little before this taken the "Solemn League and Covenant" on bended knee in the high kirk of Carrickfergus.

of his column, and by his side was Lorcan, looking twenty years younger than when we last saw him, and grasping with the vigor of lusty manhood the long spear which for old times' sake he still used in war. Like a sturdy oak of his own woods was Lorcan, hale, strong and vigorous even in decay. And how lovingly the old man clutched his spear as he thought of his murdered Connor and wished he had lived to see that day!

And as he wished, he raised his eyes towards the altar, and lo! what sight was there that enchained his wandering glance? Two female figures wrapt in sable drapery knelt close behind Father Pheliny, their faces concealed by deep riding-hoods.

"Lord save us!" ejaculated Lorcan, "are the spirits come in broad daylight? I suppose, now, nobody sees them but myself, for sure the sight of them would make more of a scatterment than Monroe's cavalry. Well! who knows but they come for me at last—indeed one of them puts me in mind of my poor dead sister, Eveleen O'Cahan—and they're welcome as the flowers in May, if that be their errand—let me only have a few hours' good hard fighting with those Scotch devils below and see them fairly taken to their legs, and I'll go with all my heart wherever God pleases."

Lorgan's surmise appeared correct, for no one but himself appeared to notice the shadowy forms. For himself, he could hardly take his eyes off them though he struggled hard to avoid so grievous a distraction, especially as he was preparing to receive the holiest of sacraments. But the sight of the dark motionless figures, fresh from the world of spirits, was more than Lorcan's piety could resist, and do as he would his eyes were ever turning stealthily in their direction, whilst his lips and his heart prayed with fervor and his fingers told the beads of his Rosary.

It was a solemn sight, take it altogether, when the soldier-bishop offered up the Atoning Sacrifice of the New Law in sight of that valiant army on the banks of the Blackwater—when every head was bowed in adoration, and every heart raised to heaven. It was a goodly sight, too, to see the rough warriors of the mountains, the kerns and gallowglasses of many a clan, kneeling in whole battalions in the light of the morning

sun, with the rich rays playing on their shining arms and accoutrements, and the fresh breeze sporting with the plumes which
shaded noble brows and rustling in the banners above the
simple altar, whilst the Sacred Host was elevated between earth
and heaven by the bishop's consecrated hands. No less solemn
or imposing was the sight when, at the Communion, the General
and all his officers advanced in regular order and received the
Bread of Life, the musicians striking up at the moment a soft
and plaintive air. Many a glorious scene had old Avon Dhu
witnessed on its banks, but never one more glorious than that.
Oh! the ineffable grandeur which encircled the brow of Owen
Roe as he stepped forward first of all, making a sign to Sir
Phelim to take his place by his side. It was not that the
chieftain looked exalted in his own estimation, for his demeanor
was that of an humble and sincere Christian, calm and collected
—no, but the effect of his example was such, and so striking,
that there was not a man on the hill of Benburb that hour who
did not bow down in spirit before so great and good a man.

After the *Ite Missa Est* Father Eugene, putting on his stole,
ascended the steps of the altar (they were formed of mountain
heather closely packed together beneath many folds of tent-
canvas) and gave the solemn Papal benediction. That done,
there was a mighty rushing sound and a deafening clang of
arms; it was the men rising from their knees and each grasping
his weapon. Then arose on the morning air a wild enthusiastic
cheer from those thousands and thousands of brave hearts; it
was for his Holiness Innocent X., the friend and protector of
the oppressed Catholics of Ireland. That cheer echoed far and
wide over the country, and pealed on the ears of Monroe's grim
Puritans as a challenge to mortal combat. They had witnessed
from afar the morning devotions of the Irish, and the sight of
the altar filled them with fury; the cheers of the Catholics were
answered by them with howls of execration, and cries of
" Death to the worshippers of idols!—wo to the followers of
Baal! The sword of the Lord and Gideon!"

Monroe had effected a junction on the previous day with
Hamilton's forces, and the presence of that savage leader was
speedily detected by the Clan O'Rourke, who testified their joy

by shouts of fierce exultation. Our old acquaintance, **Manus**, had risen to the rank of captain, and his company was composed of his own kinsmen, every man of them sworn to deadliest revenge on the murderer of their youthful Tanist. The blood-stained flag of the Hamiltons waving on the right flank of the Scottish army was early in the day pointed out by Manus to his men, and even the calm chieftain himself, noble and chivalrous as he was, could not help expressing his satisfaction that the day so long wished for was come at last.

Never did two armies face each other with more stern determination or greater ardor for the fight than on that day at Benburb. On the part of the Scotch there was the fanatical desire to clear the land of the old idolatrous natives, the "Ammonites" and "Moabites," of their Scriptural cant. Fancying themselves, like the Hebrews of old, commissioned to destroy and exterminate a race so odious to their God, they stood glaring on the Irish enemy across the watery barrier which, as yet, they might not pass. They had tried the bridge early in the morning, but were repulsed by its gallant defenders in a style that fully justified Owen's choice. The serried pikes of the Rapparees were found as a wall of iron which no Scottish steel might penetrate. Again and again the attempt was made, and again and again did the exulting shout of the Rapparees mark the enemy's discomfiture. Loudly laughed the woodsmen, and fondly they patted their trusty pikes, vowing that they should make a closer acquaintance with " the murdering Scotch" before noonday. It was long since they felt their hearts so light—

> " The fearless Rapparees!
> Oh! the jewel were you, Rory, with your Irish Rapparees!"

But the covenanters were too fiercely athirst for Papist blood to be so easily baulked, and Monroe, urged by Hamilton and others of his officers, resolved to march along the river edge to Kinard and there effect a passage.

Leaving them to accomplish this design, marvelling much at what they considered the neglect of O'Neill in leaving the ford at Kinard undefended, we will return again to the Irish army and to Lorcan Maguire at the close of the apostolic benediction.

He had bowed his head reverently to receive the blessing, and
his first glance on raising it again was towards the supposed
spirits. They had vanished, and Lorcan crossed himself devoutly, muttering between his teeth :

" Heaven's rest to you, Eveleen Maguire !—but I wonder who
the other is—maybe my own fair Una !"—meaning the wife of
his youth lost in the first year of their marriage—" pity Connor
wasn't with them—but I suppose he wasn't allowed. No matter,
no matter, *I'll see them all soon*, and, through God's mercy, for
ever more !"

The old man little dreamed that the supposed spirits had
merely emerged from the wood to hear Mass, or that Owen Roe
and Father Phelimy had been trying in vain to exorcise them
hours before the first cock-crow. The most stubborn of ghostly
creatures, they refused to quit the place come what might.
Surrounded by a small party of the Rapparees commanded by
Angus Dhu, they busied themselves in making what preparations their poverty permitted for the relief of those who should
be wounded in the battle, whilst a cross formed of two branches
was nailed to the trunk of a tree, as though to sanctify the place.
Who that saw Emmeline Coote when she reigned supreme over
Dublin drawing-rooms, and bestowed prizes with smiling grace
on those who shed the most of Papist blood, could have recognized her in the sad companion of Judith O'Cahan that day,
raising her soul-lit eyes ever and anon to the rude emblem of
salvation the while she prayed for success to the Catholic arms ?
Yet Emmeline herself it was, and not even Judith was more
wildly anxious for the overthrow of the Puritans than that
daughter of the bloody Cootes.

Apprised by the faithful Rapparees of the expected collision
of the hostile armies, the two ladies with their aged protector
had journeyed with all haste to the neighborhood of Charlemont,
as the probable scene of the coming conflict. Father Phelimy
having once joined the army, determined to remain for the
spiritual succor of the soldiers, but he shrank, and so did Owen
Roe, at the thought of the dangers to which Judith and Emmeline voluntarily exposed themselves.

But Judith would not hear of danger. "Your turn is come

now," said she to Owen, as at midnight the four stood together
looking out through an opening of the wood upon the motionless columns of the army, as they knelt in preparation for confession ; " God is with you—the shadow of His presence is over
your army—fear not, oh! first of the sons of Ireland! the Albinach is delivered to the swords of our avengers, so sure as
yonder moon walks the heavens in light !"

" First of the sons of Ireland !" repeated Owen to himself with
a thrill of joy ; aloud he said : " An' we conquer, the lady Judith
hath no small share in our success ; much hath she done of late
in nourishing the flame of patriotic ardor."

" I pray you name it not," said Judith hastily, as she turned
away ; " I did nothing—the Scottish murderers did all—all!
Come, Emmeline, let us retire !—God keep you, general ! Bless
us, father, before you go to enter on your sacred office !"

Not to rest but to prayer did the ladies retire, and Malachy's
signal found them still kneeling before their cross.

CHAPTER XXXI.

" Our rude array's a jagged rock to smash the spoiler's power,
  Or need we aid, His aid we have who doom'd this gracious hour
  Of yore He led His Hebrew host to peace through strife and pain,
  And us He leads the self-same path, the self-same goal to gain."
                                                        C. G. DUFFY.

" Like lions leaping at a fold, when mad with hunger's pang,
  Right up against the English line the Irish exiles sprang,
  Bright was their steel, 'tis bloody now, their guns are fill'd with
        gore ;
  Thro' shatter'd ranks, and sever'd files, and trampled flags they
        tore ;
  The English strove with desperate strength, paused, rallied, stag-
        ger'd, fled—
  The green-hill side is matted close with dying and with dead ;
  Across the plain and far away pass'd on that hideous wrack,
  While cavalier and fantassin dash in upon their track,
  On Fontenoy, on Fontenoy, like eagles in the sun,
  With bloody plumes the Irish stand—the field is fought and won."
                                                        THOMAS DAVIS.

IT was high noon that day when Owen Roe O'Neill appeared
again before the anxious watchers in the wood. He was paler
than his wont, and when he spoke his voice trembled slightly,
but his manner was even more collected than usual.

"Judith !" said he, " the final moment is well nigh come.
They have crossed at Kinnard, and driven back Colonel O'Farrel from the defile where I had placed him. They are rapidly
approaching."

"You mean to wait for them, then ?"

"Assuredly I do—my position here is well worth keeping—
but—but—I came to say *farewell*—should we meet no more—
God in heaven protect you and this noble damsel who hath left
her own to cling unto us—once more, let me persuade you to
remove from a place so fraught with danger—do, for God's
sake, ere yet the enemy is upon us."

"I have told you I will not go," said Judith loftily, "and

Emmeline is resolved as I am. Whither, in God's name, should
we go—our hopes are here, and here our safety lies, for if, which
God forfend! Monroe is the victor to-day, no spot on Ulster
ground will be safe for us henceforth. Away, then, Owen!
away to your post, and may the just Lord God watch over your
precious life, for a day of carnage, yea, a bloody day is before
you,—howsoever the battle goes, the slaughter will be fearful—
where revenge strikes on one side, and fanatic hatred on the
other, mercy will have no place."

"It is true, Judith, too true," said the chieftain sadly, then
turning to Angus who stood near leaning against a tree, he said
earnestly, "Angus, my brave lad, I know you well. I know
you will guard these ladies as you would the apple of your eye.
Hence it is that I leave them with you. But mark me!—if the
battle goes against us, take them to Charlemont without delay
—wait not till all is over, for then it will be too late, but go
before your retreat is cut off. Mark my words, I say again! as
you shall answer it to me at the last great day!"

"Never fear, General! never fear!" said Angus with emotion,
"but before you go, I would ask you one question. Where
have you placed Sir Phelim?"

"Yonder on the right wing—why do you ask, Angus?"

"Oh, nothing in life, general, only that I'd wish to know."

Once more O'Neill turned to the fair companions. Emmeline
was pale as death, and trembled in every limb as she gave him
her hand at parting, but on Judith's noble brow there was no
trace of fear; no dark misgiving smote her heart. Her usually
pale cheek was tinged with a roseate hue, and her dark blue
eyes gleamed through their long lashes like the sapphires in a
royal crown. O'Neill looked at her and his heart-pulse quickened. Like the genius of the land she stood in that hour, beautiful and stately, bearing on her features the imprint of sorrow
and suffering, yet radiant with the light of hope and the inner
life which passes show.

"Go forth to conquer!" said the lady as she placed her hand
on the chieftain's arm; "son of Niall, the daughter of Cooey-na-
gall stakes her life on your success. Go forth—and the God of
battles be your aid, and Mary the Help of Christians!"

Strong in the righteous cause for which he fought, strong in
the encouragement of her whom he regarded as in some sort
inspired, and strong above all in the might of Him whose corporal presence was within him, Owen Roe *did* go forth, and
mounting his war-steed, reached the centre division of his
army just as the Scottish columns planted their standards in
the plain beneath. O'Farrel's regiment, somewhat the worse
for its encounter with the Scottish vanguard,* was placed in
the rear with the *reserved corps*, and then the general, with his
staff, rode along the line amid the enthusiastic cheers of the
soldiers, while

The *generale's* beating on many a drum,

and the pipes strike up the various clan tunes. These after a
few bars are all merged in the noble and warlike strain, known
then as Planxty Sudley,† the grandest, the most inspiriting that
ever broke on warrior's ear. And the hearts of the bold clansmen throbbed high with joy and hope as they listened, and
their feet beat time to the gladsome strain, and the very horses
pranced and danced as though they, too, were eager for the
fray. Oh! sight of joy for Erin, who would not wish to see it!

> " When hearts are all high beating,
> And the trumpet's voice repeating
>   That song, whose breath
>   May lead to death,
> But never to retreating.
> Oh! the sight entrancing,

* " As they (the Scots) advanced they were met by Colonel Rich
ard O'Farrel, who occupied a narrow defile through which it was
necessary for the Scotch troops to pass in order to face the Irish.
The fire of Monroe's guns compelled O'Neill's officer to retire."—
Confederation, p. 149.

† This noble war-tune is happily preserved to us by the artistic
zeal of Sir John Stephenson. Through the delightful medium of
Moore's verse, it is known, I hope, to many of my readers as " Oh!
the sight entrancing!" I pity the Irish heart that is not stirred to
its depth by that glorious strain, so full of the martial fire which ran
in the veins of our Celtic fathers.

When morning's beam is glancing
O'er files array'd
With helm and blade,
And plumes in the gay wind dancing.

" Yet, 'tis not helm or feather—
For ask yon despot, whether
His plumed bands
Could bring such hands
And hearts as ours together.
Leave pomps to those who need 'em—
Give man but heart and freedom,
And proud he braves
The gaudiest slaves
That crawl where monarchs lead 'em.
The sword may pierce the beaver,
Stone walls in time may sever,
'Tis mind alone,
Worth steel and stone,
That keeps men free for ever."‡

Those words of fire were as yet unbreathed, but their spirit throbs in every vein of those saffron-coated warriors who stand skilfully ranged in order of battle beneath the flags of the Ulster chiefs—those flags which at dawn canopied the sacred elements.

As Owen O'Neill rode slowly along the line, he was joined by Bishop McMahon, who had been surveying the ground and the different arrangements with the eye of a veteran soldier. "Owen!" said he, "our position here is every way admirable, but how shall we manage the sun yonder, shining full in our eyes?"

" I have thought of that, my Lord," said the general with an anxious glance at the too brilliant luminary; " would the enemy but keep quiet for a few hours all were well, but an' they *will* attack us, we must e'en keep them in play till the sun begins to descend. How, now, Rory?"—he was passing the Fermanagh men at the moment, and the young chief stepped forward, indicating by a sign that he wished to speak.

" I fear for my poor uncle," said Rory; " he hath made up his mind that he is to die this day, but not till he hath worked out

‡ Moore's *Irish Melodies.*

some conceit of his own, the which I take to be so perilous that
it *may* well end as he forebodes. Could you not send him to
keep guard in the wood yonder?"

"An' he did, too," said Lorcan at his elbow, "I would not go.
Others can keep guard in the wood as well as I, and I might
thereby lose my chance of revenge. For shame, Rory! plotting
against your old uncle!"

"But, uncle, you do not know——"

"Lorcan! it were a post of honor, an' you knew but all!"

"Small thanks to either of you," said the old man snappishly;
"I know enough to take care of my *own* honor—in the van I'll
be, I tell you that—it wasn't to hide myself in the wood that I
got the sight I did this morning!"

"Steady, men, steady!" cried Owen O'Neill, "they are advancing rapidly. Keep your ground—obey your officers—they
know my plans."

"The cavalry! the cavalry!"—"oh! the hell-hounds! a warm
welcome to them!"

On they went, Lord Ardes at their head, their terrible clay-
mores flashing in the sun. Heaven help the Irish kern, with
only their barradhs and glib-locks to protect their heads! Yet
firm as a rock they stand with their pikes and bayonets firmly
clasped, prepared to resist the shock. But on and still on they
come, Monroe's bloody troopers—hurrah! mid-way on their
course they are greeted by a scathing fire from the bushes on
either side—they reel—they attempt to rally—Lord Ardes waves
his sabre and urges them on—thick and fast comes the deadly
volley from the brushwood—down go the Scots one after one,
man and horse rolling over down the hill-side—a panic seized
the troopers, and their officers losing all command of them, they
hastily made their retreat to the sheltering columns of the army.
Loud and long was the laugh that pealed after them, and Owen
Roe riding once more to the front, cried out:

"Bravely done, my faithful Rapparees! I knew it was in
you?"

"Methinks Lord Ardes will scarcely try it again, Owen," said
Phelim coming forward at a gallop. "Who may we thank for
that?"

"Captain Donogh and his brave comrades," said Owen, "they are the boys for the scrogs and bushes! But back—back, Phelim! as I live they're opening a cannonade!—Heavens! what a peal! Spare, oh, Lord! spare our brave fellows! Ha! Our Lady shields us well!"

Again the shout of mirthful mockery burst from the Irish ranks as shot after shot boomed in quick succession from the enemy's guns without so much as harming a single man.*

"Oh! the darling were you, Owen Roe!" "The Lord be praised! isn't he the wonderful man!" "See that, now!"

Amid these exulting shouts and cries of admiration, and the dull roar of the heavy cannonade, a cry of anguish was heard so loud and shrill and piercing that every eye was turned in the direction of the altar whence the sound appeared to proceed. Few could see what was going on there, but those that did found it hard to keep their places in the ranks in obedience to the stern voice of the general calling out at the moment:

"Stir not a man of you, on pain of death!"

But the cry went round "Poor Malachy na Soggarth!" and soon it reached the McMahons, and the Bishop himself was quickly on his knees beside the bleeding body of his humble friend, for Malachy indeed it was. The poor fellow, in making some new arrangement about the altar preparatory to the grand celebration of thanksgiving to which he looked forward, had incautiously ascended the steps, and, thus exposed, became a mark for some deadly shot, the Puritans, doubtless, taking him for a priest. Fitting death surely for *Malachy na Soggarth!*

Judith and Emmeline were already on the spot supporting the inanimate form between them and endeavoring to stanch the blood that flowed profusely from the breast.

"My poor, poor Malachy!" said the bishop in a choking voice as he leaned over him; "is there life in him, think you?" Laying his hand on the poor fellow's heart, he shook his head

---

* Rinuccini and other good authorities state that in this first cannonade of the Scotch but one man of the Irish was slain, owing to the admirable disposition of the army by the skill and foresight of Owen Roe.

mournfully—" Alas! alas! Malachy!" he murmured while the tears streamed from his eyes, "it will never beat again! God rest your soul in peace! Let us lay him here on the steps, my daughters! till we see how the battle goes! *Your* lives are not safe here, and *I* must away where duty calls——"

"But can we do nothing for *him*, my lord?" said Judith anxiously.

"Nothing, nothing!—my poor Malachy is beyond mortal succor!"

"For Heaven's sake, Judith! let us go!" said the more timid Emmeline, shrinking with terror as a cannon-ball raked up the ground within a few feet and went bounding away towards the wood.

"She is right," said the bishop; "haste away, I implore—I command you!"—and then tenderly he laid the body of his late sacristan on the lowest step of the altar, saying: "Rest you there, Malachy! till I return, if return I do or may."

By this time Angus and some others of the Rapparees were hurrying the ladies back to the wood, and seeing Malachy's body they would have taken it too, but hearing that the bishop had placed it where it was, they reluctantly left it behind.

"Poor Malachy na Soggarth! are you the first?" sighed Angus; "God knows who will be the last—you'll be well revenged, anyhow, before night!"

Back to the post of danger flew the bishop, and he found the Clan McMahon busily engaged in a skirmish with the enemy whilst Owen Roe himself and young Rory Maguire were charging with well-feigned impetuosity; indeed all along the line the Irish forces were more or less in action, now advancing, now retiring, yet still maintaining their ground, with all the disadvantage of a strong sun shining full in their faces, and the wind blowing the smoke of the Scottish guns right against them. Still they had the counter advantage of position, posted as they were between two hills with the wood on their rear, whereas the Puritans were hemmed in between the river and a widespreading bog. Little recked they, in their pride, that the saffron-coated kern held the hill-sides above them—were they not delivered unto them? yea, even the elements lent their aid against them, and the sun himself struck them, as it were, with blindness—verily, God's judgments were upon those idolators, and their strength must wither like grass before the wrathful eyes of the elect.

With this impression on their minds, the Puritan generals made charge after charge on the Irish columns, now with horse, now with foot, and again with both. Somehow, "the idolaters" were not quite so easily overcome, as they, in their fanatical faith, had believed. It is true they seemed to fight rather shy, as though fearing to come in too close contact with the swords of the righteous, but with the agility of mountain-goats and the cunning of foxes they managed to elude the furious onslaught of the Puritans. Truly was Owen Roe styled the Fabius of his country, for such generalship has rarely been displayed in any age—such consummate skill and prudence, as the field of Benburb witnessed that day.

It was a strange and a curious sight to see the way in which Owen kept Monroe and his legions in play for full four hours on the bright June day, until the patience of his own people was all but worn out, and the Scotch, who had been fighting with all their might, well nigh exhausted and frenzied with disappointment.

Monroe's shrill voice was heard full often urging on his officers, and O'Neill's made, as it were, a mocking echo. It was "Cunningham forward on the right"—"McMahon to the front'!'—"Hamilton advance!"—"O'Rielly forward!"

Much grumbling was heard amongst the O'Rourkes on finding that the O'Reillys, not they, were in front of the Hamiltons, and Sir Phelim O'Neill could hardly restrain his indignation that he was left out of the count and reduced to a state of inactivity, which he deemed a grievous wrong. Owen Roe smiled as he heard these complaints, and told them all to have patience. "Wait till you can see them," said he, "and then, men of Erin, you may, perchance, have your way!"

It was fortunate that the army had such boundless confidence in the wisdom of its general, for there lived not the man on Irish ground, save Owen himself, that could have kept the clans back so long, and to rush headlong on the Scotch with the dazzling sun and the drifting smoke striking full upon them, would have been certain destruction.

Old Lorcan Maguire was on thorns. Although perfectly comprehending the cause of Owen's holding back, he still could not restrain his impatience, and many an angry glance he gave through his closed eyelids at the provokingly bright sun that would not let him see what most he wished to see.

"Rory!" said he at last to his nephew, "your eyes are younger and stronger than mine—can you tell me whereabouts Blayney is—they say he's with the cavalry."

"Why, to be sure, uncle! there he is with his troop on the left flank close by Hamilton's dragoons. I have my eye on him never fear!" .

"That's well, my boy, that's well—God bless you, Rory!" A ball whizzed past the old man's ear at the moment, but so wrapped was he in his own thoughts that he heeded it not, although it drew from his nephew an exclamation of alarm. A very short time after that a stir was perceptible amongst the Irish. The sun was, at length, behind them, and the wind suddenly changing, the smoke of all the artillery was blown in the faces of the Scotch, stunning them with the effect of a hard blow.   •

By some rapid evolutions, made at the moment, by the orders of Owen Roe, Hamilton of Leitrim found himself faced by his neighbors, the O'Rourkes, amongst whom were conspicuous the square-built, athletic figure of Manus, and the stately form of his chief. Blayney was likewise confronted by his old acquaintances, the McMahons of Uriel, headed by their own chief, whilst Sir Robert Stewart and his bloody troopers stood face to face with the stern O'Cahans of the mountains. All these changes were effected with the quickness almost of thought, and then Owen Roe, surveying with that piercing eye of his the confusion prevailing amongst the Scotch, cast another glance along his own line to see that all was to his liking. He smiled and murmured softly to himself: "Now may Christ and His Blessed Mother be our stay!" .

Ay! the moment is come at last—the Scotch are confused and bewildered—they cannot fight, it would seem, as the Irish did,

through sun and smoke—their generals see the danger—they
see the ominous movements going on amongst the Confederates
—they use every effort to restore order in their own ranks, and
in part they succeed. With oaths and curses Hamilton forces
his men into line—Monroe conjures—commands his stern Scottish veterans to stand fast for the dear sake of the Covenant, and
smite the reprobate with the strong arm of righteousness.

But the Irish—how eagerly they watch their General's eye—
how bitterly they laugh as the blasphemous exhortations of the
Scottish generals reach their ears.

> "A hundred years of wrong shall make their vengeance strong!
> A hundred years of outrage, and blasphemy, and broil;
> Since the spirit of Unrest sent forth on her behest
> The Apostate and the Puritan, to do their work of spoil."[*]

By a sudden impulse, as it were, Owen Roe threw himself
into the midst of his army, and pointing to the enemy, he cried:

"Soldiers! you have your way!—They have sun and wind
against them now as we had before. They waver already,
though Monroe is trying to rally for another charge. Strike
home now for God and Country,—for martyred priests and
slaughtered kin—for your women's nameless wrongs—the Hamiltons are *there*—remember Tiernan O'Rourke and the sacred
martyr of Sligo—remember all—*all*, my brothers—remember
all the past—think of the future that awaits your country if you
are beaten here to-day—but beaten you cannot be—you have
purified your souls in the laver of penance, you have received
the blessing sent you from the vicegerent of Christ—you are
strong—your cause is holy—you must and shall conquer. On,
then, on, to death or victory! I myself will lead the way, and
let him that fails to follow remember that he abandons his
general!"

"Cursed be he who does!" cried Sir Phelim; "I'll take care
it shan't be me!"

He threw himself from Brien's back as he spoke, and flung
the bridle to Shamus, who was close by his side. Every colonel
of the army instantly followed his example amid the applauding

* Hon. G. S. Smythe's *Catholic Cavalier*.

cheers of the men, and then waving their broadswords on high,
down they dashed on the astonished Puritans, their men bounding after and around them, with the terrible force of the cataract.
Once more the cry of "Lamh dearg aboo!" awoke the echoes
of the woods, striking terror to the hearts of the murderous
crew who had so long revelled in the blood of the Irish.   In vain
did Monroe, seeing the approaching avalanche, order Lord Ardes,
with a squadron of horse, to clear a way through the Irish foot ;
in vain—in vain—his cavalry met the rushing war-tide, and the
pikes of the kern, piercing the breasts of the horses, drove
them back, maddened and affrighted, on the ranks of their own
infantry whose bayonets met them in the rear.   Death! death!
death and fury ! where is that haughty squadron now ?   Annihilated, save a few officers who were taken prisoners, Lord Ardes
himself amongst the number.   Now Hamilton and Blayney—
Stewart and Montgomery look to it—look to the doom that is
on you !   Strong, fierce and powerful this day are those whom
so long you have hunted as beasts—the O'Rourkes are in your
midst with their terrible pikes and battle-axes—the McGuires
and McMahons are flaying you down as though each had the
strength of an hundred men—the O'Cahans are drunk with joy
as Stewart's men go down in heaps beneath their crushing blows,
and the wild aboo is ringing high over all the sounds of fight, as
the clansmen follow their valiant chiefs on and on through the
dread array, shouting as they go the words of doom.   Oh ! the
might that was in Owen's arm as, first of all, he clove his way to
the heart of the Scottish host, his plume of green and white
passing on like a meteor through the battle-cloud.   And close
behind him followed Sir Phelim, dealing death on every side
and smiling grimly at the dull inertness of the Scotch, for it
seemed as though a spell had fallen on them all and the strength
had left their arms.   Here and there, however, the generals
were making an effort to rally them, reminding them that retreat
was death.   Once the savage Hamilton encountered the knight
of Kinnard, and leaning forward in his saddle aimed such a
deadly thrust at his heart that stout Phelim's life were not worth
a straw, had not a pike at the moment pierced Hamiltons's horse
through the head, and he fell to the ground with his rider under.

It was the faithful Shamus who had dealt the blow that saved his chieftain's life, but he well nigh paid the penalty of his own, for some three or four of Hamilton's men, believing their leader slain, attacked the brave fellow with their ponderous axes.

"Come on, you hell-hounds! I'm ready for you!" cried Shamus with a flourish of his trusty pike, while Sir Phelim, turning at the sound of his voice, clove the foremost of his assailants well nigh to the belt. Alas! the tide of battle rushing on, speedily carried away the knight, and left Shamus still wedged in with the wrathful followers of Hamilton. Forgotten as he thought himself by his friends, O'Hagan faced his enemies with the courage of a lion, and two of them fell beneath his stalwart arm, but the third, a gigantic fellow, maddened by the fate of his comrades, grasped his weapon with both hands and aimed such a blow at his opponent's head as would have shattered a bar of iron. Great God! what means that piercing scream! Who is it that rushes between, receives the impending stroke, and saves the life of Shamus? It is Angus Dhu whom Shamus catches in his arms with a cry of anguish, and forgetful of his own danger, of all save the friend who has given his life for him, he makes his way with maniac force through the thick of the fight, brandishing his bloody pike in one hand, while the other arm clasps to his breast the bleeding form of the gallant young Rapparee to all appearance dead. By the time he laid his sorrowful burden on the sward beside the altar, the gay green jacket, ever worn so jauntily, was wet with the life-blood from the faithful heart, yet the youth opened his eyes for a moment, and smiled as he saw Shamus. He murmured faintly:

"Aileen has got the ring, Shamus!—the Lady Judith will find it—next the heart—that loved you best—*she* will tell you —all—"

"Judith is here," said a soft voice close at hand. "But, merciful God! Angus—Aileen, my child! is it *you*? Oh, woe! woe! was it for this you left me?"

"What else would take me—dearest lady!—but to watch—over Shamus? I know it was wrong—to leave my post—ask the general's pardon for me—he'll not refuse it to *you*. Shamus! poor Shamus! don't look so wild—be pacified—I couldn't live

forever, and what death could be more welcome to me than
this? We'll meet again—maybe soon—I'd wish to see Phelim
—but there's no time—bid him farewell for me, and tell him I
have done *my* share—in revenging—Island Magee! Pray—
pray for poor Aileen—Lord Jesus! have mercy—mercy! Mary,
Mother of Christians!—help me now—*now*——"

"Aileen! Aileen!" shouted Shamus, and he snatched the
dying girl to his breast again—"Aileen! sure it isn't dying you'd
be?—sure you wouldn't leave me after all this?" A bright
smile beamed again on the pallid face, and there it rested—
Aileen was with the dead!

It was hard to convince Shamus that all was over, but when
once he *was* convinced, he sprang to his feet, and imprinting a
long kiss on the pale lips of his betrothed, he placed her gently
in the arms of Emmeline who sat weeping by whilst Judith
knelt to offer up a prayer for the departed spirit.

"I'll leave her here," said he, "for a start till I go back to
my work. My work! ha! ha! ha! ay! my *work!* We must
make an end of it this day, anyhow! Oh! ladies! dear ladies!
look at her—wasn't she the beauty! But oh! oh! the trick
she played on me! And she telling me that time when Phelim
and me went to see her that I was never, never to go back
next or nigh her—either me or Phelim—till the war would be
over and the country free, and the Scotch murderers clean
gone!—oh Aileen! Aileen! But what am I standing here for
when there's such good work to be done? Now God direct me
to Sir Phelim!"

Away he darted with the speed of a lap-wing, nor stopped till
he made his way again to the side of his chief, thanking God
that *he*, at least, was still spared.

Just then old Lorcan Maguire was carried by bleeding profusely from a wound in the chest. The brave old man was near
his last, yet he caught Sir Phelim's eye for a moment, and he
smiled a grim smile.

"I'm done for, Phelim!" he hoarsely articulated, "but so is
he too! The villain that swore Connor's life away! I swore to
do it this day, and I've kept my word! God have mercy on
my soul!" The seer of Fermanagh spoke never more.

It was true enough for Lorcan. Blayney was found amongst the slain. His fall struck terror into the hearts of the Scotch, but their misfortunes were not at the height. All that dreadful evening the work of death went on—the fanatics falling everywhere like grass benea'h the scythe of the mower. Many hundreds had already perished, when the Rapparees, breaking from the bushes and thickets around, rushed into the contest fresh and vigorous with the terrible cry:

" Island Magee—Death to the bloody Scots!"

Like a fiery torrent on they passed, young Donogh at their head looking like one of the athletes of old, his slight figure dilated, it would seem, beyond its wonted proportions, his arm endowed with giant strength by the mightiness of his wrongs, though he knew not then that the last of his race had fallen beneath a Scottish axe but a little while before.

It was the day of awful retribution: The opportunity so long promised to the outraged clans of Ulster, and good use they made of it. The might of the oppressor was withered as grass, and the stoutest soldiers of the Covenant went down before the fiery clansmen of the north, and the legions of the tyrant were swept away like dry stubble in the flame, until the terrified survivors, as evening drew on, finding no other retreat open to them, began to precipitate themselves into the river, where many hundreds perished.* Monroe did not wait to see the end of it. He made his escape from that scene of carnage long before the set of sun, nor drew bridle, as was afterwards found, till he gained the protecting walls of Lisnagarvey—a feat quite in keeping with the man's character.

The strangest thing of all was that but seventy of the Irish were slain in that battle, whilst two thousand three hundred of the enemy were found dead on the field, exclusive of those who found a grave in the Blackwater.

---

* Protestant and Catholic historians all agree that the Battle of Benburb was one of the most tremendous victories ever gained by Irish valor. The admirable prudence and military skill displayed by Owen O'Neill are loudly extolled even by such writers as Warnor, Wright, Leland, &c.

Of the chiefs and **gentlemen of Ulster, not one fell** that day save Lorcan Maguire.   Some **were** wounded but not dangerously. When the drums sounded the recall, and all came together at the foot of the altar, by the light of the rising moon, how warmly did each press the other's hand, how fervently thank God. Bishop McMahon and the priests intoned a solemn thanksgiving, and recited the *De Profundis* for those who had fallen.   Then Owen Roe demanded of his officers what prisoners they had taken, and first of all addressed Sir Phelim.

"Prisoners!" said the stalwart knight disdainfully, "prisoners, Owen! by my word, I have not one—my object was to kill what I could!"

"I have a prisoner!" said Donogh coming forward with a bob-wig on the end of his pike, and a war-cloak carelessly over his arm; "Monroe left us these as love-tokens."

A roar of laughter greeted the trophies, indicative, as they were, of the haste wherewith the owner had decamped.   But the wig and cloak were not the only trophies of the victory. All the baggage, artillery, and ammunition of the Scotch was taken, and, likewise, all their banners.   These, with twenty-one officers, remained in the hands of the Irish, and it is graphically said by some of our historians that so great was the amount of booty taken, that "even the meanest soldier was weary with plunder."   Other matters connected with this splendid victory will be found in our next chapter.

CHAPTER XXXII.

" Hide not thy tears ; weep boldly—and be proud
  To give the flowing virtue manly way ;
  'Tis nature's mark to know an honest heart by,
  Shame on those breasts of stone that cannot melt
  In soft adoption of another's sorrow !"

AARON HILL.

" When love's well-timed, 'tis not a fault to love :
  The strong, the brave, the virtuous, and the wise,
  Sink in the soft captivity together."

ADDISON's *Cato*.

THE bonfire that blazed that night on the hill of Benburb sent
a thrill of delight through the heart of old Ulster. Its meaning
was well understood, for in rapid succession every mountain-top
sent up its pillar of fire shaming the brightness of the summer
moon. The joyous acclamations of the multitudes reached not
the ears of the victorious chieftains by the Blackwater, but they
watched, nevertheless, with swelling hearts, the beacon-fires
that were proclaiming to a grateful people the news of their
triumph. They knew that prayers were going up for them from
ten thousand happy hearts, and that hills and vales were ringing
with the joyful sounds:

" Owen Roe has beaten the Scotch !"

Oh ! it was a joyous night, a glorious night for the Catholic
people of Ulster ; and they basked in the brightness of the moment without thinking of the clouds that might yet darken the
horizon. Owen Roe himself as he stood with Bishop McMahon,
Sir Phelim and others of the chiefs, looking abroad over the
rejoicing land, could not help catching the enthusiasm of all
around, and his bosom throbbed with the buoyancy of early
youth as, turning to the Bishop, he said :

" Truly we have cause for rejoicing—blessed be His name
who hath done such great things for us ! Have I not redeemed
my word, oh ! friends and brothers—said I not well that we should
have a day of reckoning ?"

"By the soul of Nial! Owen," said Phelim with a vigorous grasp of the hand, "you have made clean work of it! A few such days as this would leave Ireland in our own hands mayhap for ever! If that rascally crew in the Pale above would only put their shoulders to the wheel as we do, we would soon send the robbers packing—that is, if any were left to pack!"

"I hope McMahon and O'Rourke are pleased now," said Owen again, as he turned to the chieftains named, "and my young friend Roderick—but where is Roderick?—I trust no harm hath come unto him!"

"Not so, general," said Bishop Heber, "not so—thank God! the young chief is well in body, but grievously troubled in mind for the loss of his good old uncle——"

"What! is Lorcan slain?"

"Ay, marry is he—methought you knew how he sought Blayney out and struck him down in the midst of his troopers, then sold his life as dearly as he could—alas! poor Lorcan!—the hero of many a field—he hath gone to the company of his friends ' the spirits!' And my poor Malachy—ah! Owen, my heart is sore for that queer, quaint, simple, and most faithful follower whose oddity diverted me full oft from grave and painful thoughts! May he rest in peace, O Lord."

"Who else hath fallen?" said Owen with emotion. He started on hearing the name of Angus Dhu. So, too, did Phelim.

"Angus Dhu!" repeated Owen in a faltering voice, "it cannot be—I left him on guard in the wood with a small party of his comrades—could he have betrayed his trust?—no, no, I will not believe it!"

"It is true, nevertheless," said the trembling voice of Father Phelimy from behind; "it is true, but blame not the youth till you have heard all!"

"Good God! father, and how fares it with—our friends?" cried Owen in an agitated voice.

"They are well, I thank my God, but much occupied in caring the wounded."

"Lead me to them, reverend father! I pray you!" said Owen in a low voice, and they turned away together. No smile was on the face of any left behind—not even Sir Phelim ventured on a jest, though all knew well who were the general's "friends." The exalted character of the Lady Judith and the immensity of Emmeline's sorrows placed them far beyond the reach of mockery or derision, and, moreover, the chieftains of Owen Roe's army looked upon both as the special objects of their protection.

An hour later and

"The mess-tents are full, and the glasses are set,"

and the chieftains and the officers all await the coming of Owen Roe to commence the banquet, but Owen Roe cared little for festivity; he still lingered in the sylvan hospital where Judith and the priests were in attendance on the wounded. In many cases the general himself assisted the doctors to dress and bind up the wounds of the sufferers, and the fervent blessings which greeted him on every side in that abode of pain were dearer to his heart than the enthusiastic cheers of his army.

It was there he found the young chieftain of Fermanagh with some gentlemen of his own blood, kneeling beside the corpse of poor Lorcan where it lay with a war cloak thrown over it in the shade of a spreading sycamore. At the opposite side was a slight female figure crouched on the ground, and wrapped in a dark mantle. It was easy to guess that this was Emmeline, whose absence from Judith's company Owen had noticed. She looked up for a moment from under her hood and met the general's eye. A slight flush suffused her cheek, and she murmured in tremulous accents:

"He is dead—Connor's uncle is dead—he who was so long my protector and companion in danger—he was more a father to me than he who bore that name—he is dead, dead—and I am desolate!" She covered her face again.

"It is even so, general!" said Roderick rising from his knees; "Lorcan Maguire is no more—look there!"—and raising the cloak which covered the body he showed the face of the stern old warrior, noble even in the fixed repose of death. "Ay! you may wail him, too, Owen O'Neil! for no truer heart followed your standard—wo! wo! for the sons of the waters!—heavy

18

will their hearts be, brother of my father! and loud the wail of
our women when Lorcan is borne home to them thus from this
field of blood!"

Owen said not a word, but he took the chieftain's hand in
silence, and he pressed it between his own, while the tears that
moistened his eye-lid showed the strength of his emotion.
Turning, he gazed a moment on the venerable face of the dead,
then knelt and bowed his head on his hand, and thus remained
for several minutes in earnest supplication for the repose of
that guileless soul.

Passing on a little farther, the general found a numerous
party of the McMahons keeping watch around the body of poor
Malachy. It lay on the velvet sward in front of the altar which
his hands had raised, with the cold pale moonlight streaming
down on the stony features. Bishop Heber knelt beside the
mortal remains of his humble friend, and the chieftain stood
leaning against the end of the altar with folded arms and a
moody brow looking down on the ghastly shell that had en-
closed so pure a spirit, so loving a heart. Owen Roe knelt to
say a short prayer for the dead, and the sight of him there
drew tears from the eyes of Art Oge, for he thought how proud
poor simple Malachy would be were he conscious of the honor
done him by "the general." And the clansmen who sat or
knelt in silence around, felt their bosoms glow and their hearts
throb with renewed affection for that chosen leader. He tarried but a moment amongst them, however, for his mind was
full of troubled thought, and his heart impelled him onward to
the place where, like a ministering angel, the lady Judith was
bending over a wounded soldier, whose tartan pointed him out
as a McDonnell from the Glynns.

Owen O'Neill spoke not, but he stood a moment looking on
the beautiful picture of Christian charity and his shadow falling
over the wounded, and (as it appeared) dying man, Judith was
made aware of his presence. She looked up with a sad smile,
and said almost in a whisper:

"He is passing away, I fear—Father Eugene administered to
him a little while ago. Ah! my friend! such is the price of
victory!"

"God help us all, so it is!—but, Judith, can I have speech of you a moment?"

One of the doctor's attendants came up just then, and Judith, giving the man in charge to him, walked on by the general's side. They were still in sight of all, but not in hearing, when O'Neill stopped and so did the lady, and their eyes met. A glow was on the cheek of each, but it was the glow of enthusiasm and not of passion.

"Judith!" said Owen Roe, "are you so far content?"

"How could I be otherwise? Heaven be praised! you have done marvellously well. An' this day's work be followed up as it ought to be, the Puritans will speedily betake themselves whence they came, to avoid utter annihilation. Then, Owen,"—she stopped as if overcome by the strength of her own vivid imaginings. Her dark thoughtful eyes were suffused with tears, but they were tears of joy and fervent hope.

"And then?"—O'Neill repeated in a tone of eager expectation all unusual with him.

"Why, need I tell you what will follow?—surely, Owen Roe can well picture to himself the joy, the peace, the happiness of a people ransomed from slavery—the glory that will shine on our ancient hills when the Lord of Hosts manifests His power on behalf of His so-long afflicted people, and the pride of the tyrant will be humbled—yea for ever!"—she fixed her gaze on the starry firmament where the queen of night was shining in lonely splendor, and a dreamy, yet tender look stole over her noble features—"yea for ever—for ever," she slowly ejaculated; "no more such pitiful murders—no more such sights as I have seen—and this will *you* do, Owen O'Neill—you yourself," she added with sudden animation, turning her kindling eye on the chieftain. "Who but you is in all things fitted for so great a work!"

"Your commendation is sweet to mine ear," said Owen, "ay, truly, and balm to my heart—but, Judith, sister, friend, counsellor! you have given me leave to hope that a yet closer tie may one day bind us to each other. When will the day come?"

"When the last link is broken of Ireland's galling chain," Judith promptly replied "when the dark valley of blood and death is passed, and the halcyon settles down on the storm-tossed waters,—when the sons and daughters of Ireland are free to worship God in open day without let or hindrance, then, Owen O'Neill! my hand shall go with my heart to him whose plume waved the highest, whose arm struck the heaviest in this day's fight—to him whose matchless skill and wisdom have brought about, under God, this glorious result—the precursor, I trust in Heaven's mercy! of yet greater things to come."

Owen O'Neill was no passionate lover,—neither was Judith O'Cahan the woman to inspire or to feel what is commonly called *love*—no, the heart of each was engrossed by higher and holier aspirations than any purely selfish feeling could ever elicit—they were both chastened and refined by the pure flame of patriotism commingled with religion—yet was there in the depth of either heart an enthusiastic appreciation of the other, and a sympathy had from the first existed between them more strong and enduring than mere love could ever be. The esteem and approbation of Judith were amongst the strongest inducements which Owen had in view, as the lofty enthusiasm of her character and the womanly grace and delicacy of her demeanor threw a charm around the brief moments of their intercourse and diffused a halo of poetic light over the dreary toils of warfare. Few were the souls with which Owen O'Neill held communion, and of those few Judith O'Cahan's was the first. The effect of such words as she had just spoken, then, may well be imagined.

He took the hand which she held out to him, and held it fast, and he looked long and earnestly on the faded but still beautiful face of his betrothed, and he read as in a book through the soft clear eyes, the loving and gentle, yet high and holy thoughts that were passing within. He felt that as far as Judith's heart was accessible to human love it was his, and he asked no more. He was well content that God should hold the first place in the heart of that perfect creature of His hands.

"Judith!" he said still holding her hand between his own, "Judith! I am content to wait until the work of redemption be accomplished—like you I feel that the present is not the time for selfish enjoyment—no, no, we could not be happy even in each other, whilst our friends are falling around us,

martyrs to the holy cause. Go back now, beloved, to your
thrice-blessed ministry of mercy—and I will return to the
duties of mine office, cheered and refreshed by these few
moments—alas! how few and brief! spent in your sweet
company."

Yet another fond pressure of the hand, another wistful, lingering look and Owen Roe was hurrying away to see after the
condition of his prisoners, when a low moaning struck painfully
on his ear, and starting he said:

"Good God, Judith! are there yet other mourners hereabouts?"

"Truly yes, Owen! mayhap the most heartstruck of all—
an' you heard not of this before, prepare yourself for a pitiful
sight!"

"Mother of Heaven! my brave Donogh—and Shamus Beg!
—who—who is the dead?"

"The one that was known to you as Angus Dhu," said the
Rapparee Captain rising slowly from his half-recumbent posture.

"Angus Dhu!" repeated Owen in faltering accents; "surely,
surely, he is not dead—the bravest, noblest, gentlest heart"—
he could say no more.

"God bless you, general!" said Donogh in a choking voice;
"Angus was all you say, but he is dead for all that——"

"Ay, dead, dead and cold," muttered Shamus in a dreary,
dreamy tone, without raising his head from between his hands
where he sat on the ground near the head of the corpse. "And
I'm here alive, God forgive me!"

The body was laid on a couch of fresh green fern, and over
it was thrown, whether by accident or design, one of the flags
captured from the enemy, a costly piece of snow-white silk,
emblazoned with the arms of Blayney, and tinted in many places
with a crimson hue, suggestive of the death struggle in which
it was lost and won. Slowly and reverently Owen Roe raised
the covering from the face of the corpse, but seeing it, he
started back amazed and bewildered! it was the face of a young
and handsome female—it was that, too, of Angus Dhu, wanting
the light of the dark flashing eyes, and softened into feminine
gentleness by the smile that rested on the features. The form

was arrayed in the ghastly habiliments of the grave, and this
was, of itself, not the least of the marvels that struck Owen's
sight.

"Donogh!—Lady Judith!" he exclaimed, "who is this?—
what do I behold?"

"You behold my sister Aileen, General!" said Donogh in
tremulous accents; "she and I were all of our family that
escaped alive from Island Magee. It was Shamus there that
saved *her* at the risk of his own life (there was a promise of
marriage between them long before), and as he and I both
thought, we left her in a place of safety till the war would be
over. The poor colleen made us promise at our off-going that
we wouldn't either of us go next or nigh her till the Scots were
cut off root and branch, and the ancient faith established once
more in Ulster. She had taken it in head, you see, General,
to be with us herself, without our knowing it, and to do what
she could, be it less or more, against the cursed crew that had
shed the blood of our aged parents and all our kin.* And sure,
sure it was little myself thought when I used to see Angus
slashing away at the bloody Puritans, cutting them down right
and left, that it was our light-hearted little Aileen that was in it
all the time—Aileen that we never could get to kill a chicken—
Aileen that wouldn't crush a worm——"

"You didn't tell how she came by her death," broke in

---

* Let no reader suppose this an improbable occurrence in a time
of such universal excitement, when all ages, and both sexes were
drawn, whether voluntarily or involuntarily, into the vortex of stormy
passion. Grose, in the second volume of his *Irish Antiquities*, relates an affecting instance of this kind which occurred in 1642, in the
battle fought near Ballintubber, in the County Roscommon: "It is
recorded," says he, "that a young Irish gentleman behaved on this
occasion with singular bravery; for, after his party fled, he placed
himself at the corner of a ditch, where he defended himself with his
pike against five horsemen, who fired on him: a gigantic English
soldier, getting behind him, slew him. Being stripped, and his mon-
tero taken from his head, long tresses of flaxen hair fell down; this
farther exciting curiosity, it was at length discovered that this gallant
youth was a female."

Shamus with a wild glance around; "tell the General, can't you! that the life I saved for her she gave up for me—how she came between me and the stroke of death—and got it herself—but now that you have heard so much, General!" he added, jumping suddenly to his feet, "I must tell you the rest—do you see those stains on the banner there?" pointing to the one that covered the body.

"I do, Shamus!" said Owen Roe very gently; "what be they?"

"I'll just tell you that," and approaching him, he laid his hand on his arm and whispered in quite a confidential way, still pointing at the ghastly object, "that's the heart's-blood of *Lindsay*—Lindsay, you know, that was foremost in the chase of Aileen and me that night—Lindsay that swore he'd have her in spite of hell—ho! ho! ho! when I had him in my power once before, honor and your bidding tied my hands—but I met him to-day, after I left Aileen here *dead*, and there's no use saying what I did, but—but—*there's the stain on the flag he had in his hand*—that tells the story! But oh! Aileen, Aileen!"—with a sudden burst of grief—"sure that doesn't bring *you* back to me—how can I live at all and you dead and gone from me!—oh! Blessed Virgin! is it dreaming I am or what— or what?" And with that poor Shamus sank again into the listless apathy of woe.

"Heaven's mercy on her soul!" ejaculated Judith as she carefully smoothed back the dark tresses which the raising of the strange pall had slightly ruffled on poor Aileen's marble brow. "It is long since she told me her secret, and the heroic soul which dwelt within that slight form was mayhap better known to me than to any other human being. Emmeline, too, was of late in her confidence, and it was our privilege to prepare her for decent burial ere yet any of the soldiers had returned from the field."

"May Heaven reward your ladyship, for we can not!" said Donogh fervently; "the poorest of the poor are we Rapparees— and yet we are rich in love and gratitude, would our Lord permit us to prove it!"

"I doubt it not, Donogh," said Judith kindly, "but you owe

me nothing, I do but pay a debt of long standing—oh! would that I *could* do aught for the ever-faithful Rapparees who were friends to *us* when we had no other friends!"

Here a pressing message from Colonel O'Reilly, who had charge of the prisoners, called Owen Roe away, and Judith hastened to resume her duties in their sylvan hospital.

During the course of that night and the following morning many additional prisoners were brought in, some of these had been found hiding in the bushes and thickets, others were caught when attempting to make their escape.

A solemn scene took place on the day following that "famous victory." The Catholics who had fallen, to the number of seventy, were borne to their final rest in the consecrated mould of Eglish. On ordinary occasions, those slain in battle are consigned to the earth which their last footsteps pressed—

> "And every turf beneath his feet
> *Becomes* the soldier's sepulchre,"

but not so after the battle of Benburb. Each clan insisted on carrying its own dead to Eglish, but a few miles distant, and the general was not the man to offer any objection. But even Eglish, old and venerable and hallowed in its associations, was not deemed a meet resting-place for Lorcan Maguire. His honored remains were borne by Roderick and his clansmen home to the ancient burial-place of his family near the blue waters of their own Lough Erne. They laid the old warrior down to rest by the side of his fair-haired Una,

> "And the church-shadow falls o'er his place of rest
> Where the steps of his childhood bounded."*

Happier than his martyred nephew is "Lorcan of the Spirits" in that his body awaits the resurrection amongst the brave and noble of his own race.

Not so poor Malachy *na soggarth*—not so poor Aileen Magee. Far from their kindred dust they were laid to rest, but not by stranger hands, nor yet amongst strangers. They had company enough on their death-march, and those they loved best bore

---

* Landon's Poem of *The Soldier's Grave.*

them to the graves prepared for them amongst the departed sons and daughters of Tyr-Owen. And the churchyard bell rang clear and loud that day as none ever heard it ring before, or perchance ever again.

It was a solemn, yet scarcely a sorrowful sight, for even the crowds of country people who raised the *caoins* as the mighty funeral passed along, were heard to mingle somewhat of exultation with the doleful strain. Why should they mourn those who had fallen in defence of their country and their faith?—why should they grudge them the glory of the martyrs death? Was it not well for them to die as they did, were it only to have Owen Roe and Sir Phelim, and the Lord of Iveagh, and O'Reilly and McMahon, and those chiefs of high renown walking after them to the grave, and no less than a bishop blessing the clay that was to be their bed till the end of time? Truly, they were not to be pitied, those heroes of Benburb—

"Whose death-wound came amid sword and plume
Where the banner and the ball were flying."*

Before the army moved from Benburb a Requiem Mass was said at poor Malachy's altar for the souls of those who had fallen in the battle, and as the joyful news of the great victory sped on through the country, the Atoning Sacrifice was offered up for them at every altar, and in the great cathedrals of the four provinces, their obsequies were celebrated with clouds of incense and "pealing anthems," and the solemn mourning of the church.

The thunders of the cannon of Benburb echoed from shore to shore and filled the whole island, for no such victory had yet crowned the confederate arms. The Norman lords heard it in Kilkenny and it hushed their cabals awhile. It reached Castlehaven and Netterville in the Viceregal halls of Dublin Castle, and the swaggering peer was driven to his wit's end for some plausible innendo against Owen Roe O'Neill. None, however, could he find, for the glorious victory of the Blackwater was too stubborn a fact to be twisted one way or the other. "There it was," as Netterville observed in a disconsolate tone, "staring

* Landon's Poem of *The Soldier's Grave.*

you in the face, turn which way you would. It was well to
hear of the Scotch getting their due, but an' it went to pamper
the overbearing pride of the Irishry, particularly those of the
north, he would be content to leave Monroe as he was a while
longer."

Castlehaven administered a faint rebuke to this unworthy admission, but so very faint was it that Netterville laughed and
tossed his head, as much as to say : " I understand your lordship—a blind man may see how the land lies !"

It was in " Limerick of the Ships" that the news from Benburb reached the Nuncio. He had gone thither some weeks
before with the chief men of the Supreme Council to superin-
tend in person the siege of Bunratty, a strong Castle belonging
to the Earl of Thomond. Glamorgan having failed in this important enterprize, Muskerry had been appointed in his place,
and the noble-hearted Italian himself accompanied the army—
and, in fact, directed its operations. It pleased Heaven to
prosper his efforts, and, after a vigorous siege of twelve days, the
garrison was compelled to surrender, and one of the strongest
places on the Shannon was in the hands of the Confederates.*

The flush of this great victory had not yet subsided when the
news of the still greater one of Benburb reached Limerick. It
was Saturday afternoon, and the pious prelate was kneeling
in prayer before an image of the Virgin Mother, when word was
brought him that O'Neill had conquered at Benburb, and that
whole battalions of the Puritans had been cut to pieces.

" Blessed be the Lord of Hosts !" said Rinuncini, bowing his
head reverently, " and thou, Mary, Help of Christians ! receive
my thanks for thy gracious aid !"

So saying he calmly resumed his orisons, as though dismissing
the subject from his thoughts. Some half an hour after he was
listening, his face radiant with joy, to Father Hartigan's vivid
description of the battle of which he had been an eye-witness.

" Truly, our Ulster campaign doth begin well," he said cheerily, after taking notes of the principal details, " but say, good

---

* Meehan's *Confederation*, p. 146.

father! how fares it with our noble friends?—hath Owen O'Neill
escaped unhurt, and the valorous knight, his kinsman?"

"They are well, most reverend father!"

"And our right reverend brother of Clogher?"

"In most excellent bodily health, and uplifted beyond measure in spirit at the great things achieved by our northern
army."

"Went he forth to battle?" the Nuncio asked with a smile.

"Sooth to say he did, and I would your Grace had seen how
he wielded his broad claymore that day!—suffice it, he fought
at the head of the McMahons by the side of their valiant chief,
as became a son of his princely line—that he escaped unhurt is
little short of a miracle."

"Our Lord be praised for these His signal mercies!" said the
Nuncio, with a fervor all his own. "How the noble heart of
Innocent will rejoice at these tidings! But the trophies, good
father! what said you of trophies?"

"Yea, my good lord! trophies we have in abundance. Our
noble general, whose days may Heaven prolong! desiring above
all to pleasure your Grace, hath sent hither with what dispatch
we could make, the standards captured at Benburb. They
await your inspection."

The citizens of Limerick witnessed next day one of the grandest scenes of that long-protracted struggle. At the close of the
Vesper service, the trophies from Benburb were borne in solemn
procession from the abbey church of St. Francis, where they
had been placed on the previous day, to St. Mary's Cathedral,
where the Nuncio had already deposited the banners taken at
Bunratty. Who may describe the enthusiasm of the mighty
multitude that thronged the streets when they saw thus borne
in triumph no less than *thirty-two* standards bearing the arms
of the principal Puritan generals and the most notable Scottish
"undertakers" of Ulster. The Chichesters, Montgomerys, and
Coles, the Blayneys, the Stewarts, and the Hamiltons, were all
and each represented there by their several heraldric devices.

And these thirty-two banners were borne by a like number of
the Confederate Chieftains, Skerrin, Dunboyne, Louth, Howth,
Fingal, Slaney, and Netterville, the Dillons, and the Plunkets,

and many another magnate of the Pale, nothing loath to share with their brethren of the old blood the high honor purchased for them by the rare generalship of Owen Roe and the bravery of his Celtic followers. Yet even there the difference between the races was plainly discernible, for the exultation visible on the faces of the Irish chiefs, and the joy of their hearts, manifested in the bounding lightness of their step, was too strongly contrasted by the clouded brows and grave demeanor of the Norman Confederates. It was easy to see that the former identified themse ves with the victory of Benburb, whilst the latter grudged the glory of it to an Irish chieftain.

Stately and grand as became his high office, calm and collected as a Christian priest ought to be, Rinuccini walked after the standard-bearers, accompanied by the Archbishop of Cashel, with the bishops of Limerick, Clonfert, and Ardfert. Then came the mayor and aldermen of the city, with the multitude of citizens in their gala dress. At the head of the procession, preceding the trophies, marched the soldiers of the garrison with the national colors—the white and green of the Confederates waving proudly above the stately column.*

Having reached St. Mary's Cathedral, the procession came to a stand, the banners, torn and bloody as they were, were carried up the aisle to the high altar, at the foot of which they were laid, whilst the Nuncio, and the bishops, and all the priests, and the nobles of the Pale, and the Celtic chiefs, and all the vast assemblage of soldiers and citizens intoned together the hymn of thanksgiving, till crypt, and nave, and chancel echoes the joyous sound—

> " As thro' the long-drawn aisle and fretted vault
>   The pealing anthem swells the note of praise."

Truly, it was a glorious, a soul-stirring scene, and no heart in all that countless throng felt its inspiration more vividly than that of the Nuncio, Rinuccini. The people's cries of " O'Neill for ever!—glory to the Red Hand!" found an echo in his generous heart.

* When shall we see a Maclise, or a Barry, giving Ireland a fitting representation of such scenes as that above described? When shall the history of our country be illustrated on canvas by the genius of her sons?

CHAPTER XXXIII.

"Strike—till the last arm'd foe expires ;
Strike for your altars and your fires ;
Strike for the green graves of your sires ;
God, and your native land !"
FITZ-GREEN HALLECK.

"While the tree
Of freedom's wither'd trunk puts forth a leaf
Even for thy tomb a garland let it be."
BYRON's *Childe Harold.*

THE glories of Benburb and of Limerick passed away like a
dream. O'Neill was not suffered to follow up his victory in
Ulster, for the Nuncio found it necessary to recall him to Leinster with his victorious army to keep Preston and the Ormondists
in check. The Council was bent on concluding the peace on
Ormond's terms, and Rinuccini was just as bent on preventing
it for the dear sake of religion. Armed with the power of the
Church, and strengthened by the firm adhesion of the Ulster
general, who had given his army the distinctive title of CATHO-
LIC, to the great offence of Preston and the others—the Nuncio
carried matters with a high hand. The struggle which followed
brought out in strong relief the indomitable energy of that
prelate, his burning zeal for religion, his uncompromising ho-
nesty and singleness of purpose, together with a love for Ireland
and a devotion to the interests of her Catholic people never
entertained by any foreigner. For three long years did this
high-souled and generous stranger combat the narrow selfishness, the unworthy prejudices, and the cold indifference of the
English or Ormond faction. With the clergy on his side, and
the old Irish, and money and war-supplies in abundance, Rinuccini felt himself strong enough to set the Ormondists at defiance,
and to threaten them with the severest penalties in case they
dared to persist in their fatal course. Persist they did, nevertheless, making use of every effort to thwart the Nuncio's views
and to advance those of Ormond, the arch-enemy of their faith.

Enraged by the undisguised favor in which the Nuncio held
Owen Roe and the "Irishry," Preston and Castlehaven, and
Mountgarret and Muskerry, cared little what measures they
took or what party they joined, so that the too-formidable
Ulster general was humbled and his power destroyed. Hotter
and fiercer grew the contest. Ormond and his infatuated
henchman, Father Peter Walsh, buoying up their party in the
Council with delusive hopes of advantageous compromise, the
while they embittered them more and more against the Nuncio,
and O'Neill, and the old Irish. On the other hand, the Catholic
party in the General Assembly was sustained and invigorated
by the commanding talents and untiring zeal and lofty patriotism of Bishop French, who, through all that miserable period
of storm and strife, and low intrigue and shameless partizanship,
stood ever in the van of the clergy, their mouthpiece, their
standard-bearer, so to speak.* His word was law with the
Catholic party, whilst the highest and proudest of his adversaries were compelled to yield him a measure of respect. Ormond
and his "shadow," Father Walsh, were especially obnoxious to
the far-seeing, clear-headed prelate, for he saw in them the
roots of all the evils that were coming upon the Confederates,
and the Marquis and his party in turn both feared and hated
Nicholas French.

Rinuccini, French, O'Neill! guardian spirits of the rapidly-
decaying Confederation! how grandly and boldly do your
figures stand out on the dark back-ground of that stormy time,
your genius, your faith, your lofty self-devotion, the anchor and
stay of the Confederacy, the beacon and example unto all.

* Mr. McGee, in his *Gallery of Irish Writers*, has done ample
justice to the character of this great man, in all respects one of the
most illustrious prelates that ever adorned the Irish Church. "He
had been," says he, "an Ambassador to four different Courts. He
had ruled with episcopal power in four different countries. As a
public man and an ecclesiastic there can be no doubt of his powers,
his address, the extent of his accomplishments, nor of the greatness
of his labors. He was the leader of all work to the Catholic Confederacy. He was one of the best known Christian bishops of his
age."

With three such men at their head the Catholics could not fail to command success had they been all of the same mind, all equally devoted to the cause of freedom. But Ormond and Father Peter had long ago undermined the union that should have existed, and by sowing dissensions, fomenting jealousies, and fanning the small flame of private piques into public conflagrations, had dried up the sap from the stately tree that had promised so fair for Ireland, till they made it a useless and withered thing, cumbering the ground and tottering to its fall.

It were sad to tell how fiercely the partizans of Ormond in the Council resisted the noble efforts of Rinuccini and Bishop French. How Preston and O'Neill became open foes, and when sent to besiege Ormond in Dublin with two noble armies, took to quarrelling between themselves, and allowed the common enemy to escape the ruin which their joint attack would have been to him. That saddest of sights was seen on the Liffey's banks, just when the Confederates had the capital all but surrounded, when one vigorous and simultaneous effort would have made them masters of the city. Failing in that, they failed in all, and missed an opportunity which never came again. The bond of union so rudely rent asunder was never again to be cemented —thenceforth, "O'Neill and the old Irish"—"Preston and the new Irish" stood as openly arrayed against each other as any two parties amongst the belligerents. In vain did Rinuccini put forth all the powers wherewith nature and religion had endowed him; in vain did he exhort, entreat, menace—the Mountgarrets and Muskerrys, with the tribe of Plunkets and Butlers, were encased in triple folds of envy, self-conceit, and self-interest (perhaps thickest of all!), which rendered them proof against the Nuncio's exertions. The peace with Ormond was signed on his own terms, and the affairs of the Catholics left once more to the king's discretion. Seeing this the Nuncio had recourse to an expedient which set all Ireland in a blaze. He caused the refractory members of the Council to be imprisoned in Kilkenny, and new members elected in their place. By this arrangement more of the bishops and fewer of the laymen were in the Council, the generals were all brought under its control, and Rinuccini after a little time was placed at the head

of the provisional government. It was a strange state of affairs,
but stranger still was to come, ay! strange beyond all belief.
Ireland became one wide battle-field; the distinction of parties
was at times all but lost, so frequent were the changes and
transitions from one side to the other amongst the great captains.
Thus Ormond had been forced to fly from Dublin, and the city
was left in the hands of Jones, the Parliamentarian General.
Jones was in turn surrounded by the armies of the Confederates,
and Owen Roe, with his army, sat down at Trim, watching
him so closely that he dared not stir beyond the walls of the
metropolis.

Strangest and most unnatural of all was the truce proposed by
Inchiquin to the Confederates—Inchiquin still reeking with the
blood of slaughtered Catholics, abominable from his sacrilegious crimes, and of all men living the most feared and hated
by those of the old faith. This man, finding it his interest to
unite with the king's troops, desired a truce with the Confederates, and the Ormandists gladly embraced his offer, with the
avowed expectation of his alliance being profitable to their
patron. Rinuccini declared vehemently against so unholy a
compact, but his admonitions were disregarded and his opinions
overruled. The chiefs of Irish blood were his sole dependence,
and first of all Owen Roe, his faithful and devoted friend, the
confidant of all his projects for the good of religion, the able
and judicious counsellor, the zealous executor of his will. During all those dreary years of heart-wearing struggle and
fierce dissension, when all within and without the Confederation was discord, storm, and strife, Owen Roe stood firm as a
rock by the side of his illustrious patron, his very name an
intimidation to the internal and external enemies of the cause.
Second to Owen Roe in command was the heroic Bishop of
Clogher, a kindred spirit if there was one in Ireland, as far as fervent patriotism, and singleness of purpose, and devotion to the
interests of religion went, yet not to be compared to Bishop
French in statesmanlike qualities, for which, indeed, that prelate was famous amongst the men of his time. Nevertheless,
Heber of Clogher was one of the firmest pillars of the Confede-

racy, his bold, uncompromising, and somewhat fiery spirit making him a special favorite with the Nuncio.

Then O'Reilly, "the green-mantled chief of Breffny," McMahon and Maguire, O'Rourke and Magennis, and honest Phelim O'Neill, and, indeed, all the Ulster chiefs were true and staunch, full of that noble enthusiasm which fired them on the field of red Benburb; opposed as ever to the selfish and traitorous practices of the Normans, and prodigal as ever of their own blood where religion and love of country beckoned them on to deeds of daring.

Alas! there were fearful odds against the national party. The Scots were rapidly recruiting their shattered strength in Ulster and burning to wipe out the disgrace of Benburb. Preston was willing to unite even with Inchiquin provided the alliance would enable him to crush Owen O'Neill—that chieftain had removed his quarters to Dunamase, and in the ancient Castle of the O'Moores, looking forth from their embattled rock* over the plains of Leix, he awaited the decision of the Council with regard to Inchiquin's truce. He was not alone in that eyrie-like fortress—he had Phelim and Tirlogh O'Neill, Bishop McMahon and Art Oge, O'Reilly, Magennis, and the brave young chieftain of Fermanagh. How often their hearts swelled as they thought of Rory, the rightful lord of that princely domain over which their eyes wandered, as they remembered the infant days of the Confederacy, and his noble enthusiasm in the cause! —how bitterly they cursed the narrow prejudice of the Pale lords which had given to the choleric and unstable Preston the command of that army which should have been his, and thereby driven him from their ranks at the first tug of war!

All at once came the astounding intelligence that the truce with Inchiquin was completed, that "Murrogh of the Burnings"

---

* Dunamase, the ancient stronghold of the O'Mores, is one of the most remarkable places, perhaps, in Ireland. The rock is of great height, and presents the appearance of an embattled fortress. Its top is crowned by the once proud Castle of Dunamase, where the chiefs of Leix, the noble and chivalrous O Mores, dwelt of old in princely state.

was the ally of the Confederate Catholics, Murrogh still reeking with the blood of the Cashel massacre, Murrogh accursed of God and man on account of his sacrilegious crimes.*

The burning indignation of the chiefs was beyond all bounds, and they had well nigh made up their minds to march with all speed against the madmen who were wantonly casting from them the barest possibility of success. But the Nuncio—they must await his decision, and see what course he would have them take. Great Heavens! what tremendous tidings were the next that came from Kilkenny. Who could have dreamed that even Rinuccini would have had recourse to so terrible an expedient.

A few days after the publication of the truce the stern representative of Innocent X. caused to be posted on the doors of St. Canice's Cathedral a sentence of excommunication against all the abettors and observers of the truce, and declaring at the same time all towns, cities or villages wherein it was observed,

---

* Some of the noblest flights of Rinuccini's eloquence were directed against this fatal truce. "Make no truce with this man," said the Nuncio, "he has three times changed sides. If the massacre at Cashel has left no trace on your memories, recollect that a month ago he pillaged the town of Carrick and slew the inhabitants, who were Catholics, palliating the atrocity by asserting that he could not restrain his soldiers. Remember, too, that he has driven the Catholic clergy out of the Cathedral of Callan, and introduced those who do not profess your religion. Talk not of your inability to carry war into his quarters. . . . . . Inchiquin has not more than 3,000 men in Munster; they are naked and hungry, and you fear him when you ought to despise him. In Connaught and Ulster, the Scotch are able to do little more than commit robberies for their sustenance. At the present moment, Owen O'Neill has an army of more than 6,000 men. He is ready to act against Inchiquin in the South, and I will supply money to pay his troops, and thus rid you of those scruples with which the ravages of his soldiers have so long afflicted you. I exhort you to union of heart and purpose; and remember that your rulers of England have never treated you, Catholics, with respect, except when you stood in a united and formidable league."—Rinuccini's *Relatione*, pp 312, 420.

as solemnly interdicted. Amongst the old **Irish this, of course,** put an end to the truce with Inchiquin, but **the Ormondists faith-**fully observed it, in utter disregard of the **dread anathema of the** Church, some of **them even boasting that they were "ex-communication proof."** Preston, however, was made to feel that his soldiers, at least, were not so, for immediately on the promulgation of the decree 2,000 of them deserted to O'Neill's army.

At last the time came when Rinuccini had to call on Owen Roe and the Irish chiefs to unfurl their banners and draw their swords against the recreant Catholics who had already broken the oath of Confederation by accepting treaties and making various agreements with the enemy without the consent of the entire body. Many brilliant achievements shed lustre on the arms of these true **sons of the Church** led on by **Owen Roe and** fighting under the **immediate direction of the Nuncio. At the** pass of Ballaghmore, **this** great tactician **defeated and foiled no** less than five **generals who had** united their **forces against him.*** When any other commander of the Catholic **party failed in an** enterprize, O'Neill was **called into action, and seldom indeed** did he fail to effect his object.

But what availed all his valor and military skill? what availed all the talents and all the energy of Rinuccini and French? Preston was not ashamed to let his rancorous jealousy carry him so far as to form a league with Murrogh O'Brien for the avowed object of crushing O'Neill. Conspiracy, dark and dire, was at work. Plots were even formed amongst the quondam Confederates and their new allies against the very life of the Nuncio, whom they branded as the disturber of the peace, the arch-agitator whose influence alone kept the old Irish from ac-cepting peace on Ormond's terms, and turning their arms with him against the king's enemies. Even some of the bishops were won over to oppose the Nuncio's policy, on the plea of condemn-ing "the censures." That fatal measure, however necessary it might have appeared to a man of Rinuccini's temperament so situated, was eventually the cause **of yet** more fearful dissensions

---

* **Meehan's** *Confederation,* **p. 223.**

in the Confederate camp, seeing that it divided the clergy into two distinct parties. Things came at last to such a pass that the bishops on either side were, of necessity, escorted to and from Kilkenny by detachments from their respective armies. Yet still Rinuccini kept his ground, and by his side Nicholas French —they did not quite despair so long as Owen Roe had an army in the field, and together they toiled, struggling against all odds, exhorting, persuading, anathematizing when all else failed. In vain, in vain, " the national spirit only survived in the hearts of O'Neill and the clergy,"* and the chiefs of the old blood, for they alone were willing to sacrifice all for the cause now rapidly becoming hopeless.

At the storming of the Castle of Drumruisk on the Connaught boundary, the Irish army sustained a heavy loss in the brave and chivalrous Roderick Maguire, who fell at the head of his regiment—meet death for the brother of Connor Maguire, the nephew of gallant old Lorcan—that fiery young chieftain who, in the first outbreak of the rebellion, had inflicted such severe chastisement on the robber-planters of Fermanagh! He fell, like his martyred brother, in the flower of his years, his death no less heroic than that of Connor. The chieftains by whose side he had so often fought, and the general whose fortunes he had so faithfully followed, mourned him, as well they might. Could any amongst them have looked but one short year into the future they would have envied the fate of their gallant friend. As it was they only saw in his premature death the loss of one of their truest hearts and strongest arms—one of the first of the Confederate Chieftains, one of whom it might truly be said, from the dawn of the Confederacy, that

> " Never then, nor thence, till now, hath falsehood or disgrace
> Been seen to soil *Maguire's* plume, or mantle on his face.'

Another laurel for " the sons of the waters," but, alas ! too dearly purchased.

Would that pen of mine could do justice to the memory of those who upheld the banner of faith and nationality through

---

* Meehan's *Confederation*.

the disastrous times which followed, under the leadership of
that holy and zealous prelate who had adopted the cause of
poor Ireland as his own, and loved her patriotic and faithful
sons with all the capacity of his great heart. But my tale has
already far exceeded the bounds which I had prescribed for it,
and I must draw a veil, however reluctantly, over that most
eventful period.

In 1648 the final peace was concluded which virtually dis-
solved the Confederation. The false-hearted Norman peers who
had come so reluctantly into the Union were the ultimate ruin
of the cause. In order to leave their great patron, Ormond, at
liberty to carry out his own plans, they accepted the bare toleration which he chose to give them, instead of the complete
restoration of their faith to its ancient independence, according
to the just demands of Rinuccini and Owen Roe, the clergy, and
the chiefs of the old blood. For ever execrated be the memory
of those craven Catholics, unworthy the name, who threw the
game into the hands of the enemy, and bartered away the rights
of their country and religion for less than "the shadow of a
shade!"

About the same time that witnessed the final fall of the once
powerful Confederation, the truckling and hollow-hearted
Charles ended his life on the scaffold, a victim no less to his
own want of principle and disregard of justice than the bloody
fanaticism of his Puritan subjects.

It was a dismal year for Ireland, the year '49. Almost at its
opening, the old City of the Tribes witnessed a mournful scene.
The Nuncio Rinuccini, worn out at last by the heart-wearing
cares and troubles of his office, and despairing of effecting the
liberation of a country whose sons were so split up into factions,
and so embittered against each other, made up his mind to
return to Italy, at least for a time, until some favorable change
might take place in Ireland.

In vain did Owen Roe and the bishops who were his friends
seek to dissuade him from this step, reminding him of all he had
done for the cause, and imploring him not to give it up whilst
success was still possible. The Nuncio shook his head with a
melancholy smile, and pointed to his shrunken cheek and his

hollow chest. The hint was more than sufficient for the true friends who surrounded Rinuccini. They knew that his health had been undermined by the superhuman labors of mind and body, which for tour long years he had unceasingly undergone, and worse than all, the grief of seeing his mighty efforts thrown away, and that Ireland, which he hoped to leave free and prosperous, in no better condition than when he landed on her shore.

"Ask me not to stay, kind friends!" he said mournfully, "my doing so could not now benefit Ireland—if it could, there were no need to ask me, for the shattered remnant of my strength were well employed in the service of your faithful nation. But so long as you are cursed with such Catholics as Clanrickarde, Muskerry and Mountgarret, and that young Netterville who is now Ormond's aid-de-camp, and Castlehaven who doth assuredly serve that lord with more zeal than he ever served the Confederacy, all you or I—or any man living could do to recover your national and religious independence were not worth a feather."

"What, then," said Bishop French with some show of resentment; "would your Grace have us give up at once?"

"Not so, my reverend lord," said Rinuccini with a kindly smile, and turning he laid his hand on Owen Roe's shoulder; "there is hope for Ireland whilst O'Neill lives—darkness will never quite overshadow the land so long as the Red Hand banner is afloat—when that goes down, the cross goes down with it, and the hoof of the fanatic will crush the heart of Ireland—oh faithful, long-enduring Ireland! when, when shall the Sabbath of peace dawn for you?"

He then turned and thanked the assembled crowd for the gallant stand made by the citizens of Galway against the fatal peace,* and as they fell on their knees with tears and sobs, he extended his hand and gave the apostolic benediction.

* Galway, in common with many others of the principal cities, totally refused to have "the peace" proclaimed within its walls. "It would be idle," says Rev. Mr. Meehan, "to imagine that this peace gave satisfaction to the people of Ireland. On the contrary, it was soon ascertained that it gave them no guarantee for those rights

"To you," said he, "people of Galway, and to all true and faithful Catholics in this land of Ireland. Be ye blessed for ever, and your children throughout all time! Were your faithless nobles like unto you in devotion to the Church, my mission would have had a different result——"

Turning to Owen Roe and Bishop French, he took a hand of each and said with much feeling: "Beloved fellow-laborers! farewell!—blame me not if my mission hath been unsuccessful —you know I did all I could to free the Church of Ireland— you know how my best endeavors were met and thwarted at every move by those who had sworn to defend the ancient faith at all hazards nor lay down their arms till its shackles were all broken—you know how recreant Catholics have maligned and traduced me—yea, even at the Court of Rome—and that some amongst them have even conspired against my life—all this you know, noble and right trusty friends, but you do not know —cannot know—all the love that I cherish in my heart for you and yours! My lord of Clogher, your hand! I may never see the face of any one of you again, but—but—I will not forget you! I will do what in my power lies to advance that sacred cause the which I leave, for the present, in your hands! Be firm and faithful as you have been, and leave the issue to God!"

"May Heaven requite your Grace an hundred-fold," said Nicholas of Ferns with strong emotion, "for all you have done in behalf of poor bleeding Ireland!"

"Say rather, my dear good brother, *for what I meant to do,* and would have done, were it not for the treachery of those amongst you who have made Ormond their idol. Pray Heaven they discover that man's hollowness ere it be too late!"

which aroused them to take up arms and maintain a war of so many years duration. It was indignantly rejected by the whole province of Ulster, the cities of Waterford, Limerick, Clonmel, and Dungarvan. Twenty of the great Irish families in the province of Munster signed a protest against it. Galway . . . . refused to receive it: and, in the province of Leinster, it was treated with contempt by all the heads of the old Irish."—*Confederation,* p. 159. .

Rinuccini departed, and with him went the sun of Ireland's prosperity; from that day forth, the Ormondists had it all their own way, at least in three of the provinces; their arms were devoted, as their hearts had been, to the advancement of his views, and, as they fondly believed, the upholding the falling throne of the Stuarts. Little did they dream, until sad experience forced conviction on them, that their patron was all along playing a double game—coquetting with the rebellious Parliament, both before and after the execution of his royal master, the while he kept Preston, and even the astute Clanrickarde, and indeed the whole body of the Anglo-Irish Catholics dangling after him as most approved good servants of his mightiness, James Butler. It was not till he had delivered Dublin into the hands of the Parliamentarians, and sent his son Richard to them as a hostage for the fulfilment of his compact with them, that the duped Catholics began to see their error, and mourn when too late the share they had taken in breaking up that powerful Confederation which, had all its members been true to its principles, must and would have prevailed. They found that even Ormond himself did not attach the same importance to their adhesion as when they formed a part of that magnificent body whose influence was felt in every corner of the island. Ah! dismal retribution! Mountgarret, waiting in Ormond's antechamber, found himself only " my Lord Mountgarret"—and the old man groaned in spirit as he thought of the days when, as President of the Supreme Council, his name and office commanded respect. Muskerry, too, was doomed to realize Rinuccini's prophetic words. When, some years after, he lay extended on his bed of death, and the past appeared to him in its true colors, viewed by the ghastly light of the tomb, he said in a contrite spirit to those who were in attenda·ce upon him, " that the heaviest fear that possessed his soul, then going into eternity, was his having confided so much in his Grace (meaning Ormond), who had deceived them all, and ruined his poor country and countrymen."*

* Dr. French's *Unkind Deserter*, quoted by Meehan.

Well for you, Donogh McCarthy! you who might have helped to make Ireland

"———Great, glorious, and free"

by joining heart and hand with the other chieftains of your own blood and your own faith. You chose rather to sell yourself body and soul to James Butler of Ormond, one of the bitterest enemies of Catholicity that Ireland ever produced, and so he treated you in the end, O degenerate son of the McCarthys, unworthy the name you bore! May Heaven forgive the share you had in the failure of that grand attempt to free Ireland and her Church from foreign thrall!

But in Ulster the spirit of the Confederation still lived. There no slavish Norman peers threw their icy shadows athwart the popular enthusiasm—there the chieftains were still loyally devoted to the cause—there the clans were burning to rush again on the Puritan foe who had so often quailed before them —there O'Rielly and McMahon, Magennis and O'Rourke of Leitrim, were still up and stirring, and there the RED HAND still waved over many a tower and town. Sir Phelim was hot as though no reverse had come to cool his ardor, and Owen Roe was as powerful to do and dare as when he swept Monroe's proud army at Benburb like chaff before the wind. No, all hope was not lost—the Red Hand still waved on the northern horizon!

19

CHAPTER XXXIV.

"Wail, wail ye for the Mighty One!   Wail, wail ye for the dead;
Quench the hearth, and hold the breath—with ashes strew the head.
How tenderly we loved him!   How deeply we deplore!
Holy Saviour! but to think we shall never see him more.

"Sagest in the council was he,—kindest in the hall,
Sure we never won a battle—'twas Owen won them all.
Had he lived—had he lived—our dear country had been free;
But he's dead, but he's dead, and 'tis slaves we'll ever be.

　　*　　　　*　　　　*　　　　*　　　　*　　　　*

"Wail, wail him through the Island!   Weep, weep for our pride'.
Would that on the battle-field our gallant chief had died!
Weep the Victor of Benburb—weep him, young man and old;
Weep for him, ye women—your Beautiful lies cold!

"We thought you would not die—we were sure you would not go,
And leave us in our utmost need to Cromwell's cruel blow—
Sheep without a shepherd, when the snow shuts out the sky—
O, why did you leave us, Owen!   Why did you die?

"Soft as woman's was your voice, O'Neill! bright was your eye.
O, why did you leave us, Owen?   Why did you die?
Your troubles are all over, you're at rest with God on high;
But we're slaves, and we're orphans, Owen!—why did you die?"

THOMAS DAVIS.

LIKE unto these were the piteous cries that pierced the gray
November sky around Cloughoughter Castle* on the sixth day
of November, of the same year of '49.   Along the lake shore lay
encamped the main body of O'Neill's army, making as gallant a
show as it did on that day three years gone by when the columns were forming on the heights of Benburb under the eye of
its valiant chief.   There was none to take pride in the marshalled
host that day by dull Lough Oughter's shore—mournfully

---

* This Castle, now a ruin, is situate on a small islet near the shore
of a lake in the county Cavan. The country around it is very picturesque, abounding in wood and water.

drooped the banners flapping heavily in the gray damp air—voiceless was pipe and drum and trumpet—nought was heard save the voice of human sorrow—the wail that rose from a thousand breaki g hearts.

" Talk not of grief till thou hast seen the tears of warrior-men."*

And no wonder the sternest warrior there " hid his face and wept,"—no wonder—it were strange if he did not, for within that gray old castle of the O'Reillys, there by the lake shore, lay the idolized leader of the Irish clans—the valiant, the wise, the noble, the kind—Owen Roe lay there dead—Owen Roe the hope of Ireland—the terror of the Puritan enemy—the greatest captain of his age—he who had stood like some stately column firm and unmoved whilst all around was desolation. He whose name was the watchword of Irish freedom,—whose banner was the beacon of his country's hope—*Owen Roe was dead.* Yes !

" Weep for him through the Island ! weep, weep for our pride !"

Ay ! well may ye weep, Clan-Owen ! for since Hugh was laid in Italian mould far away from the land he loved, no son of Nial has brought with him to the tomb so much glory, so much promise, or left behind him so drear a void ! Well may ye weep, Clan-Owen ! this day, for he that made your name glorious is gone,
> " Like a summer-dried fountain,
> When your need was the sorest !" †

He that was wont to cheer you on with his beaming smile and his bland sweet voice, he is gone and forever—never more shall you hear from his lips those words that stirred you up to deeds of noblest daring—" sons of my heart, advance !" Ah ! yes, sons of his heart you were—he breathed his spirit into you, and moved you at will,—but he is dead, that voice is hushed forever, and that arm that so often waved you on to victory is stiff now and cold !

In the flower of his days the great chieftain died, and in the zenith, too, of his glory. By a signal stroke of retribution, even Ormond himself was compelled to mourn his death, and

* Mrs. Hemans.   † Sir W. Scott.

Preston, and Castlehaven, and all those unworthy Catholics who
had so lately conspired against his life. He died just when Cromwell had been sent to Ireland by the Parliament as Lord Lieutenant*—already had the torrent of blood burst forth from the
heart of Ireland beneath that butcher's sword—that torrent
which was to drench the land

> " With the mingled blood of the brave and good, of mother, and maid,
> and child."

The massacre of Drogheda had reached Owen's ears, and the
cries of the women of Wexford—slaughtered by the tyrant's
orders—had penetrated to his far northern home and moved
his chivalrous soul with pity. He had vowed to stop the murderous career of the regicide in Ireland, or he, and all who bore
his name, should perish. Ormond, baffled at every turn, straitened in means, and seeing in the ruthless republican general a
military genius of the highest order, before whom all obstacles
vanished like mist—seeing him sweeping the country like a
furious whirlwind destroying all that dared to oppose him,
Ormond began to look around for aid, and in all the land of
Ireland he saw but one man whom he deemed able to cope
with Cromwell. That man was Owen Roe O'Neill, to whom he
sent off without delay, beseeching him to come to the rescue,
and that all his former demands should be conceded. After holding a council of war, Owen agreed, smiling pleasantly to himself at the thought that Ormond was humbled indeed when he
could stoop to sue so abjectly for his assistance. It was hard
to persuade Sir Phelim to make common cause with Ormond,
who, according to him, " would betray his old Popish grandfather, Walter the Rosary, were he back again in the flesh."
Some of the other chiefs objected to the alliance on various
grounds, but Owen, with his calm, clear reasoning, speedily convinced them all.

"I have no more faith in my lord of Ormond," said he, " than
hath any one here, but in the present instance, we have the
strongest guarantee of his sincerity, in that his *interest* binds
him to us. He knows that this Cromwell is not a man to be put

---

* Lord Ormond still holding that office for the Royalist party.

down—*by him at least*—and he knows, too, that all his courtly
arts of intrigue would be thrown away on the stern ill-mannered
Puritan! Believe me, friends and brothers, Ormond is in earnest *now* in seeking our alliance, for on it his safety depends, as
he knoweth full well!"

"Well! well! Owen," cried Sir Phelim, "have it your own way
—for a man that talks little, you talk wondrous well—my opinion
is that you could coax the birds off the bushes had you no better employment for that oily tongue of yours!"

Owen Roe smiled and laid his hand caressingly on the great
brawny shoulder of his rough kinsman just as a keeper of animals would fondle a pet bear. "It is easy to persuade men
like you, Phelim, to do what religion and patriotism dictate.
You all here present have perceived at a glance that our best
chance for eventual success is now to join with Ormond—let us
do it, then, in God's name, for the sake of that cause to which
we are devoted for weal or woe. Ormond cannot impose on us
—we know him all too well—but if by uniting our forces with
his, we can oppose an effectual barrier to the murderous designs
of the Parliament of England and send back its psalm-singing,
hypocritical blood-hounds to hunt down their employers at
home, we shall assuredly have the best of the bargain. Let us
once get rid of this gloomy regicide Cromwell who esteems the
shedding of Papist blood nothing more than a godly pastime,
and we can easily hold our own with the marquis."

In pursuance of this resolution, cheerfully adopted by the
chiefs, the vanguard of the army was sent southward immediately to join Ormond and Castlehaven, whilst Owen himself
prepared to follow with the main body. His last charge, to
O'Rourke who commanded the vanguard, was characteristic:

"I have chosen you, Owen," said he, "for this post of danger, not because you are braver, but because you are cooler
than any of these. Were this sturdy kinsman of mine somewhat
less fiery than he is, I would have sent him forward, but knowing his hot haste when the foe is before him, and knowing, too,
that Cromwell is the coolest and most calculating of generals, I
feared for my brave Phelim whom we could ill afford to lose,
and, therefore, I chose you, Owen O'Rourke, the coolest officer

in my army. Go forth, then, in God's name, but I charge you,
Owen, avoid an engagement with this formidable fanatic until
we come together again. Keep to the passes and defiles and
try his patience—the winter is setting in and it will befriend us
—by the time Oliver and his canting knaves are getting sick of
our rain and sleet, we can come down on them all together like
a sledge hammer."

What wonder was it that even the rejected Phelim, choleric
as he was, had nothing to say in opposition to this appointment,
whilst the other chiefs, catching up the martial fire that burned
in their leader's heart and sparkled in his eyes, shook off the
supineness that had of late been creeping over them and longed
to meet the tyrant sword in hand.

It was the day before that appointed for the march of the
army and Owen Roe stood once more with Judith O'Cahan in
the roofless church of Dungiven by the side of a new-made grave
—it was that of Father Phelimy who had been buried there but
a week before. At a little distance from where they stood fair
Emmeline knelt in prayer, looking up with faith-inspired eyes at
the cold blue heavens above the ruined altar whereon "the
clean oblation" of the New Law had been made of old. With
her exception, there was no human being near, and the voice of
the wind and the roar of the torrent made a chorus of unearthly
music in and around the ancient church of the O'Cahans. The
place was lonely, wild and desolate, yet there was grandeur in
its loneliness and utter desertion, and to souls like those of Owen
and Judith, its silence was eloquent with voices from the past.

Having made up his mind to go south next day with the army,
Owen had journeyed to Dungiven to say farewell to Judith, and
on reaching the poor dwelling which she and Emmeline had of
late shared with Father Phelimy, he found in it only the aged
crone who had been maid of all work to the comfortless household. Then it was that Owen first heard of the old priest's
death, and was told that the ladies had just gone to visit his
grave "in the church above."

It was a strange surprise when Judith raised her eyes as she
knelt by the grave of her aged protector to see General O'Neill
standing by her side, looking down with tearful eyes on the

brown bare heap which engrossed her own sad thoughts. Emmeline was there, too, but she soon wandered away to the roofless chancel where we have seen her.

"So *he* is gone, too," said Owen, pointing downwards as Judith arose from her knees.

"Even so, Owen! those we loved are dropping off in quick succession."

"God help you, Judith!—that noble heart of yours is sorely tried—may their souls all rest in peace! I know not whether the news I bring will give you joy or sorrow—mayhap both."

"What is it, I pray you? Fear not to speak—I can hear anything."

Owen then told her of his treaty with Ormond, and ended by saying that he came to bid her farewell.

"Farewell!" repeated Judith somewhat wildly; "fare-well! it is a sad word over a new-made grave—*fare-well!*" she said again, slowly and abstractedly, "I like not the word"— and she shuddered.

"Why, Judith," said Owen Roe surprised and no little disappointed by her unwonted dejection; "why, Judith! an *you* speak so drearily, to whom must I go for hope, and faith, and fervor in the cause?"

Hearing this, Judith, by a strong effort, shook off her strange depression, and walking away a few steps from the grave beckoned Owen to follow. She then placed her hand in his, and said with something like her former spirit:

"God be with you, Owen, till we meet again! May He strengthen your arm and nerve your soul to yet more heroic efforts—may He bless all who will go up with you to battle for His name. And He will—but—but—why this is strange!"— she stopped as if gasping for breath, and pressed her hand on her bosom—"there is something wrong here—here. Ah! Owen, there is a weight on my heart—beware of Ormond, Owen! his duplicity is well nigh as dangerous as Cromwell's sword——"

"With aid from above, Judith," said O'Neill, "I fear neither one nor the other. Be you but of good heart and pray for our success—Emmeline too," as that lady approached them, "in the silence and solitude of this ruined fane, with the dead be-

roes of your race around you, invoke the God of battles for us.
A fierce struggle is before us, Judith, my best beloved!—the
might of England is now indeed to be arrayed against us, and
Cromwell and Ireton are just the men to carry out the designs
of the fanatics in our regard. An' we fail now, Judith"—he
paused and looked her steadily in the face as though to read
the depth of her soul, if perchance any sad foreboding lurked
there—"*an' we fail, Judith*"—he repeated slowly.

"An' you fail," said Judith with a shudder, her voice trembling with emotion, "Heaven help the children of the Gael, for
your past triumphs will but whet the sword of Cromwell : failure
now were ruin!"

"Your thought is mine," said Owen with a bright look of
affection; "bless you, Judith, bless you! and may Mary our
Mother shield you from harm! should we meet no more, pulse
of my heart! I would have you demand protection, both you and
Emmeline, from the Marchioness of Ormond. She hath a noble
spirit, and will compassionate your forlorn state——"

"Heaven bless her! I know it well," said Emmeline, "and
yet methinks I would be hard driven for shelter when I applied
to her after my open abandonment of home and early friends.
Rather a thousand times for me a nook in some desolate ruin
where the short remnant of our days might be passed in peace."

"And for me," said Judith drawing herself up, "my father's
daughter were brought lower than she ever will be when she
humbled herself before Elizabeth Preston, the wife of a man
whose intrigues have ruined our cause—or at least broken up the
Confederation. I little expected, Owen O'Neill! to hear such counsel from your lips. No, if God willed that you should fall—which
I will not, cannot, dare not think—Emmeline and myself must
take our chance with the Catholic daughters of this land. Be
not troubled on our account, Owen," she added in a softened
tone as she met his reproachful eye, "we have a good Father to
protect us, and a Mother, too—and you will be back to us,
Owen! your brow wreathed with laurels—surely, surely you
will! you have ever conquered—you *must* conquer now, for
there is only you fit to measure swords with Cromwell, and your
defeat by him would leave our poor country at his feet heart-

broken and helpless—oh, God! I will not, must not think of it!"

"And that reminds me, dear one!" said Owen sadly, yet with kindling enthusiasm, "that while I stand here forgetting all but the happiness of seeing you, the horrors of Drogheda or of Wexford may be renewed. Judith! stay of my life! I must say farewell!"

He took the hand which she freely gave, but it was cold, cold as ice, and her face was bloodless as that of a corpse. Her eyes, too, when she raised them to Owen's face, had a wild, haggard look in them which made the chieftain tremble, brave and fearless as he was. Twice the thin pale lips parted and Judith seemed about to speak, but they closed again with a convulsive motion, and only for the restless glance of the spirit-like eyes, the face would have been rigid as one of marble.

"Judith!" said Owen at length, "I can stand this no longer—speak but a word—a word of benediction—and I am gone!"

Slowly the pale lips opened again, and a heavy sigh came forth, and then whispered words that sounded like, "Oh, my country!" and then the blood rushed to the pale cheek, and Judith beat down into her heart the dark presentiment that had for a moment overcome her, and she said in her own clear, musical voice:

"Go, then, Owen!—your suffering country calls—religion commands—what are Judith's wishes, Judith's womanish fears? With the blood of heroes in my veins—ay! even the blood of *Cooey-na-gall*, how can I yield to puerile weakness? Go forth to conquer, sword of the Gael!—lead the clans to battle as before, and the host of heaven will aid you!"

"There spoke my own chosen one," said Owen cheerfully; "now can I set forth with a hopeful and right good heart, but your sadness weighed on me like lead—God in heaven be your safeguard till I return, and then, Judith——"

"Then, Owen! if you have prevailed over Cromwell, the Church will have peace and the country rest,—the hero of a hundred fights may well look forward to the poor reward of Judith's dowerless hand."

"Enough! I desire no more—farewell! Judith!—if I live, Drogheda and Wexford shall not go unrevenged—Cromwell and myself shall soon come together—the shock of our meeting will make the island quake, and one or the other of us will be dashed to pieces—but for *God and my right* I fear not to face him were he an hundred king-killers! Emmeline! child of our adoption, my blessing be upon you—should the day of my happiness ever come, Judith's home and mine shall be yours—weep not, fair maiden! this is no time for tears—see! Judith hath none to give——'

The words stuck in his throat, and he moved away abruptly. Emmeline caught his cloak and when he turned back looked timidly up into his face.

" What would you, Emmeline ?" said the chief.

" A word—just a word. In the storm of battle you may meet Sir Charles Coote—dare I ask you to spare his life should you have the power——"

O'Neill frowned. " No, Emmeline, not even to you can I make such a promise—it were a cruel betrayal of my own people to spare one of the Cootes in battle——"

" Oh ! say not so, General O'Neill ! say not so, I implore you ! —it is for my mother's sake not for his—bad as he is I can forgive him now through divine grace, but I would not ask you to spare the life of such as he were it not for the mother that bore him and me—and—and—his wretched soul——"

" Fair Mistress Emmeline ! I may never have the opportunity you speak of—but if I had—justice would demand its victim at my hand. No more—no more—farewell!—Judith! I will live on the hope of our next meeting !"

" It will be in heaven !" said Judith half aloud, as she stood leaning against the dilapidated wall and watched him mounting his war-steed. Once again the chieftain turned, and smiled a fond farewell as he met Judith's glance, then spurred his prancing steed and cantered down the slope. Did he murmur to himself like Roderick Dhu leaving Ellen Douglas :

" It is the last time—'tis the last, that angel voice shall Roderick hear ?"

Not so, for no dark misgiving weighed on Owen's heart. Health glowed on his cheek, life was coursing warm and ardent through his veins—how could he think of death being at hand?

'The sense of right and the power to smite are the spirit that commands.'

Was not this *spirit* his? True, Cromwell was no ordinary adversary—true, his legions were full of his own fanatical spirit, and every man was inflamed with his leader's thirst for Papist blood—but Owen Roe was as strong, and as valiant, and as wise, as when he conquered at Benburb—his army was the same that had swept Monroe's battalions into the Blackwater—their hearts clung around him as ivy round the oak—the blessing of the Pontiff was on their arms—why should he fear that ultimate, nay, immediate, success would crown their heroic efforts?

Words cannot describe the enthusiasm of that gallant army when Owen placed himself again at its head. What was the terror of Cromwell's army to men who marched under the banner of Owen Roe O'Neill, that glorious banner with the cross and keys interwoven with the Red Hand on its snowy surface? The more danger the more honor, and the more terrible the advancing foe the greater need of stopping his course. Fear indeed, had no place in their hearts—

> " High, high are their hopes, for their chieftain has said
> Tha: whatever men dare *they* can do.
>
> *   *   *   *   *
>
> And proudly they follow *that* chief to the field
> Where their laurels were gather'd before.'' *

Great Heavens! the first day's march was not completed when the general was seized with a sudden and violent disease which rendered him unable to keep his seat on horseback.† Struck

---

* Scotch ballad.

† This sudden and fatal illness of Owen Roe at such a critical juncture is very generally attributed to poison—a pair of poisoned boots, some will have it, which caused a defluxion of blood from the knees. Whether it be so or not, God alone knows. It is probably one of those historical secrets which man can never fathom, and on which the shroud of mystery will for ever rest. One thing is certain, that it was the current belief at the time that poison had been administered, and various parties were suspected of the heinous deed. It were worse than useless now to mention these names, some

with terror and consternation the whole army came to a stand
—Bishop McMahon and the chiefs would fain persuade the
general to send forward the army and remain behind, but of
this Owen would not hear—whilst God spared him life he would
go with his men—what would they do without him? Besides,
his illness could not last long.

"Not as it is now," said the bishop significantly to the chiefs
who stood around in speechless terror; "an' it continue so, it
will soon end——"

"For the love of God, my lord, don't say that!" whispered
Sir Phelim in a broken voice, and stooping down he said
anxiously:

"How are you now, Owen?——"

"Much the same, Phelim, much the same—I'll be better
soon, however—with the help of God"—then turning suddenly
to the bishop he asked:

"Are they getting that litter ready for me? I depend on
your lordship to hurry them."

"My dear son," said the bishop, "make your mind easy—
better wait a day or two till you are over the worst——"

"My lord of Clogher," said the chieftain raising himself on
his elbow, "how can you talk of a day or two, when there is
question of meeting Oliver Cromwell—you know the stern necessity that doth urge us on!"

"I know, my son, I know, but—but——"

"But what—I pray your lordship say it out—be it what it
may—I am not the man, I thank my God, to shrink from pain
or sickness——"

"Ay, but, Owen—there be worse than pain or sickness——"

"Humph!" said Owen contemptuously, "you would not
have me think that there is danger of death—I have been sick
ere now."

"Not with such sickness as this. Owen, Owen, be persuaded
—let the army march on with McMahon, and O'Rielly, and Sir
Phelim, if you will—let all go, but myself——"

of them still holding high position in Ireland. It is also certain,
that the voice of tradition invariably ascribes this disastrous event to
poison.

" And wherefore you, my lord ?"

" I—I—am a skilful nurse, Owen, and, moreover, somewhat of a leech——"

Owen smiled and muttered strangely to himself, then suddenly starting with renewed animation, gave positive orders for the litter to be made ready, alleging that he felt much better even as it was, and to move again at the head of his army would speedily restore him to health.

His wishes were obeyed, and Owen Roe was carried to the front amid the deafening cheers of his faithful followers. On one side of the litter rode the bishop and Sir Phelim, on the other, McMahon and O'Rielly, while Sir Con Magennis and O'Rourke of Breffny followed clo e behind. Oh! how fervent were the prayers put up by each in his own heart for the preservation of that precious life, so all-important in that hour! The fear that was gathering in raven darkness over them all, no one dared to communicate —they even shrank from meeting each other's eyes, but rode on silently, wrapt in gloomy thought. And still the general's voice was heard at intervals urging his officers to speed the army on. Nevertheless, his sufferings increased to such a degree in consequence of the motion of the litter, that he was obliged to give in at last.

" I can go no farther," said he ; " God's will be done !"

It so happened that they were then within sight of the gray waters of Lough Oughter, where O'Reilly's old Castle looked down in sullen grandeur on the wintry flood. On being told of this, Owen Roe smiled sadly.

" Here, then, will I rest. Beneath the roof-tree of O'Reilly, I can lay down my head in peace."

At his own urgent request, the last Sacraments were administered without delay.

" Lose not a moment, my dear lord !" he said to the bishop in a failing voice ; " that is the only affair that imports me now —my heart is breaking for the woes of Ireland, but I cannot serve her now—my own soul—eternity—death—judgment— haste, my lord! lest I go forth unshriven on my long journey !"

With a heavy heart Bishop McMahon set about his doleful task, and when all his spiritual wants were supplied, the chief-

tain rallied for a short time. He conversed calmly with his
friends on the affairs of the country, advised them as to the
prosecution of the war, and charged Sir Phelim to keep the
Red Hand afloat as long as there was the slightest possibility of
success.

"Now, Phelim," said he with startling energy, "may I depend
on you? So long as the Red Hand of Tyr-Owen is up, the
clans of the north will rally around it—you know that, son of
the Hy-Nial—there is but you now to keep the old flag unfurled
—will you do it, Phelim! for God and our bleeding country?—
will you fight manfully to the last, nor give in while a chance of
success remains?"

"I will, Owen—brother of my heart, I will!" said poor
Phelim, bursting into tears like a very child. "So help me
God, I will! The Red Hand shall never be furled whilst I live,
unless our lawful demands are conceded."

"It is well, Phelim! give me your hand on that!" Sir Phelim
did, but at the touch of Owen's hand his grief burst forth anew,
for it was already clammy and cold.

"Oh! the villains! the cowardly, black-hearted villains!" cried
the knight waxing furious at the thought of what had caused
this so dire calamity; "they couldn't conquer you by fair means,
so they must needs——"

"Don't say it, Phelim!" said the dying chieftain; "it matters little how my death cometh, so long as it is come. We
have no certainty touching the poison, and it is a fearful crime
wherewith to brand any man—yet it is none too black for my
enemies," he said musingly; "it may well be so—but even an'
it were, chieftains of the Gael! I charge ye let the matter
rest. We have no proof, I say again, as to who is the culprit—
if one there be—as my God shall judge me, then, I desire to die
in peace with all men, in that I bear no ill-will to any for this
thing, or, indeed, for any other matter of a personal nature. I
fought while I was able, and would fight again, for the sacred
rights of my country and religion—and my heavy grief is now
that I die when my services are most needed—but private malice
bear I none, for which blessing I thank my God."

Some of the chiefs conversing together in low whispers, the

name of *Preston* caught Owen's ear, whereupon he turned his
head quickly and said with surprising energy :

"Who talks of Preston? Be his name unnamed here! He
hath much to answer for in regard to our common cause—he
hath done Ormond's work not ours—so have all the Norman
lords and gentlemen—all—all—may God forgive them is my
dying prayer—but let no man name *Thomas Preston* in connection with my death—name *no* names, once more I tell you! I
would speak with Donogh the Rapparee, in private."

What passed between the two, the chiefs could but guess, but
Donogh remained by the bed-side until the last struggle was
over. The brave fellow was so overcome with sorrow that he only
roused himself from his stupor when Owen spoke to him, as he
often did, and then he bent over him to catch the faintly breathed
words of love and pity to be wafted to Judith when he was no
more. "My peerless love—spouse I may well call her—the
lone mourner in far Dungiven—the winter-winds sighed when I
bade her farewell, and there was *death* between us, Donogh!
She felt it, though I did not. Tell her I blessed her with my
dying breath—and mind, Donogh, charge her by the love I bore
her to leave this land at once with Emmeline—the money I
gave you will suffice to take them to France or Spain—tell her
there is a fearful time coming—she *must* go hence, Donogh!
and you must go to watch over her—for my sake you will—I
know you will!"

The loud wailing of the soldiers without breaking suddenly on his ear, Owen started from a heavy trance-like slumber,
and a groan of anguish burst from his heart. "My brave
fellows!" he murmured, "Heaven help you all this day! Never
again will Owen Roe lead you on to victory! Well may ye
weep, for I loved ye well—proud I was of you—and good reason
I had."

Calling to him Bishop McMahon he then begged him to give
his blessing to all his soldiers and his thanks for their faithful
service—he also charged them to follow the standard of Sir
Phelim O'Neill, on whom the chief command devolved.

Having taken leave of the sorrowing friends who surrounded
his bed, and of all the officers of his army, Owen closed his eyes

in what seemed at first the sleep of death. But just as the bishop was about to commence the prayers for the dying, his lips were seen to move, and like low, faint music words came forth :

"Benburb!—Rinuccini!—Rome!—Ireland!—I could do no more. Sweet Jesus! mercy!—Mary! receive thy child——"

A shudder, a long heavy sigh, and the noblest of Ireland's sons had ceased to breathe—the Fabius of his country—the sword of the Gael—Owen Roe was dead.

Weep, Ireland, weep!—your hero, your pride is gone, and ages may roll away before you look upon his like again. The greatest, the bravest, the wisest of your CONFEDERATE CHIEF-TAINS lies stark and cold in that desolate castle on Lough Oughter's shore !

CONCLUSION.

> " 'Tis come—*their* hour of martyrdom
>   In IRAN's sacred cause is come ;
>   And though their life hath pass'd away
>   Like lightning on a stormy day,
>   Yet shall their death-hour leave a track
>   Of glory, permanent and bright,
>   To which the brave of after-times,
>   The suff'ring brave shall long look back
>   With proud regret, and by its light
>   Watch thro' the hours of slavery's nigh
> For vengeance on th' oppressor's crimes."
>   MOORE's *Lalla Rookh.*

YES, so it was! whilst the banners he had so gloriously won at Benburb were waving in triumph in an old fane of the Eternal City,* Owen Roe was stricken down,

"And he died at Lough Oughter upon St. Leonard's Day."

"He died, and took with him to his grave the lingering hopes of Irish independence." He died and left Ireland in her greatest need, with Cromwell and his Ironsides† already sweeping the land like the red thunderbolt charged with death.

Of the noble northern army, some few officers joined Ormond with the men under their command, chiefly because it had been the last move of Owen Roe to effect a junction with that "slippery politician;" some other battalions broke up or scattered away over the country in search of homes, but the greater portion kept together under the command of Sir Phelim O Neill. Most of the veterans who had shared Owen Roe's victorious

---

* Rinuccini had sent the banners to Rome where they were received with great rejoicing, and the Holy Father himself assisted at the TE DEUM sung in honor of the victory of Benburb.

† By this characteristic name Oliver was wont to address his soldiers.

career, and the Kinel-Owen to a man, still gathered around their
ancient standard, and to do Sir Phelim justice, he bore it
bravely and steadily as became the head of the Hy-Nial race.
For three long years did he keep that flag afloat, his chance of
success diminishing month by month and year by year, manœuv-
ring so as to elude the Puritans where their strength was far
beyond his own, and giving them battle where there was even
a chance of success. He had learned a lesson from his illustrious kinsman, and displayed during that trying and perilous
time a coolness and tact little to be expected from his natural
character. During those three years of bloody and unequal
contest, when the clans of Ulster were struggling, not alone for
freedom, but for life itself, some feats of chivalric bravery were
performed not unworthy of the heroes of ancient story. On
the hill of Tullymangan, in their own border-country, the sons
of Breffny-O'Reilly met and defeated the iron warriors of
Cromwell, reviving for a moment the fading memory of Benburb,
and adding another bright name to the records of Irish valor.
In the south and west, the native tribes everywhere made a gallant resistance to the terrible power of Cromwell. In some
places they refused to receive assistance from Lord Ormond,
preferring rather to take their chance in opposing the Puritans
single-handed rather than have any connection with a man
whom they knew to be at heart their bitter enemy. This was
especially the case in Waterford, Limerick, and Clonmel. The
former city was besieged by Cromwell himself, but the heroic garrison, commanded by General Farrel, defended the town with such
determined bravery that the tyrant was forced to retreat with
loss, leaving to the citizens that proud motto which has ever
since graced their arms : URBS INTACTA—the *Unconquered City.*
Clonmel was defended with equal success by some fifteen hundred Ulstermen under Hugh O'Neill,* a nephew of Owen Roe,
who had come over from the Continent a short time before.
The brief career of this gallant young officer, during the bloody

---

* This defence of Clonmel by Hugh O'Neill is equal to anything of
the kind on record. It forms, indeed, one of the most memorable
events of the eleven years' war.

days of Cromwell, form another glorious page in the Annals of the princely O'Neills, and it must have gladdened the stout heart of Sir Phelim to find his own efforts in the north so nobly seconded by another champion of the Red Hand.

These were truly " the days that tried men's souls." Limerick, like Clonmel and Waterford, would have baffled the efforts of Cromwell, for Hugh O'Neill was within its walls, and the townsmen fought like heroes, but treachery undid their work. A certain Colonel Fennel was there, who betrayed the city to Ireton. It is true the plague was raging within the walls, but more fatal was the treachery of Fennel.* He had twice before betrayed the Catholic party, viz., at Killaloe and at Youghal, but Ireton, to his honor be it said, gave the traitor his deserts. " It is satisfactory to know," says a Protestant historian, " that of the 24 persons excepted from pardon, by way of example, upon this occasion, one of the first led out to execution was this infamous traitor."† But alas! from the same gibbet hung the heroic Bishop of Emly, Terence Albert O'Brien, executed for his noble defence of the city in conjunction with Hugh O'Neill. Forever memorable is the prediction made by this venerable soldier of Christ when, Ireton having passed sentence of death upon him, he summoned that ruthless tyrant to meet him at the bar of divine justice in the space of three days. The haughty Puritan laughed his words to scorn, but he found them true to his cost, for the plague that was decimating the citizens, laid hold on his iron frame, and *he was dead* at the time specified by the martyred prelate.

In those days, too, died Heber McMahon, the illustrious Bishop of Clogher, the friend of Owen Roe and Rinuccini, and Nicholas French. His end was the same as that of the two prelates just mentioned. After maintaining, in conjunction with Sir Phelim O'Neill, the struggle for freedom in Ulster, until every hope of success had well nigh vanished, displaying in his military career

---

* It seems very probable that this unprincipled wretch was the very same *Colonel Fennel* who was branded by Owen Roe as "the cowardly cock with the feather."

† Smith's *Ireland*, Vol. II., p. 62.

so many noble qualities and varied abilities as to command the
respect of all parties,* he was captured by a certain Major King
of Coote's division, and hanged by order of that savage general,
the worthy son of his father! The patriot prelate had been defeated in a bloody engagement but the day previous, the victory
being entirely owing to the enemy's superior cavalry. When
attacked he had with him only a small party of horse—"he defended himself with heroic bravery," says a Protestant writer
of our own day, "and it was not till after he was disabled by
numerous wounds that he was taken prisoner."† Yet they
hung that heroic bishop, that great and gifted man!

Oh! the nobleness of such a life, and the glory of such an
end! If the Maguires have their Connor and their Roderick to
boast of well may the McMahons exult in the name of HEBER!
Malachy O'Kelly, Terence Albert O'Brien, Boetius McEgan and
Heber McMahon, illustrious martyrs to Ireland's faith and Ireland's freedom, the world has never seen men of greater worth,
or of loftier souls, or more fervid zeal for the faith of Christ!
An Archbishop and three bishops martyred for justice' sake!
Oh! Church of Ireland! venerable Mother of Saints! for thee
they suffered, fought and died! may thy children never forget
the honor due to their thrice-hallowed names!

Meanwhile, Preston and Castlehaven‡ had betaken themselves beyond seas—the latter, indeed, long before the death of
Owen Roe, and was doing amateur fighting in France during
the war of the League, whilst the priests and prelates of Ireland
were in battle-harness for the faith. Mountgarret, old and
broken in spirit, died a contrite and humble man in one of his
own castles near Kilkenny, and those who visit the Cathedral
of St. Canice may see in the nave thereof a stately monument

---

* He discharged his new functions with vigor and skill, against the
Parliamentary troops, which he contrived to annoy in every quarter
of the Province, by skirmishing parties of all dimensions.—Wills'
Illustrious and Distinguished Irishmen, Vol. IV., p. 183.

† *Ibid.*

‡ "Since the rebellion of 1641," says he in his Memoirs, " I had
nothing but war and trouble, until the peace of 1646. Then I went
for France." Oh! chivalrous and patriotic Castlehaven!

to the memory of *Richard, third Viscount Mountgarret, obit A. D.* 1651. In the south transept of that same venerable edifice there is another tomb far more interesting to the Catholic or the patriot. It is that of *David Rothe,* the learned, and zealous, and patriotic Bishop of Ossory in the stormy days of the Confederation—the aged prelate whom we have seen sharing so largely in the toils and cares, and also in the glories of that legislative body which for a brief space—alas! too brief!—swayed the destinies of Ireland. Norman by blood, he was Irish in heart, and labored with all the might that was in him to effect the liberation of his native land, and the restoration of her ancient worship. Peace be with thee, David Rothe! simple, guileless soul, patriarch of the Confederation! may thy glory in heaven be commensurate with thy good deeds!

All this time Ormond had been intriguing with one party and another in the vain hope of recovering that power which had passed from his hand for ever. When all else failed him, the baffled politician was fain to have recourse to the prelates of the national party, that is to say, those who had been the supporters of Rinuccini and of Owen Roe. But they knew him too well to trust him then with the bitter experience of a ten years' fruitless struggle weighing on their minds. The Catholic prelates of Ireland could only see in Ormond the main cause of the ruin which had come upon their noble Confederation, and they knew it was his pressing necessities which induced him to make any advances to them. They saw in him the founder and protector of Protestant ascendancy,* the man who had never conceded any measure of justice to Catholics when he had the power, and the man, too, whose insidious counsels had, in all probability, kept up the breach between the ill-fated sovereign who trusted him so blindly, and the Catholic subjects who would have been his most faithful and devoted adherents. The prelates rejected with scorn the overtures of the once-pow-

---

* The Irish fabric of **Protestant ascendancy** in Church, State, and property, was thus mainly **raised by** James Butler, twelfth Earl, and first Duke of Ormond—a fatal labor preceded by one civil war, and followed by another.—Smith's *Ireland,* Vol. II, p 95.

erful dictator of Ireland, and the consequence was that Ormond,
having no other move to make, was forced to leave the country
in company with Lord Inchiquin, whose troops had mutinied
and left him without a man to command. Admirable companionship in ignoble flight! James Butler of Ormond, and
Murrough O'Brien of Inchiquin! "So far," says the candid
Protestant, G. L. Smith, "the Roman Catholic party was
revenged, if not righted. Ormond would not yield them religious freedom, and their prelates drove him out of the country."
Was ever a more signal instance of divine retribution? Defeated as they were, and by his machinations, the hierarchy
of Ireland had still power enough to drive their arch enemy
from the land which he had ruled with all but kingly power!

At Ormond's departure, he appointed Lord Clanrickarde his
deputy, hoping thereby to conciliate the Catholics, but, alas!
Clanrickarde was just as much distrusted by his co-religionists as
Ormond himself, and as he had kept coldly aloof from them
when his aid might have perchance crowned their efforts with
success, so now they looked on with stoical indifference whilst
he vainly struggled to check the power of Cromwell and the
Puritans. Sir Phelim O'Neill, however, was at last induced to
join him with what forces he had yet at his command, but their
joint efforts were of no avail. On and on swept the destroying
host, laying waste all the land, and sparing neither man, woman
nor child in its fanatical fury. The new Lord Lieutenant and
his ally were driven back, back into the far north, still fighting
against fearful odds; they succeeded in taking Ballyshannon
and Donegal, but lost both again, and were at last surrounded
on all sides. Lord Clanrickarde was so fortunate as to effect his
escape but Sir Phelim was captured and taken in chains to
Dublin on account of the reward offered for his apprehension.

The last scene in Sir Phelim's life was as noble as any we
have witnessed during the whole of that long-protracted struggle. His capture was justly considered as a death-blow to the
national cause, and although he had the semblance of a trial,
his condemnation was more from his well-known character as a
Catholic leader than any evidence brought against him. There
was a distinctive feature in his case, nevertheless, which some-

what delayed the execution of his sentence. **The horror where-with** the execution **of** Charles the First **was regarded by all** Europe, and even **by the greater part** of the English realm, **had** driven the **regicide parliament to look around for plausible pre-tences to justify their crime, and finding Sir Phelim O'Neill at last in their clutches, they remembered** the **royal** commission **which, at the first rising in Ulster, he had exhibited to** his **fol-lowers. This was ostentatiously alluded to on his trial,** but to **the surprise of all, Sir Phelim boldly declared that the** so-called **royal commission was an ingenious device of his own, and that his gracious majesty, Charles the First, had no more to do with his making war than the great Mogul or the Caliph of Bagdad. He was asked, how then did he come by the commission, to which he frankly replied that when he took the Castle of Charlemont in the year of '41, he found in an old cabinet in a** certain room **of that edifice, a patent with the broad seal of** England appended, and immediately **conceiving the idea of** counterfeiting a royal commission, he then and there cut off the seal and had it transferred to a document prepared by him.*

This statement, so humiliating **and yet so** praiseworthy, was more galling to the regicide **Puritans than can well be imagined. Some of their most eminent officials in Ireland visited Sir Phe-lim in his prison, and made use of every art to induce him to criminate** *the late man, Charles Stuart.* **But Sir Phelim was firm as a rock. Truth was truth, and not to save his life would he, the descendant of a princely line, the champion of Catholic rights, prevaricate in that final hour.**

His fate was sealed, and he stood on the scaffold. Let the Protestant minister, Warner, tell of his last moments.† He is

---

* It will be remembered that Sir Phelim O'Neill was a member of the legal profession.

† Yet this same Warner, in the very same paragraph, speaks of this very Sir Phelim as " profligate to the last degree"—in God's name, how could a man manifesting so much heroism, such a conscientious regard for truth in his last moments, be considered as " profligate to the last degree ?" Truly, this is a fair specimen of Protestant logic as regards Catholics and their religion.

quoting the testimony of a certain Dean Ker, no friend, surely, of poor Phelim O'Neill :

" Hoping still that they should prevail with Sir Phelim O'Neill, when the terrors of death were nearer, the Dean deposeth further, that he was present and very near Sir Phelim when he was upon the ladder at his execution ; and that two Marshals came riding to the place in great hurry, calling aloud ' stop a little,' and having passed through the crowd, one of them whispered him some time, and Sir Phelim O'Neill answered him, in the hearing of the Dean and several hundreds round him, ' I thank the Lieutenant-General—meaning Fleetwood—for this intended mercy ; but I declare, good people, before God and His holy Angels, and all you that hear me, that I never had any commission from the King for what I have done in levying or prosecuting this war.' "

He also expressed himself truly sorry for any unnecessary bloodshed or outrage of any kind which, in furtherance of their lawful and conscientious war, his followers might have committed, and commending his soul to God, the fatal drop was lowered and Stout Phelim—stout and staunch to the last, was launched into eternity—the martyr of truth, as he has been aptly styled.

The death of Sir Phelim O Neill is assuredly no less noble or heroic than that of Lord Maguire or Costelloe McMahon. If in that one instance he had swerved grievously from the path of rectitude, he nobly expiated his fault, a fault which was certainly extenuated, if not justified, by the motive he had in view. The hatred which the Puritans bore to his name was manifested after his death. His head was placed over the gate at the Bridge-foot in Dublin,* and the four quarters of his body sent to various cities for similar exhibition. and the greater intimidation of all traitors.

And this was the end of Sir Phelim O' Neill. *In-felix Felix*, the most hated and calumniated of all the Confederate Chieftains —the first who raised their standard in Ulster, and the last to let it fall. His name and his memory should be dear to the Catholics of Ireland, and they, at least, should remember that

---

* See Gilbert's *Dublin*, Vol. I., p. 325.

the heroic devotion of so many years to a great cause, and the nobleness of his end, should efface the memory of any human frailties to which he was subject. He was a man of strong passions, and nature had cast him in a rough mould, but we have ample evidence in the facts already mentioned that there was an innate nobleness and elevation of character beneath that ungracious exterior.

" Why is his name unsung, O! minstrel host?
Why do you pass his memory like a ghost?
Why is no rose, no laurel, on his grave?
Was he not constant, vigilant, and brave?
Why, when that hero-age you deify,
Why do you pass ' In-felix Felix by?'

" He rose the first—he looms the morning star
Of that long, glorious, unsuccessful war?
England abhors him! Has she not abhorr'd
All who for Ireland ventured life or word?
What memory would she not have cast away
That Ireland hugs in her heart's heart to-day?

" He rose in wrath to free his fetter'd land,
' There's blood—there's Saxon blood—upon his hand.'
Ay! so they say!—three thousand less or more,
He sent untimely to the Stygian shore—
They were the keepers of the prison-gate—
He slew them, his whole race to liberate.

" O! Clear-eyed Poets, ye who can descry,
Thro' vulgar heaps of dead, where heroes lie—
Ye to whose glance the primal mist is clear—
Behold there lies a trampled Noble here.
Shall we not leave a mark? shall we not do
Justice to one so hated and so true?

" If even his hand and hilt were so distain'd,
If he was guilty, as he has been blamed,
His death redeem'd his life—he chose to die,
Rather than get his freedom with a lie;
Plant o'er his gallant heart a laurel tree,
So may his head within the shadow be.

" I mourn for thee, O, hero of the North—
God judge thee gentler than we do on earth!
I mourn for thee, and for our Land, because
She dare not own the martyrs in her cause.
But they, our poets, they who justify
They will not let thy memory rot or die."*

* If Ireland owed no other debt of gratitude to Thomas D'Arcy M.Gee than the above spirited stanzas, it would be no trifling one.

20

It was well for Rory O'More that his generous heart was
spared the misery of those tragic scenes. He died, we are told,
in Flanders, "of a broken heart," on hearing of the fatal dissensions tearing asunder the glorious Confederation which his genius had planned.* Well for him that he lived not to witness
the utter ruin of the cause, the bloody extinction of the nation's
hopes, but late so fair and rich in promise! Well for him that
he was taken hence before the infuriate followers of Cromwell
were left to work their will on faithful, devoted Ireland.

A terrible picture of the bloody Cromwellian period is found
in the truthful pages of George Lewis Smith to which I have so
often referred : " The cruelties of the Puritans," says he, " during their uncontrolled occupation of Ireland, are not to be
outmatched in the long catalogue of enormities by which the
history of Christian Europe has been blackened. Fanaticism
never exhibited itself in a mood at once so stern and wild.
Vindictive interpreters of the spirit of the Old Testament, they
imbibed a blasphemous conviction that God had punished an
idolatrous people by subjecting their lives and properties to the
despotic authority of a ' purer race elect.' As Joshua used the
Gideonites so the Puritans scourged their Irish serfs with rods of
iron. At least 40,000 Irishmen were transported as slaves to
the West Indies. The peasantry were strictly forbidden to stir
out of their respective parishes without leave ; they were not
allowed to assemble for religious worship or any other purpose ;
their priests were commanded to fly the country under pain of
death ; and when it was discovered that some faithful pastors,
unmoved by these frightful denunciations, still administered the
consolations of religion in caverns, hid amidst the wild fastnesses
of uncultivated mountains, or in turf-covered huts, pitched upon

There have been few amongst us to do justice to the memory of this
gallant but unfortunate chieftain—let us hope that after times and
after generations of Catholics may give him credit for his unexam-
pled devotion to the cause of his country and her ancient faith.

* Some writers say that it was in Kilkenny Rory O'More ended his
mortal pilgrimage, but I am rather inclined to the opinion of those
who lay the scene of his death abroad.

the cheerless centre of some deserted bog, bloodhounds were
employed to track the martyrs to their retreats, and priest-
hunting became one of the field sports of the country."*

Such was the dismal condition to which the suicidal policy of
the Norman nobles, and the bickerings and dissensions within
the Catholic body had consigned Ireland—such the state of
things which followed on the final overthrow of THE CONFEDER-
ATE CHIEFTAINS!

Those of my readers who take an interest in the fortunes of
Judith O'Cahan and her young friend Emmeline, will be glad to
know that they were safely conducted to Madrid by Donogh the
Rapparee, in pursuance of the last solemn injunction of Owen
Roe. Long before the horrors of the last tragic era had commenced—before Cromwell had crimsoned one field of Ulster
with the blood of its heroic children—whilst Phelim and Heber
were yet masters of the north, and the Red Hand was still in
its power, the betrothed of Owen Roe and of Connor Maguire
were sheltered beneath the roof of a Spanish Dominican convent, where the greatness of their sorrows commanded respect,
and won tender sympathy. There,

"The world forgetting, by the world forgot,"

they spent the remaining years of their earthly sojourn in the
practice of penance, and the soothing exercise of that devotion
which souls purified by suffering can alone appreciate. The
memory of the loved and lost never faded from their minds—
identified as they were with all that was great and noble, but
the wild excitement of the stormy war-time gradually blended
with the past, and seemed through the mist of years no more
than the troubles of a feverish dream.

As for Donogh he was nearly alone in the world—Shamus
Beg had fallen in the vain effort to save his chief from the hands
of Coote's troopers—most of his brave associates had dropped
one after another in their ceaseless encounters with the enemy,
but the few who remained were resolved to fight the Crom-
wellians whilst an Irish banner was on the breeze, and Donogh,

* *Ireland, Historical and Statistical*, Vol. II., p. 65.

himself of the same mind, contrived to make his way back from
Spain just in time to see the end of it. He was slain a few
months after the tragical end of Sir Phelim;—whilst he and a
few of his gallant Rapparees were conveying an aged priest
through the fastnesses of Donegal on their way to Connaught,
they were suddenly beset by a party of Montgomery's horse, and
every man of them fell fighting around the priest who was then
hung from the crag of a neighboring rock.

Clanrickarde reaped the reward of his worldly wisdom. On
the restoration of the Stuarts, he retired to his English estates,
where he spent the few remaining years of his life in what the
world calls " dignified retirement." Peace, we can hardly think
he enjoyed with the groans of Cromwell's victims ringing in his
ears, and the blood of thousands of martyrs weighing on his soul.

There remains but one of the prominent characters of our
tale to be noticed—the great, the learned, the saintly Nicholas
French. After doing all that man could do with his voice and
with his pen for the liberation of his country, he was destined
to outlive nearly all the associates of his arduous toils. He had
gone abroad before the breaking up of the Confederacy for the
purpose of soliciting yet more liberal aid from the Catholic
sovereigns of Europe, and he never returned, for the utter ruin
of the cause and the bloody persecution going on in Ireland,
made it well for him to be abroad. Yet though absent from
Ireland his heart was there, and in the seclusion of various uni-
versities where his fame and his learning made him an honored
guest, he devoted his powerful pen to the service of his oppressed country.

At the conclusion of the Life of Bishop French, in McGee's
Gallery of Irish Writers, we find the following beautiful and
most vivid account of the end of that patriotic prelate :

" On the 23d of August, in the year of grace, 1678, the vast
Cathedral of Ghent saw a melancholy sight. In its basilica
was laid the corpse of a bishop. Many lights gleamed around
—the mitre and the staff were by his side, the shoes on his
feet, and the purple over his cold bosom. Whoever looked
upon that face, newly inanimate, might perceive the lines
of thought, and the lineaments of high resolve and noblest

courage imprinted upon it. It was the mortal form and face
of the great exiled Irish bishop. He had yielded up his soul
to God, and his memory to his country. His monument and
grave are under the roof of that sombre Cathedral. His character and his fame are our inheritance. Let us consider how to
appreciate their value."*

As for Luke Wadding there is reason to think that his heart
was broken by the failure of the Catholic cause in his native
land, that cause for which he had done so much and labored
so devotedly. He died in 1657 in Rome, honored and beloved
by the highest dignitaries of the Church, and the greatest lite-
rati of that age, for Wadding was a distinguished scholar and
an eminent writer, as well as an illustrious patriot. "His funeral
was solemnly celebrated; his grave is in St. Isidore's, and over
it a tomb, raised to his memory by a noble Roman, who was
his friend through life. . . . It bears a brief inscription in
Latin."†

And Rinuccini—did he forget Ireland on his return to Italy?
Not so—he did all that in his power lay to advance her cause,
but he did not long survive the close of his Irish nunciature,
and died, Heaven be praised! before the dark days came again
upon that Church of Ireland, for whose freedom he had labored
so strenuously. It is recorded that on his return to Rome he
caused a series of frescoes to be painted in his palace at Fermo,
illustrating the principal battles fought in Ireland during his
nunciature.‡ No better proof could be given of his love for that
country than thus perpetuating on canvas the glories of Benburb,
Bunratty (where himself had commanded), and Ballaghmore!

Their souls are, we trust, with God, those illustrious *Confederates*, and their ashes spread abroad over many lands, but so
long as the children of Ireland are true to their ancient faith,
so long will their names be a rich inheritance, their deeds and
their virtues a glorious model for all after times!

* Gallery of Irish writers, p. 163.   † *Ibid*, p. 101.
‡ Meehan's Confederation, p. 227

THE END.